COLLECTABLES

HANDBOOK & PRICE GUIDE

COLLECTABLES
HANDBOOK & PRICE GUIDE

Judith Miller

MILLER'S

Miller's Collectables Handbook & Price Guide 2021-2022
By Judith Miller

First published in Great Britain in 2021 by Miller's, a division of Mitchell Beazley,
imprints of Octopus Publishing Group Ltd., Carmelite House,
50 Victoria Embankment, London, EC4Y 0DZ
www.octopusbooks.co.uk

An Hachette UK Company
www.hachette.co.uk

Miller's is a registered trademark of Octopus Publishing Group Ltd.

ISBN 978 1 78472 666 9

A CIP catalogue record for this book is available from the British Library.

Printed and bound in China

1 3 5 7 9 10 8 6 4 2

Publisher Alison Starling
Editorial Co-ordinator Kathryn Allen
Proofreader John Wainwright
Indexer Hilary Bird
Design Ali Scrivens, TJ Graphics
Assistant Production Controller Serena Savini

Photographs of Judith Miller, **by Chris Terry**

CONTENTS

LIST OF CONSULTANTS 7
HOW TO USE THIS BOOK 7
INTRODUCTION 8

ADVERTISING 9
ANTIQUITIES 14
AMUSEMENT MACHINES 16
ASIAN CERAMICS & WORKS OF ART 17
AUSTRIAN BRONZES 31
AUTOMOBILIA 36
BOOKS 41
BOXES 47
CAMERAS 51
CANES 53
CERAMICS
    Beswick 57
    Blue & White 68
    Burmantofts 71
    Carlton 75
    Clarice Cliff 78
    Coalport 89
    Cobridge 90
    De Morgan Tiles 91
    Dennis Chinaworks 92
    Doulton 94
    Royal Doulton 96
    Fulper 106
    Goldscheider 107
    Kevin Francis / Peggy Davies 110
    Lenci 111
    Lladró 112
    Lorna Bailey 114
    Martin Brothers 115
    Meissen 116

    Minton 117
    Moorcroft 119
    Bernard Moore 132
    George Ohr 133
    Parkinson Pottery 135
    Poole Pottery 136
    Rookwood 139
    Roseville 141
    Royal Crown Derby 142
    Royal Worcester 143
    Ruskin 144
    Scandinavian Ceramics 147
    Troika 150
    Charles Vyse 151
    Wade 152
    Wedgwood 153
    Wemyss 154
    West German Stoneware 157
    Other Ceramics 162
    Studio Pottery 170
CLOCKS 178
COMICS & ANNUALS 181
DOLLS 185
FANS 199
FASHION 201
FILM & TELEVISION 215
FORNASETTI 221
GLASS
    Bottles 222
    Czech Glass 223
    Lalique 226
    Loetz 227
    Mdina / Isle Of Wight 230
    Monart 232

Murano	234	Motor Racing	351
Scandinavian Glass	239	Olympics	352
Steuben	242	Rugby	354
Stevens & Williams	243	Tennis & Other Racket Sports	355
Webb	244	TAXIDERMY	356
Whitefriars	245	TECHNOLOGY	357
Other Glass	247	TEDDY BEARS & STUFFED TOYS	359
Studio Glass	253	TOYS & GAMES	
GUITARS	256	Tinplate	365
JEWELLERY		Corgi	367
Jewellery	258	Dinky	370
Costume Jewellery	265	Other Vehicles	375
LIGHTING	269	Clockwork	378
MECHANICAL BANKS	273	Britains	380
MECHANICAL MUSIC	274	Other Toys	382
METALWARE	276	Ventriloquist Dummies	385
MILITARIA	279	Games	386
PAPERWEIGHTS	283	Trains	387
PENS & WRITING	286	Boats	394
PICTURE FRAMES	294	Pond Yachts & Model Planes	395
POSTCARDS	295	Steam	396
POSTERS	299	TREEN & CARVINGS	398
RAILWAYANA	307	TRIBAL ART	403
ROCK & POP	308	WEIRD & WONDERFUL	409
SCENT BOTTLES	313	WINE & DRINKING	410
SCIENTIFIC INSTRUMENTS	319	WRISTWATCHES	413
SCULPTURE	321		
SEWING	324	KEY TO ILLUSTRATIONS	418
SILVER	328	DIRECTORY OF CENTRES, MARKETS,	
SMOKING	337	SHOPS & SHOWS	419
SPORTING		DIRECTORY OF SPECIALISTS	420
Football	342	DIRECTORY OF AUCTIONEERS	422
Boxing	346	INTERNET RESOURCES	425
Cricket	347	DIRECTORY OF CLUBS & SOCIETIES	426
Equestrian	348	INDEX	427
Golf	349		

LIST OF CONSULTANTS

CERAMICS

Will Farmer
Fieldings Auctioneers
www.fieldingsauctioneers.co.uk

Wayne Chapman
Lynways
www.lynways.com

Michael G. Lines
John Newton Antiques
www.johnnewtonantiques.com

David Rago
Rago Arts, USA
www.ragoarts.com

COSTUME JEWELLERY

Gemma Redmond
www.gemmaredmondvintage.co.uk

FASHION

Sophie Higgs
Fellows Auctioneers
www.fellows.co.uk

GLASS

Will Farmer
Fieldings Auctioneers
www.fieldingsauctioneers.co.uk

Mike & Debby Moir
M&D Moir, www.manddmoir.co.uk

Wayne Chapman
Lynways, www.lynways.com

SPORTING

Graham Budd
Graham Budd Auctions
www.grahambuddauctions.co.uk

We'd also like to thank our friends and colleagues who have helped and supported us in many ways with this book including: Laura Dove from Adam Partridge, James Street from Aldridges of Bath, Keith Butler from Arthur Johnson & Sons, Karolina Wegrzyn from Aston's, Ian Jackson from Bearnes Hampton & Littlewood, Amelia Randle from Bellmans, Sarah Jones from Brightwells, Caroline Hodges from Boldon Auction Galleries, Jackie from British Toy Auctions, David Parker from The Canterbury Auction Galleries, Sarah Flynn from Cheffins, Sarah Beer from Chorley's, Glen Chapman from C&T, Mark Hill and Aubrey Dawson from Dawson's, Lynn Strover from Duke's, Andrew Ewbank from Ewbank's, Alexandra Whittaker and Liam Bolland from Fellows, June Emery from Fieldings, Kevin Mullins from Fonsie Mealy, Andrew Lubas from Freeman's, Mark Gilding from Gildings, Michael Duce from Graham Budd, Simon Turner from G.W. Railwayana Auctions, Jill Gallone from Hansons, Emma from Hartleys, Emilie Ferraud from Ivoire France, Tom Warren and James Welch from John Nicholson's, Geoff Shepherd from Kingham & Orme, Helen Robson and Rachel Coomber from Lacy Scott & Knight, Rachael Salter from Lawrences, Michal Kosakowski from Leitz Photographica Auction, Chris Elmy from Lockdales, Sally Ellis from Locke & England, Cathy Marsden and Alex Dove from Lyon & Turnbull, Andy Ebbage from M&M Auctions, Nigel Kirk from Mellors & Kirk, Sarah Stoltzfus from Morphy Auctions, Deirdre Pook Magarelli from Pook & Pook, Kathy from Potteries Auctions, Anthony Barnes from Rago Arts, Peigi Mackillop from Roseberys, Hugo Marsh from SAS, Kelsie Jankowski from Swann Galleries, Diane Baynes from Sworders, Chris Markwick from Tayler & Fletcher, Max Sobolevskij from Tennants, Travis Hammond from Theriaults, Louise Harker at Vectis, Tim Brophy from W&H Peacock, John Macdonald from Waddington's, James from Wallis and Wallis, and Clare Durham from Woolley & Wallis.

HOW TO USE THIS BOOK

The object The collectables are shown in full colour. This is a vital aid to identification and valuation. With many objects, a slight colour variation can signify a large price differential.

Source code Every item has been specially photographed at an auction house, a dealer, an antiques market or a private collection. These are credited by a code at the end of each caption, and can be checked against the Key to Illustrations (see p.418).

Quick reference Gives key facts about the factory, maker or style, along with stylistic identification points, value tips and advice on fakes.

The price guide These price ranges give a ballpark figure for what you should pay for a similar item. The great joy of collectables is that there is not a recommended retail price. The price ranges in this book are based on actual prices, either what a dealer will take or the full auction price.

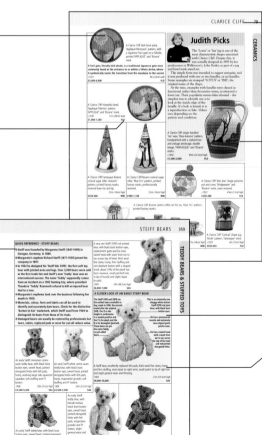

Subcategory heading Indicates the subcategory of the main heading.

Page tab This appears on every page and identifies the main category heading as identified in the Contents List on pages 5-6.

Judith Picks Items chosen specifically by Judith, either because they are important or interesting, or they might be a good investment.

Closer Look Does exactly that. Here we show identifying aspects of a factory or maker, point out rare colours or shapes, and explain why a particular piece is so desirable.

Caption The description of the item illustrated, including when relevant, the period, the maker or factory, medium, the year it was made, dimensions and condition. Many captions have **footnotes** that explain terminology or give identification or valuation information.

INTRODUCTION

Welcome to the new 'Miller's Collectables Handbook & Price Guide', in which I am proud to present more than 4,000 completely new, specially selected photographed collectables. Representative of the domestic and international market, they range from advertising to automobilia, ceramics to clocks, glass to guitars, metalware to militaria, paperweights to posters, teddy bears to tribal art. All collecting fields, tastes and passions are catered for.

Preceded by a list of contents, and a user-friendly explanation of how to use this book, every collectable depicted has a descriptive caption and a price guide.

A near-mint Dinky Toys 'VOLKSWAGEN KARMANN GHIA COUPE', no.187, in original panel box. £85-95 LSK

Many are also accompanied by detailed footnotes that highlight interesting aspects of the item. You will also find additional information in the 'Closer Look' and 'Judith Picks' features, as well as in the 'Quick Reference' boxes, which provide helpful introductions to particular collecting areas, designers or makers. At the back of the book, the practical aspects of collecting – buying and selling – are supported by directories of auction houses, specialists, fairs and societies.

A Royal Copenhagen tiger and two cubs, printed backstamp, numbered '4687' verso. 6in (15cm) high £500-600 LSK

So, what has happened to the collectables market since our last guide? As always some areas have strengthened, some have weakened. Ceramics have continued to be a particularly popular area. Clarice Cliff remains desirable, particularly rare patterns and interesting shapes. Lladró, Lenci, Royal Copenhagen and Moorcroft continue to have devoted followers. One area that reflects the whole market is Doulton. The 19thC Doulton Lambeth stoneware has had a quiet time, except for pieces by George Tinworth whose charming mice and frogs have continued to fetch record prices. The figurines and character jugs have to be early and rare to get top prices. Flambé animals continue to excite collectors.

Nostalgia underpins many developments in the collectables market. For example, on the BBC's 'Antiques Roadshow' we see a large number of postcards, many in quite elaborate albums. The majority are worth, at most, a few pounds. However, as you can see in this guide, early photographic representations of village shops and rare images of railway stations are as much in demand as liners and football teams and, as always, Louis Wain. In this edition we also have included some suffragette postcards. Of course, one generation's nostalgia isn't necessarily another's: Clockwork and Tinplate can be replaced with Dinky and Corgi. In these areas, condition is vital; collectors aim to buy mint examples.

There is also the influence of changing aesthetics. What once appeared fresh and pleasing to the eye gradually diminishes, and is replaced by a different look. Ultimately this is a matter of fashion and explains why, for example, the naturalistic form and decoration of Victorian ceramics and glass is generally fetching lower prices, while more geometric or abstract Art Deco and Mid-Century Modern equivalents, especially Scandinavian and Murano glass, are forging ahead. Meanwhile, 18thC blue and white porcelain is growing increasingly affordable, with many pieces now sold at auction in 'job lots'.

A Clarice Cliff Fantasque Bizarre 365 vase, 'House and Bridge' pattern, printed factory mark. 7in (20cm) high £1,800-2,200 WW

Of course, at some point these trends may reverse. Predicting that tipping point is far from an exact science. I am often asked what people should buy as an investment. My answer is absolutely nothing! Do some research, look in books, go to fairs, auctions and museums. Find an area you like and start collecting. Buy something that you love. My advice is: if you see something you can nearly afford – buy it. You will only regret it if you don't. Happy collecting!

A Kosta 'Winter' glass vase, by Vicke Lindstrand, engraved signature 'Kosta LH'. 1950s 7¼in (18.5cm) high £4,500-5,500 FLD

A suffragette postcard, by Millar & Lang, reading 'SUFFRAGETTES ATTACKING THE HOUSE OF COMMONS'. £60-70 LOCK

Judith Miller

QUICK REFERENCE - ADVERTISING

- Most of the advertising memorabilia available to collectors today dates from the 20thC.
- In general, collectors tend to focus either on a particular kind of advertising item, such as enamel signs or posters, or a particular brand or range of products. Food and drink advertising remains popular, as does tobacco advertising. Signs in mint condition tend to fetch the highest prices.
- The advertising collectables market is driven by a combination of nostalgia and availability. The brands that collectors know well, such as Cadbury's Chocolate or Colman's Mustard, are often popular, as are large brands such as Coca Cola, Shell or Michelin, which have produced a large range of advertising items over a long period of time.
- Items that clearly represent a subject area, artistic movement or time period are also highly collectable, whether from a well-known brand or not. Art Deco advertising items are very popular. 1950s-60s 'vintage' pieces have increased in popularity over the past decade. A design by a major artist will also increase an item's value.
- While good condition does increase value, advertising items have often been used over many years, sometimes in outdoor settings, so condition should be consistent with age and use. Reproductions are common in this market, so examine items especially carefully.

A vintage Allied Breweries Ltd. framed advertising mirror, 'DOUBLE DIAMOND BEER'.

34in (86.5cm) wide

£70-80   PSA

A single-sided enamel sign, 'ASSOCIATED MOTORWAYS BOOKING OFFICE', with map showing England and Wales.

34¾in (88.5cm) high

£900-1,100   FLD

A Bates cardboard advertising shop display sign, 'Bates SUPER RUBBER CORD TYRES', slight damage.

1930s   *31¼in (79.5cm) high*

£550-650   FLD

An enamel advertising sign, 'BENSKINS ESTABLISHED AT WATFORD SINCE 1750 ', in a cast iron frame.

17in (43cm) high

£250-300   LOCK

A 19thC C.H.Flooks two-sheet watchmaker's advertising poster, 'C.H.FLOOKS 49, PONTMORLAIS CIRCUS, MERTHYR'.

59¾in (152cm) high

£200-250   SWO

A Carter pictorial tile advertising panel, 'SPORTS BOOKS'.

22in (56cm) high

£2,000-2,500   CHOR

A Carter pictorial tile advertising panel, 'ART AND COLOUR BOOKS', slight stain to one of the tiles, grouting missing in places, the letter 'R' in the word 'COLOUR' may have been re-grouted.

22in (56cm) high

£2,000-2,500   CHOR

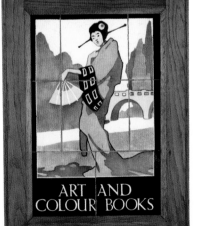

ADVERTISING

QUICK REFERENCE - CARTER

- In 1873, Jesse Carter, a builder and ironmonger, bought James Walker's struggling pottery near Poole harbour, forming Carter's Industrial Tile Manufactory. The company was then renamed Carter & Co.
- Carter & Co. became known for its advertising panels and mosaic flooring, supplying breweries, hospitals, retailers, and schools with glazed decorative and painted tiles. In 1895, Carter purchased the Architectural Pottery in Hamworthy. When Carter retired in 1901, his sons, Charles and Owen, took over the business. In 1921, a subsidiary company, Carter Stabler and Adams, was set up by Charles Carter's son Cyril, silversmith Harold Stabler and potter John Adams focusing on decorative pottery and tableware. In the 1920s, Carter & Co. created a series of tile advertising panels for WHSmith shops.
- Pilkington Tiles Ltd bought Carter & Co, along with its subsidiary, in 1964, creating Poole Pottery Ltd.

A French early to mid-20thC 'CHOCOLAT RÉVILLON' tolework advertising clock, in an oeil-de-boeuf or bullseye shape, with original brass wind-up pendulum movement.

23¼in (59cm) high

£650-750　　SWO

A Carter pictorial tile advertising panel, 'TRAVEL BOOKS', damaged.

22in (56cm) high

£2,000-2,500　　CHOR

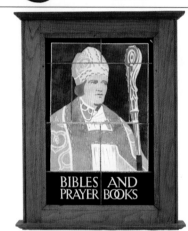

A Carter pictorial tile advertising panel 'BIBLES AND PRAYER BOOKS'.

22in (56cm) high

£950-1,100　　CHOR

A 'CHURCHMAN'S No2' cigarette card advertising sign, 'The Cigarette with a pedigree'.

26¾in (68cm) high

£120-180　　LOCK

A Carter textual tile advertising panel, for newspaper and periodical deliveries.

25in (63.5cm) high

£1,400-1,800　　CHOR

A large 'COLEMAN'S D.S.F MUSTARD' enamel sign.

38¼in (97cm) wide

£200-250　　FLD

A large ceramic model of the Dulux dog.

13in (33cm) high

£100-150　　LOC

A vintage framed 'Dewar's SPECIAL WHISKIES' advertising mirror.

36¼in (92cm) high

£40-60　　PSA

ADVERTISING

A 'DUNLOP' cardboard advertising shop display sign, slight damage.

1930s 30in (76cm) high

£600-700 **FLD**

A Fry's shop display figure, of a boy holding a large block of Fry's Chocolate, on a plinth with 'JOLLY GOOD! -and a lot for the money', some retouching, wear/flaws.

38½in (98cm) high

£4,000-5,000 **BBR**

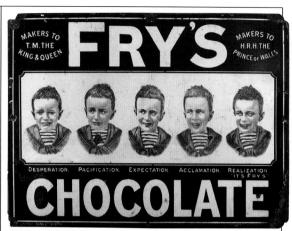

A 'FRY'S CHOCOLATE' pictorial enamel sign, by Chromo, with five different expressions to a boy's face, areas of damage and rust.

30in (76cm) wide

£1,400-2,000 **CHEF**

An early 20thC Edwardian oak fishing tackle display cabinet, with later gilt lettering.

37¾in (96cm) wide

£3,000-3,500 **L&T**

A vintage Holt, Plant & Deakin framed advertising mirror, 'HOLT PLANT & DEAKIN LTD HOLTS TRADITIONAL ALES'.

38¼in (97cm) wide

£220-280 **PSA**

A Hudson's pictorial enamel sign, 'A Pail of Water WITH A VERY LITTLE HUDSON'S GOES A VERY LONG WAY', restored.

13in (33cm) high

£150-200 **FLD**

A Hudson's Soap enamel advertising sign, 'FOR THE PEOPLE HUDSON'S SOAP', worn.

7in (17.5cm) high

£160-200 **LOCK**

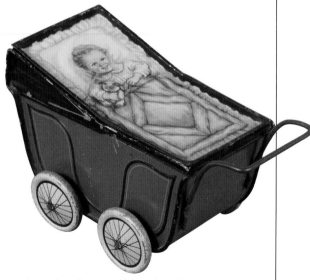

A Huntley & Palmers biscuit tin, likely produced by Huntley, Boorne and Stevens, in lithographed tinplate.

c1930 8¼in (21cm) long

£2,000-2,500 **CHEF**

JOHN BULL
—THE LONG SERVICE TYRE

An enamel advertising sign, 'JOHN BULL – THE LONG SERVICE TYRE'.

48in (122cm) wide

£350-400   **FLD**

An enamel advertising sign, 'JOULES STONE ALES', wear to edges.

1920s   *22in (56cm) high*

£200-250   **PSA**

A vintage framed Malony's advertising mirror, 'MALONY'S IRISH WHISKEY'.

37¾in (96cm) high

£55-65   **PSA**

A French 'MATHIS' automobile enamel sign, some damage.

27½in (70cm) diam

£200-250   **BELL**

An enamelled 'NECTAR TEA' advertising sign, further stamped 'Patent Enamel Co. Ltd. B'ham & London'.

21in (53.5cm) wide

£220-280   **APAR**

An American mid-20thC carved and painted Northern Pike fish trade sign.

55in (139.5cm) long

£1,500-2,000   **POOK**

An early to mid-20thC enamel advertising sign, 'HOUSE & ESTATE AGENTS AUCTIONEERS & VALUERS RD. & J.B. FRASER', made by Patent Enamel Co., Ltd., some restoration.

30in (76cm) high

£400-500   **LOCK**

A 'Rowntree's ELECT Cocoa' cardboard show card.

19in (48.5cm) high

£120-180   **FLD**

A vintage advertising mirror, 'THE SHAMROCK WHISKY DUBLIN'.

39in (99cm) high

£150-200   PSA

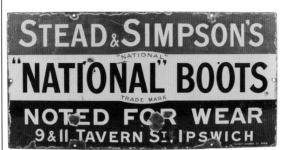

A 'STEAD & SIMPSON'S' enamel advertising sign, '"NATIONAL" BOOTS NOTED FOR WEAR'.

12in (30.5cm) high

£200-250   LOCK

A double-sided enamel WHSmith advertising sign, 'The Newsboy', framed and with hanging chain.

44½in (113cm) high

£1,000-1,500   CHOR

A WHSmith enamel advertising sign, 'MAKERS W. H. SMITH & Co. LTD. WHITCHURCH'.

14¼in (36cm) high

£50-60   LOCK

An Art Deco shipping line advertising wall calendar, 'CIE DE NAVIGATION PAQUET', by J. Tonelli, perpetual day, date and month window with levers to side, mounted on a wooden board.

19in (48.5cm) high

£450-550   DUK

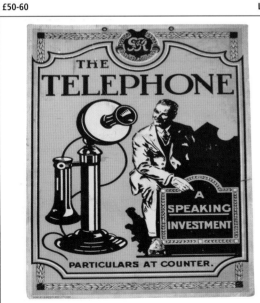

A George V 'THE TELEPHONE' cardboard advertising sign, with further motto 'A SPEAKING INVESTMENT'.

14¾in (37.5cm) high

£200-250   APAR

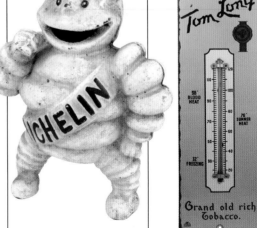

A painted metal 'MICHELIN' Man advertising figure.

6in (15cm) high

£50-60   LOCK

An advertising thermometer, 'SMOKE Tom Long Grand old rich Tobacco'.

22¾in (58cm) high

£200-250   LOCK

ANTIQUITIES

QUICK REFERENCE - ANTIQUITIES

- Antiquities are items belonging to ancient civilisations predating the Middle Ages, such as the Ancient Greeks, the Romans and the Ancient Egyptians.
- The earliest glass objects discovered date from c2500 BC. In the 1stC BC, glassblowing was invented, with the glassblowing furnace invented in AD 1. Prior to this, glass vessels were usually opaque due to air bubbles and impurities in the material being common.
- Many Roman glass vessels were buried underground in the intervening centuries since their production, with the exposure to sand, soil, heat and minerals causing iridescence – the rainbow effect often seen on the vessels' surfaces.

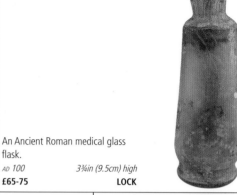

An Ancient Roman medical glass flask.
AD 100   *3¾in (9.5cm) high*
£65-75   **LOCK**

A Roman marble-effect glass cup, with finger rim to body.
AD 2ndC-4thC   *2¾in (7cm) diam*
£400-500   **FLD**

A Roman glass bowl, with traces of iridescence and internal central line band.
AD 2ndC-4thC   *5in (12.5cm) wide*
£350-400   **FLD**

A Roman amber glass beaker, some damage.
AD 2ndC-4thC   *3in (7.5cm) high*
£100-140   **FLD**

A Roman iridescent glass beaker, with slashed ribs to the base.
AD 2ndC-3rdC   *2¾in (7cm) high*
£320-380   **FLD**

A Roman glass bowl, with ribbed body and applied lattice decoration, slight damage.
AD 2ndC-4thC   *3in (7.5cm) high*
£400-500   **FLD**

A Roman miniature cobalt blue glass flask, decorated with white beehive-style bands.
AD 2ndC-4thC   *1½in (4cm) high*
£300-350   **FLD**

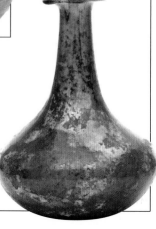

A Roman miniature glass flask.
AD 2ndC-4thC   *2½in (6.5cm) high*
£350-400   **FLD**

A Roman iridescent deep amber glass jug, with applied clear ribbed handle.
AD 2ndC-4thC   *5¼in (13.5cm) high*
£550-650   **FLD**

A Roman miniature glass jug, with yellow zig-zag bands of decoration to the shoulder.
AD 2ndC-4thC   *3in (7.5cm) high*
£950-1,100   **FLD**

An Ancient Roman terracotta oil lamp, depicitng a lion.
c AD 200
£200-250   **LOCK**

A Roman gold ring, the band consisting of four plaited wires, set with a jasper intaglio engraved with a reclining figure, possibly a Genius or personification of a river.
AD 1stC-4thC   *0.12 oz*
£1,000-1,400   **HAN**

A Roman olive glass pendant, impressed with a standing lion and glass bangle.
AD 2ndC-4thC   *2½in (6.5cm) diam*
£80-90   **FLD**

A Roman string of glass beads.
AD 2ndC-4thC   *16¼in (41.5cm) long*
£130-200   **FLD**

A Roman string of speckle millefiori coloured glass beads.
AD 2ndC-4thC   *9¼in (23.5cm) long*
£120-160   **FLD**

A Roman string of lapis lazuli blue beads, with a spiral lentoid section.
AD 2ndC-4thC   *9½in (24cm) long*
£95-110   **FLD**

A Roman string of iridescent and lunar drop beads, with interspaced blue stones and central fantail pendant.
AD 2ndC-4thC   *17¼in (44cm) long*
£400-500   **FLD**

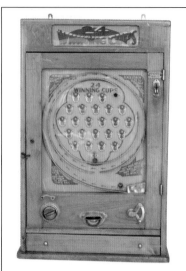

An Allwins oak-cased '24 WINNINGS CUPS' amusement machine, one penny operation.

35in (89cm) high

£500-600   FLD

An electro-mechanical 'WIZARD!' pinball machine, serial no.3335, model no.1027, by Bally, designed by Greg Kmiec, artwork by Dave Christensen based on the Ken Russell movie 'Tommy', original back glass with Roger Daltrey and Ann-Margret pictured, cabinet and playfield, with original schematic.

The WIZARD! was Bally's first mega-hit pinball, breaking the 10,000 production mark - 10,005 units were built, five units were distributed to the five top executives of Bally with the 10,005th going to Tom Neymens, Head of Sales. The artwork was franchised from the film Tommy, a rock musical fantasy based on The Who's 1969 rock opera about a 'seemingly disabled' boy who becomes a pinball champion. It had an important impact on pinball games as it was the first machine to use a popular theme to great success. Nearly every arcade had a WIZARD! and most were placed next to the door to attract players. This pinball machine was sold with a six month warranty for parts and labour for mainland UK buyers, with one free call-out visit.

1975

£4,000-5,000   ROS

A Bryans 'ELEVENSES FOUR-SQUARE' penny arcade game, the top section with four coin-operated games, mounted on a later square base with cigarette holders to the corners and painted sides 'FUN FAIR' and '2p A Go!'.

1930s   *30in (76cm) wide*

£2,500-3,500   L&T

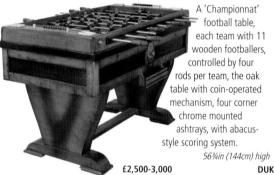

A 'Championnat' football table, each team with 11 wooden footballers, controlled by four rods per team, the oak table with coin-operated mechanism, four corner chrome mounted ashtrays, with abacus-style scoring system.

56¾in (144cm) high

£2,500-3,000   DUK

A painted iron penny table-top basketball trade stimulator, PEO Mfg. Corp., with original paper, from the William Seibt Confectionary Store in St Louis, Missouri, has the door key, no basketballs, some wear.

c1930   *14½in (37cm) high*

£450-550   POOK

A miniature 'BASEBALL WORLD CHAMPION' penny table-top trade stimulator, PEO Mfg. Corp., with nickel front panel, upper painted panel with pop-up runners, from the William Seibt Confectionary Store in St Louis, Missouri, has door key.

c1930   *17in (43cm) high*

£700-900   POOK

A Santa Claus fairground ball game, with bust of Santa Claus with open mouth above the playing area, with painted numbers and instructions, on a painted wooden base.

30in (76cm) high

£400-500   DUK

A Jennings Nevada Club 25-cent light-up slot machine.

60½in (153.5cm) high

£1,300-1,600   POOK

A Chinese Wanli period blue and white shipwreck porcelain 'Peacock' dish.

Produced from the Wanli period (1573-1619), 'Kraak' is the Dutch term for Chinese blue and white wares named after the Portuguese ships called 'carracks', which were used to export the ware from China.

10¾in (27.5cm) diam

£100-140   **JN**

A Chinese 19thC blue and white porcelain snuff bottle, with a hard stone/jadeite stopper and ivory spoon, the base with a four character Yongzheng mark.

3¼in (8.5cm) high

£180-220   **JN**

A Chinese 19thC blue and white underglaze red porcelain snuff bottle, depicting the scene of a five claw dragon, the base with a six-character Qianlong mark.

3¼in (8.5cm) high

£250-300   **JN**

A Chinese early 19thC export blue and white meat plate, slight damage.

10in (25.5cm) long

£60-70   **FLD**

A Chinese 19thC blue and white porcelain snuff bottle.

3¼in (8.5cm) high

£80-100   **JN**

A Chinese 19thC landscape decorated plate, four-character mark to base, nip to outer rim.

16in (40.5cm) diam

£220-280   **PSA**

QUICK REFERENCE - CHINESE BLUE AND WHITE CERAMICS

- Dating from the Tang dynasty, the use of blue underglaze decoration in China became increasingly important in the late 13thC and 14thC.
- During the late 14thC, Ming Emperor Hongwu imposed a trade embargo, reducing the availability of foreign cobalt. Copper oxide, which fires red, was used more widely.
- Imported cobalt became widely available again during the early 15thC. Cobalt imported from Persia produced a darker blue than locally-sourced ores.
- Blue and white wares in the 19th and 20thC often imitated that of the Ming dynasty, with precisely spaced decoration.

A Chinese early 19thC porcelain platter, small chip to top left edge.

14¾in (37.5cm) wide

£90-120   **PSA**

A Chinese Tongzhi period (1862-74) bowl, painted with scrolling lotus above false gadroon borders, six-character Tongzhi mark.

1862-74   *6¼in (16cm) diam*

£2,000-2,500   **SWO**

A Chinese 19thC vase, painted with vignettes depicting figures, double ring mark to base and bearing old paper label 'No.149/10', riveted repair and cracks, small chip to foot rim.

13in (33cm) high

£650-750　　　　　　　　**APAR**

A Chinese 19thC blue and white 'Rouleau' porcelain vase, the base with a four-character Kangxi mark.

4¾in (12cm) high

£200-250　　　　　　　　**JN**

A Chinese 19thC blue and white tea caddy, decorated with landscape scenes.

4½in (11.5cm) high

£50-60　　　　　　　　**JN**

A Chinese perhaps 19thC or Republican 'Bats and Peaches' saucer dish, Yongzheng six-character mark within double circle, the exterior with pairs of bats each incorporating a shou medallion.

The Republican period covers c1911–1949, when the Republic of China was a sovereign country. The Republic of China formed following the Xinhai Revolution, which overthrew the Qing dynasty.

8½in (21.5cm) diam

£2,500-3,000　　　　　　　　**DN**

A Chinese 19thC blue and white prunus porcelain spill vase.

4¾in (12cm) high

£20-30　　　　　　　　**JN**

A Chinese early 20thC blue and white porcelain bottle vase, with decoration of a dragon, with a Ruyi-style border, the base with a double blue ring.

8¼in (21cm) high

£140-180　　　　　　　　**JN**

A set of four Chinese early 20thC blue and white porcelain framed panels, depicting landscape scenes, the frames with handles and carved and pierced panels of bats.

30¾in (78cm) high

£350-400　　　　　　　　**JN**

A pair of Chinese Republican period (1911-49) vases, with fruiting and flowering sprays of the 'Three Abundances' – pomegranate, fingered citron and peach – the base with a six-character Qianlong seal mark.

9¼in (23.5cm) high

£2,200-2,800　　　　　　　　**L&T**

A Chinese late 20thC decorative Yen Yen vase, unmarked.

15½in(39.5cm) high

£50-60　　　　　　　　**APAR**

QUICK REFERENCE - FAMILLE ROSE

- Created in the 18thC, famille rose ware typically features flowers, foliage, figures and symbols in shades of pink and carmine. Painters blended and shaped colours using opaque yellow and white. Gold was often use for embellishments. The colours were seen as foreign in China, as they were introduced from Europe in the 17thC.

- Famille rose was popular among wealthy Europeans, with large numbers of dinner services exported to Europe. This palette was copied by European factories including Meissen and Chelsea.

- Famille verte ware, characterised by green, iron red, blue, purple and yellow, was produced during the Kangxi period (1661-1722). The use of a yellow ground with this palette is called famille jaune, while the use of a green-black ground is called famille noire.

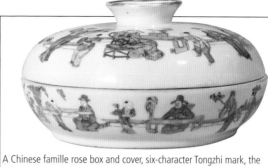

A Chinese famille rose box and cover, six-character Tongzhi mark, the interior divided into six compartments.

c1862-74

£750-850 WW

A famille rose snuff bottle, painted with military figures by the gate of a fortified city, four-character Xianfeng iron red seal mark.

1851-61   *3in (7.5cm) high*

£600-700 L&T

A Chinese 19thC famille rose porcelain bottle vase, painted with ducks in a lotus pond, the neck interior and base turquoise.

13in (33cm) high

£400-500 JN

A Chinese 19thC famille rose jardinière and stand, with Canton enamelling.

7in (18cm) high

£450-500 TRI

A Chinese 19thC famille rose ginger jar and lid, decorated with cartouches of birds.

9in (23cm) high

£400-450 TRI

A pair of Chinese 19thC porcelain famille rose baluster vases.

7½in (19cm) high

£600-700 WW

A Chinese 19thC Canton famille rose porcelain vase/lamp, lamp fittings to interior.

21in (53.5cm) high

£350-400 JN

A Chinese 19thC celadon famille rose porcelain bowl, the base with an iron-red four-character mark.

8¼in (21cm) diam

£180-220 JN

ASIAN CERAMICS

A Chinese 19thC famille rose porcelain bowl, with decoration of Chinese symbols, the base with a blue stylised seal mark.

8in (20.5cm) diam

£60-70   **JN**

A Chinese late 19thC famille rose pedestal dish, exterior sides painted with six immortal gods.

2¾in (7cm) high

£180-220   **FLD**

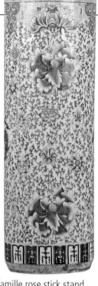

A Chinese famille rose stick stand.

c1900   *26in (66cm) high*

£500-600   **BELL**

A Chinese 20thC famille rose porcelain figurine, modelled as a standing official, seal marks.

15½in (39.5cm) high

£500-600   **DUK**

A Chinese early 20thC famille rose large porcelain vase, the verso with Chinese calligraphy.

22½in (57cm) high

£140-180   **JN**

A Chinese early 20thC famille rose footed diamond-shaped dish, decorated with panels with alternate figures and sprays of flowers.

14¼in (36cm) long

£300-350   **FLD**

A Chinese Republic period famille rose vase, iron-red four-character Shen De Tang zhi (made for the Hall of Prudent virtue) mark to base, there is a shallow indentation to one side, done at time of manufacture, which has been painted over with a pomegranate.

16in (40.5cm) high

£1,300-1,600   **BELL**

A Chinese Republican-style famille rose porcelain panel/tile, the upper right section with Chinese calligraphy/poem and seal.

12½in (32cm) high

£400-500   **JN**

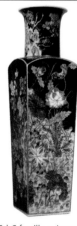

A Chinese 19thC famille noire vase, the base with a scroll mark.

19¾in (50cm) high

£500-600   **WW**

A Chinese early 19thC celadon vase, with lying dog decoration to handles, some damage, hairline crack to the body.

First used during the Song dynasty, celadon is a semi-opaque, green-tinted glaze. Between c960-1126, celadon produced in northern China had a thin olive-green glaze, while the later southern celadon had a thicker, cooler green glaze.

24¾in (63cm) high

£350-450   **PSA**

A Chinese 19thC vase, with blue and yellow glazed ground with applied relief details depicting vases, other ceramic wares, insects and flowers, handles missing, major crack to neck.

22¾in (58cm) high

£180-220   **FELL**

A Chinese 19thC double-bodied vase, with floral and dragon decoration, Chien Lung square mark to the base, on stand.

13in (33cm) high

£220-280   **PSA**

A Chinese 19thC sang-de-boeuf stoneware vase.

Chinese porcelain of the 19thC included Ming-style blue and white wares and monochromes. Most export, imperial and domestic porcelain of the 19thC and 20thC was given reign marks.

11in (28cm) high

£650-750   **LSK**

A Chinese claire-de-lune porcelain dragon vase, with high-relief moulded dragons, the base with a six-character mark.

21½in (54.5cm) high

£750-850   **JN**

A Chinese 20thC sang-de-boeuf Fanghu porcelain vase, with streaked glaze.

10in (25.5cm) high

£300-350   **JN**

A Chinese 20thC vase, with branches of peaches and bats, gilt rim, seal mark.

17in (43cm) high

£1,500-2,000   **GWA**

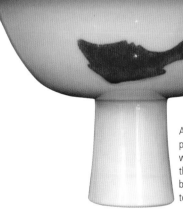

A Chinese Republic period stem cup, the white glazed body with three burnt-red carp, blue six-character mark to the pedestal inner.

4½in (11.5cm) high

£100-150   **FLD**

A Chinese Tang dynasty water pot, with a spotted Sancai glaze stopping short of the foot.

The Tang dynasty period is from AD 618 to c906.

£350-400   WW

A pair of Chinese early 19thC armorial oval dishes, decorated with the arms of Hay with the motto 'Spare Nought', the rims with confronting dragons chasing sacred jewels.

11in (28cm) wide

£450-550   WW

A Chinese pottery figure of Guanyin.

12in (30.5cm) high

£400-500   JN

A pair of Chinese 19thC pottery 'Scholar' figures.

15in (38cm) high

£500-600   JN

A pair of Chinese 19th/20thC huge glazed porcelain Buddhistic temple/lion dogs on stands.

42½in (108cm) high

£850-950   JN

A Chinese 19thC Kangxi-style Sancai porcelain official seated in a dragon chair, with a carved and fitted hardwood stand with carved lion dog head feet.

11¼in (28.5cm) high

£800-900   JN

A Chinese 19thC Yixing teapot and cover, the base with three lines of calligraphy, signed 'Yigong Zhi'.

£900-1,000   WW

A Chinese 19thC Yixing Zisha teapot and cover, with a turquoise glaze, one seal to base reads 'Shilin He shi' and another to underside of cover reads 'Xinzhou'.

Produced in the Jiangsu Province, Yixing ware is red stoneware. It was exported to Europe from the mid-17thC to the late 18thC, with the most popular ware being teapots and cups. From the late 17thC, potteries in Staffordshire produced Yixing imitation ware.

6½in (16.5cm) long

£850-950   SWO

A Chinese 19thC Yixing teapot and cover, the base inscribed with a short poem and with a Meng Chen mark.

£700-800   WW

A Chinese pale jade abstinence plaque/pendant, carved in low relief with a 'grass script' text, the other side with a scholar.

2in (5cm) high

£2,500-3,000   HAN

A Chinese late Qing dynasty (1644-1911) jade plaque, in the shape of a dragon with engraved archaic scrolls.

2¾in (7cm) long

£250-300   SWO

A Chinese 19thC red-overlay glass 'carps' snuff bottle.

2½in (6.5cm) high

£650-750   WW

A Chinese overlay snuff bottle, with emblems.

£300-400   JN

A Chinese late 19thC to early 20thC enamelled silver wine cup, maker's marks to base.

1¼oz

£150-200   JN

A Chinese early 20thC hexagonal silver bowl, by Kwan Ho, decorated with a plum tree, a dragon, floral display, interior of a house, bamboo and Chinese warriors.

3in (7.5cm) high

£550-600   MART

A Chinese silver-metal vase, possibly made for the Straits Chinese market, embossed with dragon and phoenix panels, unmarked.

12in (30.5cm) high

£700-800   JN

A Chinese 20thC silver bowl, with a dragon wrapped around the body, incised with the initials 'B D A' and with a commemorative note in Chinese to the reverse, a punch mark to the base.

8oz

£700-800   WW

A Chinese Republic period lobed Paktong teapot and cover, two impressed marks of 'yunbai' (Paktong from Yunnan Province) and 'qiutianbao' (hallmark) to the base.

Qiutianbao was one of the oldest Chinese jewellery brands in existence, the first shop opened in the 1820s in Shanghai.

6in (15cm) long

£350-400   DN

A Chinese 20thC bronze censer and cover, the cover surmounted with a guardian lion, the body with phoenix birds.

9in (23cm) high

£500-600   LC

A Chinese bronze ding censer, with tauti mask decoration, archaistic-style four-character mark.

8in (20.5cm) high

£550-600   LC

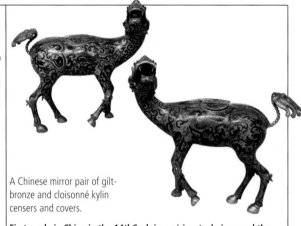

A Chinese mirror pair of gilt-bronze and cloisonné kylin censers and covers.

First made in China in the 14thC, cloisonné is a technique and the resulting ware, in which enamel is fired into compartments (or 'cloisons') made from metal wires fixed onto a metal surface. The early palette was limited to dark green, cobalt blue, red, yellow and white, on a turquoise background.

10in (25.5cm) long

£650-750   JN

A Chinese late Qing cloisonné ewer and stand, with red and green enamelled dragon handle, some damage.

12in (30.5cm) high

£900-1,100   DN

A Chinese 20thC cloisonné plaque, depicting a landscape.

23in (58.5cm) high

£1,300-1,600   DN

A Chinese late 19thC cloisonné enamelled vase, decorated with dragons and floral scenes.

5½in (14cm) high

£55-65   PSA

A Chinese carved soapstone 'Dog of Fo', on wooden base.

7¾in (19.5cm) high

£100-150   PSA

A Chinese Shoushan stone mythical lion seal, in hardwood box, with collector's label on box.

box 3¾in (9.5cm) high

£500-600   DN

A Chinese Qing dynasty or later boxwood carving of a carp.

8in (20.5cm) high

£450-500   WW

QUICK REFERENCE - SATSUMA

- Produced from the mid-19thC in the Japanese towns of Satsuma and Kyoto, Satsuma designs incorporate a cream ground, a finely crackled glaze and enamelled or gilded decoration. The town of Satsuma was important to porcelain production from 16thC but is best known for these designs. The decoration often includes depictions of landscapes or scenes, with elaborate borders. Most Satsuma ware is signed on the base.

A pair of Japanese Meiji (1868-1912) Satsuma 'cockerel' vases, hen and chicks among flowers and rockwork, gilt and impressed Kinkozan mark.

11½in (29cm) high

£1,200-1,600   L&T

QUICK REFERENCE - KINKOZAN

- The Kinkozan family have been producing ceramics since c1645 in Kyoto. From the late 19thC to the early 20thC, the Kinkozan studio became a significant producer of Satsuma ware.
- The studio was run by the Kinkozan family, with Kinkozan Sobei IV (1824-84) and his son exporting their work overseas. Kinkozan produced panelled wares, with scenes of everyday activities.
- The studio closed in 1927 after the death of Kinkozan V (1868-1927).

A Japanese Meiji Satsuma vase, by Kinkozan, painted with mandarin ducks on a stream, signed 'Kinkozan zo' in gilt to the base.

11¾in (30cm) high

£2,500-3,000   WW

A Japanese Satsuma koro and cover, by Kinkozan, the stylised lion finial above floral and pierced cover, twin elephant mask handles, the main body decorated with panels of figures, signed to base, tiny chip to lion, minor rubbing to the gilding.

5¼in (13.5cm) high

£1,000-1,400   APAR

A Japanese Meiji period Satsuma 'chicken' vase, Kinkozan mark, signed on the base in gilt 'Kinkozan zo'.

7in (18cm) high

£2,000-2,500   L&T

A Japanese Satsuma vase, by Kinkozan, decorated with figures among clouds, signed, minor rubbing to the gilding.

7½in (19cm) high

£1,000-1,200   APAR

A Japanese Satsuma vase, by Kinkozan, painted with figures in a landscape, signed within the decoration, neck has been broken off and restored, minor rubbing to the gilding.

9in (23cm) high

£800-900   APAR

A Japanese Meiji Satsuma earthenware dish, depicting a Daimyo's procession, Kinkozan seal mark.

A Daimyo was a feudal lord in shogunal Japan, subordinate only to the Shogun.

11in (28cm) diam

£1,100-1,500   JN

A Japanese Satsuma vase, by Gyokurui and Koshida, decorated with fish beside a rock with a further fish leaping towards branches, signed to base, minor rubbing to the gilding.

4¼in (11cm) high

£600-700   **APAR**

A pair of Japanese Meiji period Satsuma millefleur vases, enamelled with butterflies hovering above blossoming chrysanthemum sprays, signed 'taizan', also signed 'Dai Nippon Taizan' to the base.

12in (30.5cm) high

£1,200-1,600   **L&T**

A Japanese Meiji period Satsuma vase, signed by Yozan, panels depict characters in a wooded setting, a village scene before a mountainous backdrop.

The artist is referred to in the Louis Lawrence Satsuma book 'The Romance of Japan'.

10in (25.5cm) high

£2,200-2,800   **K&O**

A Japanese Meiji Satsuma vase, decorated with chrysanthemums below a ryui head and ogee border, eight-character mark.

5¼in (13.5cm) high

£280-340   **K&O**

A Japanese Meiji period Satsuma millefleur bowl, decorated with thousand flowers decoration highlighted with gilt, the base with a seal mark.

3½in (9cm) diam

£40-50   **JN**

A Japanese Meiji period Satsuma porcelain plate, decorated with figures by a riverside with temple buildings, the base with a black seal signature mark.

7½in (19cm) diam

£80-90   **JN**

A Japanese 19thC Meiji Imperial Satsuma teapot and cover.

2½in (6.5cm) high

£1,000-1,400   **HANN**

QUICK REFERENCE - IMARI

● Imari porcelain, named after a town on the island of Kyushu, has two different interpretations; in Japan, Shoki and Ko Imari refer to blue and white wares produced in Arita.

● In the West, Imari refers to export porcelain, usually decorated with an underglaze blue, iron-red and gilding, but may also include green, brown, yellow and turquoise. There are also sub-categories such as green family and Kenjo Imari within Imari wares. Some Imari wares of the late 17thC and 18thC are inscribed with imitation Chinese reign marks.

A Japanese blue and white Arita-style porcelain bowl, the outer glaze apple green.

7in (18cm) diam

£40-60 JN

A Japanese Arita Imari jar and cover, the cover with a Buddhist lion knop.

c1720 *24in (61cm) high*

£320-380 SWO

A Japanese Edo period large Imari vase, decorated with chrysanthemums and birch.

17in (43cm) high

£350-400 JN

A pair of Japanese 18thC Imari porcelain fluted-rim vases, highlighted with gilt.

10½in (26.5cm) high

£250-300 JN

A Japanese 18thC Imari porcelain sake bottle.

7½in (19cm) high

£200-250 JN

A Japanese Edo period Arita blue and white porcelain dish, the base with a single blue ring enclosing a factory seal.

The Edo Period began in 1603 and ended in 1868 with the Meiji Restoration. This was a political revolution, which overthrew the military government, returning Japan to imperial control. The Meiji period ran from 1868 to 1912.

8in (20.5cm) diam

£180-220 JN

A Japanese 19thC Imari porcelain dish, with blue and white bamboo decoration and panels of landscape scenes, with panels of iron-red decoration, the base with a four-character mark.

8¼in (21cm) wide

£300-350 JN

A Japanese Meiji period Fukagawa-style Arita porcelain bottle vase, the top section decorated with Imari palette, the base with an iron-red seal mark.

8in (20.5cm) high

£80-120   JN

A Japanese Meiji period Tokyo School Imari porcelain charger, with ladies underneath hanging foliage having tea.

15¾in (40cm) diam

£150-200   JN

A Japanese Meiji period Imari porcelain dish, the base with a blue seal mark.

11½in (29cm) wide

£50-70   JN

A Japanese 19thC Imari Arita blue and white dish, with arrays of ikebana and prunus blossom borders.

11¾in (30cm) wide

£80-120   JN

A Japanese 20thC Imari porcelain baluster vase, with three claw dragon in relief around neck, unmarked, with associated hardwood cover.

36¼in (92cm) high

£200-250   APAR

A pair of Japanese Edo period Kakiemon-style dishes, blue fuku mark, one dish has a riveted repair to the rim, the other with a minor chip and some nicks to the rim.

Made predominantly between 1603 and 1867, Kakiemon porcelain is a type of Arita ware made by the Sakaida family. Kakiemon ware includes small dishes, bottles, bowl and vases, often in octagonal or square shapes.

9½in (24cm) wide

£700-800   BELL

A pair of Japanese Meiji period Nabeshima fan-shaped porcelain dishes.

Between the late 17thC and c1870, Nabeshima porcelain, named after the Nabeshima clan, was produced in the Okawachi region, north of Arita. It was made for the ruling Shogun (military ruler) and feudal lords.

9in (23cm) wide

£350-400   JN

A Japanese cloisonné enamel charger with central scene of bird perched on cherry blossom tree, hairlines and surface scratches.

First made in China in the 14thC, cloisonné is a technique and the resulting ware, in which enamel is fired into compartments (or 'cloisons') made from metal wires fixed onto a metal surface.

14½in (37cm) diam

£75-85   **APAR**

A Japanese 19thC cloisonné enamel dish, with flowers and birds.

12in (30.5cm) diam

£55-65   **JN**

A Japanese Meiji/Taisho period cloisonné dragon fish vase, by Ando, with a dragon fish crashing through waves of water, the rims silvered, the base with the Ando factory mark.

9in (23cm) high

£300-400   **JN**

A Japanese early 20thC cloisonné vase, of musen shippo style with a blossoming prunus tree.

7¼in (18.5cm) high

£220-280   **SWO**

A pair of Japanese white ground cloisonné enamel vases, with coloured bamboo.

7½in (19cm) high

£180-220   **JN**

A Japanese Meiji period cloisonné vase, with scrolling vine and flora, possibly gold wire.

9in (23cm) high

£110-150   **JN**

A Japanese Meiji period cloisonné vase, with wired decoration of birds among native flora, mounted with silver/silvered mounts.

4¾in (12cm) high

£80-120   **JN**

A Japanese Meiji/Taisho period cloisonné temple vase, by Ando, with temples among clouds in moonlight, the moon silver, the rims silver mounted, the base with the Ando factory mark.

9¾in (24.5cm) high

£500-600   **JN**

ASIAN WORKS OF ART

QUICK REFERENCE - NETSUKE

● Netsuke are decorative toggles used to secure possessions, including pipes and tobacco pouches, to traditional Japanese clothing, which didn't feature pockets. By the early 20thC, with the spread of Western dress, these items became obsolete.

● Netsuke were predominantly made from wood and ivory, with some inlaid or lacquered. Designs vary, with the natural world, mythology and religion acting as inspiration.

A Japanese 19thC mask netsuke, of a long-nosed man, pale boxwood, unsigned with kaô.

Peter E. Müller Japanese Mask Collection no.12.

2in (5cm) high

£1,500-2,000   **MAB**

A Japanese 19thC mask netsuke of Beshimi, pale boxwood, unsigned.

Peter E. Müller Japanese Mask Collection no.71.

1½in (4cm) high

£550-600   **MAB**

A Japanese early 20thC mask netsuke of Okina, by Ryumin, dark stained boxwood, signed 'Ryumin saku'.

Ryumin and Hozan have characteristics in common.

2in (5cm) high

£1,500-2,000   **MAB**

A Japanese 19thC mask netsuke of Shikami, stained boxwood with gold lacquer teeth and eyes, unsigned.

Peter E. Müller Japanese Mask Collection no.62.

1¾in (4.5cm) high

£800-900   **MAB**

A Japanese mid-19thC mask netsuke of karasu-tengu, by Jogetsu, dark wood, signed 'Jogetsu to'.

Peter E. Müller Japanese Mask Collection no.219.

1½in (4cm) high

£800-900   **MAB**

A Japanese Edo/Meiji period wood netsuke, carved as a puppy, with the eyes inlaid in horn, signed 'Ransen'.

1½in (4cm) high

£850-950   **WW**

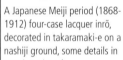

A Japanese Meiji period (1868-1912) four-case lacquer inrō, decorated in takaramaki-e on a nashiji ground, some details in aogai, unsigned.

2½in (6.5cm) high

£550-650   **WW**

A pair of Japanese early 20thC bronze rats.

3in (7.5cm) wide

£350-400   **CHEF**

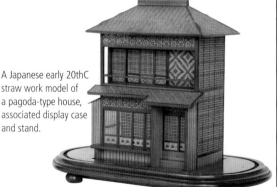

A Japanese early 20thC straw work model of a pagoda-type house, associated display case and stand.

16½in (42cm) high

£500-600   **FLD**

A Japanese Meiji/Taisho era silver vase, in the form of a koro, decorated in relief and kebori with sparrows and a boat on a river, incised signature.

5in (12.5cm) high

£1,500-2,000   **DN**

A cold-painted bronze model, by Franz Bergman, of an Arab riding a camel, foundry stamp, with part of a Nam-Greb signature, some paint loss to the rear leg.

Bergman signed his bronzes with either a letter 'B' in an urn-shaped cartouche or 'Nam Greb' – Bergman in reverse.

5in (12.5cm) high

£800-900   **GORL**

An Austrian cold-painted bronze coffee seller, in the style of Franz Bergman.

9in (23cm) high

£800-900   **BRI**

An Austrian cold-painted bronze model of a Levantine carpet seller, by Franz Bergman, the underside inscribed with a 'B' and 'GESCH' within an urn in the maquette.

c1900   *6in (15cm) long*

£650-750   **DN**

An Austrian cold-painted cast group, by Franz Bergman, circular mark.

4½in (11.5cm) high

£700-800   **JN**

An Austrian cold-painted bronze dancer, by Franz Bergman, with hinged skirt, barefoot on a draped carpet base, foundry mark.

7¼in (18.5cm) high

£1,500-2,000   **HT**

QUICK REFERENCE - AUSTRIAN BRONZES

- From the late 19thC onwards, miniature and table-top bronze figures were created in Vienna, Austria. Around 50 manufacturers were present in Vienna at the time. Vienna bronzes were considered luxury pieces that quickly attracted the attention of collectors. They depicted life-like subjects including pets, farm, forest or exotic animals, and travel-inspired subjects that reflected aspects of the Orient.
- Vienna bronzes required a high level of craftsmanship. The casting moulds that were used to produce the bronzes were designed by artists who simply sold their work to bronze manufacturers and had no further influence on the production of the figures. Sometimes, a bronze figure was cast in separate parts and then welded together.
- Cold-painting, one of the main elements of Austrian bronzes, is a technique that involved applying several layers of lead-based paint to the bronze. The cold-painting determined to a significant extent the quality and desirability of the final piece.
- Franz Bergman was the most well-known maker of the day. He took over from his father and was the main instigator of the Vienna bronze boom. Carl Kauba is another collectable bronze maker who is perhaps not as well-known as Bergman. His most impressive pieces depict Native Americans and cowboys.

An Austrian cold-painted cast group, of two Arab men on a rug.

7in (17.5cm) high

£600-700   **JN**

AUSTRIAN BRONZES

A Franz Bergman cold-painted bronze figure group, cast as four Arabic boys, on a palm tree, cast maker's mark '4888'.

c1910   *9.75in (25cm) wide*

£3,000-4,000   **PC**

An erotic bronze study of an owl and nude, by Franz Bergman, the owl with sprung door, opening to reveal a gilt bronze nude, signed 'Namgreb' in the bronze, stamped 'B' within urn symbol.

7¾in (19.5cm) high

£4,000-5,000   **PC**

An Austrian cold-painted cast man reading a book.

4¼in (11cm) wide

£850-950   **JN**

An Austrian cold-painted cast man, smoking a hookah pipe.

2¼in (5.5cm) wide

£250-300   **JN**

An Austrian cold-painted bronze Arab man sitting on a prayer mat.

4¼in (11cm) wide

£140-200   **LOCK**

An Austrian Bergman-style cold-painted bronze figurine of a water carrier.

8in (20.5cm) high

£400-500   **BRI**

A late 19thC to early 20thC Austrian cold-painted bronze lamp, with a palm tree above a partial stone building with an arch and small glazed door and two Moors with prayer rugs, the interior accommodating a light bulb, wired for electricity.

15in (38cm) high

£700-800   **L&T**

QUICK REFERENCE - FRANZ BERGMAN

● Franz Bergman (1861-1939) was one of the most important makers of bronze figures in Vienna from the end of the 19thC. The Bergman factory was founded in 1860 by his father, also called Franz Bergman, (1838-94), and was taken over by Franz Bergman junior after his father's death.

● Bergman was one of the key instigators of the Vienna bronze boom in the late 19thC and early 20thC. His factory produced a range of bronze sculptures, including Oriental figures, birds and animals, and a line of erotic models. The bronzes were highly detailed and cold-painted with vibrant colours.

● Bergman bronzes were stamped with a capital 'B' within a twin-handled urn or vase. Like many other Austrian bronzes of the time, Bergman models were often inscribed 'Geschutzt', German for 'protected' or 'copyrighted'. Erotic and other figures were sometimes marked 'Namgreb', which is Bergman backwards.

A cold-painted bronze cockerel, by Franz Bergman, impressed amphora mark, '4263' and 'GESCHUTZT'.

6¾in (17cm) high

£2,000-2,500   L&T

A late 19thC cold-painted bronze inkwell, by Franz Bergman, stamped 'GESCHUTZT' and initialed 'F B'.

2½in (6.5cm) high

£750-850   HUTC

A cold-painted bronze kingfisher, by Franz Bergman, on veined marble dish, impressed marks to cast, broken at ankles.

4¾in (12cm) long

£350-450   WW

A cold-painted bronze bird's nest, by Franz Bergman, stamped 'Geschutzt'.

6¼in (16cm) wide

£250-300   WHP

A 19thC cold-painted bronze inkwell and pen holder, by Franz Bergman, a starling on a branch, stamped 'Geschutzt', numbered '459'.

4¼in (11cm) high

£300-400   HUTC

An early 20thC Austrian cold-painted bronze model of an owl, in the manner of Bergman, on a marble plinth.

6in (15cm) high

£500-600   WW

A late 19thC Austrian cold-painted bronze sculpture, attributed to Franz Bergman, on marble base, back of tail stamped 'GAZSHUTZT 4268'.

7½in (19cm) high

£850-950   HUTC

An early 20thC Austrian cold-painted bronze bird and nest, in the manner of Bergman, stamped 'Geschutzt, Depose'.

4¼in (11cm) wide

£300-350   MOR

AUSTRIAN BRONZES

An early 20thC Austrian cold-painted bronze robin, stamped to the tail 'GESCHUTZT'.

2¼in (6cm) long

£180-220   FLD

A late 19thC cold-painted bronze sculpture, by Franz Bergman, formed as a partridge with three young, stamped 'GESCHUTZT' and 'DEPOSE' to tail feathers and base.

2½in (6.5cm) high

£750-850   HUTC

An early 20thC large Austrian cold-painted bronze setter, by Franz Bergman, impressed maker's marks, numbers and marked 'GESCHUTZT'.

11¾in (30cm) long

£1,500-2,000   L&T

A CLOSER LOOK AT A BERGMAN BRONZE BIRD

The bronze is superbly and naturalistically modelled. ——

The paint appears to be original. These figues have often been repainted.

The base also appears to be original. There are fixing screws extending beneath the birds feet, showing it was clearly designed to have a base.

The bronze is stamped to the underside of the tail feathers with the 'B' inside an urn, for the Bergman manufactory.

An Austrian cold-painted bronze model of a game bird, by Franz Bergman, on a wooden base, stamped 'B' within urn.

c1900   *10½in (26.5cm) high*

£2,500-3,000   DN

A late 19thC Austrian cold-painted bronze bulldog, by Franz Bergman, with teeth exposed.

6in (15cm) long

£350-400   HANN

A late 19thC cold-painted bronze inkwell, attributed to Franz Bergman, of a recumbent dog, with hinged head, stamped '503 Geschutzt' and with 'Déposé' stamp and registration mark to base.

3½in (9cm) high

£650-750   HUTC

An Austrian cold-painted bronze setter.

9½in (24cm) long

£350-400   BRI

A late 19thC Austrian cold-painted bronze bulldog.

7in (18cm) long

£350-400   HANN

A late 19thC cold-painted bronze bulldog, paint finish dirty.

7¼in (18.5cm) long

£650-750   GORL

A 19thC Austrian cold-painted bronze bulldog, stamped 'VIENNA ST. B'.

4in (10cm) high

£400-500   HUTC

An Austrian cold-painted cast bronze dog inkwell, with hinged head, Victorian registration stamp.

7in (18cm) long

£400-500   JN

An early 20thC Austrian cold-painted bronze cat, by Franz Bergman, foundry mark, light wear.

3in (7.5cm) wide

£300-350   APAR

A 19thC cold-painted bronze stoat, attributed to Franz Bergman, stamped 'Geschutzt' and numbered '2865'.

2½in (6.5cm) high

£650-750   HUTC

An early 20thC Austrian cold-painted bronze model of a hare, on onyx dished base.

4¾in (12cm) diam

£300-350   WW

An early 20thC Austrian cold-painted bronze lizard.

7¼in (18.5cm) long

£750-850   WW

A late 19thC to early 20thC Austrian cold-painted bronze snake.

11¾in (30cm) long

£550-650   L&T

AUTOMOBILIA

QUICK REFERENCE - AUTOMOBILIA

QUICK REFERENCE - AUTOMOBILIA

- Automobilia can refer to any motoring memorabilia. There is a market for car badges, fuel cans, scale models, car accessories, instruction manuals, car mascots and much more.
- Popular from the 1920s to 1950s, car mascots are small sculptural models fitted to the front of a car, often to the radiator grille. They were chiefly made of glass or metal, usually zinc, pewter or aluminium. They declined in popularity in the 1960s due to safety restrictions.
- While some car mascots were added by owners to personalise their cars, many were produced by car manufacturers and fitted as standard to new models. Manufacturers commissioned sculptors and designers to create mascots to become part of the company's brand.

A bronze model of a hare, made for an Alvis car, with the remains of painted decoration.

4½in (11.5cm) high

£150-200   LC

A Bentley 'Flying B' nickel-silver mascot, of the type used with 4½-, 6½- and 8-litre models, with the 'B' insignia, detailed wings, a rusting threaded mounting stud, mounted.

8½in (21.5cm) wide

£850-950   LC

A 'Flying Hornet' accessory mascot, red glass eyes, tooling to the wings, separately mounted wings and legs in the correct method, nickel-plated, display mounted, inscribed 'Asprey'.

7¾in (19.5cm) wide

£750-850   LC

A 1920s to early 1930s Casimir Brau 'Leaping Gazelle' mascot, nickel-plated on bronze, signed 'C. Brau', stamped 'Depose', finish a little rubbed.

6in (15cm) long

£1,200-1,600   LC

A rare Bentley 'Icarus' nickel-plated mascot, designed and inscribed by F. Gordon Crosby, believed to have been commissioned by W.O. Bentley as an alternative to the 'Flying B' design.

Frederick Gordon Crosby (1885-1943) was a self-taught British automotive artist and illustrator. He worked for 'Autocar' magazine.

1920s   *5½in (14cm) high*

£1,800-2,200   LC

A 1920s to early 1930s Casimir Brau 'Leaping Lion' mascot, nickel-plated on bronze, signed 'C. Brau', stamped 'Depose', finish a little worn.

This is one of the popular set of Casimir Brau-designed leaping animal mascots.

8in (20.5cm) long

£1,300-1,600   LC

A 'Leaping Jaguar' mascot, often fitted to Jaguar SS100 cars, chromium-plated, mounted on a period Jaguar threaded radiator cap, usually retailed by Desmo.

This mascot did not find favour with William Lyons and by December 1937 F. Gordon Crosby had designed a new mascot for the marque, making these mascots largely redundant.

1930s   *7½in (19cm) long*

£120-160   LC

A John Hassall (1868-1948) 'Policeman' brass car mascot, with ceramic moveable head, signed 'Hassall'.

5¼in (13.5cm) high

£120-180   DUK

A 'Running Hare' mascot, by Augustine & Emile Lejeune, nickel-plated, in German silver, with fur detail and facial expression, with 'AEL' and 'Copyright' engraved at the rear, display mounted.

3½in (9cm) high

£400-500   LC

A Telcote Pup 'Bonzo' mascot, by Augustine & Emile Lejeune, depicting the cartoon character, a hollow-cast bronze body, with diamond-cut red glass eyes, 'Bonzo' stamped on the side, 'Telcote Pup' impressed in his collar and 'AEL Copyright' at the rear, the larger of two sizes available in the 1920s, not mounted.

Augustine and Emile Lejeune established AE Lejeune in 1910. The company produced ornamental bronze items, including car mascots. The couple's son took over in 1933, renaming the company Louis Lejeune Ltd. It was then bought by Sir David Hughes in 1978 and passed to his son in 1998.

mid-1920s   *5½in (14cm) long*

£950-1,100   LC

A Rolls-Royce 'Spirit of Ecstasy' mascot, as mounted to 1914 40/50hp motorcars, in German silver, embossed 'Rolls-Royce Ltd. Feb 6 1911', original mounting stud.

£2,000-2,500   LC

A Rolls-Royce trade gift engine-turned and decorated desk inkwell, with a miniature Rolls-Royce mascot on the lid, mounted onto an onyx base with a pen holder and chamfered corners, bun feet and brass base.

6in (15cm) long

£300-350   LC

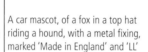

A car mascot, of a fox in a top hat riding a hound, with a metal fixing, marked 'Made in England' and 'LL' for Louis Lejeune.

5in (12.5cm) long

£320-400   LC

A Sabino vaseline glass 'Leaping Gazelle' mascot, mounted on a nickel-silver base, intaglio 'Sabino Paris' on the side, small chip on the foot.

4in (10cm) high

£250-350   LC

A 'Cock-A-Snook' car mascot, sometimes called a 'Devil' mascot, of a satyr-like figurine with original red enamel finish and black tail, designed to be fitted to the rear of a vehicle, display mounted.

1920s

£350-450   LC

A chrome-plated car mascot, of a horse jumping a fence, with a screw attachment to the base.

6¼in (16cm) long

£100-150   LC

AUTOMOBILIA

A seven-colour chrome-plated Brooklands Automobile Racing Club full member's badge, designed by F. Gordon Crosby, with the member's access bridge, numbered '979'.

1930   *5in (12.5cm) high*

£650-750   **LC**

A first issue type-1 Circle of 19thC Motorists badge, with enamels within an escutcheon, with '1900' intaglio at the apex, with a winged wheel supporter, with 'MEMBER' raised and a dashboard mount, plated in nickel-silver, the reverse inscribed 'Claude Gouldesbrough', in distressed condition.

The Circle of 19thC Motorists, founded in 1927, was the most exclusive of English Motoring Clubs, where to be a member you were required to prove that you had driven a car extensively before the turn of the 20thC. The number of members never exceeded 220, and with the passing of time the membership reduced to a point where the last meeting was a Memorial Lunch in 1952. While most of the members names are recorded, Claude Gouldesbrough does not appear to be on any known lists of members.

1927   *4¼in (11cm) high*

£200-250   **LC**

A St Christopher car badge, by J.R. Gaunt London, enamel on chrome, 'Made in England'.

£35-45   **PSA**

A J.R. Gaunt of London chrome and enamel car badge, on original card with details to the reverse of the card, boxed.

£40-50   **APAR**

A pair of B.R.C. 'Alpha' self-contained brass Boa-Rodrigues & Company acetylene gas headlamps, factory-made for Maison Labourdette, with parabolic nickel-silver reflectors with mirror lenses, both numbered '135', the generators retain their gas taps, carbide of calcium cylinders and bayonet locking.

1903-10   *14in (35.5cm) high*

£2,500-3,000   **LC**

A self-contained German-manufactured motorcycle acetylene gas lamp, nickel-plated, with front lens cover, shatter-proof front glass, burner and component parts, with a rear storage cover, in working order.

c1908

£250-300   **LC**

A pair of Lucas 'Kings Own' side lamps, in black enamel and with nickel-plated fittings, marked 'F141'.

8¼in (21cm) high

£100-150   **LC**

An early 20thC Dietz of New York brass lamp, with manufacturer's and patent stamps, general wear.

13½in (34.5cm) high

£90-120   **APAR**

A pair of early 20thC brass car lamps, each with two sides with bevelled glass panels.

11in (28cm) long

£90-120   FLD

A Cicca of France four-trumpet car horn, no.9511, nickel-plated.

c1920s   26¾in (68cm) long

£250-300   DUK

A Bentley chromed radiator hip flask, by Ruddspeed Ltd., no.909777.

8in (20.5cm) high

£400-500   FLD

A Rolls-Royce floor mat, purported to have come from Rolls-Royce Head Office, inscribed 'Sunlight', rubber backed with small 'studs' for grip.

45in (114.5cm) long

£70-80   APAR

A Birglow 'Auto Single Hand' indicator, fitted to the right-hand side of a car, with a multi-directional control for signalling.

£250-300   LC

A Lucas Ltd. polished brass 'Motor Oiler', no.38, discus-shaped, as used in fitted tool boxes.

£110-150   LC

A Ford 'Moto-Lita' steering wheel.

13½in (34.5cm) diam

£55-65   APAR

'MOTORING ANNUAL', third edition, with advertisements, the cover rubbed and a loose spine.

1903

£65-75   LC

AUTOMOBILIA

An MG Car Company promotional nickle-plated vesta case, inscribed 'Distinctive Coachwork Designs', with a profile of a c1926 14/28 MG bullnose Salonette on the front, and 'The Morris Garages, Oxford' and armorial on the reverse, signs of wear.

£180-220   LC

An unusual flip sign, cast in alloy, with a hinging half-moon shape for altering the wording to, 'WAITING LIMITED TO 20MINS IN ANY HOUR'.

20in (51cm) diam

£250-300   LC

A cast alloy sign, single-sided, with cat's eye glasses, one missing, some original paint.

27½in (70cm) wide

£180-220   LC

A vintage 'Ferrari' painted wood wall sign.

71in (180.5cm) long

£250-350   DUK

An oil on canvas motor racing scene, by Dion Pears, showing the 1930 Le Mans with Sir Henry 'Tim' Birkin driving the Bentley 4.5-litre Blower being overtaken by Woolf Barnato in the Bentley Speed 6, signed, framed, damaged.

British artist, Dion Pears (1929-85) was born in Richmond, UK. His paintings were commissioned by car manufacturers, including Renault, Bentley and Ferrari, and motor racing drivers.

35½in (90cm) wide

£800-1,000   APAR

A Sadler OKT42 novelty teapot, so-called 'Mabel Lucie Attwell' example, with a transfer underglaze design, impressed 'Made in England - Registered No 820236', and a six-hole strainer and a seven bar radiator grille variant, with orange hubs and cockpit outline.

1930s

£250-300   LC

An Austin pedal car, restored with correct parts, triple chrome plating in Sheffield, some rust.

1950s   60¾in (154.5cm) long

£1,800-2,200   APAR

QUICK REFERENCE - BOOKS

● The first print run of a first edition will always be the most valuable. A copy from the first print run of a first edition of a hardback book is called a 'true' first edition. Paperback first editions tend to fetch lower prices than hardback first editions. The quantity of the first print run of a book affects the value of its first editions. Iconic titles may well be sought-after, but more obscure works or those from an author's early career, which were printed in smaller quantities, are often more expensive. An author's signature often adds value to a first edition. To identify a first edition, check that the publishing date and copyright date match and confirm the original publishing date and publisher with a reliable source. Also, look for the number '1' in the series of numbers on the imprint/copyright page. The first editions that fetch the highest prices are undamaged and come with the original dust jacket.

Buchan, John, 'The Dancing Floor', first edition, published by Hodder and Stoughton, London, 8vo., blue cloth, dust jacket repaired and soiled, some foxing, 311 pages, four leaves of adverts.
1926   *7½in (19cm) high*
£350-450   **L&T**

Burnett, W.R., 'Little Caesar', first edition, published by Lincoln MacVeagh, The Dial Press, original blue cloth, in original issue pictorial dust jacket, small scattered chips, with the '$2.00' price at head of front flap.
1929
£5,500-6,000   **FRE**

Blixen, Karen, 'Out of Africa', first edition, published by Putnam, London, 8vo, original red cloth gilt, a little foxing, facsimile dust jacket.
1937
£350-450   **L&T**

Chandler, Raymond, 'The Long Good-Bye', first edition, first printing, preceding the first American edition by a few months, dust jacket designed by Fritz Wegner, slight foxing, 8vo.
1953
£120-160   **DN**

Churchill, Sir Winston Spencer, 'My African Journey', published by Hodder and Stoughton, London, first edition, 8vo., frontispiece, 3 maps, 46 leaves of plates with 60 photographs, original red pictorial cloth gilt, a little foxing, slight fading to covers and spine, endpapers.
1908
£350-450   **L&T**

Dickens, Charles, 'A Christmas Carol', first edition, later issue with 'Stave One', title printed in red and blue, original cloth, lower joint splitting, with crack across, slightly worn at extremities, Chapman and Hall, London.
1843
£1,800-2,200   **DN**

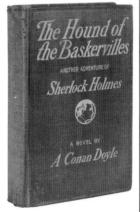

Doyle, A. Conan, 'The Hound of the Baskervilles', first American edition, third state, published by McClure, Phillips & Co., New York, 12mo., Green & Gibson A26 c.ii.
1902
£140-180   **FRE**

Forster, E.M., 'A Passage To India', first edition, 8vo., published by Edward Arnold, page tops foxed, spine dulled, slight chipping to corners, original cloth, three-page advertisement at end.
1924
£4,000-4,500   **BELL**

BOOKS

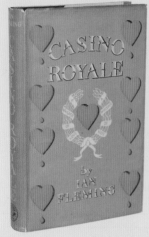

Fleming, Ian, 'Casino Royale', first edition, published by Jonathan Cape, London, first issue without Sunday Times Review, 8vo., dust jacket, not price clipped, inscribed by Ian Fleming, reading 'Alastair, from the Author - Read & Burn', slight wear to jacket spine and corners.

The Alastair in the inscription has been identified in pencil as Alastair McKinley. This matches other works signed by Fleming.
1953
£55,000-60,000   L&T

Fleming, Ian, 'Goldfinger', first edition, published by Jonathan Cape, London, 8vo., signed 'Best wishes, Honor Blackman, Pussy Galore'.
1959
£1,500-2,000   L&T

Fleming, Ian, 'Live and Let Die', first edition, published by Jonathan Cape, London, first issue, inscribed 'To Robert Bartlett from the Author 1954', some slight edge-wear.

Robert Bartlett was the artist who provided the pencil sketch of Fleming for the rear cover of the dust jacket of 'Casino Royale'. Bartlett was a fellow officer of Fleming's during World War II, both men serving in the Naval Intelligence Division.
1954
£30,000-35,000   L&T

Fleming, Ian, 'From Russia, with Love', published by Jonathan Cape, first edition, first impression, 8vo., original black cloth with gun and rose motif, dust jacket with chipping, some foxing stains, small closed tear, light internal marks.
1957
£600-700   L&T

Fleming, Ian, 'For Your Eyes Only', first edition, published by Jonathan Cape, London, 8vo.
1960
£750-850   L&T

Fleming, Ian, 'The Spy Who Loved Me', first edition, published by Jonathan Cape, London, 8vo., original black cloth with silver dagger motif, dust jacket not price clipped.
1962
£350-450   L&T

Fleming, Ian, 'Diamonds are Forever', first edition, published by Jonathan Cape, London, first impression with 'Boofy' for 'Dolly' on p.134, 8vo.
1956
£2,500-3,000   L&T

Fleming, Ian, 'The Man with the Golden Gun', first edition, published by Jonathan Cape, London, with 18s. net price on inner flap, minor discolouration to golden gun motif.

Only around 940 copies of the first issue of 'The Man with the Golden Gun' were produced before the cost of adding the golden gun motif to each upper board became too great. It is consequently rare to find a copy of this work, particularly one including its intact dust wrapper.
1965
£5,000-6,000   L&T

Golding, William, 'Lord of the Flies', first edition, published by Jonathan Cape, London, 8vo., original cloth, some browning, spotting and small tears, price intact '12s 6d', bookplate of Desmond Young.
1954

£2,500-3,000   LC

Grahame, Kenneth, 'The Wind in the Willows', first edition, published by Methuen & Co., half title, frontispiece by W. Graham Robertson, 8vo.
1908

£1,200-1,600   LC

QUICK REFERENCE - THE NEGRO TRAVELERS' GREEN BOOK

- This book was once a travel guide for African-American families, from a time when long-distance travel and finding lodging and gasoline would be a cause for apprehension. Friendly service stations, hotels, nightclubs and restaurants are arranged by state across the country.
- The cover of this edition states 'Carry your Green Book with you . . . You may need it!' This copy was clearly used by its original owners. The entries for the YMCA in Manhattan and a hotel at Niagara Falls are underlined, and a three-page article on parks has several sections underlined as well, particularly regarding national parks' non-discriminatory policies – Yellowstone and Mesa Verde are marked as potential destinations. The last 'Green Book' was printed in 1966. The recent award-winning film 'Green Book' features a copy of the book as a plot point.
- It was first published in 1936 and publication stopped in 1966. This copy is a relatively late spring 1958 issue, and sold for much more than expected.
- Victor Hugo Green, a New York mailman, launched the book, which grew to cover most of North America, including parts of Canada, Mexico, the Caribbean and Bermuda.

Hemingway, Ernest, 'A Farewell to Arms', first trade edition, first issue without legal disclaimer, published by Charles Scribner's Sons, New York, 8vo., some tears and small nicks to spine panel tips.
1929

£1,000-1,300   SWA

Ransome, Arthur, 'We Didn't Mean to go to Sea', first edition, published by Jonathan Cape, London, 8vo., original cloth, dust jacket, not price clipped.
1937

£200-250   L&T

Green, Victor H. (Editor), 'The Negro Travelers' Green Book', original coloured wrappers, original owner's signature on front wrapper, worn and detached, moderate damp staining, vertical fold, staple holes in upper corner, other minor wear.
1958

£17,000-20,000   SWA

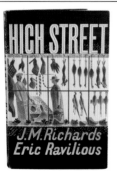

Richards, J.M., 'High Street', first edition, illustrated by Eric Ravilious, published by Country Life, London, printed at the Curwen Press, with 24 colour lithographic plates, woodcut vignette title page, publisher's pictorial boards.
1938

£2,400-3,000   HAN

Sassoon, Siegfried, 'Memoirs of a Fox-Hunting Man', published by Faber and Faber, London, with illustrations by William Nicholson, no.139 of 300 copies, signed by the author and artist, seven full-page plates and other illustrations, original full vellum, top edge gilt, others uncut, 8vo.
1929

£500-600   LC

Wells, H.G., 'The Country Of The Blind And Other Stories', published by Thomas Nelson & Sons, seemingly first edition, in rare original dust jacket, mark at base of front cover.
c1911

£4,000-4,500   CUTW

Yeats, William Butler, 'Poems', first edition, published by T. Fisher Unwin, London, one of 750 copies, half title, decorated title page, tissue guard, original cloth decorated gilt, untrimmed, spine dulled, 8vo.
1895

£300-400   LC

Artzybasheff, Boris, 'As I See', first edition, published by Dodd, Mead & Company, New York, 4to., in original dust jacket.
1954
£65-85   FRE

Brown, Margaret Wise, 'Goodnight, Moon', first edition, published by Harper & Brothers, New York, oblong 8vo., illustrated by Clement Hurd, lacking dust jacket, minor wear to spine.
1947
£950-1,100   FRE

Brown, Palmer, 'The Silver Nutmeg', first edition, published by Harper & Brothers, New York, 8vo., 138 pages, original dust jacket, price clipped, light toning to text.
1956
£120-160   FRE

Brunhoff, Jean de, 'Histoire de Babar le petit elephant', first edition, published by Editions du Jardin de Modes, Paris, first issue, with no elephant to copyright page, illustrated in colour, moderate wear, boards lightly rubbed.

The adventures of Babar, known as the most famous Frenchman in the world, continue to this day.
1931
£500-600   FRE

Burton, Virginia Lee, 'Katy and the Big Snow', first edition, published by Houghton Mifflin Company, Boston, oblong 8vo.
1943
£60-70   FRE

Burton, Virginia Lee, 'Mike Mulligan and His Steam Shovel', first edition, published by Houghton Mifflin Company, Boston, oblong 8vo., inscribed by Burton on front free endpaper 'Greetings from Virginia Lee Burton'.
1939
£450-550   FRE

Dahl, Roald, 'Charlie and the Chocolate Factory', first edition, first issue, published by Knopf, New York, illustrated by Joseph Scindelman, 8vo.
1964
£900-1,100   FRE

Dulac, Edmund (Illustrator), 'Sinbad the Sailor & Other Stories from the Arabian Nights', published by Hodder & Stoughton, some wear and dirt to exterior, some foxing.
£120-180   APAR

Grahame, Kenneth, 'Dream Days', published by John Lane, The Bodley Head, London and New York, illustrated by Maxfield Parrish, 8vo., 228 pages, without adverts at rear, spine stamped in gilt with 'John Lane Company', pictorial endpapers, markings in ink at heads of endpapers.
c1902
£110-160   FRE

Johnson, Crockett, 'Harold and the Purple Crayon', first edition, published by Harper & Brothers, New York, with Library of Congress catalog card no.55-7683 to title page, in early issue dust jacket with no price to top of front flap, with code '30-60/No.5671A', some light foxing.

One of several variants of the first edition of this book.
1955
£450-550 FRE

Lang, Andrew, 'The Red Fairy Book', first edition, published by David McKay Company, Philadelphia, large 8vo., illustrated by Gustaf Tenggren, with eight colour plates.
1924
£90-120 FRE

MacDonald, George, 'At the Back of the North Wind', first edition, published by David McKay, Philadelphia, 4to., illustrated by Jessie Willcox Smith, signed by Smith, very lightly worn.
1919
£110-160 FRE

Milne, A.A., 'The House At Pooh Corner', first trade edition, published by Methuen & Co. Ltd., London, small 8vo., illustrated with frontispiece and text illustrations, ownership signature on half title, very lightly rubbed.
1928
£200-300 FRE

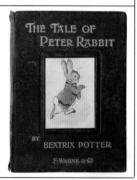

Milne, A.A., 'The House at Pooh Corner', first edition, published by Methuen & Co. Ltd., London, illustrated by Ernest W. Shepard. first printing, 8vo., spine faded and slightly cocked.
1928
£400-500 FRE

Potter, Beatrix, 'The Tale of Peter Rabbit', published by Frederick Warne and Co., London, first trade edition, fourth impression, with owner's inscription to half title, pale grey leaf-patterned endpapers, colour pastedown illustration to upper board, colour frontispiece, and a further 30 colour illustrations throughout.
1902
£360-400 HAN

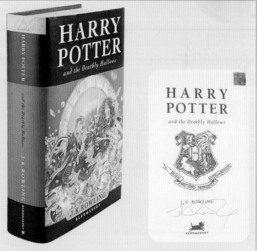

Rowling, J.K., 'Harry Potter and the Goblet of Fire', published by Bloomsbury, signed by Rowling on the dedication page, with golden ticket for the 'Hogwart's Express Book Tour' signing event in York laid in.
2000
£850-1,000 HT

Rowling, J.K., 'Harry Potter and The Deathly Hallows', first edition, published by Bloomsbury, London, 8vo., signed on title page by Rowling and with small holograph sticker dated '21/07/07' at top of title page, original cloth, dust wrapper.
2007
£1,800-2,200 L&T

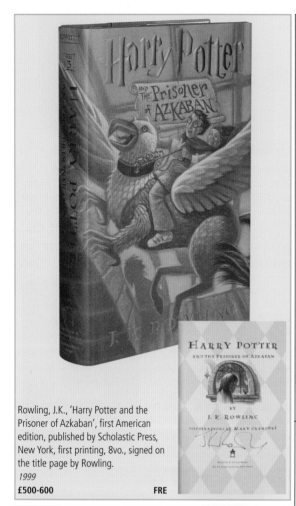

Rowling, J.K., 'The Tales of Beedle the Bard', first edition, for Children's High Level Group, 8vo., with hologram sticker to front marbled free endpaper, presentation copy inscribed 'Christmas 2008. To Di, with lots of love, J.K. Rowling (Jo) x' on half title, original brown calf binding embellished with metal skull, corner pieces and clasp incorporating replica blue gemstones, maroon morocco bag, with envelope of Collector's Edition Prints containing ten prints, housed in a velvet-lined brown calf box, lettered and decorated on upper cover, with the publisher's lightly rubbed and creased white card sleeve printed in black to the upper panel 'This Side Up'.

J.K. Rowling produced a deluxe copy of 'The Tales of Beedle the Bard' in aid of the charity Children's High Level Group (now Lumos). Rowling signed 100 copies of this book and they were randomly distributed to buyers on Amazon.com, who were surprised to receive a special copy of the book in the post. This book is an out-of-series copy, signed by Rowling.

2008
£5,500-6,000   L&T

Rowling, J.K., 'Harry Potter and the Prisoner of Azkaban', first American edition, published by Scholastic Press, New York, first printing, 8vo., signed on the title page by Rowling.
1999
£500-600   FRE

Schulz, Charles M., 'A Charlie Brown Christmas', first edition, published by The World Publishing Company, Cleveland and New York, square 8vo.
1965
£350-450   FRE

Sendak, Maurice, 'In the Night Kitchen', first edition, published by Harper & Row, New York, small 4to., lightly worn.
1970
£60-80   FRE

Seuss, Dr (Theodor Seuss Geisel), 'Green Eggs and Ham', first edition, Younger and Hirsch 27, published by Beginner Books, INC., New York, second state with the '50 Word Vocabulary' box printed on front panel of dust jacket, 8vo., 62 pages.
1960
£180-220   FRE

Travers, P.L., 'Mary Poppins Opens the Door', first edition, published by Reynal & Hitchcock, New York, 8vo. 239 pages, signed by Travers.
1943
£400-500   FRE

Wagner, Richard, 'The Rhinegold & the Valkyrie', first trade edition, published by William Heinemann and Doubleday, Page & Co., London and New York, illustrated by Arthur Rackham, translated by Margaret Armour, 8vo., 161 pages.
£600-700   FRE

QUICK REFERENCE - TEA CADDIES

- Tea first came to Europe in the early 17thC, but was imported in large chests and sold loose, so buyers required a smaller method of storage. Early tea caddies were made of European or Chinese porcelain, with the lid used as a measure.
- Most tea caddies on the market are from the 18thC and 19thC, when it was common to lock up tea to prevent spillage or theft by servants. Tea was still a relative luxury, meaning that many tea caddies were produced to high standards and made of expensive materials such as ivory, tortoiseshell and exotic woods.
- It is worth checking the condition of boxes carefully. Replaced locks, panels or hinges can reduce the value. Prestigious makers or high-quality locks often add value.

A two division tea caddy, with silk embroidered panels, one glass panel to lid is broken, the silk panels are heavily stained.

c1780s   *7½in (19cm) long*

£700-800   **APAR**

A Chinese 19thC export scarlet, gilt and black lacquer tea caddy, with pewter twin-lidded interior, lacquer rubbed, one foot replaced.

10in (25.5cm) wide

£500-600   **BELL**

A 19thC large inlaid mahogany tea caddy, with marquetry detail to the cover 'Tea', with two canisters centred by a later mixing bowl.

13½in (34.5cm) wide

£150-200   **FLD**

An early Victorian coromandel and mother-of-pearl inlaid tea caddy, the lid enclosing two dome coromandel lidded tea boxes with central reservoir set with associated bowl.

13¾in (35cm) wide

£120-160   **APAR**

An early Victorian rosewood tea caddy, with two rosewood veneered lidded tea boxes, associated glass bowl.

13¾in (35cm) wide

£85-100   **APAR**

A 19thC tortoiseshell two division tea caddy, with pewter stringing, small cracks to lid, small chips to the tortoiseshell lids to the interior, handles replaced.

6¼in (16cm) wide

£200-250   **APAR**

A 19thC tortoiseshell tea caddy, with ivory stringing, with two lidded compartments, on four silvered ball feet, slight damage.

5½in (14cm) high

£450-550   **FLD**

An Edward VII hallmarked silver tea caddy, by Henry Bourne, with stoneware body, some of the silver applied decoration lifts in parts, crazing and surface wear.

1908   *5¼in (13.5cm) high*

£90-110   **APAR**

BOXES

A late George III oak and mahogany crossbanded and inlaid candle box, with front centred with an inlaid bird, the back section hinge has been replaced, some damage.

20in (51cm) high

£75-85   **APAR**

A George III oak spoon rack and salt box, general wear.

10in (25.5cm) wide

£150-200   **APAR**

A late Georgian mahogany candle box, with pierced backplate.

9¼in (23.5cm) wide

£50-60   **APAR**

A late Victorian carved oak wall-mounted letter box, the shaped back rail inscribed 'LETTERS', old crude repair to backplate, general surface wear.

17in (43cm) wide

£100-140   **APAR**

A 19thC burr maple string box, on brass ball feet.

4in (10cm) high

£200-250   **LC**

A 19thC turned lignum vitae string box, the screw-on lid centred with a blade, small losses to the base section of the lid.

5¼in (13.5cm) diam

£120-160   **APAR**

A 19thC fruitwood string box, with screw-on rear section and metal blade attached to the 'tap', general wear.

4¼in (11cm) long

£140-180   **APAR**

A 19thC turned lignum vitae box and cover, signs of woodworm to the body.

5¼in (13.5cm) diam

£100-150   **APAR**

A Scandinavian 19thC pine lidded box, with traces of incised floral decoration and original paintwork, surface wear.

8¾in (22cm) diam

£180-220   **APAR**

A Victorian mahogany sewing box, with a fabric lined interior, with two base drawers, with twin brass lion mask ring handles, overall wear and tear.

18¼in (46.5cm) wide

£200-250   APAR

An early Victorian rosewood and mother-of-pearl inlaid sewing box, with fitted interior with cotton reels, small jars and accoutrements with further sewing related items to the base, some losses to the mother-of-pearl, a split to base.

14¾in (37.5cm) wide

£600-700   APAR

A 19thC Killarney ware inlaid arbutus twin-lidded box, with swing-over handle.

Killarney ware, produced in Killarney and the Gap of Dunloe, Ireland, in the mid-to-late 19thC, is often made out of local wood such as arbutus. The ware can feature local buildings/sites or traditional Irish symbols.

9½in (24cm) wide

£400-450   BELL

A Victorian amboyna and rosewood crossbanded sewing box, with related sewing tools.

10in (25.5cm) wide

£90-120   APAR

A mid-Victorian figured walnut travelling cabinet, with pen tray and inkwell to the front.

12¼in (31.5cm) high

£100-150   APAR

An early Victorian rosewood and mother-of-pearl inlaid travelling case or vanity box, with lift-out tray revealing a jewellery compartment, three splits to the top, dents and surface scratches.

10¾in (27.5cm) wide

£80-100   APAR

A 19thC teak and brass bound gentleman's travelling box, the lid set with a folding mirror, the interior with lift-out tray with a hip flask, razor, scissors, a pewter measure and a pewter bowl, wear as expected from a campaign piece.

7in (18cm) wide

£120-160   APAR

A late 19thC mahogany miniature bureau, on clear glass feet.

12¼in (31cm) high

£120-160   APAR

An early 20thC mahogany shop display cabinet, for 'J. & P. COATS SEWING COTTON'.

21¼in (54cm) wide

£250-300   LOCK

A 19thC mahogany apothecary box, with seven bottles, a measuring jug and a further drawer of bottles.

10in (25.5cm) wide

£400-500   **FLD**

An H. Bahlsen sheet-metal biscuit box, designed by Emanuel Josef Margold, inscribed with exhibition history.

c1911-12   *7½in (19cm) long*

£350-400   **QU**

An early 20thC enamelled glass glove casket, attributed to Moser, decorated with songbirds, on gilt brass wirework legs, unmarked.

13in (33cm) wide

£900-1,100   **L&T**

A 19thC lighthouse keeper's brass tinder box, one cover stamped 'US LIGHT HOUSE ESTABLISHMENT', the other 'US L H DEPOT 3 DIST. LAMP SHOP, STATEN ISLAND', the interior fitted with a tray, a box and holders for wicks, matches, oil and funnels.

12¼in (31cm) long

£1,100-1,500   **NA**

A 19thC travelling tradesman's gilt-metal mounted tortoiseshell veneered vitrine.

14¼in (36cm) high

£300-400   **BELL**

A mid-19thC Jennens & Bettridge writing box, with patent inlaid gems, with a fitted interior and a gilt decorated papier mâché frame.

Gem laying was introduced by Theodore Jennens in 1847.

13¾in (35cm) wide

£160-200   **BELL**

A Victorian brass bound mahogany artist's box, inscribed 'COLOURS FOR HERALDIC & MISSAL PAINTING C. ROWNEY & CO.' on inside of lid.

10in (25.5cm) wide

£220-300   **BELL**

A 19thC birdcage, in the American 'Tramp Art' manner.

32¼in (82cm) wide

£400-500   **BELL**

A German St Bernard sweet container, in white and brown artificial silk plush, glass eyes, oil-cloth collar and head removed to reveal sweet container.

1930s   *12in (30.5cm) long*

£250-300   **SAS**

An Agfa Super Isolette 120 CRF camera, with Solinar 75mm f3.5 lens and 'Ever Ready' case.
£350-400   AST

A Canon Pellix camera with FL 50mm f1.4 lens.
£80-100   AST

A Canon VI L Rangefinder camera, working, with Canon 28mm f2.8 lens and clip-on finder.
£450-550   AST

A Corfield Periflex 1 camera, with Lumar-X 50mm f3.5 lens, no.3434, with torpedo finder and case.
£200-250   AST

A 3B Quick Focus Kodak camera, for postcard-sized prints.

In use, the focus distance is pre-set on the side-mounted scale and when a button is pressed the front lens board springs forward.
£100-140   AST

A Kodak Regent II Medium Format Rangefinder camera, fitted with Xenar 10.5cm f3.5, shutter linkage needs adjustment.
£550-650   AST

A Leica M2 N0 10108277 camera, Elmar 5 cm f2.8 no.1590916, with original leather case and instructions.
£750-850   DUK

A rare Leica M4 Rangefinder chrome camera, serial no.331A, with Leitz Summicron-M f/2 50mm lens, serial no.3357940.

The top plate of the camera with serial no.331A indicates that this was originally part of a dummy camera and therefore the body and top plate may not be original to each other.

A Leica IIIC no. 465037 camera, collapsible Elmar 50 mm f2.8 no.1669820 lens cap and original leather case.
£300-400   DUK

£1,500-2,000   GORL

CAMERAS

A Meyer Planovista Primarette folding 6x4.5cm camera.

A Leica model 1a camera, serial no.32019, with Letz Elmar1:3,5 F=50mm lens, in fitted leather case, with a cased Excelsior light meter.
£500-600 FLD

A Mamiya RZ67 120 professional camera, serial no.101027, with Mamiya Sekor Z f=90mm 1:35 lens, with instructions.
£400-500 FLD

This is designed like two cameras one on top of the other, the top for viewing and the bottom for taking.
£400-500 AST

A Mycro leather-cased IIIA miniature camera, with Mycro Una 1:4.5 F=20mm lens.
£20-30 APAR

A Nikon F5 film camera body, in maker's box.
£200-300 AST

A Penta Asahiflex camera, named for the South African Market, no.230406, slight wear to chrome.

In 1959, Pentax were in dispute with Zeiss so their cameras for the South African market could not use the Pentax name. Their problems did not last long, so only a few had the Penta name before the Pentax name could legally be used. They are now very difficult to find.
£250-300 AST

A Ross & Co., London, plate camera, with a leather bellows and a leather and brass mounted case, 8 x 5 rapid symmetrical brass lens, within fitted case with two Thornton-Pickard roller shutters, leather cased Zeiss Convertible Anastigmat 14in lens and other accessories.
£500-600 WHP

An uncommon Shew Twin Lens Xit.

This looks like a stereo camera, but one lens enables viewing on ground glass screen, the other is the taking lens.
£1,500-2,000 AST

A Seaside Photographer's camera and Taylor Hobson Lens, based on a Thornton Pickard Reflex plate cameras, no.30, with a Taylor Hobson Wide Angle 6 1/4inch f6.5 lens.

This was probably converted in the late 1940s by Sunbeam Photos, Margate, to accept rolls of photographic paper.
£140-180 AST

QUICK REFERENCE - CANES

● Decorated canes first became popular during the 16thC, but reached their golden age in terms of variety and quality in the late 18thC and 19thC. Favoured by the upper classes and the bourgeoisie, they largely went out of fashion after World War I. As well as being of practical use, they acted as a status symbol.

● The shaft is usually made from wood. The handle or pommel can be made from ivory, bone, silver, gold or wood. The tip of the stick or cane is typically tipped in metal to prevent it being worn.

● Most canes found today date from the Victorian or Edwardian period and can be divided into two types – decorative canes and gadget canes. The latter have a second function, such as containing something useful like a small bottle or a telescope. Some canes cross into folk art and can attract large sums, particularly for rare and desirable American examples.

● In all instances, the quality of the decoration or objects inside, and of the material used, counts greatly towards value. Also consider the age and place of manufacture. Many sticks do not bear maker's marks, but may bear hallmarks if in a precious metal, or a retailer's mark such as Swaine & Adeney. Condition is also important – always examine carving all over to ensure parts are not missing.

A George III gold and enamel mounted walking cane, the handle with initials 'SB' within chased laurel leaf borders, interspersed with oval paterae and with five oval panels decorated 'en grisaille' with the muses, with an indistinct maker's mark, with an ebony tapering shaft.

37¾in (96cm) long

£1,800-2,200   WW

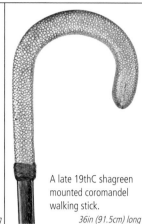

A late 19thC shagreen mounted coromandel walking stick.

36in (91.5cm) long

£200-250   BELL

A Russian ebony cane, with a T-shaped handle designed to dispense coins of three different sizes, the handle is engraved with niello work.

35in (89cm) long

£1,500-2,000   SWO

A Russian cloisonné enamel and silver-mounted walking cane, the handle decorated with leaves and flowers, the silver marked '84', with a Malacca shaft.

35in (89cm) long

£500-600   WW

A late 19thC Continental gold-mounted snakewood walking cane.

36¼in (92cm) long

£950-1,100   BELL

A late 19thC Continental ivory walking cane, the handle in the form of a military gentleman, wearing the Order of the Golden Fleece and the Order of St Esprit, with malacca shaft and bone ferrule.

32¾in (83cm) long

£500-600   ROS

An Edwardian walking stick, with bone carved handle, after DALI.

£150-200   JN

A Victorian folk art treen blackthorn walking cane, the handle carved with a grotesque bust of Punch, with glass eyes.

42in (106.5cm) long

£500-600   WW

A rare 19thC sharkskin boxed tortoiseshell walking cane, Toledo work handle with a Ducal crown on the end and initials for the Duke of Bivona, the ferrule is also in Toledo work, the sharkskin case with three metal fasteners and lined in satin, a small piece of wooden core is visible at the bottom of the stick.

box 38½in (98cm) long

£3,500-4,000   CHOR

CANES

A CLOSER LOOK AT A WALKING CANE

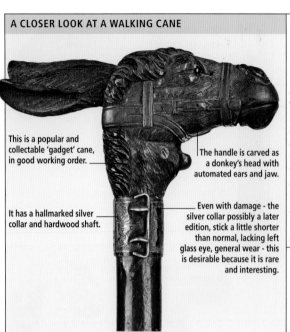

This is a popular and collectable 'gadget' cane, in good working order.

It has a hallmarked silver collar and hardwood shaft.

The handle is carved as a donkey's head with automated ears and jaw.

Even with damage - the silver collar possibly a later edition, stick a little shorter than normal, lacking left glass eye, general wear - this is desirable because it is rare and interesting.

A late 19thC Black Forest walking cane.

32½in (82.5cm) long

£1,000-1,500   BELL

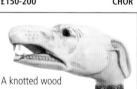

A malacca walking stick, with silver collar, the ivory handle carved as a pug head with glass eyes.

This stick contains an element of pre-1947 ivory or other organic material that may be subject to export restrictions.

£150-200   CHOR

A knotted wood walking stick, with brass collar and greyhound handle with beaded eyes.

This stick contains an element of pre-1947 ivory or other organic material that may be subject to export restrictions.

£180-220   CHOR

A rosewood walking stick, with gilt copper collar and carved ivory bullmastiff handle.

This stick contains an element of pre-1947 ivory or other organic material that may be subject to export restrictions.

£150-200   CHOR

A thorn wood walking cane, the handle modelled as the head of a dog, with white metal collar to neck with engraved initials, handle and cane associated.

34½in (87.5cm) long

£200-300   FELL

A late 19thC silver-mounted blackthorn walking stick, the handle carved as a dog's head, in a silver muzzle, indistinctly hallmarked 'London 18??'.

34½in (87.5cm) long

£220-280   BELL

A late 19thC Black Forest novelty walking cane, the carved cat's head pommel with automated jaw, glass eyes, white metal collar and hardwood shaft.

37in (94cm) long

£300-350   BELL

A silver-mounted bamboo walking cane, the handle cast as a dog's head with inset glass eyes, hallmarked London 1889.

34in (86.5cm) long

£180-220   BELL

An Edwardian carved ivory walking cane, modelled as a bulldog's head, with engraved silver band.

This stick contains an element of pre-1947 ivory or other organic material that may be subject to export restrictions.

34in (86.5cm) long

£300-350   JN

A walking stick, with plated collar and ivory handle carved as a hound.

This stick contains an element of pre-1947 ivory or other organic material that may be subject to export restrictions.

£180-220   CHOR

A late-Victorian novelty silver-mounted walking cane, maker's mark WH?, the handle modelled as a horse's head, the hinged cover opens to reveal a vesta compartment and hinged striker, and a hole, possibly for a lighting cord, carved wooden shaft.

1887   36¼in (92cm) long

£1,200-1,800   WW

A rosewood walking stick, with silver collar, the ivory handle carved as the hare and tortoise, the hare has a slight crack from eyes to the base of head, slight staining, stick slightly scatched, with no stop end.

This stick contains an element of pre-1947 ivory or other organic material that may be subject to export restrictions.

35in (89cm) long

£400-500   CHOR

A rosewood walking stick, the ivory handle with python and elephant finial, elephant is split and neck and trunk re-glued, minor splits to elephant back, some minor straining throughout.

This stick contains an element of pre-1947 ivory or other organic material that may be subject to export restrictions.

35½in (90cm) long

£180-220   CHOR

A rosewood walking stick, with silver collar, the ivory handle carved as a horse with foal, stick is scratched and pitted, no stop end.

This stick contains an element of pre-1947 ivory or other organic material that may be subject to export restrictions.

35¾in (91cm) long

£1,500-2,000   CHOR

A Malacca shafted cane, concealing a horse measurer up to 17 hands, with a silver knop, the measuring arm concealing a spirit level.

1895   37in (94cm) long

£450-500   SWO

An early 20thC Black Forest carved wooden bulldog umbrella handle, with automated mouth and ears, with a gilt metal collar, bamboo handle and silk shade.

36¾in (93.5cm) long

£250-300   BELL

An Edwardian novelty silver-mounted carved wooden umbrella/pencil, by Charles Dumenil, retailed by Brigg, London, the handle carved as a snake head, set with green eyes, also with a pull-out fully marked silver pencil.

1908   36¾in (93.5cm) long

£400-450   WW

A 19thC painted brass combination walking cane and telescope, by G Willson, London, the stepped cylindrical case with painted detail as simulated bamboo, some losses and damage throughout.

34in (86.5cm) long

£350-400   KEY

CANES

A 19thC Malacca mandarin cane, with a large silver cap, when unscrewed it releases a matching knife, fork and a pair of chopsticks, the cap is engraved 'To master Seaman Houghton from Colonel Raveunull'.

34½in (87.5cm) long

£1,300-1,600   **SWO**

A triple function dog owner's cane, with a tapered ebony cane and cast handle including a whistle and a spring-loaded collar catch, with Ackwell's patent.

c1895   34¾in (88.5cm) long

£750-850   **SWO**

A cane, with a Brigg silver handle and a cab-hailing whistle, the forward part of the handle containing a press fit cap with a small tube holding a pencil, the handle hallmarked London and marked with initials on the cap, marked '69 St George's Square SW' on the stem.

1893   36¼in (92cm) long

£750-850   **SWO**

An Edwardian gold-mounted whistle walking cane, with a 9ct gold L-shaped handle, inscribed 'Rd No 31680 J C Vicery 181-183 Regent St', with an ebonised shaft and horn ferrule.

1906   34½in (88cm) long

£500-600   **ROS**

A Victorian umbrella, modelled as an Alsatian's head, Black Forest carved wood handle, with glass eyes and bone teeth.

30¼in (77cm) long

£400-500   **JN**

A walking stick, with a silver knop, concealing a sword marked on one side of the blade 'Defence not Defiance', and the other 'Peace with Honour', the sword with a twist/release action.

1891   35¾in (91cm) long

£750-850   **SWO**

A stout square section stiletto cane, with four silver straps at intervals along the length, with a silver cap, engraved 'Lieut. Col. Thomas Brooke who carried the cane during the Peninsular War', with a concealed 'flick' dagger in the handle.

35in (89cm) long

£800-900   **SWO**

A black knurled sword cane, with a short 12½in (32cm) blade, mounted atop a silver-plated watch that unscrews from the shaft, and is rewound by rotating the bezel in an anticlockwise direction, time adjustment is achieved by raising the hinged glass cover and rotating the centre knob.

c1900   35¼in (89.5cm) long

£2,000-2,500   **SWO**

An unusual watch cane, possibly manufactured in Russia, with a French clock decorated with an enamel surround below the cap, the shaft of ebonised mahogany, the time is altered by rotating the rim of the watch after depressing a small catch, and it is rewound by rotating the outer rim in an anticlockwise direction.

c1890   34in (86.5cm) long

£2,500-3,000   **SWO**

QUICK REFERENCE - BESWICK POTTERY

- The Beswick Pottery was founded in Loughton, Staffordshire, in 1894, by James Wright Beswick and his sons John and Gilbert. It initially focused on tableware and vases, then began to produce figurines from 1900.
- Beswick was sold to Royal Doulton in 1969, but production continued under the name 'Beswick' until 1989, when Beswick and Doulton animal figurines were combined as 'Royal Doulton'. The name 'Beswick' returned to use in 1999, until the factory closed in 2002.
- Produced from 1900, Beswick's animal figurines remain its most sought-after wares. By 1930, these figurines were very successful and a major part of the factory's production – aided by the company's introduction of high-fired bone china in 1934. Beatrix Potter figurines, produced from 1946, and Disney figurines produced from 1952, are also popular.
- Prices for Beswick wares rose after the closure of the factory in 2002 and prices for rare figurines remain high. Early pieces, limited edition or prototype figurines fetch the highest prices. However, it is difficult to identify early pieces, as figurines were not backstamped or numbered until 1934. Limited editions, even from the 1990s can be valuable if the edition was small and you have documentation.

A rare Beswick 'Foal', designed by Arthur Gredington, model no.763, first version, blue gloss-glazed.

First version has long ears. Second version has short ears.

1940-Unknown   *3½in (9cm) high*
£550-650   **PSA**

A rare Beswick 'Shire Mare', designed by Arthur Gredington, model no.818, first version, piebald gloss-glazed.

8½in (21.5cm) high
£2,500-3,000   **PSA**

A rare Beswick 'Shire Mare', designed by Arthur Gredington, model no.818, first version, chestnut gloss-glazed.

1958-67   *8½in (21.5cm) high*
£1,500-2,000   **PSA**

A Beswick 'Shire Mare', designed by Arthur Gredington, model no.818, first version, black gloss-glazed.

In recognition of 50 years of production of model no.818, a black gloss shire mare was commissioned by the Beswick Collectors Circle in 1990. Approximately 135 of these were issued with a gold backstamp for Circle Members.

1990   *8½in (21.5cm) high*
£700-800   **PSA**

A rare Beswick 'Shire Mare', designed by Arthur Gredington, model no.818, first version, skewbald gloss-glazed.

8½in (21.5cm) high
£4,000-5,000   **PSA**

A Beswick 'Foal', designed by Arthur Gredington, model no.836, in rocking horse grey, with early hint of blue colours.

5in (12.5cm) high
£650-750   **PSA**

A Beswick 'Stocky Jogging Mare', designed by Arthur Gredington, model no.855, third version, black gloss-glazed, Royal Doulton backstamp 'DA44', produced for the Beswick Collectors Club.

Model no.855 third version was transferred to the Royal Doulton backstamp (DA44) in 1989.

2005   *6in (15cm) high*
£120-180   **PSA**

A Beswick 'Stocky Jogging Mare', designed by Arthur Gredington, model no.855, third version, rocking horse grey gloss-glazed.

c1947-62   *6in (15cm) high*
£550-650   **PSA**

A rare Beswick 'Huntsman on Rearing Horse', designed by Arthur Gredington, model no.868, style one, rocking horse grey gloss-glazed, restoration to back legs, tail and one front leg.

1940-52   *10in (25.5cm) high*
£1,500-2,000   **PSA**

CERAMICS

A Beswick 'Huntsman on Rearing Horse', designed by Arthur Gredington, model no.868, second version, painted white gloss, slight crazing.

1965-71   *10in (25.5cm) high*

£400-500   **PSA**

A Beswick large 'Shire Foal', designed by Arthur Gredington, model no.951, chestnut gloss-glazed.

1958-67   *6¼in (16cm) high*

£550-650   **PSA**

A Beswick 'Cantering Shire', designed by Arthur Gredington, model no.975, black gloss-glazed, Collectors Club Special, boxed.

Model no.975 was transferred to the Royal Doulton Backstamp (DA45) in 1989.

1996   *8¾in (22cm) high*

£200-250   **PSA**

A Beswick 'Cantering Shire', designed by Arthur Gredington, model no.975, palomino gloss-glazed.

1961-70   *8¾in (22cm) high*

£550-650   **PSA**

A rare Beswick 'Woolly Shetland Mare', designed by Arthur Gredington, model no.1033, chestnut gloss-glazed, restoration to one ear.

5¾in (14.6cm) high

£4,500-5,000   **PSA**

A Beswick 'Racehorse and Jockey', designed by Arthur Gredington, model no.1037, brown gloss-glazed, with stripes on saddlecloth, one broken leg.

Colourway no.1 has stripes on the saddlecloth. Colourway no.2 has a number on the saddlecloth.

1945-Unknown   *8½in (21.5cm) high*

£220-280   **PSA**

A Beswick 'Grazing Shire', designed by Arthur Gredington, model no.1050, in grey gloss.

5½in (14cm) high

£400-500   **PSA**

A Beswick 'Knight in Armour - The Earl of Warwick', designed by Arthur Gredington, model no.1145, grey gloss-glazed.

1949-73   *10¾in (27.5cm) high*

£600-700   **PSA**

A Beswick 'Swish Tail Horse', designed by Arthur Gredington, model no.1182, first version, chestnut gloss-glazed.

1958-67   *8¾in (22cm) high*

£400-500   **PSA**

A Beswick 'Pony', designed by
Arthur Gredington, model no.1197,
with head up, rocking horse grey
gloss-glazed.
c1951-62   *5½in (14cm) high*
£450-550   **PSA**

A Beswick 'Suffolk Punch
Champion – Hasse Dainty',
designed by Mr Orwell, model
no.1359, dark chestnut
gloss-glazed.
Unknown-1971   *8in (20.5cm) high*
£200-250   **PSA**

A rare Beswick 'Suffolk Punch Champion – Hasse Dainty', designed by
Mr Orwell, model no.1359, grey gloss-glazed, three chips to rear hoof.
1965   *8in (20.5cm) high*
£2,500-3,000   **PSA**

A Beswick 'Pinto Pony',
designed by Arthur
Gredington, model
no.1373, first version,
palomino gloss-glazed.

**The tail of the first
version is attached to the
hind leg from the hock
down.**
1961-70
6½in (16.5cm) high
£900-1,100   **PSA**

A Beswick 'Canadian
Mounted Cowboy',
designed by Mr Orwell,
model no.1377, palomino
gloss-glazed, tail
restored.
1955-73   8¾in (22cm) high
£400-450   **CHT**

A Beswick 'Mounted Indian',
designed by Mr Orwell, model
no.1391, skewbald gloss-glazed.
1955-90   8½in (21.5cm) high
£280-360   **PSA**

A rare Beswick 'Girl's Pony',
designed by Arthur Gredington,
model no.1483, rocking horse grey
gloss-glazed.
1957-62   5in (12.5cm) high
£750-850   **PSA**

A Beswick 'Girl on Pony', designed
by Arthur Gredington, model
no.1499, skewbald gloss-glazed.

**The pony used for model no.1499
was also available separately as
model no.1483 'Girl's Pony'.**
1957-65   5½in (14cm) high
£300-350   **PSA**

A rare Beswick 'Girl on Pony',
designed by Arthur Gredington,
model no.1499, with light green
jacket.
5½in (14cm) high
£1,500-2,000   **PSA**

CERAMICS

A rare Beswick model of a boy on chestnut pony, designed by Arthur Gredington, model no.1499, with green jacket.

5½in (14cm) high

£1,500-2,000 **PSA**

A rare Beswick 'Huntsman', designed by Arthur Gredington, model no.1501, on rocking horse grey horse, restoration to all legs.

8¼in (21cm) high

£1,000-1,500 **PSA**

A Beswick 'Appaloosa Spotted Walking Pony', designed by Arthur Gredington, model no.1516, gloss-glazed.

1957-66 *5¼in (13.5cm) high*

£400-450 **PSA**

A Beswick 'Horse', designed by Pal Zalmen, model no.1549, first version, chestnut gloss-glazed.

The tail of the first version is angled towards the off-hind hock.

1958-67 *7½in (19cm) high*

£600-700 **PSA**

A Beswick 'Fell Pony - Dene Dauntless', designed by Arthur Gredington, model no.1647, black gloss-glazed.

This model is part of the 'Mountain and Moorland Ponies' series.

1961-82 *6¾in (17cm) high*

£120-180 **PSA**

A Beswick 'Huntswoman', designed by Arthur Gredington, model no.1730, style two, grey gloss-glazed.

1960-95 *8¼in (21cm) high*

£200-250 **PSA**

A Beswick horse, 'Arab Bahram', designed by Arthur Gredington, model no.1771, chestnut gloss-glazed.

From the 'Connoiseur Horses' series.

1961-67 *7½in (19cm) high*

£600-700 **PSA**

A rare Beswick 'Thoroughbred Foal', designed by Arthur Gredington, model no.1817, piebald gloss-glazed.

3¼in (8.5cm) high

£300-400 **PSA**

A Beswick 'Horse and Jockey', designed by Arthur Gredington, model no.1862, style two, light dapple grey gloss-glazed, ear re-stuck.

1963-83 *8in (20.5cm) high*

£150-200 **PSA**

A Beswick 'Horse and Jockey', designed by Arthur Gredington, model no.1862, style two, brown gloss-glazed.
1963-84
£180-220   8in (20.5cm) high
£180-220   **PSA**

A Beswick 'Dun Stallion', model no.2007, limited-edition Collectors Club piece, boxed.
£150-200   **PSA**

A small Beswick 'T'ang Horse', designed by Graham Tongue, model no.2137, green/bronze gloss-glazed.
1967-72   8in (20.5cm) high
£280-340   **PSA**

A large Beswick 'T'ang Horse', designed by Graham Tongue, model no.2205, green/bronze gloss-glazed.
1968-72   13in (33cm) high
£350-400   **PSA**

A Beswick 'Highwayman on Rearing Horse', designed by Albert Hallam, model no.2210, bay matt, on a wooden plinth.

From the 'Connoisseur Horses' series.
1970-75   13¾in (35cm) high
£400-500   **PSA**

A Beswick 'Norwegian Fjord Horse', designed by Albert Hallam, model no.2282, dun gloss-glazed.
1970-75   6½in (16.5cm) high
£200-300   **PSA**

A rare Beswick 'White Horse Whisky', designed by Alan Maslankowski, model no.2514, white gloss-glazed.

This model is part of the 'Advertising' series.
1974   6¾in (17cm) high
£550-600   **PSA**

A Beswick 'Red Rum with Brian Fletcher Up', designed by Graham Tongue, model no.2511, bay matt, on a wooden base.

From the 'Connoisseur Horses' series.
1975-82   12¼in (31cm) high
£300-350   **PSA**

A Beswick 'Lifeguard', designed by Graham Tongue, model no.2562, style two, black gloss-glazed, on a wooden base.

This is from the 'Connoisseur Horses' series. Model no.2562 was transferred to the Royal Doulton backstamp (DA22) in 1989.
1977-89   14½in (37cm) high
£110-150   **PSA**

A Royal Doulton 'Chestnut Punch Peon' galloping shire horse, designed by W.M. Chance, model no.HN2623.

1950-60   *7½in (19cm) high*

£160-200   **PSA**

A Beswick 'Rearing Cancara', designed by Graham Tongue, model no.3426, black matt, made for the Beswick centenary, on a wooden base, boxed.

Model no.3426 was transferred to the Royal Doulton backstamp (DA234) in 1989. It reverted to the Beswick backstamp in September 1999. Modelled from the 'Downland Cancara' graded Trakehner stallion famous for advertising Lloyds Bank.

1994   *16½in (42cm) high*

£160-200   **PSA**

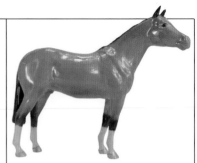

A Beswick 'Stallion', model no.BCC2007, dun gloss-glazed, produced for the Beswick Collectors Club.

2007   *7½in (19cm) high*

£100-150   **PSA**

A Beswick Connoisseur 'Champion Welsh Mountain Pony', designed by Graham Tongue, black gloss-glazed, produced for the Beswick Collectors Club, boxed.

The 'Champion Welsh Mountain Pony' was issued in a limited edition of 580. Model DA247 was transferred from the Royal Doulton backstamp in September 1999.

1999   *8¼in (21cm) high*

£200-250   **PSA**

A Beswick 'Shetland Pony - Hollydell Dixie', designed by Amanda Hughes-Lubeck, model no.H185, skewbald gloss-glazed, produced for the Beswick Collectors Club, boxed.

1995   *5¼in (13.5cm) high*

£150-200   **PSA**

A Beswick 'Shetland Pony', designed by Amanda Hughes-Lubeck, dapple grey gloss-glazed.

The 'Shetland Pony' model was transferred from the Royal Doulton backstamp (DA185) in September 1999.

1992-99

£100-150   **PSA**

A Beswick 'Warlord's Mare - Another Bunch', designed by Graham Tongue, bay/brown gloss-glazed.

This was the second in a series of specially commissioned models for PR Middleweek & Co. from the John Beswick Studios,limited to 1,500 models.

1997   *6in (15cm) high*

£50-70   **PSA**

Judith Picks

Kruger was the last pit pony to work at the Chatterley Whitfield Colliery and was retired in 1931.

The first model from this set of four was presented to H.R.H. Princess Royal on her visit to Chatterley Whitfield Mining Museum to open the New Pit on 13 October 1987.

A rare Beswick 'Spirit of Whitfield', by Graham Tongue, modelled after 'Kruger', some tarnishing to the metal plaque.

9½in (24cm) high

£6,000-7,000   **PW**

A Beswick 'Hereford Cow', designed by Arthur Gredington, model no.948, first version, restored horn.
1941-c1957   *5in (12.5cm) high*
£50-80   **PSA**

An early Beswick 'Hereford Bull', designed by Arthur Gredington, model no.949, brown and white gloss-glazed.
c1941-57   *5¾in (14.5cm) high*
£100-150   **PSA**

A rare Beswick Lincoln Red Bull, model no.1363A, red gloss-glazed, stamped 'Beswick England', minor crazing to glaze.
4½in (11.5cm) high
£4,000-4,500   **CHT**

A Beswick 'Dairy Shorthorn Calf', desiged by Arthur Gredington, model no.1406C, brown and white with shading gloss-glazed, restored ears.
1956-73   *3in (7.5cm) high*
£150-200   **PSA**

A Beswick 'Dairy Shorthorn Bull - CH Gwersylt Lord Oxford 74th', designed by Arthur Gredington, model no.1504, brown and white with shading gloss-glazed.
1957-73   *5in (12.5cm) high*
£350-400   **PSA**

A Beswick 'Dairy Shorthorn Cow - CH Eaton Wild Eyes 91st', designed by Arthur Gredington, model no.1510, brown and white with shading gloss-glazed, restored front legs.
1957-73   *4¾in (12cm) high*
£350-400   **PSA**

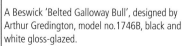

A Beswick 'Galloway Bull', designed by Arthur Gredington, model no.1746A, black gloss-glazed.
1962-69   *4½in (11.5cm) high*
£750-850   **PSA**

A Beswick 'Belted Galloway Bull', designed by Arthur Gredington, model no.1746B, black and white gloss-glazed.
1963-69   *4½in (11.5cm) high*
£750-850   **PSA**

A Beswick 'Silver Dunn Galloway Bull', designed by Arthur Gredington, model no.1746C, fawn and brown gloss-glazed.
1962-69   *4½in (11.5cm) high*
£700-800   **PSA**

CERAMICS

A Beswick 'Aberdeen Angus Calf', designed by Arthur Gredington, model no.1827A, black gloss-glazed.

1985-89   *3in (7.5cm) high*

£85-100   **PSA**

A Beswick 'Black Galloway Cow', designed by Robert Donaldson, model no.4113B, gloss-glazed, produced for the Beswick Collectors Club.

2002   *5¼in (13.5cm) high*

£120-180   **PSA**

A Beswick 'Middlewhite Boar', designed by Robert Donaldson, model no.4117, white gloss-glazed.

This model is part of the 'Rare Breeds' series.

2001-02   *8in (20.5cm) high*

£100-150   **PSA**

A Beswick 'Berkshire Boar', designed by Robert Donaldson, model no.4118, black and grey gloss-glazed.

This model is part of the 'Rare Breeds' series.

2001-02   *3¼in (8.5cm) high*

£120-160   **PSA**

A Beswick 'Shetland Cow', designed by Robert Donaldson, model no.4112, black and white gloss-glazed.

This model is part of the 'Rare Breeds' series.

2001-02   *5¼in (13.5cm) high*

£85-100   **PSA**

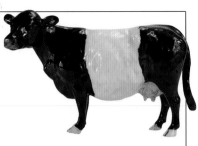

A Beswick 'Belted Galloway Cow', designed by Robert Donaldson, model no.4113A, gloss-glazed.

2001-02   *5¼in (13.5cm) high*

£110-150   **PSA**

A Beswick 'Merino Ram', by Arthur Gredington, model no.1917, grey with white face gloss-glazed, oval mark.

1964-67   *4¼in (11cm) high*

£500-600   **FLD**

A Beswick 'Tamworth Pig', designed by Amanda Hughes-Lubeck, model no.G215, brown gloss-glazed.

Transferred from the Royal Doulton backstamp (DA215) in September 1999.

1999-present   *6in (15cm) high*

£60-80   **PSA**

A Beswick 'Gloucester Old Spot Pig', designed by Amanda Hughes-Lubeck, model no.G230, pink with black markings gloss-glazed.

Transferred from the Royal Doulton backstamp (DA230) in September 1999.

1999-present   *3in (7.5cm) high*

£100-150   **PSA**

A Beswick 'Seagull on Rock', designed by Arthur Gredington, model no.768, gloss-glazed, beak and wing tip restored.

1939-54   *8½in (21.5cm) high*

£450-550   **PSA**

A rare Beswick 'Grebie', designed by Arthur Gredington, model no.1006.

This model is part of the 'Stylistic Model' series.

1945–54   *5¼in (13.5cm) high*

£1,200-1,500   **WM**

A Beswick 'Barnacle Goose', designed by Arthur Gredington, model no.1052, dark grey-blue and white gloss-glazed.

1943-68   *6½in (16.5cm) high*

£250-300   **PSA**

A Beswick 'Mandarin Duck', designed by Arthur Gredington, model no.1519-1, approved by Peter Scott.

1958-71

£100-150   **PSA**

A Beswick 'Budgerigar', designed by Arthur Gredington, model no.1216B, second version, yellow gloss-glazed.

This version has no flowers on the base.

1970-72   *7in (18cm) high*

£450-550   **PSA**

A Beswick 'Kookaboro', model no.1159.

£60-80   **PSA**

A Beswick 'Fantail Pigeon', designed by Arthur Gredington, model no.1614, white gloss.

1959-69   *5in (12.5cm) high*

£180-220   **PSA**

A Beswick 'Sussex Cockerel', designed by Arthur Gredington, model no.1899, black, white and pink gloss-glazed, minor crazing to glaze.

1963-71   *7in (18cm) high*

£350-400   **WM**

A Beswick 'Turkey', designed by Albert Hallam, model no.1957, white gloss-glazed.

1964-69   *7¼in (18.5cm) high*

£450-550   **PSA**

CERAMICS

A Beswick 'Gamecock', designed by Arthur Gredington, model no.2059, gloss-glazed.
1966-75   *9½in (24cm) high*
£250-300   FLD

A Beswick 'Pair of Partridges', designed by Albert Hallam, model no.2064.
1966-75   *5½in (14cm) high*
£220-280   PSA

A Beswick 'Cedar Waxwing', designed by Graham Tongue, model no.2184, gloss-glazed.
1968-73   *4½in (11.5cm) high*
£150-200   PSA

A Beswick 'Penguin Chick', designed by Graham Tongue, model no.2398, gloss-glazed.
1971-76   *7in (18cm) high*
£200-300   PSA

A Beswick large 'Penguin', designed by Albert Hallam, model no.2357, black and white gloss-glazed.

This model is part of the 'Fireside Model' series.
1971-76   *12in (30.5cm) high*
£400-500   PSA

A Beswick 'Penguin Chick', designed by Graham Tongue, model no.2434, sliding, gloss-glazed.
1972-76   *8in (20.5cm) wide*
£400-450   PSA

A Beswick 'Staffordshire Bull Terrier - Bandits Brintiga', designed by Arthur Gredington, model no.1982A, dark brindle gloss-glazed.
1964-69   *4¾in (12cm) high*
£200-250   PSA

A Beswick large 'Fireside Labrador Dog', designed by Graham Tongue, model no.2314, gloss.
1970-89   *13½in (34.5cm) high*
£100-150   PSA

A Beswick 'Labrador', designed by Alan Maslankowski, model no.3062B, chocolate brown gloss-glazed, produced for the Beswick Collectors Club (BCC), boxed.

Produced for the BCC with a special BCC backstamp.
1993   *5in (12.5cm) high*
£300-400   PSA

A Beswick 'Cat Scratching Ear', designed by Albert Hallam, model no.1877, grey Swiss roll colourway gloss-glazed.

1964-66   *6½in (16.5cm) high*
£150-200   **PSA**

A Beswick 'Moose', designed by Arthur Gredington, model no.2090, dark brown gloss-glazed.

1967-73   *6¼in (16cm) high*
£500-600   **PSA**

A Beswick 'Stylised Bull', designed by Colin Melbourne, brown and black colourway, one horn re-stuck.

7in (18cm) high
£150-200   **PSA**

A rare Beswick Beatrix Potter 'Tailor of Gloucester', modelled by Arthur Gredington, model no.1108, stamped 'BP1a'.

1949-2002   *3½in (9cm) high*
£4,000-5,000   **CHT**

A rare Beswick Beatrix Potter 'Duchess with flowers', designed by Graham Orwell, model no.1355, style one, stamped 'BP2a'.

1955-67   *3¾in (9.5cm) high*
£850-950   **PSA**

A Beswick Beatrix Potter 'Pickles', modelled by Albert Hallam, model no.2334, stamped 'BP3b'.

1971-82   *4½in (11.5cm) high*
£60-80   **PSA**

A Beswick Beatrix Potter 'Sir Isaac Newton', modelled by Graham Tongue, model no.2425, stamped 'BP3b'.

1973-84   *3¾in (9.5cm) high*
£100-150   **PSA**

A Beswick Beatrix Potter 'Simpkin', modelled by Alan Maslankowski, model no.2508, stamped 'BP3b'.

1975-83   *4in (10cm) high*
£85-100   **PSA**

A Beswick Beatrix Potter 'Ginger', modelled by David Lyttleton, model no.2559, stamped 'BP3b'.

1976-82   *3¾in (9.5cm) high*
£85-100   **PSA**

CERAMICS

An Arts and Crafts painted ceramic mug, with text 'Some people are always grumbling because roses have thorns; I am so glad that thorns have roses' A. Kapp, the base reads 'To be kept for some of A.M.'s best printing for B. or/or R. or M.', signed, dated.

1916   *3¼in (8.5cm) high*

£180-220   **DUK**

QUICK REFERENCE - TRANSFER-PRINTED WARES

- A cheaper and quicker alternative to painting ceramics by hand, transfer-printing was developed between 1757 and 1758 at the Worcester factory.
- A design was engraved on a copper sheet and covered in ink. The design could then be transferred to the ceramics surface using paper and then sealed under a clear glaze.
- Transfer-printed wares were traditionally blue and white, as a cobalt blue underglaze was, at the time, the only one that could withstand the heat of the kiln.
- By the 1770s, printed blue and white ceramics were being mass produced by factories across England, including at Worcester and Spode. Makers in Staffordshire used this printing method on inexpensive pottery, eventually undermining the porcelain industry.

An early 19thC dish, perhaps by John Rose, Coalport, transfer-printed in underglaze blue, 'Dragon' pattern, with twin shell-form handles, unmarked, restored handle.

12in (30.5cm) wide

£100-150   **HALL**

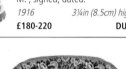

A Baker, Bevans and Irwin meat plate, 'Ladies of Llangollen' design, three small restored rim chips.

19in (48.5cm) wide

£150-200   **CHOR**

An early 19thC Davenport blue and white pap boat, printed mark.

4¼in (11cm) long

£180-220   **HAN**

A 19thC blue Staffordshire English scenery pitcher and basin, small worn spot to tip of handle.

pitcher 8¾in (22cm) high

£350-450   **POOK**

A Staffordshire nine-piece supper set, 'Lace Border' design, with a mahogany two-handled tray of a later date, one lid has a small chip and another a hair crack.

21¼in (54cm) diam

£350-450   **CHOR**

A 19thC Staffordshire footbath, printed to the interior with a large vase of flowers, against a seeded ground scattered with flowers, printed mark 'Semi-China'.

7¾in (19.5cm) high

£1,500-2,000   **BELL**

An early 19thC creamware 'Frederick Duke of York' commemorative mug, entitled 'His Royal Highness FREDERICK DUKE of YORK', painted 'X' to base, some damage.

4¾in (12cm) high

£90-120   **FLD**

A 19thC Staffordshire pearlware mug, with a transfer Chinoiserie scene, unmarked, slight damage.

5½in (14cm) high

£35-45   **FLD**

A 19thC Staffordshire platter, 'Christiansburg Danish Settlement on the Gold Coast of Africa' design.

20¾in (52.5cm) wide

£1,000-1,500   **POOK**

A 19thC Staffordshire platter, 'America & Independence' design, impressed Clews.

16¾in (42.5cm) wide

£1,500-2,000   **POOK**

A 19thC Staffordshire platter, 'Winter View of Pittsfield, Massachusetts' design, marked Clews, light staining to underside.

14½in (37cm) wide

£550-650   **POOK**

A 19thC Staffordshire platter, 'Landing of Lafayette' design, impressed Clews.

17in (43cm) wide

£600-700   **POOK**

A 19thC Staffordshire cup plate, eagle and shield design.

3¾in (9.5cm) diam

£1,500-2,000   **POOK**

A 19thC Staffordshire undertray, 'Woodlands Near Philadelphia' design, shallow chip to base.

10½in (26.5cm) wide

£750-850   **POOK**

A 19thC Staffordshire platter, depicting 'Military School, West Point, New York', rim repair.

17½in (44.5cm) wide

£1,000-1,500   **POOK**

A 19thC Staffordshire fruit bowl, 'State House, Boston' design.

11¼in (28.5cm) wide

£2,500-3,000   **POOK**

CERAMICS

A 19thC Staffordshire soup tureen, with camel and attendant, the lid with a rabbit, both handles with a few spots of glaze loss, small flake to finial.

10¼in (26cm) high

£650-750   POOK

A 19thC Staffordshire soup tureen, depicting NW view of La Grange, the residence of the Marquis Lafayette, with a grapevine pattern ladle, repaired breaks to ladle, repair to rim of tureen.

15in (38cm) wide

£500-600   POOK

A Staffordshire fruit bowl, 'Esplanade and Castle Garden, New York' design, one small hairline crack.

10in (25.5cm) wide

£3,000-3,500   POOK

A 19thC Staffordshire Quadrupeds reticulated tray, with fox and rooster design, inscribed 'J Hall'.

12¼in (31cm) wide

£2,500-3,000   POOK

A 19thC Staffordshire pitcher, 'America & Independence' design.

6¾in (17cm) high

£1,500-2,000   POOK

A Lawrence Mansion Staffordshire transfer-printed wash basin, 'Boston (Boston Athenæum)' design, Ralph Stevenson (& Son), Cobridge, impressed 'STEVENSON', with the spire of the Octagon Church in the background.

Apparently this view only appears on wash basins, one version with a regular rim, the other the rarer example with white moulded gadrooned rim, as on this piece.

1810-35   *12¾in (32.5cm) diam*

£1,000-1,500   NA

A 19thC Staffordshire pitcher, 'Welcome Lafayette' design, rim flake, firing indent to spout.

5¾in (14.5cm) high

£750-850   POOK

A Staffordshire gravy boat, 'Catholic Cathedral' design.

7¾in (19.5cm) wide

£1,000-1,500   POOK

A Staffordshire transfer-printed caster, Enoch Wood & Sons, with four figures in a rowboat.

1818-46   4¼in (11cm) high

£1,500-2,000   NA

QUICK REFERENCE - BURMANTOFTS

- In the late 19thC, Burmantofts Faience Pottery began as a side project to James Holroyd's brickworks company, and an art pottery studio was opened in Leeds, using local deposits of clay. The company specialised in handthrown and handpainted ceramics.
- Burmantofts was influenced by the Aesthetic Movement and produced a range of detailed ceramics between 1881 and 1904, when its production of art pottery ceased.
- Many wares were hand modelled, often using the French Barbotine technique, where thick slip is used to paint and model ceramics. Some lines, such as the fantastical grotesques and 'Partie-Colour', were made from moulds, then embellished and painted by hand. Burmantofts monochrome wares of blue, red and orange-yellow are especially distinctive.
- The breadth and variation of Burmantofts' designs demonstrate the freedom the designers had to explore their own ideas. Designer Joseph Walmsley's (1865-1956) repertoire includes 'Partie-Colour' and lustre-glazed wares.

A Burmantofts Faience 'Anglo-Persian' vase, by Leonard King, impressed marks, painted 'LK' monogram, small glaze nick.

5in (12.5cm) high

£400-500   WW

A Burmantofts Faience vase, designed by Joseph Walmsley, model no.2048, impressed and painted marks.

12in (30.5cm) high

£300-350   WW

A Burmantofts Faience lustre wall plaque, by Joseph Walmsley, painted with an Egyptian queen and hieroglyphs, impressed marks, painted 'JW' monogram.

14½in (37cm) diam

£400-500   WW

A Burmantofts Faience 'Anglo-Persian' jug, by Leonard King, model no.90, impressed marks, painted 'LK' monogram, D.527.

8in (20.5cm) high

£350-450   WW

A Burmantofts Faience 'Anglo-Persian' vase, by Leonard King, model no.D221, impressed marks, painted marks and 'LK' monogram, professionally restored.

10in (25.5cm) high

£400-500   WW

A Burmantofts Faience 'Partie-Colour' vase, by Joseph Walmsley, impressed marks.

12¼in (31cm) high

£450-550   WW

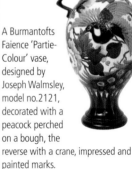

A Burmantofts Faience 'Partie-Colour' vase, designed by Joseph Walmsley, model no.2121, decorated with a peacock perched on a bough, the reverse with a crane, impressed and painted marks.

20½in (52cm) high

£1,000-1,500   WW

A Burmantofts Faience lustre vase, by Joseph Walmsley, model no.1327, impressed marks, painted 'JW' and 'No1', fine crazing to the ground.

12¼in (31cm) high

£450-550   WW

A Burmantofts Faience lustre vase, by Joseph Walmsley, painted 'JW' monogram.

8½in (21.5cm) high

£450-550   WW

CERAMICS

A Burmantofts Faience large jardinière, model no.1306, impressed marks, minor glaze chip to top rim.

17¼in (44cm) high

£500-550   WW

A Burmantofts Faience jardinière and stand, the jardinière modelled in relief with classical winged cherub, the base with three seated griffins, impressed marks, chips, glaze loss from water damage to the interior.

34in (86.5cm) high

£350-450   WW

A Burmantofts Faience jardinière and stand, model no.2155, modelled in relief with Art Nouveau waterlily flowers, impressed and painted marks, two stress crack lines in the bowl's side.

41¼in (105cm) high

£450-550   WW

A Burmantofts Faience 'Veritas' oil stove and cover, cast with Moorish fan-shaped flower panels, cast 'Burmantofts Faience' and 'Veritas', light chips and losses.

32¼in (82cm) high

£500-600   WW

An unusual Burmantofts Faience 'Partie-Colour' wall plaque, slip decorated with flag iris, impressed marks, incised '2309'.

12in (30.5cm) diam

£400-500   WW

A Burmantofts Faience large floor vase, model no.649, impressed factory marks.

21¼in (54cm) high

£500-600   WW

A Burmantofts Faience stick stand, model no.808, impressed mark, a small glaze chip to the rim.

24in (61cm) high

£300-400   WW

A Burmantofts Faience pierced Koro cover and stand, the cover with a grotesque anthropomorphic creature, in a sang-de-boeuf glaze, impressed 'Burmantofts Faience'.

10in (25.5cm) high

£600-700   WW

A Burmantofts Faience 'Barbotine Pilgrim' flask, model no.298, impressed marks, original paper label, restored chip to foot.

The design on this flask is just to one side.

11¾in (30cm) high

£220-280   WW

A Burmantofts Faience 'Partie-Colour' vase, impressed marks.

18¼in (46.5cm) high

£400-450   WW

A Burmantofts Faience 'Partie-Colour' vase, model no.2063, impressed and painted marks.

18¼in (46.5cm) high

£550-650   WW

A CLOSER LOOK AT A VASE

This is a good example of a Faience tyg vase with three handles.

It is model no.2203, of waisted cylindrical form.

It is incised with dogs running between foliage on sinuous Art Nouveau stems.

See Jason Wigglesworth, 'The History of Burmantofts Pottery', p.54, for this vase illustrated.

A Burmantofts vase, impressed marks.

10in (25.5cm) high

£500-600   WW

A Burmantofts Faience 'Egyptianesque' vase, with hieroglyphs, impressed marks.

12¼in (31cm) high

£500-600   WW

A Burmantofts Faience grotesque lizard vase, model no.741, impressed and incised marks, some light wear.

7½in (19cm) high

£500-600   WW

A Burmantofts Faience grotesque alligator chamberstick, model no.884, impressed marks.

4¼in (11cm) high

£300-400   WW

A Burmantofts Faience model of a lizard, model no.1993, modelled coiled around a shell eyeing up a spider, with applied glass eyes, impressed marks.

4½in (11.5cm) wide

£650-750   WW

A Burmantofts Faience model of a scaly fish, model no.2166, with sang-de-boeuf glaze, with applied glass eyes, impressed marks, restored tail fins.

7in (18cm) wide

£650-750   WW

CERAMICS

A Burmantofts Faience model of a monkey, model no.797, impressed marks, small hairline to vase.

6in (15cm) high

£500-600   **WW**

A Burmantofts Faience model of a monkey, model no.2000, with applied glass eyes, impressed marks.

3¼in (8.5cm) high

£400-500   **WW**

A Burmantofts Faience grotesque ibex creature ewer, model no.555, the horns forming a handle, impressed marks, restoration to handle.

13in (33cm) high

£350-400   **WW**

A Burmantofts Faience grotesque crocodile ewer, model no.554, impressed marks, some minor glaze frits.

11¾in (30cm) high

£450-550   **WW**

A Burmantofts Faience grotesque dragon, impressed marks, restoration to feet.

5¼in (13.5cm) wide

£400-450   **WW**

A Burmantofts Faience grotesque creature, model no.583, impressed marks, small glaze chip to one foot.

7½in (19cm) wide

£450-550   **WW**

A Burmantofts Faience grotesque creature, model no.1906, impressed marks, chips to all four feet, painted to conceal.

6½in (16.5cm) wide

£350-400   **WW**

A Burmantofts Faience model of a Kirin, model no.522, impressed marks, restoration to crest on head, tail and an ear.

7¾in (19.5cm) high

£400-500   **WW**

A Burmantofts Faience model of a Kirin, model no.1174, impressed marks and incised marks, re-stuck tail, small frit to the glaze on tail and ear.

4¾in (12cm) wide

£400-500   **WW**

QUICK REFERENCE - CARLTON WARE

- The Wiltshaw & Robinson Company was founded in 1890 in Stoke. It was soon operating under the trade name Carlton Ware.
- The founder's son, Frederick Cuthbert Wiltshaw, took over in 1918. With the help of design director Horace Wain and later Enoch Boulton, Wiltshaw launched a range of lustre projects featuring flower and animal designs.

A 1920s Wiltshaw and Robinson Carlton Ware ginger jar and cover, 'Barge' pattern, printed mark, some damages to cover.

10¼in (26cm) high

£70-80   FLD

An Art Deco Carlton Ware Tomb jar and cover, 'Chinaland' pattern no.2948, highlighted in gilt, printed and painted factory marks, hairline to top rim.

14½in (37cm) high

£250-350   WW

A Carlton Ware ginger jar and cover, 'Dragon and Cloud' pattern.

10½in (26.5cm) high

£100-150   PSA

A Carlton Ware ginger jar and cover, 'Sunflower Geometric' pattern no.3334, printed and painted, printed factory mark, applied Carlton Ware paper label, cover restored.

The Michael Burningham Collection.

8in (20.5cm) high

£650-750   WW

A Carlton Ware ginger jar and cover, 'Devil's Copse' pattern, printed and painted in enamels, highlighted in gilt, printed factory mark, remains of painted mark, original paper retailer's label.

6¾in (17cm) high

£300-400   WW

A Carlton Ware ginger jar and cover, 'Chinese Bird and Cloud' pattern no.3327, designed by Violet Elmer, printed and painted in colours highlighted in gilt, printed and painted marks.

10¼in (26cm) high

£400-500   WW

A Carlton Ware ginger jar and cover, 'Mandarins Chatting' pattern no.3675, printed and enamelled in colours and gilt, printed and painted marks, original paper label.

10½in (26.5cm) high

£450-550   WW

A Carlton Ware ginger jar, 'Tutankhamun' pattern no.2711, designed by Enoch Boulton, printed and enamelled in colours with hieroglyphs, printed factory marks and special Tut mark.

The 'Tutankhamun', or more correctly 'Tut', pattern was introduced by Carlton Ware in 1923, the year after Howard Carter discovered the King's tomb in November 1922. Egyptomania spread rapidly across Europe through architecture and the decorative arts.

10¼in (26cm) high

£400-500   WW

CERAMICS

A CLOSER LOOK AT A CARLTON WARE VASE

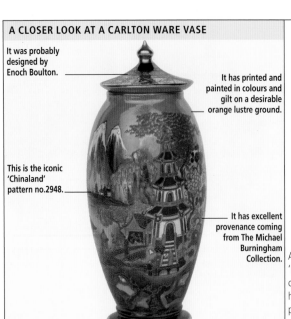

It was probably designed by Enoch Boulton.

This is the iconic 'Chinaland' pattern no.2948.

It has printed and painted in colours and gilt on a desirable orange lustre ground.

It has excellent provenance coming from The Michael Burningham Collection.

A Carlton Ware vase and cover, printed and painted factory marks.

7½in (19cm) high

£650-750   **WW**

An Art Deco Carlton Ware vase, 'Bluebells' pattern, enamelled in colours on a Rouge Royale ground, highlighted in gilt, printed and painted marks.

14in (35.5cm) high

£250-350   **WW**

A Carlton Ware vase, 'Hollyhocks' pattern.

4¾in (12cm) high

£70-90   **PSA**

A Carlton Ware vase, 'Mandarin's Chatting' pattern no.3653, printed and painted marks.

7¼in (18.5cm) high

£400-500   **WW**

A Carlton Ware vase, 'Wagonwheels' pattern no.3814, printed and painted marks, professional restoration to base.

7½in (19cm) high

£400-500   **WW**

A Carlton Ware vase, 'Forest Tree' pattern no.3244, printed and painted marks.

12¼in (31cm) high

£300-400   **WW**

An Art Deco Carlton Ware vase, 'Devil's Copse' pattern, with an indented collar neck, gilt and enamel decoration, printed script mark.

1930s   8in (20.5cm) high

£150-200   **FLD**

An Art Deco Carlton Ware vase, 'Palm Blossom' pattern, printed script mark.

1930s   8in (20.5cm) high

£450-550   **FLD**

An Art Deco Carlton Ware vase, 'Chinaland' pattern, by Wiltshaw and Robinson, printed mark.

1920s   8¼in (21cm) high

£120-180   **FLD**

An Art Deco Carlton Ware preserve pot, cover and stand, 'Feathertailed Bird and Flower' pattern, printed script mark.

1930s   *stand 4in (10cm) diam*

£100-150   **FLD**

An Art Deco Wiltshaw and Robinson Carlton Ware footed bowl, 'Barge' pattern, printed mark.

1930s   *12¼in (31cm) long*

£100-150   **FLD**

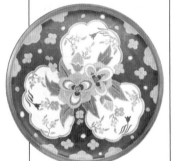

A Carlton Ware handcraft wall plaque, decorated with flowers.

12½in (32cm) diam

£45-65   **PSA**

An Art Deco Carlton Ware tray, 'Fan' pattern no.3557, highlighted in gilt, printed and painted marks.

14¼in (36cm) wide

£250-300   **WW**

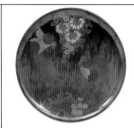

A rare Carlton Ware charger, 'Fighting Cocks' pattern no.4161.

See Dr Czes and Yvonne Kosniowski 'Carlton Ware The Complete Guide', page 228, for the original design illustrated.

12½in (32cm) high

£300-400   **WW**

A Carlton Ware bowl, 'Jazz' pattern no.3361, designed by Enoch Boulton, printed and painted marks, hairline to rim.

8in (20.5cm) diam

£400-500   **WW**

A rare Carlton Ware advertising wall plaque, of a toucan next to a pint of Guinness.

Carlton Ware produced ceramics used by Guinness, such as toucans and small animal figurines, for advertising purposes. The toucan was based on John Gilroy's creation of the hapless zoo keeper and his unruly animals for Guinness adverts in the 1920s-1960s. Many fakes of the pieces have since been created.

7in (18cm) high

£1,500-2,000   **PSA**

A Carlton Ware 'Martell Brandy' ceramic advertising figure.

Cognac house Martell was founded in 1715 by Jean Martell. This Carlton Ware advertising piece states, 'Make friends with Martell'.

8¼in (21cm) high

£250-300   **PSA**

CERAMICS

MARKET REPORT

The market in Clarice Cliff is now one of the most established in the field of 20thC ceramics, from its early beginnings in the 1970s through to its meteoric rise towards the millennium! Post 2000, there was a significant re-adjustment in the market that previously had been driven by the search for knowledge: regardless of what the object was, if it bore Clarice Cliff's name, it was assured to fetch large sums.

Today, the market is much more educated and aware of her story and the products she created and there has been a definite divide and separate between basic, better and best! The lower entry level market has settled down to the point where a basic banded or plain piece of Clarice can be snapped up for as little as a few pounds. However, at the other end of the spectrum prices continue to rise!

Collectors now know exactly what they want, be it pattern, shape or - better still - the perfect combination of both. Rare patterns, especially in unusual colour variants are still the must-have among collectors and nowadays the market can be divided into four main categories of Landscapes, Abstracts, Fruits and Florals and Novelty wares. For many years, the Abstracts and Landscapes have always been the most significantly sought after with pieces regularly fetching four and even five figure sums. However, for me, the Florals perfectly display Clarice Cliff's unique talent for taking simple floral motifs and turning them into bold, bright and iconic pieces of 1930s ceramics.

It was thought some time ago that we had seen all there was to discover and found all that we were going to find. However, new patterns still emerge, even if not as regularly as 30 years ago, and collectors are still left speechless at a new abstract or landscape pattern.

Will Farmer, Fieldings Auctioneers, Stourbridge

A Clarice Cliff Bizarre Stamford 'Alton' teapot and cover, printed factory marks.

4¾in (12cm) high

£500-600   **WW**

A Clarice Cliff Bizarre fern pot, 'Appliqué Avignon' pattern, printed and painted factory marks.

3in (7.5cm) high

£650-750   **WW**

A Clarice Cliff plate, 'Appliqué Blossom' pattern, handpainted with stylised flowers and foliage over a patterned ground, printed 'APPLIQUÉ' and 'Bizarre' mark.

c1931   8in (22.5cm) wide

£1,000-1,200   **FLD**

A Clarice Cliff plate, 'Appliqué Caravan' pattern, handpainted with a scene of a caravan below a fruiting tree, handpainted 'APPLIQUÉ' and 'Bizarre' mark.

c1931   9in (25cm) wide

£2,000-3,000   **FLD**

A rare Clarice Cliff Bizarre 265 vase, 'Appliqué Etna' pattern, painted with two mountain scenes, printed and painted marks.

6¼in (16cm) high

£4,500-5,500   **WW**

A Clarice Cliff Bizarre plate, 'Appliqué Etna' pattern, printed and painted marks, impressed date mark.

1931   10in (25.5cm) diam

£3,000-3,500   **WW**

A Clarice Cliff wall plaque, 'Appliqué Idyll' pattern, with a crinoline lady below a flowering tree, signed 'Clarice Cliff' to the front and to the reverse 'The Property of Threlfalls Brewery', printed 'APPLIQUÉ' and 'Bizarre' mark.

13in (33cm) diam

£1,500-2,000   **FLD**

A Clarice Cliff dish-form plate, 'Appliqué Monsoon' pattern, with a Japanese Torii gate on a hillside, printed 'APPLIQUÉ' and 'Bizarre' mark.

A Torii gate, literally bird abode, is a traditional Japanese gate most commonly found at the entrance to or within a Shinto shrine, where it symbolically marks the transition from the mundane to the sacred.

c1931   *9in (23cm) wide*
£5,000-6,000   **FLD**

A Clarice Cliff 'Hiawatha' bowl, 'Appliqué Palermo' pattern, 'APPLIQUÉ' and 'Bizarre' mark.
c1930   *11in (28cm) wide*
£1,000-1,500   **FLD**

Judith Picks

The 'Lotus' or 'Isis' jug is one of the most characteristic shapes associated with Clarice Cliff. Despite this, it was actually designed in 1919 by her predecessor at Wilkinson's, John Butler, as part of a jug and bowl wash stand set.

The simple form was intended to suggest antiquity, and it was produced with one or two handles, or no handles. Some examples are stamped 'LOTUS' or 'ISIS', the original name of the shape.

At the time, examples with handles were classed as functional rather than decorative wares, so attracted a lower tax. Their popularity means fakes abound – the simplest way to identify one is to look at the inside edge of the handle. If a hole is found, it is a reproduction or fake. Values vary depending on the pattern and condition.

A Clarice Cliff single-handled 'Isis' vase, 'Blue Autumn' pattern, handpainted with a stylised tree and cottage landscape, double image, 'FANTASQUE' and 'Bizarre' marks.
c1930   *9¾in (24.5cm) high*
£1,500-2,000   **FLD**

A Clarice Cliff Fantasque Bizarre conical sugar sifter, 'Autumn' pattern, printed factory marks, restored base rim and tip.
5½in (14cm) high
£350-400   **WW**

A Clarice Cliff Bizarre conical sugar sifter, 'Blue Firs' pattern, printed factory marks, professionally restored.
5½in (14cm) high
£900-1,100   **WW**

A Clarice Cliff 'Bon Jour' shape preserve pot and cover, 'Bridgewater' and 'Bizarre' mark, cover restored.
c1933   *4¼in (11cm) high*
£220-280   **FLD**

A Clarice Cliff Bizarre Lynton coffee set for six, 'Blue Firs' pattern, printed factory marks.
7in (18cm) high
£3,000-4,000   **WW**

A Clarice Cliff 'Conical' shape jug, 'Broth' pattern, 'Fantasque' mark.
c1929   *6in (15cm) high*
£550-650   **FLD**

QUICK REFERENCE - CLARICE CLIFF

- Clarice Cliff (1899-1972) was born in Stoke-on-Trent and began her career as an apprentice enameller at Linguard Webster & Co. in 1912.

- In 1916, she moved to A.J. Wilkinson. In the mid-1920s, Wilkinson gave Cliff her own studio, Newport Pottery. Here she began to work on her earthenware designs, first experimenting by handpainting decoration on blank defective wares.

- Her Bizarre and Fantasque ranges were launched in 1928, covering a range of patterns and shapes. The majority of her wares were tableware, although she also designed vases, candlesticks, figurines and other items.

- She trained a group of female decorators to paint her designs by hand. They became known as the 'Bizarre Girls'.

- Clarice Cliff wares were handpainted in thickly applied bright colours, often with thin black outlines around coloured elements. Her bold designs include stylised floral patterns, landscapes, geometric and abstract shapes. Many patterns come in a variety of colours. Orange is commonly found, with pastels and blue and purple being scarcer. There is often variation within one pattern, as the 'Bizarre Girls' had the freedom to slightly vary the designs.

- In general, the market for Clarice Cliff has remained strong, especially for rarer shapes and patterns. Rare landscapes such as the 'Appliqué' range, 'May Avenue', 'Luxor' and unusual colour variants of classic patterns such as 'Red Autumn' or 'Green House' continue to perform well. Geometric patterns such as 'Café', 'Sunspots', 'Football' and 'Tennis' remain strong.

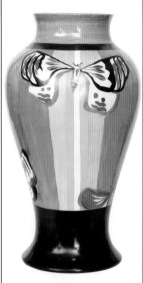

A Clarice Cliff large shape 14 'Mei Ping' vase, 'Butterfly' pattern, Fantasque mark.

16in (41cm) high

£2,500-3,000   **FLD**

A Clarice Cliff shape 368 stepped fern pot, 'Orange Chintz' pattern, 'Bizarre' mark.

c1932   *9in (23cm) high*

£250-300   **FLD**

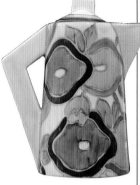

A Clarice Cliff 'Conical' shape coffee pot, 'Blue Chintz' pattern, 'Bizarre' mark with gold 'Lawleys' backstamp.

c1932   *7in (18cm) high*

£360-400   **FLD**

A large Clarice Cliff 'Perth' shape jug, 'Circle Tree (RAF Tree)' pattern, 'Fantasque' mark.

c1929   *5½in (14cm) high*

£350-450   **FLD**

A Clarice Cliff globe-shaped teapot, 'Circle Tree (RAF Tree)' pattern, 'Fantasque' mark, small restoration to the spout.

c1929   *4in (10.5cm) high*

£500-600   **FLD**

A Clarice Cliff 'Humpty' shape sugar bowl, 'Coral Firs' pattern, 'Bizarre' mark.

c1933   *3in (8cm) high*

£200-250   **FLD**

A Clarice Cliff Bizarre part-conical tea set, 'Delecia Nasturtium' pattern, comprising milk-jug and sugar basin, one conical cup, saucer and side plate, printed factory marks.

£900-1,200   **WW**

A Clarice Cliff shape 630 vase, 'Delecia Pansies', handpainted 'PANSIES' and 'Bizarre' mark.

c1933   *6in (16.5cm) high*

£250-300   **FLD**

QUICK REFERENCE - CONICAL SUGAR SIFTER

- The 'Conical' sugar sifter is one of Clarice Cliff's most iconic and recognisable designs. It was designed by Cliff herself and issued in 1931 in one height.
- It was produced in large quantities and was decorated with a huge number of handpainted and transfer-printed patterns until around 1938. As a result, some collectors choose to focus on collecting this shape exclusively.
- Always examine the edges and particularly the top for damage or restoration as any damage will affect the value.

A Clarice Cliff Fantasque Bizarre conical sugar sifter, 'Farmhouse' pattern, printed factory marks, minor frits to paintwork on the tip.

5¾in (14.5cm) high

£750-850   **WW**

A pair of Clarice Cliff 'Football' 'Meiping' vases, printed marks, both restored.

The vendor's grandmother recalls that these were purchased, direct from the factory, on the family's return journey from their summer holiday to Cornwall in around 1930. Subsequently, they were passed down through the family.

14¼in (36cm) high

£4,000-5,000   **SWO**

A rare Clarice Cliff miniature vase, 'Double V' pattern, printed Newport Pottery mark,

These miniature vases were made as tradesman's sample vases taken to show prospective stockists of Clarice's new and vibrant ware.

2¾in (7cm) high

£650-750   **WW**

A Clarice Cliff shape 187 vase, 'Honolulu' pattern, 'Bizarre' mark.

c1933   *7in (18cm) high*

£1,000-1,500   **FLD**

A Clarice Cliff Bizarre 362 vase, 'Honolulu' pattern, printed factory marks.

8in (20.5cm) high

£1,800-2,200   **WW**

A Clarice Cliff Fantasque Bizarre 365 vase, 'House and Bridge' pattern, printed factory mark.

7in (20cm) high

£1,800-2,200   **WW**

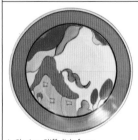

A Clarice Cliff shape 360 vase, 'Geometric Flowers' pattern, gold 'Fantasque' mark.

c1929/30   *8in (20.5cm) high*

£2,200-2,800   **FLD**

A Clarice Cliff dish-form plate, 'Green House' pattern, handpainted with a stylised tree and cottage landscape, 'FANTASQUE' and 'Bizarre' mark.

c1931   *9in (23cm) wide*

£1,000-1,500   **FLD**

A Clarice Cliff 'Coronet' shape jug, 'Orange House' pattern, 'FANTASQUE' and 'Bizarre' mark.

c1930   *7in (18cm) high*

£800-900   **FLD**

A Clarice Cliff shape 14 'Meiping' vase, 'Inspiration Bouquet' pattern, handpainted 'INSPIRATION' and 'Bizarre' mark, small restoration to the foot.

c1930   *14in (36cm) high*

£1,100-1,500   **FLD**

A Clarice Cliff Bizarre 'Meiping' vase, 'Inspiration Caprice' pattern, painted factory mark, chips to rims.

See Peter Wentworth-Sheilds and Kay Johnson, 'Clarice Cliff', L'Odeon London (1976), page 49, plate 13, for illustration.

14in (37cm) high

£800-900   **WW**

A Clarice Cliff shape 370 'Globe' vase, 'Inspiration Clouvre Flowers' pattern, handpainted 'CLOUVRE', printed 'Bizarre' mark.

c1930   *6in (15cm) high*

£2,800-3,200   **FLD**

A Clarice Cliff shape 386 'Mallet' vase, 'Inspiration Clouvre Waterlily' pattern, handpainted 'INSPIRATION' and 'Bizarre' mark, restored.

c1929   *12in (31cm) high*

£600-700   **FLD**

A Clarice Cliff shape 370 'Globe' vase, 'Inspiration Rose' pattern, handpainted ochre 'INSPIRATION' mark only, restored.

c1930   *6in (15cm) high*

£800-900   **FLD**

A Clarice Cliff 'Leda' shaped plate, 'Yellow Japan' pattern, with 'A.J. Wilkinson' mark only.

c1934   *9in (25cm) wide*

£220-280   **FLD**

A large Clarice Cliff wall plaque, 'Latona Red Roses' pattern, handpainted 'LATONA' and 'Bizarre' mark.

c1930   *13¼in (33.5cm) wide*

£1,200-1,500   **FLD**

A Clarice Cliff Bizarre 'Meiping' vase, 'Latona Tree' pattern, printed and painted marks.

12in (30.5cm) high

£1,100-1,500   **WW**

A Clarice Cliff advertising bowl, 'Limberlost' pattern, handpainted with the words 'Bizarre by Clarice Cliff', 'Bizarre' mark.
6in (16cm) high
£400-500   **FLD**

A Clarice Cliff wall plaque, 'Luxor' pattern, 'Bizarre' mark.
c1930   13in (33cm) high
£1,500-2,000   **FLD**

A CLOSER LOOK AT A 'MAY AVENUE' JUG

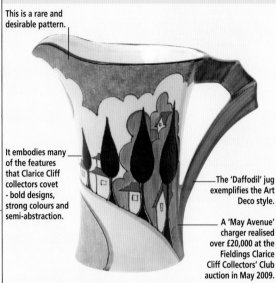

This is a rare and desirable pattern.

It embodies many of the features that Clarice Cliff collectors covet - bold designs, strong colours and semi-abstraction.

The 'Daffodil' jug exemplifies the Art Deco style.

A 'May Avenue' charger realised over £20,000 at the Fieldings Clarice Cliff Collectors' Club auction in May 2009.

A rare Clarice Cliff Bizarre 'Daffodil' jug, 'May Avenue' pattern, painted in colours, printed factory mark.
6in (17cm) high
£2,500-3,000   **WW**

A Clarice Cliff dish-form wave-edge plaque, 'Marigold' pattern, handpainted 'MARIGOLD' and 'Bizarre' mark.
c1930   12¼in (31cm) wide
£900-1,200   **FLD**

A rare Clarice Cliff Bizarre 'Meiping' vase, 'May Avenue' pattern, printed factory marks.
6¼in (16cm) high
£3,000-4,000   **WW**

A Clarice Cliff shape 196 vase, 'Melon' pattern, 'FANTASQUE' and 'Bizarre' mark.
c1930   2½in (6.5cm) high
£500-600   **FLD**

A large Clarice Cliff jardinière, 'Melon' pattern, 'FANTASQUE' and 'Bizarre' mark, slightly damaged.
c1929   8in (20cm) high
£600-700   **FLD**

A large Clarice Cliff shape 356 'Kidney' vase, 'Pastel Melon' pattern, 'FANTASQUE' and 'Bizarre' mark, small restoration to the rim.
c1930   6¾in (17cm) high
£400-500   **FLD**

A 'Conical' shape coffee service, 'Melon' pattern, 'Fantasque' mark.
c1929-30
£3,000-4,000   **FLD**

A Clarice Cliff 'Bon Jour' sugar sifter, 'Moonlight' pattern, partial 'Bizarre' mark.

c1933   *5in (12.5cm) high*
£450-550   **FLD**

A Clarice Cliff 'Bon Jour' preserve pot, 'Newlyn' pattern, with a tonal blue 'Delecia' effect sky, script signature.

c1935   *4in (10cm) high*
£300-400   **FLD**

A Clarice Cliff 'Humpty' sugar pot, 'Oasis' pattern, 'FANTASQUE' and 'Bizarre' mark.

c1933   *8in (20.5cm) high*
£90-120   **FLD**

A Clarice Cliff shape 369A vase, 'Orange L', handpainted with a repeat abstract linear and block design, 'Bizarre' mark, some damages.

c1930   *7in (19.5cm) high*
£1,000-1,500   **FLD**

A Clarice Cliff shape 269 vase, 'Original Bizarre' pattern, partial gold 'Fantasque' mark.

c1929   *5in (14.5cm) high*
£250-300   **FLD**

A Clarice Cliff shape 120 vase, 'Original Bizarre' pattern, gold 'Bizarre' mark.

c1928   *10½in (26.5cm) high*
£500-600   **FLD**

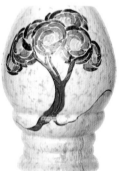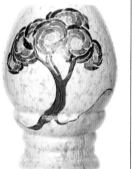

A Clarice Cliff shape 362 vase, 'Blue Patina Tree' pattern, decorated with a blue splatter effect, printed 'PATINA' and 'Bizarre' mark.

c1932-33   *7in (20cm) high*
£400-500   **FLD**

A Clarice Cliff single-handled 'Lotus' jug, 'Petunia' pattern, handpainted with a yellow and brown stippled 'Café au Lait'-style ground, 'Bizarre' mark.

c1933   *11in (29cm) high*
£350-450   **FLD**

A Clarice Cliff 'Conical' bowl, 'Red Gardenia Café Au Lait' pattern, 'Bizarre' mark.

c1931   *8in (20cm) wide*
£600-700   **FLD**

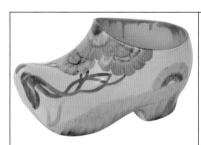

A Clarice Cliff large sabot or clog, 'Rhodanthe' pattern, large script signature.
c1935   *5in (14cm) high*
£200-250   **FLD**

A Clarice Cliff 'Bon Jour' vegetable tureen, 'Rhodanthe' pattern, script signature and Biarritz mark.
c1936   *7¾in (20cm) wide*
£200-250   **FLD**

A Clarice Cliff Fantasque Bizarre conical sugar sifter, 'Orange Roof Cottage' pattern, printed factory marks, tip restored.
5½in (14cm) high
£400-500   **WW**

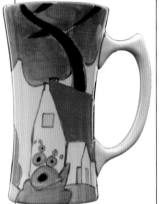

A Clarice Cliff waisted cylindrical mug, 'Red Roofs' pattern, 'FANTASQUE' and 'Bizarre' mark, restored.
c1931   *4¾in (12cm) high*
£250-300   **FLD**

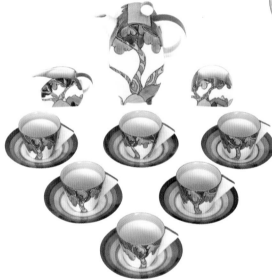

A Clarice Cliff 'Bon Jour' coffee service, 'Rudyard' pattern.
c1933
£2,500-3,000   **FLD**

A Clarice Cliff shape 54 fruit bowl, 'Secrets' pattern, 'FANTASQUE' and 'Bizarre' mark.
c1933   *19in (48.5cm) wide*
£200-250   **FLD**

A Clarice Cliff shape 472 bonbon dish, 'Solitude' pattern, 'FANTASQUE' and 'Bizarre' mark.
c1933   *9½in (24cm) wide*
£200-300   **FLD**

A unique Clarice Cliff Bizarre large floor vase, 'Sliced Fruit' pattern, printed factory marks.
'Clarice Cliff Giants' by Len Griffin, October 1989, discusses a comparable example of this large vase decorated in the 'Branch & Squares' pattern, which was exhibited at L'Odeon's Clarice Cliff exhibition, loaned by Midwinter and now in the Wedgwood collection, after Midwinter closed in 1986.
27½in (70cm) high
£2,500-3,000   **WW**

A large Clarice Cliff tumbler, 'Summerhouse' pattern, 'Fantasque' and 'Bizarre' marks.
c1932   *4½in (11.5cm) high*
£300-400   **FLD**

CERAMICS

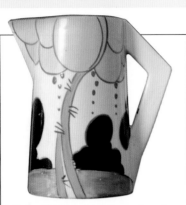

A Clarice Cliff 'Conical' jug, 'Summerhouse' pattern, 'Bizarre' mark.
c1932   *4½in (11.5cm) high*
£350-450   **FLD**

A large Clarice Cliff 'Bee Hive' honey pot, 'Summerhouse' pattern, 'Bizarre' mark.
c1932   *4¼in (10.5cm) high*
£450-550   **FLD**

A Clarice Cliff shape 14 'Meiping' vase, 'Summerhouse', 'FANTASQUE' and 'Bizarre' marks, some damages.
c1931   *9in (23cm) high*
£850-950   **FLD**

A Clarice Cliff Fantasque Bizarre 365 vase, 'Summerhouse' pattern, printed factory marks.
                                    8in (20.5cm) high
£1,800-2,200   **WW**

A Clarice Cliff shape 120 vase, 'Summerhouse' pattern, 'FANTASQUE' and 'Bizarre' mark.
c1932   *10¼in (26cm) high*
£1,000-1,500   **FLD**

A Clarice Cliff Bizarre 'Conical' teapot and cover, 'Sunray' pattern, printed factory marks, paint flakes.
                                      4in (12cm) high
£1,100-1,500   **WW**

A Clarice Cliff globe-shaped teapot, 'Sunray (Night and Day)' pattern, matched cover, 'Bizarre' mark.
c1929   *6in (15cm) high*
£450-550   **FLD**

A Clarice Cliff 'Heath' shape fern pot, 'Sunray (Night and Day)' pattern, 'Bizarre' mark.
c1929   *3in (9.5cm) high*
£650-750   **FLD**

A Clarice Cliff side plate, 'Tennis' pattern, handpainted with an abstract design with stylised tennis net, 'FANTASQUE' and 'Bizarre' mark.
c1931   *7in (17.5cm) wide*
£500-600   **FLD**

A Clarice Cliff Fantasque Bizarre 'Meiping' vase, 'Orange Trees and House' pattern, with printed factory mark.

8in (22.5cm) high

£1,100-1,500 WW

A Clarice Cliff shape 278 vase, 'Red Trees and House' pattern, 'Fantasque' mark.

c1929 *6in (15cm) high*

£550-650 FLD

A Clarice Cliff tankard-shape coffee service, 'Red Trees & House' pattern, full and partial 'Fantasque' marks.

c1930

£2,000-2,500 FLD

A Clarice Cliff Fantasque Bizarre wall charger, 'Red Trees and House' pattern, printed factory marks.

17¾in (45cm) diam

£4,000-5,000 WW

A Clarice Cliff shape 269 vase, 'Red Trees and House' pattern, 'Fantasque' mark, restored.

c1929 *6in (15.5cm) high*

£350-450 FLD

A Clarice Cliff shape 565 vase, 'Tulips' pattern, 'Bizarre' mark.

c1934 *11½in (29cm) high*

£400-450 FLD

A large Clarice Cliff plate, 'Windbells' pattern, 'Bizarre' mark.

c1933 *9in (23cm) wide*

£300-350 FLD

A Clarice Cliff 'Isis' vase, 'Windbells' pattern, 'FANTASQUE' and 'Bizarre' mark.

c1933 *9¾in (25cm) high*

£1,200-1,800 FLD

CERAMICS

QUICK REFERENCE - BRANGWYN PANELS

● In 1926, Frank Brangwyn was commissioned by Lord Iveagh to paint a pair of large canvases to be displayed in the Royal Gallery at the House of Lords, Westminster. The paintings were to commemorate peers and their family members who had been killed in World War I. Accordingly, Brangwyn painted two battle scenes, which included a scene of life-size troops advancing into battle beside a British tank. When the paintings were unveiled in 1928, the Lords rejected the panels considering them too grim and disturbing. They recommissioned Brangwyn to produce a series of panels that would celebrate the beauty of the British Empire and the Dominions. Over the next five years, Brangwyn completed 16 panels (that covered 3,000sq ft), which would be known as the British Empire Panels. Five of the panels were displayed in the Royal Gallery for approval by the Lords, but were again refused on the ground of being 'too colourful and lively'. In 1934, the 16 panels were purchased by Swansea Council and are now housed in the Brangwyn Hall, Swansea.

A Clarice Cliff Wilkinson's vase, in the form of a closed book.

7¼in (18.5cm) high

£60-80   WHP

An early Clarice Cliff figurine, 'Mrs Puddleduck', on an enamelled base, 'A.J.Wilkinson' mark.

6¼in (16cm) high

£200-250   FLD

A Clarice Cliff framed charger, handpainted after the original from the British Empire Panel with African figures, the reverse with the handpainted mark 'The Brangwyn panels designed for the Royal Gallery of the House of Lords 1925, First Exhibited at Olympia 1933. Painted by Clarice Cliff from one of the panels. A.J. Wilkinson, Royal Staffordshire Pottery Burslem, Staffordshire', numbered '17' and signed Frank Brangwyn.

12¾in (32.5cm) diam

£1,500-2,000   FLD

An early Clarice Cliff figurine, 'Mr Puddleduck', on an enamelled base, 'A.J. Wilkinson' mark.

6¼in (16cm) high

£180-220   FLD

A Clarice Cliff novelty candlestick, modelled as an Arab in pantaloons with sash and turban holding a basket.

6in (15cm) high

£150-200   FLD

A Clarice Cliff 'United Service' salt pot, printed mark.

4in (10cm) high

£180-220   WW

A rare Clarice Cliff Bizarre 'Age of Jazz' table centrepiece, model no.436, modelled as a Jazz piano player and a banjo player, printed factory mark, professional restoration to piano.

5in (13.5cm) high

£12,000-15,000   WW

A Clarice Cliff face mask, 'Chahar', 'Bizarre' mark.

11in (28cm) high

£1,200-1,600   FLD

A Coalport figurine, 'Time', limited edition from 'The Millennium Ball' collection, boxed with certificate.
£80-100 PSA

A Coalport figurine, 'Rain', limited edition from 'The Millennium Ball' collection, boxed with certificate.
£80-100 PSA

QUICK REFERENCE - COALPORT

● John Rose established the porcelain factory and began production at Coalport in c1796. It was the first factory established in the Ironbridge Gorge, Shropshire.

● The Coalport factory began by manufacturing low-cost enamelled copies of Chinese patterns, as well as supplying plain white porcelain to independent china painters for decoration. This resulted in a huge variety of designs on Coalport porcelain. By the mid-19thC, Coalport employed in-house decorators.

● Porcelain from the factory was also referred to as Coalbrookdale porcelain. In the 1860s, Coalport moved into domestic ware.

● In 1967, the Coalport brand was bought by the Wedgwood Group. The original factory buildings at Ironbridge now house the Coalport China Museum.

A Coalport figurine, 'Sun', limited edition from 'The Millennium Ball' collection, some small nips to base edge.
£80-100 PSA

A Coalport Guinness advertising figurine, 'Elephant and Keeper', boxed with certificate.
£100-150 PSA

A Coalport ewer, gilded and handpainted, with scenes of Loch Awe by E. Ball.
7½in (19cm) high
£75-85 PSA

A Coalport vase, handpainted with castle scene.
6¾in (17cm) high
£110-140 PSA

A late 19thC Coalport pâte-sur-pâte vase, painted in white slip with winged putti dancing above a river, with gilt and 'jewelled' arabesques and stylised motif, signed 'A. Handley', green printed mark.
17¾in (45cm) high
£2,000-2,500 DUK

A mid-19thC Coalport porcelain bowl, painted with stag hunting scenes.
10¼in (26cm) wide
£200-250 DUK

A Coalport trinket box, with a painted scene of sheep, the lid interior stamped 'Coalport AD 1750'.
2¾in (7cm) wide
£90-110 DUK

CERAMICS

QUICK REFERENCE - COBRIDGE

- Based in Stoke-on-Trent, Cobridge stoneware operated between 1998 and 2005. It was part of Moorcroft Pottery.
- After the company's closure, its moulds were acquired by Burslem Pottery – owned by Tracey Bentley, a former employee at Cobridge.
- Cobridge designer and decorator Anita Harris also worked for Poole Pottery.

A Cobridge stoneware vase, signed Nicola Slaney.

10½in (26.5cm) high

£100-150   PSA

A Cobridge stoneware vase, 'Land of the Pharaohs' pattern, impressed and painted marks, painted 'Trial 16.11.04', signed Shirley Hayes, boxed.

10¼in (26cm) high

£150-200   FLD

A Cobridge stoneware high-fired vase, impressed marks.

10¾in (27.5cm) high

£200-250   FLD

A Cobridge stoneware high-fired barrel vase, impressed marks.

10in (25.5cm) high

£180-240   FLD

A Cobridge stoneware high-fired vase, impressed marks.

7¼in (18.5cm) high

£120-160   FLD

A pair of Cobridge stoneware vases, designed by Paul Adiamec, 'Caledonian Sunset' pattern, impressed marks, limited edition, one numbered 6/25 and the other 8/25, dated.

2003   *10in (25.5cm) high*

£250-350   LSK

A pair of Cobridge stoneware vases, designed by Emma Bossons, 'Witching Hour' pattern, impressed, monogrammed and dated verso.

2002   *11¾in (30cm) high*

£150-200   LSK

A Cobridge stoneware charger, designed by Jackie Strode, 'Cobbled Court' pattern, impressed marks, dated, numbered 11/25 verso.

2003   *14¼in (36cm) diam*

£60-80   LSK

QUICK REFERENCE - DE MORGAN

- William De Morgan (1839-1917) studied at the Royal Academy Schools, before meeting and working with William Morris, designing and producing decorative tiles.
- De Morgan was inspired by Iznik pottery of the 15thC and 16thC and specialised in Persian ware.
- From 1882-1900, P&O Cruises commissioned De Morgan to supply decorative tiles for 12 of their new liners. In 1888, De Morgan set up a pottery at Sands End, London. Here, he developed his 'Moonlight' and 'Sunlight' series.
- De Morgan began writing at the age of 65, producing best-sellers, but his work in ceramics had dwindled by 1904.
- At the beginning of the 20thC, De Morgan's pottery had become less popular and he is thought to have said, 'All my life I have been trying to make beautiful things … and now that I can make them nobody wants them.'

A pair of William De Morgan plastic clay tiles, Fulham, decorated with Persian flowers and foliage, impressed mark.

each 9in (23cm) square

£1,800-2,200   **FLD**

A pair of William De Morgan tiles, impressed marks for Merton Abbey.

c1885   *6¼in (16cm) square*

£250-350   **L&T**

A pair of William De Morgan 'Arabia' tiles, Sands End Pottery, with stylised Persian pattern, impressed marks, minor chips.

These tiles were commissioned for the P&O Liner 'Arabia'.

9in (23cm) square

£3,500-4,000   **WW**

A William De Morgan tile, Sands End Pottery, depicting a galleon in full sail, framed.

c1890   *6in (15cm) square*

£700-800   **L&T**

A William De Morgan plastic clay tile, Sands End Pottery, decorated with a handpainted galleon at sea, impressed mark.

6in (15cm) square

£650-750   **FLD**

A William De Morgan ruby lustre 'Wild Boar' tile, Merton Abbey, impressed mark.

6in (15cm) square

£2,500-3,000   **WW**

A William De Morgan triple lustre 'Hoopoe' tile, impressed late-Fulham period mark.

6in (15cm) square

£3,500-4,000   **WW**

A William De Morgan two-tile snake and flower panel, Merton Abbey, impressed mark, chips, mirror glaze nibbles.

1882-88   *8¼in (21cm) square*

£8,500-9,500   **SWO**

CERAMICS

QUICK REFERENCE - DENNIS CHINAWORKS

- Dennis Chinaworks was founded in 1993 in Somerset, UK, by Sally Tuffin and Richard Dennis.
- Tuffin graduated from the Royal college of Art and co-ran design house Foale & Tuffin. Between 1986 and 1993, Tuffin was Partner and Design Director of the Moorcroft Pottery.
- Richard Dennis trained with Sotheby's, before establishing an antique glass and ceramic business and publishing house.
- At Dennis Chinaworks, a single decorator works on each pot, with their signature marked on the item's base along with the number, company name, date and thrower's mark.

A Dennis Chinaworks 'Illyria' vase, designed by Sally Tuffin, B&W Thornton retailer exclusive, limited edition, numbered '4/12', impressed and painted marks.

14¼in (36cm) high

£750-850   **FLD**

A Dennis Chinaworks jug, designed by Sally Tuffin, impressed marks and painted 'S.T.des No. 83'.

8¾in (22cm) high

£100-150   **FLD**

A Dennis Chinaworks 'Moonlight Hare' vase, designed by Sally Tuffin, potted by Rory Mcleod, no.10, impressed and painted marks, dated.

2005   *13½in (34.5cm) high*

£350-400   **WW**

A Dennis Chinaworks 'Carp' vase, designed by Sally Tuffin, impressed and painted marks, dated.

2003   *12½in (32cm) high*

£180-220   **WW**

A Dennis Chinaworks 'Penguin' jar and cover, designed by Sally Tuffin, impressed and painted marks, dated.

2000   *6¼in (16cm) high*

£140-200   **WW**

A Dennis Chinaworks 'Beetle Scarab' Etruscan vase, designed by Sally Tuffin, impressed and painted marks, limited edition, dated.

2004   *11¾in (30cm) high*

£200-250   **WW**

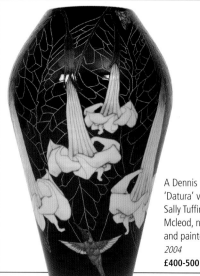

A Dennis Chinaworks large 'Datura' vase, designed by Sally Tuffin, potted by Rory Mcleod, no.16, impressed and painted marks, dated.

2004   *18¼in (46.5cm) high*

£400-500   **WW**

A Dennis Chinaworks 'Koala' vase, designed by Sally Tuffin, impressed and painted marks, dated.

2001   *10½in (26.5cm) high*

£250-350   **WW**

A Dennis Chinaworks 'Slipper Orchid' vase, designed by Sally Tuffin, painted and impressed marks, dated.

2004   *10¾in (27.5cm) high*

£140-200   **WW**

A Dennis Chinaworks 'Koi Carp' circular charger, designed by Sally Tuffin, thrown by Rory Mcleod, limited edition no.21, impressed and painted marks.
14¼in (36cm) diam
£200-250   DUK

A Dennis Chinaworks 'Phoenix' trial vase, designed by Sally Tuffin, thrown by Rory Mcleod, deocrated by Adam White, impressed and painted marks.
c2014   12¾in (32.5cm) high
£250-350   DUK

A Dennis Chinaworks 'Hare' vase, designed by Sally Tuffin, impressed and painted marks, dated.
2005   13¾in (35cm) high
£200-300   WW

A Dennis Chinaworks 'Beer Lugger Night Time' trial vase, designed by Sally Tuffin, thrown by Rory Mcleod, decorated by Adam White, impressed and painted marks.
c2011   11¼in (28.5cm) high
£200-250   DUK

A Dennis Chinaworks 'Tulip' trial vase, designed by Sally Tuffin, thrown by Rory Mcleod, painted by Teresa Brooker, impressed and painted markings.
c2010   13in (33cm) high
£300-350   DUK

A Dennis Chinaworks vase, by Sally Tuffin.
12½in (32cm) high
£150-200   WHP

A Dennis Chinaworks 'Egyptian Head' jar and cover.
8in (20.5cm) high
£200-250   PSA

A Dennis Chinaworks 'Butterfly' jar and cover.
8in (20.5cm) high
£150-200   PSA

CERAMICS

QUICK REFERENCE - DOULTON LAMBETH

- The Doulton Factory was founded in Lambeth, London, in 1815 by John Doulton, Martha Jones and John Watts. Doulton first focused on everyday stoneware such as inkwells and bottles.
- When John Doulton's son Henry joined the firm in 1835, the business expanded and began to make and supply drainpipes to various cities around the world. Henry's success allowed the factory to switch their focus to decorative wares from 1871.
- Doulton worked closely with the Lambeth School of Art, and many Doulton pieces were designed and decorated by students. These Doulton Lambeth pieces are often in the Art Nouveau style.
- Most are signed with artists' monograms. Significant designers include the Tinworth brothers, Arthur (dates unknown) and George (1843-1913), and the Barlow siblings, Hannah (1859-1913), Florence (d.1909) and Arthur (d.1909).
- Doulton prices have declined over the past 15 years, especially for late 19thC and early 20thC Victorian-style stoneware. The most valuable pieces tend to be those by notable designers, such as Mark Marshall or the Barlow or Tinworth siblings. Unusual patterns, shapes, sizes or styles, especially Moorish or Art Nouveau-style pieces, can also fetch high prices.

A late 19thC Doulton Lambeth vase of footed baluster form, by Arthur Barlow, impressed mark, incised initials.

1873   *10¾in (27.5cm) high*

£250-300   FLD

A Doulton Lambeth vase, by Hannah Barlow, decorated with goats on a mottled blue-green ground.

13in (34cm) high

£450-500   WHP

A Doulton Lambeth vase, decorated by Hannah Barlow, sgraffito decoration depicting sheep, impressed marks.

c1900   *15in (38cm) high*

£360-400   K&O

A Doulton Lambeth stoneware vase, by Frank Butler, impressed marks, dated.

1882   *19¼in (49cm) high*

£280-340   K&O

A Doulton Lambeth lamp base, decorated by Edith Lupton, on brass base.

13in (33cm) high

£120-160   PSA

A Doulton Lambeth faience vase, handpainted with yellow blossoms and a butterfly, impressed marks to base, restoration to neck, dated.

1877   12in (31.5cm) high

£100-150   FELL

A Doulton large flambé Sung vase, with mottled glaze, by Fred Moore.

£120-160   PSA

A Doulton Burslem Artwares large flambé Qingdao charger plate, boxed with certificate.

£160-200   PSA

A CLOSER LOOK AT A GEORGE TINWORTH GROUP

This is a complex and rare group by George Tinworth. His mice and frog figures are very collectable.

It is modelled as mice watching and performing a 'Punch and Judy' puppet show.

There are six mice in the group. A large number of mice will tend to increase the value.

The appealing subject will also increase desirability.

A Doulton Lambeth stoneware group, 'Play Goers', by George Tinworth, incised and printed marks.

6in (15cm) high

£8,000-9,000   K&O

A Doulton Lambeth stoneware group, 'Sculptor', by George Tinworth, of a mouse sculpting, incised title and monogram.

3¼in (8.5cm) high

£4,000-4,500   K&O

A Doulton Lambeth stoneware group, 'The Ox and the Frogs', by George Tinworth, depicting an Aesop's fable, incised title and monogram, inscribed 'H. Doulton Lambeth'.

1881   *3¼in (8.5cm) high*

£5,500-6,000   K&O

A Doulton Lambeth stoneware rabbit bibelot, designed by Harry Simeon and Vera Huggins, impressed marks.

4in (10cm) wide

£200-250   WW

A Doulton Lambeth stoneware soap dish, designed by Harry Simeon, stamped marks 'X8978'.

5½in (14cm) high

£400-500   SWO

A Doulton Lambeth stoneware vase, 'Double base and Cello', by George Tinworth, modelled as mice playing musical instruments, incised title and monogram.

5¼in (13.5cm) high

£4,000-4,500   K&O

A Doulton Lambeth stoneware vase, 'Painting', by George Tinworth, modelled as mouse painting a model, beside a trumpet vase, incised title and monogram.

5¼in (13.5cm) high

£3,000-4,000   K&O

QUICK REFERENCE - GEORGE TINWORTH

- George Tinworth (1843-1913) was born in Walworth, London, and studied at the Lambeth School of Art in the evenings.
- At the age of 21, Tinworth went on to study at the Royal Academy School (Royal Academy of Arts).
- J.C.L. Sparkes, Tinworth's headmaster at Lambeth School of Art which worked closely with Doulton, persuaded Henry Doulton to employ Tinworth.
- Around the time that Tinworth joined Doulton in the late 1860s, the company was starting to move away from everyday ware into decorative pottery.
- Tinworth become known for his decorative jugs, vases and humorous figurines, particularly those depicting anthropomorphised mice in humorous situations. Unusually for Doulton designers, Tinworth signed his initials on the body of his works.
- The 1893 Chicago Exhibition saw Doulton exhibit 1,500 pieces, including Tinworth's 'History of England Vase' (1872). It was one of only two thought to have been made.

A Doulton Lambeth stoneware group, 'Scandal', by George Tinworth, modelled as a tea party with monkey and bird above, incised marks.

6in (15cm) high

£4,000-5,000   K&O

CERAMICS

QUICK REFERENCE - ROYAL DOULTON FIGURINES

- Doulton first produced figurines in the 1880s under George Tinworth, then under Charles Noke from 1889 onwards.
- Doulton was known as Royal Doulton after receiving a royal warrant in 1901.
- All figurines were assigned a 'HN' number, from 1912. 'HN' stood for Harry Nixon, who ran the painting department. Over time, more than 4,000 HN numbers were assigned. The first model to be assigned a HN number, HN1 'Darling', was allegedly named after Queen Mary called the figurine 'a darling' on a visit to the factory in 1913.
- Significant designers of Royal Doulton figurines include Leslie Harradine, who worked closely with Noke in the 1920s-50s, Mary Nicoll and Peggy Davies, who produced the majority of the figurines in the 1950s-60s, and Alan Maslankowski, who worked at Royal Doulton from 1968-2006.
- In general, collectors focus on type, colour or designer. Figurines that were produced only for a short time are rarer and more valuable, as are those with unusual colourways. Many Royal Doulton figurines were produced in a range of colourways, which can vary dramatically in price.
- In general, the most desirable and sought-after figurines are those produced before World War II.

A Royal Doulton figurine, 'The Jester', model no.HN45, signed C.J. Noke to base.
1915-38   *9½in (24cm) high*
£1,500-2,000   **PSA**

A Royal Doulton titanian figurine, 'Spook', model no.HN51, designed by H. Tittensor, painted marks, 'No.30'.
1916-36   *7in (18cm) high*
£1,800-2,200   **K&O**

A Royal Doulton figurine, 'Mephistopheles and Marguerite', model no.HN775, designed by C.J. Noke, mounted on wood mirror shelf.
1925-49   *7¾in (19.5cm) high*
£400-500   **PSA**

A Royal Doulton 'Angela' figurine, model no.HN1204, designed by L. Harradine.
1926-40   *7in (18cm) high*
£350-400   **K&O**

A Royal Doulton figurine, 'Lido Lady', model no.HN1220, designed by L. Harradine.
1927-38   *6¾in (17cm) high*
£220-280   **JN**

A rare Royal Doulton figurine, 'Scotch Girl', model no.HN1269, designed by L. Harradine, head re-stuck.
1928-38   *7½in (19cm) high*
£450-550   **PSA**

A Royal Doulton figurine, 'The Alchemist', model no.HN1282, designed by L. Harradine.
1928-38   *11¼in (28.5cm) high*
£200-250   **PSA**

A Royal Doulton figurine, 'Snake Charmer', model no.HN1317, designer unknown.
1929-38   *4in (10cm) high*
£450-500   **PSA**

A Royal Doulton figurine, 'Iona', model no.HN1346, designed by L. Harradine.
1929-38   *7½in (19cm) high*
£550-600   **PW**

A Royal Doulton figurine, 'The Parson's Daughter', model no.HN1356, designed by H. Tittensor.
1929-38   *9¼in (23.5cm) high*
£250-300   **PSA**

A Royal Doulton figurine, 'Love Locked In', model no.HN1474, designed by L. Harradine, restoration to lady's neck and hairline crack to cupid's arm.
Also called 'Love in the Stocks'.
1931-38   *5in (12.5cm) high*
£450-550   **PSA**

A Royal Doulton figurine, 'Gloria', model no.HN1488, designed by L. Harradine.
1932-38   *7¼in (18.5cm) high*
£400-450   **PSA**

A Royal Doulton figurine, 'Bonnie Lassie', model no.HN1626, designed by L. Harradine.
1934-53   *5¼in (13.5cm) high*
£150-200   **FLD**

A Royal Doulton figurine, 'Miranda', model no.HN1819, designed by L. Harradine.
1937-49   *8½in (21.5cm) high*
£350-400   **FLD**

A Royal Doulton figurine, 'Antoinette', model no.HN1851, designed by L. Harradine, small hairline crack to base of pillar.
1938-49   *8in (20.5cm) high*
£200-250   **LOCK**

A Royal Doulton figurine, 'Annabella', model no.HN1875, designed by L. Harradine.
1938-49   *4¾in (12cm) high*
£120-160   **PSA**

A Royal Doulton figurine, 'Sir Walter Raleigh', model no.HN2015, designed by L. Harradine.
1948-55   *11½in (29cm) high*
£120-160   **PSA**

A Royal Doulton Prestige figurine, 'St George', model no.HN2067, designed by S. Thorogood.

1950-79   *15¾in (40cm) high*

£800-1,000   **PSA**

A Royal Doulton large Prestige figurine, 'Jack Point', model no.HN2080, designed by C.J. Noke.

16in (40.5cm) high

£450-550   **PSA**

A large Royal Doulton figurine, 'Jack Point', model no.HN2080, with painted 'P.S' and dated '1.12.80' in black.

Produced after the 1918 original by Charles Noke, in the 'Prestige' series.

1980   *17in (43cm) high*

£600-700   **GWA**

A pair of Royal Doulton figurines, 'Oliver Hardy', model no.HN2775 and 'Stan Laurel', model no.HN2774, designed by W.K. Harper, limited edition of 9,500.

1990   *10in (25.5cm) and 9¼in(23.5cm) high*

£160-200   **PSA**

A Royal Doulton figurine, 'Lord Olivier as Richard III', model no.HN2881, designed by E.J. Griffiths, limited edition of 750, marked 'Exhibition only' to base.

1985   *11½in (29cm) high*

£180-220   **PSA**

A Royal Doulton figurine, 'Flower Arranging', model no.HN3040, designed by D. Brindley, limited edition of 750, in velvet box with wood base and certificate.

From the 'Gentle Arts' series.

1988   *7¼in (18.5cm) high*

£140-180   **PSA**

A Royal Doulton figurine, 'Queen Elizabeth I', model no.HN3099, designed by P. Parsons, from a limited edition of 5,000, boxed.

From the 'Queens Of The Realm' series.

1987   *9in (23cm) high*

£80-120   **PSA**

A Royal Doulton figurine, 'Queen Victoria', model no.HN3125, designed by P. Parsons, from a limited edition of 5,000, with certificate.

From the 'Queens Of The Realm' series.

1988   *8in (20.5cm) high*

£80-120   **PSA**

A Royal Doulton figurine, 'Queen Anne', model no.HN3141, designed by P. Parsons, limited edition of 5,000, boxed with certificate.

From the 'Queens Of The Realm' series.

1988   *9in (23cm) high*

£60-80   **PSA**

A Royal Doulton figurine, 'Mary Queen of Scots', model no.HN3142, designed by P. Parsons, boxed with certificate.

A limited edition of 5,000 from the 'Queens Of The Realm' series.

1989   *9in (23cm) high*

£80-120   **PSA**

A Royal Doulton figurine, 'Henry VIII', model no.HN3458, designed by P. Parsons, limited edition of 9,500, boxed.

1994   *9¼in (23.5cm) high*

£140-180   **PSA**

A set of Royal Doulton figurines, Henry VIII and his six wives, Henry model no.3458, Catherine of Aragon model no.3233, Jane Seymour model no.3349, Anne of Cleves model no.3356, Anne Boleyn model no.3232, Catherine Parr model no.3450, Catherine Howard model no.3449, designed by P. Parsons, limited editions of 9,500.

1990-94

£650-750   **PSA**

A Royal Doulton figurine, 'Lady Jane Gray', model no.HN3680, designed by P. Parsons, limited edition of 5,000, boxed.

1995   *8¼in (21cm) high*

£150-200   **PSA**

A Royal Doulton figurine, 'Margaret Tudor', model no.HN3838, designed by P. Parsons, limited edition of 5,000, boxed with certificate.

1997   *6½in (16.5cm) high*

£160-200   **PSA**

A Royal Doulton figurine, 'Edward VI', model no.HN4263, designed by P. Parsons, numbered 273 from a limited edition of 5,000, printed mark.

     8¼in (21cm) high

£260-300   **FLD**

A Royal Doulton figurine, 'King Arthur', model no.HN4541, designed by S Ridge, from a limited edition of 950, boxed.

2003   *9in (23cm) high*

£250-300   **PSA**

A Royal Doulton prototype figurine, 'Peggy Davies'.

c1960s   *7¼in (18.5cm) high*

£700-800   **PSA**

A Royal Doulton prototype figurine of period seated lady in garden, marked not for resale.

     8¼in (21cm) high

£120-180   **PSA**

QUICK REFERENCE - CHARACTER JUGS

- Having experimented with stoneware jugs in their early days, Doulton saw the idea revived in the early 1900s when Charles Noke produced 'The Kingsware Huntsman', among other Toby jugs portraying various figures from literature, politics and folklore, and began producing character jugs.
- Unlike Toby jugs, which depict the entire figure, character jugs just portray the head and shoulders. These jugs come in three sizes: large, small, and miniature.
- Harry Fenton was a prominent designer of Doulton's character jugs, modelling 26 character jugs and 15 Toby jugs. Following Fenton's death in 1953, Max Henk began modelling jugs with a focus on incorporating the handle into the design to a greater degree.

A large Royal Doulton 'Red-Haired Clown' character jug, model no.D5610, designed by Harry Fenton.

1936-42   *7½in (19cm) high*
£1,100-1,300   **PSA**

A Royal Doulton large character jug, 'Cavalier with Goatee Beard', model no.D6114, designed by Harry Fenton.

1949-50   *7in (18cm) high*
£450-550   **PSA**

A Royal Doulton small character jug, 'The Jester', model no.D5556, designed by Charles Noke, with special Darley & Son Souvenir backstamp.

1936-60   *3¼in (8.5cm) high*
£200-250   **PSA**

A Royal Doulton large character jug, 'White Haired Clown', model no.D6322, designed by Harry Fenton.

1951-55   *7½in (19cm) high*
£180-220   **PSA**

A Royal Doulton large character jug, 'The Poacher', model no.D6429, designed by Mark Henk, different colour painted scarf and hat.

1955-95   *7in (18cm) high*
£140-180   **PSA**

A Royal Doulton large character jug, 'Field Marshal Smuts', model no.D6198, designed by Harry Fenton.

1946-48   *6½in (16.5cm) high*
£400-500   **PSA**

A Royal Doulton large double-sided character jug, 'Punch and Judy', model no.D6946, designed by Stanley J. Taylor, with certificate.

Created exclusively for the Royal Doulton International Collectors Club in a limited edition of 2,500.

1994   *7in (18cm) high*
£80-100   **PSA**

A Royal Doulton prototype character jug, 'The Clown', model no.D6834, designed by Stanley J. Taylor, in a different colourway, 'GT original sample' to base with 'Property of Royal Doulton' backstamp.

£450-500   **K&O**

A Royal Doulton large two-handled character jug, 'King Henry VIII', model no.D6888, designed by William K. Harper, boxed.

Issued in a limited edition of 1,991 to commemorate the 500th anniversary of the birth of Henry VIII.

1991   *7in (18cm) high*
£140-180   **PSA**

A Royal Doulton large three-handled character jug, 'King Charles I', model no.D6917, designed by William K. Harper, limited edition of 2,500, with certificate.

1992   *7in (18cm) high*
£90-120   **PSA**

A Royal Doulton large character jug, 'Phantom of the Opera', model no.D7017, designed by David B. Biggs, from a limited edition of 2,500.

1995   *7in (18cm) high*
£280-340   **PSA**

A Royal Doulton large character jug, 'Marley's Ghost', model no.D7142, designed by David B. Biggs, from a limited edition of 2,500, boxed.

1999   *7½in (19cm) high*
£360-400   **PSA**

A Royal Doulton large character jug, 'Lord Kitchener', model no.D7148, designed by David B. Biggs, to commemorate the 150th anniversary of his birth, limited edition of 1,500.

2000   *7¼in (18.5cm) high*
£160-200   **PSA**

A Royal Doulton large character jug, 'Noah', model no.D7165, designed by David B Biggs, limited edition of 1,000.

2001   *7¼in (18.5cm) high*
£160-200   **PSA**

A Royal Doulton large character jug, 'Boudicca', model no.D7221, designed by Caroline Dadd, from 'The Great Military Leaders' series, limited edition of 250, with certificate.

2005   *5¾in (14.5cm) high*
£250-300   **PSA**

A Royal Doulton large character jug, 'Genghis Khan', model no.D7222, designed by Caroline Dadd, from 'The Great Military Leaders' series, limited edition of 250.

2005   *6¾in (17cm) high*
£300-350   **PSA**

A Royal Doulton large character jug, 'Alexander the Great', model no.D7224, designed by Caroline Dadd, from 'The Great Military Leaders' series, limited edition of 250.

2005   *6½in (16.5cm) high*
£200-250   **PSA**

CERAMICS

A Royal Doulton large character jug, 'Attila The Hun', model no.D7225, designed by Caroline Dadd, from 'The Great Military Leaders' series, limited edition of 250, with certificate.

£300-350   PSA

A Royal Doulton large character jug, 'Emperor Kaiser', model no.D7233, from the 'World War One Military Leaders' series, limited edition.

£400-500   PSA

A Royal Doulton large character jug, 'John F. Kennedy', model no.D7246, special commission for Pascoe and Company, boxed.

£150-200   PSA

A Royal Doulton character jug, 'Joseph Stalin', model no.D7284, from the 'World War II Politicians' series, limited edition of 100, with certificate.

2009

£400-500   PSA

A Royal Doulton large character jug, 'Yuri Andreyevich Zhivago', model no.D7286, from 'The Literary Characters' series, limited edition with certificate.

£280-340   PSA

A Royal Doulton large character jug, 'Erwin Rommel', model no.D7290, from 'The Great Generals' series, limited edition.

£500-600   PSA

A Royal Doulton large character jug, 'Lord Chamberlain', model no.D7296, limited edition with certificate, Pascoe and Company backstamp.

£220-280   PSA

A small Royal Doulton prototype 'James Dean' character jug, 'Property of Royal Doulton' backstamp.

This was designed for the 'Celebrity Film Star' collection but never put into production.

2005

£2,000-2,500   K&O

A Royal Doulton large prototype character jug, 'Maori', 'Property of Royal Doulton' backstamp.

£4,500-5,000   K&O

QUICK REFERENCE - BUNNYKINS

- Bunnykins earthenware figurines were introduced in the 1930s. Only six were originally made and the range was discontinued just before World War II. The original six included 'Billy', 'Mary', 'Freddie' and 'Reggie' Bunnykin as well as a 'Farmer' and 'Mother' Bunnykin. They remain rare.
- Charles Noke, the Art Director responsible for the HN range of Royal Doulton figurines is believed to have modelled them, as they resemble some of his character animals.
- After Royal Doulton took over the Beswick factory in 1969, a new Bunnykins range was introduced in 1972 with the DB pattern numbers. A new look was developed by Harry Sales, the Design Manager of the Beswick factory, in the 1980s. From then on, the figurines reflected children's interests. The first such figurine depicted a guitar-playing bunny called 'Mr. Bunnybeat Strumming' (DB16) and a space traveller 'Astro Bunnykins Rocket Man' (DB20).

A set of rare Royal Doulton Bunnykins figurines, from the 'Oompah Band', in a green colourway, with Sousaphone model no.DB105, Trumpet model no.DB106, Cymbals model no.DB107, Drummer model no.DB108 and Drum Major model no.DB109.

£700-800   **PSA**

A rare Royal Doulton Bunnykins figurine, 'Boston College Touchdown', model no.DB29, designed by Harry Sales, in purple colourway.

1985   *3¼in (8.5cm) high*
£350-400   **PSA**

A Royal Doulton Bunnykins figurine, 'Harry the Herald', model no.DB115, designed by Harry Sales, special limited colourway, signed Michael Doulton.

1991   *3¼in (8.5cm) high*
£180-220   **PSA**

A Royal Doulton Bunnykins figurine, 'Clown', model no.DB129, designed by Denise Andrews.

From a limited edition of 250, signed Michael Doulton.

1992   *4¼in (11cm) high*
£200-250   **PSA**

A Royal Doulton Bunnykins figurine, 'Sergeant Mountie', model no.DB136, designed by Graham Tongue, limited edition of 250.

1993   *4in (10cm) high*
£400-500   **PSA**

A Royal Doulton prototype Bunnykins figurine, 'The Jester', model no.DB161, designed by Denise Andrews, in a trial yellow and black colourway.

1995   *4½in (11.5cm) high*
£220-280   **PSA**

A Royal Doulton prototype Bunnykins figurine, 'The Piper', designed by Martyn Alcock, decorated in a different colourway, not for resale backstamp.

1995   *4¼in (11cm) high*
£250-300   **PSA**

A Royal Doulton prototype Bunnykins figurine, 'Shopper', designed by Warren Platt, decorated in a different colourway, not for resale backstamp.

2001   *4½in (11.5cm) high*
£200-250   **PSA**

A Royal Doulton Bunnykins teapot, designed by Charles Noke.

4¾in (12cm) high
£450-500   **LOCK**

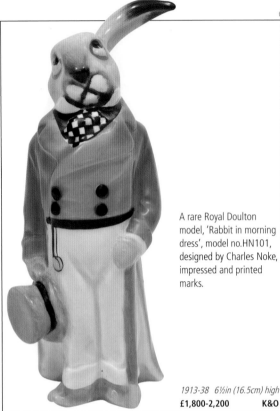

A Royal Doulton model, 'Red Admiral Butterfly', model no.HN2607, on embossed floral base, small loss to edge of one petal.

1941-46   *2in (5cm) high*

£200-250   **PSA**

A rare Royal Doulton prototype puppy, playing with ball of string attached to its tail.

1930/40s   *4in (10cm) high*

£550-650   **PSA**

A rare Royal Doulton model, 'Rabbit in morning dress', model no.HN101, designed by Charles Noke, impressed and printed marks.

1913-38 *6½in (16.5cm) high*

£1,800-2,200   **K&O**

A Royal Doulton figurine, 'Terrier Puppies in a Basket', model no.HN2588.

1941-58   *3in (7.5cm) high*

£40-50   **JN**

A Royal Doulton porcelain spaniel, model no.HN1987.

£30-40   **JN**

A Royal Doulton figurine, 'Cocker Spaniel Chewing Handle of Basket', model no.HN2586.

1941-85 *2¾in (7cm) high*

£40-50   **JN**

A Royal Doulton large flambé stalking fox, model no.HN147A.

1912-62   *12½in (32cm) long*

£150-200   **PSA**

A medium Royal Doulton figurine, 'English Setter', model no.HN1050.

1931-85   *5¼in (13.5cm) high*

£40-50   **JN**

A rare Royal Doulton flambé model of cat lying down, model no.HN233.

1920-36   *3in (7.5cm) high*

£750-850   **PSA**

QUICK REFERENCE - FLAMBÉ

- Taking inspiration from Asian ceramics, Royal Doulton experimented with flambé glaze, applying it to animal figurines in the early 1900s.
- Using copper and iron oxide in a glaze, fired in a kiln without oxygen, the vibrant red finish with streaks of purple or blue is achieved.
- The resulting pattern of this technique is uncontrollable, meaning pieces with the glaze are not identical.
- Noke experimented with variations of the red flambé glaze, creating the mottled Sung, Chang and Chinese Jade finishes.
- While the Chang glaze, produced 1925-39, was the brainchild of Noke, Harry Nixon did most of the decorating, with his monogram often appearing on the base. Several layers of thick glazes were applied to heavy bodies and dripped freely, forming a painterly effect.
- Joseph Ledger, art director at Royal Doulton from the 1950s, also experimented with flambé glazes, creating a Mandarin glaze of mottled blue and green, which he used on pieces in his Chatcull series.

A Royal Doulton flambé seated Alsation dog, model no.HN899.

1926-46   *3¾in (9.5cm) high*
£280-320   **PSA**

A Royal Doulton large veined flambé dragon, model no.2085, initialled to base 'AM'.

11in (28cm) long
£140-180   **PSA**

A Royal Doulton flambé pair of snoozing pigs, model no.HN802, signed Noke.

1912-36   *7in (18cm) long*
£300-350   **PSA**

A Royal Doulton large veined flambé owl, model no.2249, designed by A. Maslankowski.

1973-96   *12in (30cm) high*
£150-200   **PSA**

A Royal Doulton prototype flambé model of a group of otters, 'Tumbling waters', never put into production with a flambé glaze, printed marks.

14¼in (36cm) high
£3,000-4,000   **K&O**

An early 20thC Royal Doulton flambé Sung vase, signed Noke and initialled Fred Moore, decorated mottled and veined tonal glazes over the red ground, printed mark and painted Sung.

6¾in (17cm) high
£250-300   **FLD**

A very rare Royal Doulton flambé group of hugging apes, printed marks.

c1910   *5¾in (14.5cm) high*
£3,000-4,000   **K&O**

A Royal Doulton flambé Sung pumpkin vase.

6¾in (17cm) high
£400-450   **PSA**

CERAMICS

A Fulper large urn, blue and ivory flambé glaze, raised racetrack mark, some darkened crazing lines.
1920s   *14½in (37cm) high*
£600-700   **DRA**

A rare Fulper six-handled incense burner, mahogany-ivory-Flemington green flambé glaze, rectangular ink stamp, with original lid.
1910s   *11½in (29cm) high*
£2,500-3,000   **DRA**

A Fulper salamander vase, cat's eye flambé glaze, rectangular ink stamp, some efflorescence.
c1910   *8in (20.5cm) high*
£600-700   **DRA**

A Fulper vase, Flemington green flambé glaze, rectangular ink stamp, spider firing line to base, grinding flakes around foot.
1910s   *14in (35.5cm) high*
£420-480   **DRA**

A rare Fulper jardinière, leopard skin crystalline glaze, vertical racetrack ink stamp, long crack to waist with related glaze losses to interior, possibly in the making.

The Fulper Pottery Co., based in Flemington, New Jersey, was incorporated in 1899, having been established c1814. At the turn of the 20thC, under the direction of William H. Fulper II, the company became known for its Arts and Crafts pottery. Ceramics engineer Martin Stangl was employed by Fulper in 1910 and designed the 'Vasekraft' lamps. By 1924, Stangl was Vice President of the company. In 1935, he closed the original Fulper factory, shifting production focus to handpainted dinnerware.
1910s-20s   *15in (38cm) diam*
£800-1,000   **DRA**

A Fulper vase, cucumber green crystalline glaze, vertical rectangular ink stamp, a few minor grinding chips.
1910s   *12½in (32cm) high*
£850-950   **DRA**

A Fulper vase, in green, blue, and brown flambé glaze, oval incised mark.
1917-27   *10in (25.5cm) high*
£200-250   **DRA**

A Fulper vase, brown and black flambé over mustard matt glaze, glazed-over mark.
1910s-20s   *7in (18cm) high*
£950-1,100   **DRA**

A Fulper vase, in blue flambé glaze, rectangular ink mark.
1909-17   *9in (23cm) diam*
£180-220   **DRA**

QUICK REFERENCE - GOLDSCHEIDER

- Friedrich Goldscheider (1845-97) founded the Goldscheider Manufactory & Majolica Factory in Vienna in 1885. Goldscheider opened retail outlets in Paris, Leipzig and Florence.
- The Goldscheider factory, with sculptors such as Josef Lorenzl (1892-1950) and Stefan Dakon (1904-92), produced Art Deco figurines, tobacco jars, jardinières and wall masks.
- The Art Deco figurines, which portrayed fashionable, carefree women or avant-garde dancers using vivid colours and fine details, are highly collectable.
- The factory closed in 1953, with the brand name sold on to Carstens which continued production until 1963. In the late 1980s, Friedrich's great-grandson, Peter Goldscheider, produced a small number of figurines and objects.

A Goldscheider figurine of a pair of Spanish dancers, designed by Josef Lorenzl, model no.5775, impressed and printed marks.

17in (43cm) high

£3,000-3,500   K&O

A Goldscheider figurine of a nude woman, by Josef Lorenzl, black printed marks, stamped '5802/489/4', some restoration, crazed all over.

c1926   *11¼in (28.5cm) high*

£450-550   BELL

A Goldscheider 'The Egyptian Dancer' figurine, designed by Josef Lorenzl, model no.5281, with eight photographic postcards depicting the dancer Miss Maud Adams in exotic Egyptianesque costume, impressed marks and printed Goldscheider mark, impressed Lorenzl facsimile signature.

See Pinhas, Ora, 'Goldscheider', Richard Dennis Publications, pp.108-109 for six examples of this figurine illustrated in different colours.

11¼in (28.5cm) high

£1,400-2,000   WW

A Goldscheider figurine of a butterfly girl, by Sailor, model no.5840, stamped and printed marks, extensively restored.

Provenance: The Barbra Streisand Collection of Decorative and Fine Arts and Memorabilia, Part II, 4 March 1994, Christie's.

19¼in (49cm) high

£3,000-4,000   SWO

A Goldscheider figurine of a dancer, model no.6399, stamped and printed marks, restored left wrist.

11½in (29cm) high

£700-800   SWO

A Goldscheider large model of a woman in exotic costume, designed by Josef Lorenzl, model no.5927, headdress and purple cape, on domed octagonal base, impressed factory marks, printed marks and impressed facsimile signature, small glaze chip to cloak rim.

17½in (44.5cm) high

£6,500-7,500   WW

An Art Deco Goldscheider figurine of a female dancer, by Josef Lorenzl, model no.6693/49/7, printed and impressed marks, small chip to top, some crazing.

c1930   *7in (18cm) high*

£300-350   BELL

CERAMICS

An Art Deco Goldscheider figurine, after Josef Lorenzl, model no.7058, impressed with model number and '2' and '4' to base, some restoration to arms, some crazing.

13in (33cm) high

£850-950   **PW**

A Goldscheider figurine of a couple ballroom dancing, by Stephan Dakon, model no.7059, stamped and printed marks, restored lady's right arm, left-hand finger retouched, base of plinth chipped.

12in (30.5cm) high

£1,200-1,600   **SWO**

A Goldscheider figurine, by Stephan Dakon, model no.7256, stamped and printed marks, restored and damages.

14½in (37cm) wide

£2,200-2,600   **SWO**

A Goldscheider figurine, by Stephan Dakon, model no.7257, stamped and printed marks, small chip to edge of dress.

12¼in (31cm) high

£650-750   **SWO**

A Goldscheider figurine of an ice skater, by Stephan Dakon, model no.7849, incised on plinth 'Dakon', with original silver label, stamped and printed marks.

10¾in (27.5cm) high

£1,300-1,800   **SWO**

A Goldscheider figurine of a dancer, by Stephan Dakon, model no.7857, with remnants of original label, stamped and printed marks, remnants of the label, small flake to left hand.

15¾in (40cm) high

£1,200-1,600   **SWO**

A Goldscheider figurine of a dancer, by Stephan Dakon, model no.8126, stamped 'L', printed marks.

15½in (39.5cm) high

£950-1,100   **SWO**

A Goldscheider figurine of a dancer, probably by Stephan Dakon, model no.8129, stamped and printed marks, crack to underside of dress, foot restored.

13in (33cm) high

£450-550   **SWO**

A rare Goldscheider figurine of a dancer, model no.8746, stamped, with 'Wiener Manufaktur J. Schuster' printed mark.

15½in (39.5cm) high

£1,000-1,400   **SWO**

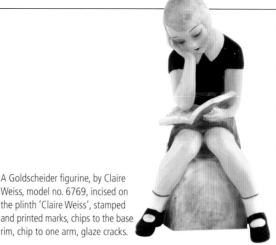

An Art Nouveau Goldscheider large bust, by Gambeauche, model no.2437, impressed marks, artist signature to shoulder.

23¼in (59cm) high

£1,500-2,000   WW

A Goldscheider figurine, by Josef Lorenzl, model no.7064, incised facsimile signature, stamped and printed marks, minor glaze cracks to cuff.

10¾in (27.5cm) high

£4,000-5,000   SWO

A Goldscheider figurine, by Claire Weiss, model no. 6769, incised on the plinth 'Claire Weiss', stamped and printed marks, chips to the base rim, chip to one arm, glaze cracks.

Hungarian-born Claire Weiss (1906-97), who was also known as Claire Weiss-Herczeg or Klára Herczeg, studied at the Budapest Academy before moving to Paris and Berlin in the late 1920s. Her speciality at Goldscheider was figurines of elegant women, but she also modelled lamps and figurines of children. She also designed large sculptures for public displays and worked for Rosenthal and Bing & Grøndahl.

8in (20.5cm) high

£750-850   SWO

A Goldscheider figurine of a girl and a rabbit, model no.7201, stamped and printed marks.

8½in (21.5cm) high

£500-600   SWO

A Goldscheider craft pottery figurine, possibly modelled by Kurt Goebel, model no.7845, stamped and printed marks.

10¼in (26cm) high

£400-500   SWO

A Goldscheider mask, printed mark 'Goldscheider, West Germany', numbered '12', mould '544'.

8¾in (22cm) high

£250-350   SWO

A Goldscheider wall mask, by Stephan Dakon, model no.7412, incised and printed marks.

10in (25.5cm) high

£200-300   SWO

A Goldscheider wall mask, by Stephan Dakon, model no.7412, stamped and printed marks, restored.

10in (25.5cm) high

£120-160   SWO

A Goldscheider wall mask of a lady holding a cup, faint printed mark.

8¾in (22cm) high

£120-160   SWO

A Peggy Davies Rita Hayworth 'Covergirl' figurine, limited edition.
£100-150   PSA

A Peggy Davies 'Putting on the Ritz' figurine, limited edition.
£150-200   PSA

A Peggy Davies 'Isadora' figurine, artist's proof by M. Jackson.
£180-220   PSA

A Peggy Davies large 'The Whisperer' grotesque bird figurine, modelled by Robert Tabbenor, limited edition.
£100-150   PSA

A Kevin Francis/Peggy Davies 'Lolita Erotic' figurine, in unusual colourway, original artist's proof by M. Jackson.
£350-450   PSA

A Kevin Francis/Peggy Davies Ceramics 'Isadora' erotic figurine.
£160-200   PSA

A Kevin Francis/Peggy Davies 'Clarice Cliff, The Artisan' figurine, in red and blue special colourway.
£80-100   PSA

QUICK REFERENCE - KEVIN FRANCIS AND PEGGY DAVIES

- Kevin Francis was founded by Kevin Pearson and Francis Salmon in 1985. It specialised in handpainted, limited edition figurines and Toby jugs.
- Before partnering with Peggy Davies Ceramics (established in 1981), Kevin Francis relied on commissions from Royal Doulton.

A Kevin Francis/Peggy Davies 'Clarice Cliff' figurine, decorating a cup, numbered '1 of 1', signed 'Victoria Bourne'.
£160-200   PSA

A Kevin Francis/Peggy Davies Ceramics 'Bubbles' erotic figurine, by Victoria Bourne, limited edition, artist's proof.
£200-250   PSA

QUICK REFERENCE - LENCI

- Lenci was established in Turin, Italy, in 1919, by Helen (Elena) König Scavini and her husband Enrico di Scavini.
- The company originally produced felt dolls, but from 1928, they also made earthenware and porcelain figurines, mostly of women.
- Distinguishing features of these figurines include elongated limbs, bright yellow hair, and a combination of matt and glossy glazes.

A Lenci 'Maternita' figurine, designed by Helen König Scavini, painted factory marks, paper retailers label, professional restoration.

12½in (32cm) high

£1,600-2,000   WW

A Lenci 'Il Grattacielo' pottery figurine, by Abele Jacopi, modelled as a young lady with a compact and powder puff, painted mark 'Lenci Made in Italy, Torino, 28', some minor chips.

The figurine, titled 'Il Grattacielo' – Italian for skyscraper – was first shown at the Turin International Exhibition in 1928, around the time that skyscrapers were cropping up across Europe's cities. Designer Abele Jacopi (1882-1957) took inspiration for the figure's outfit from 'Vogue' magazine. The figurine sold for a record price for Lenci.

c1930   *17¼in (44cm) high*

£40,000-45,000   BOL

An Art Deco Lenci porcelain wall mask plaque, probably after a design by Helen König Scavini, minor surface wear and dirt, signature and marks are blurred.

13¾in (35cm) high

£950-1,100   APAR

A Lenci 'A Teatro' figurine, designed by Helen König Scavini, inscribed 'Lenci torino made in Italy', with a flower possibly for Giovanni Ronzan.

11¾in (30cm) high

£750-850   SWO

A Lenci 'Giovinezza' figurine, possibly by Sandro Vacchetti, model no.442, inscribed 'Lenci Torino 4 (XII) made in Italy TK'.

7¾in (19.5cm) wide

£4,500-6,500   SWO

A Lenci 'Madonna' bust, signed 'Lenci Made in Italy'.

c1930s   *8¾in (22cm) high*

£400-500   FLD

A Lenci 'Madonna and Child' earthenware figurine, designed by Sandro Vacchetti, signed 'Lenci, IVA, Made in Italy, 31-10-1936'.

8¾in (22cm) high

£550-650   ROS

CERAMICS

QUICK REFERENCE - LLADRÓ

- Lladró was founded in 1953 near Valencia, Spain, by bothers Juan, José and Vicente Lladró. The company started out modelling plates, vases and ceramic figurines.
- In the 1960s, Lladró founded its Professional Training School, and in 1969 opened its current headquarters in Tavernes Blanques, Valencia.
- Figurines from 1954 to the mid-1960s were stamped with decimal point serial numbers.
- Lladró was bought by Spanish investment fund PHI Industrial Group in 2017.

A Lladró 'Romeo and Juliet' figurine group, model no.4750.

18½in (47cm) high

£300-350 APAR

A Lladró 'Alice in Wonderland' figurine, privilege gold, dated.

2009 *8¼in (21cm) high*

£400-500 PSA

A Lladró figurine group, marked 'J. Puche & Angeles Cabo no.83', with wooden plinth stand, loss of one flower.

23¾in (60.5cm) high

£650-750 WM

A Lladró 'Antique Car' figurine group, model no.1146, on a wooden base.

24in (61cm) wide

£900-1,100 APAR

A pair of Lladró figurines, 'Pocket Full Of Wishes' model no.7650, and 'A Wish Come True' model no.7676, printed marks.

10¾in (27.5cm) high

£100-140 FLD

A pair of Lladró figurines, 'Basket Of Love' model no.7622, and 'Innocence In Bloom' model no.7644, printed marks.

10in (25.5cm) high

£50-60 FLD

A pair of Lladró figurines, 'Afternoon Promenade' model no.7636, and 'Now & Forever' model no.7642, printed marks.

10¾in (27.5cm) high

£70-80 FLD

A pair of Lladró clown figurines, 'Circus Sam' model no.5472, and 'Sad Sax' model no.5471, printed marks, slight damage.

9in (23cm) high

£60-70 FLD

A pair of Lladró figurines, 'Jazz Horn' model no.5832, and 'Jazz Sax' model no.5833, both with damage.

£110-150   PSA

A Lladró 'Big Sister' figurine, model no.5735.

7in (18cm) high

£180-220   PSA

A Lladró 'Sancho Panza' figurine, model no.6633, printed mark.

10in (25.5cm) high

£45-55   FLD

A Lladró 'Birth of Venus' figurine group, designed by Antonio Ramos, no.32 of an addition of 1,000, with wood base.

2001   *33½in (85cm) wide*

£1,600-2,000   PW

A Lladró 'Two Horses' figurine group, model no.4597.

17¼in (44cm) high

£250-300   APAR

A Lladró large 'Horse with Lady Rider' figurine group, factory marks to base.

17¾in (45cm) high

£180-220   WM

A Lladró 'Pensive Clown' bust, model no.5130, printed mark.

10¾in (27.5cm) high

£90-110   FLD

A Lladró 'Penguin Love' figurine, model no.2519, matt glazed.

9in (23cm) high

£160-200   PSA

CERAMICS

QUICK REFERENCE - LORNA BAILEY

- Lorna Bailey (b.1978) worked as a painter at her father's firm LJB Ceramics, in Stoke-on-Trent.
- At the age of just 17, her 'House and Path' and 'Sunburst' patterns were put into production.
- In 2003, LJB Ceramics was renamed Lorna Bailey Artware. Taking inspiration from the Art Deco period, Lorna Bailey Artware produced a range of handcrafted and handpainted domestic and decorative wares.
- Lorna Bailey retired in 2008.

A Lorna Bailey 'Iggy The Cat' prototype.

£45-65   PSA

A Lorna Bailey 'Christmas Mayhem The Cat' prototype.

£110-150   PSA

A Lorna Bailey 'House and Path' bulbous vase.

7in (18cm) high

£40-50   LOCK

A Lorna Bailey 'Poolfields' conical shape sugar sifter.

5¼in (13.5cm) high

£28-34   LOCK

A Lorna Bailey 'Ashcroft' jug, signed on base.

7in (18cm) high

£45-55   LOCK

A Lorna Bailey 'Brampton Cottage' vase, signed on base.

6¾in (17cm) high

£45-55   LOCK

A Lorna Bailey 'Bridge and Stream' vase, signed on base.

6¾in (17cm) high

£40-50   LOCK

A Lorna Bailey 'Pagoda Garden' jug, signed on base.

6¼in (16cm) high

£40-50   LOCK

QUICK REFERENCE - MARTIN BROTHERS

● Martin Brothers, comprising Robert (1843-1923), Charles (1846-1910), Walter (1857-1912) and Edwin (1860-1915), was established in 1873, in Fulham. It moved to Southall in 1877, and production continued until 1923.

● Robert Martin's range of birds and grotesques are popular with collectors, as are sgraffito-decorated vases.

● Each brother had a role at the business; Robert modelled the figures, Walter threw the pots, Edwin painted and decorated and Charles ran the shop and gallery.

A Martin Brothers grotesque 'Fish' vase, signed 'Martin Bros, London and Southall'.

c1890   *3¼in (8.5cm) high*

£1,800-2,200   **K&O**

A Martin Brothers salt-glazed stoneware vase, incised with a frieze of grotesque birds and a serpent, incised maker's marks 'R. W. MARTIN & BROS. LONDON & SOUTHALL 6.1894', chip to rim.

1894   *9in (23cm) high*

£1,500-2,000   **L&T**

An early 20thC Martin Brothers stoneware vase, moulded and decorated with a man in medieval dress, incised to the base 'Martin Bros, London & Southall', some damages, dated.

1903   *9½in (24cm) high*

£700-800   **FLD**

A Martin Brothers stoneware a 'Aquatic' miniature vase, by Edwin and Walter Martin, incised '11 Martin Bros London'.

1911   *2¼in (5.5cm) high*

£2,000-2,500   **WW**

A Martin Brothers stoneware vase, incised mark 'Martin ... London & Southall 1-1902'.

2¾in (7cm) high

£1,200-1,600   **SWO**

A Martin Brothers stoneware vase, inscribed '21.5.85, Martin Bros., London & Southall'.

8¼in (21cm) high

£750-850   **CHEF**

A Martin Brothers stoneware vase, decorated with anthropomorphic fish, eels, a jellyfish and seaweed, incised 'Martin Bros. London and Southall, 8-1894', restored.

1894   *8¼in (21cm) high*

£1,100-1,400   **SWO**

A Martin Brothers stoneware miniature vase, by Edwin and Walter Martin, incised '12-1903 Martin Bros London', dated.

1903   *2¼in (5.5cm) high*

£550-650   **WW**

CERAMICS

QUICK REFERENCE - MEISSEN

- Meissen was founded in 1710 by Augustus the Strong, Elector of Saxony, in its namesake town in Germany. Its signature of the crossed swords was introduced in 1722. Meissen porcelain was heavily influenced by Asian styles and designs.
- In the early 1720s, under the direction of porcelain painter Johann Gregorius Höroldt, Meissen developed the enamelling process, increasing the range of colours. From the early 1730s, Meissen produced figurines and table services.
- Key modellers include Johann Gottlieb Kirchner (1706-68), Johann Joachim Kändler (1706-75), Peter Reinicke (1715-68) and Michel Victor Acier (1736-99).
- New production facilities, still used today, were built in Triebischtal, Germany, from 1861. During World War II production was hindered and stopped in 1945, with the company returned to the German Democratic Republic in 1950 by occupying Soviet forces.
- Since 1991, the company has been owned by the State of Saxony.

A 20thC Meissen 'The Pastry Seller' porcelain figurine, after the original by Peter Reinicke from the 'Cris de Paris' series, underglaze blue crossed sword mark, incised 'No.60220', further numbered '179'.

5¼in (13.5cm) high

£300-400   LSK

A 20thC Meissen 'Woman with Triangle' porcelain figurine, after the original by Peter Reinicke from the 'Cris de Paris' series, underglaze blue crossed sword mark, incised 'No.60223', further numbered '102'.

5¼in (13.5cm) high

£300-400   LSK

A 20thC Meissen 'Boy with Flute and Drum' porcelain figurine, after the original by Peter Reinicke from the 'Cris de Paris' series, underglaze blue crossed sword mark, incised 'No.5', further numbered '127'.

6in (15cm) high

£300-400   LSK

A 20thC Meissen 'The Fruit Seller' porcelain figurine, after the original by Peter Reinicke from the 'Cris de Paris' series, underglaze blue crossed sword mark, incised 'No.60225', further numbered '126'.

6in (15cm) high

£300-400   LSK

A 20thC Meissen 'The Carp Seller' porcelain figurine, after the original by Peter Reinicke from the 'Cris de Paris' series, underglaze blue crossed sword mark, incised 'No.60229', further numbered '733'.

5¼in (13.5cm) high

£350-450   LSK

A 19thC/20thC Meissen allegorical 'Broken Bridge' figurine group, after the model by Acier, blue crossed swords mark, incised 'F63', small amount of restoration.

9¾in (24.5cm) high

£600-700   WW

An early 20thC Meissen 'Four Seasons' figural group, painted mark to base.

11½in (29cm) high

£350-450   FLD

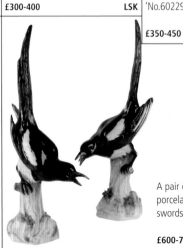

A pair of late 19thC Meissen porcelain magpies, blue crossed swords marks.

21in (53.5cm) high

£600-700   DUK

A pair of 20thC Meissen peacock figurines, blue crossed swords marks, one lacking its crest, the other with a small chip to its beak.

5½in (14cm) wide

£300-350   WW

QUICK REFERENCE - MINTON

- Minton was established in 1793 by Thomas Minton (1765-1836) and Joseph Poulson in Stoke-on-Trent. After Thomas' death, he was succeeded by his son, Herbert Minton (1793-1858).
- The factory traded under various names, becoming Mintons in 1873. Various parts of the company traded under different names, with its subsidiary tile business separating into Minton & Co. and Minton, Hollins & Co.
- Léon Arnoux, Art Director from 1849, developed the tin-glaze used for Minton's tin-glazed majolica range.
- Under the direction of Léon Solon, Art Director from 1900–09, the company developed a range of Art Nouveau earthenware, decorated with tube-lining and influenced by the Vienna Secession.
- The company became part of the Royal Doulton Tableware Group in 1968.

A Minton plaque, painted freehand with a cherub, signed L. Boullemier (Lucien Emile), in an oak frame.

£180-220   PSA

A 19thC/20thC Minton cabinet plate, handpainted with a young woman, by A. Boullemier, gilded to the ribbon edge.

9½in (24cm) diam

£300-350   PSA

A Minton's Art Pottery Studio charger, painted by Rebecca Coleman, signed, printed Kensington Gore mark with date code, painted '739' and monogram 'WSC', dated.

Rebecca Coleman was the sister of William Stephen Coleman, who was the Art Director at Minton's Art Pottery Studio from 1871-73.

1872   *16½in (42cm) diam*

£2,500-3,000   SWO

A Minton bicentenary pâte-sur-pâte dish, with cupids lighting candles, gilded rim.

4¾in (12cm) diam

£110-160   PSA

A Minton fruit bowl, heavily gilded.

11½in (29cm) diam

£100-150   PSA

An early 20thC Minton pâte-sur-pâte cup and saucer, decorated with portrait panels and raised gilded.

£550-650   PSA

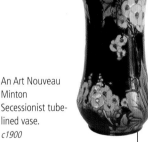

An Art Nouveau Minton Secessionist tube-lined vase.

c1900

£110-160   PSA

An early 20thC Minton Secessionist vase, decorated with tube-lined stylised flowers, printed mark with 'No.7'.

5½in (14cm) high

£250-350   FLD

A Minton Secessionist jardinière, hairline crack from top rim.

8¾in (22cm) high

£80-120   PSA

QUICK REFERENCE - MAJOLICA

- Majolica (the anglicised term derived from the Italian 'maiolica' meaning tin-glazed pottery) was inspired by Italian Renaissance pottery and the work of Bernard Palissy (c1510-90), as well as Staffordshire-based Thomas Whieldon (1719-95) and Ralph Wood (1715-72).
- Minton & Co., Wedgwood and George Jones & Sons dominated majolica production. Leon Arnoux, at Minton & Co., developed the glaze formulas for the pottery's majolica. Minton & Co. presented their majolica range to the public at London's Great Exhibition of 1851.

A 19thC Minton majolica monkey teapot, in ochre, cobalt and green glazes, the interior glazed turquoise, impressed shape no.1844 and date code.

This is the original that the others were inspired by.

1860s   *6in (15cm) high*

£400-500   FLD

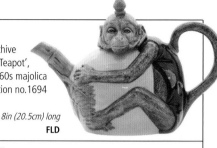

A boxed Minton Archive Collection 'Monkey Teapot', modelled on the 1860s majolica original, limited edition no.1694 of 1,793.

8in (20.5cm) long

£120-160   FLD

A boxed Minton Archive Collection 'Cat and Mouse Teapot', modelled on the late 19thC majolica original, limited edition no.612 of 2,500.

7½in (19cm) long

£250-300   FLD

A boxed Minton Archive Collection 'Chinaman Teapot', modelled on the 1870s majolica original, limited edition no.571 of 2,500.

8¼in (21cm) long

£140-200   FLD

A boxed Minton Archive Collection 'Cockerel Teapot', modelled on the late 19thC majolica original, limited edition no.197 of 2,500.

8¾in (22cm) long

£100-140   FLD

A boxed Minton Archive Collection 'Fish Teapot', modelled on the late 19thC majolica original, limited edition no.646 of 2,500.

9in (23cm) long

£200-250   FLD

A boxed Minton Archive Collection 'Cockerel and Monkey Teapot', modelled on the 19thC majolica original, limited edition no.577 of 1,000.

8¾in (22cm) long

£150-200   FLD

A boxed Minton Archive Collection 'Tortoise Teapot', modelled on the 1870s majolica original, limited edition no.111 of 2,500.

8in (20.5cm) long

£110-140   FLD

QUICK REFERENCE - MOORCROFT

- William Moorcroft (1872-1945) studied at the Royal College of Art, London. He began his career at the Staffordshire pottery manufacturers James Macintyre & Co. in 1897, and soon ran the company's art pottery studio.
- Moorcroft patterns were often inspired by the natural world. His early designs included the distinctive 'Aurelian' and 'Florian' wares, decorated with stylised floral and foliate Art Nouveau designs. The later 'Hesperian' design portrays fish, and landscapes appeared in patterns such as 'Claremont', 'Prunus', 'Hazeldene', 'Dawn' and 'Eventide'.
- He founded W Moorcroft Ltd. in 1913. With the backing of Liberty of London and other major retailers, the company was quickly successful. In 1928, William Moorcroft was appointed 'Potter to HM The Queen'.
- The designs were produced through 'tube-lining'. Outlines of a pattern were piped onto the surface, leaving a low-relief outline design. The spaces within the pattern were then filled in with coloured glazes.
- On William's death, his son Walter (1917-2002) took over the company. Moorcroft is still open today and operates from the same factory in Stoke-on-Trent where it was originally founded.
- Early ranges from the 1900s-20s, such as 'Florian' or 'Claremont' tend to be the most valuable, while common patterns, such as 'Anemone' and 'Pomegranate' are, in general, more affordable. In 2013, a 'Claremont' pattern loving cup (c1905) sold for £18,000 at Clars Auction Gallery in Oakland, California. The piece included mounts by the Californian jeweller Shreve & Co.
- Many collectors are increasingly interested in contemporary pieces from the 1990s onwards, by designers such as Rachel Bishop, Emma Bossons, Philip Gibson, Sian Leeper and Sally Tuffin. Large pieces from limited editions tend to fetch the highest prices.

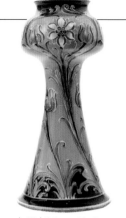

An early 20thC James Macintyre & Co. vase, by William Moorcroft, 'Alhambra' pattern, printed mark.

8in (22.5cm) high

£600-700   FLD

An early William Moorcroft Macintyre 'Aurelian' ware gilded vase.

5¼in (13.5cm) high

£120-180   PSA

An early 20thC James Macintyre & Co. 'Florian' ware vase, by William Moorcroft, 'Cornflower' pattern, printed mark and signed in green.

13in (33cm) high

£450-550   FLD

A William Moorcroft Macintyre 'Florian' vase, 'Cornflower' pattern.

6¼in (16cm) high

£1,200-1,600   PSA

A William Moorcroft Macintyre funnel vase, 'Forget-me-nots' pattern.

10in (25cm) high

£500-600   PSA

A William Moorcroft small vase, 'Hazeldene' pattern, turquoise green ground, underglaze green signature and date, printed Liberty mark.

c1908   4in (10cm) high

£1,100-1,500   K&O

A James Macintyre vase, designed by William Moorcroft, 'Hazeldene' pattern, printed marks 'Made for Liberty & Co.', 'Rd no 397964' and 'W. Moorcroft des' in green, crazing to the body.

6¼in (16cm) high

£1,200-1,800   SWO

An early 20thC Moorcroft vase, 'Hazeldene' pattern, tube-lined green, blue and yellow streaked colours, signed in green 'W. Moorcroft Des', restoration to foot rim.

10in (25.5cm) high

£2,600-3,000   ROS

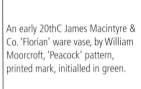

An early 20thC James Macintyre & Co. 'Florian' ware vase, by William Moorcroft, 'Peacock' pattern, printed mark, initialled in green.

A William Moorcroft Macintyre vase, 'Pansy' pattern.

9in (24.5cm) high

£1,000-1,400   **PSA**

11in (28cm) high

£500-600   **FLD**

An early 20thC James Macintyre & Co. 'Florian' ware vase, by William Moorcroft, 'Poppy' pattern, printed mark and signed in green, restored.

9in (25cm) high

£250-300   **FLD**

A Moorcroft vase, 'Rose Garland' pattern, model no.M2837/3, with gilt highlights, signed, printed marks.

11½in (29cm) high

£250-300   **DUK**

A William Moorcroft Macintrye vase, 'Wisteria' pattern, restoration to top rim, dated.

1913   *9in (24.5cm) high*

£1,300-1,600   **PSA**

An early 20thC Moorcroft 'Florian' vase, 'Lilac' pattern, printed marks, signed.

5½in (14cm) high

£700-800   **FLD**

A Moorcroft 'Florian' ware ewer, with William Moorcroft signature to the base and inscribed 'Made for Liberty & Co.', extensive crazing, some rim restoration.

8in (20.5cm) high

£250-300   **APAR**

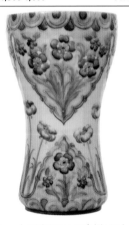

An early 20thC Moorcroft 'Florian' vase, decorated with tube-lined poppies and forget-me-nots, printed mark to base, signed.

8in (20.5cm) high

£300-400   **FLD**

A Macintyre Moorcroft ewer, model no.M2837/3, 'Peacock' pattern, printed and painted marks, some glaze running.

8in (22.5cm) high

£700-800   **CHEF**

QUICK REFERENCE - MOORCROFT MINIATURES

- Small is often considered beautiful by Moorcroft collectors.
- Miniature versions of Moorcroft's pieces, measuring only around 2½in -3½in (6.5cm-9cm), can fetch significant prices.
- In the 1970s, miniatures sold for around £30; in the Kingham & Orme sale in June 2019, a series of rare Moorcroft-Macintyre miniatures, some of which are featured on this page, sold for four-figure prices.
- Condition of the miniatures can vastly affect price. At the Kingham & Orme sale, a 'Harebells' double gourd vase (c1903) with a small flaw sold for £1,600 less than another version of it in good condition.
- To collectors pattern is important as is ground colour but, as stated, the most important consideration is condition.

A William Moorcroft for James Macintyre miniature vase, 'Yellow Poppy' pattern, printed mark and underglaze green monogram.
c1904   *3in (7.5cm) high*
£4,000-5,000   **K&O**

A William Moorcroft for James Macintyre miniature vase, 'Orange Poppy' pattern, printed mark and underglaze green monogram.
c1903   *3in (7.5cm) high*
£1,600-2,000   **K&O**

A William Moorcroft for James Macintyre miniature vase, 'Blue Poppy' pattern, printed mark and underglaze green monogram.
c1904   *3in (7.5cm) high*
£1,100-1,600   **K&O**

A William Moorcroft for James Macintyre miniature scent bottle, 'Blue Poppy' pattern, with gold screw stopper.

A Macintyre scent bottle is a great rarity although the market has softened recently.

c1904   *1½in (4cm) long*
£3,600-4,000   **K&O**

A William Moorcroft for James Macintyre miniature vase, 'Poppy Garland' pattern, printed mark and underglaze green monogram.
c1904   *2½in (6.5cm) high*
£1,200-1,600   **K&O**

A William Moorcroft for James Macintyre miniature vase, 'Cornflower' pattern, printed mark and underglaze green monogram.
c1910   *3¼in (8.5cm) high*
£2,000-2,500   **K&O**

A William Moorcroft for James Macintyre miniature vase, 'Blue Harebell' pattern, printed mark and underglaze green monogram.
c1903   *3¼in (8.5cm) high*
£3,000-4,000   **K&O**

A William Moorcroft for Liberty and Co. miniature vase, 'Hazeldene' pattern, printed mark and underglaze green signature.
c1912   *3in (7.5cm) high*
£1,800-2,200   **K&O**

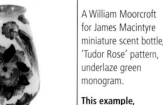

A Moorcroft miniature vase, 'Hazeldene' pattern, designed by William Moorcroft, impressed marks, painted green signature.
3¼in (8.5cm) high
£2,000-2,500   **WW**

A William Moorcroft miniature vase, 'Hazeldene' pattern, impressed Burslem marks and underglaze green signature.
c1914   *3¼in (8.5cm) high*
£900-1,100   **K&O**

A William Moorcroft miniature vase, 'Persian' pattern, impressed mark and underglaze green monogram.
c1914   *3in (7.5cm) high*
£1,800-2,200   **K&O**

A William Moorcroft for James Macintyre miniature scent bottle, 'Tudor Rose' pattern, underlaze green monogram.

This example, although still valuable, has seen a dramatic downturn in price achieved. It sold for close to £5,000 a decade ago.

c1904   *2½in (6.5cm) long*
£2,000-2,500   **K&O**

CERAMICS

QUICK REFERENCE - 'CLAREMONT'

- Instantly recognisable from the toadstool motif, 'Claremont' was introduced in October 1903 and named by Liberty. Produced for nearly 40 years, early examples were produced in green and mottled blue backgrounds.
- By the 1920s, colouring had become darker and stronger and the drawing had become bolder. During the 1920s and 30s, it was also produced with desirable flambé glazes and in light colours on pale matt grounds.
- Despite being so successful, it is considered scarce, particularly when compared to ranges such as 'Pomegranate'. Always desirable, early pieces in unusual and strong forms, from the mid-late 1910s, are highly sought-after.

A William Moorcroft vase, 'Claremont' pattern.

2¾in (7cm) high

£1,000-1,400   PSA

A Moorcroft vase, designed by William Moorcroft, 'Claremont' pattern, impressed factory marks.

3in (7.5cm) high

£1,200-1,600   WW

A Moorcroft vase, 'Claremont' pattern, with a ruby lustre glaze, signed to base.

5½in (14cm) high

£400-500   FLD

A Walter Moorcroft large vase, 'Clematis' pattern.

8½in (21.5cm) high

£140-180   PSA

A Moorcroft vase, 'Revived Cornflower' pattern, signed 'W. Moorcroft XII - 1913' to the base.

9½in (24cm) high

£1,100-1,500   FLD

A Moorcroft vase, designed by William Moorcroft, 'Dawn' pattern, painted blue signature.

9in (23cm) high

£1,500-2,000   WW

A Moorcroft vase, designed by William Moorcroft, 'Dawn' pattern, with a light flambé glaze, impressed factory marks.

2¾in (7cm) high

£500-600   WW

A Moorcroft plate, 'Dawn Landscape' pattern, impressed to base, restored.

6¾in (17cm) diam

£200-250   FLD

A Moorcroft flambé vase, 'Dawn' pattern, impressed mark, initialled, restored.

9in (23cm) high

£1,400-1,800   FLD

A Moorcroft vase, designed by William Moorcroft, 'Eventide' pattern, impressed marks, painted blue signature.

6¼in (16cm) high

£1,200-1,600   **WW**

A 1930s Moorcroft vase, 'Fish' pattern, facsimile signature and Royal Warrant.

12¼in (31cm) high

£900-1,200   **WAD**

A rare Moorcroft matt glaze vase, 'Fish' pattern, painted and impressed marks.

c1930   *12in (30.5cm) high*

£5,000-6,000   **CHEF**

A rare Moorcroft vase, with a flambé glaze, painted and impressed marks, glaze chip to footrim, some glaze runs.

c1930   *12in (30.5cm) high*

£6,500-7,500   **CHEF**

A William Moorcroft for Liberty & Co. vase, 'Hazeldene' pattern, signed 'W. Moorcroft', printed marks.

c1907   *4in (10cm) high*

£2,200-2,800   **K&O**

A Moorcroft flambé vase, 'Leaf and Berries' pattern, small glaze fault.

3½in (9cm) high

£180-220   **PSA**

A Moorcroft flambé vase, 'Leaf and Berries' pattern, with a lustred glaze.

4¼in (11cm) high

£220-280   **PSA**

A William Moorcroft flambé vase, 'Leaf and Berries' pattern.

14¼in (36cm) high

£550-650   **PSA**

A William Moorcroft tray, 'Moonlit Blue' pattern, impressed mark.

13½in (34cm) wide

£1,000-1,400   **FLD**

CERAMICS

A William Moorcroft vase, 'Moonlit Blue' pattern, signed 'WM', impressed marks.

c1925   *7in (18cm) high*

£1,400-1,800   **K&O**

A Moorcroft 'Tudric' pewter-mounted sugar caster, 'Moonlit Blue' pattern, impressed marks, painted initials, cover stamped 'TUDRIC 13'.

c1925   *6¾in (17cm) high*

£800-1,000   **WAD**

A Walter Moorcroft flambé vase, 'Orchid' pattern, small nick to base edge.

6¼in (16cm) high

£300-400   **PSA**

A William Moorcroft small vase, 'Pansy' pattern.

2¼in (5.5cm) high

£400-450   **PSA**

A pair of William Moorcroft vases, 'Pansy' pattern, impressed marks, signed in green.

10½in (26.5cm) high

£850-950   **FLD**

A Moorcroft vase, 'Pansy' pattern, impressed factory mark 'MOORCROFT BURSLEM 1914', painted signature 'W. MOORCROFT', dated.

1914   *8¼in (21cm) high*

£550-650   **L&T**

QUICK REFERENCE - 'POMEGRANATE'

- In the early 'Pomegranate' designs, introduced in 1910, the decoration was usually constrained to a particular area, for example a band circling the piece or just covering the shoulder.
- The rest of the piece was usually decorated in a mottled or pale colour. In the early pieces, this was in yellows or greens, but had changed to purples and blues by 1916.
- 'Pomegranate', sold widely by Liberty, was produced until the 1930s and became one of Moorcroft's most popular designs.

A William Moorcroft Burslem milk jug, 'Pomegranate' pattern.

5in (12.5cm) high

£400-500   **PSA**

A William Moorcroft Burslem tankard, 'Pomegranate' pattern, marked to base 'Made for Liberty & Co'.

3in (9.5cm) high

£600-700   **PSA**

A William Moorcroft Burslem tankard, 'Pomegranate' pattern, marked to base 'Made for Liberty & Co'.

4½in (11.5cm) high

£300-400   **PSA**

A Moorcroft vase, 'Pomegranate' pattern, impressed and painted marks to base, overall crazing.

12½in (32cm) high

£700-800   PW

A William Moorcroft vase, 'Pomegranate' pattern, signed 'W. Moorcroft'.

c1913   *6¾in (17cm) high*

£1,000-1,400   K&O

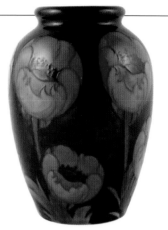

A Moorcroft vase, 'Poppy' pattern, impressed mark and painted signature to base.

9in (23cm) high

£1,400-1,800   PW

A William Moorcroft salt-glazed vase, 'Big Poppy' pattern, impressed mark, signed in blue.

7in (19cm) high

£550-650   FLD

A William Moorcroft vase, 'Poppy' pattern.

8in (21cm) high

£400-500   PSA

A William Moorcroft bonbonnière vase, in the rare green 'Spanish' pattern, ½in (1.5cm) firing crack to top rim.

7in (18cm) high

£400-500   PSA

An early 20thC William Moorcroft for Liberty & Co. vase, 'Tudor Rose' pattern, signed in green, scratched out Liberty & Co. mark.

7in (20cm) high

£600-700   FLD

A Moorcroft pottery vase, 'Waving Corn' pattern, impressed marks, painted signature.

12½in (32cm) high

£700-800   WW

A William Moorcroft vase, 'Yacht' pattern, impressed mark and initialled in blue.

1930s   *4in (12cm) high*

£200-300   FLD

CERAMICS

QUICK REFERENCE - SALLY TUFFIN

- Sally Tuffin (b.1938) studied at Walthamstow Art School and the Royal College of Art.
- In the 1960s and 70s, she co-ran a fashion design business, Foale & Tuffin, with her colleague Marion Foale.
- In 1986, in an attempt to preserve the security of the Moorcroft pottery, Sally Tuffin, her husband Richard Dennis, and their friends Hugh and Maureen Edwards jointly purchased a 76% stake in the company.
- From 1986-93, Tuffin worked as art director and designer for Moorcroft. Her numerous pattern designs include 'Balloons', 'Bramble', 'Peacock' and 'Sunflower'.
- In 1993, she founded Dennis Chinaworks with her husband, Richard Dennis (see pp.92-93).

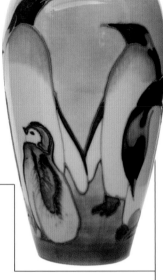

A Moorcroft vase, designed by Sally Tuffin, 'Penguin' pattern, painted and impressed marks, numbered '61' of 350.

10in (25.5cm) high

£220-280   FLD

A Moorcroft vase, designed by Sally Tuffin, 'Red Tulip' pattern, impressed and painted marks, boxed.

8in (20.5cm) high

£200-250   FLD

A Moorcroft vase, designed by Sally Tuffin, 'Polar Bear' pattern, numbered '51' of 250.

This vase is believed to have been made for the Canadian market.

6¾in (17cm) high

£200-250   FLD

A Moorcroft table lamp, designed by Sally Tuffin, 'Bramble' pattern, with wooden plinth, marks obscured.

11¾in (30cm) high

£150-200   FLD

A Moorcroft dish, designed by Sally Tuffin, 'Finches' pattern, impressed and painted marks.

10¼in (26cm) diam

£100-150   FLD

A Moorcroft year plate, designed by Sally Tuffin, 'Carp' pattern, with certificate, numbered '101' from an edition of 250, boxed.

1989   *8¾in (22cm) diam*

£85-95   FLD

A Moorcroft mantel clock, designed by Sally Tuffin, 'Bramble' pattern, impressed mark, the clock movement marked for Wedgwood.

6¼in (16cm) high

£100-150   FLD

A CLOSER LOOK AT A MOORCROFT JARDINIÈRE

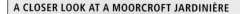

Grand statement jardinière and stand, in the 'Tree Bark Thief' pattern.

Designed by Rachel Bishop, dated 1998.

An elaborate design painted in colours on a yellow ground.

From a limited edition of 50 pieces, with original paper certificate.

A Moorcroft jardinière and stand, impressed marks, painted signature and number.

1998   *33½in (85cm) high*

£2,500-3,000   **WW**

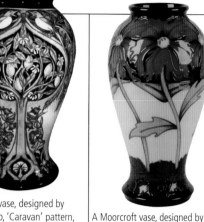

A Moorcroft vase, designed by Rachel Bishop, 'Caravan' pattern, limited edition no.52 of 100, marked 'Moorcroft', signed, with a retail label for Watsons of Salisbury, dated.

2003   *16¾in (42.5cm) high*

£950-1,100   **LC**

A Moorcroft vase, designed by Rachel Bishop, 'Crown of Flowers' pattern, limited edition no.13 of 50, signed, painted and impressed markings.

c2013   *10¼in (26cm) high*

£180-220   **DUK**

A modern Moorcroft vase, decorated by Rachel Bishop, 'England' pattern, impressed and painted marks.

9in (23cm) high

£100-150   **FLD**

A Moorcroft Prestige vase, designed by Rachel Bishop, 'Flanders Field' pattern.

Rachel Bishop joined Moorcroft as a designer in 1993 at the age of 24, after receiving a Bachelor of Arts in design (ceramics) at Staffordshire University. Bishop's numbered edition 'In Flanders Field' and her 'Chocolate Cosmos' and 'Phoebe Summer' ranges demonstrate her interest in floral designs.

18½in (47cm) high

£850-950   **PSA**

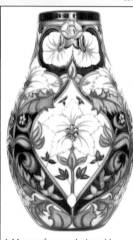

A Moorcroft vase, designed by Rachel Bishop, 'Kelmscott Dream' pattern, printed marks, numbered '23' of a limited edition of 25.

The 'Kelmscott Dream' pattern was designed as a limited edition only available via the Locked Room page on the Moorcroft website.

10in (25.5cm) high

£180-220   **FLD**

A Moorcroft vase, designed by Rachel Bishop, 'Pavion' pattern, impressed and painted marks, numbered '191' from a limited edition of 200, signed.

11¾in (30cm) high

£350-450   **FLD**

A Moorcroft vase, designed by Rachel Bishop, 'Phoenix' pattern, impressed and painted marks.

10½in (26.5cm) high

£180-220   **FLD**

A Moorcroft large vase, known as the 'Absentee Pot', designed by Sian Leeper, signed to the base and numbered '4', impressed marks.

The Absentee Pot was awarded to an employee in the production departments, on the day the factory closed for Christmas, who had not been absent all year. If a number of staff had not been absent all names were put into a hat and one picked out; it was awarded to a different member of staff each year. This has been confirmed by Moorcroft Pottery.

10¾in (27.5cm) high

£600-700   **FLD**

A Moorcroft ginger jar and cover, 'Giant Pandas' pattern, in limited edition of 150, signed Sian Leeper, with box, dated.

This is a Collectors Club piece.

2004   8¼in (21cm) high

£400-500   **PSA**

A pair of modern Moorcroft vases, designed by Sian Leeper, 'Isabella' pattern, signed and dated, limited edition numbered '139' of 250 and '228' of 250.

2004   10in (25.5cm) high

£400-500   **LSK**

A Moorcroft vase, designed by Sian Leeper, 'Ranthambore' pattern, no.136 of a limited edition of 400, impressed and painted marks on the base, signed, dated.

10.25in (26cm) high

£500-600   **FLD**

A Moorcroft vase, designed by Sian Leeper, 'Shamwari' pattern, limited edition no.173 of 300, marked 'Moorcroft, '173/300', signed 'Sian Leeper', with box, dated.

Having graduated with a Bachelor of Arts in 3D-design from the University of Brighton in 1988, Sian Leeper worked for Moorcroft briefly before going freelance. She returned to Moorcroft as a designer, with her first catalogue design, 'Pride of Lions', appearing in 2000.

2006   10½in (26.5cm) high

£700-800   **LC**

A Moorcroft ewer, designed by Sian Leeper, 'Shimba Hills' pattern, impressed mark, painted 'Trial 8.8.05', signed.

12¼in (31cm) high

£450-550   **FLD**

A Moorcroft vase, designed by Sian Leeper, 'Tamarin Monkey' pattern, limited edition no.265 of 300, signed, painted and impressed markings.

10¾in (27.5cm) high

£250-300   **DUK**

A Moorcroft vase, designed by Vicky Lovatt, 'Farm Cove' pattern, model no.49, with sailing yachts in a harbour, signed, printed and impressed markings.

c2015   4½in (11.5cm) high

£180-220   **DUK**

A Moorcroft vase, by Nicola Slaney, 'Talwin' pattern, Glasgow School-style motifs, printed and impressed marks, with box.

7in (18cm) high

£200-250   **FLD**

CERAMICS

A Moorcroft vase, designed by Kerry Goodwin, 'Cheviot Sheep' pattern, limited edition. **This vase is part of the Countryside Collection.**

6in (15cm) high

£250-300   PSA

A Moorcroft vase, designed by Kerry Goodwin, 'Gardeners' pattern, impressed mark verso, signed, limited edition numbered '23' of 200, dated.

2003   14½in (37cm) high

£250-300   LSK

A Moorcroft vase, designed by Kerry Goodwin, 'Sichaun Giant Pandas' pattern, trial 16/11/16.

Having joined Moorcroft as a painter in 2000, Kerry Goodwin soon became a designer. Goodwin has become known for her humorous or quirky designs, for example 'Potteries in Recession', which depicts a Lowry-like scene of the 2008 recession.

2016   15¾in (40cm) high

£400-500   PSA

A Moorcroft vase, designed by Kerry Goodwin, 'Lest We Forget' pattern, signed.

9½in (24cm) high

£250-300   PSA

A Moorcroft vase, designed by Philip Gibson, 'Moonlight' pattern, impressed mark verso, signed, limited edition numbered '116' of 250, dated, boxed with outer sleeve.

Philip Gibson studied at the Newcastle School of Art and The North Staffordshire Polytechnic, earning a Masters degree in ceramic design. Before going freelance, he worked for Moorcroft and Wedgwood.

2003   12¼in (31cm) high

£180-220   LSK

A Moorcroft vase, designed by Philip Gibson, 'Hidcote' pattern, impressed and painted marks, numbered '7' from a limited edition of 75, signed.

18½in (47cm) high

£800-900   FLD

A Moorcroft biscuit barrel and cover, designed by Philip Gibson, 'Puriri Tree' pattern, impressed mark verso and dated.

From the New Zealand Collection.

2004   6in (15cm) high

£250-300   LSK

A Moorcroft table lamp base, designed by Philip Gibson, 'Trout' pattern, with a wooden plinth, marks obscured, retains original Moorcroft shade.

8¾in (22cm) high

£300-400   FLD

A Moorcroft vase, designed by Emma Bossons, 'Bellahouston' pattern.

8¼in (21cm) high

£100-150   PSA

A Moorcroft vase, designed by Emma Bossons, 'Sweet Betsy' pattern, limited edition no.29 of 50, signed E Bossons, impressed and painted marks.

16¾in (42.5cm) high

£550-650   FLD

A Moorcroft vase, designed by Emma Bossons, 'Hidden Dreams' pattern, numbered '29/50', impressed 'Moorcroft Made in Stoke on Trent England', painted signatures for Emma Bossons and Rachel Bishop, dated.

Emma Bossons (b.1976) joined Moorcroft at the age of 20 as a painter before becoming a designer. Her 'Hepatica' range of 2000 and her 2001 'Queen's Choice' proved very successful. At the age of 24, Bossons became the youngest female member of the Fellowship of the Royal Society of Arts. She has looked widely for inspiration for her designs, travelling to Australia, North America, Fiji, New Zealand and Kiribati. The Queen allowed the use of the Royal Cypher on the base of each piece in Bossons' 2002 Golden Jubilee collection.

2005   *26¾in (68cm) high*

£1,700-2,000   BE

A Moorcroft vase, designed by Paul Hilditch, 'Charles Dickens' pattern, limited edition no.43 of 75, marked 'Moorcroft', signed 'Paul Hilditch', with box. 2012.

Paul Hilditch joined Moorcroft as a painter in 1999. His intricate designs convey pictorial scenes, requiring him to research historical periods or figures. Many of Hilditch's designs are recognisable by a fine raised tube-lining on the surface.

11¼in (28.5cm) high

£750-850   LC

A Moorcroft vase, designed by Paul Hilditch, 'Cornish Cove' pattern, limited edition no.81 of 200, marked 'Moorcroft', signed 'Paul Hilditch', with box.

2008   *7½in (19cm) high*

£600-700   LC

A Moorcroft vase, designed by Paul Hilditch, 'High Society' pattern, signed, painted and impressed marks, limited edition no.69 of 100.

c2012   *12¼in (31cm) high*

£250-300   DUK

A Moorcroft vase, designed by Paul Hilditch, 'Merchants of Venice' pattern, trial 26/7/16.

2016   *12¼in (31cm) high*

£450-550   PSA

A Moorcroft jug, designed by Paul Hilditch, 'Snowdrift' pattern, printed and painted marks, numbered '37' from a limited edition of 50, signed.

10¾in (27.5cm) high

£260-300   FLD

A Moorcroft plate, designed by Anji Davenport, 'Woodside Farm' pattern, painted marks.

10in (25.5cm) diam

£250-300   FLD

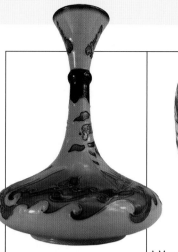

A Moorcroft vase, 'Blue Nautical' pattern, signed 'J. Moorcroft', dated.

1997   *9½in (24cm) high*

£140-180   **PSA**

A Moorcroft vase, 'Bronwyns Bouquet' pattern, dated.

This is a Collectors Club piece.

2000   *10in (25.5cm) high*

£180-220   **PSA**

QUICK REFERENCE - LISE B. MOORCROFT

- Lise B. Moorcroft is the fourth generation of the Moorcroft dynasty; great granddaughter of Thomas Moorcroft, granddaughter of factory founder William Moorcroft and daughter of Walter Moorcroft OBE. The family situated their famous factory in Burslem, Stoke-on-Trent in August 1913 and were involved in its operations until 1987.

- Lise studied at London's Central School of Art and Design, graduating with honours before setting up an independent studio in Stoke, continuing the traditions favoured by her illustrious forebears yet adding her individual flair.

- Lise's designs, predominantly derived from nature and local environs, are sketched freestyle in pencil onto the clay making every piece a unique, one-off bespoke piece of art. It is then tube-lined onto the surface with coloured slip followed by several firings, possibly up to ten. These can include, firstly, bisque, then numerous applications of under glaze, handpainted glazes and lustres. Using this method enables a build up of colours over many firings so Lise can achieve the deep colour and texture intensity on the surface. Some pieces are then enhanced further by precious metal foils, gilding the surface, which is then sealed to protect it.

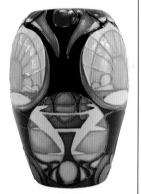

A Moorcroft vase, 'Rising Sun' pattern, trial 11/10/16.

2016   *5¼in (13.5cm) high*

£140-180   **PSA**

A Moorcroft vase, 'Winter's Feed' pattern.

8¾in (22cm) high

£450-550   **PSA**

A Lise B. Moorcroft Studio Pottery vase, decorated with penguins.

4¼in (11cm) high

£60-80   **PSA**

A Lise B. Moorcroft Studio Pottery vase, decorated with toadstools.

4¾in (12cm) high

£80-100   **PSA**

A Lise B. Moorcroft Studio Pottery vase, 'Tall Trees' pattern.

4¼in (11cm) high

£90-120   **PSA**

A Lise B. Moorcroft Studio Pottery vase, decorated with pansies.

4¼in (11cm) high

£80-100   **PSA**

CERAMICS

QUICK REFERENCE - BERNARD MOORE

- Known for his use of coloured glazes, Bernard Moore was a potter born in 1850 in Longton, UK.
- Moore worked at his father's pottery company, Samuel Moore & Son, taking it over upon his father's death in 1867. The firm changed its name to Moore Brothers, exhibiting in the USA in the early 1880s and 1890s.
- Moore experimented with flambé and sang-de-boeuf glazes on stoneware in the 1890s.
- In 1905, Moore Brothers closed, and Moore opened his own studio in Stoke-on-Trent. He died in 1935.

A pair of Bernard Moore high-fired vases, speckled sang-de-boeuf and purple flambé glaze, signed.

3½in (9cm) high

£200-300   HAN

An early 20thC Bernard Moore flambé vase, with an upper band of painted flowers and foliage with patterned banding below, the neck interior with a blood red glaze, signed.

10¾in (27.5cm) high

£600-700   FLD

A Bernard Moore sang-de-boeuf bottle vase, of chimney form, part glazed in red with matt turquoise rim and shoulder, signed.

5¼in (13.5cm) high

£200-250   HAN

A miniature Bernard Moore aventurine glazed bottle vase, signed.

2½in (6.5cm) high

£350-400   HAN

A Bernard Moore mottled flambé vase.

8in (20.5cm) high

£60-80   PSA

A Bernard Moore high-fired flambé vase, decorated with panels of birds, bats, flowers and trees, glaze fault to foot rim.

4¼in (11cm) high

£180-220   PSA

A Bernard Moore flambé vase, decorated with Art Nouveau-style trees, chip to base.

3¾in (9.5cm) high

£70-90   PSA

A Bernard Moore small red flambé bust, with original glass eyes.

2¼in (5.5cm) high

£160-200   PSA

QUICK REFERENCE - GEORGE OHR

● From 1880 to c1907, the Biloxi Pottery in Mississippi was worked solely by owner George Ohr (1857-1918). The eccentric Ohr became known as 'the mad potter of Biloxi'. Ohr's work is characterised by thin walls, a manipulated and pinched asymmetrical form with ridges and glazing, usually in brown, green and red. During his lifetime, Ohr sold very little, despite producing a vast number of pieces. On his death, his work was left to his family, and later bought by antiques dealer James Carpenter, who introduced Ohr's work into the ceramics market.

A George Ohr large double-sided vessel, indigo, raspberry, and green glaze, body incised 'Marie Evans and Walters' (illegible), base stamped 'G.E. OHR., Biloxi, Miss.', partially overglazed mark incised 'Sept 189' (illegible).

1897-99   *6¼in (16cm) high*
£40,000-45,000   **DRA**

A George Ohr vase, multicolour sponged-on glaze, stamped 'G.E. OHR. Biloxi, Miss.'.
1897-1900   *5in (12.5cm) high*
£10,000-12,000   **DRA**

A George Ohr vase, raspberry and turquoise mottled glaze, stamped 'G.E. OHR Biloxi, Miss.'.
1897-1900   *4½in (11.5cm) wide*
£4,500-5,500   **DRA**

A George Ohr vase, brown and black speckled and sponged-on glaze, stamped 'G.E. OHR Biloxi, Miss.'.
1897-1900   *5¼in (13.5cm) high*
£5,000-6,000   **DRA**

A George Ohr vase, with blister glaze, stamped 'G.E. OHR, Biloxi, Miss.', some scratches, kiln flaw to shoulder.
1897-1900   *6in (15cm) high*
£2,500-3,000   **DRA**

A George Ohr vase, with sponged-on glaze, incised 'OHR BILOXI', some chips.
1896-1910   *6in (15cm) high*
£1,000-1,500   **DRA**

A George Ohr vessel, with sponged-on glaze, stamped 'GEO. E. OHR BILOXI MISS.', restoration to rim.
c1895-96   *5in (12.5cm) wide*
£700-800   **DRA**

A George Ohr tall vase, mahogany, gunmetal and aventurine glaze, stamped 'G.E. OHR., Biloxi, Miss.'.
1897-1900   *6in (15cm) high*
£4,000-5,000   **DRA**

A George Ohr vessel, mahogany and gunmetal glaze, stamped 'G.E. OHR. Biloxi, Miss.'.
1897-1900   *4in (10cm) high*
£6,500-7,500   **DRA**

A George Ohr vase, green and gunmetal glaze, script signature, museum deaccession number 'L.S.OC.HK.', two grinding chips.
1898-1910   *6½in (16.5cm) high*
£8,000-9,000   **DRA**

A George Ohr bi-colour vase, stamped 'G.E. OHR Biloxi, Miss.', a few minor touch-ups to ruffles.
1897-1900   *8in (20.5cm) high*
£6,500-7,500   **DRA**

A George Ohr vase, gunmetal and indigo sponged-on glaze, stamped 'GEO. E. OHR BILOXI, MISS.'.
1895-96   *3¾in (9.5cm) high*
£3,000-3,500   **DRA**

A George Ohr vessel, green, gunmetal and raspberry glaze, stamped 'G.E. OHR BILOXI'.
1895-96   *4½in (11.5cm) wide*
£9,000-10,000   **DRA**

A George Ohr pinched vase, with two faces, aventurine glaze, stamped 'G.E. OHR, Biloxi, Miss.', a few light scratches.
1897-1900   *4in (10cm) wide*
£6,500-7,500   **DRA**

A George Ohr vessel, green and ochre glaze, stamped 'G.E. OHR BILOXI'.
1895-96   *4in (10cm) wide*
£3,000-3,500   **DRA**

A George Ohr two-sided teapot, deep indigo and speckled green and gunmetal glaze, stamped 'G.E. OHR, Biloxi, Miss.'.
1897-1900   *6in (15cm) high*
£4,000-4,500   **DRA**

A George Ohr top hat novelty vase, stamped 'G.E. OHR Biloxi, Miss.'.
1897-1900   *3¼in (8.5cm) high*
£1,500-2,000   **DRA**

A George Ohr Cadogan teapot, 'Branch' pattern, script signature, dated.
1900   *5in (12.5cm) high*
£3,500-4,000   **DRA**

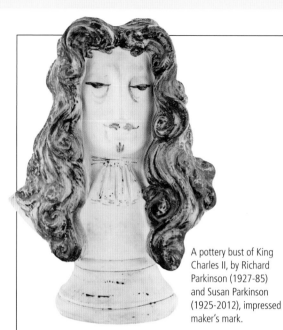

A pottery figurine of three musicians, by Richard and Susan Parkinson, impressed maker's marks.

1950s   *9in (23cm) high*

£400-500   **L&T**

A pottery bust of King Charles II, by Richard Parkinson (1927-85) and Susan Parkinson (1925-2012), impressed maker's mark.

Richard and Susan Parkinson set up Richard Parkinson Pottery in an oast house near Ashford Kent, in 1951. The work was split, with Richard doing the slip-casting, firing and designing of the functional tableware, while Susan (who trained at the Royal College of Art) designed and decorated the more ornamental pieces, including figurines. The company closed in 1963.

c1950s   *13¼in (33.5cm) high*

£950-1,100   **L&T**

A pottery figurine, 'Adam and Eve', by Richard and Susan Parkinson, indistinct moulded marks.

c1950s   *7½in (19cm) high*

£600-700   **L&T**

A Richard Parkinson Pottery model of a policeman, designed by Susan Parkinson, model no.85, impressed factory marks.

c1958   *12in (32cm) high*

£450-550   **WW**

A 'Woman Knitter' figurine, model no.110, by Susan Parkinson, impressed marks to feet.

These slightly larger figurines from the early 1960s were 'made for a more discerning market' according to Carol Cashmore's 2004 book.

c1960s   *7½in (19cm) high*

£400-500   **ROS**

A Richard Parkinson Pottery bust of a lawyer, painted in monochrome, impressed and printed marks.

13in (33cm) high

£500-600   **CHEF**

A Richard Parkinson Pottery figurine, 'Golfer', model no.70, designed by Susan Parkinson, impressed marks.

15½in (39cm) high

£400-500   **WW**

CERAMICS

QUICK REFERENCE - POOLE POTTERY

- Poole Pottery was established in 1873 as Carter & Co., trading as Poole Pottery from 1963.
- Based in Poole, Dorset, the company combined traditional hand-throwing techniques with handpainted colourful modern designs.
- Key designers include John Adams, Anita Harris, Truda Adams (formerly Truda Carter), Ruth Pavely and Alan White. Harris also worked at Cobridge Stoneware Pottery, and created designs for Liberty, Harrods and Tiffany.
- The company produced many successful ranges, such as 'Handcraft' in the 1920s, Truda Carter's 'Twintone' in the 1940s, 'Contemporary' in the 1950s and 'Delphis' in the 1960s. The 'Contemporary' range, designed by Alfred Burgess Read, used geometric or curving linear patterns. The brightly coloured 'Delphis' range was created by Robert Jefferson, Guy Sydenham and Tony Morris. The second half of the 20thC also saw the 'Atlantis' and 'Aegean' ranges.
- Factory production was moved away from the Poole quayside in 1999 to the Sopers Lane, Poole, site, which closed in 2006. The company was acquired by Denby Holdings in 2011.

A Poole Pottery 'Bush Velt' vase, designed by John Adams, painted by Anne Hatchard, 'LZ' pattern, with a lion attacking an antelope, impressed and painted marks.

24½in (62cm) high

£10,000-14,000   DUK

A Poole Pottery 'Bush Velt' vase, designed by John Adams, painted by Ruth Pavely, 'EZ' pattern, shape no.916, painted and impressed marks.

14½in (37cm) high

£1,000-1,500   DUK

An Art Deco Poole Pottery vase, designed by Truda Carter, 'GPA' pattern, impressed and painted marks.

6in (15cm) high

£80-100   WW

A Poole Pottery 'Leaping Gazelle' vase, designed by Truda Carter, painted by Gwendoline Selby, 'TZ' pattern, impressed marks, painted artist cipher and mark.

8½in (21.5cm) high

£350-400   WW

A Poole Pottery glazed red earthenware vase, possibly by Truda Carter, with unusual black and mauve stylised tulips, impressed maker's mark, incised '700 X', painted '/YR'.

c1921-34   9¼in (23.5cm) high

£350-400   ROS

A Poole Pottery 'Persian Deer' vase, designed by Truda Adams, with printed factory marks, firing flaw to base.

13in (33cm) high

£220-280   WW

A Poole Pottery vase, designed by Truda Adams, painted by Anne Hatchard, 'PU' pattern, shape no.337, impressed and painted marks.

9¾in (24.5cm) high

£200-250   DUK

A Poole Pottery 'Persian Deer' charger, designed by Truda Adams, painted by Anne Hatchard, 'VU' pattern, shape no.528, decorated with a deer, painted and impressed marks.

15in (38cm) diam

£400-500   DUK

A Poole Pottery 'Galleon' bookend, designed by Harold Stabler, modelled by Harry Brown, impressed marks.

10½in (26.5cm) high

£350-400   DUK

A Poole Pottery charger, designed by Arthur Bradbury, painted by Ruth Pavely, inscribed with 'The Ship of Harry Paye Poole 1400', painted and impressed marks.

c1938   *15in (38cm) diam*

£400-500   **DUK**

A Poole Pottery vase, painted by Anne Hatchard, 'ZW' pattern, shape no.684, impressed and painted marks.

14½in (37cm) high

£200-300   **DUK**

A Poole Pottery vase, painted by Margaret Holder, 'BR' pattern, shape no.429, impressed and painted marks.

10in (25.5cm) high

£180-220   **DUK**

A Poole Pottery vase, painted by Ruth Pavely, 'ER' pattern, impressed and painted marks.

14¼in (36cm) high

£200-250   **DUK**

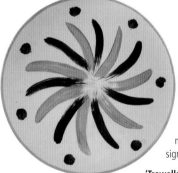

A Poole Pottery bowl, painted by Pat Summers, 'UI' pattern, shape no.686, impressed and painted marks.

9in (23cm) diam

£150-200   **DUK**

A Poole Pottery four-panel tile, designed by E.E. Stickland, 'Farmyard' series, made for Dewhurst butchers, impressed marks with painted 'FY' mark.

12in (30.5cm) square panel

£250-300   **WW**

A Poole Pottery 'Freeform' peanut vase, painted by Gwen Haskins, 'WL' pattern, shape no.701, impressed, painted and printed marks.

12½in (32cm) high

£120-150   **DUK**

A Poole Pottery 'Trewellard red' charger, by Sir Terry Frost RA, printed marks, facsimile signature to verso.

'Trewellard Red' was inspired by the colours of the sunset as seen from Trewellard on the north coast of Cornwall near Land's End. Terry decided to paint this special charger to celebrate his 80th birthday. Part of a limited edition of 100, this actual charger was painted by Sir Terry himself at the Poole Pottery Studio.

16in (40.5cm) diam

£350-400   **DUK**

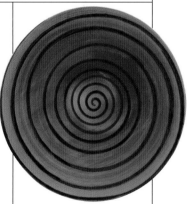

A Poole Pottery 'Arizona Blue' charger, by Sir Terry Frost RA, limited edition of 100, painter's marks only.

16in (40.5cm) diam

£250-300   **DUK**

CERAMICS

A Poole Pottery 'Freeform' Yo Yo vase, designed by Alfred Read, painted by Gwen Haskins, 'HYT' pattern, shape no.719, impressed and painted marks.

12½in (32cm) high

£250-300   **DUK**

A Poole Pottery 'Contemporary' jardinière, designed by Alfred Read and Guy Sydenham, 'HOL' pattern, printed and painted marks.

7¼in (18.5cm) high

£200-300   **WW**

A Poole Pottery 'Freeform' footed vase, 'FST' pattern, shape no.772, impressed and painted marks.

c1950   *9½in (24cm) high*

£90-120   **FLD**

A Poole Pottery 'Freeform Skittle' vase, 'PRP' pattern, shape no.698, impressed and painted marks.

15¾in (40cm) high

£100-150   **FLD**

A Poole Pottery 'Atlantis' vase, designed and thrown by Guy Sydenham, impressed marks.

9½in (24cm) high

£150-200   **DUK**

A Poole Pottery studio charger, with printed 'Poole Studio England' mark.

13½in (34.5cm) diam

£130-180   **WW**

A Poole Pottery exhibition standard 'Atlantis' vase, designed by Guy Sydenham and Beatrice Bolton, impressed marks.

12in (30.5cm) high

£600-700   **DUK**

A Poole Pottery studio charger, with printed 'Poole Studio England' mark.

13½in (34.5cm) diam

£150-200   **WW**

A later 20thC Poole Pottery studio plaque, by Tony Morris, printed and painted marks to the reverse.

16¼in (41.5cm) diam

£250-350   **FLD**

A Rookwood vase, by Lenore Asbury, iris glaze, with Queen Anne's lace, flame mark '/VIII/1126C/LA', fine crazing, two firing lines do not go through.

1908 *8½in (21.5cm) high*

£800-900 **DRA**

A Rookwood banded scenic vase, by Ed Diers (1871-1947), iris glaze, flame mark '/XI/1658F/ED/W', fine overall crazing.

1911 *6½in (16.5cm) high*

£1,300-1,600 **DRA**

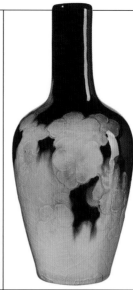

A rare Rookwood 'Black Iris' cabinet vase, by Fred Rothenbusch (1876-1937), flame mark '/765L/ FR', crazing over flowers.

Rookwood Pottery was established by Maria Longworth Nichols in Cincinnati, Ohio, in 1880. Nichols saw the business as an artistic venture, not a commercial one. Japanese artist Kataro Shirayamadani joined Rookwood in 1887. The factory patented their vellum glaze in 1904. In the late 20thC, Rookwood changed ownership multiple times. In 2009, production moved to the current facility at Race Street, Cincinnati.

1900 *5¼in (13.5) high*

£1,000-1,200 **DRA**

A Rookwood vase with tulips, by Fred Rothenbusch, iris glaze, flame mark '/II/935C/FR'.

1902 *8¾in (22cm) high*

£750-850 **DRA**

A Rookwood vase, by Sara Sax (1870-1949), iris glaze, with crocuses, flame mark '/VI/904CC/ SX'.

1906 *9¾in (24.5cm) high*

£1,200-1,600 **DRA**

A Rookwood vase, by Josephine Zettel (1874-1954), iris glaze, flame mark '/II/932D/JZ/W', fine overall crazing.

8¾in (22cm) high

£650-750 **DRA**

A Rookwood jewel porcelain baluster vase, by Margaret McDonald, shape no.6211, flame mark, artist cipher, 'XXXVI'.

1936 *10½in (26.5cm) high*

£500-600 **DRA**

A Rookwood matt vase, by Anna Marie Valentien (1862-1947) with daffodils, flame mark '/IV/187BZ/V/ AMV', fine crazing.

1904 *11½in (29cm) high*

£1,200-1,500 **DRA**

A Rookwood decorated matt vase, by Margaret McDonald, flame mark, dated, model and artist's cipher.

1928 *7½in (19cm) high*

£350-400 **DRA**

CERAMICS

A Rookwood painted matt vase, by Harriet Wilcox (1869-1943), flame mark '/II/192CZ/H.E.W.'.

The companion piece to this vase is in the permanent collection of the Metropolitan Museum of Art, New York.

1902   *10in (25.5cm) high*
£15,000-16,000   **DRA**

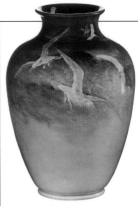

A Rookwood sea-green vase, by Sturgis Laurence (1870-1961), 'The Fishers', flame mark '/814/A/G', incised 'The Fishers, SL, hb. '97'.

1897   *9½in (24cm) high*
£1,300-1,600   **DRA**

A Rookwood tall vase, by Lenore Asbury, standard glaze, flame mark, dated, model and artist's cipher, professionally restored base.

1903   *14¼in (36cm) high*
£650-750   **DRA**

A Rookwood scenic vellum vase, by Lenore Asbury, flame mark '/XIX/30F/V/LA', fine overall crazing.

1919   *7in (18cm) high*
£800-900   **DRA**

A Rookwood small winter scenic vellum vase, by Sallie Coyne (1876-1939), flame mark '/XXIII/1096V/SEC'.

1923   *5in (12.5cm) high*
£1,000-1,500   **DRA**

A Rookwood double vellum vase, by William Hentschel (1892-1962), with flowers, flame mark '/XXX/900D/', artist cipher.

1930   *7in (18cm) high*
£600-700   **DRA**

A Rookwood double vellum vase, by Elizabeth Lincoln (1880-1957), with oak branch and acorns, flame mark '/XXIX/130/LNL', glaze imperfection to widest part of body.

1929   *6½in (16.5cm) high*
£500-600   **DRA**

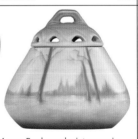

A rare Rookwood winter scenic vellum pot pourri jar, by Elizabeth McDermott (1875-1944), flame mark '/XVII/2337/V/EFM', fine overall crazing, firing line to inner rim in the making.

1917   *4¼in (11cm) high*
£900-1,100   **DRA**

A Rookwood vellum vase, by Sara Sax, with nasturtium border, flame mark, dated, model and artist's cipher.

1908   *9in (23cm) high*
£400-500   **DRA**

A Roseville 'Sunflower' jardinière and pedestal, unmarked, jardinière with a couple of small glazed-over chips in the making, pedestal with one small glaze chip.

Established in 1892 in Roseville, Ohio, Roseville Pottery began producing art wares in 1898. It had produced stoneware since 1890. Roseville launched its first art pottery range, 'Rozane', after hiring Ross Purdy in 1900. The 'Della Robbia' line was designed by Frederick Hurten Rhead (1880-1942) and introduced in 1906. The popular 'Futura' line was introduced in 1928. Production ceased in 1954.

1925   28½in (72.5cm) high
£1,500-2,000   DRA

A Roseville matt green jardinière and pedestal, unmarked, three tight hairlines.

c1910   12in (30.5cm) high
£800-900   DRA

A Roseville 'Brown Pine Cone' jardinière and pedestal, stamped.

1935   29in (73.5cm) high
£650-750   DRA

A Roseville 'Mostique' jardinière with pedestal, unmarked.

1915   10in (25.5cm) high
£850-950   DRA

A Roseville 'Pauleo' vase, with roses, unmarked, restored base.

c1915   16in (40.5cm) high
£200-250   DRA

A Roseville 'Rozane' ware 'Della Robbia' vase, with stylized feathers, raised seal, body incised 'E.D.', several chips and touch-ups to high points throughout body.

c1910   8½in (21.5cm) high
£5,500-6,000   DRA

A Roseville 'Rozane' ware 'Chief Richards' portrait vase, by Arthur Williams, with war paint, marked, professionally restored.

13½in (34.5cm) high
£250-300   DRA

A Roseville 'Green Rosecraft Nude Panel' fan vase, 'RV' blue ink stamp.

1920   8in (20.5cm) high
£300-350   DRA

A Roseville 'Ivory Morning Glory' lamp base, unmarked.

1935   19in (48.5cm) high
£300-350   DRA

CERAMICS

QUICK REFERENCE - ROYAL CROWN DERBY

- The Derby china works was established by Andrew Planché in c1750. The factory was purchased by William Duesbury and John Heath in 1756. After George III granted Duesbury permission to use the royal crown in the company's backstamp in 1775, it became known as Crown Derby.
- The company received a royal warrant and became The Royal Crown Derby Porcelain Co. in 1890.
- The factory changed hands and sites multiple times over the years. In 2016, businessman and former chief executive of Royal Doulton Kevin Oakes acquired 100% of the share capital in Royal Crown Derby.

A Royal Crown Derby 'Spirit of Peace' paperweight, limted edition no.129 of 150, with gold stopper, boxed.

This paperweight was made as an exclusive edition commissioned by Wheelers of Loughborough to commemorate the 50th anniversary of VE Day.

9in (23cm) high

£550-650   FLD

A Royal Crown Derby 'Brown Pelican' paperweight, with gold stopper, boxed.

£40-60   PSA

QUICK REFERENCE - ROYAL CROWN DERBY PAPERWEIGHTS

- Royal Crown Derby introduced paperweights in 1981 at Chatsworth House, Derbyshire. These paperweights were the 'Duck', 'Owl', 'Penguin', 'Quail', 'Rabbit' and 'Wren', and they continued the Derby tradition of rich decoration. The range became very popular.

A Royal Crown Derby 'Nanny Goat' paperweight, with gold stopper, boxed.

£75-100   PSA

A Royal Crown Derby 'Puppy' paperweight, with gold stopper, boxed.

£50-70   PSA

A Royal Crown Derby Jubilee 'Black Swan' paperweight, limited edition no.140 of 2,002, with a gold stopper, boxed, with certificate.

£150-200   PSA

A Royal Crown Derby 'Cheshire Cat' paperweight, commissioned by John Sinclair, limited edition no.80 of 500, complete with certificate of authenticity and original presentation box.

c1996   *5¼in (13.5cm) high*

£450-550   DUK

A Royal Crown Derby 'Thorpe' vase, in the 'Old Imari 1128' design, boxed.

11½in (29cm) high

£500-600   PSA

A Royal Crown Derby 'Kettle Teapot', in the 'Old Imari 1128' design, boxed.

7in (18cm) high

£450-550   PSA

A Royal Crown Derby large candlestick, in the 'Old Imari 1128' design, boxed.

10¾in (27.5cm) high

£300-400   PSA

QUICK REFERENCE - ROYAL WORCESTER

- The Worcester factory was founded in 1751 at Warmstry House, Worcester. After a visit from George III, it was awarded a royal warrant in 1788.
- The name and owner of the factory changed multiple times throughout the late 18thC. By 1862, the company was known as Royal Worcester.
- The company produced a range of ceramics, including tableware and figurines. Key artists include James Hadley, George Owen and Charles Toft.
- Hadley established a school at Worcester in 1896, using local painters to develop new traditions in porcelain painting. From c1900, painters were allowed to sign their work. Charles Baldwyn painted birds and swans in flight, while Harry Davis (1885-1970) painted fish, sheep, landscapes and architecture.
- Davis (1885-1970) started working for Royal Worcester at the age of 13, becoming foreman of the 'Men Painters' department in 1928 and retiring in 1969.
- The Stintons were also well-known painters. Harry Stinton painted Highland cattle, James Stinton painted birds and John Stinton Junior painted landscapes, castles and cattle.
- Royal Worcester went into administration in 2008. The brand name and intellectual property was bought by Portmerion Pottery Group in 2009.

A framed Royal Worcester plaque, by Harry Davis, with sheep in a mountainous landscape, signed 'H Davis', puce mark to reverse.

plaque 4¼in (11cm) diam

£2,000-2,500 GWA

A Royal Worcester pot pourri, signed 'H Ayrton', with printed black marks, includes inner lid.

10¼in (26cm) high

£2,000-2,500 K&O

A Royal Worcester 'Stroller and Marion Coakes' figurine, by Doris Lindner, model no.RW3872, limited edition no.537 of 750, with wooden plinth and framed certificate.

11¼in (28.5cm) high

£300-400 FELL

A Royal Worcester 'Mill Reef' porcelain figurine, modelled by Doris Lindner, with black printed marks, numbered '150', with wooden plinth.

1974 *9¾in (24.5cm) high*

£400-500 FELL

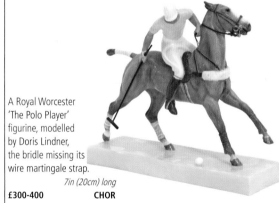

A Royal Worcester 'The Polo Player' figurine, modelled by Doris Lindner, the bridle missing its wire martingale strap.

7in (20cm) long

£300-400 CHOR

A Royal Worcester 'Appaloosa Stallion' figurine, modelled by Doris Lindner, on wooden plinth, with certificate.

1969 *10¾in (27.5cm) long*

£350-400 WM

A Royal Worcester 'Hereford Bull' figurine, modelled by Doris Lindner, on wooden plinth.

1959 *10in (25.5cm) long*

£250-300 WM

A Royal Worcester 'Charolais Bull' figurine, modelled by Doris Lindner, black printed mark and script signature, on a wooden plinth.

11.5in (29cm) long

£350-400 FLD

CERAMICS

QUICK REFERENCE - RUSKIN POTTERY

- Ruskin Pottery was established in 1898 by Edward R. Taylor and William Howson Taylor, in Sandwell, near Birmingham.
- Early products included a range of ornamental and useful ware, such as vases, tableware, buttons and cuff links.
- Inspired by Chinese ceramics, William Howson Taylor experimented with glaze techniques, including sang-de-boeuf, flambé, soufflé and lustre glazes.
- Shortly before William's death and the factory's closure in 1935, notes and documentation for the unique Ruskin glazes and pottery were deliberately destroyed.

A Ruskin Pottery high-fired vase and cover, decorated with a deep sang-de-beouf glaze, with lavender patches and copper green spotting, impressed mark, dated.

1909　　　*10in (25.5cm) high*

£1,600-2,000　　　**FLD**

A Ruskin Pottery high-fired Meiping vase, decorated with a sang-de-boeuf glaze, impressed mark, dated.

1913　　　*10¾in (27.5cm) high*

£1,500-2,000　　　**FLD**

A Ruskin Pottery crystalline vase, decorated in a streaked green over a mottled dark blue with faint crystalline flecks, impressed marks.

15¼in (39cm) high

£350-450　　　**FLD**

A Ruskin Pottery high-fired vase, decorated in a sang-de-boeuf glaze, impressed mark, dated.

1933　　　*4in (10cm) high*

£600-700　　　**FLD**

A Ruskin Pottery high-fired vase, decorated in a sang-de-boeuf glaze, with lavender mottling, impressed marks, dated.

1920　　　*4in (10cm) high*

£300-350　　　**FLD**

A Ruskin Pottery high-fired pot pourri and cover, in a sang-de-boeuf glaze with dove grey mottling to the upper half and a flambé red with lavender patches to the lower half, impressed mark, dated.

1927　　　*3½in (9cm) high*

£450-550　　　**FLD**

A Ruskin Pottery high-fired flower jug, in sang-de-boeuf glaze, with a dove grey body beneath with darker veining, impressed mark, dated.

1933　　　*9in (23cm) high*

£550-650　　　**FLD**

A Ruskin Pottery high-fired pagoda-topped scent bottle, in a sang-de-boeuf glaze with copper green spotting and lavender patches, impressed mark, restored, replacement cover.

5in (12.5cm) high

£500-600　　　**FLD**

A Ruskin Pottery high-fired 'Lily' vase, in a sang-de-boeuf and lavender glaze, impressed mark, painted glaze code 'E16' to the base, dated, restored.

1926   *9¾in (24.5cm) high*

£600-800   **FLD**

A Ruskin Pottery high-fired 'Elephants Foot' vase, in a sang-de-boeuf glaze, with deep lavender streaks and copper green spotting, impressed West Smethwick mark, dated, restored.

See Atterbury, Paul, and Henson, John, 'Ruskin Pottery', Baxendale Press (1993), page 59.

1903   *8in (20.5cm) high*

£1,200-1,600   **FLD**

A Ruskin Pottery high-fired stoneware vase, by William Howson Taylor, in a sang-de-boeuf and flambé glaze with fine turquoise speckles, impressed marks, dated.

1925   *8in (20.5cm) high*

£400-500   **WW**

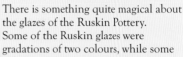

Judith Picks

There is something quite magical about the glazes of the Ruskin Pottery. Some of the Ruskin glazes were gradations of two colours, while some were textured multicolour patterns.

These glazes included misty soufflé glazes, ice crystal-effect glazes – 'crystalline', lustre glazes resembling metallic finishes, and sang-de-boeuf and flambé glazes, which produced a blood red effect. The sang-de-boeuf glazes were created using a reduction of copper and iron oxides at high temperature.

William Howson Taylor's glazes were leadless, and the decoration was handpainted.

A Ruskin Pottery high-fired vase, with a flambé and tonal lavender glaze, with copper green spotting and dove grey patches, impressed mark.

15½in (39.5cm) high

£3,000-4,000   **FLD**

A Ruskin Pottery high-fired stoneware vase, by William Howson Taylor, in a mottled sang-de-boeuf and silver-grey glaze, impressed marks, dated.

1933   *5¼in (13.5cm) high*

£750-850   **WW**

A Ruskin Pottery high-fired stoneware carafe vase, by William Howson Taylor, in a fissured sang-de-boeuf glaze over white impressed marks, dated, professional restoration to neck.

1922   *9¼in (23.5cm) high*

£400-500   **WW**

A Ruskin Pottery high-fired vase, in a celadon green with lavender and copper green spotting and sang-de-boeuf patches and pooling, impressed mark, dated, restored.

1910   *8¼in (21cm) high*

£600-700   **FLD**

A Ruskin high-fired vase, silver-grey and red glaze, impressed marks, dated.

1924   *11½in (29cm) high*

£750-850   **K&O**

A Ruskin Pottery vase, decorated in a Kingfisher blue glaze, impressed marks and dated.

1918   *10in (25.5cm) high*

£1,100-1,500   **FLD**

CERAMICS

A Ruskin high-fired flambé vase and cover, in purple and white with turquoise specks, impressed marks, dated.

1906   *14in (35.5cm) high*
£5,000-6,000   **SWO**

A Ruskin Pottery candlestick, in a Strawberry Crush soufflé glaze, impressed oval 'West Smethwick' mark, dated.

1906   *7in (18cm) high*
£90-120   **FLD**

A miniature Ruskin Pottery high-fired vase, in a tonal purple and green glaze with copper green spotting, unmarked, slight damage.

2¾in (7cm) high
£300-400   **FLD**

A Ruskin Pottery high-fired vase, with lavender and red patches over the dove grey ground, impressed mark, dated.

1921   *6in (15cm) high*
£650-750   **FLD**

A Ruskin Pottery vase, matt black with handpainted silver foliate decoration, impressed mark, dated.

See Atterbury, Paul, and Henson, John, 'Ruskin Pottery', Baxendale Press (1993), page 59.

1916   *6¼in (16cm) high*
£2,000-3,000   **FLD**

A Ruskin Pottery high-fired pot pourri and cover, in a green speckled glaze with lavender and dove grey patches beneath, impressed mark, dated.

1911   *3½in (9cm) high*
£1,400-1,800   **FLD**

A Ruskin Pottery high-fired vase, in a speckled green with red and purple fissuring, impressed oval 'West Smethwick' mark, also impressed '423', dated.

1905   *8in (20.5cm) high*
£4,000-5,000   **FLD**

A Ruskin Pottery high-fired vase, in a flambé glaze against the white ground with copper green spotting, impressed mark, dated.

1932   *12¼in (31cm) high*
£2,500-3,000   **FLD**

A Ruskin Pottery high-fired stoneware vase, by William Howson Taylor, in a fissured purple and blue glaze over white, with flambé patches, impressed marks, dated, professional restoration to neck.

1920   *8in (20.5cm) high*
£650-750   **WW**

A 1950s Michael Andersen & Sons earthernware pitcher, attributed to Marianne Starck, design no.5552, from the 'Tribal' range.

This range was originally called the 'Negro' range and later become known as the 'Tribal' range. Each piece was initially moulded, then hand-carved, meaning that no two pieces are ever the same.

7in (18cm) high

£165-195   LYN

A Swedish Gustavsberg faience studio footed bowl, designed by Stig Lindberg, decorated by Helinä Pitkänen, with impressed mark, and painted 'SWEDEN 158.T.82', with 'G. & hand' cipher, and decorator's yellow flower motif.

Established in Sweden in the 1820s, Gustavsberg porcelain factory was run by Wilhelm Kåge (1889-1960) and then Stig Lindberg (1916-82). In 1994, the Dutch company N.V. Koninklijke Sphinx acquired Gustavsberg. The firm is now owned by Villeroy & Boch AG. In its later years, the company moved away from porcelain production to sanitary wares.

1950s   6½in (16.5cm) high

£150-200   DAWS

A Gustavsberg Studio 'Farsta' vase, by Wilhelm Kage, turquoise drip-glazed with incised decoration in segmented panels, impressed marks and paper labels.

This vase was reputedly exhibited at the 1955 'Stockholmia 55' Exhibition.

8in (20.5cm) high

£1,200-1,600   DUK

A Kähler Keramik stoneware 'Leda & The Swan' figurine, made by Kai Nielson, incised signature 'Danmark'.

Danish sculptor Kai Nielsen (1882-1924) worked for various factories including Royal Copenhagen and Bing & Grøndahl.

£120-160   LC

QUICK REFERENCE - ROYAL COPENHAGEN

- **Royal Copenhagen began in Denmark in 1775 as the Royal Porcelain Factory, under the patronage of the Royal family.**
- **The Danish Court ran the Royal Porcelain Factory until the late 1860s, when it moved into private hands. The company began producing a Christmas plaque series in 1895, with the design changing annually.**
- **In 1972, Royal Copenhagen acquired the Georg Jensen Silversmithy and in 1985 it merged with Holmegaard Glassworks. It then became part of the Royal Scandinavia group. The company's flagship store is located on Amagertorv, in Copenhagen.**
- **Royal Copenhagen ware is marked with three handpainted waves, symbolising Denmark's three important waterways, a crown, showing the royal patronage and the maker's mark. The crowns changed over time.**

A Nymolle ceramic, designed by Bjørn Wiinblad.

£80-100   LYN

A Rörstrand olive green glazed vase, by Carl-Harry Stålhane, impressed marks to base.

7¼in (18.5cm) high

£120-160   APAR

A Royal Copenhagen Mandarin ducks figurine, modelled by Peter Herold, numbered '1863', with printed marks.

8¼in (21cm) wide

£250-350   SWO

A pair of Royal Copenhagen herons, designed by Theodor Madsen, with printed backstamps, numbered '532' and '138'.

largest 11¼in (28.5cm) high

£500-600   LSK

A Royal Copenhagen eagle, signed by Vilhelm Theodor Fischer (1857-1928), marked to base, no.2033, some firing imperfections, dated.

1919   21in (53.5cm) high

£850-950   APAR

CERAMICS

A Royal Copenhagen porcelain Icelandic falcon, printed backstamp, numbered '109', monogrammed 'DR' verso.

16in (40.5cm) high

£300-400 **LSK**

A Royal Copenhagen Hyacinth Macaw parrot, design attributed to Armand Petersen, model no.2235, impressed, printed and painted marks.

16¼in (41.5cm) high

£450-550 **WW**

A Royal Copenhagen barn owl, designed by Thomsen, model no.273, marked 'Royal Copenhagen, 273, Denmark'.

8½in (21.5cm) high

£250-300 **LC**

A Royal Copenhagen seal, designed by Theodor Madsen, model no.265, printed mark with date code.

1938 *11½in (29cm) high*

£120-160 **FLD**

A Royal Copenhagen seal with pup, printed backstamp, numbered '090' verso, surface scratches to glaze.

7¾in (19.5cm) high

£70-90 **LSK**

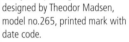

A Royal Copenhagen polar bear attacking a seal, printed backstamp, numbered '1108', monogrammed 'OF' verso.

9in (23cm) high

£350-400 **LSK**

A Royal Copenhagen polar bear, printed backstamp, numbered '060', monogrammed 'SM' verso.

12½in (32cm) high

£120-160 **LSK**

A Royal Copenhagen bull, designed by Knud Kyhn, incised signature, printed backstamp, numbered '1195', small glaze fault.

8in (20.5cm) high

£250-300 **LSK**

A Royal Copenhagen goat, designed by Christian Thomsen, printed backstamp, numbered '466' verso.

11in (28cm) long

£200-250 **LSK**

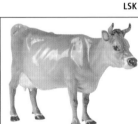

A Royal Copenhagen Jersey cow, printed backstamp, numbered '4678', the udder nipples are three unglazed and one glazed.

10¼in (26cm) long

£300-350 **LSK**

A Royal Copenhagen elk, model no.2813, marked to base.

8¼in (21cm) high

£200-250   **CHOR**

A Royal Copenhagen leopardess, printed backstamp, numbered '805' verso.

7in (18cm) high

£120-160   **LSK**

A Royal Copenhagen tiger and two cubs, printed backstamp, numbered '4687' verso.

6in (15cm) high

£500-600   **LSK**

A Royal Copenhagen 'The Wave and Rock' figurine, by Theodor Lundberg, marked to base.

17¾in (45cm) high

£450-550   **CHOR**

A Royal Copenhagen 'Pan' figurine, printed and painted marks to base, numbered '2113'.

7in (18cm) high

£200-250   **APAR**

A Royal Copenhagen vase, by Axel Salto, model no.21474, with matt brown 'Sung' glaze, printed and painted marks, impressed 'Salto' mark, with paper label.

Born in Copenhagen, Axel Salto (1889-1961) studied at the Royal Danish Academy of Fine Arts and worked for Bing & Grøndahl, Saxbo and Royal Copenhagen.

3½in (9cm) high

£250-300   **WW**

A Royal Copenhagen lobster moulded shallow bowl, painted and printed marks to the base, numbered '3498', surface dirt.

7¾in (19.5cm) long

£45-60   **APAR**

A Soholm vase, by Sven Aage Jensen, with sunflower decoration, shape 2057-2.

1950s   *8½in (21.5cm) high*

£85-95   **LYN**

A Soholm vase, designed by Einar Johansen, shape no.3325, with unglazed neck, with factory, designer and shape marks.

7in (18cm) high

£75-90   **LYN**

A Soholm vase, with geometric raised design, shape 2057-2.

1950s   *8½in (21.5cm) high*

£60-70   **LYN**

CERAMICS

QUICK REFERENCE - TROIKA

- Troika was founded in 1962 in St Ives, Cornwall, by potter Benny Sirota, painter Lesley Illsley and architect Jan Thompson. Thompson left in 1965.
- In 1968, Troika ware was sold for the first time by Heal's and Liberty in London. A year later, the company moved to a larger site in Newlyn.
- Troika wares were slip-moulded and decorated by hand. Early pieces had gloss glazes, but textured matt finishes were predominant from 1974. Designs were influenced by Scandinavian ceramics and the Cornish landscape.
- The company closed in 1983 following economic troubles and tension between the founders.

A Troika totem vase, by Alison Brigden, signed to base.

8¾in (22cm) high

£160-200 HAN

A Troika pottery wheel vase, by Penny Black, one side decorated with a stylised Mosque, the opposing side with raised geometric motifs, painted 'Troika England' mark and artist monogram 'PB' verso.

1970s *8in (20.5cm) high*

£200-300 LSK

A Troika Pottery wall plaque, by Simone Killburn, painted marks and artist monogram.

12in (30.5cm) high

£550-650 WW

A Troika pottery wheel vase, by Sue Lowe, signed 'Troika Cornwall SL'.

1976 *6½in (16.5cm) high*

£250-300 BELL

A rare Troika Pottery 'Thames' wall plaque, designed by Benny Sirota, with the meandering river and buildings, painted 'Troika' marks and artist cipher.

10in (25.5cm) high

£750-850 WW

A rare Troika Pottery 'Love' plaque, designed by Benny Sirota, with stylised couples, painted 'Troika' marks, trident mark, artist cipher to back.

14½in (37cm) wide

£800-1,000 WW

A Troika Pottery cube form table lamp base, decorated by Annette Walters, painted marks 'Troika Cornwall' and 'AW'.

8in (20.5cm) high

£200-300 FLD

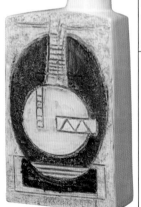

A Troika Pottery chimney vase, signed to base.

8in (20.5cm) high

£250-300 FLD

A Troika marmalade pot, signed to base 'Troika Cornwall SK'.

3½in (9cm) high

£100-150 LOCK

QUICK REFERENCE - CHARLES VYSE

- Charles Vyse (1882-1971) began his career as an apprentice modeller and designer at Doulton in Burslem at the age of 14, and was trained by Charles Noke. He studied at the Royal College of Art and Camberwell School of Art. He was an early pioneer of British studio pottery, experimenting with high-fired stoneware vessels based on medieval Chinese prototypes and producing technically highly accomplished wares throughout the 1930s. After a spell at the Royal College of Art he produced designs for Doulton in the inter-war period, for example the figurine 'Darling'. Vyse is, however, best-known for the moulded and hand-decorated pieces produced by a studio pottery at Cheyne Walk in Chelsea, which he started in 1919 with his wife Nell. Here, they produced figurines based on ordinary people seen around London.
- After the Blitz damaged his studio, Vyse taught at Farnham School of Art and continued producing figurines, before retiring in 1963.

A Charles Vyse 'Barnet Fair' Chelsea figurine, incised maker's marks 'C. VYSE/ CHELSEA'.

1920s   *10¼in (26cm) high*

£3,000-4,000   **L&T**

A Charles Vyse 'The Shawl' Chelsea figurine, painted maker's marks under base 'CV / CHELSEA / 1926', dated.

1926   *10¾in (27.5cm) high*

£600-800   **L&T**

A Charles Vyse 'The Piccadilly Rose Woman' Chelsea figurine, painted mark and date to base, minor losses to petals.

1923   *8¼in (21cm) high*

£450-550   **WW**

A Charles Vyse 'The Lavender Girl' Chelsea figurine, painted maker's marks under base 'CV / CHELSEA / 1922', dated.

1922   *9in (23cm) high*

£500-600   **L&T**

A Charles Vyse 'Saturday Night' Chelsea figurine, painted maker's marks under base 'CV / CHELSEA / 1927', dated.

1927   *10in (25.5cm) high*

£600-800   **L&T**

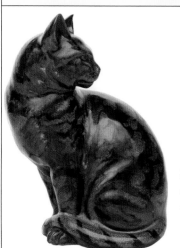

A Charles Vyse 'Seated Tabby Cat' stoneware figurine, painted in shades of tenmoku and ochre, incised 'C Vyse Chelsea'.

8¾in (22cm) high

£3,000-3,500   **WW**

A Charles Vyse stoneware vase, glazed to the foot with a green celadon, with running iron splashes, incised 'C Vyse'.

4½in (11.5cm) high

£400-450   **WW**

CERAMICS

A Wade 'Sunshine' underglaze figurine.

Wade was established in 1810 in Stoke-on-Trent, where the company began producing ceramics for the textile and wool spinning industries and bottles for breweries. In 1910, as Sir George Wade joined, the company moved into the Manchester Pottery in Burslem, Staffordshire. In 1930, designer Jessie Van Hallen, known for producing ceramic figurines of celebrities, joined the company. The Wade Whimsies were introduced in 1954. The company opened a new factory in 2010 and production continues today.

6½in (16.5cm) high

£100-150   **PSA**

A Wade 'Old Nannie' underglaze figurine.

1930s   *9½in (24cm) high*

£120-180   **PSA**

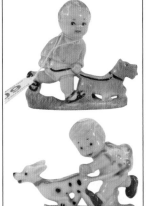

A pair of Wade 'Sarah and Sam' porcelain figurines, from the Mabel Lucie Attwell series.

£50-60   **PSA**

A rare Wade underglaze model of a spaniel dog, Wade porcelain label to base.

6¼in (16cm) long

£400-450   **PSA**

A Wade model of a polar bear, by Faust Lang, signed to base 'Wade 1939 Polar Bear', hairline crack.

c1939   *7in (18cm) high*

£350-400   **LOCK**

A Wade 'Running Spoof' underglaze model, by A.G. Fiddes Watt.

5¼in (13.5cm) high

£280-350   **PSA**

A Wade 'Baby Scruple' ceramic glazed model, designed by A.G. Fiddes Watt, printed marks.

5¼in (13.5cm) long

£600-700   **DUK**

A set of Wade 'Snow White and the Seven Dwarfs' figurines, some light wear to applied detail.

£55-65   **APAR**

A set of five Wade pig money banks, with Wade plaque.

£25-35   **APAR**

QUICK REFERENCE - WEDGWOOD

- The Wedgwood Pottery was founded in 1759 in Staffordshire by Josiah Wedgwood. Thomas Bentley soon joined Wedgwood as business partner.
- Jasperware, an unglazed vitreous fine stoneware, was developed in c1774.
- Key 20thC designers include Daisy Makeig-Jones (1881-1945), Keith Murray (1892-1981), John Skeaping (1901-80) and Eric Ravilious (1903-42).
- Ravilious, a painter, illustrator, designer and wood-engraver, worked for Wedgwood between 1936 and 1940. His work included commemorative wares, dinner and tea ware and nursery ware. In 1942, Ravilious was lost in active service during World War II.
- The company went into administration in 2009 and is now part of WWRD Ltd. and the Fiskars Group. Today, Wedgwood pieces are designed in the Wedgwood Design Studio, England, with production facilities across Europe and Asia.

A Wedgwood coronation mug, designed by Eric Ravilious, with a printed design and highlighted in yellow and pink, printed mark.

1953   *4in (10cm) high*

£300-400   **SWO**

A Wedgwood commemorative King George VI and Queen Elizabeth coronation bowl, designed by Keith Murray, in grey glaze.

1937   *10¼in (26cm) diam*

£200-250   **PSA**

A rare Wedgwood Queensware 'The Boat Race' bowl, by Eric Ravilious, with scenes from three stages of the boat race and a mermaid, the inside with an oval view of Piccadilly Circus.

£1,000-1,500   **HAN**

A 20thC Wedgwood Jasperware crimson vase.

3½in (9cm) high

£60-70   **PSA**

A Wedgwood Queensware 'Country Lovers' figural group, by Arnold Machin.

12¼in (31cm) high

£200-250   **PSA**

A prestige Wedgwood Jasperware 'Four Seasons' engine-turned coffee set, limited edition no.5 of 50, boxed with certificate.

£1,000-1,500   **PSA**

A Wedgwood Pottery ribbed spherical vase, designed by Keith Murray, printed factory mark and facsimile signature.

6¼in (16cm) high

£200-250   **WW**

A Wedgwood conical bowl, by Keith Murray, printed and impressed marks, a hairline crack to the rim and two small glaze bubbles.

6¼in (16cm) high

£200-300   **CHEF**

QUICK REFERENCE - WEMYSS WARE

- Established by Robert Methven Heron (1833-1906) in the 1880s in a pottery in Kirkcaldy, Fife, Wemyss Ware was designed and painted by Karel Nekola. Edwin Sandland succeeded Nekola. The company was patronised by Dora Wemyss of Wemyss Castle.
- The company closed in 1930 following financial struggles, but production of Wemyss Ware was transferred to Bovey Tracey Pottery Co. in Devon and supervised by Joseph Nekola, Karel's son. Production continued there until 1957.
- Joseph's apprentice Esther Weeks (née Clark) became head decorator after Joseph's death in 1952.
- In 1994, Griselda Hill Pottery in Fife acquired the Wemyss Ware trademark.

An early 20thC Wemyss Ware model of a pig, painted maker's mark 'Wemyss' in black script, crazed all over.

18¼in (46.5cm) long

£1,700-2,000   **BELL**

A Wemyss Ware pink glazed model of a pig, impressed 'Wemyss Ware R.H. & S.' mark, restored.

6¼in (16cm) long

£200-300   **FLD**

An early 20thC Wemyss Ware model of a pig, 'Shamrocks' pattern, painted and impressed mark 'WEMYSS'.

17in (43cm) long

£4,000-5,000   **L&T**

A Wemyss Ware decanter, modelled as a pig, with black sponged patches, small cork nose, unmarked.

6¼in (16cm) long

£500-600   **FLD**

A Wemyss Ware money box, modelled as a pig, with handpainted clover leaves and flowers, impressed, restored.

6in (15cm) long

£550-650   **FLD**

A Wemyss Ware model of a cat, decorated with handpainted clover leaves and painted features, with inset green glass eyes, painted 'Wemyss' to base.

13½in (34.5cm) high

£1,200-1,800   **FLD**

A Wemyss Ware heart-shaped tray, 'Brown Cockerel and Hens' pattern, impressed mark 'WEMYSS', printed retailer's mark 'T. GOODE & CO.'.

c1900   *11½in (29cm) long*

£1,200-1,800   **L&T**

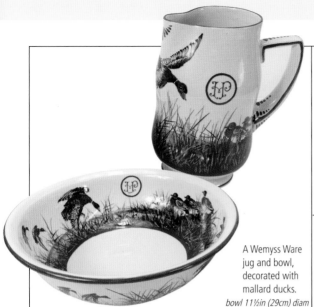

A Wemyss Ware
jug and bowl,
decorated with
mallard ducks.
bowl 11½in (29cm) diam

£3,000-4,000   **PSA**

A Wemyss Ware porridge bowl,
decorated by Karel Nekola,
with inscription 'WILLIE
GARDNER HIS PORRIDGE
PLATE', impressed mark
'WEMYSS WARE R.H. & S.',
painted mark 'WEMYSS/ KN/
1915'.
1915   *6½in (16.5cm) diam*

£1,400-2,000   **L&T**

A pair of Wemyss Ware
large geese flower holders,
impressed marks 'WEMYSS
WARE/ R.H. & S.', one with
printed retailer's mark 'T.
GOODE AND CO.'.
c1900   *8in (20.5cm) high*

£800-1,000   **L&T**

A Wemyss Ware button, decorated by Karel Nekola, depicting a bee,
impressed 'WEMYSS'.
c1900   *1½in (4cm) diam*

£550-650   **L&T**

A Wemyss Ware gordon
dessert plate, 'Damsons'
pattern, impressed mark
'WEMYSS WARE/ R.H. & S.'.
c1900   *8in (20.5cm) diam*

£750-850   **L&T**

An early 20thC Wemyss Ware letter rack, 'Purple Plums' pattern, painted
maker's and retailer's mark 'WEMYSS/ T. GOODE & CO.', hairline.
9in (23cm) wide

£400-500   **L&T**

An early 20thC Wemyss
Ware loving cup,
'Carnations' pattern,
impressed mark
'WEMYSS'.
8¼in (21cm) diam

£750-850   **L&T**

CERAMICS

A near pair of Wemyss Ware candlesticks, 'Carnations' pattern, impressed marks 'WEMYSS WARE/ R.H. & S.'.
c1900   *12in (30.5cm) high*
£1,200-1,600   **L&T**

A 20thC Wemyss Ware basin, 'Campanula' pattern, impressed mark 'WEMYSS', hairlines.
15½in (39.5cm) diam
£1,400-1,800   **L&T**

A Wemyss Ware loving cup, 'Tulips' pattern, impressed mark 'WEMYSS WARE/ R.H. & S.'.
c1900   *10in (25.5cm) diam*
£1,200-1,600   **L&T**

An early 20thC Wemyss Ware Kenmore vase, decorated by Karel Nekola, 'Cabbage Roses' pattern, impressed mark 'WEMYSS', painted retailer's mark 'T. GOODE & CO./ LONDON'.
14¼in (36cm) high
£1,500-2,000   **L&T**

A Wemyss Ware gypsy jardinière, decorated by Karel Nekola, with cabbage roses and butterflies, painted mark 'WEMYSS/ KN/ 1915'.
1915   *8¾in (22cm) diam*
£2,500-3,000   **L&T**

An early 20thC Wemyss Ware quaich, decorated by Edwin Sandland, 'Strawberries' pattern, painted and impressed mark 'WEMYSS'.
10¼in (26cm) diam
£1,200-1,600   **L&T**

An early 20thC Wemyss Ware 'Fifies' mug, painted with fishing boats on the Fife coast of the Firth of Forth, impressed mark 'WEMYSS', printed retailer's mark 'T. GOODE AND CO.'.
3½in (9cm) high
£1,000-1,500   **L&T**

QUICK REFERENCE - WESTERWALD STONEWARE

- Westerwald stoneware is a type of salt-glazed pottery from the Ransbach-Baumbach and Höhr-Grenzhausen areas of Westerwaldkreis in Rheinland-Pfalz, in West Germany.
- The Westerwaldkreis area has large clay quarries of unusually rich and pure quality. These quarries have long encouraged locals to turn to pottery, and there is evidence of ceramic production in the area since 1000 BC.
- Traditional salt-glazing was first developed in the mid-15thC when changing technology allowed kilns to be heated to higher temperatures. The 1960s-70s saw a revival of traditional techniques. These new designs were influenced by Japanese and other Asian ceramics.
- Key artists of the mid-to-late-20thC movement include Elfriede Balzar-Kopp, Klotilde Giefer-Bahn, Görge Hohlt, Walburga Külz, Wim Mühlendyck, Gisela Schmidt-Reuther and Wendelin Stahl.

Thanks to Michael G. Lines, John Newton Antiques.

A Westerwald pottery jug/floor vase, decorated in the studios of Elfriede Balzar-Kopp, design in sgraffito, signed to base.
c1960/70   16¼in (41.5cm) high
£450-500   JNEW

A Westerwald pottery figurine of a badger, decorated in the studios of Elfriede Balzar-Kopp, signed 'BK' to base.
c1960/70   3¾in (9.5cm) high
£275-350   JNEW

A Westerwald lidded jug, decorated by Elfriede Balzar-Kopp, with a sgraffito design on a cobalt ground, signed with initials.

Born in Berdorf, Luxembourg in 1904, Elfriede Balzar-Kopp studied and worked at the State Majolica Factory in Karlsruhe, before opening his own studio in 1927. In 1974, he won the Federal Cross of Merit. Balzar-Kopp died in 1983.
c1940s   16½in (42cm) high
£350-400   JNEW

A scarce Westerwald pottery figural group, decorated in the studios of Elfriede Balzar-Kopp, signed to base.
c1960/70s   10¼in (26cm) high
£750-850   JNEW

A Westerwald pottery figurine of a rooster, decorated in the studios of Elfriede Balzar-Kopp, signed 'BK' to base.
c1970   10¼in (26cm) high
£275-325   JNEW

A vase, decorated in the studios of Elfriede Balzar-Kopp, with a design in traditional enamels and salt-glaze.
c1970   9in (23cm) high
£140-160   JNEW

A figurine of a fish, decorated in the studios of Elfriede Balzar-Kopp.
c1970   6¼in (16cm) high
£180-200   JNEW

A studio pottery plaque, by Elfriede Balzar-Kopp, decorated with a Modernist design of an owl in sgraffito.
c1970s   11¾in (30cm) diam
£250-275   JNEW

A Modernist studio pottery jug, by Heinz Theo Dietz, with sgraffito decoration.

Heinz Theo Dietz (born 1938 in Cologne, Germany) studied ceramic engineering in Höhr-Grenzhausen, before opening his pottery in 1965. In 1969, he moved to Königswinter and set up a new pottery with his wife, Katherina Dietz. He retired In 2003 and the pottery transferred to Dietz's daughter.
c1960-70   *9in (23cm) high*
£325-375   **JNEW**

A studio pottery figurine, made by Heinz Theo Dietz, of a 'hybrid creature'.
c1980   *10in (25.5cm) high*
£1,000-1,200   **JNEW**

A Modernist studio pottery jug, by Heinz Theo Dietz, decorated in sgraffito.
c1960-70   *9in (23cm) high*
£350-400   **JNEW**

A salt-glaze jug, made in the studios of Klotilde Giefer-Bahn, decorated in sgraffito with a retro bird design, signed to base.

Klotilde Giefer-Bahn was born in Koblenz, Germany, in 1924. She trained as a ceramicist and opened her own studio in 1947 in Höhr-Grenzhausen (Rhineland-Palatinate). Following her death in 2008, her son, Roland Giefer, took over her studio.
c1960/70   *12½in (32cm) high*
£375-450   **JNEW**

A Modernist studio pottery jug, by Heinz Theo Dietz, with owls in sgraffito.
c1970s
£120-150   **JNEW**

A scarce Westerwald pottery figurine of a rabbit, decorated in the studios of Klotilde Giefer-Bahn, with cobalt and traditional glaze and enamels, signed 'Giefer Bahn' to base.
c1960s   *4¾in (12cm) high*
£225-275   **JNEW**

A Westerwald pottery figurine of a fox, decorated in the studios of Klotilde Giefer-Bahn, with a traditional salt-glaze and enamels, signed 'Giefer Bahn' to base.

Klotilde Giefer-Bahn's son Roland Giefer produced another version of this figurine in the 1980s, but the later version has paler enamels and is signed Roland Giefer.
c1970   *5¾in (14.5cm) high*
£225-275   **JNEW**

A Modernist salt-glaze vase, by Klotilde Giefer-Bahn, decorated with an abstract design of a tree, in cobalt blue and earthy enamels, signed to base.
c1970s   *9¾in (24.5cm) high*
£275-350   **JNEW**

A Westerwald pottery figurine of a toucan, decorated in the studios of Klotilde Giefer-Bahn by her son Roland Giefer, with cobalt and traditional salt-glaze and enamels, signed 'Giefer Bahn' to base.
c1980   *7¾in (19.5cm) high*
£225-275   **JNEW**

A studio vase, made by Gerhard Liebenthron, with layered erupted/pitted earthy glaze, with Liebenthron's monogram and year code to base.

Born in 1925 in Neustrelitz, Germany, Gerhard Liebenthron studied at the North German Art College, before opening his own workshop in 1952 in Bremen. He was a member of the Arts and Crafts Working Group in Bremen. Liebenthron died in 2005.

1962   *7in (18cm) high*
£125-150   JNEW

A studio vase, made by Gerhard Liebenthron, with a flowing layered glaze, with Liebenthron's monogram and year code to base.

1963   *6¼in (16cm) high*
£175-225   JNEW

A studio vase, made by Gerhard Liebenthron, with a flowing layered glaze, with Liebenthron's monogram and year code to base.

1973   *10in (25.5cm) high*
£200-250   JNEW

A studio vase, made by Gerhard Liebenthron, with a layered glaze, with Liebenthron's monogram and year code to base.

1977   *10¼in (26cm) high*
£175-225   JNEW

A studio vase, made by Gerhard Liebenthron, with a flowing layered glaze giving the illusion of looking out onto an exotic landscape, with Liebenthron's monogram and year code to base.

1979   *5in (12.5cm) high*
£200-250   JNEW

A Modernist studio pottery jug, made by Gerhard Liebenthron, with a multi-layered flowing earthy glaze, with Liebenthron's monogram and year code to base.

1980   *10¾in (27.5cm) high*
£275-325   JNEW

A studio pottery vase, made by Gerhard Liebenthron, with a multi-layered flowing glaze, with a calligraphy-type design, with Liebenthron's monogram and year code to base.

1983   *7in (18cm) high*
£175-225   JNEW

A Modernist/Space Age-inspired studio vase, made by Gerhard Liebenthron, with a layered glaze, with Liebenthron's monogram and year code to base.

1984   *9¾in (24.5cm) high*
£200-250   JNEW

A stoneware vase, made by Gerhard Liebenthron, painted with a graffiti design, in the style of Picasso, with an earthy glaze, with Liebenthron's monogram and year code to base.

1991   *15¾in (40cm) high*
£600-750   JNEW

CERAMICS

A stoneware jug, by Wim Mühlendyck, decorated in sgraffito, salt-glaze and earth enamels.

Born in 1905 in Porz, Cologne, Wim Mühlendyck studied at the State Ceramic Technical School in Höhr-Grenzhausen, before training as a teacher in Cologne. He opened his own workshop in 1931 in Höhr-Grenzhausen. Mühlendyck worked closely with his wife, Bita Mühlendyck, and Elfriede Balzar-Kopp. Wim Mühlendyck died in 1986.

c1950   *7½in (19cm) high*
£125-150   **JNEW**

A stoneware salt-glaze lidded decanter, by Wim Mühlendyck, decorated in sgraffito, with a traditional study of forest animals, with Mühlendyck's signature and studio mark.

c1960   *14in (35.5cm) high*
£400-450   **JNEW**

A Westerwald salt-glazed jug, decorated in sgraffito by Wim Mühlendyck, with a stylised design of a leaping horse, signed to base.

c1960   *9¼in (23.5cm) high*
£325-375   **JNEW**

A salt-glazed stein, by Wim Mühlendyck, decorated in sgraffito, with a stylised elephant.

c1960/70   *6¼in (16cm) high*
£150-175   **JNEW**

A Westerwald salt-glazed pottery jug, decorated in sgraffito by Wim Mühlendyck, with owls, signed to the base.

c1960/70s   *11in (28cm) high*
£250-300   **JNEW**

A stoneware lidded tankard, by Wim Mühlendyck, decorated in sgraffito, with a wild boar, finished with a metallic oxide and salt-glaze, signed 'Wim Mühlendyck'.

c1960s   *5¾in (14.5cm) high*
£150-175   **JNEW**

A German stoneware jug, by Wim Mühlendyck, decorated in sgraffito, with a leaping stag, finished with rich salt-glaze, with Mühlendyck's studio mark.

c1960s   *13in (33cm) high*
£250-275   **JNEW**

A salt-glazed and cobalt blue-ground jar and cover, by Wim Mühlendyck, decorated in sgraffito, with stylised seahorses.

c1970   *4in (10cm) high*
£150-175   **JNEW**

A globular-shaped tea caddy, by Wim Mühlendyck, decorated with a stylised design in sgraffito, with a cobalt blue and salt-glazed ground.

c1970   *4in (10cm) high*
£150-175   **JNEW**

A salt-glaze liquor flask, made in the studios of Wim Mühlendyck, decorated with a Modernist Space Age design, studio mark to the base.

c1970   *6¼in (16cm) high*

£150-175   **JNEW**

A salt-glazed and cobalt blue-ground cigarette-ash jar and cover, by Wim Mühlendyck, decorated in sgraffito, with stylised fish.

c1970   *3in (7.5cm) high*

£150-175   **JNEW**

A stoneware lidded tobacco jar, by Wim Mühlendyck, decorated with stylised owls in sgraffito and rich enamels, with Mühlendyck's signature and studio mark to the base.

c1970   *6in (15cm) high*

£225-250   **JNEW**

A Westerwald salt-glazed 'Milk Churn' jug, decorated in sgraffito by Wim Mühlendyck, with a stylised leaping horse, signed to base, dated.

1973   *9½in (24cm) high*

£250-275   **JNEW**

A Westerwald salt-glazed jug, decorated in sgraffito by Johannas Mühlendyck, with a stylised design and rich glaze, bears the studio mark 'MJ' for Johannes Mühlendyc.

Born in 1933 to Wim and Bita Mühlendyck, Johannes Mühlendyck studied at the College of Ceramics in Landshut, Germany, before working in his parents' pottery studio from 1956-86. He died in 2013.

6¼in (16cm) high

£150-175   **JNEW**

A Westerwald salt-glazed jug, decorated in sgraffito by Johannes Mühlendyck, with musical instruments.

c1970   *8½in (21.5cm) high*

£175-225   **JNEW**

A studio pottery vase, made by Rudi Stahl, with a variegated earthy blue glaze, signed to base.

Born in 1918 in Westerwald, Germany, Rudi Stahl studied pottery under Wim Mühlendyck, before attending the State Ceramic Technical School in Höhr-Grenzhausen. In 1938, he founded his own pottery in Höhr-Grenzhausen. Stahl died in 1987.

c1960   *11in (28cm) high*

£250-275   **JNEW**

A studio pottery vase, made by Rudi Stahl, with a variegated earthy glaze, decorated with a Greek key-type design, signed to base.

c1960s   *9¾in (24.5cm) high*

£250-300   **JNEW**

A studio pottery vase, made by Rudi Stahl, with a variegated earthy glaze, decorated with a Greek key-type design, signed to base.

c1960s   *8in (20.5cm) high*

£250-300   **JNEW**

CERAMICS

A Bing & Grøndahl figurine of a cow, modelled by Lauritz Jensen, numbered '2161', with artist's monogram.

9½in (24cm) long

£220-280   SWO

A pair of Black Ryden pottery vases, designed by Kerry Goodwin, 'Summers End' pattern, impressed mark verso, signed, limited edition no.12/100 and no.14/100, dated.

2003   *14in (35.5cm) high*

£200-250   LSK

A late 19thC to early 20thC painted terracotta boxer, by Bernard Bloch, impressed '4380/ BB'.

9¼in (23.5cm) high

£500-600   L&T

A C.H. Brannam Barum Pottery 'Mr Punch' money box, possibly retailed by Liberty & Co., incised 'C.H. Brannam, Barum, 1901', incised 'rd' mark, dated.

1901   *3½in (9cm) high*

£750-850   WW

QUICK REFERENCE - BRETBY ART POTTERY

- In c1883, Henry Tooth and William Ault set up the Bretby Art Pottery in Derbyshire, producing decorative and novelty wares. Bretby also created ceramic pieces imitating other materials, such as copper and pewter. The company traded as Tooth & Co. Ault left the business to set up his own pottery in 1887.

- After c1920, production shifted away from decorative and novelty ware and after changing hands multiple times the factory closed in c1996.

An early 20thC Cantagalli maiolica charger, decorated with Renaissance-style roundel depicting St Martin of Tours, painted cockerel mark.

18½in (47cm) diam

£1,200-1,600   FLD

A pair of Bretby Art Pottery glazed earthenware bookends, model no.3072, impressed Pottery marks.

c1930   *8in (20.5cm) high*

£70-80   ROS

A Caulden handled vase, by S. Pope.

8in (20.5cm) high

£50-70   PSA

A pair of Compton Potters' Art Guild bookends, depicting St Joan on horseback.

c1920   *7½in (19cm) high*

£350-450   L&T

A British W.T. Copeland & Sons stoneware beer jug, with 'ARCTIC EXPEDITION 1875' transfer crest, with maker's transfer anchor mark on the base, impressed '12', inscribed 'DISCOVERY', chip to the rim on the left of the spout.

For this expedition, which was led by Sir George Strong Nares, Copeland produced special services for both HM Ships 'Alert' and 'Discovery' in stoneware and porcelain using either blue or sepia transfers. Sent by the Admiralty in an attempt to reach the North Pole by way of Smith Sound, it culminated in Commander Albert Hastings Markham's Farthest North of 83° 20'26"N (12 May 1876), a record latitude at the time.

1875   *8in (20cm) high*

£1,500-2,000   CM

A late 19thC Walter Crane dust-pressed tile, decorated with 'Mary Mary Quite Contrary', from 'The Baby's Opera', painted onto a Minton Hollins blank.

1877   *6in (15cm) square*

£150-200   **FLD**

A Max Emanuel & Co. ceramic pig spill vase, by Louis Wain, painted in colours, signed on the body 'LOUIS WAIN', with printed maker's marks and moulded registration mark.

Louis Wain (1860-1939) was an English artist and illustrator, best-known for his depictions of anthropomorphised cats. His work appeared in children's books, journals and on postcards. Wain struggled with his mental health and was diagnosed with schizophrenia. In 1924, he was admitted to Springfield Mental Hospital and later moved to Bethlem Royal Hospital.

c1914   *4¾in (12cm) high*

£500-600   **L&T**

A Karl Ens 'Emperor Penguins' ceramic figural group.

1930s

£110-150   **PSA**

A Della Robbia terracotta bottle vase, by Charles Collis, base numbered '573', drilled.

13½in (34.5cm) high

£500-600   **WHP**

A Max Emanuel & Co. ceramic cat spill vase, by Louis Wain, signed on the body 'LOUIS WAIN', with printed maker's marks and registration mark 'RD NO 638317', printed mark 'MADE IN ENGLAND'.

c1914   *5¼in (13.5cm) high*

£400-500   **L&T**

An Italian Marcello Fantoni bottle vase, signed 'Fantoni, Italy', slight scratches to the base.

1960s   *15in (38cm) high*

£250-350   **DAWS**

A Bourne Denby stoneware hot water bottle.

10in (25.5cm) wide

£40-50   **PSA**

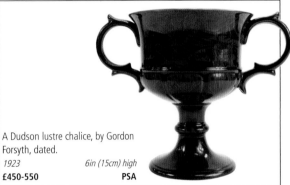

A Dudson lustre chalice, by Gordon Forsyth, dated.

1923   *6in (15cm) high*

£450-550   **PSA**

A Della Robbia vase, painted by Annie Smith, incised by Harry Fletcher, incised marks to base.

11in (28cm) high

£550-650   **PW**

A Fielding's 'Fairy Castle' Crown Devon vase, designed by Enoch Boulton, pattern no.2414, printed and painted marks, restored.

Simon Fielding established an earthenware manufacturer in c1870 at The Railway Pottery, Stoke. The company became known as S. Fielding & Co. The Crown Devon line of pottery was developed. In the early 20thC, the factory was renamed the Devon Pottery. The pottery was knocked down in 1987.

9in (23cm) high

£220-280   WW

A Fielding's 'Crown Devon' charger, pattern no.2130, printed and painted marks.

15½in (39.5cm) diam

£180-220   WW

An early 20thC Gallé-style pottery cat, with inset glass eyes.

13¾in (35cm) high

£600-700   BE

An early 20thC Gallé-style faience 'Barrister' pug, with inset glass eyes.

12½in (32cm) high

£750-850   BE

An early 20thC Gallé-style nodding pottery cat, with inset glass eyes.

11in (28cm) long

£650-750   BE

An Austrian Gmundner Keramik pottery figurine, model no.359, impressed marks, remnants of paper label, some crazing.

c1930   8¼in (21cm) high

£150-200   BELL

A 'Flesh Pots' jug, designed by Morris Rushton, printed factory mark.

'Flesh Pots' was a small, humorous pottery launched in Stoke on Trent in 1978 by founder Morris Rushton. Although small and short lived, it influenced, among others, Next, the high street retailer, with its avant garde designs, while also producing a more traditional range retailed by the National Trust.

9¼in (23.5cm) high

£300-350   WW

A Fulham Pottery bowl, decorated by Quentin Bell, with an incised portrait of Virginia Woolf, incised 'Fulham Pottery, Quentin Bell'.

5¾in (14.5cm) wide

£400-500   FLD

Judith Picks

William Henry Goss (1833-1906) studied at the School of Design at Somerset House, before working for William Taylor Copeland. In c1858, Goss established his own porcelain business. At the turn of the century, Goss' pieces were hugely popular. Following a decline in popularity after World War I, Goss sold the factory in 1929, but production continued there until the late 1930s. We are often asked on the 'Antiques Roadshow' how we decide on our valuations. There are many factors but rarity and desirability are critical. Many Goss pieces can be purchased for under £20 but this tiger is a rare model and hence the price achieved.

A W.H. Goss model of a tiger.

3¾in (9.5cm) high

£800-900   PSA

QUICK REFERENCE - GRUEBY

- William Henry Grueby (1867-1925) trained at the Low Art Tile Works, before founding the Grueby Faience Company in Boston, Massachusetts, in 1894.
- Most of the pottery was handmade and decorated by a team of young women from Boston's Museum of Fine Arts and other schools.
- Grueby experimented with glazes and developed a distinctive matt finish, in contrast to the glossy glazes popular at the time. Grueby received much critical acclaim for his art pottery, but the company struggled financially in the early 1900s, reducing its decorative pottery production, and filing for bankruptcy.
- Grueby then founded the Grueby Faience and Tile Company, which was bought out by the C. Pardee Works in the late 1910s.

A Grueby vase, circular pottery stamp, incised 'FR', some hairlines, some flecks to leaves.
c1905   *8in (20.5cm) high*
£3,000-4,000   DRA

A Hancock & Sons 'Morrisware' vase, designed by George Cartlidge, model no.C99-1, printed factory mark, painted mark 'C99-1'.

Founded in Tunstall, Staffordshire in the mid-to-late 1800s, Sampson Hancock & Sons produced tableware, home ware and crested china. Following Sampson Hancock's death in c1900, his sons took over the business. Key designers include George Cartlidge, F.X. Abraham and Edith Gater. The company closed in 1937.

11in (28cm) high
£550-650   WW

A Hancock & Sons 'Morrisware' table lamp base, by George Cartlidge, model no.C20-6, printed mark, slight damage.

13½in (34.5cm) high
£220-280   FLD

A Grueby lobed vase, by Ruth Erickson, with yellow buds, circular pottery stamp 'RE/BL/13-08', one touched-up chip, minor nicks.
c1905   *8½in (21.5cm) high*
£2,000-2,500   DRA

A Hancock & Sons 'Morrisware' flower bowl, designed by George Cartlidge, model no.C19-28, printed factory mark, facsimile signature.
11in (28cm) diam
£150-200   WW

An early 20thC Hancock & Sons 'Morrisware' pot pourri, by George Cartlidge, model no.C56-1, decorated with the tube-lined verse 'Essences of Past Summers', lacks cover, printed mark, restored.
8in (20.5cm) high
£200-250   FLD

A Grueby vase, circular 'Faience' stamp.
c1902   *7in (18cm) high*
£2,500-3,000   DRA

A Hancock & Sons 'Morrisware' vase, designed by George Cartlidge, model no.C17-10, printed factory mark, painted facsimile signature.

See Tony Johnson, 'The Morris Ware, Tiles and Art of George Cartlidge', MakingSpace (2004), page 97, catalogue no.264, for comparable vases.

11¾in (30cm) high
£350-450   WW

A Howson high-fired flambé vase, dated.
1911   *8in (20.5cm) high*
£70-90   PSA

CERAMICS

QUICK REFERENCE - HERTWIG AND CO., KATZHÜTTE

- Christoph Hertwig, Benjamin Beyermann and Carl Birkner founded the Hertwig and Co. porcelain factory in 1864 at the Lower Hammer Mill in Katzhütte, Germany. Production started in 1865.
- After Birkner quit and Beyermann died, Hertwig ran the business until 1886, when his sons took over.
- By 1890, the factory had a workforce of over 300 people as well as homeworkers in surrounding villages, producing decorative ceramics, dolls and stoneware. Production of porcelain figurines began in 1900.
- Sculptor Stefan Dakon worked at the factory as a designer. Dakon produced Art Deco-style bronze figurines and ceramics, and also worked for Goldscheider and Keramos.
- The Katzhütte factory was passed down the Hertwig family, and by 1937 was run by Christoph Hertwig's grandsons.
- Production was limited to decorative ceramics after nationalisation in 1958. The factory closed in 1990.

A Katzhütte 'Ballet Russes' figurine, printed maker's marks, impressed 'Germany'.

c1920   *8¾in (22cm) high*

£250-300   **ROS**

A Katzhütte Pottery large figurine, by Stephan Dakon, printed factory mark, impressed Dakon.

17in (43cm) high

£450-550   **WW**

A Katzhütte figurine, printed factory mark.

9¾in (24.5cm) high

£150-200   **WW**

An Art Deco Katzhütte figurine, of a lady walking her Borzoi hound, green stamp below, chain lead is loose.

12½in (32cm) high

£350-400   **CHOR**

An Austrian Keramos 'Junge Frau im Kleid' (Young Woman in a Dress) figurine, printed and painted mark 'R17', restoration to bonnet.

c1920   *15¾in (40cm) high*

£200-250   **BELL**

A Plichta model of a cat, with handpainted thistle decoration, with inset glass eyes, with printed mark.

Jan Plichta ran a glass and pottery wholesalers in London in the early-to-mid-1900s. He commissioned pieces from the Bovey Pottery, the Elton Pottery and sold some Wemyss Ware. Some of these pieces were marked 'Plichta'. Records of Plichta after the 1950s are vague.

10¼in (26cm) high

£120-160   **FLD**

A rare Morris and Co. 'Cinderella in the Kitchen' tile, designed by Edward Burne-Jones, glaze chips and small hairline to base rim.

6in (15cm) high

£3,500-4,000   **WW**

A Plichta model of a pig, decorated by Joseph Nekola, printed mark with Nekola Pinxt in script.

6¼in (16cm) high

£250-300   **FLD**

A 19thC Portobello pottery figurine, of a seated Scotsman in kilt and tam-o'-shanter, on stepped base.

9¼in (23.5cm) high

£900-1,000   **GWA**

A pair of Royal Bonn pottery vases, printed and impressed marks, one handle reset.

15¾in (40cm) high

£400-500   SWO

A Meissen-style 'Nodding Chinaman' seated figurine, possibly by Samson of Paris.

9½in (24cm) high

£300-400   JN

QUICK REFERENCE - WILEMAN & CO.

- Based in Staffordshire and known as Wileman & Co. until the early 20thC, as well as Foley Potteries, Shelley Potteries produced ceramics until 1966.
- Joseph Ball Shelley joined the firm in 1862, leaving his son Percy Shelley in charge after his death in 1896. The company became known for its Art Deco fine bone china teaware.
- Percy Shelley took on ceramic designer Frederick Rhead as art director in 1896.
- Rhead produced the 'Intarsio' and 'Urbato' ranges of decorative earthenware, before leaving the company in 1905. Rhead was succeeded by Walter Slater and, by 1914, the company was moving into the production of dinnerware.
- In 1925, Percy Shelley trademarked the name Shelley, after failing to trademark Foley years previously.
- In the 1920s, illustrator Hilda Cowham designed a range of nursery ware for the company, depicting children playing and seaside scenes. Another illustrator, Mabel Lucie Attwell, joined Shelley Potteries in 1926, producing designs featuring children, the 'Boo Boo' elves, and animals.
- In the 1930s, Shelley stopped producing earthenware, to focus on fine bone china. Shelley Potteries changed its name to Shelley China in 1965 and traded until 1966, when it was bought out by the Allied English Potteries.

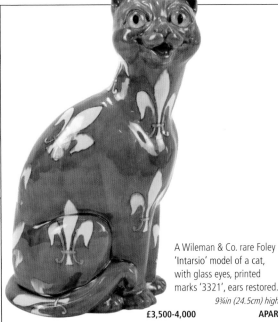

A Wileman & Co. rare Foley 'Intarsio' model of a cat, with glass eyes, printed marks '3321', ears restored.

9¾in (24.5cm) high

£3,500-4,000   APAR

A Shelley Art Deco preserve jar, 'Melody' pattern.

4¼in (11cm) high

£40-50   PSA

A pair of Foley 'Intarsio' vases, designed by Frederick Rhead, pattern no.3159, printed factory marks to base.

12¼in (31cm) high

£650-750   WW

A Shelley 'Boo Boo' milk jug, by Mabel Lucie Attwell, printed mark.

6in (15cm) high

£70-90   FLD

A Shelley lustre ginger jar, designed by Walter Slater, unmarked, wear and scratches.

13in (33cm) high

£95-120   WW

CERAMICS

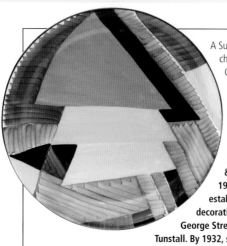

A Susie Cooper wall charger, Grays Pottery Galleon mark.

Susie Cooper (1902-95) studied at the Burslem School of Art before joining AE Gray & Co. in 1922. By 1929, Cooper had established a ceramic decoration company at George Street Pottery in Tunstall. By 1932, she was designing her own shapes, produced by Wood & Sons, in Staffordshire, where she had her own production unit called Crown Works.

1930s   *15½in (39.5cm) wide*

£950-1,100   **FLD**

An Art Nouveau Spencer Edge pottery ewer, printed factory mark.

10in (25.5cm) high

£150-200   **WW**

A Spode cup, commemorative of Great Britain's entry into the Common Market, limited edition no.341 of 500, with certificate signed by Lord Harlech, in a fitted case.

£65-75   **CHOR**

A plate, printed 'by Susie Cooper' mark.

1930s   *8in (20.5cm) diam*

£250-300   **FLD**

A Wiener Werkstätte earthenware figurine, by Michael Powolny, impressed marks.

8in (20.5cm) long

£700-800   **DUK**

An earthenware 'Sherwood Forest' wall plaque, handpainted and signed 'UKC Wallace', in gilt frame.

14½in (37cm) high

£50-70   **PSA**

A 19thC Yorkshire-type Toby jug, the handle formed as a ship's figurehead, painted '2G1 Black' to the base.

10¼in (26cm) high

£300-350   **FLD**

An early 20thC Continental figurine of a dog, with 'Votes For Women' moulded to the base, unmarked.

3¼in (8.5cm) high

£120-160   **FLD**

A French 20thC Art Deco earthenware group.

11¾in (30cm) high

£150-200   **BELL**

A Czechoslovakian wall mask, model no.1172, printed and moulded marks.

10in (25.5cm) high

£160-200   SWO

A Czechoslovakian double wall mask, model no.15187, printed and moulded mark, crack to back, some minor paint flakes.

11¾in (30cm) high

£160-200   SWO

A Czechoslovakian wall mask, modelled as a female jester, printed 'Czechoslovakia', impressed '15175'.

1930s   *7¼in (18.5cm) high*

£150-200   FLD

A Czechoslovakian wall mask, printed 'Made in Czechoslovakia', impressed '15380', slight damage.

1930s   *8¾in (22cm) high*

£100-150   FLD

A late 20thC Crown Devon handpainted wall mask, 'Dorothy Ann', printed mark.

11in (28cm) long

£35-45   FLD

QUICK REFERENCE - ROYAL DUX

- In 1860, Eduard Eichler founded E. Eichler Thonwaren-Fabrik – which would become Duxer Porzellan-Manufaktur, then Royal Dux – in Dux, Bohemia, now Duchcov, Czech Republic.
- Eichler ran the company until his death in 1887.
- By the late 19thC/early 20thC, the firm was focussing on porcelain statues, figurines, Art Nouveau busts, masks and vases.
- Production was interrupted by the World Wars, with the company struggling financially. However, it maintained its popularity. Royal Dux is now a member of the Czech Porcelain Group.

A Goebel wall mask, modelled as a female with side glancing eyes, impressed crown mark 'FX 61/2', slight damage.

1930s   *6¾in (17cm) high*

£120-180   FLD

A Keramos Pottery wall mask, designed by Stephan Dakon, model no.2058, stamped and printed 'Keramos Wien'.

12¾in (32.5cm) high

£300-400   SWO

A Royal Dux wall mask, printed mark, impressed 'CZECHOSLOVAKIA' and illegible number.

1930s   *6¼in (16cm) high*

£300-350   FLD

CERAMICS

QUICK REFERENCE - STUDIO POTTERY

- The term 'studio pottery' is used to describe pieces made by the pottery owner or by others under his or her supervision. Studio potteries are typically small in size. Early studio pottery-type establishments were founded in the 19thC.
- Each piece can be both handmade and hand-decorated. Many designs hark back to traditional pottery or techniques such as slipware glazes, or Asian designs, particularly from China and Japan. Much is derived from the pioneering work of Bernard Leach (1887-1979) and Shoji Hamada (1894-1978). Leach's and Hamada's influence continues to be felt today.
- The most important and often valuable work was made by a first generation of studio potters, which included Leach and his family, Hamada, Lucie Rie (1902-95), and Hans Coper (1920-81).
- The work of a second generation, such as Alan Caiger-Smith MBE (b.1930) and Michael Cardew (1901-83) is also highly collected. In some cases, their works are perceived as the 'antiques of the future'. Many contemporary potters, such as Grayson Perry (b.1966) use pottery to convey a message.
- Look at the base of a studio pot for an impressed, printed, painted or incised mark, which may be in the form of a motif, monogram or signature. This will help to identify the potter and may help to date the pot. Always look for skill and quality in terms of potting, form and overall design.

An Aldermaston Pottery tin-glazed pottery bowl, by Alan Caiger-Smith MBE, printed factory mark, painted monogram, date mark.

1961   *18in (47cm) diam*

£750-850   **WW**

A stoneware casserole dish and cover, by Michael Cardew, brush detailing to a cream ground, impressed marks to base, slight blemishes to glaze.

7in (18cm) high

£550-650   **CHOR**

An Aldermaston pottery red lustre bowl, by Alan Caiger-Smith MBE, painted mark, date code, a few minor pits in glaze.

The Aldermaston Pottery operated in Berkshire, England, from 1955-2006. It was founded by Alan Caiger-Smith MBE, who studied ceramics at Central School of Arts and Crafts in London, and was joined a year later by Geoffrey Eastop (1921-2014).

1983   *11in (28cm) diam*

£1,200-1,600   **DN**

A large stoneware crock jar and cover, by Richard Batterham (b.1936), with a celadon-green ash glaze, unsigned, incised 'WF' to base, applied paper label numbered 30, small chips.

15½in (39.5cm) high

£750-850   **WW**

A large platter, by Dylan Bowen, slip decorated earthenware.

Dylan Bowen makes slip-decorated earthenware using both traditional and contemporary materials and techniques. The clay can be thrown, handbuilt, carved, or assembled. Dylan then pours, trails or brushes on slips depending on what is suggested by the form. He aims to capture some of the spontaneity and action of the making process in the finished work. Dylan lives and works in Oxfordshire and is a Fellow of the Craft Potters Association.

17¼in (44cm) diam

£300-350   **FLD**

A Winchcombe Pottery earthenware wall vase or pocket, by Michael Cardew, impressed seals to base.

c1930-40   *9in (23cm) high*

£120-180   **ROS**

QUICK REFERENCE - PETER BEARD

- Peter Beard obtained a degree in Industrial and Furniture Design at Ravensbourne College of Art, London and, on graduating, immediately began a career in ceramics. He has been working professionally since 1973 and during his career has taken part in many one-person shows and group exhibitions around the world. Beard's work is represented in many public and private collections and he has held masterclasses in many countries. Beard is a Fellow of the Craft Potters Association and is currently serving on its council, as well as serving a three-year period as the Chair of Ceramic Art London. He has been granted various international awards and been invited to partake in residencies in several countries, including the USA, Japan and Hungary.

A porcelain vessel, by Peter Beard.

8¾in (22cm) high

£750-850   **FLD**

An owl figurine, produced by Cinque Ports, Rye.

When Richard and Susan Parkinson closed their pottery in 1963, the moulds were purchased by George Gray of Cinque Ports Pottery. Most of these moulds are believed to have been destroyed.

c1960s

£150-200   **FLD**

A late 20thC to early 21stC wood-fired globular jar, by Nic Collins, signed to base.

19¾in (50cm) high

£300-400   **ROS**

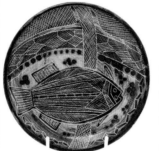

A saucer dish, designed by Carl Cooper (1912-66), with an aboriginal design of a fish, with earth-glazes, signed and dated.

1954   6¾in (17cm) diam

£200-300   **HAN**

A porcelain vase, by Joanna Constantinidis (1927-2000), in a pale cleadon glaze with cobalt blue swirl, impressed seal mark, hairline crack.

7¼in (18.5cm) high

£800-900   **WW**

A stoneware vase, by Hans Coper, glazed with iron manganese to rim and white slips to body, impressed seal mark.

5¼in (13.5cm) high

£18,000-22,000   **WW**

A large vase, by Tony Dasent, with slip decoration, makers mark.

14½in (37cm) high

£150-200   **BELL**

A thrown bowl, by Derek Davis, with pinched-out edge, copper with barium and ash glaze, signed.

1980s   7in (18cm) diam

£400-450   **BELL**

A lidded celadon glazed porcelain jar, by Edmund de Waal (b.1964), on a wooden base, impressed marks, lid restored.

c1998   12¼in (31cm) high

£2,000-3,000   **ROS**

CERAMICS

A Winchcombe Pottery stoneware vase, by Ray Finch, with Tenmoku glaze.

13¾in (35cm) high

£150-200   CHOR

A high-fired stoneware flask, by Robert Fournier.

13in (33cm) high

£200-250   BELL

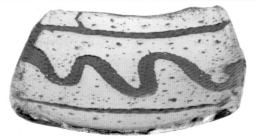

A late 20thC David Frith dish, with a brown wave and linear design, twin seal mark.

14½in (37cm) wide

£180-220   FLD

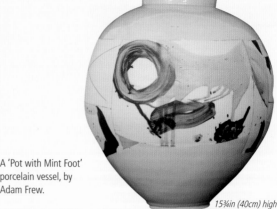

A 'Pot with Mint Foot' porcelain vessel, by Adam Frew.

15¾in (40cm) high

£800-900   FLD

A late 20thC David Frith studio pottery shallow dish, with a brown tenmoku border edge, twin seal mark.

12½in (32cm) diam

£230-300   FLD

A stoneware vase, by Henry Hammond (1914-89), with a celadon glaze, painted in rust with a willow tree design, impressed seal mark, some restoration.

1990   *9in (23cm) high*

£400-500   WW

A 'Small Round Pot', carved raku, by Ashraf Hanna, handbuilt.

7in (18cm) diam

£650-750   FLD

A 'Bowl Form' handbuilt vessel, by Ashraf Hanna, surface treatment terra sigillata slips.

15¾in (40cm) wide

£1,200-1,500   FLD

A 'Disc with Blue Wave' raku, by Peter Hayes.

Peter Hayes creates sculptures using ceramics, bronze, glass, marble and stone from his studio on Bath's Cleveland Bridge. During his career, he has created commissions for office spaces, hotels, yachts and private homes. His work has been exhibited globally. Having lived and travelled in Africa and India, he is naturally drawn to the shapes of artefacts and objects from other cultures and other times but that remain timeless.

19in (48.5cm) high

£800-900   FLD

A 'Bowl with Disc and Blue Wave' raku, by Peter Hayes.

10¾in (27.5cm) high

£400-500   FLD

A Margaret 'Margi' Hine (1927-87) earthenware platter, slip decorated with a flying angel, signed and dated.

1951   *15½in (39cm) wide*

£700-800   WW

A Margaret 'Margi' Hine 'Girl on a Horse' stoneware sculture, painted signature, minor professional restoration.

17in (43cm) high

£5,000-6,000   WW

A porcelain bowl, by Don Jones, painted cobalt blue with pink, gold and white stripes.

18¼in (46cm) diam

£400-500   CHOR

A monumental stoneware garden vase, by Jenifer Jones (b.1940), impressed seal mark, garden patinantion.

25½in (65cm) high

£7,000-8,000   WW

A contemporary conical bowl, by Tony Laverick, initialled, dated.

2009   *6in (15cm) diam*

£130-180   FLD

A large handbuilt stoneware vase, by Janet Leach, the form having open cracks, multiple incisions and marks.

By repute this was the funerary jar that Janet Leach made to commemorate the life of her husband Bernard Leach.

c1980s   *11½in (29cm) high*

£300-350   ROS

CERAMICS

A Muchelney Pottery wood-fired burnished stoneware vase, by John Leach, decorated with a smoked, wave design, stamped marks to base.

9in (23cm) high

£120-180   **WW**

A Lowerdown Pottery Willow stoneware vase, by David Leach OBE (1911-2005), with a tenmoku willow tree, under thick and running Dolomite glaze, impressed seal mark.

11in (28cm) high

£2,000-2,500   **WW**

An Ainstable Pottery stoneware bottle vase, by Jim Malone, incised with willow tree motif, glazed in hakeme, under a celadon glaze, impressed seal marks.

16in (40.5cm) high

£400-500   **WW**

An early pottery flowerhead wall plaque, by Kate Malone (b.1959), impressed seal marks and date.

1933   *8¼in (21cm) diam*

£300-400   **WW**

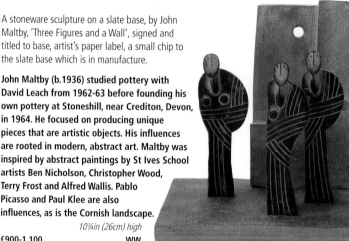

A stoneware sculpture on a slate base, by John Maltby, 'Three Figures and a Wall', signed and titled to base, artist's paper label, a small chip to the slate base which is in manufacture.

John Maltby (b.1936) studied pottery with David Leach from 1962-63 before founding his own pottery at Stoneshill, near Crediton, Devon, in 1964. He focused on producing unique pieces that are artistic objects. His influences are rooted in modern, abstract art. Maltby was inspired by abstract paintings by St Ives School artists Ben Nicholson, Christopher Wood, Terry Frost and Alfred Wallis. Pablo Picasso and Paul Klee are also influences, as is the Cornish landscape.

10¼in (26cm) high

£900-1,100   **WW**

A tall spade vase, by John Maltby, 'Small Suffolk Seaport', painted to one side with houses, the reverse with a boat, painted 'Maltby' to base.

1991   *8in (20.5cm) high*

£2,000-2,500   **WW**

A John Maltby stoneware sculpture, painted with graveyard crosses, signed.

Produced in a limited edition of two for an exhibition at the New Craftsman Gallery, St Ives. It is believed this example was kept by John Maltby.

22in (56cm) high

£4,000-5,000   **WW**

A contemporary sculpture, by John Maltby, entitled to the base 'Bird and Five Fish', seal mark to the side, hand-written title, dated.

2011   *16½in (42cm) high*

£600-700   **FLD**

A cut-sided stoneware bottle vase, by William 'Bill' Marshall (1923-2007), in a pitted celadon green ash glaze, impressed seal mark.

19in (48.5cm) high

£1,300-1,600   **WW**

QUICK REFERENCE - PICASSO POTTERY

- In the latter part of his life, Pablo Picasso (1881-1973) became interested in creating pottery. In 1949, he met and began working with Georges and Suzanne Ramié, owners of the Madoura pottery.
- Producing over 3,500 ceramic designs, Picasso combined techniques of painting, sculpture and printmaking. Human and animal faces appear frequently on his pieces. His second wife, Jacqueline Roque, also appeared on and inspired his ceramic works.
- The pieces were not only decorative, but functional too. Picasso used his plates and bowls in his home.
- Each piece is marked or stamped, however these changed over time. The edition number also appears on some pieces.

A Madoura 'Pichet Têtes' earthenware jug, by Pablo Picasso, from a limited edition of 500, stamped and marked.

designed 1956   4¾in (12cm) high

£3,000-4,000   **DN**

A swollen cylindrical stoneware vase, by Katharine Pleydell-Bouverie, with incised vertical petal motif, impressed seal mark, painted glaze mark.

6¾in (17cm) high

£350-400   **WW**

A stoneware vase, by Katharine Pleydell-Bouverie, impressed seal, glaze codes to base.

c1930-40   7in (18cm) high

£200-250   **ROS**

QUICK REFERENCE - LAURENCE MCGOWAN

- Laurence McGowan was born in Salisbury in 1942. After an earlier career in land surveying he resolved to become a potter. Receiving workshop training, first with Pru Greene at Alvingham Pottery, Lincolnshire, and then with Alan Caiger-Smith at Aldermaston. In 1979, he returned to his native Wiltshire and established his own workshop at Collingbourne Kingston.
- Trained in the traditional majolica or in-glaze technique of pottery decoration, McGowan now applies this knowledge to enhance his thrown stoneware pots with ever-changing brushwork patterns distilled from plant and animal forms.

A Laurence McGowan earthenware owl, tin glazed and painted, signed marks.

8¼in (21cm) high

£300-400   **DUK**

A Fulham Pottery tile, by John Piper (1903-92), with a stylised face in green, impressed Fulham Pottery mark.

6¼in (16cm) square

£160-200   **HAN**

A porcelain bottle vase, by Dame Lucie Rie, with sgrafitto or 'knitted' decoration, impressed personal seal.

Having studied at the Vienna School of Arts and Crafts, Lucie Rie (1902-95) emigrated to the UK in 1938. She set up a studio in Paddington and, during the World War II, produced ceramic buttons for the fashion industry. She was joined in the studio by Hans Coper in 1946. Initially, the studio produced functional tableware, with Rie moving on to make stoneware and porcelain, including bowls, urns and vases. She became known for her decorative yet functional domestic ceramics, as well as the delicate appearance of her pieces contrasting to the durable material from which they are made.

9½in (24cm) high

£22,000-28,000   **BE**

CERAMICS

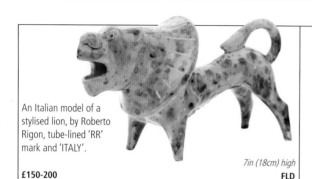

An Italian model of a stylised lion, by Roberto Rigon, tube-lined 'RR' mark and 'ITALY'.

7in (18cm) high

£150-200 FLD

A porcelain vase, by Julian Stair (b.1955), impressed seal mark.

8¼in (21cm) high

£1,500-2,000 WW

A porcelain bowl, by Alan Spencer-Green (1932-2003), incised with leaves, unsigned.

7in (18cm) diam

£150-200 SWO

A flared stoneware bowl, by William Staite Murray (1881-1962), with abstract brushed and resist decoration, impressed seal to foot.

c1930

3¾in (9.5cm) high

£300-400 ROS

QUICK REFERENCE - CLARE SUTCLIFFE

- Clare Sutcliffe (1943-2019) spent 27 years making traditional wood-fired stoneware pots. She trained at Wenford Bridge Pottery, Cornwall, as Seth Cardew's first student and worked in the Leach/Cardew tradition. She made her own glazes from different wood ashes and local stream clays, and fired her pots in a wood-burning kiln to 1,300°C with a firing cycle of up to twenty hours. During the course of the glaze firing, additional wood ash was drawn on the flame through the kiln, where it settled on the pots, melting to create soft colours and incidental effects making each pot unique.

- Sutcliffe had an earlier career as an actress appearing in such films as 'The Ploughman's Lunch', 'I Start Counting' and 'The Best Pair of Legs in the Business', but was regularly seen on television in, 'Play for Today', 'Coronation Street', 'Z Cars', 'Softly Softly' and 'On the Buses'.

A stoneware globular vase, by William Staite Murray, impressed seal to side of foot.

c1930-40   6½in (16.5cm) high

£280-320 ROS

A rimmed bowl, by Clare Sutcliffe, with reed design and copper red glaze, maker's mark.

12½in (32cm) diam

£150-200 BELL

A vase, by Clare Sutcliffe, with shino glaze, maker's mark.

7½in (19cm) high

£120-160 BELL

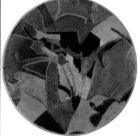

An earthenware bowl, by Sutton Taylor (b.1943), on narrow foot, paper label no.44, with a hairline crack.

18¼in (46.5cm) diam

£900-1,100 WW

QUICK REFERENCE - CRAIG UNDERHILL

- Craig Underhill's slab-built vessels are essentially three-dimensional canvasses for his richly abstract painting and marking. These objects explore clay as a strong ground for his resourceful interpretations of landscape – objects that evoke the colour, space and texture of our changing environment. Born in Scotland, Underhill studied ceramics in Derbyshire, Harrow College and Portsmouth Polytechnic. He now works and teaches in Stourbridge in the West Midlands.
- Underhill's pots mark out a world affected by time, geological movement and our own human imprint, and his work shows a sensitive appreciation of a broader field of abstraction, from Antoni Tàpies to William Scott and Patrick Heron, effectively brought into the realm of intimate clay objects and through his own imaginative filter.

A slab-built 'Plans' vessel, by Craig Underhill, with engobes (slips), glazes, oxides and stains.

£450-500   **FLD**

A slab-built 'Pink Fields' vessel, by Craig Underhill.

£450-550   **FLD**

A stoneware vessel, by John Ward (b.1938), impressed mark.

5¾in (14.5cm) high

£3,000-4,000   **CHOR**

A John Ward handbuilt stoneware tulip vase, impressed seal mark.

8¼in (21cm) high

£1,700-2,000   **WW**

An ovoid stoneware vase, by John Ward, impressed seal mark, scratching to inside.

8¾in (22cm) high

£1,500-2,000   **CHOR**

An Avoncroft stoneware vase, by Geoffrey Whiting (1919-88), with a rust glaze, with running tenmoku to the shoulder, impressed marks.

13½in (34.5cm) high

£130-180   **WW**

A porcelain bowl, by Peter Wills (b.1955), incised signature to base.

10¾in (27.5cm) diam

£250-300   **CHOR**

A pair of raku sparrows, by Rosemary Wren, maker's mark.

4in (10cm) high

£300-350   **BELL**

CLOCKS

A 19thC 'Black Forest' cuckoo mantel clock, carved oak, in a dome-shaped Gothic-style case.

25¼in (64cm) high

£650-750 FLD

An Aesthetic Movement oak and enamelled mantel clock, after a design by Lewis Day.

13½in (34.5cm) high

£250-300 SWO

QUICK REFERENCE - AESTHETIC MOVEMENT

- Thriving in Europe and the USA between the 1860s and late 1880s, the Aesthetic Movement was a decorative arts movement with a strong influence from Japanese art and culture.
- It focused on producing art that was aesthetically pleasing, rather than meaningful or practical.
- Key artists of the movement include Dante Gabriel Rossetti, Edward Burne-Jones, William Morris, E.W. Godwin and Christopher Dresser.

An Arts & Crafts brass wall clock, attributed to Peter Wylie Davidson, with eight-day movement, dial with inscription 'TIME TIDE', with swallows and a longboat.

c1900   *17in (43cm) high*

£700-800 L&T

An Aesthetic Movement Howell & James ceramic mantel clock, by Fred Miller, with twin-train movement, painted inscription under base 'PAINTED FOR HOWELL, JAMES & CO BY FRED MILLER LONDON 1880'.

1880   *10¾in (27.5cm) high*

£400-500 L&T

A gilded bronze 'Crocodile Tears' clock, modelled as a crocodile with a timepiece in its mouth, two crystal tears beside each eye, the enamel clock dial with an applied donkey.

23¼in (59cm) long

£3,000-4,000 DUK

A Wilemand & Co./Foley 'Intarsio' mantel timepiece, the case inscribed 'Carpe Diem' beneath the dial, with side panels with Art Nouveau decoration, printed marks 'Rd.342317?. 3160', some crazing and rubbing, the clock and dial are replacements.

11½in (29cm) high

£1,000-1,500 APAR

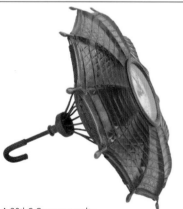

A 20thC German novelty mantel clock, with a moulded glass and brass case in the form of an umbrella.

6¾in (17cm) wide

£150-200 WHP

A 20thC gilt-bronze book-form clock, signed 'H. BENOIT-GUBELIN', the spine engraved 'LIVRE D'HEURES', the movement cover marked '15 Jewels', serial no.2845.

5¼in (13.5cm) high

£700-800 L&T

A massive 'Signs of the Zodiac' brass and copper clock dial, centred with an electric clock movement, the middle ring with twelve panels depicting the signs of the zodiac.

67¼in (171cm) diam

£1,500-2,000 SWO

A Valery patinated metal and onyx mantel clock garniture, surmounted with a bronze lion, with two en-suite vases, dial signed 'Valery, Limoges'.

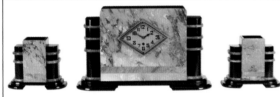

19in (48.5cm) wide

£250-300   **WW**

An Art Deco marble and onyx mantel clock, mounted with a lady and a dog, inscribed 'Desoleil-Seneghal Berch...'.

21in (53.5cm) wide

£400-500   **SWO**

An Art Deco marble and chrome mantel clock garniture, with garnitures mounted with lights, each with frosted stands.

16in (40.5cm) wide

£400-500   **SWO**

An Art Deco clock garniture, with central panel of yellow and rose variegated marble, and two conforming vases.

clock 18½in (47cm) wide

£400-500   **CHOR**

An Art Deco mantel clock, mounted with two mountain ibex, one lacking horns, the dial inscribed 'A Ploquet Valognes'.

21¾in (55cm) wide

£200-250   **SWO**

A French Art Deco marble clock garniture, mounted with 'The Promise' depicting a gilt metal couple in an embrace, with a pair of vases.

13¼in (33.5cm) wide

£200-250   **SWO**

An Austrian Werkstätte Hagenauer Wien carved wood and ebonised figural clock, no hands, impressed maker's roundel, 'Atelier Hagenauer Wien'.

Werkstätte Hagenauer Wien was founded by Carl Hagenauer (1872-1928) in Vienna in 1898 and produced metalware and other handcrafted decorative items. Carl's son Karl (1898-1956) joined the firm in c1918. After Karl's death in 1956, his son Franz (1906-86) took over. The workshop closed in 1987.

c1930   *6¼in (16cm) high*

£1,500-2,000   **ROS**

A chrome eight-day 'tennis racket' desk clock, by C.M. Depose.

c1930s   *9in (23cm) long*

£500-600   **GBA**

CLOCKS

An Art Deco Harrods chrome travelling timepiece, with Swiss eight-day movement, with original case stamped 'Harrods, London'.

3½in (9cm) high

£200-250   **WW**

An Art Deco walnut and coromandel inlaid mantel clock, with Westminster movement.

13in (33cm) wide

£200-250   **SWO**

A French electric mantel clock, dial stamped 'Cartier Electric', cast 'Made in France 420' to base, modern battery movement.

8¾in (22cm) high

£160-200   **WW**

A WWII period F.W. Elliot Ltd. RAF Sector clock, with RAF wings and eight-day fusée movement, the clock is numbered on movement '5174', dated, the dial replaced about 50 years ago.

1938

£3,000-3,500   **CHOR**

QUICK REFERENCE - JAEGER-LECOULTRE ATMOS CLOCK

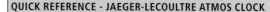

- In c1928, watchmaker Jaeger-LeCoultre presented the Atmos clock, which did not need to be wound manually. The mechanism for the clock was developed from the prototype and designs of engineer Jean-Léon Reutter.
- Variations in temperature cause a mixture of gases within the clock's sealed capsule to expand and contract, winding the mechanism. The clock's design has developed over time, but the mechanism is kept visible.

An unused Jaeger-LeCoultre 'Atmos du Millenaire' mantel clock, designed by Robert Kohler, no.698665, with rhodium-plated 13-jewel 556-calibre single-train movement operating via typical Atmos barometric aneroid mechanism and regulated by torsion escapement, limited edition, inscribed 'JAEGER-LECOULTRE ATMOS', with original packaging, boxed manual and guarantee, numbered quality control card.

10¾in (27cm) high

£10,000-14,000   **FELL**

A Jaeger-LeCoultre 'Atmos' clock, calibre 526-5, in a lacquered brass case, numbered '485458', in original box, with guarantee and instructions.

9in (23cm) high

£750-850   **SWO**

A Jaeger-LeCoultre novelty clock, in the form of a Parisian street lamp, the clock with alarm, the lamp post with street sign for Rue Jeanne d'Arc.

11in (28cm) high

£900-1,100   **LSK**

A rare Guillerme et Chambron oak longcase clock, with ebonised spear numerals, the top of the pendulum bar broken off.

Artists Robert Guillerme and Jacques Chambron met during World War II and founded the Votre Maison company in 1949, working with Émile Dariosecq. The company produced Guillerme et Chambron furniture, with Guillerme as the main designer. Hervé Chambron, Jacques' son, took over the company in 1983.

c1970   *75½in (192cm) high*

£1,000-1,200   **CHEF**

QUICK REFERENCE - MARVEL

- Marvel Comics' precursor, Timely Comics, began in October 1939. Its first publication was called 'Marvel Comics no.1' and featured the 'Human Torch'. Several other superheroes were added to the company's repertoire in the 1940s, including 'Captain America' and 'Miss Marvel' – this was the 'Golden Age' of comic books. In 1951, Timely Comics became Atlas Magazines. In the early 1960s, Atlas Magazines became Marvel Comics.

- Many Marvel comics were created by Marvel's head writer and editor, Stan Lee, and illustrated by artist Jack Kirby. In the 1960s, they worked together to create famous superhero figures such as 'The Fantastic Four', 'The Incredible Hulk', 'The Amazing Spider-Man' and 'The X-Men'. The 'Silver Age' refers to comics produced between c1956 and c1969. In 2009, the Walt Disney Company bought Marvel's parent company. The success of the Marvel film franchise has pushed up prices for key comic book issues.

'The AMAZING SPIDER-MAN, "RETURN of DOCTOR OCTOPUS!"', volume 1, no.11, 'Silver Age', edge wear and creases, yellowed.
1963
£100-150   **VEC**

'The AMAZING SPIDER-MAN, "The GOBLIN And The GANGSTERS!"', volume 1, no.23, 'Silver Age', early 'Green Goblin' appearance, edge wear tears and creases, yellowed.
1963
£80-100   **VEC**

'The AMAZING SPIDER-MAN, "SPIDER-MAN GOES MAD!"', volume 1, no.24, 'Silver Age', edge wear and creases, yellowed.
1963
£80-100   **VEC**

'The AMAZING SPIDER-MAN, "THE MAN IN THE CRIME-MASTER'S MASK!"', volume 1, no.26, 'Silver Age', edge wear and creases, yellowed.
1963
£60-70   **VEC**

'The AMAZING SPIDER-MAN, "THE THRILL OF THE HUNT!"' volume 1, no.34, 'Silver Age', edge wear and creases, yellowed.
1963
£50-60   **VEC**

'The AMAZING SPIDER-MAN, "THE SINISTER SHOCKER!"', volume 1, no.46, 'Silver Age', edge wear and tears, creases, front page is creased top to bottom, yellowed.
1963
£75-90   **VEC**

'The AMAZING SPIDER-MAN, "RHINO ON THE RAMPAGE!"', volume 1, no.43, 'Silver Age', edge wear and tears, creases, front page is creased top to bottom, yellowed.
1963
£80-100   **VEC**

'The AMAZING SPIDER-MAN, "WOULD'JA BELIEVE ... KRAVEN THE HUNTER!"', volume 1, no.47, 'Silver Age', edge wear and tears, creases, yellowed.
1963
£60-70   **VEC**

'The AMAZING SPIDER-MAN, "SPIDEY and the GREEN GOBLIN...BOTH UNMASKED!"', volume 1, no.39, 'Silver Age', edge wear and creases, yellowed.
1963
£120-150   **VEC**

'TALES OF SUSPENSE', no.48, with story by Stan Lee, featuring the first appearance of 'Iron Man's' new armour drawn by Steve Ditko, UK variant.
1963
£50-60   AST

'FANTASTIC FOUR, "AMONG US HIDE ... THE INHUMANS!"', volume 1, no.45, 'Silver Age', script by Stan Lee, cover pencils by Jack Kirby, inks by Joe Sinnott, first appearance of the 'Inhumans', edge wear and tears, creases, yellowed.
1964
£90-110   VEC

'The AMAZING SPIDER-MAN, "SPIDEY SAVES THE DAY!"', volume 1, no.40, 'Silver Age', edge wear and creases, yellowed.
1963
£80-100   VEC

'The AMAZING SPIDER-MAN, THE VULTURE'S BACK ... AND SPIDEY'S GOT 'IM', volume 1, no.48, 'Silver Age', edge wear and tears, creases, yellowed.
1963
£60-70   VEC

'Fantastic Four, "THOSE WHO WOULD DESTROY US!"', volume 1, no.46, 'Silver Age', script by Stan Lee, pencils by Jack Kirby, inks by Joe Sinnott, second appearance of the 'Inhumans', wear and tears, creases, yellowed.
1964
£60-70   VEC

'THE MIGHTY THOR, "WHOM THE GODS WOULD DESTROY!"', volume 1, no.126, 'Silver Age', title previously 'Journey Into Mystery With Thor', script by Stan Lee, pencils by Jack Kirby, inks by Vince Colletta, wear and tears, creases, yellowed.
1964
£50-60   VEC

'THE AVENGERS', no.4, featuring Jack Kirby cover art of 'Captain America' joining the 'Avengers' in his first 'Silver Age' appearance, wear to the spine and a small back cover section missing, UK variant.
1964
£140-160   AST

'TALES OF SUSPENSE', no.49, featuring 'Iron Man' drawn by Steve Ditko, first 'X-Men' crossover, first 'Avengers' crossover and second appearance of 'The Watcher', UK pence variant.
1964
£60-70   AST

'Fantastic Four, "THE COMING OF GALACTUS!"', volume 1, no.46, 'Silver Age', script by Stan Lee, pencils by Jack Kirby, inks by Joe Sinnott, first appearance of 'Galactus' and the 'Silver Surfer', wear and tears, creases, yellowed.
1964
£180-220   VEC

'The AMAZING SPIDER-MAN, "RETURN of DOCTOR OCTOPUS!"', no.11, featuring the first appearance of 'Bennett Brant' and the second appearance of 'Doctor Octopus', art by Steve Ditko, UK variant.
1964

£100-140   AST

'The AMAZING SPIDER-MAN, "UNMASKED BY DR. OCTOPUS!", no.12, UK variant.
1964

£90-110   AST

'The AMAZING SPIDER-MAN, "SPIDEY BATTLES DAREDEVIL!"', no.16, art by Steve Ditko, UK variant.
1964

£80-100   AST

'The AMAZING SPIDER-MAN, "KRAVEN, THE HUNTER!"', no.15, art by Steve Ditko first appearance of 'Kraven the Hunter', first mention of 'Mary Jane Watson', UK variant.
1964

£180-220   AST

'HERE COMES ...DAREDEVIL, THE MAN WITHOUT FEAR!', no.1, the first appearance of 'Daredevil', written by Stan Lee, illustrated by Bill Everett, UK cover version, wear on the edges, slight mark above 'Daredevil's' arm, tear on the back cover, the pages have been chipped.
1964

£500-600   AST

'STRANGE TALES OF SUSPENSE, SECRETS OF THE UNKNOWN', no.38, with art by Jack Kirby, featuring 'Thor' and the lead story from 'Journey into Mystery' no.84.
1966

£20-30   AST

'THE INVINCIBLE IRON MAN', no.1, featuring the origin of 'Iron Man', with art by Gene Colan, UK cover stamped.
1968

£100-120   AST

'EXCITING COMICS', no.46, with cover art by Alex Schomburg, 'Golden Age', cover is loose.
1946
£50-60   AST

'THE BEANO', no.452, including the first appearance of 'Dennis the Menace', duotone illustrations, original colour printed wrappers.

'The Beano' is the longest running British children's comic and is published by DC Thomson. The first issue was published in the 1930s and by the 1950s its weekly circulation was near to two million copies. The 1950s also saw the introduction of characters such as 'Roger the Dodger', 'The Bash Street Kids' and 'Minnie the Minx'. In 2015, the 3,800th issue of 'The Beano' was published.
1951
£260-300   LOCK

'THE BEANO BOOK', personalised inscriptions on inside cover, some minor marks to the covers.
1951
£150-200   LOC

'THE FLASH, "THE BIG FREEZE!"', no.114, 'Silver Age', cover edges are worn with some tears, creasing, yellowed.

DC began in the 1930s as National Allied Publications, founded by Malcolm Wheeler-Nicholson. Following the company changing hands and a series of mergers, the name 'DC Comics' was officially adopted in 1977. 'Superman' appeared in 1938 and 'Batman' in 1939. Today, DC's parent company, DC Entertainment, is a subsidiary of Time Warner Inc.
1960
£35-45   VEC

'THE FLASH, "INVASION of the CLOUD CREATURES!"', no.111, 'Silver Age', cover edges worn, tears, back page has tape repair, creasing, yellowed.
1960
£30-35   VEC

'BATMAN', no.181, with art by Carmine Infantino, first appearance of 'Poison Ivy', with centrefold pin-up page of 'Batman' and 'Robin'.
1966
£260-300   AST

'DETECTIVE COMICS', no.359, first appearance of new-look 'Bat-Girl' (Barbara Gordon), UK cover stamped.
1967
£260-300   AST

A French early 19thC papier-mâché doll, with painted hair and features, the rigid body with leather arms, stitched fingers and separate thumbs, with original clothing, all embroidered in red with 'VI', and with a period dress.

c1835   *14¼in (36cm) high*

£300-350   LC

A mid-Victorian papier-mâché doll, with moulded hair and painted features, fabric body with painted wood lower limbs, in original dress.

10in (25.5cm) high

£450-550   HT

An English 19thC poured wax doll, with implanted hair, glass eyes, smiling mouth, with a fabric body and leather lower arms.

c1865   *17in (43cm) high*

£250-300   LC

A poured wax child doll, inserted hair in ringlets, stuffed body with wax limbs, Princess-line silk dress with bustle and train, underclothes and brown shoes, hair sparse on top of head, some fraying to silk, a later hat.

1870s   *24½in (62cm) high*

£800-900   SAS

A French 19thC bisque-head fashion doll, with fixed blue eyes, closed mouth and pierced ears, with a leather body, a dress and hat, marked 'H5', impressed '6'.

Bisque (or biscuit) is porcelain or earthenware that has been fired, but not glazed. Features of bisque dolls appear very realistic. Bisque-head dolls were manufactured in Germany in the 1850s, selling throughout Europe. From the 1860s to the 1890s, French bisque dolls became popular.

15½in (39.5cm) high

£800-900   LC

A Bru Bébé bisque-head doll, in the 'Circle/Dot' style, with glass paperweight eyes, open mouth and sheepskin wig, on original leather body with bisque forearms, the shoulder incised '4'.

16in (40.5cm) high

£6,000-7,000   MORP

A French fashion doll, in the style of Barrois, with glass eyes, closed mouth and later mohair wig, on wooden articulated body, in 1870s-style walking dress, the head incised '4', green stamp on leather collar attaching shoulder to body reading 'Poupee Passage de L'Opera Paris'.

Madame Barrois was a maker of china and bisque dolls in Paris, France, active between 1844-77. In the late 1870s, the company was bought by Aristide M. Halopeau.

16in (40.5cm) high

£2,500-3,000   MORP

A French 19thC fashion doll, possibly by Barrois, with fixed eyes, painted closed mouth and pierced ears, with a bisque shoulder plate and a leather body and arms, in a period clothing, marked on the side of each shoulder '00'.

10in (25.5cm) high

£900-1,100   LC

A DEP closed-mouth child doll, with fixed eyes, closed mouth, pierced ears, jointed papier-mâché French body, floral sprig printed dress, black velvet coat and matching hat, Ermin muff, pink corset, underclothes and leather shoes.

19in (48.5cm) high

£1,500-2,000   SAS

DOLLS

A Simon & Halbig for Heinrich Handwerck 'Bébé Cosmopolite' doll, with weighted eyes, open mouth and jointed composition body, with a Bébé Cosmopolite box, probably original, marked 'Simon & Halbig, Heinrich Handwerck, 2½'.

21in (53.5cm) high

£450-500   LC

A Simon & Halbig for Heinrich Handwerck child doll, with sleeping eyes, pierced ears, synthetic wig, jointed composition body.

29½in (75cm) high

£300-350   SAS

A German Heinrich Handwerck/S. & H. bisque-head doll, with weighted glass eyes, real lashes, open mouth, upper teeth, pierced ears, on a fully jointed wood and composition body, with original clothing.

c1910   31½in (80cm) high

£400-500   C&T

A German Imhoff bisque mechanical walking doll, patented 1899.

12in (30.5cm) high

£250-300   BER

QUICK REFERENCE - JUMEAU

- Jumeau (1842-99) was founded near Paris, France, in the 1840s by Pierre François Jumeau (1811-95) and Louis-Desire Belton. It designed and manufactured high-end bisque dolls, with detailed clothing.
- In 1855, Jumeau produced the first Bébé doll – a doll modelled as a little girl.
- The company's dolls were highly acclaimed, receiving medals at the 1851 London Great Exhibition and the 1878 Exposition Universelle. In 1875 Jumeau's son, Emile, took over the firm.
- Jumeau dolls remain popular with collectors today and those with original costumes in good condition can fetch high prices. In the 1890s, Jumeau joined Société Française de Fabrication de Bébés et Jouets.

A French Jumeau doll, with open mouth, fixed eyes, pierced ears, jointed composition body, with contemporary clothing, marked '12'.

27in (68.5cm) high

£550-650   LC

A French Jumeau doll, with glass paperweight eyes, pierced ears, jointed composition body, marked 'Depose Tete Jumeau Bte SGDG 9'.

19in (48.5cm) high

£600-700   LC

A CLOSER LOOK AT A JUMEAU BÉBÉ

The doll has a pale bisque head with fixed blue eyes and closed mouth.

It has the original wig over a replaced cork pate.

The doll has a fully jointed body, with clothing and original leather Jumeau size 9 shoes.

It is marked in red 'Tete Jumeau, Depose, SGDG, 9', and also stamped on the body in blue.

A Jumeau Bébé bisque-head doll.

20in (51cm) high

£2,500-3,000   LC

A Bébé Jumeau bisque-head doll, with fixed glass paperweight eyes, open mouth and teeth, pierced ears, mohair wig, jointed composition limbs and body, marked '11', in original box with label and lid.

23in (58.5cm) high

£450-550   HT

A Jumeau kiss-throwing and walking doll, the bisque head with fixed eyes, open mouth with upper teeth, with pierced ears and composition body, with clothing and antique shoes, marked on the neck '8'.

21in (53.5cm) high

£650-750   LC

A Jumeau small bisque-socket-head child doll, with glass eyes, mohair wig, on articulated body, in antique (if not original) silk and lace dress, the head stamped 'Depose Tete Jumeau 5', the body stamped 'Bébé Jumeau Paris', the shoes impressed '5 Paris Depose'.

14½in (37cm) high

£2,500-3,000   MORP

A Tete Jumeau Bébé no.11, with jointed papier mâché and wood body with blue ink stamp, restoration to head, chipping to fingers.

25in (63.5cm) high

£750-850   SAS

A Tete Jumeau bisque-head Bébé doll, with later wig, on a fully jointed wood and composition body, with marked size 11 Jumeau shoes, one firing line.

c1890   *25in (63.5cm) high*

£550-650   C&T

A Simon & Halbig for Kämmer & Reinhardt child doll, with lashed sleeping eyes, pierced ears, mohair wig, jointed composition body, printed pink cotton body, dirty face.

Kämmer & Reinhardt (1886-c1940) was founded in Waltershausen, Germany, in 1886, by designer Ernest Kämmer and entrepreneur Franz Reinhardt. Kammer designed the heads until his death in 1901, when Simon & Halbig took over production, working from Kämmer's designs. In 1909-14, Kämmer & Reinhardt produced popular character dolls, with painted eyes, closed mouths and mohair wigs. The character child dolls are especially collectable.

20½in (52cm) high

£200-250   SAS

A Kämmer & Reinhardt bisque-head doll, with glass sleeping eyes, open mouth and teeth, pierced ears, later blonde mohair wig, jointed composition limbs and body, marked 'K&R SIMON & HALBIG 70'.

27in (68.5cm) high

£250-300   HT

A Simon & Halbig for Kämmer & Reinhardt doll, with weighted eyes, open mouth and pierced ears, marked 'Simon & Halbig, K & R'.

12½in (32cm) high

£150-200   LC

A Simon & Halbig for Kämmer & Reinhardt doll, with weighted eyes, open mouth with tongue and pierced ears, marked 'Simon & Halbig, K & R, 403, Germany'.

25in (63.5cm) high

£250-300   LC

A Kestner bisque-head doll, with glass sleeping eyes and open mouth, with later mohair wig, marked '16 1/2 171'.

Kestner & Co. was founded in 1816 in Thuringia, Germany, by Johannes Daniel Kestner. The company was later taken over by his grandson, Adolphe Kestner. It became known for its child dolls, with high quality bisque heads, mohair wigs and blown-glass sleeping eyes. The comparatively rare '200' series, produced c1910, are especially sought after by collectors. Kestner dolls were distributed by George Borgfeldt in the USA. Kestner & Co. merged with Kämmer & Reinhardt in 1930.

c1910   *32in (81.5cm) high*

£500-600   HT

A German bisque-head Oriental doll, possibly Kestner, with glass sleeping eyes, open mouth and teeth, mohair wig, jointed composition limbs and body, marked '164 Germany 36'.

14in (35.5cm) high

£650-750   HT

A Kestner bisque-head doll, with glass sleeping eyes, open mouth and teeth, mohair wig, marked '192'.

31in (78.5cm) high

£900-1,000   **HT**

An Armand Marseille bisque-head doll, marked 'AM, Germany'.

Armand Marseille was founded in Thuringia, Germany, by Armand Marseille and was active between 1885 and 1930. The company manufactured bisque dolls' heads until the 1930s, also supplying other manufacturers. Armand Marseille merged with Koppelsdorf in 1919 to form the Koppelsdorf porcelain factory.

36in (91.5cm) high

£100-150   **JN**

An Armand Marseille bisque-head doll, with articulated body.

25in (63.5cm) high

£120-180   **JN**

An Armand Marseille '370' doll, with weighted eyes and open mouth, with original clothing and shoes, impressed marks 'AM, 370, Dep'.

20in (51cm) high

£120-160   **LC**

An Armand Marseille Oriental 'Ellar' doll, with weighted eyes, closed mouth and bent limb body, marked, 'AM, Ellar, Germany, 2K'.

10in (25.5cm) high

£150-200   **LC**

An Armand Marseille '390' walking doll, with fixed eyes and open mouth, with a mechanism to move the head as the legs move, impressed marks '390', 'Armand Marseille', 'Made in Germany'.

23in (58.5cm) high

£140-180   **LC**

An Armand Marseille '390' doll, with weighted eyes and open mouth, impressed marks 'Armand Marseille', '390', '12'.

28in (71cm) high

£150-200   **LC**

A Porzellanfabrik Mengersgereuth bisque-head character doll, with glass sleeping eyes, open mouth and teeth, mohair wig, marked 'P.M. 94 14'.

£150-200   **HT**

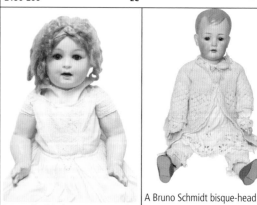

A Bruno Schmidt bisque-head boy doll, with glass sleeping eyes, closed mouth, moulded hair, jointed composition limbs and body, marked '2048'.

21in (53.5cm) high

£400-450   **HT**

A Schoenau & Hoffmeister 'PB Star' bisque-head doll, no.1909, size 7.5.

25in (63.5cm) high

£120-160   JN

An SFBJ Paris '301' bisque-head doll.

The Société Française de Fabrication de Bébés et Jouets (SFBJ) was formed in 1899, as an association of leading French doll manufacturers. It formed as a response to increasing competition from German doll manufacturers. SFBJ was based at the Jumeau factory. Despite incorporating highly-acclaimed companies, such as Jumeau and Bru Jeune & Cie (1866-83), the need to keep costs down resulted in reduced quality. Character dolls, produced from c1911, were of slightly better quality and proved more successful than the bébé dolls. Production ceased in c1950.

26in (66cm) high

£150-200   JN

A large SFBJ, Paris '301' bisque-head doll, with white lace bonnet and dress.

£200-250   JN

An SFBJ Paris '60' doll, with weighted eyes, open mouth and jointed composition body, marked 'SFBJ, 60, Paris, 2/0'.

15in (38cm) high

£150-200   LC

An SFBJ '60' Trouville fisherwoman, with sleeping eyes, mohair wig, pierced ears, jointed composition body, original costume, sabots with 'TROUVILLE' written on them.

13½in (34.5cm) high

£220-280   SAS

A Simon & Halbig bisque-head doll, model no.121, with open-close eyes and jointed composition body in lace edged dress.

Based in Thuringia, Simon & Halbig (c1869-c1930) produced bisque dolls and bisque doll parts, which they supplied to other manufacturers, such as Kämmer & Reinhardt and Jumeau.
Simon & Halbig's early dolls has fixed glass eyes, closed mouths and solid, domed heads. Their later dolls had open mouths and socket heads. The company was bought by Kämmer & Reinhardt in c1920 and production continued until the early 1930s. The Simon & Halbig factory was then renamed Keramisches Werk Gräfenhain and production continued until 1943.

22½in (57cm) long

£150-200   FLD

A Simon & Halbig doll, with weighted eyes, open mouth and pierced ears, marked 'S & H, 1079, Dep, Germany, 9'.

22in (56cm) high

£180-220   LC

A Simon & Halbig child doll, with sleeping eyes, mohair wig, jointed composition body, impressed 'S & H H X I'.

16in (40.5cm) high

£150-200   SAS

A Simon & Halbig bisque-head musical automaton doll, with glass eyes, open mouth and teeth, mohair wig, on a base with spinning top action, marked 'SH 1300 DEP'.

c1900   18in (45.5cm) high

£1,000-1,400   HT

DOLLS

A British National Dolls 'Dollie Walker' hard plastic doll, with original box.

1950s *21in (53.5cm) high*
£50-60 **VEC**

An early 20thC velvet and mohair golly doll, probably by Chad Valley.

11½in (29cm) long
£300-400 **WW**

A Character Novelty Co. 'Mickey Mouse' doll, with original corduroy pants, missing one shoelace.

10½in (26.5cm) high
£150-250 **POOK**

A Martha Chase cloth boy doll, small sporadic surface flakes and minor sporadic rubs.

40in (101.5cm) high
£200-250 **POOK**

A Crolly Irish composition doll, musical key-wound mechanism plays 'When Irish Eyes are Smiling', weighted eyes, five piece jointed body, original clothing, with card swing label to wrist 'CROLLY DOLLIES FACTORY CROLLY CO DONEGAL'.

1940s *15in (38cm) high*
£150-200 **VEC**

QUICK REFERENCE - CELLULOID

- Celluloid is a form of plastic, made from camphor and cellulose nitrate. Companies in Japan (where camphor was relatively easily attainable from the native camphor trees), Germany, the USA (where celluloid was patented), France and Italy used the material to make dolls. The Rhineland Rubber & Celluloid Co. (1873-c1930) produced celluloid dolls from 1873. Kämmer & Reinhardt, Kestner & Co. and Jumeau followed suit. Celluloid proved popular as it did not flake, however it was highly flammable, had a tendency to crack, fade or dent, and was difficult to restore.

A Japanese celluloid walking doll, carrying a small baby doll in carriage while holding umbrella, with ringing bell and key-wound walking movemnet, with box.

9¼in (23.5cm) high
£850-950 **BER**

A Lantiner Cherie child doll, with fixed eyes, open mouth with moulded top teeth, pierced ears, jointed papier-mâché body.

20in (51cm) high
£130-160 **SAS**

A mint R. John Wright Genevieve artist-designed felt doll, fully jointed, dress made from custom-printed silk, straw bonnet with felt flowers, hand-cobbled shoes, holding a doll made of resin with cotton stuffed body, with original box, outer sleeve.

This doll was made for the United Federation of Doll Club's Region 14 Conference 2009, limited to 150 pieces, complete with certificate. Second in the Victorian Children series, made as a companion to the Abigail doll.

11½in (29cm) high
£150-200 **VEC**

A Gotz 'Jennie' vinyl artist doll, by Sissel-Bjorstad Skille, swing label certificate, with three additional Gotz cardigans. **Designed by Gotz for Trisha Plant's shop KR Bears and Dolls, limited edition no.13 of 100.**

26in (66cm) high

£300-350 VEC

A rare Harwin World War I 'Tommy' felt doll, the face with central seam, boot button eyes, painted moustache, eyebrows and hair, jointed body, khaki green felt uniform, oil-cloth Sam Brown, shoes and hat band, small holes, slightly discoloured and missing some brass buttons.

13in (33cm) high

£450-550 SAS

A mint Heidi Plusczok 'Li Wang' vinyl artist designed doll, limited edition 5 of 120, with swing label and certificate, with box, outer trade carton.

12in (30.5cm) high

£180-220 VEC

A Lenci pressed felt boy doll, with side glancing eyes, sad expression, mohair wig, swivel head, jointed body, original felt traditional Italian costume, with cloth label on waistcoat and card tag on leg, slight fading.

1930s *19in (48.5cm) high*

£200-250 SAS

A Kathy Kruse doll, with original hang tag.

15in (38cm) high

£80-110 POOK

A near-mint Annette Himstedt 'Kleine Leleti' club mini vinyl artist designed doll.

2003 *13½in (34.5cm) high*

£300-350 VEC

A mint Neue Munchner Kinderpuppen H255 artist designed doll, by Elisabeth Pongratz, '83B5111P' to sole of left foot and 'NEUE MUNCHNER KINDERPUPPEN ELISABETH PONGRATZ' to sole of right foot, hand-carved wood five-way jointed body, handpainted eyes, handmade costume, with sewn-in cloth Pongratz embroidered labels.

Elisabeth Pongratz first started to make dolls in 1979.

14in (35.5cm) high

£600-700 VEC

A mint Neue Munchner Kinderpuppen H 199 artist designed doll, by Elisabeth Pongratz, '83B4802P' to sole of left foot and 'NEUE MUNCHNER KINDERPUPPEN ELISABETH PONGRATZ' incised to sole of right foot, hand-carved wood five-way jointed body, handpainted eyes, costume is handmade.

14in (35.5cm) high

£950-1,100 VEC

A Lenci '300' series boy and girl, with pressed felt face with side glancing eyes.

17½in (44.5cm) high

£900-1,100 SAS

DOLLS

A Pedigree 'Captain Scarlet' original doll, with gun and cap with metal headset attached, in original box, loss to clear peak on cap.

Between 1945 and the 1950s, hard plastic was used to manufacture dolls by companies such as Pedigree, Rosebud and British National Dolls Ltd.

1967

£400-500   LOCK

A pair of British Pedigree hard plastic vintage dolls.

1950s   *tallest 20in (51cm) high*

£50-70   VEC

A pair of British Pedigree hard plastic vintage dolls, baby is in original clothing, other doll is in handmade clothing.

1950s   *tallest 18in (45.5cm) high*

£75-95   VEC

A Pedigree 'Sindy Pretty Pose' vintage doll, with original jumper and jeans, missing shoes, within Fair box.

From the 1950s, vinyl was used. 'Barbie' was launched in 1959 by Mattel and in 1962 Pedigree made the vinyl doll 'Sindy'.

£45-55   VEC

A Pedigree 'Sindy' vintage doll.

£20-25   VEC

A near-mint Pedigree 'Active Sindy' vintage doll, marked '033055' to back of head, original clothing, within Fair box.

11in (28cm) high

£55-65   VEC

A mint Heidi Plusczok 'Candy' vinyl artist designed doll, limited edition 28 of 120, with swing label certificate, with box, outer trade carton.

10¼in (26cm) high

£150-200   VEC

A Plush 'Uncle Wiggly' cloth rabbit doll, in original outfit, some fading.

17in (43cm) high

£90-120   POOK

A Trendon 'Sasha Gregor' boy doll, in original wool sweater and denim jeans.

£50-60   SAS

A Trendon 'Sasha' doll, probably original white boots.

Swiss designer Sasha Morgenthaler created the vinyl doll 'Sasha' in c1970.

£40-50   SAS

A Sebastian of London fashion doll, with closing eyes, in a faux leather coat and a pair of faux leather boots.

c1969   *2in (56cm) high*

£60-70   LOCK

A Steiff 'Little Red Riding Hood' doll, in original box, small break to plastic box lid.

18in (45.5cm) high

£110-160   POOK

A Norah Wellings fairy doll, with a label to the wrist 'Made in England by Norah Wellings'.

18½in (47cm) high

£300-400   ROS

A set of three 'Wynken', 'Blynken' and 'Nod' cloth artist designed baby dolls, by Jan Shackelford, limited edition 2 of 30, each signed on the torso by the artist, with cloth tag stating 'JAN SHACKELFORD ORIGINALS, INC', cotton stockinette, dated.

1996   *17in (43cm) high*

£50-70   VEC

A vintage 'Action Man' doll, dressed in camouflage.

£25-35   WHP

A vintage 'Action Man' doll, dressed as a lancer.

£45-55   WHP

A rare Moritz Göttschalk large dolls' house, brick and stone external papers, three storeys with attic rooms, hanging two-storey celestial window to either side, dormer windows, front opening to reveal six rooms, central staircase with generous hall and landings, mainly original wall papers and door bell mechanism on the second floor, some overpainting to balconies, front steps replaced, lacks glazing, other damage and repairs, some slight worm.

This house appears in the reproduced 1895 catalogue on page 33 of 'Ciesliks Reprints "Moritz Göttschalk 1892-1931"'.
German dolls' house manufacturer, Mortiz Göttschalk specialised in French-style dolls' houses. Produced from c1880-1910, Göttschalk's blue roof series used blue lithographic printed paper to imitate slate tiles. Dolls' houses with red roofs were more frequently produced by the company from 1910. Göttschalk was one of the few makers to create a Modernist house. After Göttschalk's death in the early 1900s, the company remained in the family until its closure in the late 20thC.

c1895   *58in (147.5cm) high*
£5,000-6,000   **SAS**

A Moritz Göttschalk furnished blue-roof dolls' house, with brick and stone façade, two rooms with original papers, furniture and chattels including soft metal upright piano, single bed, dressing table and tinplate and soft metal fireplace, Erhard fender, wall clock and Rococo chair, two bisque shoulder-head dolls and other items.

20½in (52cm) high
£1,800-2,200   **SAS**

A Göttschalk red-roof front-opening dolls' house, lithographed paper floor, furnished with several pieces of painted cardboard and wood Göttschalk furniture, electrified, side railing incomplete.

15¼in (38.5cm) high
£400-500   **POOK**

A German red-roof border control dolls' house, possibly Göttschalk, with central office with desk and shelving, 'Contor' and 'Spedition' sign, storage loft, slight wear.

18¾in (47.5cm) wide
£200-250   **SAS**

A G. & J. Lines 'The Clock House' dolls' house, no.34, timbered to left and clock dormer with working clock, front opening in the middle to reveal four rooms with fireplaces and range, original interior papers, some restoration.

G. & J. Lines was founded by Joseph and George Lines in the 1870s. The company produced dolls' houses from c1895. Joseph Lines' son established Lines Brothers in 1919, selling modern-style dolls' houses under the name Triang from the mid-1920s. When Joseph Lines died in the early 1930s, Lines Brothers acquired the G. & J. Lines trade name and marks. Lines Brothers was put into liquidation in 1971.

c1910   *32in (81.5cm) high*
£150-200   **SAS**

A G. & J. Lines dolls' house, no.32, two-storey large bay to left and three windows to right with balustraded garden, mansard roof with dormer window and widow's walk and two chimneys, front opening in the middle to reveal four rooms with fireplaces and dresser, completely restored.

c1909   *33½in (85cm) high*
£200-300   **SAS**

An unusal German Moko dolls' house, windows with printed paper shutters, dormer window with four shuttered windows and front opening to reveal an attic room, with two rooms with original wall and flower papers, Moko label to base, one chimney replaced, general wear.

24¾in (63cm) wide
£250-350   **SAS**

A late 19thC/early 20thC six-room painted-wood dolls' house, the façade with rusticated corner stones, with arched front door with lead light window and steps to two doors, on turned feet, the two doors opening to rooms around a central flight of stairs over three levels, each room fitted with a fire place, panel doors and wall paper to interior, with a collection of furniture and figures.

This doll's house was owned by the Duke of Bedford. This item includes documentation and letters between a previous owner and the Duke, explaining that he had sought to build a collection of dolls' houses and games in order to amuse the younger visitors to Woburn, but with the rise in value of his collection of Japanese porcelain he thought it wise to display that in the cases reserved for the toys, hence his decision to sell the dolls' houses.

62½in (159cm) high
£4,500-5,500   **ROS**

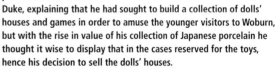

A contemporary double-fronted three-storey dolls' house, Regency style, with basement and attic rooms, opening sash windows and doors, with internal staircases, fitted internal lighting but lacking transformer.

48in (122cm) high
£2,500-3,000   **FLD**

An early to mid-20thC dolls' house, damaged.

21¾in (55cm) wide
£25-35   **LOCK**

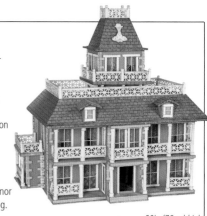

A handcrafted six-room plantation-style dolls' house, with removable front, widow's walk or observatory, of lithographed paper on wood construction, with wood railing, trim and miniature tile cornerstones, unmarked, a few minor pieces need re-gluing.

30in (76cm) high

£150-200   **POOK**

A rare English mahogany two-room dolls' house, 'The Travelling Baby House', of the type mentioned in Jonathan Swift's 'Guilliver's Travels', the windows are painted on the reverse with glazing bars and curtains, and there are two inlaid lozenges of mother-of-pearl, with brass finials, brass lion mask ring handles and a brass carrying handle on the roof, the front is hinged at one side, there are two rooms, one above the other, each with dark green painted walls, wooden dado and white painted fire surrounds.

From the Vivien Greene Collection. Purchased at Bonham's Sale, December, 1998, by the children's charity Tara's Palace Trust and displayed at Powerscourt House, Enniskerry.

c1810   *17¼in (44cm) high*

£45,000-50,000   **FOM**

A German red-roof wooden dolls' house, with brick-paper façade, front door with steps to veranda, gable and front opening to reveal two rooms with original papers, repainted roof and other restoration.

23in (58.5cm) high

£150-200   **SAS**

An Asian-themed miniature music room box, attributed to Robert Bernhard, with oriental paper-covered walls and mirrors, furnished with Rosemarie Torre chinoiserie handpainted, signed and dated pieces, to include collectors chest on stand, a side table, a trinket chest on stand and two armchairs, with a cello, a violin, a harp, guitars, a shamisen, and a Steinway spinet piano by Ralph Partelow.

From the Carolyn Sunstein Collection.

1981   *25in (63.5cm) wide*

£500-700   **POOK**

A German large-scale room box, with lithographed folding card walls, silk upholstered and wood stained furniture, to include a day bed with canopy, mirrored cupboard, four chairs, table, and mantel cabinet, with ormolu accessories including a mirror, rare figural E.P. mantel clock, and two oval portraits, some light wear to bed drapes and upholstery.

21½in (54.5cm) wide

£1,000-1,500   **POOK**

A Georgian dining room diorama, attributed to Robert Bernhard, with inlaid parquet flooring, corner cupboards, a panoramic lithographed panelled wallpaper scene, and a crystal chandelier, furnished with fine artisan furniture, to include a Federal-style sideboard, three-pedestal table, Chippendale side and arm chairs, and a cellarette, with a bisque gentleman, with numerous porcelain, china, silver, and metal accessories, figurines, and a birdcage with a tiny wax bird.

From the Carolyn Sunstein Collection

28in (71cm) wide

£3,000-4,000   **POOK**

A German painted composition butcher shop, with a figural butcher at a butcher block, with a cut of meat and sausage with a cat below, the window with various cuts of meat and bread, the back wall with carcasses and ducks, the pediment inscribed 'D. CAIRNS BUTCHER & POULTERER'.

8½in (21.5cm) high

£1,300-1,800   **POOK**

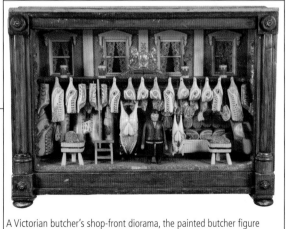

A European-style butcher shop diorama, with two carved and painted butchers, two butcher blocks and rows of carcasses of various cuts of meat, with a painted brick façade with potted plants, age cracks to façade of shop.

21¾in (55cm) high

£7,500-8,500   **POOK**

A Victorian butcher's shop-front diorama, the painted butcher figure standing to the centre with his display before a four-window building, surmounted by a gilt Royal coat of arms, all in a glazed wood case, scuffs and light damages to case, much of the internal leather fringing now lost.

26¾in (68cm) wide

£20,000-25,000   **CHEF**

DOLLS

A rare Rock & Graner dolls' house tinplate half-tester bed, painted grained finish, with gold painted Classical scroll motif.

1870s   *7¾in (19.5cm) high*

£400-500   **SAS**

A mid-19thC Victorian stained beech dolls' half-tester bed, with a moulded canopy, footboard with knob finials, feather pillows, eiderdowns and hair mattress.

39in (99cm) high

£300-400   **L&T**

A rare Rock & Graner dolls' house tinplate square piano, painted grained finish, three keys that should pluck three metal strings, slight flaking, one leg soldered.

1870s   *5¼in (13.5cm) wide*

£750-850   **SAS**

A toy/doll's upright piano, of grained wood, brass carrying handles, candle sconces, bone keys and inside lid printed with musical scales, missing one sconce.

c1900   *15¾in (40cm) wide*

£80-90   **SAS**

A rare Rock & Graner dolls' house tinplate secrétaire, painted grained finish, yellow painted interior and serpent legs.

1870s   *5in (12.5cm) high*

£300-400   **SAS**

A rare Rock & Graner dolls' house tinplate desk, painted grained finish.

1870s   *6¼in (16cm) high*

£300-350   **SAS**

A miniature tilt-top breakfast table, with burr walnut top inlaid with boxwood stringing and carved tripod legs.

5½in (14cm) high

£55-75   **SAS**

A Marklin painted tin doll carriage, with flower and pinstripe stenciling, fabric replaced, some paint wear.

8in (20.5cm) high

£800-1,000   **POOK**

A German all-bisque dolls' house doll, with glass eyes, closed mouth, mohair wig, socket head, peg-joints at shoulders and hips, original clothing, impressed '4', arms and head need restringing.

4½in (11.5cm) high

£300-350   **SAS**

A Davenport dolls' part dinner service, printed and impressed marks 'DAVENPORT' and '7-64', with 2 soup tureens with covers, 1 with broken ladle, 2 platters with covers, 5 ashets, 2 platters, 2 sauce boats, 6 soup plates, 6 side plates, 11 dinner plates and 6 dessert plates.

c1860

£300-400   **L&T**

An 18thC fan, with pierced ivory sticks with cherubs and swags, the leaf painted figures in a landscape, in a gilt glazed case, minor tears to leaf where there are folds.

Contains an element of pre-1947 ivory so export restrictions may apply.

£3,500-4,000 CHOR

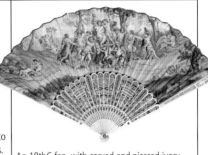

An 18thC fan, with carved and pierced ivory guards and sticks, double paper leaf showing a mythological procession.

11¾in (30cm) long

£3,500-4,000 K&O

A late 18thC bone fan, the guards pierced and carved, the sticks centred by an Aesop's Fable panel, the paper leaf painted with a side-to-side Arcadian scene, in a card box.

10¾in (27.5cm) long

£850-950 DN

A miniature Italian Grand Tour fan, with carved and pierced ivory guards and sticks, the double leaf painted recto with the bay of Naples with Vesuvius smoking in the background, to the fore are ships and figures with the city beyond, in contemporary box.

c1800 *6¾in (17cm) long*

£3,500-4,000 K&O

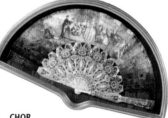

A 19thC fan, the leaf printed with an 18thC 'fête champêtre', with pierced and gilt mother-of-pearl sticks, in a gilt-glazed case.

£950-1,100 CHOR

A Chinese mid-19thC Canton export black lacquer 'Applied Faces' or 'Mandarin' fan, painted in two colour gilt with figures and building, the paper leaf painted with figures with applied ivory faces and silk robes.

15½in (39.5cm) long

£1,000-1,400 DN

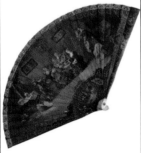

A 19thC ivory brisé fan, painted with 'An Allegory of the Five Senses' after David Teniers the Younger.

7in (18cm) long

£150-200 DN

A Japanese 19thC Shibayama white metal lacquered fan, inlaid with mother-of-pearl, decorated with cockerels in a landscape, metal tarnished.

15¾in (40cm) wide

£6,500-7,500 ECGW

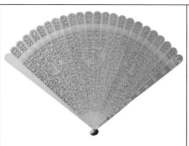

A Cantonese 19thC ivory fan, foliate carved and pierced decoration with a Chinese landscape flanked by two pagodas, stick guard.

10¾in (27.5cm) wide

£750-850   **BELL**

A Japanese late 19thC ivory fan, with three female figures representing 'speak no evil, hear no evil, see no evil', stick guard, with a Japanese ivory Shibayama comb.

9½in (24cm) wide

£950-1,100   **BELL**

A Chinese 19thC ivory fan, pierced and carved with Chinese figures and animals, stick guard.

17¾in (19.5cm) wide

£550-650   **BELL**

A paper fan, with wooden sticks commemorating the Battle of Trafalgar, printed and hand-coloured with Nelson's coat of arms and his baronial arms, with a portrait of Nelson, the reverse with a plan of the Battle of Trafalgar and a caption 'Plan of the Brilliant Action of Trafalgar'.

c1805   *8in (20.5cm) long*

£1,200-1,600   **FLD**

An early 19thC fan, the leaf with adults and children in a cottage tavern, in a glazed gilt frame.

19¾in (50cm) wide

£450-550   **BLEA**

A Chinese Qing dynasty painted bamboo lacquer and paper fan, with a courtly scene with ivory-faced figures with their clothes made of silk, and reverse painted with vignettes of country scenes, Macao.

c1860   *21¼in (54cm) wide*

£850-950   **DN**

A Chinese Qing dynasty lacquered bamboo brisé fan, painted on both sides in colours with figures, pagodas and foliage, Macao.

c1860   *9in (23cm) wide*

£1,300-1,600   **DN**

A mother-of-pearl fan, the paper leaf painted in gouache with a hunt in full cry, signed 'Van Garden', the reverse with a hunting trophy ferns and foliage, in a card box from Duvelleroy.

Van Garden worked at the famous French fan factory Duvelleroy. He also painted fan leaves for the Henrik Wigstrom workshop for retailing by Fabergé.

c1900   *15½in (39.5cm) long*

£850-950   **DN**

A tortoiseshell and gilt metal inlaid-handle fan, painted with pastoral and allegorical figures in a landscape, within a glazed gilt frame.

According to a pencil note to the reverse, 'This fan belonged to Ellen Terry'.

25¼in (64cm) wide

£2,000-2,500   **CHEF**

A Christian Dior sillk scarf, with the maker's monogram print in black on a cream background.

30¾in (78cm) wide

£180-220 **FELL**

A Gucci cotton scarf.

34¾in (88.5cm) square

£80-120 **FELL**

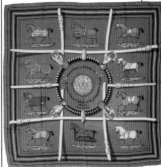

A Hermès 'Couvertures Et Tenues De Jour' silk scarf, designed by Jacques Eudel.

c1970 *35½in (90cm) square*

£180-220 **DUK**

A Gucci cotton scarf, with a nautical theme.

35in (89cm) wide

£80-120 **FELL**

A Hermès 'Petits Chevaux' silk scarf, designed by Jacques Eudel.

c1974 *33½in (85cm) square*

£150-200 **DUK**

A Hermès 'Chasse À Vol' silk scarf, designed by Henri de Linares, boxed.

c1962 *35½in (90cm) square*

£130-160 **DUK**

A Hermès 'Rouages' silk scarf, designed by Francois Heron, with 55¼in (140.5cm) of Hermès brown gift ribbon.

c1966 *35½in (90cm) square*

£180-220 **DUK**

A Hermès 'Faune Et Flore Du Texas' silk scarf, designed by Kermit Oliver.

c1992 *35½in (90cm) square*

£90-120 **DUK**

A Hermès 'République Française Liberté Égalité Fraternité 1789' silk scarf, designed by Joachim Metz, first issued in 1989.

35½in (90cm) square

£300-350 **FELL**

A Hermès 'Cheval Turc' scarf, originally designed in 1969 by Christiane Vauzelles.

35½in (90cm) wide

£100-150 **FELL**

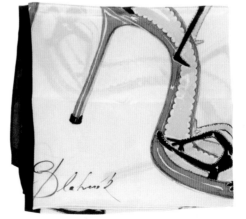

A Manolo Blahnik for Liberty scarf.

32¼in (82cm) long

£300-400 **FELL**

A Louis Vuitton limited edition 'Yayoi Kusama Monogram Dots' cotton scarf.

21¾in (55cm) square

£350-400　　　　FELL

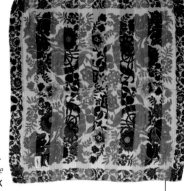

An Yves Saint Laurent silk scarf.

33½in (85cm) square

£50-80　　　　DUK

An Austrian sterling silver and guilloche enamel novelty powder compact, modelled in the form of a lady's dressing mirror, impressed marks.

4in (10cm) long

£500-600　　　　WM

An Art Deco Richard Hudnut 'Deauville Idie Aiuviolioie' powder compact, with enamelled silhouette, the hinged cover lifts to enclose spring-loaded mirror, impressed marks, with lipstick holder and chain.

One of the first American cosmetic manufacturers, Richard Hudnut began selling perfumes and cosmetics from his father's pharmacy in New York in the late 19thC. He went on to form his own company, Richard Hudnut's Pharmacy Co., which sold perfumes and cosmetics in pharmacies and department stores.

5in (12.5cm) long

£110-150　　　　WM

A rare Art Deco Richard Hudnut 'Three Flowers' powder compact, the hinged cover lifts to enclose spring loaded mirror, impressed marks.

c1930　　*2¼in (5.5cm) diam*

£180-220　　　　WM

A George VI hallmarked silver and enamel powder compact, made by Deakin & Francis Ltd.

1947　　*3in (7.5cm) diam*

£180-220　　　　WM

An Art Deco Evans Of America sterling silver compact.

4in (10cm) diam

£200-250　　　　WM

A German 935 Rodica butterscotch guilloche enamel powder compact, cover with silver border, with perfume bottle.

2½in (6.5cm) long

£750-850　　　　WM

A pair of Cartier Aviator sunglasses, stamped 'Cartier 62 12', with maker's pouch.
£450-550   FELL

A pair of Fendi rimless sunglasses, with maker's FF zucca-patterned acetate arms.
£120-180   FELL

A pair of Ray-Ban Traditional B&L sunglasses, with imitation tortoiseshell acetate frames, signed 'Ray-Ban, Style B 54 18', with maker's case.
£90-120   FELL

A pair of Tiffany & Co. sunglasses, with nude brown acetate frames, with maker's case.
£150-200   FELL

A pair of Dunhill gentleman's jade and silver cufflinks, of tortoise form, inscribed 'ALFRED DUNHILL', in a fitted case.
£350-450   DUK

A pair of Dunhill gentleman's silver cufflinks, of Scottish terrier form, inscribed 'dunhill', in a fitted case.
£350-400   DUK

A Dunhill gentleman's alligator and silver cufflinks, inscribed 'dunhill', with clip connections, in a fitted case.
£130-180   DUK

A silver and enamelled buckle, by Liberty & Co.
1908   *4¾in (12cm) wide*
£500-600   SWO

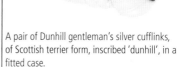

A set of six Liberty & Co. silver and enamel buttons, attributed to Jessie M. King, London, stamped maker's marks, hallmarked for Birmingham, with original box.
1906   *each 1in (2.5cm) diam*
£550-600   L&T

FASHION

A Balenciaga logo wallet, with a black leather exterior, with multiple card slots and slip pockets, with maker's care card and box.

4¼in (11cm) wide

£120-180 **FELL**

A Patek Philippe leather card holder, with the maker's logo crest, with maker's box.

4in (10cm) long

£120-180 **FELL**

A Louis Vuitton 'Eye-Trunk' iPhone 7 Plus case, designed to replicate the maker's trunks, with maker's cleaning cloth and care guides.

6½in (16.5cm) long

£450-500 **FELL**

A Cartier black leather belt, with silver-tone hardware, with garnet cabochon details, stamped 'Cartier Paris', with maker's box and authenticity card.

£180-220 **FELL**

A Chanel black leather and gilt metal coin belt, buckle stamped 'Chanel Paris', size marked '85/34'.

2in (5cm) wide

£700-800 **ROS**

A pair of Hermès gentleman's brown alligator skin penny loafers.

size 8 (UK)

£450-500 **DUK**

A pair of Gianni Versace patent leather shoes, loafer-style, with gold chain and medallion trim.

size 6½ (UK)

£75-110 **DUK**

A pair of Dolce & Gabbana embellished leather gloves, with rhinestones and sequins on soft beige leather, labelled 'Dolce & Gabbana', with maker's box.

size 7½

£350-400 **FELL**

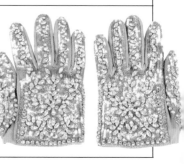

An Armani Collezioni three quarter-length virgin wool coat with fur trim, labelled 'Armani Collezioni'.

size 48

£65-85   **FELL**

A Burberry women's classic trench coat, with buttoned epaulettes, a storm flap on the left side, labelled 'Burberrys'.

size 12

£200-250   **FELL**

QUICK REFERENCE - BURBERRY

- Burberry was founded in 1856 by Thomas Burberry, who went on to develop gabardine, a waterproof and breathable fabric. The company patented the fabric.
- In 1912, gabardine was used to make the Tielocken coat, which was a predecessor to the trench coat. The Tielocken coat was worn during the Boer War and, after further development, Burberry supplied around 500,000 to the Armed Forces during World War I. A single strap and buckle fastened the Tielocken coat.
- The Burberry check (or nova check) was introduced in the 1920s as a coat lining. It is now trademarked.

A Burberry wool and camel hair knee-length coat, labelled 'Burberrys'.

chest 42in (106.5cm)

£100-150   **FELL**

A Chanel cream satin and black velvet camellia dress, look no.49 from the Fall 2014 Runway, front CC button accents, slip pockets at sides and concealed zip closure at the rear, labelled 'Chanel', with maker's hanger and dust bag.

size 50

£250-300   **FELL**

A Jean Paul Gaultier blue denim jacket, with black leather trim, labelled 'JPG Jeans'.

size 10

£110-150   **FELL**

QUICK REFERENCE - JOHN GALLIANO

- Having studied at St Martin's School of Art, John Galliano (b.1960) started his own fashion label in East London and despite financial trouble, he went on to win the British Fashion Council Designer of the Year in 1987, 1994, 1995 and 1997 (the latter award was shared with Alexander McQueen).
- Galliano was appointed Head Designer of Givenchy in 1995 and then Designer in Chief at Dior in 1996.
- In 2011, Galliano was accused of making racist remarks and was fired from Dior and his namesake fashion house. Galliano briefly retired from the public eye, before collaborating on an Oscar de la Renta collection in 2013 and then taking up the role of Creative Director at Maison Margiela.

A John Galliano silk bias cut shoestring strap dress.
1990s

£350-450   **SWO**

A Michael Kors white double-breasted virgin wool pea coat, with two decorative style pockets, labelled 'Michael Kors'.

size 10

£60-80   **FELL**

An Yves Saint Laurent fur-lined, knee-length coat, with black metallic leather with black fur lining, labelled 'Yves Saint Laurent Fourrures'.

chest 34in (86.5cm)

£650-750   **FELL**

FASHION

A Missoni three quarter-length wool-blend coat, lined with a multicoloured foliate-patterned fabric, labelled 'Missoni'.

size 12

£110-160   FELL

A Love Moschino longline coat, with gold-tone front button fastenings, labelled 'Love Moschino', with maker's original tags attached.

size 14

£110-160   FELL

A Loro Piana shearling cape, with a brown leather exterior, hkahi wool lining, labelled 'Loro Piana'.

one size

£400-500   FELL

QUICK REFERENCE - EMILIO PUCCI

- Emilio Pucci (1914-92) began his fashion career in the late 1940s. He became known for his vividly printed silk jersey clothing, as well as his so-called 'Pucci pants'. These lightweight vivid prints were popular in the 1960s and were revived in the 1980s and '90s.
- In 2000, French conglomerate LVMH acquired 67% of the Pucci company.

An Emilio Pucci cotton jacket, with the maker's psychedelic colourful print, front zip fastening and optional foldout hood, labelled 'Emilio Pucci'.

size 8

£110-160   FELL

A Valentino 'Red' black three-quarter length coat, with a Peter-Pan collar, labelled 'Red Valentino'.

size 12 (UK)

£150-200   FELL

A Vivienne Westwood striped shirt dress, with long sleeves, full-length button fastening and a gathered ruffle detail to the front, labelled 'Vivienne Westwood'.

size 40

£80-120   FELL

A Vivienne Westwood and Malcolm McLaren 'Devil' white linen vest top, with a printed design of a stylised dog barking the word 'devil' in different languages, Velcro fastening to the reverse, with original Worlds End label, 'Born in England'.

£350-450   SWO

A lady's vintage blonde mink fur long coat.

size 10/12

£100-150   **PSA**

A lady's vintage grey mink fur jacket, label 'Firs of Canada'.

size 10/12

£250-300   **PSA**

A dark ranch mink shawl, with mink tail tasselled trim and one hook and eye front fastening.

May be subject to export restrictions.

one size

£200-300   **FELL**

A full-length mink and silver fox fur coat, labelled 'Faulkes Edgbaston Birmingham'.

size 10

£400-500   **FELL**

A knee-length green cashmere and mink lined coat, with a lapel collar, labelled 'Habsburg'.

size 16

£800-900   **FELL**

A cream hooded jacket, with mink fur trim, wool, angora and cashmere blend jacket, labelled 'Jan-Rone Paris'.

chest 50in (127cm)

£130-180   **FELL**

A knee-length tapestry coat, with a large brown beaver lamp notched lapel collar.

chest 32in (81.5cm)

£180-220   **FELL**

An English embroidered linen stomacher, embroidered with exotic blooms and pods in floss silks, annotated in pencil 'R.A.C. 1778'.

c1710

£650-750   **KT**

A handpainted organza ballgown, with black tulle petticoat, additional dark red taffeta skirt and inner skirt of black linen.

1950s   *UK size 6*

£80-120   **CHEF**

FASHION

QUICK REFERENCE - HANDBAGS

- Handbags have become a desirable fashion accessory. Collectors will pay hundreds or even thousands of pounds for new or vintage examples by designers such as Chanel, Hermès, Judith Leiber, Louis Vuitton and Gucci. Sometimes second-hand luxury bags, which are still in production, change hands on the vintage market for more money than they would if they were new.
- However, many bags by less well-known makers are equally desirable and do not have such a high price tag.
- If you want to collect designer handbags, it's important to buy them from a reputable source as there are many fakes and copies on the market.

An Aspinal of London snakeskin letterbox saddle handbag, with gold-tone hardware accents, with maker's dust bag and box.

10in (25.5cm) wide

£250-300   FELL

A Berluti leather 'Deux Jours' briefcase, optional shoulder strap, with maker's dust bag and box.

15¾in (40cm) wide

£1,000-1,400   FELL

A Bottega Veneta 'Intrecciato Knot Grosgrain' clutch, cream lizard skin trim, with maker's dust bag and care card.

9¼in (23.5cm) wide

£450-550   FELL

A Bottega Veneta 'Nappa Intrecciato Veneta' hobo handbag, in calfskin leather, with maker's small hand mirror, slight wear to the base corners.

19in (48.5cm) wide

£550-650   FELL

A Burberry 'Nova Check' hobo handbag, top zip fastening and one interior side pocket, with maker's dust bag.

16½in (42cm) wide

£250-350   FELL

A vintage Cartier top handle 'Happy Birthday Bordeaux' handbag, with a twist-lock fastening and two interior side pockets, with maker's authenticity card, dust bag and box.

11in (28cm) wide

£650-750   FELL

A Céline khaki leather 'Trapeze' handbag, with optional suede side wings, with maker's dust bag and care cards, some scuffs and scratches.

12½in (34cm) wide

£400-500   FELL

MARKET REPORT

The demand for high-end handbags and accessories (such as scarves) is really high.

Auction is a great way to get your hands on items that are incredibly sought-after yet very hard to come by. Designer bags made from good quality materials will stand the test of time. They might also retain their value over time.

In terms of trends and prices, if the piece is very worn, it will be reflected in the estimate. The more pristine an item, the higher price it commands. The material it is made of will also be a factor. The exotic leathers demand a much higher price than the standard ones.

Limited edition pieces also tend to surpass their estimates. Auction is a good way to get your hands on a piece that was released in limited quantities or items such as Hermès Birkin bags, which are hard to come by. According to a 2016 study, Birkin handbags have increased in value year on year. Indeed, the Birkin's value has never fluctuated downwards and it offers an average annual increase in value of 14.2%. Even at its lowest annual increase in 1986, the value of a Birkin went up from 1985 by 2.1%.

As far as record-breaking lots are concerned, Fellows Auctioneers broke a house record for the price achieved on a Louis Vuitton Neverfull handbag in February 2019 – the limited edition 'Pumpkin Dot Neverfull MM' handbag more than doubled its estimate and sold for £2,041.60.

Furthermore, in October 2016 Fellows sold a 'Rouge Porosus Crocodile Birkin 35' handbag by Hermès for a full price of **£22,968.** Other brands to look out for are Chanel, Louis Vuitton and Gucci.

Sophie Higgs, Specialist for The Designer Collection, Fellows Auctioneers

QUICK REFERENCE - CHANEL

- Gabrielle Chanel (1883-1971) opened her first shop in Paris, Chanel Modes, in 1910, and her first couture house in Biarritz, in 1915. The Chanel brand produced many bags, which remain instantly recognisable today.
- In 1955, Chanel launched the '2.55' bag (referring to the month and year the bag was introduced) combining quilted leather and a gold chain. An iconic design, the bag was also practical, with various compartments and a shoulder strap allowing women to keep their hands free. Celebrities of the time, including Elizabeth Taylor, Brigitte Bardot and Jane Fonda, were seen wearing Chanel's bag.
- The brand continued after Gabrielle Chanel's death in 1971, with Karl Lagerfeld (1933-2019) becoming Artistic Director in 1983.
- Lagerfeld's 2011 '11.12' version of the '2.55' bag, saw a more rigidly structured design and featured a more heavy-duty chain. Lagerfeld also introduced the interlocking Cs logo, known as the mademoiselle lock.
- Under Lagerfeld's direction, Chanel created more instantly recognisable bags, including the 'Grand Shopping Tote', the 'Chanel Gabrielle', and the 'Boy' bag.

A Chanel 50th anniversary limited edition '2.55' reissue quilted 'Classic Flap' handbag, antique gold-tone chain strap and mademoiselle turn-lock fastening, with maker's dust bag and box, metalwork purposefully distressed from gold to silver.

In 2005, this commemorative 50th anniversary edition marked the official relaunch of the '2.55' bag.

10in (25.5cm) wide

£2,000-3,000   FELL

A small Chanel 'Classic Double Flap' handbag, serial no.1403263, featuring maker's iconic black quilted lambskin leather exterior with gold-tone hardware, with maker's authenticity card.

1989-91   *9in (23cm) wide*

£2,000-3,000   FELL

A beaded Chanel 'Camellia Flap' lambskin leather handbag, serial no.16503618, with beaded and embroidered camellia flower embellishments, 'CC' fastening, silver-tone hardware, with maker's authenticity card, care pamphlet and dust bag, signs of light use.

10¼in (26cm) wide

£3,000-3,500   FELL

A vintage Chanel 'Medium Classic Double Flap' handbag, with quilted lambskin leather exterior, with maker's authenticity card.

10in (25.5cm) wide

£1,500-2,000   FELL

A Chanel small quilted duffle bag, of soft black lambskin leather, with maker's authenticity card.

11¾in (30cm) wide

£1,000-1,500   FELL

A Chanel suede quilted handbag, serial no.3581503.

11¾in (30m) wide

£800-900   ROS

A Chloe 'Madeleine' lambskin-leather handbag, with 'Chloe Authenticity card BOFMX8' and dust cover.

13½in (34.5cm) wide

£500-600   DUK

A Coyard 'Chevron Okinawa PM' handbag, with maker's dust bag.

14¼in (36cm) wide

£1,000-1,500   FELL

A Christian Dior 'Cannage Quilted Lady Dior MM' handbag, with maker's dust bag, care guide and authenticity card.

9in (23cm) wide

£1,200-1,800   FELL

A Dunhill prototype alligator document briefcase, inscribed 'Alfred Dunhill'.

15¾in (40cm) wide

£1,200-1,800   **DUK**

A Fendi '3Jours' leather bicolour handbag, with maker's dust bag and care guide.

13¾in (35cm) wide

£450-550   **FELL**

A Gucci 'Horsebit' hobo handbag, serial no.232961 213317, made from maker's 'GG' canvas, minor wear.

14in (35.5cm) wide

£300-400   **FELL**

A Gucci 'Unskilled Worker Matelassé Marmont' camera handbag, an online exclusive in collaboration with Unskilled Worker for the 2017 'Capsule' collection, with maker's care guide, dust bag and box.

9½in (24cm) wide

£800-900   **FELL**

QUICK REFERENCE - HERMÈS

- **Hermès was founded in 1837 and is best-known for its handbags, most famously the 'Kelly', designed in the 1930s and used by Grace Kelly from 1956, and the 'Birkin', designed for actress Jane Birkin in 1984, adapted from a 1894 design.**
- **Hermès bags are produced in a wide variety of different leathers and skins. Depending on the bag and its material, prices can vary from under £100 to over £100,000.**
- **Condition can affect value considerably. Fakes are common and can be extremely good, so if in doubt it is worth taking a bag to Hermès for identification.**

A Hermès tan 'Epson Birkin 35' handbag, with tan stamped-grain leather and rolled leather handles, with polished silver-tone turn-lock fastening, minor wear.

c2007   *13in (33cm) wide*

£7,000-8,000   **FELL**

A Hermès 'Kaba' red handbag, date stamp 'U', minor scratches.

c1991   *15in (38cm) wide*

£1,000-1,500   **FELL**

A Hermès 'Birkin 35' handbag, maker's padlock with detachable clochette and keys and four protective base feet, with maker's dust bag and box.

2008   *13¾in (35cm) wide*

£7,000-8,000   **FELL**

A Hermès 'Padded Berline' messenger bag, with the 'Kelly' strap closure with central turn-lock fastening, with maker's dust bag, blind stamp 'T'.

c2015   *11in (28cm) wide*

£3,000-4,000   **FELL**

A Hermès Kelly Sport MM black leather bag, date letter 'W' within circle for 1993.

1993   *9½in (24cm) wide*

£1,500-2,000   **ROS**

A Miu Miu matelassé crystal leather handbag, with silver-tone hardware, with maker's care card and dust bag.

13in (33cm) wide

£600-700   **FELL**

QUICK REFERENCE - MULBERRY

- Founded by Roger Saul in 1971, Mulberry began designing buckled leather belts, before moving on to accessories, bags and womenswear in 1979. Saul's sister designed the iconic tree logo.
- Mulberry opened its first factory, The Rookery, in 1989 in Chilcompton, Somerset, with just 100 employees. The Rookery now employs nearly 300 skilled workers. The Willows, Mulberry's second UK factory, opened in 2013 in Bridgewater.
- Mulberry Green, the company's signature colour, was created in 2015. It is used on Mulberry's packaging, shoe insoles and outerwear linings. Now, the company has over 120 shops worldwide.

A Mulberry mini Boston 'Roxanne' leather handbag, internal pocket with zip, wear and scuffing.

7in (18cm) wide

£140-200   **CHEF**

A Mulberry 'Mocha' ostrich-leather handbag, serial no.1706018, with a detachable embossed key fob.

14¼in (36cm) wide

£250-350   **DUK**

A Mulberry ostrich-leather handbag, silver tone hardware with the Mulberry tree logo, with a detachable embossed key fob.

14¼in (36cm) wide

£800-900   **DUK**

A Mulberry embossed 'Bayswater' handbag, serial no,656188, with postman's lock fastening, minor wear.

14¼in (36cm) wide

£900-1,100   **FELL**

A Prada backpack, with a black leather-trimmed quilted velvet exterior, with maker's dust bag, care card and authenticity card, dusty exterior.

11in (28cm) high

£600-700   **FELL**

A Prada caramel saffiano leather handbag, with gold-tone hardware, with maker's authenticity card and dust bag.

14¼in (36cm) wide

£650-750   **FELL**

A Valentino Garavani leather flower handbag, some wear.

15in (38cm) wide

£180-220   **FELL**

FASHION

A Louis Vuitton 'Damier Neverfull MM' handbag, with maker's archive details, date code 'GI4112', faint marks to red canvas lined interior.

18¼in (46.5cm) wide

£800-1,000   **FELL**

A Louis Vuitton 'Monogram Montsouris' backpack, serial no.SP1907, minor marks, wear and tarnishing to hardware, lining faded.

c1997   *11in (28cm) high*

£450-550   **FELL**

A Louis Vuitton 'Ribera MM' lady's handbag, in Damier Ebene canvas leather, a mobile phone pocket and another to the interior.

13in (33cm) long

£250-350   **CHEF**

A Louis Vuitton 'Monogram Graffiti Pochette Accessoires' handbag, serial no.AR0051, with maker's dust bag, minor scratches to gold-tone hardware.

8in (20.5cm) wide

£220-280   **FELL**

A Louis Vuitton 'Cherry Blossom Sac Retro' handbag, serial no.CA0023, with maker's dust bag, minor scattered water marks.

c2003   *11in (28cm) wide*

£350-450   **FELL**

A Louis Vuitton 'Multicolor Monogram Accessories Pochette' handbag, serial no.SL0053, with bolt key holder, signs of light use, with maker's dust bag.

5in (21.5cm) wide

£250-350   **FELL**

A Louis Vuitton 'Epi Gobelins' backpack, serial no.VI1909, with maker's dust bag, padlock and keys, some minor scuff marks.

c1999   *13in (33cm) high*

£500-600   **FELL**

A Louis Vuitton 'Monogram Vernis Alma GM' handbag.

15in (38cm) wide

£900-1,100   **FELL**

A Louis Vuitton 'Speedy' Epi leather handbag, with two keys, hardware and padlock stamped 'Louis Vuitton'.

£500-600   **DUK**

QUICK REFERENCE - LOUIS VUITTON

- Louis Vuitton (1821-92) founded his namesake fashion company and retailer in 1854.
- The company's success sparked from its 'Trianon' trunk, produced in 1858. This trunk was waterproof, canvas covered and airtight. Previously, trunks had domed or sloping tops to allow water to run off, but as Vuitton's trunk was already waterproof it could have a flat top. This allowed it to stack when being transported.
- In 1876, Louis Vuitton introduced beige and brown striped canvas in order to differentiate its products from competitors and imitators. Its checked 'Damier' was introduced in 1888, followed in 1896 by the 'LV' monogram canvas, which is still used by Louis Vuitton today.
- Vintage Louis Vuitton pieces are highly popular today. Specially commissioned pieces or those with niche uses, such as musical instrument cases, can fetch especially large sums.

A Louis Vuitton attaché case, serial no.1030479, with two keys.

17¾in (45cm) wide

£800-900   **BELL**

A 20thC Louis Vuitton vanity case, serial no.915955, the lid with internal mirror, with two keys.

16in (40.5cm) wide

£1,200-1,600   **ROS**

A Louis Vuitton 'Boite Chapeaux 50' hat box, with leather card holder and two keys.

19¾in (50cm) diam

£1,500-2,000   **BELL**

A Louis Vuitton monogram 'Pégase 65' rolling suitcase, a canvas-lined interior with removable garment cover, heat stamped initials to leather tag.

25½in (65cm) high

£1,500-2,000   **FELL**

A Louis Vuitton cigar humidor, of briefcase form, the lockplate stamped with London and Paris addresses and '082946', the interior with hygrometer.

15¾in (40cm) wide

£2,500-3,000   **CHOR**

An early 20thC Louis Vuitton leather trunk, with leather banding and brass fittings, the lock stamped with serial no.023361, the interior with paper label and stamped no.151369, the side with monogram 'K.C.K.'

24in (61cm) wide

£6,000-7,000   **L&T**

An early 20thC Louis Vuitton wooden and leather-bound travelling trunk, the brass flip-catch signed '70. Champs Elysees, Paris, Louis VUITTON, London 149 New Bond Street', with affixed iron wheels to the underside.

40in (101.5cm) wide

£8,500-9,500   **T&F**

An early 20thC Louis Vuitton leather touring trunk, the lockplate stamped '70 CHAMPS ELYSEES PARIS LOUIS VUITTON LONDON 149 BOND STREET', the relined interior with paper trade label.

30¼in (77cm) wide

£7,000-8,000   **L&T**

A Louis Vuitton 'Epi Keepall 55' luggage bag, a few creases to the exterior.

18in (45.5cm) wide

£600-700   **FELL**

A Cartier 'Must De Cartier' travel vanity case, the emblazoned suede and leather box with gold-tone hardware accents, interior mirror missing, with maker's dust cover.

12in (30.5cm) long

£600-700   **FELL**

An early 20thC Goldsmiths & Silversmiths Co. Ltd. crocodile-skin suitcase, with gilt embossed maker's name and address '12 REGENT STREET LONDON W.'.

24in (61cm) wide

£700-800   **L&T**

A Mulberry Scotchgrain and tan leather suit carrier and a holdall ensuite, both with detachable shoulder straps.

£220-300   **CHEF**

An early 20thC small crocodile-skin Gladstone bag, stamped 'J.C. VICKERY 179, 181 & 183 REGENT ST. W.' and 'TO THEIR MAJESTIES THE KING AND QUEEN'.

Contains material that may be subject to import/export restrictions, especially outside the EU, due to CITES regulations.

13¾in (35cm) wide

£500-600   **L&T**

A Goyard steamer trunk, leather bound chevron fabric with brass fittings, the interior with cream linen-covered drawers with leather tab handles to one side, extending chrome rail and four original clothes hangers, stamped 'Goyard Aine, Monte-Carlo, Biarritz, Paris', one strap handle missing.

c1900   *22in (56cm) wide*

£13,000-18,000   **ROS**

A leather-covered and brass-bound shipping trunk, the lid decorated with a painted vignette of a sailing ship being towed by a steam-powered tugboat, inscribed 'The Barque Marion Johnstone', further inscribed 'Joshua Brown: Master', dated.

1847   *61½in (156cm) long*

£1,100-1,400   **DUK**

A stitched leather suitcase, stamped 'Churchill' below a crown.

26½in (67.5cm) wide

£100-150   **FLD**

A 20thC leather car trunk, with gilt-metal hardware and original lined interior.

33¾in (85.5cm) wide

£500-700   **L&T**

A vintage Kenner 'Star Wars' vinyl cape 'Jawa' figure, small pin hole in cape.

3¾in (9.5cm) high

£1,000-1,400   VEC

A Kenner 'Star Wars' vintage 'Imperial Gunner' figure.

3¾in (9.5cm) high

£120-160   VEC

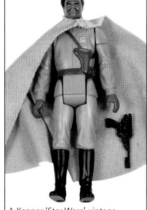

A Kenner 'Star Wars' vintage 'Lando Calrissian General' figure.

3¾in (9.5cm) high

£150-200   VEC

A Kenner 'Star Wars' vintage 'Luke Skywalker Stormtrooper' figure, yellow paint on inside of helmet.

3¾in (9.5cm) high

£150-200   VEC

A Hasbro 'Star Wars' 'Han Solo' modern hard copy prototype figure head.

12in (30.5cm) high

£250-350   VEC

A Hasbro 'STAR WARS, RETURN OF THE JEDI, SCOUT WALKER AT-ST', the vintage collection, near-mint packaging.

£75-85   VEC

A vintage Kenner 'STAR WARS, RETURN OF THE JEDI, JABBA THE HUTT, ACTION PLAYSET', missing pipe, within near-mint packaging, with instructions and inserts.

£180-220   VEC

A vintage Kenner 'STAR WARS, LAND SPEEDER'.

£120-150   VEC

A vintage Kenner 'STAR WARS, RETURN OF THE JEDI, Han Solo' figure, near-mint, creasing of 65C back punched card.

figure 3¾in (9.5cm) high

£250-300   VEC

A vintage Kenner 'STAR WARS, Han Solo, LARGE SIZE ACTION FIGURE', mint, within scuffed sealed packaging.

figure 12in (30.5cm) high

£400-500   VEC

A vintage Palitoy 'STAR WARS, THE EMPIRE STRIKES BACK, AT-AT ALL TERRAIN ARMOURED TRANSPORT', missing chin guns, with inserts.

£130-160   VEC

A near-mint vintage Palitoy 'STAR WARS, BLASTER PISTOL', within scuffed packaging, includes Acrylic display case.

£900-1,100   VEC

A vintage Palitoy/General Mills 'STAR WARS, RETURN OF THE JEDI, HOTH WAMPA ACTION FIGURE', with insert.

£180-220   VEC

A vintage Palitoy/General Mills tri-logo 'STAR WARS, RETURN OF THE JEDI, RANCOR MONSTER FIGURE', with insert and poster, creased packaging.

£120-160   VEC

A vintage Palitoy/General Mills tri-logo 'STAR WARS, RETURN OF THE JEDI, Sy Snootles and the Rebo band', broken microphone.

£180-220   VEC

A vintage Palitoy/General Mills 'STAR WARS, RETURN OF THE JEDI, MILLENNIUM FALCON VEHICLE', with instructions.

£180-220   VEC

A vintage Palitoy/General Mills tri-Logo 'STAR WARS, RETURN OF THE JEDI, Artoo-Detoo (R2-D2) with pop-up Lightsabre'.

figure 3¾in (9.5cm) high

£300-400   VEC

A vintage Palitoy/General Mills tri-logo 'STAR WARS, RETURN OF THE JEDI, Yak Face' figure, mispackaged with 'Sand People' weapon.

figure 3¾in (9.5cm) high

£1,400-1,800   VEC

A 'Star Wars' floor-standing life-size 'Ewok' figure, complete with bow, quiver with feather arrows.

The 'Ewok' is a character played by Warwick Davis in 'Star Wars'. The 'Ewoks' became very popular, having their own film 'Caravan of Courage: An Ewok Adventure'.

44in (112cm) high

£250-300   AST

QUICK REFERENCE - LEGO 'STAR WARS'

- LEGO signed a licensing agreement with LucasFilm Ltd., producer of the 'Star Wars' films, in 1998 to produce LEGO versions of the film's characters, locations, starships and other vehicles.
- This line of products was launched in 1999 at the International Toy Fair, New York. In the same year, LEGO's first new male hair piece in 20 years was designed for 'Qui Gon Jinn' and the first specially designed minifigure head was made for 'Jar Jar Binks'.
- In 2011, the 'UCS Super Star Destroyer' was launched. At a length of 124cm it was the longest LEGO product ever made.
- In 2013, the world's largest LEGO model of the X-Wing Starfighter went on display in Times Square, New York.
- In 2017, LEGO launched its 'Ultimate Collector Series Millennium Falcon #75192'. It had 7,541 pieces.

A 'LEGO, STAR WARS, 10143, Death Star II', in dusty box with some undulation, box seals have been broken.

£750-850   AST

A 'LEGO, STAR WARS, 4483, AT-AT', box with some undulation and creasing.

£140-180   AST

A 'LEGO, STAR WARS, 10188, Death Star', box seals have been broken.

£280-320   AST

A 'LEGO, STAR WARS, 10236, Ewok Village', sealed in box.

£200-250   AST

A 'LEGO, STAR WARS, 10030, IMPERIAL STAR DESTROYER', box seals have been broken.

£750-850   AST

A 'LEGO, STAR WARS, 10240, Red Five X-wing Starfighter', box has been opened.

£150-200   AST

A 'LEGO, STAR WARS, 7964, Republic Frigate', box has been opened.

£60-80   AST

A 'LEGO, STAR WARS, 10225, R2-D2', box has been opened.

£180-220   AST

A Universal Studios Lon Chaney 'The Hunchback Of Notre Dame' diorama, assembled resin 1:6 scale Garage Model Kit.
1923   *12in (30.5cm) high*
£150-200   **VEC**

A Universal Studios Boris Karloff as 'The Mummy' diorama, assembled resin 1:6 scale Garage Model Kit, sculpted by Jeff Yagher for the Janus Company, painted by Darren Kefford.
                                        17in (43cm) high
£250-300   **VEC**

A Universal Studios Boris Karloff 'The Mummy' diorama, assembled resin 1:6 scale Garage Model Kit, painted by Darren Kefford.
                                      12in (30.5cm) high
£150-200   **VEC**

A Universal Studios 'King Kong' diorama, assembled resin 1:6 scale Garage Model Kit, painted by Darren Kefford.
1933   *11in (28cm) high*
£150-200   **VEC**

A Universal Studios Lon Chaney Jnr as 'The Wolf Man' with Harry Talbot diorama, assembled resin 1:6 scale Garage Model Kit, sculpted by Mike Hill for the Janus Company, painted by Darren Kefford.
                                      12in (30.5cm) high
£150-200   **VEC**

A Universal Studios Bela Lugosi as 'Dracula' diorama, assembled resin 1:6 scale Garage Model Kits creating one diorama, sculpted by Mike Hill for the Janus Company.
c1999   *22in (56cm) high*
£250-300   **VEC**

A Hammer Films 'Dracula' diorama, starring Christopher Lee and Veronica Carlson, assembled resin 1:6 scale Garage Model Kit, painted by Darren Kefford.
2005   *16in (40.5cm) high*
£150-200   **VEC**

A mimeographed manuscript shooting script for 'The Quiet Man', by Frank Nugent, from a story by Maurice Walsh, 146 pages, legal folio.

Acquired from a cast member.
1951
£4,000-4,500   **WHYT**

A 'The Horror of Frankenstein' script, from the sound department's boom operator Keith Batten, 124 pages detailing the screenplay by Jimmy Sangster and Jeremy Burham for Hammer Film Productions Ltd., signed, with underlinings but without annotations, a loose additional dialogue page for scene 70 p.66.
£180-220   **AST**

A Lone Star 'JAMES BOND 007, MOONRAKER SPACE GUN', some wear, opened packaging, one torn flap.

£100-150   **VEC**

A 'James Bond: Moonraker' laser rifle, created for the film, features a telescopic sight with rotating grid metal trigger guard.

This is one of only a few surviving examples of these props. This item belonged to the late Brian Bailey who worked with Cubby Broccoli at Pinewood Studios. Bailey was the Production Accountant and is named in the end credits of 'Moonraker'.

1979   *20in (51cm) long*

£27,000-30,000   **AST**

A 'James Bond: The World is Not Enough' Russian cylinder-shaped screen-used barrel, with certificate of authenticity.

£70-80   **AST**

A Wentoy's 'James Bond 007' toy pistol, in unopened German packaging.

£40-50   **VEC**

A Swatch 40th Anniversary 'James Bond 007' watch, unused, includes instructions.

£50-70   **VEC**

An original 'Jurassic Park' production-made velociraptor claw, directed by Steven Spielberg, all the life-sized animatronic dinosaurs were created by the Stan Winston Studios.

This item was made during production, but unfinished so never screen used. It is constructed from a type of resin and remains in an excellent production-used condition.

1993   *4½in (11.5cm) long*

£400-450   **AST**

A 'Blade Runner' special edition box set, containing cinema poster, screen play, film cell and DVD.

2002

£25-30   **LSK**

An original 'Planet of the Apes' chimp helmet, directed by Tim Burton, made from fibreglass, with a chinstrap and chain mail, with a foam interior lining.

2001   *18in (45.5cm) long*

£400-500   **AST**

A Marx Toys vintage 'The Black Hole' bagatelle.

£65-75   **VEC**

FILM & TELEVISION

An original 'Garfield: The Movie!' animation maquette, made by Rhythm and Hues Studio, with production markings on the bottom of the maquette 'CB-03'.
2004   *9in (23cm) high*
£400-450   **AST**

A 'Corpse Bride' character head maquette for 'The Maid', production used, made of resin, with photocopied certificate.
2005   *4in (10cm) wide*
£90-110   **AST**

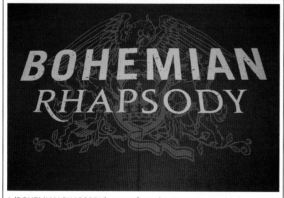

A 'BOHEMIAN PHAPSODY' carpet, from the Queen-inspired light installation switch-on in celebration of the release of the film 'Bohemian Rhapsody' on 21 October 2018 at Carnaby Street, London.
192.5in (489cm) wide
£60-80   **AST**

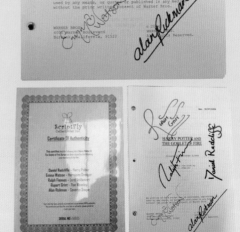

A 'Harry Potter and the Goblet of Fire' original script, signed by Daniel Radcliffe as 'Harry Potter', Emma Watson as 'Hermione Granger', Ralph Fiennes as 'Lord Voldemort', Rupert Grint as 'Ron Weasley' and Alan Rickman as 'Severus Snape', the script is dated '30/07/2004', screenplay by Steven Kloves, with a letter from Warner Bros. Pictures concerning the provenance of the script.
2004
£500-600   **AST**

A Jakks Pacific large-scale DC Comics 'Batman' figure, mint, with box.
31in (78.5cm) high
£30-40   **VEC**

A Dapol 'Doctor WHO, DAVROS, Creator of the Daleks' black card figure, BBC Enterprises Ltd., CAS graded 75 C80 B70 F80, real grade 76.4, upon punched card, with certificate.
1987
£40-50   **VEC**

A Dapol 'Doctor WHO, THE FOURTH DOCTOR' black card figure, BBC Enterprises Ltd. series two, AFA graded 80NM C80 B80 F85, upon punched card.
1988
£65-75   **VEC**

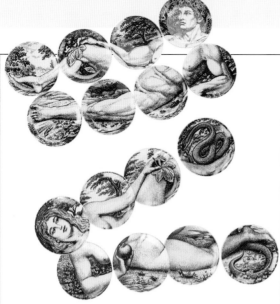

A set of 16 Fornasetti 'Adam and Eve' coasters, in two original boxes, marked 'Fornasetti Italy'.

Piero Fornasetti (1913-88) was an Italian artist and designer of furniture, ceramics, glass and homeware. He attended and was expelled from Milan's Brera Art Academy. Fornasetti's designs were highly decorative and often featured Surrealist imagery. He died in 1988 in Milan, Italy.

c1965   *4in (10cm) diam*

£1,000-1,500   **DRA**

A pair of Fornasetti 'Astrolabio' and 'Melodramma' plates, designed by Piero Fornasetti, printed and gilt, printed mark 'Weihnachten 1967' and 'Melodramma 15', gilt wear to both.

largest 10½in (26.5cm) diam

£400-500   **SWO**

A Fornasetti porcelain inkwell and penholder, decorated with classical verse on a gold lustre ground, printed marks.

2¾in (7cm) high

£140-180   **SWO**

A Fornasetti waste bin, lithographed with a repeating design of a soldier on horseback, with a brass collar, printed 'Fornasetti Milano Made in Italy'.

11in (28cm) high

£1,100-1,500   **SWO**

A Fornasetti transfer-printed and brass-bound umbrella stand, 'Losanghe' pattern, printed mark 'Fornasetti Milano, Made in Italy'.

c1950s   *22¾in (58cm) high*

£850-950   **ROS**

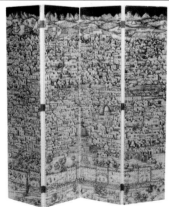

A Fornasetti four-fold 'Jerusalem' lacquer screen, transfer-printed and painted, the reverse with playing cards, factory label, some scuffs.

78¾in (200cm) high

£11,000-15,000   **DN**

A Fornasetti four-fold dressing screen, printed to one side with 'The Clockmaker's Shop' design, the reverse in plain painted finish, unmarked.

c1950s   *51¼in (130cm) high*

£2,000-2,500   **FLD**

GLASS

An 'Onion' bottle, patches of iridescence to the green ground.
c1680-1700   *5½in (14cm) high*
£650-750   **FLD**

An 18thC olive green glass wine bottle, of mallet form, applied lip.
                              14½in (37cm) high
£700-800   **FLD**

A Haywards amber glass hand fire grenade.
                              6in (15cm) high
£100-140   **FLD**

A Harden Star cobalt blue glass fire grenade, unopened.
                              7in (18cm) high
£70-80   **FLD**

A French amber 'Unic' glass fire grenade.
                              5½in (14cm) high
£90-110   **FLD**

Judith Picks

The Coca Cola bottle shown here is no ordinary Coca-Cola bottle. For nearly a decade after its introduction in the mid-1880s, Coca-Cola was sold by the glass from shop-installed soda fountains, but as its popularity grew the owners of the company realised bottling it was the best way to further expand the business. They were right: by 1915 there were some 1,000 contracted or sub-contracted bottling plants in existence.

There was, however, a problem: diversity in the types of bottles used, together with inconsistent labelling, made it easy for the brand to be confused with a growing number of imitations from competitors. What was needed was a standardised and highly distinctive, indeed unique bottle, so the company asked several large glass manufacturers to submit potential designs.

Conceived by Earl R. Dean, working at the Root Glass Company, the winning design, with its contoured sides that made it distinguishable even in the dark, was confidentially tested and, after reducing the centre diameter to make it more stable on a conveyor belt, went into national production in 1917.

Now it had been long thought that all the pre-1917 prototypes of these bottles had been broken and discarded at the bottling plants. Until, that is, this bottle (made in 1915 at the Atlanta, Georgia, plant) surfaced among the collection of Coca-Cola artefacts of a retired bottling plant employee. Its huge current value is testament to not only an iconic design, but also one of the world's biggest and most enduring brands.

A Coca-Cola Root Glass Co. modified prototype bottle.
                              7¾in (19.5cm) high
£90,000-100,000   **MORP**

An early 20thC Harrach cameo glass vase, cased in blue over pale pink and cut with trailing flowers, cameo signature to body.

10¼in (26cm) high

£300-400   **FLD**

A late 19thC Harrach cameo glass pot pourri, with pierced gilt-metal fitting, the body cased in ruby over a citron rose and acorn air trap ground, numbered to base.

9in (23cm) high

£2,000-2,500   **FLD**

QUICK REFERENCE - HARRACH

- In the early 18thC, Elias Müller (1672–1730) took over operation of the glassworks on the Harrach estate in Neuwelt (now Nový Svet in the Czech Republic). There had been a glassworks in the area since the mid-17thC, founded by Count Harrach.
- Coloured glass, high-quality tableware and milk glass were produced from the 18thC. In 1764, Graf Ernst Guido Harrach ran the company.
- In the early 19thC, Johann Pohl managed the glassworks. It produced Lithyalin glass (a polished opaque glass), as well as Hyalith, engraved, enamelled, cut and cameo glass.
- The glassworks became a pioneer of Art Nouveau glass ware under the management of Jan Mallin in the early 20thC. It produced glass for Czech companies, including J. & L. Lobmeyr and Moser.
- The company was nationalised in 1948, becoming part of The Glassworks of Železný Brod, then The Glassworks of Nový Bor and finally Crystalex Nový Bor in 1974. In 1993, the glassworks were bought by František Novosad. To support the glassworks' production of luxury and decorative glassware, a microbrewery was built in 2002.

A pair of late 19thC Harrach lizard vases, in pale cinnamon with applied blue crimped handles, rustic form feet and lizards, unmarked.

11½in (29cm) high

£350-450   **FLD**

A pair of Harrach uranium green over red drip vases.

c1890   *5in (12.5cm) high*

£250-350   **M&DM**

A Harrach 'Chinoiserie' vase, with birds flying over mountains.

c1895   *6in (15cm) high*

£250-350   **M&DM**

A late 19thC Harrach glass vase, with collar neck in maroon cased over opal, printed propeller mark to base.

6¾in (17cm) high

£500-600   **FLD**

A Harrach cameo and intaglio-cut vase, blue over clear and gilded.

c1900   *14in (35.5cm) high*

£500-600   **M&DM**

A Harrach 'Lilies and Sun' cameo vase white on green, gilded.

c1899   *4in (10cm) high*

£1,000-1,200   **M&DM**

GLASS

A pair of late 19thC Kralik glass vases, of propeller form, with a crackle finish over the graduated ruby and silvered ground and overlaid with green trails.

The Wilhelm Kralik Söhne glassworks was originally founded by Josef Meyr in Bohemia in 1815 under the factory name Adolfshütte. It passed to his son and then his son's nephews, Josef Taschek and Wilhelm Kralik. After Kralik's death in 1877, the company's factories were divided into what became the Wilhelm Kralik Söhne glassworks and the Meyr's Neffe glassworks. Wilhelm Kralik Söhne, known as Kralik, continued production until World War II.

9in (23cm) high

£150-200   FLD

A late 19thC Kralik bronze ware vase, decorated with random whiplash lines over the iridescent ground.

6¼in (16cm) high

£100-150   FLD

A Kralik large vase, with applied green flower.

c1900   *14in (35.5cm) high*

£450-550   M&DM

A pair of Kralik vases, by Franz Tomschick.

c1925   *8in (20.5cm) high*

£400-500   M&DM

A Kralik giant cut-to-clear/cameo vase.

This is one of the few pieces of Kralik to be documented, pattern no.5089/6.

c1935   *13in (33cm) high*

£500-600   M&DM

A Moser 'Alexandrit' trio of dishes, signed 'Moser Alexandrit'.

Colour change glass depending on light - goes from purple to blue.

Ludwig Moser (1833-1916) founded a glassworks in Karlsbad, Bohemia (now Karlovy Vary, Czech Republic) in 1857. The company specialised in polishing, engraving and cutting glass, and began making their own glass from 1893. In the 1930s, the Depression caused Moser difficulties and the family sold their shares in 1938. The company was nationalised in 1948, changed hands multiple times and became Moser a.s. in 1991.

c1929   *2in (5cm) high*

£300-400   M&DM

A late 19thC Moser spirit flask, cased in amber over clear crystal and cut with wild poppies, gilded handle and thumb lift cover.

9in (23cm) high

£250-300   FLD

A Moser 'Alexandrit' vase, designed by H. Hussmann.

The glass changes colour from pink to blue, depending on light.

c1928   *5in (12.5cm) high*

£300-350   M&DM

A Moser cameo bowl, by Otto Tauschek, signed.

c1915   *6in (15cm) diam*

£1,000-1,200   M&DM

A pair of Moser jewelled vases, on Loetz blanks, pink shading to clear, faintly signed.

c1890   *10in (25.5cm) high*

£1,000-1,200   M&DM

A Czech Borské Sklo 'Expo 58' vase, designed by Jaroslav Lebeda for the 1958 World Exposition in Brussels.

A similar, but smaller, shape was included in the commemorative supplement for the Brussels Expo produced by Czechoslovak Glass Review in 1958.

designed 1957   12in (30.5cm) high
£550-650   **DAWS**

A rare late 1950s Czechoslovakian Borské Sklo cased, cut, enamelled and gilded 'Expo '58' bottle, designed by Jaroslav Lebeda in 1957, the red-pink core overlaid with opaque white glass and cut through with mitre cut curving lines in a grid pattern, yellow and gilt embossed foil 'Expo '58' paper label, light rubbing.

This is the most iconic form from this series of vases, bottles and bowls produced for the Czechoslovakian pavilion at the World Expo in Brussels in 1958. Each element of the design updated historic Bohemian glass traditions, from the colours to the style of the casing and cutting, and the Picasso-eques, Modern-art inspired choice of motifs for enamelling. Glass was not considered to convey a social, ideological or political message, so many artists were free to use glass as a medium to express themselves in a modern manner.

Mark Hill, Dawson's Auctioneers

12¾in (32.5cm) high
£1,200-1,500   **DAWS**

A pair of Carl Goldberg vases, silver overlaid with a silver 'Gui' (mistletoe) pattern.

c1900   4in (10cm) high
£300-400   **M&DM**

A pair of Meyr's Neffe glasses, white over clear, made for Bakalowits using Otto Prutscher designs, on an unknown designer's shape.

c1906   4in (10cm) high
£900-1,100   **M&DM**

A Meyr's Neffe liqueur set, including decanter and six shot glasses, after a design by Hoffmann.

c1907   decanter 9in (23cm) high
£800-900   **M&DM**

A Czech Novy Bor cased and cut glass conical vase, possibly designed by Karel Wünsch, with Borocrystal distributor's paper label.

1960s   15in (38cm) high
£250-300   **DAWS**

A large 'Splatter' vase, possibly Ruckl.

c1925   12in (30.5cm) high
£200-250   **M&DM**

A Welz vase, 'Octopus' pattern.

The pattern is so named because of the oval suckers.

c1925   8in (20.5cm) high
£250-300   **M&DM**

A pair of Welz 'Splatter' vases.

c1925   6in (15cm) high
£250-300   **M&DM**

A Ruckl 'Splatter' salts jar, with original lid, retailer's label 'BATH CRYSTALS Old English Lavender'.

c1925   10in (25.5cm) high
£120-150   **M&DM**

GLASS

A Lalique 'Myosotis' frosted glass scent bottle and stopper, designed by Rene Lalique, with sepia staining, etched 'R. Lalique France 611', stopper repaired.

11¾in (30cm) high

£1,800-2,200   **WW**

QUICK REFERENCE - LALIQUE

- Jewellery designer René Lalique (1860-1945) moved into glass ware production in the early 20thC, founding the Verrerie d'Alsace glassworks at Wingen-sur-Moder, Alsace, in 1921.
- The Lalique glassworks produced glass screens, lamps, car mascots, fountains, lights and vases. These were primarily mould-blown or pressed, of frosted white, opalescent glass.
- Lalique participated in the 1925 International Exposition of Modern Industrial and Decorative Arts in Paris. He was also commissioned for various projects, including decorating the Côte d'Azur Pullman Express carriages in 1929 and producing a temporary fountain for the Galerie des Champs-Elysées in Paris. In 1935, the Lalique shop at 11 Rue Royale, Paris, opened.
- In 1945, René Lalique died and was succeeded by his son Marc. René Lalique's designs remained in production after his death, but a new crystal glass was also used. Marc's daughter Marie-Claude took over management of the company in 1977 and created the fragrance 'Lalique de Lalique' in 1992.
- In 2008, Lalique was acquired by Art & Fragrance. The Lalique museum opened in 2011 and the Villa René Lalique, a restaurant and hotel, opened in 2015 in Wingen-sur-Moder.

A Lalique 'Lapin' Topaz glass seal, script-etched maker's mark 'R. LALIQUE'.

c1925   *2¼in (5.5cm) high*

£300-400   **L&T**

A late 20thC Lalique powder box, after designs by René Lalique, relief moulded with a serpent, with original box.

£250-350   **FLD**

A Lalique chameleon figurine, engraved signature.

2½in (6.5cm) long

£130-180   **FLD**

A 20thC Lalique 'Sidonie' turtle figurine, in light green with a frosted finish, engraved signature.

3¼in (8.5cm) long

£40-50   **FLD**

A Lalique 'Sainte-Christophe' clear and frosted glass paperweight/car mascot, model no.1142, intaglio moulded 'R. Lalique France'.

1928   *4½in (11.5cm) high*

£1,000-1,500   **ROS**

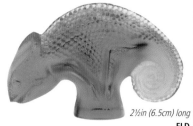

A Lalique 'Coq Nain' clear and frosted glass paperweight, designed 1928, model no.11-800, engraved 'Lalique ® France', Cristal Lalique Paris label.

post 1951   *8in (20.5cm) high*

£200-250   **ROS**

A René Lalique clear and frosted glass 'Pinsons' bowl, no.11-016, designed 1933, moulded with sparrows and foliage, engraved 'Lalique ® France', 'Cristal Lalique Paris' label.

post 1951   *9¼in (23.5cm) diam*

£250-300   **ROS**

A René Lalique clear and frosted glass 'Naiades' clock face, no.764, designed 1926, intaglio moulded with water nymphs, without movement, engraved 'R. Lalique France'.

4½in (11.5cm) square

£1,200-1,500   **ROS**

QUICK REFERENCE - LOETZ

- In 1836, Johann Eisner founded a glassworks factory in Klostermühle, Bohemia (now Klášterský Mlýn, Czech Republic). The factory was acquired by Susanne Loetz, widow of glassmaker Johann Loetz.
- In 1879, the factory, known as Johann Loetz Witwe, passed to Maximilian von Spaun. Along with Eduard Prochaska, von Spaun modernised and expanded production. Notable designers include Franz Hofstätter, Michael Powolny, Koloman Moser and Josef Hoffmann.
- After World War I, two major fires and the Depression, the factory declared bankruptcy, finally closing in 1947, having produced utilitarian glassware during World War II.
- Loetz's best-known ranges were iridescent and trailed in the Art Nouveau style.

A late 19thC Loetz 'Aesthetic' glass vase, relief enamelled and gilt oriental dragon on the tangerine to opal ground rising to a gilt band with black enamelled characters.

7½in (19cm) high

£500-600   FLD

A late 19thC Loetz bowl, with relief gilded fir boughs over a graduated white to pink Burmese-style ground, unmarked.

5¼in (13.5cm) high

£250-300   FLD

A Loetz brown-to-cream yellow vase, enamelled with birds on blooming branches, enameller's codes to base.

c1888   *4in (10cm) high*

£300-450   M&DM

A Loetz vase, 'Rubin PG 6893 Phänomen Genres' pattern, with silver to electric blue iridescent wave lines over a ruby-coloured ground, unmarked.

c1898-1900   *10in (25.5cm) high*

£2,000-2,500   FLD

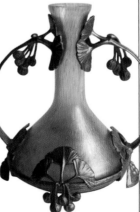

A Loetz two-handled vibrant pink bowl/vase, gilded with one of the classic French Rococo patterns.

c1893   *7in (18cm) wide*

£600-700   M&DM

A Loetz handled vase, in opal blue mountain, with enamel flowers.

c1898   *8in (20.5cm) high*

£1,000-1,200   M&DM

A Loetz 'Candia Papillon' vase, in an original gold-plated over pewter mount, decorated with ginkgo.

1898   *6in (15cm) high*

£1,800-2,200   M&DM

A Loetz 'Dec I/255' vase, on an apparently undocumented Loetz early 'Phänomen' genre, marked.

c1898   *5in (12.5cm) high*

£900-1,100   M&DM

GLASS

A Loetz 'Candia Phan 6893 85/3681' vase, made for Bacalowitz, often called 'The Broken Egg', on original bronze stand.
1899   *5in (12.5cm) high*
£2,000-2,500   **M&DM**

A Loetz 'Phan 7773' vase, with rare early signature of two crossed arrows and stars in a circle.

Only a handful of pieces have been found with this signature.
1899   *5in (12.5cm) high*
£2,500-3,000   **M&DM**

A Loetz iridescent glass vase, of shell form decorated with blue 'Papillon'.
c1900   *10¼in (26cm) long*
£300-350   **ROS**

A Loetz 'Phänomen PG 85/3780' may green vase, made for Bakalowits.
1900   *6in (15cm) high*
£1,500-2,000   **M&DM**

A Loetz silver overlay vase, with a 'PG 1/475' type ground, overlaid in silver with interlaced whiplash lines with sprays of flowers and central cabochon garnets, unmarked.
c1901   *6¾in (17cm) high*
£4,500-5,000   **FLD**

A Loetz 'Phänomen PG 2/187' vase, dark blue on opal.
1902   *4in (10cm) high*
£3,000-3,500   **M&DM**

A Loetz giant 'Medici' vase, 'Phan 2/484', spreading peach colour.

Shown with a Loetz miniature to illustrate size difference.
c1902   *14in (35.5cm) high*
£2,500-3,000   **M&DM**

A Loetz 'Green Metalin' vase, with silver overlay, with US silver marks.
c1907   *5in (12.5cm) high*
£1,500-1,800   **M&DM**

A pair of Loetz silver-mounted iridescent glass vases, green with pink tints, overlay with flowers, unmarked.

c1910   *11in (28cm) high*

£800-1,000   **DN**

An early 20thC Loetz vase, decorated in green 'Papillon' over an opalescent ground.

7¼in (18.5cm) high

£200-250   **FLD**

An early 20thC Loetz vase, decorated in a 'Phänomen' genre decor with pulled threads over a 'Papillon' ground.

9in (23cm) high

£250-300   **FLD**

A Loetz 'Titania' iridescent glass vase, the ruby body with pulled silver iridescent frieze and bubble inclusions.

c1910   *7¾in (19.5cm) high*

£1,400-1,800   **L&T**

A Loetz 'Ausfuehrung 157' vase, black piped onto orange.

1914   *8in (20.5cm) high*

£350-450   **M&DM**

A Loetz 'Propeller' iridescent glass vase, triangular section with brim top.

12½in (32cm) high

£500-600   **K&O**

A Loetz glass bowl, the shaped rim with a plain iridescent centre.

6½in (16.5cm) diam

£400-450   **SWO**

A Loetz 'Ausf 181 Mandarin Mit Schwarz' vase.

c1914   *8in (20.5cm) high*

£300-400   **M&DM**

A Loetz 'Ausf 226' atomiser, in metallic yellow and cobalt 'Papillon', with all its original fitments including the puffer with metal valve.

c1925   *6in (15cm) high*

£600-750   **M&DM**

QUICK REFERENCE - MDINA

- Mdina Glass was established in 1968 by Eric Dobson and Michael Harris in Malta. Shortly after, glassmaker Joseph Said joined the company, eventually becoming Production Manager in 1975.
- Harris left the company in 1972 and Dobson left in 1985, with Said taking over. Harris went on to establish the Isle of White Studio Glass works near Ventnor, Isle of White, with his wife. When Harris died in 1994, his son Timothy Harris took over.
- When the company went into liquidation in 2012, Michael Harris' brother bought most of the company's assets and its name and, with Timothy, set up the company again in a new location near Newport, Isle of White.

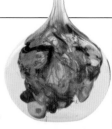

A rare late 1960s Mdina 'Cut Ice' glass vase, designed and made by Michael Harris, the colourless flat, ovoid body containing swirls in silver chloride beige, green, blue, and browny-purple, one face cut with large polished facets, the base signed 'Michael Harris Mdina Glass Malta'.

Glass signed by Michael Harris with his name is very rare, and the presence of his signature usually indicates that he made the piece. The plethora of small 'seeds' in the colourless casing and the slight green tinge, may indicate that this is an early piece. If it is early, it is almost certain that Harris made this piece due to only him having the skills and experience needed to make it at the time.

8¾in (22cm) high

£900-1,100 **DAWS**

A Mdina large 'Fish' glass vase, the central compressed globe and shaft section decorated with ochre and blue streaking over a cinnamon to ruby ground, heavily cased with clear crystal squared shoulders with angular crystal strapping, signed 'Michael Harris - Mdina Glass - Malta'.

11½in (29cm) high

£1,800-2,200 **FLD**

A Mdina 'Fish' cased glass vase, designed by Michael Harris, etched 'Mdina'.

1981   *11in (28cm) high*

£140-180 **WW**

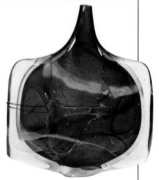

A Mdina 'Fish' cased glass vase, designed by Michael Harris, etched marks to base.

9¾in (24.5cm) high

£300-400 **WW**

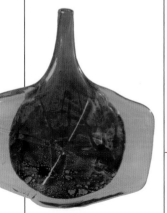

A Mdina 'Fish' glass vase, designed by Michael Harris, green mottled centre and cased in clear.

8¾in (22cm) high

£200-250 **DUK**

A Mdina large wrapped 'Fish' vase, unmarked.

9½in (24cm) high

£250-350 **FLD**

A Mdina glass vase, by Michael Harris, the green to blue swirling ground detailed with black linear designs, signed.

6¾in (17cm) high

£250-350 **FLD**

A late 20thC Mdina 'Attenuated Bottle' vase, by Michael Harris, with applied deep blue strapping over an amethyst ground, signed.

16¼in (41.5cm) high

£650-750 **FLD**

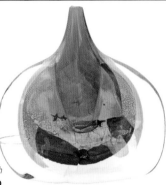

An Isle of Wight 'Fish' green azurene glass vase, the green ground with silver leaf, signed 'Michael Harris'.

7¾in (19.5cm) high

£400-500   **FLD**

A late 20thC Isle of Wight large 'Seascape Bell' vase, by Michael Harris, with veined blue patches over an opal and gold aventurine ground, numbered '46/500', signed.

This piece was formerly in the Ronald Stennett-Willson Collection.

9in (23cm) high

£750-850   **FLD**

A late 20thC Isle of Wight 'Undercliff' vase, by Michael Harris, with a stylised tree landscape over mottled ground, full engraved signature.

8¼in (21cm) high

£600-700   **FLD**

A late 20thC Isle of Wight 'Aurene' blue glass globe jar, signed by Michael Harris.

7½in (19cm) high

£100-150   **FLD**

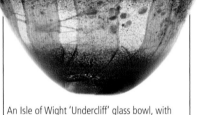

An Isle of Wight 'Undercliff' glass bowl, with blue, yellow and green concentric designs, signed 'Michael Harris'.

5in (12.5cm) high

£400-500   **FLD**

An Isle of Wight 'Seascape' glass box vase, by Michael Harris, signed.

12½in (32cm) high

£350-450   **FLD**

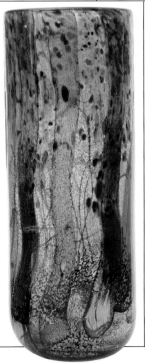

An Isle of Wight 'Undercliff' glass vase, by Michael Harris, with trees to the exterior side, picked out in brown, green and azurene, before a mottled ground, signed.

13¾in (35cm) high

£700-800   **FLD**

A late 20thC Isle of Wight 'Kyoto' glass perfume bottle.

6in (15cm) high

£120-160   **FLD**

GLASS

Judith Picks

I first came across Monart as a homesick Scot in London. Monart glass was made at the Moncrieff Glassworks in Perth, Scotland, from 1926-61. It was a collaboration between the Spanish glassmaker Salvador Ysart and Isobel Moncrieff, the wife of the factory's owner. 'Monart' comes from 'Moncrieff' and 'Ysart'. Salvador Ysart and his son Paul Ysart designed over 300 shapes, including vases, bowls, dishes and lamps. Most pieces were free-blown, and typically have vibrant colours and mottled patterns. Monart glass is not signed but bears a distinctive pontil mark. Before leaving the factory, every piece was given a sticky paper label. These were very often lost over time, so it is a great treat to a collector to discover one with the original paper label still present.

A Monart stoneware vase, of ovoid form with collar neck, shape A.
1930s   *6¾in (17cm) high*
£900-1,200   **FLD**

A Monart vase, shape CF.
c1935   *6in (15cm) diam*
£250-350   **M&DM**

A Moncrieff's Monart Ware glass vase, mottled green shoulder graduating to purple and blue with aubergine veins, cased in clear.
8in (20.5cm) high
£250-300   **WW**

A Moncrieff's Monart Ware vase, shape F, orange glass with green and ochre pulled stripes, unsigned.
8½in (21.5cm) high
£550-650   **WW**

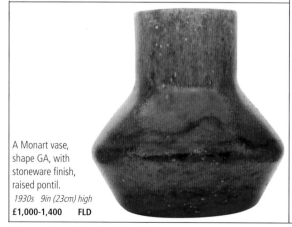

A Monart vase, shape GA, with stoneware finish, raised pontil.
1930s   9in (23cm) high
£1,000-1,400   FLD

A Monart vase, shape HF, colour 187, mottled purple and red over a cloisonné-type internally crackled turquoise body.
9½in (24cm) high
£400-500   **K&O**

A 20thC Monart cloisonné glass vase, shape MF, with crackled-surface decoration.
10¼in (26cm) high
£300-400   **ROS**

A Monart stoneware glass vase, shape N.

9½in (24cm) high

£500-600   ROS

A Monart vase, shape PA, in orange.

c1935

£350-450   M&DM

A Monart vase, shape SA.

c1935   7in (18cm) high

£300-400   M&DM

An unusual Moncrieff's Monart Ware vase, clear glass surface decorated with yellow, blue and metallic crackled patches, unsigned.

7in (18cm) high

£500-600   WW

A Monart glass vase, by John Moncrieff Ltd., 'Paisley' pattern, overlaid with swirls in silver, red and blue on a green body.

c1930   10in (25.5cm) high

£1,800-2,000   L&T

A Monart glass vase, stress cracks to base.

6½in (16.5cm) high

£250-300   WW

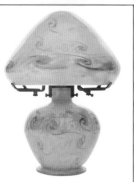

A Moncrieff's Monart Ware glass lamp base and shade, model VII, with brass tripod mount, unmarked.

See Ian Turner, 'Ysart Glass', Volo Editions (1990), pp.86-89 for two comparable mushroom-shaped lamps.

12½in (32cm) high

£2,000-2,500   WW

A Moncrieff's Monart Ware vase, decorated with yellow and lustred white stripes, applied collection label for the Ian Turner Collection.

This technique was achieved by blowing the glass into a dip mould with vertical grooves and then rolled in coloured glass powder.

5¼in (13.5cm) high

£800-1,000   WW

A Moncrieff's Monart Ware glass mushroom lamp and shade, with bronze tripod mount, applied retail paper label for Watson's China Hall, Perth.

13¾in (35cm) high

£1,600-2,000   WW

GLASS

QUICK REFERENCE - VENINI & C.

- A prominent figure in Italian glassmaking, Paolo Venini (1895-1959) founded Venini & C. in Murano in 1921, with Giacomo Cappellin.
- The company produced Art Deco glassware using Venetian glassmaking techniques.

- Designer Fulvio Bianconi (1915-96) worked with Venini, creating the Handkerchief vases in c1949. Other key designers include Napoleone Martinuzzi, Gio Ponti and Carlo Scarpa.
- In 2001, Venini was bought by Italian Luxury Industries.

A rare Venini 'Pezzato' glass vase, by Fulvio Bianconi, 'Istanbul' colour variation, with original manufacturer's label.

See 'Venetian Glass - The Nancy Olnick and Giorgio Spanu Collection', Edizioni Charta (2000), fig. 87.

c1951

£7,500-8,500　　　　　　　　　**FIS**

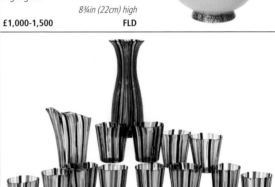

A mid-20thC Venini 'Laguna' vase, by Tomaso Buzzi, the coral-coloured body with aventurene highlights.

8¾in (22cm) high

£1,000-1,500　　　　　　　**FLD**

A set of 12 Venini 'A Canne' beakers, designed by Gio Ponti, including a jug and a carafe.

highest 10¼in (26cm) high

£4,000-5,000　　　　　　**SWO**

A Venini 'Tessuto' vase, by Carlo Scarpa, the body with a series of vertical green running lines before a segmented black and white ground, acid etched mark to base.

1950s　　　　*11½in (29cm) high*

£1,600-2,000　　　　　**FLD**

A Venini & C. 'Sommerso a Bollicine' shell, designed by Carlo Scarpa, stamped 'venini murano MADE IN ITALY'.

c1934　　　*2¾in (7cm) high*

£650-750　　　　　　**QU**

A Venini & C. 'A fili molato' vase, by Carlo Scarpa, clear glass, applied threads, unsigned.

c1942　　　*7¾in (19.5cm) high*

£4,500-5,000　　　　　**QU**

A post-war Venini glass Fazzoletto 'A Canne' vase, designed by Paolo Venini, remnant of label to base, acid-marked signature.

3¼in (8.5cm) high

£90-120　　　　　**FLD**

A post-war Italian Murano Venini glass 'Fazzoletto' vase, designed by Paolo Venini, acid-marked signature to base.

11in (28cm) high

£100-150　　　　　**FLD**

A Versace for Venini vase, with alternating panels of red, mauve and white glass, separated with vertical black lines, signed and dated to base.

c2010　　　*8in (20.5cm) high*

£450-550　　　　　**ROS**

QUICK REFERENCE - BAROVIER & TOSO

● The merging of Fratelli Barovier and Ferro Toso in 1936 formed the glassmaker that became known as Barovier & Toso in 1942. One of Barovier & Toso's leading designers was Ercole Barovier (1889-1974). Having worked at Fratelli Barovier, experimenting with new methods of bringing colour and texture to glass, Barovier produced pieces incorporating fused mosaic and 'Intarsio' glass, made up of geometric patterns in coloured glass.

A rare Barovier & Toso iridescent vase, by Ercole Barovier, thick-walled colourless glass with inserted air bubbles, decoration of stylised fish.

c1940   *11½in (29cm) high*
£5,500-6,000   **FIS**

A Barovier & Toso 'Oriente' vase, designed by Ercole Barovier, model no.24335, multicoloured ribbon rods and wavy threads, with original paper label.
1940   *10¾in (27.5cm) high*
£4,500-5,000   **FIS**

A Barovier Seguso & Ferro 'Laguna Oro' glass bowl, designed by Flavio Poli and Alfredo Barbini.
c1936   *5¼in (13.5cm) high*
£850-950   **FIS**

A Barovier & Toso blown iridescent glass vase, by Ercole Barovier.
1938   *12½in (32cm) high*
£1,300-1,600   **FIS**

A post-war Italian Murano glass vase, by Barovier & Toso, engraved signature to base.
13¾in (35cm) high
£150-200   **FLD**

An Italian 20thC Murano glass vase, in the style of Barovier, in clear crystal cased over deep red with internal trails of gold aventurine.
10in (25.5cm) high
£100-140   **FLD**

A 20thC Italian Murano glass duck, in the style of Barovier, the amber and gold aventurine interior encased with clear glass and applied black detailing to eyes, bill and neck.
11in (28cm) long
£100-150   **FLD**

A 20thC Italian Murano stylised glass bird, in the style of Barovier.
4½in (11.5cm) high
£70-100   **FLD**

A Fratelli Toso 'Murrine Redentore' vase, by Ermanno Toso, colourless glass with scattered multicoloured 'Murrine Redentore', surface acid-matted, with original label.

Fratelli Toso was established in 1854 by the Toso family. The six Toso brothers (Angelo, Giovanni, Carlo, Ferdinando, Liberato and Gregorio) were joined by Ermanno Toso in 1924. The company was known for producing colourful murrina pieces.

c1955   *13¼in (33.5cm) high*
£5,000-6,000   **FIS**

A Murano glass vase, possibly by Dino Martens for Aureliano Toso, of tapering form, with polychrome inclusions, with a label 'MADE IN ITALY', numbered '3509' in red.

See Marc Heiremans, 'Vetreria Aureliano Toso, Murano 1938-1968: Designs by Dino Martens, Enrico Potz and Gino Poli', Arnoldsche Art Publishers (2016), for similar designs by Dino Martens. The number '3509' relates to the model list and, even though this is incomplete, the date of similar numbers is 1952.

c1952   *14½in (37cm) high*
£1,200-1,600   **SWO**

A rare Fratelli Toso vase, designed by Ermanno Toso, colourless glass with re-melted murrine terrazzo, framed with 'nerox', original manufacturer's label.

1930s   *13½in (34.5cm) high*
£3,000-4,000   **FIS**

A Fratelli Toso 'Murrine Strisce con Nerox' vase, by Ermanno Toso, framed with 'Nerox', manufacturer's label.

c1930   *12in (30.5cm) high*
£6,000-7,000   **FIS**

A Fratelli Toso vase.

c1910   *8in (20.5cm) high*
£650-750   **FIS**

A Fratelli Toso 'Black Violet' glass vase, with scattered melted murrine in white and purple.

c1925   *14¾in (37.5cm) high*
£600-700   **FIS**

A Fratelli Toso vase, by Ermanno Toso, colourless glass with melted murrine no.41, manufacturer's label.

This was acquired from the sample collection of the manufactory, which makes it rare and desirable.

c1930   *10½in (26.5cm) high*
£10,000-12,000   **FIS**

A Fratelli Toso 'Millefiori' vase, by Ermanno Toso, blue and yellow murrines, before a purple ground, signed 'S. Nicola'.

1976   *6¾in (17cm) high*
£1,500-2,000   **FLD**

An Arte Vetraria Muranese (A.VE.M.) vase, by Aldo Nason, cased in translucent pink and blue over a foil aventurine ground with deep blue interior, unsigned.

10¾in (27.5cm) high

£2,500-3,000   **FLD**

An Italian A.VE.M. glass vase, designed by Giulio Radi.

1960s   *11in (28cm) high*

£200-250   **DAWS**

A rare 'Fenicio' vase, designed by Carlo Scarpa, Maestri Vetrai Muranesi, Cappellin & Co.

c1928/29   *9in (23cm) high*

£2,500-3,000   **FIS**

A Salviati 'Soffici' glass vase, by Christian Ghion, with a mitre-cut linear grid design over the black ground, with original box.

c2004   *8in (20.5cm) high*

£200-250   **FLD**

A Seguso Vetri d'Arte sommerso vase.

c1960   *9¾in (24.5cm) high*

£65-75   **FIS**

A Seguso Vetri d'Arte bowl, designed by Flavio Poli.

c1937   *4¼in (11cm) high*

£160-200   **FIS**

A pair of Seguso Vetri d'Arte vases, the clear glass decorated with mottled gold aventurine inclusions, unpolished pontil marks.

1940s   *14½in (37cm) high*

£350-400   **FLD**

An Aureliano Toso 'Trina' vase, designed by Dino Martens, in the form of a stylised chicken, slight damage.

1950   *8¾in (22cm) long*

£150-200   **FLD**

GLASS

A Murano Vistosi 'Pulcini' bird, by Alessandro Pianon, blown glass, murrines, patinated copper, unmarked, some scuffs.

1960s   *12in (30.5cm) high*
£5,000-6,000   **DRA**

A Murano Vistosi 'Pulcini' glass bird, by Alessandro Pianon, with a triangular pale blue body, dark blue spiral line and murrine glass eyes above clear crystal base with copper wire legs.

c1963   *6¼in (16cm) high*
£9,000-11,000   **FLD**

Judith Picks

And now my particular favourites! Established in Murano in 1945 by the Vistosi family, Vistosi became known for its lighting design, but also produced bright glassworks. Alessandro Pianon (1931-84) worked for Vistosi from 1956. His 'Pulcini' series of 1962 consisted of five coloured glass birds.

Each bird was hand-blown into a mould. Some had textured surfaces applied or were decorated with murrines, slices of multicoloured glass. The beaks and tails were pinched on and the metal sockets for the copper legs were set in clear glass applied after the making of the body. The 'Pulcini' birds were made in limited numbers and were very expensive. They are particularly difficult to give price ranges as prices vary considerably. They also have different personalities - some being more appealing than others!

A Murano Vistosi 'Pulcini' bird, by Alessandro Pianon (1931-84), blown glass, murrine, patinated copper, unmarked, scratches to body, pitting to chest, residue to interior.

1960s   *9½in (24cm) high*
£5,000-6,000   **DRA**

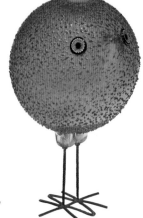

A Murano Vistosi 'Pulcino' bird, by Alessandro Pianon, with applied glass eyes standing on copper legs, unsigned.

c1960s   *8¾in (22cm) high*
£4,500-5,000   **ROS**

A Murano Vistosi 'Pulcini' glass bird, designed by Alessandro Pianon, with an olive green glass body, internal applied murrines in blue and orange, millefiori glass eyes, on copper wire feet.

This example was purchased by the vendor new directly from Vistosi in Murano on a family holiday, having driven there from the UK in 1964.

c1964   *8¼in (21cm) high*
£11,000-13,000   **FLD**

A mid-20thC Italian Murano sommerso glass stylised bear figurine, designed by Archimede Seguso, unmarked.

9½in (24cm) long
£100-150   **FLD**

A mid-20thC A.VE.M. glass model of a stylised aardvark, in the manner of Archimede Seguso, slight damage.

10in (25.5cm) long
£250-300   **FLD**

A post war Italian Murano glass stylised seagull, in the manner of Seguso, on a clear crystal stylised wave, unmarked.

10¼in (26cm) high
£150-200   **FLD**

A post-war Kosta 'Unika' glass vase, by Vicke Lindstrand, internally decorated, marked 'UNIKA 1713', engraved signature.

5in (13cm) high

£1,200-1,600   **FLD**

A Kosta 'Winter' glass vase, by Vicke Lindstrand, engraved signature 'Kosta LH'.

1950s   7¼in (18.5cm) high

£4,500-5,500   **FLD**

A Kosta 'Trees in Fog' glass vase, designed by Vicke Lindstrand, internally decorated with onyx stylised branches, acid stamped 'LIND-STRAND KOSTA LU2005'.

c1951   13¼in (33.5cm) high

£2,500-3,000   **FLD**

A Kosta Boda sommerso vase, designed by Vicke Lindstrand, marked 'LH1361'.

c1959

£275-325   **LYN**

QUICK REFERENCE - KOSTA

- ● Kosta glassworks was founded in 1742 by Anders Koskull and Georg Bogislaus Staël von Holstein in Småland, Sweden.
- ● Kosta designers include Vicke Lindstrand (1904-83), Bertil Vallien (b.1938), Elis Bergh (1881-1954), Anna Ehrner (b.1948) and Sven-Erik Skawonius (1908-81).
- ● Between 1950 and 1973, Lindstrand was Art Director at Kosta. He worked with engraved decoration on clear and coloured glass.
- ● A merging of glassworks in the areas of Kosta, Boda and Åfors bought the company under the control of the Afors Group in the early 1970s. In 1976, the company changed its name to Kosta Boda AB and became part of Orrefors Kosta Boda AB from 1989.

A Kosta crystal glass vase, designed by Vicke Lindstrand, the turquoise core surrounded by purple threads, engraved 'Kosta, LH 1720'.

c1958-62   6in (15cm) high

£400-500   **FLD**

A Kosta Boda 'Moonlanding' glass vase, designed by Monica Backström, original label, engraved signature.

c2000   8¼in (21cm) diam

£250-300   **SWO**

A late 20thC Kosta Boda 'Satellite' vase, by Bertil Vallien, original label, engraved signature.

11½in (29cm) high

£100-150   **FLD**

A late 20thC Kosta Boda bowl, designed by Bertil Vallien, 'Galaxy' pattern, no markings.

6¼in (16cm) diam

£80-120   **FLD**

A contemporary Artist's Collection Kosta Boda glass vase, designed by Bertil Vallien, engraved signature.

7½in (19cm) high

£150-200   **FLD**

GLASS

QUICK REFERENCE - ORREFORS

- Established in 1898 in Småland, Sweden, Orrefors began producing bottles and tableware. From the 1920s, the company's focus moved to art glass. It experimented with cameo glass, graal engraving and cut and engraved glass produced using a copper wheel.
- Key designers include Simon Gate (1883-1945), Edvard Hald (1883-1980), Ingeborg Lundin (1921-92), Sven Palmqvist (1906-84), Edvin Öhrström (1906-94) and Vicke Lindstrand (1904-83). Lindstrand worked for Orrefors between 1928 and 1941.
- The graal technique was developed by Knut Bergqvist. It featured internal decoration with a clear glass exterior. Graal came in various colours.
- In 1989, Orrefors merged with Kosta Boda.

An Orrefors graal vase, designed by Eva Englund, marked 'v968-75', 'Orrefors' and 'Eva Englund'.

Normally Graal vases have very thick walls; unusually, in this vase the glass is extremley thin, having the appearance of medieval or Roman glass.

6¼in (16cm) high

£220-250　　　　　　LYN

An Orrefors graal 'Fish' vase, by Edvard Hald, signed 'ORREFORS GRAAL 17980 Edvard Hald'.

c1955　　　　5in (12.5cm) high

£350-400　　　　　　BELL

An Orrefors graal fish bowl, by Edvard Hald, signed 'ORREFORS GRAAL 4390 Edvard Hald'.

c1955　　　7¾in (19.5cm) high

£400-500　　　　　　BELL

An Orrefors graal glass paperweight vase, by Edvard Hald, signed marks.

c1930　　　5in (12.5cm) high

£500-600　　　　　　DUK

An Orrefors 'Ariel' glass vase, by Ingeborg Lundin, signed 'ORREFORS No 179 E3 INGEBORG LUNDIN'.

c1973　　　6¼in (16cm) high

£400-500　　　　　　BELL

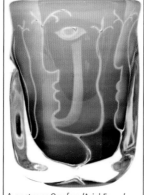

An Orrefors 'Ariel' glass vase, by Ingeborg Lundin, signed 'ORREFORS ARIEL No 718N INGEBORG LUNDIN'.

c1964　　　8in (20.5cm) high

£400-500　　　　　　BELL

A post-war Orrefors 'Ariel Faces' glass vase, by Ingeborg Lundin, internally decorated with stylised Picasso-esque faces with ariel band detailing, engraved signature.

7in (18cm) high

£3,000-3,500　　　　FLD

An Orrefors 'Ariel' glass vase, designed by Edvin Öhrström, etched signature and number '957913' with 'Orrefors Sweden' sticker.

8in (20.5cm) high

£1,200-1,600　　　　SWO

An Orrefors 'Kraka' vase, by Sven Palmqvist, with engraved signature to the base.

c1954　　　8¼in (21cm) high

£550-650　　　　　　FLD

A Flygsfors glass vase, etched mark.

17¼in (44cm) high

£100-150   SWO

A Hadeland slab-sided glass vase, by Hermann Bongaard, signed.

4¾in (12cm) high

£150-200   HAN

A Holmegaard Carnaby vase or candlestick, designed by Per Lutken.

The more common version of this vase has three layers of glass, not two, and an inner white core.

10¼in (26cm) high

£170-195   LYN

A pair of green glass 'Gulvvase' bottle decanters and ball stoppers, in the style of Holmegaard.

15½in (39.5cm) high

£200-250   SWO

A 'Stellaria' large serving bowl, designed by Tapio Wirkkala, manufactured by Iittala, Finland, signed to base.

c1960s   11½in (29cm) diam

£120-180   ROS

A post-war Iittala bamboo vase, designed by Tapio Wirkkala, engraved signature.

c1950s   6¾in (17cm) high

£300-350   FLD

A Nuutajärvi Notsjo glass 'Sieppo' or 'Flycatcher' figurine, designed by Oiva Toikka, original label, engraved signature.

c1972   5in (12.5cm) high

£300-350   FLD

A Nuutajärvi 'Ariel' glass bowl, by Kaj Frank, acid mark to the base.

4¼in (11cm) wide

£70-90   FLD

A Nuutajärvi Notsjo sommerso glass vase, designed by Kaj Franck, engraved signature, dated.

1961   4in (10cm) high

£150-200   FLD

A Steuben 'Partridge In A Pear Tree' sculpture, designed by Lloyd Atkins, signed 'Steuben' on base, with box.

designed 1968   6in (15cm) high

£700-800   **CLAR**

A 20thC Steuben blue 'Aurene' vase, marked, shallow chip to underside of base.

10½in (26.5cm) high

£750-850   **DRA**

An early 20thC Steuben 'Gold Aurene' trumpet vase, etched signature, numbered '2909', wear to iridescence, scuffs and scratches.

5¾in (14.5cm) high

£200-250   **DRA**

QUICK REFERENCE - STEUBEN

- Steuben was founded in 1903 in Corning, New York, by Frederick Carder (1863-1963). In 1918, it was acquired by Corning Glass Works, which is now Corning Incorporated.
- Carder patented an iridescent glass called 'Aurene' in 1904. It was produced in blue, brown, red and green.
- In 1933, a new formula for colourless crystal glass was introduced and Steuben moved away from producing coloured pieces.

A pair of early 20thC Steuben jade cameo glass vases, attributed to Frederick Carder, 'Bristol' pattern, unmarked, with scuffs and scratches throughout, ground down rims and bases, chip to one at body.

12¼in (31cm) high

£1,700-2,200   **DRA**

A Steuben glass vanity jar with threaded stopper, marked, acid-etched fleur-de-lis mark.

1903-33   6¼in (16cm) high

£150-200   **DRA**

A 20thC Steuben glass lion sculpture, on lacquered wood base, with original box.

7in (18cm) high

£600-700   **DRA**

A Steuben blue 'Aurene' intarsia glass vase, by Frederick Carder, unmarked, repaired crack to rim.

8½in (21.5cm) high

£120-180   **DRA**

An early 20thC Steuben gold 'Aurene' blown glass vase, on carved wood stand, etched 'AURENE 2412', wear to iridescent surface.

without stand 8in (20.5cm) high

£450-550   **DRA**

A 20thC Steuben 'Excalibur' paperweight, with sword, crystal and sterling silver, 18k gold, original box, marked, some small chips.

11in (28cm) high

£700-800   **DRA**

A late 19thC Stevens & Williams Osiris-type vase, on three clear rustic form feet.

Stevens & Williams was established in Stourbridge in 1847 and produced heavily cut crystal glass. The company's 'Rockingham' ware is especially sought-after. John Northwood was appointed Art Director in the 1880s. In 1919, Stevens & Williams received a Royal Warrant and later changed its name to Royal Brierley Crystal. The company went bankrupt in the 1990s, but in the early 2000s it was reopened under ownership of Dartington Crystal Ltd.

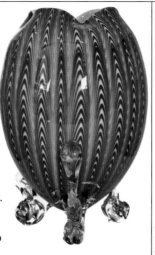

8¾in (22cm) high

£300-350 **FLD**

A late 19thC Stevens & Williams satin quilted air trap vase, slight damage.

9½in (24cm) high

£60-80 **FLD**

An early 20thC Stevens & Williams posy vase, pattern no.43686, dated.

1912 *8¼in (21cm) high*

£120-160 **FLD**

A Stevens & Williams Royal Brierley footed glass vase, designed by Keith Murray, unsigned.

14¾in (37.5cm) high

£200-250 **WW**

A Stevens & Williams glass tumbler vase.

1940s *8in (20.5cm) high*

£60-80 **FLD**

An early 20thC Stevens & Williams decanter, with silver collar, Sheffield, Hammond, Creak and Co., slight damage.

1904 *11in (28cm) high*

£550-650 **FLD**

A late 19thC Stevens & Williams 'Scrooge' decanter, collar neck with silver mounts, with a matched lobed stopper, hallmarked for Sheffield.

1898 *10¾in (27.5cm) high*

£120-160 **FLD**

A Stevens & Williams intaglio hock drinking glass, probably engraved by T.E. Wood, the bowl cut in the 'Willow' pattern.

8in (20.5cm) high

£1,100-1,400 **DUK**

A Stevens & Williams opaline glass bowl, by Will Capewell, with classical figurines in black enamel, unmarked.

1930s *6¼in (16cm) high*

£100-140 **FLD**

GLASS

QUICK REFERENCE - WEBB

● Thomas Webb & Sons was founded by Thomas Webb in Stourbridge in 1837. When Thomas Webb retired in 1869, his son Thomas Wilkes Webb took over the company. Webb employed freelance decorators, including French decorator and gilder Jules Barbe. The company became known for rock crystal-style glass, 'Cameo Fleur' glass and cameo glass. Thomas Webb & Sons became part of Webb's Crystal Glass Co., which was bought by Crown House Ltd. and then the Coloroll Group PLC. The factory closed in 1990.

A late 19thC Thomas Webb & Sons cameo glass vase, by the Thomas & George Woodall workshop, base faintly inscribed '1563'.

8in (20.5cm) high

£6,000-7,000   **FLD**

A late 19thC Thomas Webb & Sons cameo glass vase, with white metal collar to the rim.

2½in (6.5cm) high

£400-500   **FLD**

A Thomas Webb & Sons cameo glass vase, wheel-carved brambles, acanthus leaf border.

6¼in (16cm) high

£700-800   **DUK**

A Thomas Webb & Sons cameo glass vase, wheel-carved convolvulus flowers, insects and butterflies.

11¾in (30cm) high

£1,300-1,600   **DUK**

A Thomas Webb & Sons miniature cameo glass vase, wheel-carved flowers and insects.

3in (7.5cm) high

£550-650   **DUK**

A late 19thC Thomas Webb & Sons unfinished padded cameo glass vase, showing remains of the original pencil outline design.

£600-700   **FLD**

An early 20thC Thomas Webb & Sons glass vase, flash-cut with fish in reeds.

10½in (26.5cm) high

£100-140   **FLD**

A Webb cameo 'Fleur' glass vase, with textured finish, overlaid in pink with flower stems, Webb cameo signature.

8¾in (22cm) high

£200-250   **WW**

A pair of Webb Corbett Agate Flambé glass vases.

Webb Corbett Ltd. was formed in c1897 by Thomas and Herbert Webb, sons of Thomas Wilkes Webb, with George Harry Corbett.

1920s   *6¾in (17cm) high*

£100-140   **FLD**

QUICK REFERENCE - WHITEFRIARS

● In the late 17thC, a glassworks was founded at Whitefriars, off Fleet Street, in London. The site was previously a monastery of the Carmelite Fathers, known as the 'White Friars' due to their white habits. James Powell took over the glassworks in 1834, renaming it James Powell & Sons.

● In 1962, the company changed its name to Whitefriars Glass Ltd. However, glass produced from the 1830s to 1980 is usually referred to as Whitefriars.

● The factory struggled financially in the 1970s and closed in the 1980s. Scottish glassmaker Caithness bought the Whitefriars brand name.

A James Powell & Sons Whitefriars goblet, probably designed by Harry Powell, unsigned.

The melted threads relate to the Minerbi range of glass tableware designed by Harry Powell and produced by James Powell & Sons in 1906 as a 400 piece service for Count Lionel Minerbi.

8¼in (21cm) high

£1,200-1,600   WW

A James Powell & Sons Whitefriars 'Alsatian' blue glass goblet vase, designed by Harry Powell, unsigned.

8½in (21.5cm) high

£850-950   WW

A James Powell & Sons Whitefriars glass inkwell, probably designed by Harry Powell, with blue and white swirls and silver inclusions, with silver cover, stamped marks 'JP & Ss, London 1906'.

3¾in (9.5cm) high

£1,500-2,000   WW

An early 20thC Whitefriars golden amber 'Serpent' or 'Comet' vase, designed by Harry Powell, pattern no.1218.

9½in (24cm) high

£300-350   FLD

A Whitefriars ribbon-trailed bucket vase, in sea green and sapphire blue.

7¼in (18.5cm) high

£70-100   FLD

A Whitefriars footed bowl, by James Hogan, pattern no.8973.

1930s   *8in (20.5cm) diam*

£180-220   FLD

A Whitefriars 'New Studio' range vase, by Geoffrey Baxter, pattern no.9886.

Geoffrey Baxter (1922-95) joined James Powell & Sons as a designer in 1954, having studied at the Royal College of Art. Baxter became known for using unusual materials, such as nails, bark and wire, to make his initial moulds. Baxter worked for Whitefriars until the company's closure in 1980.

1970s   *7½in (19cm) high*

£200-250   FLD

A Whitefriars vase, designed by Geoffrey Baxter, pattern no.9700.

1960s   *7½in (19cm) high*

£100-150   FLD

A Whitefriars 'Swung Out' vase, designed by Geoffrey Baxter, pattern no.9650, clear crystal cased over willow.

1960s   *15¾in (40cm) high*

£200-250   FLD

A Whitefriars 'Banjo' vase, designed by Geoffrey Baxter, unsigned, in willow.

12½in (32cm) high

£650-750   **WW**

A Whitefriars 'Banjo' vase, designed by Geoffrey Baxter, unsigned, in Kingfisher blue.

12½in (32cm) high

£1,000-1,400   **WW**

A Whitefriars 'Banjo' vase, designed by Geoffrey Baxter, unsigned, paper label to base, in tangerine.

12½in (32cm) high

£850-950   **WW**

A rare Whitefriars 'Banjo' vase, designed by Geoffrey Baxter, unsigned, in aubergine.

12¾in (32.5cm) high

£2,000-2,500   **WW**

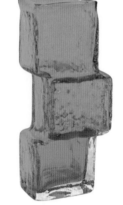

A Whitefriars reversed 'Drunken Bricklayer' vase, designed by Geoffrey Baxter, in tangerine.

8½in (21.5cm) high

£450-550   **WW**

A Whitefriars 'Drunken Bricklayer' vase, designed by Geoffrey Baxter, unsigned, in willow.

13in (33cm) high

£400-500   **WW**

A post-war Whitefriars 'Textured' range 'Bamboo' vase, designed by Geoffrey Baxter, pattern no.9669, in Kingfisher blue.

8¼in (21cm) high

£100-140   **FLD**

A Whitefriars 'Nuts and Bolts' vase, by Geoffrey Baxter, shape no.9668, in cinnamon.

10½in (26.5cm) high

£180-220   **DUK**

A Whitefriars vase, by Geoffrey Baxter, in willow, paper label.

c1967   *12¼in (31cm) high*

£250-300   **DUK**

A pâte-de-verre 'Roses/Ranunculus' glass box, by Gabriel Argy-Rousseau, model no.0108, pull-off cover, cast signature.

3¼in (8.5cm) diam

£1,000-1,500 **DUK**

An early 20thC Baccarat cameo glass vase, cased in ruby over citron and acid cut with a flowering bough with faint gilded highlights, unmarked.

6in (15cm) high

£250-300 **FLD**

An Art Deco Boom Glass 'Flamingo' vase, by Paul Heller, the black ground cut with a frieze of stylised flamingos on a silvered textured back, foil label.

11¾in (30cm) high

£500-600 **DUK**

A James Couper & Sons 'Clutha' glass vase, designed by Christopher Dresser (1834-1904), streaked green glass with air bubble inclusions and aventurine, unsigned.

15in (38cm) high

£1,500-2,000 **WW**

A James Couper & Sons 'Clutha' glass vase, by Christopher Dresser, acid-etched mark with Liberty's Lotus flower trademark, inscribed 'CLUTHA DESIGNED BY CD REGISTERED'.

c1900 *3¼in (8.5cm) high*

£800-1,000 **L&T**

A late 20thC Dartington vase, relief moulded with flower designs, all in a pale grey tint.

10in (25.5cm) high

£55-75 **FLD**

An early 20thC Daum cameo glass vase, cased in magenta over a mottled tonal red to orange ground, cut and engraved with campanula, engraved signature 'Daum Nancy', with the cross of Lorraine.

c1900 *13¾in (35cm) high*

£950-1,200 **FLD**

A Decorchemont pâte-de-cristal glass coupe, by François-Émile Décorchemont, cast with pairs of budgerigars, impressed seal mark, etched '0808' to base.

8in (20.5cm) wide

£1,200-1,600 **WW**

A French Devez cameo glass vase, the body with a sailing boat with mountains in the background, signed marks.

8½in (21.5cm) high

£400-500 **DUK**

GLASS

A Georges De Feure amethyst glass vase, made for Fauchon, relief moulded with classically dressed females, relief moulded signature.

5½in (14cm) high

£90-120 FLD

A Gallé cameo glass vase, the yellow body overlaid and acid-etched with clematis flowers and leaves, signed in cameo 'Gallé'.

c1910 *5¼in (13.5cm) high*

£650-750 ROS

A drinking glass, by Émile Gallé (1846-1904), decorated with enamelled flowers with gilt highlights, signed marks.

3¼in (8.5cm) high

£300-400 DUK

An Elizabeth Graydon-Stannus 'Graystan' glass vase, engraved signature.

1930s *7in (18cm) high*

£100-140 FLD

An early 20thC Fritz Heckert vase, possibly designed by Max Rade, hand enamelled, unmarked.

5¼in (13.5cm) high

£80-90 FLD

A Legras cameo glass vase, wheel-cut with holly leaves, berries and twigs on a yellow peach ground, signed in cameo.

11¾in (30cm) high

£500-700 DUK

An Art Deco Legras 'Neptune' glass vase, acid-etched and cut with stylised decoration, impressed marks.

17½in (44.5cm) high

£900-1,000 DUK

A Lobmeyr glass, signed.

Pieces that are produced for the Islamic market usually have Islamic calligraphy on them, but this is the only one with stylised animals.

c1885 *5in (12.5cm) high*

£1,300-1,600 M&DM

A late 19thC to early 20thC Mont Joye vase, enamel decorated with stylised flowers.

5¼in (13.5cm) high

£100-150 FLD

A Poschinger blue and purple vase, often mistaken for Loetz 'Phänomen' but equal quality.

c1900   *4in (10cm) high*

£1,500-1,800   **M&DM**

A pair of American Quezal iridescent glass bell-shaped shades, signed 'Quezal' with a 'Gold Aurene' iridescent interior.

c1910   *5in (12.5cm) high*

£250-300   **ROS**

A Richardson's 'Rich' cameo vase, with Richardson's 'Rich Cameo' mark.

1930s   *10in (25.5cm) high*

£100-200   **FLD**

A late 19thC Richardson's glass vase, in opaline with green and gilded decoration around floral panels, Richardson's mark to base.

13½in (34.5cm) high

£250-300   **FLD**

A mid-19thC Richardson's vase, decorated with Richardson's vitrified enamels, depicting Christ and the money lenders, enamelled mark.

10in (25.5cm) high

£250-300   **FLD**

A mid-19thC Stourbridge glass vase, probably Richardson's, painted in the Etruscan style, with a classical figure below a Greek key border.

9in (23cm) high

£90-120   **FLD**

A Rindskopf vase, with a tonal white and purple iridescent pulled and feathered design over the deep green ground.

13in (33cm) high

£250-300   **FLD**

An early 20thC Rindskopf vase, with a wrapped serpent in iridescent green over an iridescent apple green ground.

12¾in (32.5cm) high

£150-200   **FLD**

A large Rosenthal Studio abstract glass flower bowl, designed by Andy Warhol.

20½in (52cm) diam

£80-90   **PSA**

GLASS

An Art Deco Sabino iridescent powder box and cover, the lid decorated with three relief-moulded mermaids, marked to the lid.

1930s   *6¼in (16cm) diam*

£250-300   **FLD**

A Schneider 'Le Verre Français' cameo glass vase, decorated with dahlias, inscribed 'Le Verre Français, France', wear to base.

12½in (31.5cm) high

£500-600   **SWO**

A Schneider cameo glass vase, with mottled amber ground, cut with stylised flowers, in orange and blue.

8in (20.5cm) high

£500-600   **SWO**

A Stourbridge cameo glass vase, with images of parrots in branches, marked 'SGC' (Stourbridge Glass Co.), dated.

1983   *17in (43cm) high*

£350-400   **FLD**

A late 19thC Stourbridge glass vase, ribbed and decorated with a rainbow striped pattern.

9½in (24cm) high

£90-120   **FLD**

A late 19thC Stourbridge glass strawberry set, in pale ruby with applied white threading.

£50-60   **FLD**

A late 19thC Stuart & Sons vase, with applied clear rigger work garlands and raspberry prunts.

6½in (16.5cm) high

£75-95   **FLD**

An early 20thC Stuart & Sons glass vase.

11¾in (30cm) high

£150-200   **FLD**

A Stuart & Sons glass cocktail shaker, with chromed fittings, acid marked.

1930s   *9in (23cm) high*

£120-160   **FLD**

An early 20thC glass vase, by L.C. Tiffany, decorated with a repeat green and pearlised swirl design, full engraved signature.

5½in (14cm) high

£500-600   **FLD**

An L.C. Tiffany 'Heart and Vine' Favrile vase, decorated with murines (paperweight canes), signed.

c1902   *4in (10cm) high*

£2,500-3,000   **M&DM**

An L.C. Tiffany experimental Favrile vase, coded with an 'X', signed.

c1900   9in (23cm) high

£2,000-2,500   M&DM

A mid-20thC Val St Lambert cut glass vase, 'Bolero', by Charles Graffart, signed 'Val St Lambert'.

8in (20.5cm) high

£80-120   **ROS**

An Art Deco Val St Lambert 'Ardennes' glass vase, in an amethyst-brown tint with gilt highlight, stylised decoration.

10¼in (26cm) high

£500-700   **DUK**

A mid-20thC Val St Lambert 'Propeller' vase, engraved signature.

10¾in (27.5cm) high

£60-80   **FLD**

An Art Deco Verart glass vase, acid cut with a repeat abstract panel pattern over the cinnamon ground, signed 'VERART Paris'.

1930s   12½in (32cm) high

£150-200   **FLD**

A Walsh Walsh 'Vesta' statue, by Walter Gilbert, 'Hercules and the Cretan Bull'.

c1929   *6½in (16.5cm) high*

£700-900   **M&DM**

A late 19thC to early 20thC John Walsh Walsh 'Opaline Brocade' vase, unmarked.

11¼in (28.5cm) high

£150-200   **FLD**

GLASS

A John Walsh Walsh cut clear glass fan vase, with applied green glass teardrops cut with feather motif, unsigned.

10¼in (26cm) high

£350-400   **WW**

A WMF 'Ikora' glass vase, internally decorated with white fissuring over the tonal orange ground, unmarked.

1930s   *8¼in (21cm) high*

£75-95   **FLD**

An early 20thC WMF 'Myra Crystal' glass vase, with a gold petrol iridescence, unmarked.

3¼in (8.5cm) high

£100-140   **FLD**

A set of five mid-20thC novelty 'Mickey Mouse' band cocktail glasses, with lampworked 'Mickey Mouse'-style musician figure stems.

4in (10cm) high

£300-400   **FLD**

A late 19thC Continental glass vase, in the style of Mary Gregory with a white enamelled female figure.

10¾in (27.5cm) high

£120-160   **FLD**

A late 19thC satin quilted 'air trap' jug, in a graduated blue to maroon, with a diamond design.

9in (23cm) high

£150-200   **FLD**

A late 19thC to early 20thC twin-handled pedestal vase, engraved with classical profiles.

8in (20.5cm) high

£250-300   **FLD**

A late 19thC Bohemian ruby glass pedestal bowl, with panels of enamelled decoration of children, some damage.

7in (18cm) high

£200-250   **FLD**

A late 19thC 'Amberina' glass vase, with enamelled and gilt trailing flowers.

9in (23cm) high

£45-65   **FLD**

A contemporary studio glass vase, designed by Martin Andrews, from his 'Stone' series, with black and white mottled and linear design over a deep blue ground, unsigned.

Martin Andrews studied at West Surrey College of Art and Design, graduating in 1991 with a B.A. (Hons) Glass. In 2000, he opened a workshop at the Ruskin Glass Centre, Stourbridge. All Andrews' pieces are handmade and signed.

5½in (14cm) high

£100-150   **FLD**

A hand-blown 'Koi Glass' graal-type vase, by Vic Bamforth, cased in clear crystal with Koi carp, engraved signature, numbered 1 of 1, dated.

Vic Bamforth (b.1952) studied at Buckinghamshire Chilterns University College and Dudley International Glass Centre, graduating with a diploma in Glass Techniques and Technology and an Advanced Diploma in Glass Design. Bamforth is based at the Ruskin Glass Centre, Stourbridge.

2007   *7½in (19cm) high*

£450-550   **FLD**

A 21stC glass vase, by Guido van Besouw (b.1951), signed and numbered to base.

Guido van Besouw (b.1951) was apprenticed to glassmaker Anton Voorveld before becoming a full-time glass artist in 1980, producing windows for churches and private residences. Van Besouw set up his own studio and began making glassware in the late 1990s.

20½in (52cm) high

£400-450   **ROS**

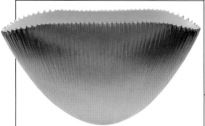

A large 'Fin' bowl, by Laura Birdsall, of compressed ovoid form, cased in olive green over white over lime green and cut with a vertical ripple line rising to a fine scalloped rim, engraved signature.

Laura Birdsall is based in North Yorkshire, where she makes blown glass vessels with strong sculptural qualities. Birdsall's inspiration is often some small detail in nature, such as a seed pod or a fish's fin.

2014   *14½in (37cm) wide*

£500-600   **FLD**

A contemporary glass sculpture, by Tim Boswell, engraved signature to base.

10¾in (27.5cm) high

£200-250   **FLD**

A glass seaform, by Dale Chihuly (b.1941), signed 'Chihuly PP97'.

8¼in (21cm) high

£2,500-3,000   **POOK**

A late 20thC studio glass vase, by Norman Stuart Clarke, with random whiplash lines over a silver iridescent ground, signed, dated.

1996   *7½in (19cm) high*

£200-300   **FLD**

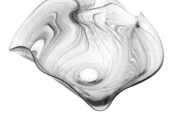

A large 'Contour' bowl, by Bob Crooks, in mixed colour palette with lattachino thread work, engraved signature.

c2000   *21in (53.5cm) wide*

£800-900   **FLD**

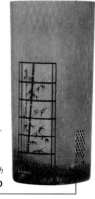

A Osiris Studio glass vase, by Iestyn Davies, cased in green over deep amethyst and acid-cut with a window revealing bamboo shoots, dated.

1986   *11½in (29.5cm) high*

£300-350   **FLD**

GLASS

A Salviati 'Goccia di Poggia' glass vase, by Christian Ghion, with original box.

c2007   8¾in (22cm) high

£220-280   FLD

An 'Aesculus' bowl, by Stephen Gillies and Kate Jones, cased in purple to the exterior and pale blue to the interior and cut with wave lines over the clear crystal ground, signed, dated.

2004   11½in (29cm) wide

£2,200-2,800   FLD

A contemporary studio glass sculpture in the form of a pumpkin, by Richard P. Golding, engraved signature.

6¾in (17cm) high

£150-200   FLD

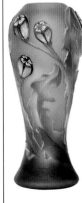

A late 20thC Okra studio cameo glass vase, by Richard P. Golding and Sarah Cowan, cased in green and opal over the red ground cut with poppy heads among leaves and detailed with enamelling, numbered 16 of 50, engraved signature.

See Charles R. Hajdamach, '20th Century British Glass', Antique Collectors' Club Ltd. (2009), for a comparable example.

1 9in (23cm) high

£300-350   FLD

A contemporary Jonathan Harris 'Unique Golden Graal' vase, decorated foliate scrolls in gold leaf over a mottled cinnamon ground, engraved signature.

The Jonathan Harris Art Glass Studios was set up in 1999 at the Coalport China Museum at the Ironbridge Gorge, near Telford, by Jonathan Harris and his wife Alison. However, Harris had been producing glassware for over 20 years, focusing on cameo and Graal glass.

2003   8in (20.5cm) high

£200-250   FLD

A large British studio glass 'Untitled' sculpture, by Sam Herman, made using the wet stick process at the Jam Factory, South Australia, with applied and melted-in, silver chloride trails, and browny-green applied mottles, the base inscribed 'Samuel J. Herman 1978 SA1853', with 'Sam Herman Glass' Lots Road studio paper label.

Sam Herman introduced the use of the wet stick technique at the Jam Factory in 1974 in order to make the largest pieces he could while working alone. After the body had been partially blown and decorated, a wet stick was forced into the mass. The heat of the glass caused the water in the stick to turn into steam, which caused the body to expand and swell, creating a random, bulbous form. This is an example in colours typical of his work in South Australia.

11½in (29cm) high

£1,200-1,800   DAWS

A Sam Herman glass vase, cased in clear glass, streaked, etched signature and date.

1970   7¼in (18.5cm) high

£250-300   WW

A Sam Herman solifleur vase, with metallic oxide pale blue streaked glass body with swollen green knop, unsigned.

11¾in (29.5cm) high

£400-500   WW

A Loco Glass unique sculptural glass vase, by Sam Herman, with silver leaf inclusions, signed.

From The Private Collection Of Samuel (Sam) J. Herman.

Sam Herman (b.1936) studied at the University of Wisconsin before gaining a Fulbright Scholarship to study at the Edinburgh College of Art in 1965. Herman then became the head of the Royal College of Art's glass and ceramics department, where he remained until 1974. Herman set up the Glasshouse in Covent Garden in 1969. In 1974, Herman opened a glass workshop at the Jam factory in Adelaide, Australia, before returning to the UK in 1979 to set up a studio in London. In 1984, Herman moved to Mallorca and focused on his painting and sculpture work. Since then he has only made glass on a handful of occasions, at Adam Aaronson's studio in West London in 2007, at Peter Layton's London Glassblowing studio in London in 2012 and at Loco Glass in Gloucestershire from 2015-16. Herman estimates that he made less than 90 pieces of glass between 1984 and 2017, making later vases such as this very rare.

15¼in (39cm) high

£2,200-2,800   DAWS

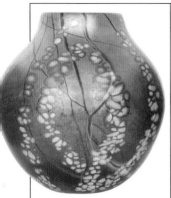

A Peter Layton chalcedony flared vase, incised signature to base.

Made at the London Glassblowing Workshop.

Peter Layton (b.1937) studied at Bradford Art College and London's Central School of Art and Design, specialising in ceramics. While teaching at the University of Iowa, USA, in 1965, Layton became interested in glass and enrolled on the University's glass blowing programme. After returning to the UK in 1968, Layton opened a glass studio in the Scottish Highlands. In 1976, he opened the London Glassblowing Workshop at Rotherhithe, before moving the studio to Bermondsey Street.

A Brideshead studio glass vase, by Siddy Langley, decorated in a petrol iridescent with white spotting and whiplash lines, engraved signature, dated.

1998   *8¾in (22cm) high*
£260-300   **FLD**

9½in (24cm) high
£300-350   **WW**

A late 20thC Peter Layton vase, cased in turquoise decorated with blue and ochre flashes over an opal interior, engraved signature.

9in (23cm) high
£220-280   **FLD**

A large contemporary studio glass 'Un-refined Arch' sculpture, by Allister Malcolm.

Featured in the 2008 International Festival of Glass British Biennale.

11¾in (30cm) high
£1,500-2,000   **FLD**

A Richard Marquis free-blown teapot, with multicoloured murrines, signed 'Marquis 1979-4CQ'.

1979   *3in (7.5cm) wide*
£2,500-3,000   **FIS**

A late 20thC studio glass vase, by Karlin Rushbrook, engraved signature.

9in (23cm) high
£150-200   **FLD**

A Melting Pot Glassworks studio glass vase, by Robin Smith and Jeff Walker, signed to base.

9¾in (24.5cm) high
£180-220   **CHOR**

A 'Garden' bowl, by Pauline Solven, engraved signature, dated.

1996   *6in (15cm) high*
£150-200   **FLD**

A contemporary 'Vertical No.35' glass piece, by Rachael Woodman, mounted to a black slate base, signed, dated.

Rachael Woodman (b.1957) studied at the Orrefors Glass School, in Sweden, and the Royal College of Art, London. Between 1986 and 2005, Woodman worked as a designer for Dartington Crystal.

2004   *6½in (67.5cm) high*
£1,400-2,000   **FLD**

GUITARS

A Danelectro DC59 12-string guitar, the lightweight hollow body with single F-hole, in black finish with white pickguard, fitted with two single-coil 'lipstick' pick ups, one master volume, one master tone and three-way selector, with padded carry bag.

c2015-16

£250-400   SWO

A Danelectro Bellzouki 7020 12-string guitar, in metallic blue finish, with two single coil lipstick pickups, three-way selector switch, volume, tone and master knobs, and chrome hardware, with soft case, with 'Andy's Guitar Workshop, 27 Denmark Street, London' label to the reverse of the headstock.

Developed in the early 1960s by American session guitarist Vinnie Bell, the electric Bellzouki was inspired by the traditional 8-string Greek Bouzouki, an acoustic instrument with a pear-shaped body. The early models of the electric Bellzouki (model no.7010) also had pear-shaped bodies, but the revised models as here (no.7020) featured four notches in the body, making the instrument more stable on the thigh when played sitting down.

c1965

£400-700   ROS

An Epiphone EB-3 bass guitar, with stained mahogany body and mother-of-pearl inlaid rosewood fretboard, serial no.1208201654, light wear and minor surface scratches as expected in the usual places, plus a dent and small area of damage to the edge upper left side of body, and pitting to the metalwork, with hard case.

2012

£150-250   APAR

A Fender Stratocaster-style electric guitar, the metallic orange body fitted with Charvel SoCal electrics, including Seymour Duncan 'Distortion' pickups, with G&G hard case and strap.

This guitar was constructed from Warmoth parts by the renowned Suffolk-based luthier Andrew Guyton, best-known for his restoration of Queen guitarist Brian May's original and iconic 'Red Special', and his internationally acclaimed authorised limited (50) edition replicas of the latter in 2004.

£500-700   SWO

A Fender Custom Shop '61 Relic Stratocaster, the alder body finished in Aztec Gold, complete with original paperwork and tags, with G&G vintage flight case.

2017

£1,500-2,000   SWO

Judith Picks

Provenance, and indeed the lack of it, can be an important factor in determining the value of musical instruments (as it is for almost all collectables). However, there's provenance, and then there's provenance. For example, the mid-1970s-made standard Fender Jazz bass with three-tone sunburst finish shown here, bought in 1981 and subsequently played by bassist Noel Redding (1945-2003), will currently cost you £3,000-4,000. In contrast, exactly the same mid-70s bass, in similar condition but without any affiliation to Noel Redding (or, indeed, any other famous rock musician), would currently set you back about £1,200-2,000. So, this particular provenance roughly doubles the price. However, and this is a big however, if the same Fender Jazz bass had been made in the mid-1960s (as many were), and if it had been the one bought by Noel Redding and played by him from 1966-69 while he was the bass player in one of the most innovative and iconic rock bands of all time, namely the Jimi Hendrix Experience, then you would have to dig significantly deeper into your pocket to buy it. Back in 1980, Noel Redding did in fact sell his original mid-60s Hendrix-period Jazz bass to a private collector, for the sum of £10,000. Forty years on, I wonder just how many more tens of thousands it would go for!

A Fender Jazz bass guitar, with three-tone sunburst finish, played by Noel Redding, formerly of the Jimi Hendrix Experience, serial no.670644, accompanied by a receipt signed 5 December 1981 by Noel Redding acknowledging payment of a deposit of £200 for the guitar.

1975

£3,000-4,000   WHYT

A Gibson SG Classic electric guitar, made in the USA, with red-stained solid mahogany body, rosewood fretboard, P90 pickups, with hard case.

2004

£500-700   SWO

A Gibson Les Paul 60s Tribute electric guitar, the weight-relieved solid mahogany body with carved maple top and tobacco sunburst finish, rosewood fretboard, P90 pickups, serial no.160055255, with hard case.

2016

£500-700   SWO

A Gibson Custom Shop 1958 Explorer re-issue, the elbow-cut mahogany body with two humbucker pickups, rosewood fretboard, white pickguard with applied Clockwork Orange sticker, with original case and certificates.

2014-18

£1,800-2,500   GHOU

A Gibson ES-335 TD 12-string semi-hollow electric guitar, made in Kalamazoo, USA, in vintage sunburst finish, its Brazilian rosewood fretboard with 22 frets, fitted with two humbucker pickups, three-way toggle pickup selector, two volume and two tone knobs, and chrome stoptail, serial no.403438, in original hard case, with CITIES licence no.580443/1.

Introduced by Gibson in 1958, and still in production, the 6-string ES-335 features a double cutaway body with arched top and back constructed of laminated maple, incorporating a sold block of maple running through its centre – a semi-solid design that produced much of the warmth of hollow body guitars, while eliminating much of the feedback associated with the latter. Notable players have included Chuck Berry, Eric Clapton, Keith Richards, and Larry Carlton. The 12-string version, as here, was originally produced 1965-70.

1966

£2,000-3,000   ROS

A Luthier-built Fender-style Telecaster, with a Hipshot 'String Bender' mechanism, maple neck, and an Asher Guitars tortoiseshell pickguard.

Invented c1968, a 'B-Bender' mechanism employs a series of levers or pulleys inside or outside the guitar body which, when activated by a pull or push of either the guitar neck, bridge, or body (as with the Hipshot mechanism), bends the B string up by as much as a minor third (three frets). The resulting change in tone sounds similar to a pedal steel guitar, and consequently the 'B-Bender' is primarily associated with Country music. However, rock musicians, notably Jimmy Page, Keith Richards and Ronnie Wood, have also used it to distinctive effect.

£400-500   SWO

A Vox V257 Mando 12-string electric guitar, made in Italy, in two-tone dark sunburst finish, with double T-bar neck, two single-coil pickups, a three-way toggle selector, volume and tone knobs, and chrome hardware, serial no.334144, with original hard case, with CITES licence No.580443/2.

In 1964, a prototype version of the guitar was given to George Harrison of The Beatles and to Brian Jones of the Rolling Stones.

c1964-66

£900-1,200   ROS

A Vox V251 guitar organ, the maple Phantom body with white polyester finish, the 21-fret maple neck with rosewood fretboard, fitted with two single-coil pickups and six organ tone generator circuits, and chrome hardware, serial no.73059, with original PSU and hard case.

Only approximately 400 of these organ guitars were made. The first, a prototype, was in 1964 given by it's inventor, Vox engineer Dick Denny, to John Lennon of The Beatles. Because of its stellar provenance, this model sold at Sotheby's in 2014 for £179,148.

c1966

£1,500-3,000   ROS

JEWELLERY

A silver-gilt and blue enamel butterfly brooch, by Child & Child, the wings engraved with veins and decorated with shaded blue enamel, the body set with demantoid garnets, maker's mark to reverse, fine hairline cracks to enamel, fitted case.

c1905   *2.5in (6cm) wide*

£7,500-8,500   **WW**

An Arts & Crafts silver brooch, attributed to Dorrie Nossiter, set with a cluster of moonstones, native-cut sapphires and zircons with matching polished bead fringe, fitted Dorrie Nossiter case.

c1930   *2¾in (7cm) high*

£4,000-5,000   **WW**

An early Victorian 15ct gold and amethyst brooch.

3in (7.5cm) long 0.67oz

£1,000-1,500   **FELL**

An early 19thC gold cameo brooch, the agate cameo carved to depict a lady in profile, with split pearl, single and rose-cut diamond surround, signed 'Pestrini', French assay marks.

2½in (6.5cm) long 0.83oz

£2,500-3,000   **FELL**

A Victorian yellow gold opal and diamond tubular scroll drop brooch, in box.

2¾in (7cm) long 0.46oz

£450-550   **PW**

A late Victorian silver and gold opal and diamond brooch, some surface scratches and wear.

1¼in (3cm) diam 0.17oz

£900-1,100   **FELL**

A late Victorian gold, diamond and enamel brooch, with a vari-cut diamond and blue enamel star-set dome, inset to the rose-cut diamond, some surface scratches and wear.

2¼in (5.5cm) long 0.57oz

£1,500-2,000   **FELL**

A 19thC oval cameo pendant/ brooch, depicting a Roman gladiator driving a chariot pulled by two prancing horses.

2¾in (7cm) long

£550-650   **BE**

A late 19thC enamelled baroque pearl and rose diamond brooch.

1¾in (4.5cm) long 0.56oz

£300-400   **BE**

An Edwardian yellow metal bar brooch, set with peridot and small pearls.

0.18oz

£90-110   **WHP**

An Egyptian yellow metal scarab beetle brooch, with hardstones including moss agate, amber, chalcedony and turquoise, each carved with a different hieroglyph to the reverse, unmarked.

7¾in (19.5cm) long 0.74oz

£350-400   **APAR**

A mid-20thC turquoise and ruby brooch, designed as a textured owl.

1½in (4cm) long 0.43oz

£650-750   **FELL**

A vintage Continental turquoise-set dragonfly brooch, gilt-metal stamped '800', the gilding is thin and worn.

This is an inexpensive example of a popular 19thC theme.

2in (5cm) long

£350-450   **CHEF**

An 18k yellow gold and enamelled frog brooch, with red and clear stone eyes.

2in (5cm) long 0.5oz

£500-600   **DUK**

An 18ct gold poodle brooch, diamond collar and ruby eyes.

0.54oz

£550-650   **LOCK**

An enamel ladybird and arrow diamond brooch, mounted in white and yellow metal testing as silver and 9ct, largest rose-cut diamond is 0.33ct, evidence the brooch is made from two pieces.

¾in (7cm) long 0.4oz

£1,500-2,000   **ECGW**

A turquoise and ruby flower head brooch, with petals, stamped '18K'.

1960s   1½in (4cm) wide

£500-600   **DN**

An enamel and diamond cluster brooch, with eight cut-diamond accents, approximately 0.35ct total, stamped '750'.

1960s   1¾in (4.5cm) diam

£600-700   **DN**

A citrine and emerald owl brooch.

1970s   1½in (4cm) long 0.79oz

£2,000-2,500   **FELL**

A cat brooch, with round cut emerald eyes, mounted in 18ct yellow gold, hallmarked London.

1980   1¾in (4.5cm) high 0.41oz

£500-600   **ECGW**

JEWELLERY

An early 19thC 18ct gold enamel locket, with inscription 'a mon amie,' to the interior, Swiss marks.

2½in (6.5cm) long 0.74oz

£850-950   **FELL**

A Victorian carved coral pendant, mounted in gold.

2½in (6.5cm) high

£220-280   **LC**

A Victorian turquoise gilt-metal set pendant.

1½in (4cm) high

£400-500   **LC**

A Revivalist gold pendant, with enamel portrait, locket compartment to the reverse, on a fine link gold chain, in the style of Falize.

c1885   pendant 1½in (4cm) high

£1,200-1,600   **WW**

A 19thC gem-set snake necklace and locket, with three cabochon turquoises and garnet cabochon eyes, with a diagonal stripe of four turquoises separated by a quatrefoil of seed pearls, bordered with black enamel.

15½in (39.5cm) long

£850-950   **CHEF**

A Victorian hairwork, coral and seed pearl pendant, unmarked yellow metal tests for gold, with light wear and tear.

2in (5cm) long 0.5oz

£400-500   **CHEF**

A late 19thC gold enamel and diamond pendant, in the manner of Riker Bros., suspending a pearl, on fine-link gold neck chain set with a diamond.

pendant 1¾in (4.5cm) long

£1,800-2,200   **WW**

A 19thC pinchbeck shell cameo necklace, with six oval shell cameo panels, with textured fancy-link connecting chains and push-piece clasp.

16¼in (41.5cm) long

£300-350   **FELL**

A late 19thC gold micro-mosaic pendant, may be worn as a brooch.

2¼in (5.5cm) long 0.96oz

£3,000-3,500   **FELL**

An Arts and Crafts gold, amethyst and opal pendant, with a gold-filled chain.

pendant 2in (5cm) long

£1,300-1,600   **NA**

An Arts and Crafts silver-gilt and enamel pendant, by Omar Ramsden, engraved to the reverse 'ELLEN MAYNARD LEWIS MAYORESS 1922-23 and OMAR RAMSDEN ME FECIT'.

pendant 1¾in (4.5cm) long

£1,200-1,600 WW

An Arts and Crafts silver and enamel pendant, attributed to Ramsden & Carr, decorated with three flowerheads each set with a garnet cabochon, enamel ground cracked.

c1905 pendant 2½in (6.5cm) high

£1,400-1,800 WW

An Art Nouveau Charles Horner silver and enamel pendant necklace, stamped marks, Chester, indistinct date code.

1¼in (3cm) wide

£350-400 WW

An Art Nouveau Murrle Bennett & Co. enamelled pendant, set with an oval-cut mother-of-pearl, with an unmarked white metal chain.

17in (43cm) long

£350-400 DUK

An early 20thC gold, sapphire and diamond pendant, with later trace-link chain, may be worn as a brooch, estimated diamond weight 0.90ct.

pendant 1½in (4cm) long 0.34oz

£900-1,000 FELL

An Edwardian Liberty & Co. gold, turquoise and pearl necklace, with fitted case.

15½in (39.5cm) long 0.36oz

£2,500-3,000 FELL

A silver and turquoise Navajo 'Squash Blossom' necklace, of white metal, with numbers to reverse '499' above '24' above '7387'.

10.16oz

£400-500 CHOR

A Cartier 18ct gold dice locket, with four internal compartments, signed 'Cartier London, _3352', partially indistinct, hallmarks for London.

1955. 1½in (4cm) long 1.09oz

£1,800-2,200 FELL

A 9ct gold triangular-link necklace.

14½in (37cm) long 1.5oz

£600-700 BE

An Indian gem-set silver and gold pendant, set with emeralds, rubies and rose-cut diamonds with a fringe of seed pearls, on a link gold chain set with ruby and emerald beads and seed pearls.

This comes with the original purchase receipt from The Gem Palace, Jaipur, dated 9 March 1998.

pendant 1½in (4cm) high

£600-700 WW

JEWELLERY

A Victorian yellow metal-hinged snap bangle, set with five old European round and oval-cut diamonds, total 1.10ct, light surface scratches.

2in (5cm) wide 0.85oz

£1,200-1,600   **APAR**

A mid-19thC citrine-set gold bangle, the oval-shaped citrine set within yellow gold ropetwist surround, with seed pearls, French marks.

2½in (6.5cm) diam 2.57oz

£1,800-2,200   **WW**

A Victorian Etruscan-style 15ct coral and pearl hinged bangle, unmarked.

£400-500   **FLD**

A 19thC Indian gold bracelet, with eight miniature paintings on ivory, depicting famous Indian temples.

7in (18cm) long

£850-950   **PW**

A Victorian hinged bangle, set with lapis lazuli and pearls, unmarked, tested as 18ct.

£750-850   **ECGW**

A lady's yellow metal pearl-encrusted bangle, with central diamond, test as 14ct gold, three pearls missing.

0.31oz

£300-350   **LOCK**

A Victorian amethyst five stone ring, set in 15ct gold.

size M½

£170-220   **LC**

A silver and green agate foliate bracelet, design no.3, stamped 'Sterling Denmark' and with maker's mark.

post-1945   *7¼in (18.5cm) long*

£1,800-2,200   **WW**

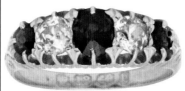

A Victorian 18ct gold, sapphire and diamond-set five stone ring, Birmingham.

1895   *size P½*

£450-500   **BELL**

A late Victorian emerald and diamond panel ring, the old cut diamonds, 0.54ct total, set in 15-18ct gold, emeralds rubbed to the crown, one emerald probably a replacement.

c1900   *size K*

£700-800   **DN**

A Chanel 'Profil de Camelia' dress ring, signed 'Chanel, 20H 2768'.

size L

£400-450 **FELL**

A pair of sapphire and diamond earrings, by Child & Child, sapphires approximately 2ct, maker's mark.

c1905 *1¼in (3cm) high*

£2,200-2,800 **WW**

A pair of diamond and sapphire pendant earrings, with Continental hook and clip fittings, white and yellow metal stamped '750'.

c1910-25 *1¼in (3cm) long*

£4,000-4,500 **CHEF**

A pair of sapphire and diamond floral earrings, estimated diamond weight 0.25ct.

½in (1.5cm) long ¼oz

£650-700 **FELL**

A pair of Kutchinsky 18ct gold diamond earrings, with vari-cut diamond line accents, signed 'Kutchinsky', estimated diamond weight 0.80ct, partial hallmarks.

1in (2.5cm) long 1oz

£2,500-3,000 **FELL**

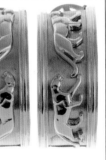

A pair of Cartier 18ct gold 'Panthere de Cartier' earrings, with walking panther motif, signed 'Cartier, 655935', French assay marks.

1½in (4cm) long 1.64oz

£2,500-3,000 **FELL**

A pair of Cartier 'Trinity' earrings, signed 'Cartier, 987509', stamped '750'.

1in (2.5cm) long

£700-800 **FELL**

A pair of Chaumet 18ct gold diamond and ruby earrings, with scattered brilliant-cut diamond and marquise-shape ruby highlights, signed 'Chaumet', estimated total diamond weight 0.40ct, import marks for London.

1968 *1¼in (3cm) long 1oz*

£2,000-2,500 **FELL**

A pair of early 20thC emerald and diamond hair clips, emeralds are all abraded or chipped.

1¾in (4.5cm) long

£550-600 **CHEF**

An Arts and Crafts silver belt buckle, by Ramsden & Carr, with an enamel monogram 'E*C*R', linked to two embossed side sections each set with a rough turquoise, London hallmarks, maker's mark, in original fitted box.

1901 *4¾in (12cm) wide*

£1,200-1,600 **WW**

JEWELLERY

QUICK REFERENCE - GEORG JENSEN

- Georg Jensen Co. was founded in Copenhagen in 1904 by silversmith and jewellery designer Georg Jensen (1866-1935). Jensen's jewellery designs were inspired by the Arts and Crafts and Art Nouveau movements.
- Georg Jensen Co. has employed many talented designers, including Johan Rohde (1856-1935), Harald Nielsen (1892-1977), Arno Malinowski (1899-1976), Henning Koppel (1918-81) and Vivianna Torun Bülow-Hübe (1927-2004).
- The company is still operational today.

A Georg Jensen silver and enamel brooch, designed by Arno Malinowski, no.284, stamped marks.

1¼in (3cm) wide

£550-650   WW

A Georg Jensen sterling silver brooch, designed by Arno Malinowski, no.250.

1½in (4cm) square

£220-280   LOCK

A Georg Jenson sterling silver cockerel/rooster brooch, no.276.

1½in (4cm) square

£220-280   LOCK

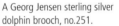

A Georg Jensen sterling silver dolphin brooch, no.251.

1½in (4cm) wide

£200-250   LOCK

A Georg Jensen silver pendant bird necklace, designed by Arno Malinowski, model no.97, stamped marks.

1½in (4cm) high

£300-350   WW

A Georg Jensen silver link necklace, model no.826S, cast with flowerhead panels, the links set with green chrysoprase, stamped marks.

17½in (44.5cm) long

£1,800-2,200   WW

A Georg Jensen silver necklace, model no.270, each link modelled as a stylised seed pod, stamped marks.

17¾in (45cm) long

£1,100-1,500   WW

A Georg Jensen silver necklace, designed by Astrid Fog, model no.122, stamped marks.

pendant 2in (5cm) long

£650-750   WW

An early 20thC Georg Jensen 18ct gold labradorite ring, maker's mark, '111', stamped 'GI, 111, 18k, 765', some surface scratches.

size L½ 0.18oz

£1,500-2,000   FELL

A pair of Balenciaga gold-plated metal, blue enamel, plastic and rhinestone earrings.
1980s   *2¼in (5.5cm) long*
£150-200   **GRV**

A pair of Chanel gilt-metal and glass earrings.
1950s   *1½in (4cm) long*
£500-600   **GRV**

A pair of Chanel gold-plated metal and Gripoix glass earrings.
1994
£400-450   **GRV**

A pair of Coppola e Toppo gilded metal and glass earrings.
1960s
£350-450   **GRV**

A pair of Christian Dior silver-tone metal and rhinestone earrings.
1990s
£150-200   **GRV**

A pair of Jomaz green glass, rhinestone and gold-tone metal earrings.
1960s   *2¼in (6cm) long*
£250-300   **GRV**

A pair of Kramer silver-tone metal and rhinestone earrings.
1950s
£75-100   **GRV**

A pair of Christian Lacroix gold-plated metal earrings, with rhinestones, velvet and faux pearls.
1990s
£250-300   **GRV**

A pair of Napier silver-tone metal and rhinestone earrings.
1950s
£75-100   **GRV**

A pair of Louis Rousselet gold-tone metal and glass earrings.
1940s
£150-200   **GRV**

A pair of Trifari gold-tone metal and enamel earrings.
1960s   *2in (5cm) long*
£75-150   **GRV**

A pair of silver, marcasite, carnelian glass and paste earrings.
1920s
£350-400   **GRV**

A Ciro sterling silver and rhinestone brooch.

1930s   *2¼in (6cm) long*

£175-225   **GRV**

A Christian Dior rhodium-plated metal, rhinestone and turquoise glass brooch.

1968   *1¾in (4.5cm) long*

£250-300   **GRV**

A Coro gold-plated sterling, enamel and rhinestone brooch.

1944

£150-200   **GRV**

A Miriam Haskell gilded metal and glass brooch.

1950s

£150-200   **GRV**

A Hobé gold-plated metal, enamel, rhinestone and glass demi-parure.

1966

£120-180   **GRV**

A Knoll and Pregizer silver and paste brooch.

1930s

£250-300   **GRV**

Judith Picks

I've always loved the glamour of Joseff of Hollywood. Eugène Joseff was born in 1905 in Chicago. In the late 1920s, he moved to Los Angeles to train as a jewellery designer and to exploit one of the few booming industries of the period: Hollywood.

Joseff soon met with incredible success, both as a designer and a supplier of jewellery to the major film studios. He developed a coppery-gold coloured matte finish (known as Russian gold), which minimised the problem of over-reflectivity when filming gold jewellery under studio lights. He leased his pieces to the studios and was able to accumulate an archive of nearly three million pieces available for hire.

From 1937, Joseff developed a retail line of jewellery, sold via some 500 'exclusive' stores throughout the USA and abroad. It is these pieces that are now so much in demand. He died in a plane crash in 1948.

A Joseff of Hollywood Russian gold-plate and glass demi-parure.

1940s

£350-400   **GRV**

A Henry Perichon silver and glass brooch.

1960s

£300-350   **GRV**

A Roger Jean Pierre silver, rhinestone and glass demi-parure.

1950s

£450-550   **GRV**

An Yves Saint Laurent gold-plated metal brooch.

1980s

£80-120   **GRV**

An Archimede Seguso for Chanel glass and gold-tone metal necklace.
1960s
£220-280   **GRV**

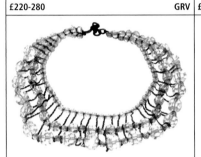

A Christian Dior 'Aurora Borealis' crystal necklace, signed.
c1950
£250-300   **SWO**

A Christian Dior gold-plated metal necklace.
1970s
£350-400   **GRV**

A Joseff of Hollywood Russian gold-plate and glass necklace.
1960s
£450-500   **GRV**

A Ciner gold-plated metal and enamel necklace.
1970s
£150-200   **GRV**

A Christian Dior by Mitchel Maer rhodium-plated metal, glass and rhinestone full parure.
1952-56
£1,000-1,200   **GRV**

A Jomaz rhodium-plated metal and rhinestone necklace.
1940s
£275-350   **GRV**

A Louis Rousselet Bakelite, glass, faux pearl and base metal necklace.
1930s   *17¼in (44cm) long*
£150-200   **GRV**

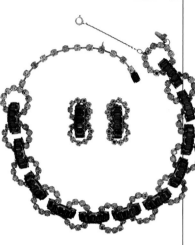

A Christian Dior gold vermeil-plated and green rhinestone necklace and earrings set, designed by Mitchel Maer.
1950s   *necklace 14½in (37cm) long*
£750-850   **GRV**

QUICK REFERENCE - LAWRENCE VRBA

● **Lawrence (Larry) Vrba worked as a designer for Miriam Haskell in the 1960s and 1970s. In the early 1980s, Vrba set up his own jewellery business. Vrba has created pieces for theatre shows, including 'Wicked' and 'Hairspray', cinema and private customers.**

A Lawrence Vrba brass, glass and plastic demi-parure.
£650-750   **GRV**

A Selro silver-tone metal, thermoset plastic and rhinestone demi-parure.

Selro was founded by Paul Selenger in the 1940s. Selenger was born in Russia in 1911 and emigrated to New York, USA, in 1927. Before setting up his own company, Selenger worked for jewellery company H. Pomerantz & Co. in New York. He also made jewellery under the name of Selini. Selro closed in the mid-1970s.

1960s

£250-350 GRV

A Czechoslovakian gilt-metal, enamel, glass and paste necklace.
1910s
£200-250 GRV

A chrome-plated metal, glass and paste necklace.
1920s
£250-350 GRV

A Piel Frères gilt-metal, enamel and glass buckle.
c1900
£750-850 GRV

A Limoges copper and enamel bracelet.
1950s
£150-200 GRV

A Jean Painlevé brass and plastic bangle.
1930s
£150-200 GRV

An Elsa Schiaparelli rhodium-plated metal and glass bracelet.
1950s
£250-300 GRV

A carved bakelite bangle.
1930s
£350-400 GRV

An Anna Greta Eker silver ring.
1970s
£250-300 GRV

A Trifari silver-tone metal and rhinestone ring.
1960s
£80-120 GRV

QUICK REFERENCE - OIL LAMPS

- An oil lamp produces light using an oil-based fuel source. The use of oil lamps began thousands of years ago.
- Oil lamps were used as an alternative to candles before the use of electric lights. Starting in 1780, the Argand lamp quickly replaced other oil lamps still in their basic ancient form. These in turn were replaced by the kerosene lamp in about 1850.
- Sources of fuel for oil lamps include a wide variety of plants such as nuts (walnuts, almonds) and seeds (sesame, olive, castor, flax). Also widely used were animal fats, including butter, fish oil, shark liver and whale blubber. Camphine, a blend of turpentine and alcohol, was the first 'burning fluid' fuel for lamps after whale oil supplies were depleted. It was replaced by kerosene after the US Congress enacted excise taxes on alcohol to pay for the American Civil War.

A Victorian oil lamp and shade.

£65-85   PSA

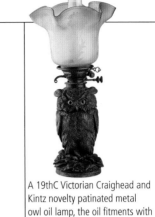

A 19thC Victorian Craighead and Kintz novelty patinated metal owl oil lamp, the oil fitments with marks 'OSBERT HENDERSON/ GLASGOW'.

19½in (49.5cm) high

£500-700   L&T

A Victorian oil lamp, with brass base and cranberry shade.

£170-200   PSA

A 19thC Victorian enamelled opaque glass and brass oil lamp, with a Palmer & Co. patent fitting and Rococo-style brass base.

35in (89cm) high

£350-450   L&T

A Jesson Birkett & Co. patinated copper ceiling light, collar set with three Ruskin Pottery turquoise stones, unsigned.

The Birmingham Arts and Crafts metalworking business of R. LL. B. Rathbone, part of which was taken over by the Faulkner Bronze Company in 1902, was reconstituted as Jesson, Birkett & Co., in 1904. This company took over more of Rathbone's business, but was liquidated in 1910.

24¾in (63cm) drop

£2,000-2,500   WW

A Continental Arts and Crafts bronze table lamp, the shade inset with glass 'jewels', the band pierced with panels depicting a hunting scene, impressed monogram.

23¾in (60.5cm) high

£650-750   DUK

An Edwardian silver Corinthian column oil lamp, made by Mappin & Webb, with diamond cut and engraved frosted glass shade, shade with two chips to bottom rim, burner has been re-plated.

1902   *30¼in (77cm) high*

£850-950   LSK

An Art Nouveau 'Le Lumiere de Nancy' silvered metal figural table lamp, with Le Verre Français glass shade, signed.

16¼in (41.5cm) high

£300-350   WW

A pâte-de-verre 'Chrysanthemum' glass lamp, by Gabriel Argy-Rousseau (1885-1953), cast signature, on a tripod bronze base, with incised geometric decoration.

6¼in (16cm) high

£900-1,200　　　　　　　　　　**DUK**

A Degué 'Cristalleries de Compiègne' cameo glass lamp, with conical glass shade, signed, on a scrolling ironwork base.

8¾in (22cm) diam

£300-350　　　　　　　　　　**CHOR**

An Art Deco Degué 'Cristalleries de Compiègne' chandelier, signed, a few shades with minor chips.

31½in (80cm) high

£450-550　　　　　　　　　　**CHOR**

A patinated metal figural table lamp, in the manner of Josef Lorenzl (1892-1950), on alabaster base, with frosted glass shade, unsigned.

8in (20.5cm) wide

£300-350　　　　　　　　　　**WW**

An Art Deco adjustable brass table lamp, the shade inset with four tinted blue glass panels.

13¼in (33.5cm) high

£220-280　　　　　　　　　　**DUK**

An Art Deco-style lamp, in the form of a metal figurine of a dancer.

25¼in (64cm) high

£220-280　　　　　　　　　　**CHOR**

An Art Deco table lamp, with a glass globe shade, chrome mounts and a reeded Bakelite column.

16½in (42cm) high

£250-350　　　　　　　　　　**SWO**

A French Art Deco table lamp, with a frosted glass shade, mounted on a cast plinth.

17¾in (45cm) high

£300-400　　　　　　　　　　**SWO**

An Art Deco cast lamp, with a moulded glass shade on a brass and silvered cast stand.

22½in (57cm) high

£300-350   **SWO**

An Italian 14-light chandelier, in the manner of Fontana Arte, with smoky glass shades.

c1950   *20in (51cm) high*

£1,500-2,000   **ROS**

A Flos 'Arco' floor lamp, by Achille and Pier Giacomo Castiglioni, the steel shade, on adjustable arm to Carrera marble base, applied label.

c1990   *86½in (220.5cm) high*

£800-900   **ROS**

Judith Picks

This is the epitomy of the Art Deco style. Lamps incorporating elegantly posed nude or barely clothed athletic ladies were typical of this period. Their poses were largely based on earlier Modernist ideals about health, exercise, and athletics. Some were, however, based on dance movements or the expensive highly fashionable bronze and ivory figurines designed by sculptors such as Ferdinand Preiss. The use of figural forms for lamps (or candlesticks) was not a new idea, from Blackamoors of the Georgian period to all manner of forms from warriors to shepherds during the Victorian period. Later examples were often made from spelter alloy, which was less expensive than bronze, lighter in weight, but more brittle. Always look for good proportions and quality in terms of pose, finishing and details such as the face and hands.

An Art Deco table lamp, modelled as a fan dancer after Guerbe, with signature, some wear to the nude, fan appears plastic not glass.

19¾in (50cm) high

£2,000-2,500   **SWO**

A pair of Fog and Mørup ceiling lights, designed by Jo Hammerborg.

18¼in (46.5cm) high

£120-160   **SWO**

A Fontana Arte Italian glass five-light ceiling light, in the style of Max Ingrand.

67in (170cm) high

£5,500-6,500   **SWO**

A pair of black lacquered and brass desk lamps, by Louis Christian Kalff.

c1950s   *15in (38cm) high*

£750-850   **ROS**

A J. Lüber AG 'SP2' ceiling light, by Verner Panton, in silvered plastic, the mount, with hanging spiral droplets.

c1969   *57½in (146cm) high*

£4,000-5,000   **ROS**

A CLOSER LOOK AT A LUMITRON LAMP

Robert Welch (1929-2000) was a leading British designer best known for his stainless steel tableware.

In 1986, Welch was commissioned by lighting company Lumitron to design a light. He was inspired by mid-century modern Scandinavian examples. This is shown by the clean lines, acrylic and silvered metal.

The range included a spherical-form ceiling light and a taller floor lamp.

Many examples were retailed through Habitat (founded by Terence Conran in 1964).

A Lumitron table lamp, designed by Robert Welch.

21in (53.5cm) high

£150-200　　**WW**

A pair of Martinelli Luce 'Pipistrello' table lamps, designed by Gae Aulenti.

34¾in (88.5cm) high

£1,000-1,500　　**SWO**

A Memphis 'Charleston' standard lamp, by Martine Bedin, with lacquered aluminium frame, with label.

c1984　　*77½in (197cm) high*

£1,200-1,500　　**ROS**

A gilt-metal ceiling light, by Oliver Messel, of sunburst form, with matching ceiling rose.

c1960　　*17¼in (44cm) diam*

£500-600　　**L&T**

A 1950s Italian Stilnovo-style chandelier, in gilt metal and enamel.

36¼in (92cm) high

£1,000-1,500　　**BELL**

A 1970s pair of large Murano glass lamps, with painted shades.

£300-350　　**SWO**

An Italian brushed steel and glass five-light chandelier, by Gaetano Sciolari.

c1970　　*27½in (70cm) high*

£400-500　　**SWO**

An Italian Stilnovo desk lamp, on brass support and metal splay feet, shade support split, adjuster screw inoperable.

1950s　　*18¼in (46.5cm) high*

£400-500　　**CHOR**

An Ives, Blakeslee & Co. 'Bulldog Savings' mechanical bank, clockwork activated, press lever and dog springs forward and bites/swallows coin from man's hands.
c1878
£2,000-3,000   BER

A Kyser & Rex 'GLOBE SAVINGS FUND' semi-mechanical bank, extensive casting effects with colourful highlights in red and gold, bronze dragons seated at roof, combination lock at front door.
c1889
£2,000-3,000   BER

A Kyser & Rex 'Organ Grinder and Performing Bear' mechanical bank, when wound the bear revolves as organ grinder turns organ handle.
c1882
£4,500-5,500   BER

A Jerome B. Secor 'FREEDMAN'S BANK' mechanical bank, the seated man thumbs his nose and gives a jeering look to depositors when clockwork is activated, minor repair to head.

This bank gains its inspiration from the Freedman's Bank for newly freed slaves as established by US Congress. Less than ten known examples of this bank still exist in what has come to be considered one of the best-known historically important banks ever made.
c1880
£100,000-150,000   BER

A Kyser & Rex cast iron 'Mammy and Child' mechanical bank, with original spoon, trap replaced.
7¾in (19.5cm) high
£1,800-2,200   POOK

A J. & E. Stevens Co. classic Americana 'Darktown Battery' mechanical bank.
c1888
£9,000-10,000   BER

A J. & E. Stevens Co. 'Calamity' mechanical bank, place a coin in the slot in front of the full back and press lever, as the players crash together at front, coin drops into the receptacle.
c1904   *7½in (19cm) high*
£3,500-4,500   BER

A J. & E. Stevens Co. 'Acrobat' mechanical bank.
c1883
£9,500-11,000   BER

A rare American 'Sewing Machine' mechanical bank, coin slot appears on table.

This bank was reportedly given away by the American Sewing Machine Co.
c1880s
£8,000-9,000   BER

MECHANICAL MUSIC

A German silver automaton musical box, the hinged lid enclosing a rotating singing bird, stamped '800', in a Tessiers Ltd. New Bond Street retail box, bellows in need of attention.

4¼in (11cm) wide

£2,000-2,500   **BE**

An early 20thC German symphonion, with 32 discs, the double combe with serial number '290472', in a walnut case with brass claw feet.

20in (51cm) wide

£900-1,200   **DUK**

A late 19thC Swiss walnut and rosewood banded music box, the mechanism playing eight airs via pinned brass cylinder and tuned steel combs, the lid with hand-written tune sheet inscribed 'no.7219', some wear.

12¼in (31cm) long

£2,000-2,500   **DN**

A Swiss filigree gilt singing bird box.

4in (10cm) long

£2,500-3,000   **JN**

A musical box, playing ten airs, eighteen-key organ section, tune card, cylinder 9¼in (23.5cm), with crossbanded rosewood lid.

26in (66cm) wide

£1,800-2,200   **FLD**

A 19thC coin-operated walnut wall-mounted polyphon, with twenty-eight 50cm-diameter disks.

49¼in (125cm) high

£2,500-3,000   **APAR**

A style 104 upright polyphon, by Nicole Frères, coin operated, carved walnut case playing 19⅝in discs on duplex combs, serial no.8931, on a later bin stand with fall front to reveal twenty-five discs.

82in (208.5cm) high

£5,500-6,000   **FLD**

A rare American Wurlitzer 'Peacock' type 850 juke box, designed by Paul Fueller, serial no.788323, amusement machine no.3738, expiring 30 June 1948, playing twenty-four 10in 78 rpm records, in veneered wooden case, the front in glass, chrome, Plexiglass and walnut veneer, coin selectors taking 25¢, 10¢ and 5¢ pieces.

Launched in 1941, just before America entered World War II, the 'Peacock' was regarded as the decorative top of the range at the time and is one of the larger and showiest jukeboxes ever made.

1940s   *68in (172.5cm) high*

£18,000-22,000   **HT**

A Continental oak-cased wind-up gramophone, with green tin horn.

1920s   *12¼in (31cm) wide*

£350-400   **FLD**

A Graphophone type Q phonograph, with small witches hat-type horn, oak case on plinth base.

10½in (26.5cm) wide

£260-300   **FLD**

A Columbia Graphophone Co. phonograph, with key-wind operation, fixed horn and original reproducer.

13½in (34.5cm) long

£150-200   **FLD**

An Edison Gem phonograph, serial no.G118804, model C reproducer with horn and six cylinders.

£250-300   **FLD**

An Edison Gem phonograph, serial no.G116835, model B reproducer and key-wind operation, with later aluminium horn.

10in (25.5cm) wide

£260-300   **FLD**

An Edison Standard phonograph, with a brass-finished horn and a group of cased cylinders, in an oak case.

£300-350   **WHP**

An Edison 'Fireside' phonograph, serial no.13685, four to two minute play, with combination model reproducer, with original fireside horn and crane, in oak case.

11½in (29cm) wide

£550-650   **FLD**

A French Pathé phonograph, later aluminium horn and stencilled walnut case.

11¾in (30cm) wide

£200-250   **FLD**

A Pye 'Stereophonic Projection System', in a mahogany case, with instructions and guarantee, working order.

1967   *22¼in (56.5cm) wide*

£200-250   **SWO**

An Akai Model X-355 Cross Field Head 4-Track stereo recorder, with original instructions.

£250-300   **SWO**

METALWARE

A pair of Victorian steel scissors, by Joseph Cousins, stamped 'J. COUSINS & SONS SHEFFIELD'.

By repute these were made for the Great Exhibition at Crystal Palace in 1851.

10½in (26.5cm) long

£350-400   **WW**

A W.A.S. Benson copper and brass hand candlestick, foliate design by George Heywood Sumner, stamped Benson shield mark to brass handle.

9in (23cm) high

£800-900   **WW**

A 19thC brass dog collar, with padlock.

3in (7.5cm) diam

£120-160   **LOCK**

A late 19thC ornate brass coal bin, with foliate scrolls and shell surmount.

£650-750   **BRI**

A late Victorian brass vesta case, modelled as a hand clasping a scroll.

For Smoking, see pp.337-341.

2½in (6.5cm) high

£45-55   **FELL**

A Keswick School of Industrial Art copper letter rack, with repoussé work, titled 'Post', stamped.

8in (20.5cm) wide

£250-300   **FLD**

A pair of Stickley Brothers hammered copper candlesticks, with brass bands, marked '131', rims bent out of form.

c1915   *12in (30.5cm) high*

£850-950   **DRA**

A World War I trench art model of a brass post office pillar box, engraved 'GR', inset with an aluminium collection time plaque.

6½in (16.5cm) high

£200-250   **FLD**

A Roycroft hammered copper and enamel vase, designed by Walter Jennings, with etched dogwood pattern and Italian enamel decoration, incised with orb and cross mark with two dots for Walter Jennings.

The Roycrofters, an Arts and Crafts community, was founded in 1895 in East Aurora, New York, by Elbert Hubbard (1856-1915). While Roycroft began as a publishers, a blacksmiths was added in 1899 and a copper shop in 1902. Copper ware was sold commercially from 1906. Roycroft pieces are patinated. Notable craftsmen include Karl Kipp and Walter Jennings. Production ceased in 1938.

c1915-20   *7in (18cm) high*

£2,200-2,800   **WES**

An Art Deco table mirror, by Émile Jacques Ruhlmann (1879-1933), on a waterfall front walnut stand.

16¼in (41cm) high

£650-700   **DUK**

An American 19thC painted tin folk art weathervane, of a firefighter, traces of original paint, extremely worn, lacking post.

30in (76cm) high

£950-1,100   **DRA**

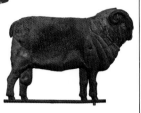

An American 19thC Merino ram molded sheet iron weathervane, horn present but detached, part of head on one side missing, wear throughout.

34in (86.5cm) long

£750-900   **DRA**

An American 'Polo Players' enamelled wrought iron weathervane, by William Hunt Diederich (1884-1953), unmarked, repainted.

46in (117in) long

£12,000-15,000   **DRA**

A Victorian painted cast iron fox head doorstop.

5¾in (14.5cm) high

£350-400   **WW**

A Victorian cast iron heraldic doorstop, of a greyhound with its paw resting on a shield, with a faint registration lozenge.

18in (45.5cm) high

£650-750   **WW**

A William IV bronze shell decorated doorstop, on a scroll weighted base.

14½in (37cm) high

£140-180   **WW**

A Victorian brass doorstop, in the form of a basket of fruit and flowers, on a weighted base.

14in (35.5cm) high

£450-550   **WW**

An early Victorian brass doorstop, of a fox emerging from foliage, with a leaf and flower scroll handle.

16½in (42cm) high

£1,300-1,600   **WW**

A 19thC brass sphinx doorstop, on a polished cast iron plinth.

15½in (39.5cm) high

£150-200   **WW**

A Victorian brass lion's paw doorstop, with weighted base.

14½in (37cm) high

£140-180   **WW**

METALWARE

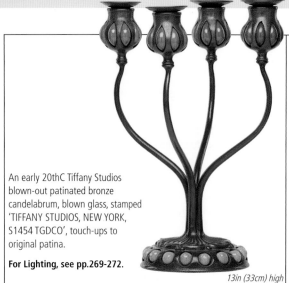

An early 20thC Tiffany Studios blown-out patinated bronze candelabrum, blown glass, stamped 'TIFFANY STUDIOS, NEW YORK, S1454 TGDCO', touch-ups to original patina.

For Lighting, see pp.269-272.

13in (33cm) high

£2,000-2,500   DRA

An early 20thC Tiffany Studios patinated bronze lamp base, stamped 'TIFFANY STUDIOS, NEW YORK, 540', rewired.

13in (33cm) high

£1,500-2,000   DRA

An early 20thC Tiffany Studios fleur-de-lis gilt-bronze candelabrum, stamped 'TIFFANY STUDIOS, NEW YORK, 1230', with cipher, some wear.

8¾in (22cm) high

£350-450   DRA

A Tiffany Studios patinated copper and glass outdoor sconce, unmarked, verdigris throughout, original screw/screw caps, all but one glass panel replaced.

c1900   *22½in (57cm) high*

£2,000-2,500   DRA

A 20thC style of Tiffany bamboo patinated and bronzed metal table lamp base, spurious mark, with mottled verdigris patina.

21in (53.5cm) high

£1,500-2,000   DRA

An early 20thC Tiffany Studios 'Seven Zodiac' acid-etched gilt-bronze desk set, all marked.

largest 9½in (24cm) long

£800-900   DRA

A Tiffany Studios 'Adam' acid-etched, enamelled and gilt-bronze picture frame, stamped 'TIFFANY STUDIOS, NEW YORK, 1610', some light wear, glass possibly replaced.

1920s   *12in (30.5cm) high*

£850-950   DRA

An early 20thC Tiffany Studios 'Pine Needle' patinated bronze and slag glass picture frame, stamped 'TIFFANY STUDIOS, NEW YORK', etched '147', a Y-line crack to one large piece of glass, few minor dents.

9¼in (23.5cm) high

£1,200-1,600   DRA

A Tiffany & Co. yellow gold champagne swizzle stick, stamped by the maker.

4¾in (12cm) high

£500-600   DRA

A Victoria Burma medal, awarded to 1418 Corp. S. Helsby 1st Bn. R.W.

£220-280   PSA

A Punjab medal, with two clasps for Chilianwala and Goojerat, named to Cornet F.C.J. Brownlow, 1st Bengal Cavy.

1849

£850-950   CHEF

An India General Service medal, with Pegu clasp, named to Lieutenant Colonel G.W. Osborne 19th Madras Native Infantry.

1854-95

£350-450   CHEF

An Army of India medal, with Ava clasp, awarded to Captain John Wilson 30th N.I., with ribbon.

1799-1826

£850-950   CHEF

An India General Service Medal, with Perak clasp, named to Lieutenant H.A.Rigg Rl. Arty., with partial ribbon.

1854-95

£250-350   CHEF

An Indian Mutiny one-clasp 'Delhi' medal, awarded to Captain G.G. McBarnet, 55th Bengal Native Infantry, in frame.

George Gordon McBarnet was the son of Donald McBarnet Kingussie and Insh, Inverness-shire, Scotland. He was born 8 October 1823 and later became captain in the 55th Bengal Native Infantry, attached to the 1st Bengal European Fusiliers. He was killed in action at the assault of Delhi during the Indian Mutiny on 14 September 1857.

1857-58

£1,300-1,600   BRI

An India medal, with Punjab Frontier 1897-98 clasp, named to 526 Sergeant J. Smith 3d Bn Rifle Brigade, with copy medal roll.

1896

£250-300   LOCK

A Malaya General Service medal, with clasp awarded to '2252647 SIGMN K.T BEAUMONT R.SIGS'.

£45-55   PSA

A South African medal, awarded to '2621 GNR. J.BIRCH. 19th Bty.R.F.A', with the following clasps, South Africa 1902, South Africa 1901, Transvaal, Orange Free State, Cape Colony.

£150-200   PSA

A Naval General Service medal, with renamed inscription for John Brookfield, Copenhagen 1801 bar and ribbon.

£650-750   HT

A British South Africa Company medal, with 'Rhodesia 1896' reverse, awarded to Trooper R. Dickson, Belingwe Column.

£400-500   LOCK

A gilt Victorian 6th Royal Warwickshire Regiment helmet plate.

£1,000-1,400 LOCK

An Austro Hungarian Empire Austrian pilot's badge, toned.

£120-180 LOCK

A small WM HP, or puggaree, of the Hong Kong Volunteer Corps Garrison Artillery, with slide. *1902-08*

£750-850 W&W

A possibly World War I London Scottish Regiment unmarked silver officer's Glengarry badge, rusty stout pin to reverse.

1⅜oz

£160-200 LOCK

A Churchill's Secret Army enamel badge, '1-202-3', fitting to the reverse.

£450-500 LOCK

A Victorian officer's gilt and silver-plated helmet plate, of The Middlesex Regiment.

£180-220 W&W

An officer's gilt and silver-plated shako plate, of The 65th 2nd Yorkshire N. Riding Regiment, shallow dents to Garter. *1861*

£250-300 W&W

A Women's Land Army distinguished service badge, inscribed on the back 'E. Brooke 27.11.19'.

This is a rare badge, awarded for outstanding devotion to duty or for an act of courage.

£220-280 LOCK

A World War I bronze death plaque, for Thomas William Young.

£90-110 PSA

An early 17thC German 'Black and White' comb morion, the base encircled with brass rosette-washers, some splits, refreshed with paint.

9¾in (25cm) wide

£1,200-1,600   TDM

A Crimean War French shako, with helmet plate and no.3 pommel, with leather sweatband liner. *c1850s*

£450-500   LOCK

An officer's white cloth tropical helmet, leather and silk headband lining, 'By Appointment' label of Military Taylor J.B. Johnston inside, spike and chin chain missing.

£1,500-2,000   W&W

A German World War I Sappenpanzer Gesichtsmaske green-painted iron 'Elephant Plate' sniper's mask, general surface wear and tear.

11in (28cm) high

£2,200-2,800   APAR

A Victorian officer's full dress embroidered sabretache, of the Second Hants Volunteer Artillery, the Royal Arms with supporters and motto, silver-plated cannon within wreath with title scrolls 'Second' above and 'Hants Volunteer Artillery' below.

13in (33cm) high

£1,000-1,200   W&W

A Victorian officer's full dress embroidered sabretache, of the Royal Bucks Yeomanry, gilt 'VR' cipher, black leather backing and pouch, three buff leather suspension straps with buckles.

£1,400-1,800   W&W

A Victorian 16th Queen's Lancers lieutenant's tunic. *c1860*

£600-700   DUK

An early Victorian officer's mess dress, with silver buttons and silver-gilt cuffs and collar, three buttons pre-cuff, with waistcoat.

£170-200   DUK

MILITARIA

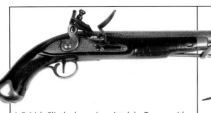

A British Flintlock service pistol, by Tower, with full walnut stock, brass trigger guard and iron swivel ramrod.
c1808   *15in (38cm) long*
£650-750   **DUK**

A 56-bore flintlock boxlock overcoat pocket pistol, with spring bayonet, signed 'Dunderdale, Mabson & Labron', the top safety and walnut slab butt with oval silver escutcheon, some wear.
c1815   *8in (20.5cm) long*
£250-350   **W&W**

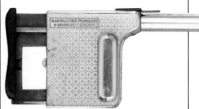

An 8mm french five-shot centre-fire gaulois patent palm pistol, by Manufacture d'armes de St Étienne, no.2512, with short barrel stamped 'Mitrailleuse'.
c1880   *5¼in (13.5cm) long*
£650-750   **TDM**

A six-shot percussion revolver, by E.M. Reilly & Co. Gun Manufacturers of London, with Bakelite grip in oak pistol case, with oil bottle and accessories.
£900-1,100   **DUK**

A Colt US 1911A1 transition model second-type pistol, .45 ACP caliber, marked 'MODEL OF 1911 U.S. ARMY'.
1924   *barrel 5in (12.5cm) long*
£3,000-3,500   **POOK**

An infantry officer's dirk, Lockwood Brothers, Sheffield, the single fuller blade signed, the scabbard set with bi knife and fork, the mounts with applied crown, badge and initials.
17¾in (45cm) long
£1,200-1,600   **L&T**

A rare 1st Royal Lanarkshire militia basket-hilted sword, by Henry Wilkinson, London, the blade numbered '16898', with regimental badge and Royal cipher, in original scabbard.
39½in (100.5cm) long
£1,400-1,800   **L&T**

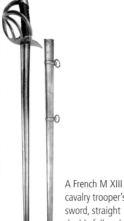

A French M XIII cavalry trooper's sword, straight double fullered blade, marked 'Mfture Imple du Klingenthal Octobre'.
blade 37½in (95.5cm) long
£1,200-1,600   **W&W**

A 1796 pattern heavy cavalry trooper's sword, in its steel scabbard with two rings, pitting overall, blade heavily cleaned.
blade 34½in (87.5cm) long
£1,400-1,600   **W&W**

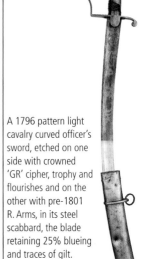

A 1796 pattern light cavalry curved officer's sword, etched on one side with crowned 'GR' cipher, trophy and flourishes and on the other with pre-1801 R. Arms, in its steel scabbard, the blade retaining 25% blueing and traces of gilt.
blade 32½in (82.5cm) long
£750-850   **W&W**

QUICK REFERENCE - BACCARAT PAPERWEIGHTS

- Although paperweights were first made in Murano, Italy, France became the prominent producer of paperweights in the 19thC, with Clichy, St Louis and Baccarat as the leading companies in the 1840s-50s.
- The Compagnie des Cristalleries de Baccarat was founded in Baccarat, France, in 1765. Baccarat produced paperweights from 1845.
- Many were made from clear crystal with canes cut to create floral designs. Millefiori paperweights were also common. Millefiori is Italian for 'thousand flowers' and refers to designs of densely packed stylised decoration often found in paperweights.
- Some Baccarat paperweights contain a signature cane, marked with the date the paperweight was made.

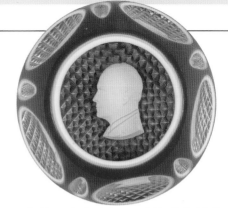

A Baccarat double-overlay faceted paperweight, with Dwight Eisenhower sulphide.

3in (7.5cm) diam

£60-80   POOK

A Baccarat flower paperweight, set with a primrose, edged with eleven leaves.

c1850   3in (7.5cm) diam

£400-500   WW

A Baccarat paperweight.

2in (5cm) wide

£100-150   JN

A Baccarat paperweight.

2¾in (7cm) wide

£100-150   JN

A Baccarat paperweight, with scrabble lacework.

2½in (6.5cm) wide

£65-80   JN

A Baccarat paperweight.

2in (5cm) wide

£350-450   JN

A Baccarat spaced millefiori glass paperweight, the canes including silhouette canes of a cockerel, a stag, a goat and a dog and the date cane 'B1848', two chips to foot rim, some surface scratches.

1848   2½in (6.5cm) diam

£550-650   BELL

A CLOSER LOOK AT A BACCARAT PAPERWEIGHT

This is a rare antique magnum Baccarat spaced millefiori and griddle canes paperweight.

With assorted complex canes of flower and animal design, including horses, dogs, deer and elephants.

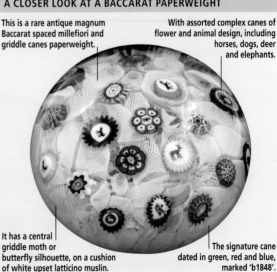

It has a central griddle moth or butterfly silhouette, on a cushion of white upset latticino muslin.

The signature cane dated in green, red and blue, marked 'b1848'.

A Baccarat paperweight, with expected scratching to edge of base.

1848   3in (7.5cm) diam

£800-1,000   MART

PAPERWEIGHTS

A Baccarat paperweight, with flower canes formed into a mushroom, with a spiral ring of white and blue threads.

c1850   3¼in (8.5cm) diam

£300-400   **FIS**

A Clichy swirl paperweight.

c1850   2½in (6.5cm) diam

£250-350   **WW**

A Clichy spaced paperweight, set with colourful canes including two Clichy roses.

c1850   3in (7.5cm) diam

£600-700   **WW**

A Clichy spaced paperweight, set with thirty-seven canes including a Clichy rose, on a twisted latticino ground.

c1850   3in (7.5cm) diam

£400-500   **WW**

A Baccarat glass paperweight, internally decorated with floral design, limited edition, numbered '211/250', dated to cane.

1977   3¼in (8.5cm) diam

£200-250   **APAR**

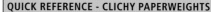

A mid-19thC Clichy faceted concentric millefiori paperweight, small chips to edges.

2in (5cm) diam

£300-400   **BELL**

QUICK REFERENCE - CLICHY PAPERWEIGHTS

- Clichy was founded by Joseph Maës in 1837. It produced paperweights from the 1840s to 1852, after which production was sporadic.
- These paperweights are rarely dated, usually marked only with a 'C'. They were mostly flat with a concave base.
- Millefiori patterns were common as were coloured swirls and flowers. One common design was a small rose-shaped cane that became known as the 'Clichy rose'.

A contemporary paperweight, by Jim D'Onofrio, depicting a snake, approaching a mouse, signed in script 'Jim D'Onofrio 01' and '1241'.

3½in (9cm) diam

£450-550   **JDJ**

A Millville mushroom footed paperweight.

3¼in (8.5cm) diam

£100-150   **POOK**

A Millville orange crimp rose footed paperweight, by Tony DePalma, stamped on base.

2¾in (7cm) diam

£50-70   **POOK**

QUICK REFERENCE - ST LOUIS PAPERWEIGHTS

- The glassworks at St Louis, Lorraine, started producing clear crystal wares in the 1780s and paperweights in c1842-45.
- Many St Louis paperweights were made with a latticinio ground, with threads of glass arranged in a lattice design, usually in pink or white. St Louis paperweights tend to have star-cut bases and high domes.
- The St Louis factory still produces paperweights today.

A 20thC St Louis glass paperweight newel post, with millefiori canes, with brass fitting, limited edition, with signature cane, original box and certificate, dated.

1974   6¾in (17cm) high
£800-900   FLD

A 20thC St Louis glass piedouche paperweight, with a central ruffle cane and nine varying millefiori rings atop a lattachino foot, limited edition, dated, signature cane, original box and certificate.

1972   3in (7.5cm) high
£600-700   FLD

A St Louis glass paperweight, with a central lampwork white flower, limited edition, dated, signature cane, original box and certificate.

1973   3¼in (8.5cm) diam
£160-200   FLD

A St Louis glass paperweight vase, the base with radial millefiori cane work below a bell-form bowl with internal latticino decoration, dated, original label and signature cane, boxed.

1973   5¼in (13.5cm) high
£500-600   FLD

A St Louis paperweight, with lacework and fruit.

2¼in (5.5cm) wide
£150-200   JN

A St Louis paperweight, set with pears, cherries and leaves in a basket of spiralling white latticinio threads, minor bruising and chips.

c1850   2¾in (7cm) diam
£300-350   BELL

QUICK REFERENCE - PAUL YSART

- Paul Ysart (1904-91) is seen by many collectors as one of the most important 20thC paperweight makers. After working at St Louis and the Leith Flint Glass Co., Paul joined his father at the Moncreiff Glassworks in Perth where he worked until 1963.
- He then moved to Caithness Glass where he worked from 1963-70.
- Ysart opened a dedicated paperweight studio in Harland, Wick, which he ran until he retired in 1979. His typically complex and finely made weights are often signed with 'PY' or 'H' canes.

A 20thC Paul Ysart glass paperweight inkwell, with a central five-flower bouquet surrounded by an alternating ring of millefiori canes, cased in clear crystal, rising to the stopper in the conforming pattern with three central flower heads.

5¼in (13.5cm) high
£600-800   FLD

A mid-19thC St Louis glass pansy paperweight, small bruise above foot rim.

3in (7.5cm) diam
£250-300   BELL

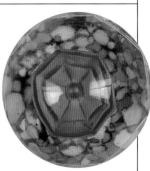

An upright red flower paperweight, probably Czechoslovakian, with a multicolour chip ground and white looping around base.

c1920   2¾in (7cm) diam
£60-70   POOK

QUICK REFERENCE - THE KB COLLECTION OF PENCILS

- The evolution of the mechanical pencil from c1822-1930 is documented in the KB Collection of Pencils, which was put together over many decades by Kenneth Bull. Bull, along with Dr David Shepherd, published a book on the collection.
- The collection includes pencils from makers such as Sampson Mordan and Co., Cartier, Tiffany and Co., among others. The majority of the collection's pencils date from 1870-90.
- While commercial production of the lead pencil dates from around 1775, a graphite pencil is documented as early as 1686, following the discovery of black lead/plumbago (graphite) near Keswick, UK, in the 16thC. Variety in the hardness of pencils was developed in the 1790s, when Nicholas Conté and Josef Hardtmuth mixed powdered graphite with china clay and fired it.
- Many of the pencils in this section come from Kenneth Bull's collection.

An early Victorian novelty silver pencil and toothpick set, by S. Mordan, modelled as pistols, engraved 'July 6, 1840', with a cartridge for leads, in a fitted velvet lined ivory box, with an oval plaque inscribed 'S. Mordan Pencil Maker'.

1840   *closed 1½in (4cm) long*
£800-900   **WW**

A Victorian novelty gold pencil, by S. Mordan and Co., modelled as a revolver, with revolving cartridge case, with diamond registration mark for 8 March 1855.

From the KB Collection of Pencils.
closed 2in (5cm) long
£400-500   **WW**

A Victorian novelty ten carat gold pencil, by S. Mordan and Co., modelled as a tennis racket, with a ring attachment, with a design registration for September 1878.

1878   closed 2½in (6.5cm) long
£650-750   **WW**

An early Victorian matched pair of novelty gold and enamel pencils, by S. Mordan, modelled as pistols, one of the butts with vari-coloured enamel decoration, the other with dark blue enamel and set with diamonds, both with ring attachments, one engraved 'July 6, 1840'.

From the KB Collection of Pencils.
1840   *closed 1½in (4cm) long*
£1,500-2,000   **WW**

An early Victorian novelty gold pencil, by S. Mordan, modelled as a pistol.

From the KB Collection of Pencils.
c1840   closed 1½in (4cm) long
£350-450   **WW**

A Victorian novelty gold pencil, by S. Mordan, modelled as a hand and sleeve, the finger with a hardstone ring, with a ring attachment, and with a coloured stone matrix terminal, marked 'S. Mordan Aug 3, 1842, no.1390', in a later fitted box.

From the KB Collection of Pencils.
c1840   closed 1½in (4cm) long
£600-700   **WW**

A Victorian novelty silver pencil, by S. Mordan and Co., modelled as a roller-skate, with a ring attachment, with a registration lozenge.

From the KB Collection of Pencils.
1879   *closed 2½in (6.5cm) long*
£1,000-1,300   **WW**

A Victorian novelty silver pencil, by S. Mordan and Co., modelled as a screw, with a ring attachment.

closed 2in (5cm) long

£400-450   **WW**

A Victorian novelty silver pencil, by S. Mordan and Co., modelled as a pistol, with a ring attachment.

closed 1¾in (4.5cm) long

£250-300   **WW**

A Victorian novelty silver pencil, by S. Mordan and Co., modelled as a bullet, with a ring attachment.

This pencil is referred to in the 1898 catalogue as 'Magazine Rifle Cartridge'.

closed 2¼in (5.5cm) long

£320-400   **WW**

A Victorian novelty silver pencil, by S. Mordan and Co., modelled as a cannon barrel, with a ring attachment, also marked 'Patent'.

closed 2¾in (7cm) long

£250-300   **WW**

A Victorian novelty silver pencil, by S. Mordan and Co., modelled as a cricket bat, with a ring attachment.

closed 2¼in (5.5cm) long

£450-550   **WW**

A Victorian novelty silver-mounted pencil, by S. Mordan and Co., the ceramic body modelled as a bird's egg, with a ring attachment.

closed 1¼in (3cm) long

£400-500   **WW**

A Victorian novelty silver and enamel pencil, probably by S. Mordan and Co., modelled as an Allsopp's India Pale Ale bottle, with enamelled label, unmarked.

c1880   *1¾in (4.5cm) long*

£320-400   **WW**

A Victorian novelty ten carat gold pencil, by S. Mordan and Co., modelled as a crucifix, with a ring attachment.

closed 1½in (4cm) long

£200-250   **WW**

A Victorian novelty silver and enamel pencil, by S. Mordan and Co., modelled as a Bass beer bottle, the enamelled label with the beer details and 'S.MORDAN & C/ London', with a ring attachment.

c1880   *2in (5cm) long*

£250-350   **WW**

PENS & WRITING

A Victorian novelty silver and enamel pencil, by S. Mordan and Co., modelled as a Royal Mail pillar box, engraved with the 'VR' cipher, the enamel panel with 'Cleared at 7am and 8pm Sundays Excepted', with a ring attachment.

From the KB Collection of Pencils.

closed 2in (5cm) long

£750-850   WW

A Victorian novelty silver pencil, by S. Mordan and Co., modelled as a broom.

From the KB Collection of Pencils.

7in (18cm) long

£800-900   WW

A Victorian novelty silver pencil, by S. Mordan and Co., modelled as a begging dog, with a ring attachment.

From the KB Collection of Pencils.

c1880   closed 1½in (4cm) long

£650-750   WW

A Victorian novelty silver pencil, by S. Mordan and Co., modelled as a railway lamp, with a ring attachment.

From the KB Collection of Pencils.

closed 2¼in (5.5cm) long

£800-900   WW

QUICK REFERENCE - S. MORDAN AND CO.

- Sampson Mordan (1790-1843) was a British silversmith. In 1822, he and his associate John Isaac Hawkins patented the first ever mechanical pencil.
- Mordan then went into partnership with Gabriel Riddle, a stationer with whom he manufactured and sold silver propelling pencils. The partnership dissolved in 1837, and Mordan continued to sell his pencils under the trading name of S. Mordan and Co., until his death in 1843, when the company passed to his sons, Sampson Mordan junior and Augustus Mordan.
- Edmund Johnson, Horace Stewart, Henry Lambert Symonds and James Pulley joined the company and production was diversified, focusing on smaller pieces. In 1884, Augustus Mordan retired and left the company to his partners.
- The company manufactured a wide variety of products, including locks, whistles, boxes and inkwells – but they were chiefly known for their propelling and telescopic pencils.
- S. Mordan and Co. became a limited liability company in 1898.
- Following the destruction of their City Road Factory by a bombing raid in 1941, the company stopped trading.
- S. Mordan and Co.'s silver and gold-cased 'Everpoint' pencils remain popular with collectors today, as do the novelty propelling pencils. These pencils were often shaped as animals, figures, tools or everyday objects. They were usually made in silver or gold.

A Victorian novelty silver pencil, by S. Mordan and Co., modelled as a railway lamp, with a ring attachment.

From the KB Collection of Pencils.

closed 2¼in (5.5cm) long

£800-900   WW

A Victorian novelty silver pencil, by S. Mordan and Co., modelled as a horse's head, with a ring attachment.

From the KB Collection of Pencils.

closed 1½in (4cm) long

£850-950   WW

A Victorian novelty silver figural pencil, by S. Mordan and Co., modelled as a man wearing a habit and holding a spear, possibly a disciple, ring attachment, with a registration lozenge.

From the KB Collection of Pencils.

1880   1½in (4cm) long

£1,200-1,600   WW

A Victorian novelty silver pencil, by S. Mordan and Co., modelled as a cat, with a ring attachment, with a registration lozenge.

From the KB Collection of Pencils.

1881   closed 1¾in (4.5cm) long

£1,200-1,600   WW

A novelty silver and enamel pencil, by S. Mordan and Co., also marked 'Pan Tan patent, sterling silver', the side enamelled 1-8 with the vari-coloured discs, the top enamelled 1-8, with a ring attachment.

From the KB Collection of Pencils.

3½in (9cm) long

£450-550   **WW**

A novelty gold pencil, by S. Mordan and Co., modelled as a shoe, also marked 'Rd199100'.

From the KB Collection of Pencils.

closed 1½in (4cm) long

£600-700   **WW**

A CLOSER LOOK AT A SENTRY BOX PENCIL

This is an extremely rare and desirable pencil by S. Mordan and Co.

It is well modelled as a sentry box.

It is enamelled with a soldier from the 17th Lancers.

The reverse is inscribed with 'A.P.K.'s compliments "Royalty" 28 Aug.1895'.

It has superb provenance coming from the KB Collection.

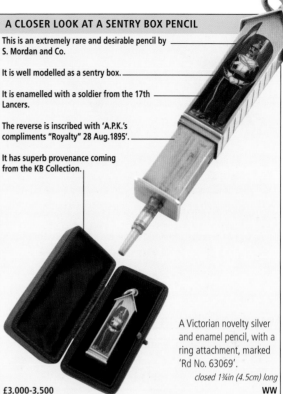

A silver-gilt pencil and aide memoire, by S. Mordan and Co., the fan formed by six ivory sheets.

May be subject to CITES regulations if exported.
From the KB Collection of Pencils.

3¼in (8.5cm) long

£650-750   **WW**

A Victorian novelty silver and enamel pencil, with a ring attachment, marked 'Rd No. 63069'.

closed 1¾in (4.5cm) long

£3,000-3,500   **WW**

QUICK REFERENCE - CARTIER

- Louis-François Cartier founded Cartier in Paris in 1847. The company was passed to Cartier's son and remained in the family until it was bought by investors in the mid-to-late 20thC. The company's headquarters remain in Paris, despite being owned by Switzerland-based Richemont Group.
- In the early 20thC, Cartier began producing writing equipment, including fountain and rollerball pens, pen holders, mechanical pencils and office accessories. Some of the writing equipment included a pen combined with a watch element.
- The writing equipment could be made from gold, silver, guilloché enamel and jade, among other materials, and some items are set with precious stones.

A rare Victorian novelty silver pencil, by Edward and Son, modelled as a sphinx, with a ring attachment, the base inscribed ' Tel-El-Kebir, 13 Sept.1882' and 'D. Martin'.

From the KB Collection of Pencils.

The battle of Tel-el-Kebir was fought between the Egyptian army, led by Ahmed Urabi, and the British military, near Tel-el-Kebir. After Egyptian officers rebelled in 1882, the British reacted to protect its financial and expansionist interest in the country, and in particular the Suez Canal, which opened to shipping in 1869.

c1882   *closed 1½in (4cm) long*

£1,500-2,000   **WW**

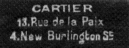

A French gold and enamel pencil, by Cartier, feather quill-form, with grey enamel decoration and a gold and white enamel bead border, with a moonstone slider, in a fitted Cartier case, the underside with 'Cartier 13, Rue de la Paix, and 4, Burlington St.'.

3¾in (9.5cm) long

£10,000-15,000   **WW**

A Victorian novelty silver figural pencil, by Leuchars, modelled as a child wearing a necklace, with a ring attachment, with a registration lozenge.

From the KB Collection of Pencils.
closed 1¾in (4.5cm) long
£850-950   WW

A Victorian novelty gold and enamel pencil, by Thornhill, enamelled with the 'Jack of Hearts', with a ring attachment, also marked '1761'.

From the KB Collection of Pencils.
closed 2in (5cm) long
£600-700   WW

A rare American novelty silver pencil, by Tiffany and Co., modelled as The Metropolitan Life Tower, together with an old postcard depicting the tower.

From the KB Collection of Pencils.
The Metropolitan Life Tower is a landmark skyscraper at One Madison Avenue, Manhattan, New York. Designed by the architectural firm Napoleon Brun and Sons, the tower is modelled after the Campanile in Venice. It was constructed in 1909, and was the world's tallest building until 1913, when it was surpassed by the Woolworth Building.
closed 3½in (9cm) long
£3,000-3,500   WW

A Victorian novelty silver pencil, by W. Thornhill, modelled as tortoise, with a ring attachment.

From the KB Collection of Pencils.
closed 1¾in (4.5cm) long
£2,500-3,000   WW

A rare novelty silver pencil, modelled as a lobster claw, with a ring handle, unmarked.

From the KB Collection of Pencils.
2in (5cm) long
£600-700   WW

A Victorian novelty silver and red enamel pencil, modelled as a heart, unmarked, with a ring attachment.

From the KB Collection of Pencils.
closed 1½in (4cm) long
£550-650   WW

A French silver-mounted enamel pencil and scent bottle, decorated with a lady and gentleman, the hinged cover opens to reveal a scent bottle, marked with a French control mark.

From the KB Collection of Pencils.
2¾in (7cm) long
£500-600   WW

A novelty papier-mâché pencil, modelled as a globe, with a ring attachment.

From the KB Collection of Pencils.
1¼in (3cm) long
£400-500   WW

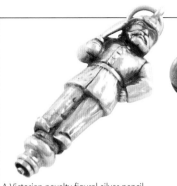

A Victorian novelty figural silver pencil, modelled as a policeman holding his truncheon, with a ring attachment, unmarked.

From the KB Collection of Pencils.

1¾in (4.5cm) long

£350-450   **WW**

A rare Victorian novelty gold pencil, modelled as an elephant, with a ring attachment, unmarked.

From the KB Collection of Pencils.

closed 1½in (4cm) long

£650-750   **WW**

A Victorian novelty parcel-gilt silver pencil, modelled as a rowing boat, with enamelled oars, a rudder formed as a ring attachment, unmarked.

From the KB Collection of Pencils.

closed 2in (5cm) long

£450-550   **WW**

A Victorian novelty silver and enamel pencil, modelled as a soda water bottle, with an enamelled label, unmarked.

From the KB Collection of Pencils.

1¾in (4.5cm) long

£400-450   **WW**

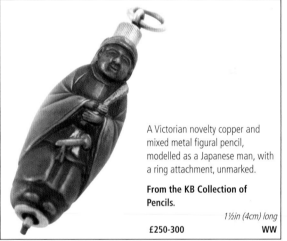

A Victorian novelty copper and mixed metal figural pencil, modelled as a Japanese man, with a ring attachment, unmarked.

From the KB Collection of Pencils.

1½in (4cm) long

£250-300   **WW**

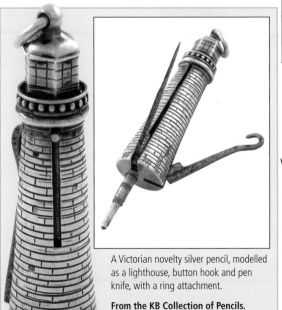

A Victorian novelty silver pencil, modelled as a lighthouse, button hook and pen knife, with a ring attachment.

From the KB Collection of Pencils.

1896   *1¾in (4.5cm) long*

£850-950   **WW**

A rare Edwardian novelty gold pencil, modelled as a frog, with gem set eyes, with a ring attachment, unmarked, one eye missing.

From the KB Collection of Pencils.

c1902   *1¼in (3cm) long*

£1,200-1,600   **WW**

PENS & WRITING

QUICK REFERENCE - FOUNTAIN PENS

- The first commercial fountain pens date from the 1880s, but the 'golden age' of the fountain pen was the 1910s-50s.
- Most collectors aim to collect one period or brand of fountain pen. The collectors' market for fountain pens has long been dominated by pens produced in the first half of the 20thC by big names such as Parker, Waterman, Montblanc and Dunhill Namiki. However, these pens have become less common in recent years, prompting some collectors to focus on lesser-known brands and contemporary limited edition pens.
- The rarity, quality and material can all affect value. Unusual celluloids or pens with complex metal overlays can be popular, as can classic models, such as the Parker 51 or 75. Limited editions, such as Montblanc's 'Lorenzo de Medici' of 1992, are also highly sought after.
- Condition is paramount. To ensure value, a pen must come with its original packaging and paperwork. Most collectors do not use the pens, or even unpack them. Uninked pens in mint condition, and pens still sealed in their cellophane, tend to fetch the highest prices.

A Dunhill 18ct yellow gold ballpoint pen, with a rope twist design barrel, stamped 18k, in a fitted presentation case.

£1,200-1,600   **DUK**

An S.T. Dupont 'Place Vendome' gold and diamond fountain pen, limited edition no.20/35, the cap and barrel reminiscent of the Vendôme Column, the cap with a clip and set with a band of eight panels of diamonds, the barrel set with conforming diamond set band, the medium nib stamped '750', cartridge filling system, uninked, with an S T Dupont box, guarantee card, instruction booklet, diamond certificate, information booklet, a box of six ink cartridges, cartridge converter and outer card packaging.

£3,500-4,000   **DN**

A Montblanc 'Patron of Art Peter the Great' fountain pen, limited edition no.292 of 888, the cap and barrel with white gold overlay, the cap with a clip and set with a band of emeralds, the medium nib stamped '750 18K', piston filling system, with a Montblanc box, international service certificate book, outer card packaging and white card sleeve.
1997

£3,500-4,000   **DN**

A Conway Stewart 'Dinkie 550' fountain pen and pencil set, green marble effect, in original box with original guarantee certificate.

£160-200   **HAN**

A Montblanc 'Patron of Art, Ludovico Sforza [Duke of Milan]' fountain pen, limited edition no.089 of 888, the lacquer cap and barrel with gold trim, stamped 'Au750', the nib stamped '18K', uninked, with related Montblanc leaflet.
2013

£2,200-3,000   **DN**

A Montblanc 'Patron of Art' fountain pen, by Andrew Carnegie, the black resin body with pistol filling system, silver Art Nouveau foliate overlay marked 'Ag 925', the twist action cap with silver coloured clip modelled as a nude female figure, and Montblanc white star emblem to terminal, the bicolour nib decorated with a lily and marked '2002, 18K 750, 4810', limited edition no.0403 of 4810, in maker's fitted lacquer box, some slight tarnishing to silver.

5¾in (14.5cm) long

£800-900   **FELL**

A Montblanc Meisterstuck Ramses II fountain pen, with certificate, booklet and cloth, in original case and outer cardboard packaging, unused.

£600-700   **LOCK**

A Montblanc 'Johannes Guttenberg 42' fountain pen, limited edition no.30 of 42, the hardwood barrel inlaid with letters, the gold coloured cap with enamel chequerboard detail, stamped '750', the medium nib stamped '18K', piston filling system, with a Montblanc box, leaflet, outer card packaging and white card sleeve.
2007

£12,000-15,000   **DN**

A Montblanc 'Meisterstuck' ball point pen, boxed, with paperwork.

£400-450   **PSA**

A Montblanc 'Meisterstuck' black fountain pen, no.149.

£250-300   **LOCK**

A rare Montblanc 'Pope Julius II' fountain pen, 2005 Patron of the Arts limited edition no.748 of 888, crafted in 18K gold fretwork encasing a guilloche enamel ground, gemstones set to the cap, five diamonds set to the clip, mother-of-pearl Montblanc star insignia to the cap cover, 18ct gold nib engraved with the emblem of the Pope, in lacquer presentation box and Montblanc branded pouch, outer cardboard box and service certificate with matching limited edition number.

Considered to be one of the most influential patrons of art, Pope Julius II consolidated the papal states and transformed Rome into the cultural centre of the Renaissance. He supported Michelangelo and Raphael, among others, and commissioned the famous frescoes in the Sistine Chapel and ordered the design and construction of St Peter's Basilica. Montblanc's tribute pen, their 2005 'Patron of the Arts' version is limited to just 888 examples.

2005

£4,000-5,000   HAN

A rare Montblanc 'Sir Winston Churchill' fountain pen, limited edition no.36 of 53, the barrel crafted in 18K pink gold, inlaid with black and brown tortoiseshell lacquer bands, the cap top ringed with 53 diamonds to commemorate the year in which Churchill was knighted and bestowed the Nobel Prize for Literature, the Montblanc star is of lustrous mother-of-pearl, the great statesman's legendary 'V for Victory' sign is echoed in the design of the clip, 18K gold nib engraved with Churchill's portrait, with pouch, in a lacquered presentation box with outer cardboard box, plain outer sleeve with two accompanying brochures, signs of light use.

£12,000-16,000   HAN

A Montegrappa 'Aphrodite' silver fountain pen, limited edition no.1318 of 1912, the resin body and cap decorated with figural silver mounts and mother-of-pearl panels, 18ct gold nib, with presentation case, outer sleeve and booklets.

£1,000-1,400   DUK

An Omas 'Harmonia Mundi' fountain pen, limited edition no. 504 of 950, the titanium cap with gold coloured clip and fittings, the cap and barrel etched with the messages of peace in various languages by Clara Halter, the nib stamped '18K 750', piston filling system, in a box, with booklet and outer card packaging.

£1,000-1,400   DN

An Onoto Magna '261 High Density' black acrylic fountain pen, with silver gilt hallmarked band, limited edition no.70 of 261, certificate of authenticity, in original case.

£250-300   LOCK

A Parker '61' custom fountain pen, boxed.

£50-70   PSA

A Parker '75 Laque Ball' point pen, boxed in tortoiseshell.

£30-40   PSA

A Parker 'Duofold' centennial fountain pen, with 18ct gold nib, blue marbled effect body with gold plated arrow clip and double band cap, cartridge filling system, medium nib.

5½in (14cm) long

£220-280   DUK

A Parker 'Duofold' fountain pen, with orange case.

£250-300   FLD

A Parker 'Duofold' blue marbled fountain and ballpoint pen set, in original fitted mahogany case.

£250-300   LOCK

PICTURE FRAMES

A leather heart-shaped photograph frame, by Child & Child, gilt centre-section with guilloche enamel ground, signed to frame.

c1900   *4¾in (12cm) wide*
£3,000-4,000   **WW**

A hallmarked silver-mounted mirror, by Goldsmiths & Silversmiths Company, London, with back stand.

1901   *12¼in (31.5cm) high*
£220-280   **FLD**

An Edwardian silver-mounted photograph frame, on a replacement oak easel reverse, hallmarked E. Jacobs & Co., Birmingham.

1903   *8in (20.5cm) high*
£300-400   **FELL**

An Art Nouveau silver embossed photograph frame, by Henry Charles Freeman, Birmingham, on oak backing, surmounted by a butterfly, stamped 'RD No.442132'.

1904   *13¼in (33.5cm) high*
£200-250   **LSK**

A matched pair of Edwardian silver-mounted photograph frames, with later cold enamel accents, by E.F. Braham Ltd. and Deakin & Francis Ltd., minor wear.

1904   *5½in (14cm) high*
£750-850   **FELL**

A pair of Edward VII Art Nouveau silver-fronted frames, by Synyer & Beddoes, with enamel flowerheads, with oak easel backs, minor tarnishing.

1904   *5½in (14cm) high*
£700-900   **APAR**

An early 20thC Arts and Crafts hammered pewter photo frame, with Ruskin-type cabochon, with oak easel back.

9½in (24cm) high
£350-450   **APAR**

A pair of Edward VII Art Nouveau silver-fronted photo frames, by William Neale, with enamel flowers, with oak easel backs.

7¾in (20cm) high
£1,500-2,000   **APAR**

A Dunhill walnut photograph frame, by David Linley, easel back, stamped marks, with original box.

12¾in (32.5cm) high
£300-400   **DUK**

A postcard, G.B. Bigwood, Gaiety House shopfront, Southend-on-Sea, Essex, with staff, facing the pier.

£24-28 LOCK

QUICK REFERENCE - POSTCARDS

- Postcards have their origins in the mid-19thC, but their golden age was arguably 1890-1910. Postcards continued to be sent throughout the 20thC, but today have largely fallen out of fashion.
- As well as being used as greetings cards, postcards in the late 19thC and early 20thC were used as a method of spreading news. People regularly sent commemorative postcards and postcards featuring photographs of fires, mining disasters, shipwrecks and train crashes.
- Postcards were so commonly sent and received in the 20thC that most vintage postcards are worth very little, sometimes only a few pence. It is only very rare postcards that can today fetch very high prices. These include postcards depicting rare or now closed railway stations, postcards of the 'Titanic', and postcards by key designers such as Louis Wain.

A real photographic postcard, of a 'H.DOWNING STEAM BAKERY' horse-drawn delivery wagon.

£36-40 LOCK

A China real photographic postcard, 'Selling food on street', franked British stamp, with British Army PO 1927 military postmark.
1927

£36-40 LOCK

A real photographic postcard, of W. Smith's 'THE FAVOURITE' dining room on Victoria Dock Road, Canning Town.

£100-120 LOCK

A real photographic postcard, of 'THE GASLIGHT & COKE COMPANY BECKTON' horse and cart.

£20-25 LOCK

A real photographic postcard, of Loudwater station, interior, C316.

£30-34 LOCK

A real photographic postcard, of Newhaven railway station.
1913

£30-35 LOCK

A postcard, of 'New Barnet Railway Station'.

£50-60 LOCK

A real photographic postcard, by Warner Gothard, of 'S.E. RAILWAY COLLISION TONBRIDGE JUNCTION MAR. 5TH 1909'.

£36-40 LOCK

POSTCARDS

A real photographic postcard, of the disaster at Greenhalgh's Dye Works and Burnley Viaduct.

£48-52   **LOCK**

A real photographic postcard, of the Lincoln typhoid disaster, 'TAKING THEIR TURN FOR WATER EASTGATE TYPHOID OUTBREAK LINCOLN 1905'.

£72-78   **LOCK**

A postcard, of the 'RMS Carpathia', the ship that rescued the 'Titanic', not as titled the 'Cunard Liner, "Juernia"'.

£100-120   **LOCK**

A postcard, reading 'THE ILL-FATED WHITE STAR LINER "TITANITC" Struck an iceberg off the coast of Newfoundland on her maiden voyage & sunk with over One Thousand and Six Hundred of her Passengers & Crew, Monday morning April 15th 1912'.

£70-80   **LOCK**

A postcard, of 'R.M.S. TITANIC', wrecked April 1912, F.G.O. Stuart 1697.

£90-100   **LOCK**

A postcard, signed in ink by 'F. Poynton England's Rd Walking Champion 1923', pictured with trophy and in his race gear.

Poynton's most successful year was 1923; he won the British 20 miles championship and the London to Brighton race.

For Sporting, see pp.342-355.

£18-22   **LOCK**

A postcard, by Crawford Edmonton, of Tottenham Hotspur FC 1919-20, black and white team photo.

For Sporting, see pp.342-355.

£60-70   **LOCK**

A real photographic postcard, of Dover Cycling Club's awards gathering.

£36-40   **LOCK**

A postcard, of Colditz, hand signed by Douglas Bader.

£48-52   **LOCK**

QUICK REFERENCE - SUFFRAGETTES

● Mary Wollstonecraft's 1792 book 'A Vindication of the Rights of Woman' first publicly advocated women's suffrage in Britain. In 1865, the first women's suffrage committee was formed in Manchester, with many following suit across the country. In the late 1800s and early 1900s, Parliament rejected nearly all major suffrage bills brought before it. However, in 1869, Parliament granted the right to vote in municipal elections to women taxpayers. In 1897, the National Union of Women's Suffrage was formed as these committees united.

● In 1903, the Women's Social and Political Union (WSPU) was formed. Emmeline Pankhurst (1858-1928) was a founding member of the WPSU. With a call for 'Deeds not Words', the WSPU undertook hunger strikes and militant action to bring attention to women's suffrage and initiate social change. In 1918, the parliamentary vote was granted to women, but only those over the age of 30 who owned land or property.

● Postcards were used by both sides; pro-suffrage organisations and publishers promoted women's right to the vote, while some commercial publishers used postcards to mock and criticise the movement.

A suffragette postcard, hand-drawn court-size, reading 'The New Woman' and 'Votes for Women'.
£30-35   LOCK

A suffragette postcard, reading 'WE ONLY WANT WHAT THE MEN HAVE GOT!!!', depicting a woman with a political rosette by a table with a banner reading 'VOTES FOR WOMEN MISS ORTOBEE SPANKDFIRST'.
£85-95   LOCK

A suffragette postcard, by Millar & Lang, reading 'SUFFRAGETTES ATTACKING THE HOUSE OF COMMONS'.
£60-70   LOCK

A suffragette postcard, by Millar & Lang, reading 'THE MARTYRS SUFFRAGETTES IN PRISON I WONDER WHAT THEIR OLD MEN ARE DOING JUST NOW'.
£60-70   LOCK

A suffragette postcard, by Millar & Lang, reading 'SUFFRAGETTES IT'S LOVE THAT MAKES THE WORLD GO ROUND'.
£60-70   LOCK

A real photographic suffragette postcard, of 'ST CATHERINE'S CHURCH HATCHAM CLEMENT BROS NUNHEAD DESTROYED BY FIRE MAY 6TH 1913', the arson disaster was said to have been started by militant suffragettes.
£40-50   LOCK

A suffragette postcard, 'There are things that even a Suffragette cannot do', with a man resting his leg up on wall to tie his shoelaces.
£25-30   LOCK

A suffragette postcard, 'I want my Vote!', sent to Mrs A. Pankhurst Dec 1908 from Alf.
£32-36   LOCK

POSTCARDS

A silk postcard, reading 'SOUTH AFRICA INFTY'.
£30-35   LOCK

A silk postcard, reading 'WAAC SOUVENIR DE FRANCE'.
£36-40   LOCK

A silk postcard, for the Royal Welsh Fusiliers.
£30-35   LOCK

A silk postcard, for the Shropshire Light Infantry.
£27-30   LOCK

An Art Nouveau postcard, by Alphonse Mucha, of a Byzantine head, 'Blonde 427'.
£250-300   LOCK

A Louis Wain postcard, by Faulkner, 'And He winked the other Eye'.
£24-28   LOCK

A Louis Wain postcard, by Davidson, 'A Cat's Matrimony'.
£29-32   LOCK

A Louis Wain postcard, by Faulkner, 'Men were Deceivers ever'.
£29-32   LOCK

A Louis Wain postcard, by Faulkner, 'Wheelbarrow race'.
£27-30   LOCK

A Louis Wain postcard, by Tuck, 'CHEER UP! You can still post me for a halfpenny!'.
£29-32   LOCK

'SCOTLAND BY "THE NIGHT SCOTSMAN"', by Robert Bartlett, lithographic poster, backed on linen, repaired tear from centre of right-hand margin into image, further minor repaired tears.

This poster was sold in April 2019 alongside 14 others advertising Scotland by rail (all but one sold). The Art Deco image and Robert Bartlett are highly rated in the poster collecting/railwayana worlds.

1932   40¼in (102cm) high

£15,000-20,000   L&T

A CLOSER LOOK AT AN ART DECO POSTER

Michel Bouchaud (1902-65) is a well-known Art Deco poster artist. He was also a painter and illustrator and designed many album covers.

This is a highly stylised Art Deco image, from the woman's hair to the suggestion of waves in the water.

A fashionable couple flirts beneath a decorative trellis, at the confluence of the bay and a pool, with the beaches and town in the distance.

Bouchaud is known to have designed one other poster, for Val d'Esquieres, another waterside resort, but it is far less Art Deco than this scene.

'LA PLAGE DE MONTE CARLO', printed by Publicité Vox, Paris, framed, small stains in image.

1929   46¼in (117.5cm) high

£3,000-4,000   SWA

'EDINBURGH', signed 'BERRY 1951', lithograph, not backed.

1951   40¼in (102cm) high

£600-700   L&T

'LINLITHGOW PALACE', by Claude Buckle, lithograph, not backed.

c1950   40¼in (102cm) high

£400-500   L&T

'DROITWICH THE BRINE BATHS SPA', designed by Leonard Campbell Taylor (1874-1969), printed by David Allen & Sons Ltd., London, extensive creases and abrasions in margins.

This poster depicts an elegant couple watching a car pass them on a driveway shrouded in shadows. The sophisticated Art Deco imagery combines a mixture of light and shadow with a contrast between the natural beauty and the architecture of this spa town. Taylor was a painter known for his portraits and interiors with figures. This is Taylor's only known poster.

1925   39in (99cm) high

£2,000-3,000   SWA

'AIR FRANCE CORSE', designd by Raoul Eric Castel (1915-97), printed by Havas, Paris, repaired tears.

1949   38in (96.5cm) high

£800-1,000   SWA

'AUSTRALIA THE WORLD'S LOVELIEST HARBOUR, SYDNEY', designed by Albert Collins (1883-1951), printed by The Moore Young Litho Co., Melbourne, losses, margins trimmed, restoration in margins and image.

1930   39½in (100.5cm) high

£1,200-1,600   SWA

'CLEAR ROAD AHEAD', designed by Terence Cuneo, printed by Waterlow & Sons Ltd., lithograph, signed, some losses, fold marks, some staining.

39½in (100.5cm) high

£900-1,100   SWO

POSTERS

'RAVELLO', designed by Domenico (Mino) Delle Site (1914-96), printed by Di Mauro, Cava, restored losses.

1950   *39in (99cm) high*

£300-400   **SWA**

'WASHINGTON MANHATTAN UNITED STATES LINES', by R. Devignes, printed in France.

                          39in (99cm) high

£400-500   **DUK**

'GENÈVE ET LE MONT-BLANC', designed by Edouard Elzingre (1880-1966), printed by Atar, Geneva, repaired tears.

1925   *43¼in (110cm) high*

£750-950   **SWA**

'RODI', designed by Florestano Di Fausto (1890-1965), paper, printed by A. Marzi, Rome, minor tears and abrasions.

1927   *39½in (100.5cm) high*

£650-800   **SWA**

'San Francisco UNITED AIR LINES', by Stan Galli, minor creases and restoration at edges.

Born in San Francisco, Stan Galli (1912-2009) was a painter, illustrator and printmaker. He was a member of the New York and California Society of Illustrators. Galli designed a series of posters for United Airlines in the 1950s and 1960s.

40¼in (102cm) high

£500-600   **SWA**

'Travel by train CANADIAN PACIFIC RAILWAY LINES', by Norman Fraser, repaired tears, restored losses.

Although Norman Fraser was by far the most prolific artist commissioned by Canadian Pacific, he has remained an elusive figure. It is known that he lived in Montreal from 1930 to 1953 and that he was commissioned to design dozens of posters in that period.

1947   *36¾in (93.5cm) high*

£1,500-2,000   **SWA**

'New York UNITED AIR LINES', designed by Stan Galli, repaired tears, creases and restoration at lower right edge.

c1960   *40in (101.5cm) high*

£450-550   **SWA**

'CARLISLE THE GATEWAY TO SCOTLAND', by Maurice Greiffenhagen, for the London Midland and Scottish Regions, Japan backed.

c1924

£1,000-1,500   **DUK**

'CHAMONIX-MONT BLANC', designed by Alo (Charles Hallo, 1884-1969), printed by Cornille & Serre, Paris, overpainting and airbrushing in margins.

In 1924, the eighth Olympic Games were held in Chamonix. One year later, 'these successful Games were retrospectively recognized at the "International Olympic Committee" Congress in Prague as the first Olympic Winter Games'. The decision to hold these winter games came in 1921, and 'triggered a period of frenzied construction as rail and road links and hotel development opened up the area to international tourism'.

1924 *42½in (108cm) high*
£3,000-4,000 **SWA**

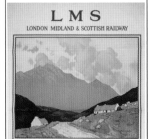

'LMS LONDON MIDLAND & SCOTTISH RAILWAY CONNEMARA "IRELAND THIS YEAR"', by Paul Henry, printed by S.C. Allen and Co., mounted on rice paper.

40in (101.5cm) high
£800-900 **WHYT**

'CROSS THE CHANNEL FROM DOVER', by Lawrence, for the Southern Region.

c1960 *39¾in (101cm) high*
£250-350 **DUK**

'By Rail across GREAT SALT LAKE Overland route Southern Pacific', designed by Maurice Logan (1886-1977), printed on thick paper, flaking and minor skinning in margins.

By the late 1920s, Logan had begun including a train into many of his designs. A particularly vivid image, of two Overland Limiteds passing as they cross the Great Salt Lake in opposite directions, summed up the campaign and the era, absorbing the drama of both the West and western railroading.

1928 *23in (58.5cm) high*
£600-700 **SWA**

'NEWQUAY ON THE CORNISH COAST', designed by Alfred Lambart (1902-70), printed by The Dangerfield Printing Co. Ltd., London, repaired tears at edges.

1937 *40¼in (102cm) high*
£3,000-4,000 **SWA**

'MERANO', designed by Franz Lenhart (1898-1992), printed by Coen & Ci., Milan, light foxing at edges.

1934 *39¼in (99.5cm) high*
£2,000-2,500 **SWA**

'LOCH LOMOND', by Alasdair Macfarlane (1902-60), lithograph, not backed.

c1950 *40¼in (102cm) high*
£600-700 **L&T**

'THE RIVER TWEED', by Jack Merriott (1901-68), lithograph, not backed.

c1950 *40¼in (102cm) high*
£650-750 **L&T**

POSTERS

'Holland-America Line', designed by Franciscus J.E. Mettes (1909-84), minor repaired tears and abrasions, vertical lines in central image.
1955   37in (94cm) high
£400-500   **SWA**

'YELLOWSTONE NATIONAL PARK-THRU GARDINER GATEWAY NORTHERN PACIFIC', designed by Louis Moen, printed on board, minor tears, creases, abrasions and skinning in margins.
22in (56cm) high
£3,000-4,000   **SWA**

'FISHGUARD–ROSSLARE', by Arthur G. Muir, printed by Waterlow & Sons Ltd.
39½in (100.5cm) high
£450-550   **DUK**

'RAILROADS ON PARADE NEW YORK WORLD'S FAIR-1939', designed by Leslie Ragan (1897-1972), framed, minor creases and abrasions.

Among the exhibits at the 1939 New York World's Fair was the Court of Railways, 'a sixteen-acre display of locomotives, trains, and the men who made them run. Twenty-seven principal railroads east of the Mississippi participated, and there were three and a half miles of track... in the yards stood the British-built John Bull locomotive of 1831 alongside a modern 140-foot Pennsylvania streamlined giant that ran continuously at sixty miles an hour on a roller bed... the highlight of the exhibit was Railroads on Parade ... a pageant about the "romance of transport" from covered wagon days to the streamlined trains of 1939', 'World of Tomorrow', pp.101-102.
1939   40¼in (102cm) high
£900-1,100   **SWA**

'ROMA', designed by Virgilio Retrosi (1892-1975) printed by Novissima, Rome, mounted on paper, minor creases.

A student of the Accademia di Belle Arti in Rome, Retrosi was a painter, designer and ceramicist.
c1930   37½in (95.5cm) high
£350-450   **SWA**

'CONSTABLE'S COUNTRY', designed by Kenneth Slil, printed by Jarrold and Sons Ltd., Norwich, paper, tears and repaired tears at edges.
c1950s   40in (101.5cm) high
£450-550   **SWA**

'CULZEAN CASTLE PRESIDENT EISENHOWER'S SCOTTISH HOME', designed by Kenneth Slil, printed by Jarrold and Sons Ltd., Norwich, paper, small tears at edges, minor creases.
1955   40¼in (102cm) high
£500-600   **SWA**

'LE HAVRE TO NEW YORK FRANCE French Line', by Laura Smith, thick paper mounted onto board, minor creases and abrasions.
1979   36in (91.5cm) high
£800-1,000   **SWA**

OVER THE SEA TO SKYE
SEE BRITAIN BY TRAIN

'OVER THE SEA TO SKYE',
by Kenneth Steel (1906-73),
lithograph, not backed.
c1950 40¼in (102cm) high
£550-650 L&T

THE ROYAL MAIL LINE
TO
NEW YORK
MAKE YOUR NEXT CROSSING BY
'THE COMFORT ROUTE'
THE ROYAL MAIL STEAM PACKET CO
ATLANTIC HOUSE, MOORGATE, E.C.2

'THE ROYAL MAIL LINE TO NEW
YORK', designed by Horace Taylor
(1881-1934), printed by The
Baynard Press, London, minor
staining, unobtrusive folds.
c1925 40in (101.5cm) high
£1,200-1,600 SWA

HOLLAND-AMERIKA
LIJN

'HOLLAND-AMERIKA LIJN',
designed by Willem Frederik
Ten Broek (1905-93), printed
by Joh. Enschedé en Zonen, The
Netherlands, margins trimmed off,
airbrushing around lower text,
abrasions and restoration in image.
1936 36in (91.5cm) high
£800-1,000 SWA

DURHAM
IT'S QUICKER BY RAIL
FULL INFORMATION FROM ANY L·N·E·R OFFICE OR AGENCY

'DURHAM IT'S QUICKER BY RAIL',
by Harry Tittensor, printed by
Waterlow, published by London &
N. Eastern Railway.
39¾in (101cm) high
£300-400 PSA

'KELSO ON THE BANKS OF THE
TWEED IT'S QUICKER BY RAIL', by
Harry Tittensor, printed by Jordison,
published by London & Eastern
Railway, dated, crease towards
lower edge.
1941 39¾in (101cm) high
£300-400 PSA

KELSO ON THE BANKS
OF THE TWEED
IT'S QUICKER BY RAIL

'NOW FLY TO Bermuda by CLIPPER FROM BOSTON
PAN AMERICAN WORLD AIRWAYS', by Adolph Treidler
(1886-1981), overpainted margins, repaired tears.

**Treidler worked on many advertising campaigns
during his career. He designed propaganda posters
during World War I, worked for the French and
Furness Lines and was employed by the Bermuda
Board of Trade to help promote the island.**
c1955 38in (96.5cm) high
£300-400 SWA

NOW FLY TO
Bermuda
by CLIPPER
PAN AMERICAN WORLD AIRWAYS

fly to RIO by Clipper

PAN AMERICAN
WORLD AIRWAYS
The System of the Flying Clippers

'Fly to RIO by Clipper PAN AMERICAN WORLD AIRWAYS', designed
by Mark von Arenburg, repaired tears and creases in margins, partial
silkscreen.
c1947 42in (106.5cm) high
£1,200-1,600 SWA

PHILADELPHIA

Go by Train
PENNSYLVANIA RAILROAD

'PHILADELPHIA Go by Train
PENNSYLVANIA RAILROAD',
designed by Harley Wood, paper,
minor abrasions in image.
40¼in (102cm) high
£300-400 SWA

GEORGIAN MILITARY
HIGHWAY

'GEORGIAN MILITARY HIGHWAY',
designed by Alexander Zhitomirsky
(1907-93), printed by Intourist,
USSR, replaced losses, repaired
tears.

**The Georgian Military Highway
is a 200km road leading from
Tbilisi to Vladikavkaz in the
Autonomous Republic of North
Ossetia-Alania within the Russian
Federation.**
1939 39in (99cm) high
£2,000-2,500 SWA

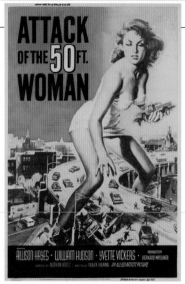

'ATTACK OF THE 50FT. WOMAN', partial silkscreen, mounted on thick paper, repaired tears, creases.

1958 *60¾in (154.5cm) high*

£2,500-3,000 SWA

'JAMES BOND 007 CONTRE Dr. NO', French one sheet poster, the first James Bond film, central fold, small hole to centre, wear to edges.

1962 *63in (160cm) high*

£300-400 WM

'LE MANS', artwork completed by Tom Jung, printed by Lonsdale and Bartholomew.

Le Mans was made in 1971 and starred Steve McQueen as Michael Delaney, a racing driver competing in the Le Mans endurance race driving for the Porsche team. His character is haunted by the memory of an accident at the previous year's race in which a competing driver was killed and highlights the interaction between himself and the driver's widow, against the background of the race. The film was directed by Lee H. Katzin and features film recorded during the 1970 race.

1971 *40¼in (102cm) wide*

£1,000-1,200 ROS

'MOTHRA MIGHTIEST MONSTER IN ALL CREATION', small repaired tears and creases.

1962 *41in (104cm) high*

£300-400 SWA

'2001 lodyssee de lespace', Stanley Kubrick, printed by Cine Poster.

1968 *61in (155cm) high*

£500-600 ROS

'CHARLIE Chaplin', repaired tears at edges, some into image.

c1930s *41in (104cm) high*

£950-1,100 SWA

'SHAFT IL DETECTIVE', printed by Rotolitografica, Rome, repaired tears, creases and restoration.

1971 *55¼in (140.5cm) high*

£800-900 SWA

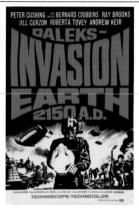

'DALEKS-INVASION EARTH 2150 A.D.', EMI Films, British one sheet rolled film poster.

The Daleks' fiendish plot in 2150 against Earth and its people is foiled when Doctor Who and friends arrive from the 20thC and figure it out. With Peter Cushing, Bernard Cribbins and Ray Brooks.

1966 *40¼in (102cm) high*

£300-400 SWO

'FRED ASTAIRE Ginger ROGERS SHALL WE DANCE', printed by Morgan Lith. Corp., Cleveland, repaired tears, creases and restoration.

1937 *39¾in (101cm) high*

£1,200-2,000 SWA

'SNOW WHITE and the SEVEN DWARFS', US insert poster, framed.

Walt Disney had entertained the idea of producing a feature-length animated film for years, and when financial troubles began to brew, Disney knew he had to come up with something new to save his company. He invested $1,500,000 and three years of hard work, along with the combined talents of 570 artists, into the production of this animation classic. The film was a huge success, earning $8,500,000 Depression-era dollars, that not only saved the company financially, but also laid the foundation for the animation empire that was to follow. The film was such a significant screen innovation that it was given a special Oscar (and seven tiny oscars) in 1939.

1937   *35½in (90cm) high*
£1,800-2,200   GORL

'STAR WARS', British Quad film poster, artwork by Tim & Greg Hildebrandt, 20th Century Fox, minor nicks/bumps to edges.

This version of the British Quad poster was issued when the film was initially released in the UK. However, following the film's release it was discontinued in favour of Tom Chantrell's version, which portrayed the film's actors more accurately.

1977   *40in (101.5cm) wide*
£5,500-6,500   ECGW

'THE GHOST BREAKERS', Paramount Pictures, Morgan Litho Corp, US one-sheet, Paramount logo and 1940 copyright, numbered '18324 05-407/278', starring Bob Hope and Paulette Goddard, unframed.

1940   *41in (104cm) high*
£300-400   BELL

'THE MAN WITH THE GOLDEN GUN', Roger Moore, printed by Lonsdale and Bartholomew Ltd.

1974   *40in (101.5cm) wide*
£400-600   ROS

'THE PLAGUE OF THE ZOMBIES', British Quad film poster, Hammer Film Production, folded, grubby marks, general creasing and handling marks.

1966   *40in (101.5cm) wide*
£3,000-4,000   ECGW

'THE TERROR OF THE TONGS', rare British quad film poster of 1910 Hong Kong-based Hammer Horror film, starring Christopher Lee, pin holes to corners, small tears.

1961   *40in (101.5cm) wide*
£800-1,100   SWO

'SEAN CONNERY "THUNDERBALL"', no.65/372, by United Artist Corporation.

1965   *59¾in (152cm) high*
£250-300   FLD

'THUNDERBIRDS are GO', printed in England by Leonard Ripley and Co. Ltd. London.

1966   *40¼in (102cm) wide*
£350-450   ROS

'YOU ONLY LIVE TWICE', designed by Robert McGinnis and Frank McCarthy, printed by Lonsdale and Bartholomew, England, framed and glazed.

1967   *39¼in (100cm) wide*
£1,200-1,600   ROS

'travel? adventure? answer - Join the Marines!', designed by James Montgomery Flagg (1870-1960), minor expertly-repaired tears.

c1918   40in (101.5cm) high

£4,500-5,500   SWA

'SEE THE WORLD AND GET PAID FOR DOING IT', designed by Alfred Leete (1882-1933), paper, small tears, unobtrusive folds.

1919   30¼in (77cm) high

£2,500-3,500   SWA

QUICK REFERENCE - CLARENCE COLES PHILLIPS

● In what is perhaps the most 'artistic' of the American World War I posters, Phillips unites the bold, direct elements of German object posters by artists such as Lucien Bernhard with the intricate swirls and patterns of American Art Nouveau in the style of William Bradley. Interestingly, while it may echo the work of European artists, the poster represents a divergence from Phillips' usual style. He was nationally known for his 'fadeaway girls,' which graced the covers of 'Life Magazine' from 1908 onward. In these images, which stylistically borrowed from both the Beggarstaff Brothers and Ludwig Hohlwein, Phillips featured attractive young women whose clothing was the same colour as the background, forcing the viewers to complete the image with their imagination.

'LIGHT CONSUMES COAL SAVE LIGHT SAVE COAL', designed by Clarence Coles Phillips (1880-1927), printed by Edwards Deutsch & Litho Co. Chicago, repaired tears and losses.

c1918   27¼in (69cm) high

£2,500-3,000   SWA

'POST OFFICE SAVINGS BANK SAVE for DEFENCE', by Frank Newbound, printed in England.

19¾in (50cm) high

£250-300   DUK

'WAR SAVINGS ARE WARSHIPS', by Norman Wilkinson, printed by J. Weiner Ltd, for HM Stationery Office.

29½in (75cm) high

£200-300   DUK

'Another call MORE MEN AND STILL MORE UNTIL THE ENEMY IS CRUSHED', printed by Hill, Sifflken and Co. London, published by the Parliamentary Recruiting Committee.

28¾in (73cm) high

£120-180   FLD

'CINÉMA Pathé Tous y mènent leurs enfants!', by Adrian Barrère (1877-1931), printed by Robert & Cie., Paris, repaired tears, minor creases and restoration.

This early film poster shows the royal families of Europe bringing their children to the cinema to watch themselves on film. This political parody/celebrity endorsement is intended to promote the cinema as good family entertainment for all. Present at this screening are Alphonse XII of Spain and his son, Edward VII (the Prince of Wales) and Leopold II of Belgium, French President Fallieres, Victor Emmanuel of Italy with his son Umberto and his daughter Yolande, and Tsar Nicolas II of Russia with his wife Alexandra and their son Alexis.

c1909   46½in (118cm) high

£7,000-8,000   SWA

'QUINQUINA DUHOMARD', designed by Dorfi (Albert Dorfinant, 1881-1976), printed by Affiches Camis, Paris, minor staining.

c1935   46¾in (118.5cm) high

£2,000-3,000   SWA

'CASINO DE PARIS MISTINGUETT', designed by Louis (Zig) Gaudin (1882-1936), printed by Central Publicité, Paris, matted and framed.

1930   23in (58.5cm) high

£1,500-2,000   SWA

A Southern Railway 'CREDITON' lamp tablet, from the former London and South Western Railway station between Exeter and Okehampton, china glass with original wooden frame.

18in (45.5cm) wide

£230-280   **GWRA**

A Southern Railway 'POOLE' enamel target sign, from the former London and South Western Railway station between Bournemouth and Wimborne.

£1,200-1,600   **GWRA**

An LNWR 'DOWN MAIN TO SEACOMBE' cast iron signal lever plate.

5½in (14cm) wide

£120-160   **GWRA**

A 'GREAT EASTERN RAILWAY TRESPASSERS WILL BE PROSECUTED' cast iron sign, appears repainted.

21in (53.5cm) wide

£100-140   **LSK**

An early 20thC London, Midland and Scottish Railway 'LMS 158' cast iron bridge plaque.

£50-80   **LOC**

A British Railways Southern Region buffer stop lamp, single aspect, with red warning ring around the red lens.

£100-140   **W&W**

An Adlake 'Non Sweating' lamp, single aspect for TSR Advance Warning Board, with applied label 'Lamp Manufacturing & Railway Supplies Ltd., Dorking, England.

£70-80   **W&W**

A pair of Great Western Railway locomotive whistles, top nuts stamped 'GWR' and in polished condition.

largest 10in (25.5cm) high

£300-400   **GWRA**

A Great Western Railway mahogany cased single line block instrument.

1947   *12in (30.5cm) tall*

£250-300   **GWRA**

A Great Western Railway ship's clock, with an 8in (20.5cm) painted dial, cast brass bezel, brass case and English lever movement, with GWR ivorine number plate 'GWR 3612', in working condition complete with key.

£1,000-1,400   **GWRA**

A 'LOVE ME DO' 7in single, by The Beatles, Parlophone, signed to the A-side in blue ink by Paul McCartney, John Lennon, Ringo Starr and George Harrison, bearing dead wax matrix number '7XCE 17144-1N', 'ZT' tax code stamp.

1962   11¼in (28.5cm) square

£3,000-4,000   WHYT

An autographed postcard, signed by the four members of The Beatles, signed by John Lennon, Ringo Starr, George Harrison, Paul McCartney to reverse.

The signatures were acquired by the vendor's boyfriend on his summer holiday in July 1963. The vendor believes they were signed on either 17 or 19 July 1963 when the band were playing at the Rhyl Ritz Ballroom in North Wales.

£4,500-5,000   AST

An original set of psychedelic posters of The Beatles, three inscribed 'Photographed by Richard Avedon for The Daily Express, Copyright by NEMS Enterprises Ltd...Limited First Edition', framed and glazed.

1971   26¾in (68cm) high

£200-£250   APAR

An album cover 'GEORGE HARRISON, ALL THINGS MUST PASS', signed by George Harrison lower left, with certificate of authenticity verso, framed and glazed.

12in (30.5cm) square

£120-160   APAR

A photograph of John Lennon, by Robert Whitaker, an outtake from the infamous 'Butcher' cover of 'Yesterday and Today', Capitol Records USA release, with annotation to back 'John Studio 1964', printed notation for Uniphoto Press Inc., mounted.

The image of John Lennon was photographed and printed in 1966 by Robert Whitaker (1939-2011). Whitaker accompanied The Beatles to Tokyo in 1966.

6¾in (17cm) wide

£350-400   ROS

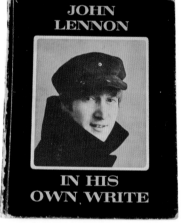

Lennon, John, 'In His Own Write', early edition, published by Jonathan Cape, London, signed by John Lennon to the opening page in blue ink, also inscribed in another hand 'Foyles Luncheon, Dorchester Hotel 23rd April 1964'.

This whimsical book of surrealist poems, drawings and short stories was the first solo endeavour by any of The Beatles. Originally published in March 1964, it was a huge success, reportedly selling 50,000 copies on the first day of its release in England. To celebrate the book's success, Lennon was invited to a literary luncheon hosted by Foyle's at the Dorchester Hotel in London, for which he took a break from filming 'A Hard Day's Night'. Unfortunately, Lennon was not aware that he was expected to make a speech and, according to his wife Cynthia, they were both painfully hungover. When the moment arrived, with the press and attendees waiting with bated breath to hear from the 'intelligent' Beatle, Lennon stood and said 'Er, thank you all very much, and God bless you'.

1964

£2,500-3,000   LSK

A Live Aid gelatin silver print, by David Bailey, of Bob Geldof and Paula Yates, signed in pen by David Bailey, and signed on reverse by Bob Geldof and Paula Yates, stamped 'ARCHIVAL DAVID BAILEY' and pencil initials 'DB3/3', framed.

Five photographs were taken by David Bailey backstage at the Live Aid concert during the summer of 1985, for a benefit auction hosted by Sotheby's later that year. Each print is signed by the photographer and the majority are signed on the reverse by the subject. Only three of each image were printed for the auction. Live Aid was a dual-venue benefit concert held on 13 July 1985, and an ongoing music-based fundraising initiative. The original event was organised by Bob Geldof and Midge Ure to raise funds for relief of the ongoing Ethiopian famine. The event was held simultaneously at Wembley Stadium in London and John F. Kennedy Stadium in Philadelphia, USA. On the same day, concerts inspired by the initiative happened in other countries, such as the Soviet Union, Canada, Japan, Yugoslavia, Austria, Australia and West Germany. It was one of the largest-scale satellite link-ups and television broadcasts of all time; an estimated global audience of 1.5 billion across 140 nations watched the live broadcast. This was nearly 40% of the world population at the time.

1985   *20in (51cm) high*
£1,500-2,000   **SWO**

A Live Aid gelatin silver print, by David Bailey, of George Michael, signed by David Bailey, and signed on reverse by George Michael, stamped 'ARCHIVAL DAVID BAILEY' and pencil initials 'DB 85 3/3', framed.

During the Live Aid concert, Michael sang 'Don't Let the Sun Go Down on Me' with Elton John on piano for the first time. The song found further success in 1991 as a duet between Elton John and George Michael, which reached number one in the UK and US charts.

1985   *20in (51cm) high*
£5,500-6,000   **SWO**

A Live Aid gelatin silver print, by David Bailey, of Status Quo, signed in pen by David Bailey, and signed on reverse by Rick Parfitt and Francis Rossi, stamped 'ARCHIVAL DAVID BAILEY' and pencil initials 'DB 85 2/3', framed.

1985   *19¾in (50cm) high*
£2,500-3,000   **SWO**

A Live Aid gelatin silver print, by David Bailey, of Spandau Ballet, signed in pen by David Bailey, and signed on reverse by Gary Kemp, Martin Kemp, Tony Hadley, Steve Norman and John Keeble, stamped 'ARCHIVAL DAVID BAILEY' and pencil initials 'DB 85 2/3', framed.

1985   *20in (51cm) high*
£2,000-2,500   **SWO**

QUICK REFERENCE - KEITH FLINT

- Keith Flint (1969-2019) was born in Redbridge, London. After being expelled from school, Flint worked as a roofer and then travelled, working for a while in Israel, before returning to the UK.
- In the late 1980s, along with Leeroy Thornhill, Liam Howlett, Sharky and MC Maxim Reality, Flint formed The Prodigy. Flint became lead vocalist in 1996.
- In 2006, Flint married Mayumi Kai, a Japanese DJ. They divorced in 2018. Flint died in 2019.
- All items on this page were part of the Keith Flint Collection.

A carved and polychrome painted wooden head study of Keith Flint.

33in (84cm) high

£3,500-4,000   CHEF

A Steve Liddard custom-built oak and steel bed, supported at each corner by entwined thorns and accessed via steps supported on the back of a crouching winged mythical beast, branded mark.

It is understood that Keith worked closely with Steve Liddard on the design of this bed.

125in (317.5cm) long

£11,000-14,000   CHEF

An Obediar Creations and Frailloop large welded aluminium and steel model ant, by Obediar Madziva and Gavin Darby, signed, dated.

When The Prodigy performed in Milton Keynes in 2010 at the Warriors Dance Festival, Frailloop were commissioned by the band's management to produce six large ant sculptures, based on the band's logo, to put on display at the venue. Each band member received one as a gift after the event.

2010   99in (251.5cm) high

£11,000-14,000   CHEF

A charcoal portrait of Keith Flint, by Kirk Andrews, framed, mounted with various inscriptions to the mount, commemorating Keith's 47th birthday in 2016.

This work was commissioned by The Prodigy Dirtchamber fan club and taken to the Leather Bottle, Keith's pub in Pleshey, where fans travelled from Europe to write messages to Keith on the mount.

22in (56cm) square

£3,500-4,500   CHEF

A pair of NME presentation awards to Keith Flint, one for Best Dance Act for The Prodigy in 1997, the other for Best Video for 'Firestarter'.

£10,000-12,000   CHEF

A Doug Murphy (PlasticGod) stretcher acrylic on canvas, Keith Flint signed and dated 'Doug Murphy/4.25.03'.

PlasticGod is the tag of Los Angeles-based artist, Doug Murphy (b.1973), also known as 'The 21st Century Warhol'. His paintings of pop icons from the world of music, art, fashion, cinema, theatre and celebrity have made PlasticGod a Pop icon in his own right.

4in (10cm) square

£2,000-3,000   CHEF

A Vivienne Westwood Anglomania Monty duffle coat, in branded suit carrier, with a Vivienne Westwood diamanté dress stud in the form of a bone.

£2,500-3,000   CHEF

A set of four MTV Music Television Awards, awarded to Keith Flint, comprising 1997 Award for Best Video, 1997 for Best Dance, 1997 Award for Best Alternative and 1996 Award to The Prodigy for Best Dance, with a framed photograph of the band at the award ceremony.

£9,000-11,000   CHEF

'ABBA', signed by all four members in ink, some wear and staining, mounted on a board.

c1977   *37¼in (94.5cm) high*

£350-400   **LOCK**

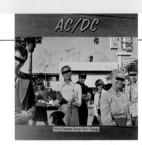

A 'Dirty Deeds Done Dirt Cheap' sleeve of the international edition of AC/DC's third studio album, released in December 1976, signed in blue ballpoint by Bon Scott, Angus Young, Malcolm Young, Phil Rudd and Cliff Williams, framed.

17¾in (45cm) square

£850-950   **WHYT**

An 'ANDROMEDA' record, RCA orange label, SF 8031.

£600-700   **LSK**

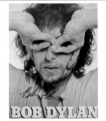

A Bob Dylan Earls Court concert programme, signed in black felt-tip pen to the front cover, mounted.

1978

£450-550   **WHYT**

A Bob Dylan magazine cutting, in blue ink, signed to the top right corner.

Acquired Albany Hotel, Birmingham, 1966.

9in (23cm) high

£200-300   **FLD**

A Tito Burns presents signed Bob Dylan '66 (Highway Revisited) tour programme, in black and white, signed on the fifth page 'To John Weston, Bob Dylan'.

Acquired from the Albany Hotel prior to the concert.

£1,800-2,200   **FLD**

A nude portrait of Marsha Hunt, by Patrick Lichfield, for the musical 'Hair', framed and glazed.

1969   17½in (44.5cm) square

£160-200   **BELL**

A Jimi Hendrix (1942-70) Polydor Records single sleeve, for 'HEY JOE', signed Jimi Hendrix, mounted together with two press clippings from the 'Musical Express'.

By repute this sleeve was signed by Hendrix at the Lauro Verde beach bar in Palma, Mallorca on 16 July 1968. The bar owner had this record signed.

the mount 16½in (42cm) wide

£1,000-1,500   **ROS**

A 'THIS WAS' record, by Jethro Tull, UK pressing, pink Island label, ILPS 9085 A.

£100-150   **LSK**

An 'IN THE COURT OF THE CRIMSON KING' record, by King Crimson, UK first pressing, pink Island Records white 'i' label ILPS-9111.

£150-200   **LSK**

ROCK & POP

A 'SHE JUST SATISFIES, KEEP MOVING' 1st press Fontana 45 single, by Jimmy Page, TF 533, 267418 TF, Mono.

Jimmy Page's first solo single was not a favourite of Page himself, who was trying to move away from session music at the time (he later claimed that it was 'better forgotten'). However, it is an interesting footnote in his career. Page undertook lead vocals and played all of the instruments except drums.

£600-700   LSK

A signed 'Sticky Fingers' LP record, by the Rolling stones, COC 59100, in zip sleeve designed by Andy Warhol, printed inside with his signature, signed in red felt-tip pen by Mick Jagger, Keith Richards, Mick Taylor and Charlie Watts.

£2,700-3,000   WHYT

A Chris Ruocco pirate print shirt, worn by George Michael in Wham's American Tour in 1985, labelled 'Tailored by Chris Ruocco'.

Chris Ruocco, tailors in Kentish Town, North London, dressed the likes of Bananarama, Spandau Ballet and Wham in the 1980s. This shirt comes with the packaging it was sent in from Andrew Ridgley.

£500-600   SWO

An 'Arnold Layne, Candy and a Current Bun' single, by The Pink Floyd, 7in original French release Columbia ESRF 1857, matrix M3 252951 7TCA 10350 21.

This 1967 debut single from The Pink Floyd was apparently about a transvestite knicker thief called Arnold Layne (B-side Candy and a Current Bun). Despite charting, the unusual subject matter shocked some radio station personnel and the song was eventually removed from airplay.

£250-300   LSK

A Rolling Stones black and white postcard, signed in black ink by Keith Richards, Brian Jones, Mick Jagger, Charlie Watts and Bill Wyman, to the reverse signed in black ink, 'Best Wishes to John from the Rolling Stones', with a Yamaha Soloist no.10 a.440 Harmonica reputedly given to the owner by Mick Jagger.

Acquired in person by the current owner at the Plaza Hansworth, 1963.

£2,500-3,000   FLD

A 'THE WHO LIVE AT LEEDS' album and cover, signed by Roger Daltrey, Peter Townshend and John Entwhistle, with a poster for The Who in concert, at the Rainbow (formerly the Astoria Theatre), Finsbury Park, 4, 5, and 6 November 1971.

£1,500-2,000   ROS

A 'THE PIPER AT THE GATES OF DAWN' record, by Pink Floyd, Columbia blue/black label SX 6157, Matrix XAX 3420 1/ XAX 3420 2, file under POPULAR sleeve, 'ROG 15.12.68' in pen to back cover.

£300-350   LSK

A 'Tommy' official souvenir brochure, signed by Paul Nicholas, Robert Powell, Pete Townshend, Tina Turner, Eric Clapton and Arthur Brown.

£150-200   FLD

A 'Led Zeppelin I', by Led Zeppelin, UK first pressing Atlantic 588171, red/maroon label with Superhype, jewel credits, 588171 A//1 118, B//1 184.

This 1969 UK first pressing of the self-titled Led Zeppelin album depicts the Hindenburg air disaster on the cover with turquoise lettering and red/maroon Superhype/Jewel label. Within weeks of its release, the cover was replaced with the orange lettering version – which was considered more Rock 'n' Roll than turquoise.

£1,500-2,000   LSK

A Victorian silver-gilt and glass scent bottle/vinaigrette, by S. Mordan and Co., the glazed front opens to reveal a silver-gilt grille, the reverse with a hinged compartment, with a chain and finger ring, the glass body is cracked.

Sampson Mordan (1790-1843) was a British silversmith. He went into business with John Isaac Hawkins in 1822 and together they invented the mechanical pencil, but Mordan later bought Hawkins out. Mordan then went into partnership with stationer Gabriel Riddle, but the partnership dissolved in 1837, and Mordan continued under the trading name of S. Mordan and Co., until his death in 1843, when the company passed to his sons. The company manufactured a wide variety of products, including scent bottles, pencils, locks, whistles, boxes and inkwells. S. Mordan and Co. became a limited liability company in 1898. The company stopped trading in 1941.

3¼in (8.5cm) long

£450-500   WW

A Victorian silver scent bottle, by S. Mordan & Co., with bright cut engraving.

2in (5cm) long

£400-500   JN

A Victorian silver-gilt mounted double scent bottle/vinaigrette, with foliate engraved split hinged covers, conforming silver-gilt heel, stamped to the underside 'S. Mordan & Co. Makers', with diamond registration mark for 1 September 1858.

1858

£500-600   FLD

A Victorian S. Mordan & Co. double-ended cut glass scent bottle, with silver-gilt mounts, London.

1876.   5in (12.5cm) long

£200-300   JN

A Victorian engraved silver scent bottle and stopper, by S. Mordan & Co., London.

1881   2in (5cm) long

£250-300   JN

A Victorian silver scent bottle, by S. Mordan & Co., with engraved Kate Greenaway decoration, hinged cover.

1883   2¼in (5.5cm) high

£400-500   WW

A Victorian silver-mounted 'fish' glass scent bottle, by S. Mordan & Co., the green glass body with gilded scales and details, red glass eyes.

1884   6¼in (16cm) long

£1,800-2,200   WW

A Thomas Webb three-layer cameo glass scent bottle, with a silver screw-fitted cap, hallmarks for S. Mordan & Co., London.

c1887   4in (10cm) high

£850-950   WW

A cut glass scent bottle, by S. Mordan & Co., with screw-off silver cap, marked in leather case 'H. W. BEDFORD, 67 REGENT STREET'.

11in (28cm) long

£300-400   JN

QUICK REFERENCE - SCENT BOTTLES

- Until the 19thC, the design of scent bottles was determined by the volatility and expense of scent. The bottles had to be airtight and impervious to light and were made to reflect the cost of the scent.
- Although glass had been used for scent bottles from Roman times, it became the most popular material for scent bottles from the end of the 18thC, with precious metals and hardstones often used previously.
- By the 20thC, perfume makers had begun to sell bottled perfume, leading collectors to generally focus on one parfumier or fashion house. Prior to this, perfume was sold to be mixed and decanted into scent bottles.

A George III silver scent bottle, by Joseph Willmore, chequer-board decoration, screw-off cover with a ring attachment.

1805   1½in (4cm) long
£300-350   **WW**

A 19thC red flash-cut lay scent bottle, with a hinged white metal cap.

                    4in (10cm) long
£120-180   **FLD**

A George IV silver 'horn' vinaigrette/scent bottle, by Nathaniel Mills, with a pierced foliate grille, engraved decoration, with a chain and screw-off scent bottle cover set with an agate cabochon.

Vinaigrettes were small hinged boxes containing a perfume-soaked sponge behind a pierced grille. Some vinaigrettes had a small ring on the exterior allowing them to be worn around the neck. In the early 1800s, vinaigrette designs became increasingly elaborate and the boxes grew in size.

1828   4in (10cm) long
£750-850   **WW**

A Victorian double-ended glass scent bottle, with silver caps.

                    5½in (14cm) long
£95-110   **JN**

A Victorian ruby glass scent bottle, with silver cap.

                    3¼in (8.5cm) long
£55-65   **JN**

A Victorian double-ended glass scent bottle, with engraved silver caps, initialled.

                    5¼in (13.5cm) long
£95-110   **JN**

A Victorian tinted glass scent bottle, with engraved silver cap.

                    3½in (9cm) long
£120-160   **JN**

A Victorian ruby facet-cut glass scent bottle, with repoussé silver cap.

                    3¾in (9.5cm) long
£100-150   **JN**

A Victorian blue tinted glass scent bottle, with repoussé silver cap and frosted glass stopper.

                    4¼in (11cm) long
£120-160   **JN**

A Victorian Bristol blue facet-cut double-ended glass scent bottle, with repoussé silver caps.

5¼in (13.5cm) long

£95-110   JN

A Victorian ruby tinted facet-cut glass scent bottle, with repoussé silver cap.

1½in (4cm) high

£70-80   JN

A Victorian cut glass scent bottle, with repoussé silver cap, glass stopper and chain.

3½in (9cm) long

£100-140   JN

A Victorian facet-cut double-ended glass scent bottle and vinaigrette.

3¼in (8.5cm) long

£75-85   JN

A Victorian hobnail cut glass folding scent bottle and vinaigrette, with repoussé silver caps and silver-gilt vinaigrette.

5½in (14cm) long

£250-300   JN

A Victorian ruby facet-cut double-ended glass scent bottle, with silver-gilt repoussé caps.

4¾in (12cm) long

£100-140   JN

A Victorian ruby glass and gold-mounted scent bottle and stopper, with a 'Mary Gregory' child.

3in (7.5cm) long

£400-500   JN

A Victorian tapering ruby glass scent bottle, with flowers and foliage in gilt, with screw-off silver cap and glass stopper.

7¾in (19.5cm) long

£250-300   JN

A Victorian silver-gilt mounted overlay scent bottle/vinaigrette, by Abraham Brownett, the cover with engraved decoration and a concealed photograph frame, inset with turquoise and pearl cabochons, the front engraved 'Lally' and opens to reveal a foliate pierced silver-gilt grille, engraved 'Registered P. & F. Schafer, 27 Piccadilly, 21st Aug 1866', the reverse with a hinged compartment and engraved 'Xmas 1916'.

1867   *3in (7.5cm) long*

£1,300-1,600   WW

SCENT BOTTLES

A 19thC clear glass perfume bottle, with silver cap, painted with a Chinese figure and deer.

4in (10cm) high

1876

£130-160   **JN**

A late19thC Russian silver-gilt and enamel scent flask, by Pavel Ovchinnikov, assay master V Savinsky, pull-out stopper.

1876   *8in (20.5cm) high*

£2,200-3,000   **WW**

A Victorian silver engraved scent bottle, with frosted glass stopper, maker 'C.M.'.

1882   *2¼in (5.5cm) long*

£150-200   **JN**

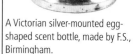

A Victorian silver-mounted egg-shaped scent bottle, made by F.S., Birmingham.

1885   *3in (7.5cm) high*

£300-350   **JN**

A Victorian glass scent bottle, made by C.M., with screw-off silver cap, Birmingham.

1886   *4in (10cm) long*

£120-160   **JN**

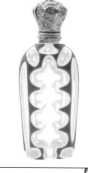

A 19thC scent bottle, the pink and white overlaid clear glass body below silver-gilt metal collar and hinged cover.

3½in (9cm) long

£220-280   **FLD**

A silver-mounted ceramic 'egg' scent bottle, by Saunders and Shepherd, screw-off cover.

1885   *2½in (6.5cm) long*

£350-400   **WW**

A Victorian cameo glass scent bottle, with screw-off silver cap, Chester.

1890   *1½in (4cm) diam*

£350-400   **JN**

A 19thC facet-cut glass 'horn' scent bottle.

1½in (4cm) long

£125-150   **JN**

A French novelty silver 'owl' scent bottle and desk seal, the hinged cover set with glass eyes, with a glass stopper.

2¼in (5.5cm) high

c1890

£250-300   **WW**

A late 19thC Russian silver-gilt and enamel scent bottle, maker's mark worn, screw-off cover.

c1890   *3in (7.5cm) long*

£500-600   **WW**

A Russian silver and enamel scent flask, by Ivan Saltykov, pull-out stopper, Moscow.

c1890   *6in (15cm) high*

£1,200-1,600   **WW**

A Russian silver-mounted scent bottle, maker's mark possibly that of A.S. Bragin, with a stopper.

1896-1908   *5¾in (14.5cm) high*

£200-250   **WW**

A novelty silver-mounted 'bird's egg' ceramic scent bottle, by Saunders and Shepherd, with a registration number, plain screw-off cover.

1897   *1½in (4cm) long*

£150-200   **WW**

A Victorian glass and silver scent bottle, maker C.M., Birmingham.

1897   *1½in (4cm) long*

£70-80   **JN**

A Victorian glass scent bottle and stopper, made by C. & G., Birmingham, with plain silver cap.

1900   *2¾in (7cm) long*

£120-160   **JN**

A late 19thC Thomas Webb & Sons large cameo glass lay scent bottle, cut with flowering boughs to one side and peace lily and cow parsley verso, gilded silver mounts stamped 'Gorham'.

5¼in (13.5cm) long

£750-850   **FLD**

SCENT BOTTLES

A Bristol blue glass facet-cut scent bottle, with silver cap.

1½in (4cm) long

£80-100   **JN**

An Italian glass spiral-shaped scent bottle, with cork stopper.

3in (7.5cm) long

£65-75   **JN**

An early 20thC Continental silver finger scent bottle, with relief-moulded flowers, with screw cap.

2½in (6.5cm) long

£90-110   **FLD**

An 20thC silver-plated glass faceted scent bottle.

5¼in (13.5cm) long

£45-55   **FLD**

An early 20thC glass scent bottle, overlaid with silver clover pattern, with a hinged silver lid, makers mark worn.

1907   *4in (10cm) high*

£180-220   **FLD**

A Webb's cameo glass scent bottle, with engraved silver cap, Birmingham.

1907   *1½in (4cm) high*

£300-400   **JN**

A George V Levi & Salaman silver framed and tortoiseshell egg-shaped scent bottle stand, the hinged body enclosing a pair of glass scent bottles.

1912   *4¼in (11cm) high*

£300-350   **APAR**

An Edward VII engraved silver scent bottle, made by D.M. & Co., with plain glass and frosted stopper, Birmingham.

1908   *2¼in (5.5cm) long*

£65-75   **JN**

A studio glass scent bottle, by Jonathan Harris, with gold leaf and mottled pastel-coloured decoration, signed and dated to base, some abrasions to the base of the stopper.

2002   *4¼in (11cm) high*

£60-80   **APAR**

A late 19thC microscope magnifier, by R. and J. Beck Ltd., London, with fitted and adjustable side lens, chimney and coloured slides over a clear glass reservoir, in mahogany case with slide box and funnel.

11¾in (30cm) high

£900-1,100   FLD

A late 19thC brass binocular microscope, by E.G. Wood, with accessories, including a brass bullseye lens and a brass adjustable night light, in a mahogany case, unsigned.

20in (51cm) high

£1,500-2,000   BELL

A brass binocular microscope, by John Browning, 63 Strand, London, no.823, in a mahogany case with a detachable part box of lenses.

John Browning (c1831-1925) was an English inventor and maker of precision scientific instruments.

16½in (42cm) high

£550-600   WHP

A C. Reichert of Wien brass monocular microscope, numbered '21798'.

£80-120   APAR

An E. Leitz Wetzlar brass and black lacquered monocular microscope, numbered '149146'.

£40-50   APAR

A 3½in (9cm) refracting lacquered brass telescope, by Secretan, Paris, signed on the back plate 'Secretan, Epry SUCr, PARIS', 44½in (113cm) main tube with star spotter, threaded 11in (28cm) eye-piece tube with rack-and-pinion fine focus, in original case with maker's label and three eyepiece accessories, with original stand.

c1880   *case 51¼in (130cm) wide*

£900-1,200   CM

A lacquered and oxidised brass theodolite, by Hildebrand & Schramm, Freiberg, the 10in (25.5cm) tube with rack-and-pinion fine focus and top sights secured to circular protractor with opposing vernier scales on a pillar with fine longitude adjustment, numbered '1558', in original case, with tripod stand.

c1880   *18¼in (46.5cm) high*

£900-1,200   CM

A pair of German Schneider 25 x 105 field binoculars, with Zeiss lenses, chrome-plated, on a wooden and chrome tripod stand.

1950s   *52¾in (134cm) high*

£2,500-3,000   DUK

A late 19thC Victorian walnut stereoscopic viewer, the base with fitted drawer containing card stereoscope slides, including examples by the London Stereoscopic and Photographic Company of The International Exhibition of 1862.

15¾in (40cm) high

£1,300-1,600   ROS

SCIENTIFIC INSTRUMENTS

A vernier octant, by Spencer, Browning & Rust, London, the scale divided to 95 degrees and stamped with 'SBR' dividing letters, with brass index arm, pinhole sight, three shades and mirrors, with signed maker's plate.

c1790   *13½in (34.5cm) radius*

£250-350   **CM**

A lean-pattern brass miner's dial, by Negretti & Zambra, 4¼in (11cm) silvered dial signed, with Diff of Hypo scale over with 7½in (19cm) sighting telescope, with rack-and-pinion fine focus top objective.

c1880   *box 13½in (34.5cm) wide*

£400-500   **CM**

A George III table-top 12in (30.5cm) terrestrial globe, by W. & S. Jones, London, 12 printed gores, labelled 'THE NEW TWELVE INCH BRITISH Terrestrial Globe REPRESENTING THE ACCURATE POSITIONS OF THE PRINCIPAL KNOWN PLACES OF THE EARTH, FROM THE DISCOVERIES OF CAPTAIN COOK AND SUBSEQUENT CIRCUMNAVIGATORS TO THE PRESENT PERIOD', with a brass meridian ring, and horizon ring with calendar and zodiac markers, on an ebonised stand, dated.

1800

£3,000-3,500   **L&T**

A dry card binnacle compass, by Hooper & Son, Portsmouth, signed engraved, wax balancing, in painted brass bowl gimbal mounted within wooden binnacle with removable glass viewing panel, oil lamp, securing rings, top handle and shaped lower edge.

c1850   *13in (33cm) high*

£500-600   **CM**

A two-day marine chronometer, by Kelvin, White & Hutton, the silvered dial signed, evacuated from Singapore on HMS Bulan, impressed with Government broad arrow mark, blued steel hands, the Mercer movement, with Harrison's maintaining power, Earnshaw escapement, bi-metallic standard balance with hellical balance spring, gimbal mounted within wooden box with ivorine maker's plate, Singapore adjuster's label inside lid for 'Sept. 1940'.

9½in (24cm) wide

£2,200-2,600   **CM**

A silver-mounted drawing set etui, by Benjamin Martin, the scissor protractor and folding rule signed, with a full set of instruments, in a silver-mounted shagreen case.

c1760   *7in (18cm) high*

£4,000-5,000   **CM**

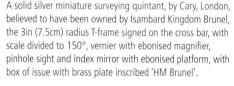

A solid silver miniature surveying quintant, by Cary, London, believed to have been owned by Isambard Kingdom Brunel, the 3in (7.5cm) radius T-frame signed on the cross bar, with scale divided to 150°, vernier with ebonised magnifier, pinhole sight and index mirror with ebonised platform, with box of issue with brass plate inscribed 'HM Brunel'.

Isambard Kingdom Brunel's sons died childless, so his collection passed down the female line via his daughter Florence Coleridge née Brunel (b.1847) who in turn had daughters Celia and Lillian. Celia Brunel (1872-1962) made the principal donation of artefacts to Bristol University in 1950. However, it seems some items were retained as her daughter, Lady Cynthia Noble Jebb (1898-1990) passed on this item as part of a group to one of her daughters, who had them evaluated when winding up her mother's estate.

c1830   *box 4¾in (12cm) square*

£4,000-5,000   **CM**

A Negretti and Zambra brass pocket barometer, no.10772, the reverse a compass with locking button, in lined crocodile skin case.

£400-500   **FLD**

An Art Deco 'Amazon' cold-painted bronze group, by Marcel-André Bouraine (1886-1948), on bronze base, signed 'Bouraine and Etling Paris'.

c1930   *10in (25.5cm) wide*

£2,000-2,500   **ROS**

An Émile Carlier patinated spelter figurine of a dancer, on veined marble stepped base, signed.

20¾in (52.5cm) high

£300-350   **WW**

An Art Deco bronze 'Egyptian Dancer' study, by Demetre H. Chiparus, on a veined marble base, with gilt Egyptian-style plaque to front, signed.

28¾in (73cm) high

£8,500-10,000   **FLD**

QUICK REFERENCE - DEMETRE H. CHIPARUS

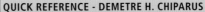

- ● **Born in Romania, Demetre H. Chiparus (1880-1950) studied in France and worked predominantly with bronze and ivory.**
- ● **Most of Chiparus' work was handled by the Etling foundry. Models were made by Chiparus for Goldscheider and Les Neveux de J. Lehmann.**
- ● **Chiparus took inspiration from the theatre, the Ballet Russes and Egyptian culture. The tomb of Tutankhamun was opened in 1922, driving an interest in Ancient Egypt.**

An early 20thC French 'La Danseuse Ayouta' ivory figurine, by Demetre H. Chiparus, patinated and cold-painted bronze figurine, on an onyx base, signed, light wear.

18¼in (46.5cm) high

£9,000-11,000   **GORL**

An Art Deco patinated bronze 'Cleopatra' figurine, by Demetre H. Chiparus, on a variegated black marble base, signed.

£6,500-7,500   **FLD**

A gilt-bronze figurine of a girl balancing two balls, by Claire Jeanne Roberte Colinet (1880-1950), on a marble base.

10in (25.5cm) high

£500-600   **JN**

A polished bronze 'The Juggler' sculpture, by Claire Jeanne Roberte Colinet, on striated onyx base, signed.

14½in (37cm) high

£650-750   **WW**

An Art Deco patinated spelter centrepiece of a girl and a borzoi, by A. Godard, on an onyx plinth.

23¼in (59cm) wide

£200-300   **SWO**

A cold-painted bronze and ivory figurine, by Josef Lorenzl, on onyx base, signed 'LORENZL'.

c1925   *8¾in (22cm) high*

£2,200-2,800   **TEN**

SCULPTURE

QUICK REFERENCE - JOSEF LORENZL

- Austrian sculptor and ceramicist Josef Lorenzl (1892-1950) trained and worked in Vienna.
- Lorenzl used bronze and ivory to sculpt figurines predominantly of slim female dancers with elongated limbs. The bronze figurines are usually cold-painted or silvered.
- The signature of 'Crejo', the craftsman who enamelled some of Lorenzl's figurines, appears on some of his work. Lorenzl also designed ceramic figurines for Goldscheider.

An Art Deco bronze figurine of a nude dancer, by Josef Lorenzl, on onyx base, signed indistinctly to cast.

c1925   *9¾in (25cm) high*

£550-650   **HAN**

An Art deco lacquered gilt-bronze nude figurine, by Josef Lorenzl, on onyx base, signed 'R. Lor, Austria'.

c1930   *8in (20.5cm) high*

£700-800   **ROS**

A silvered bronze figurine of a dancer, by Josef Lorenzl, signed, on an onyx plinth.

10½in (26.5cm) high

£500-600   **SWO**

An Art Deco cold-painted bronze and ivory figurine of a woman, by Josef Lorenzl, modelled with a scarf hanging from each wrist, on onyx plinth, engraved 'Lorenzl' on base.

c1930   *8¾in (22.5cm) high*

£1,500-2,000   **ROS**

A bronzed figurine of a nude dancing girl, by Josef Lorenzl, signed, on onyx plinth, chips to base, some wear.

11in (28cm) high

£1,500-2,000   **GORL**

A 1920s Art Deco patinated bronze figurine of a semi-clad female, by Josef Lorenzl, her robes enamelled with floral sprays, signed, on an onyx base.

12¼in (31cm) high

£1,500-2,000   **FLD**

An Art Deco patinated gilt bronze dancer, by Josef Lorenzl, on onyx base, signed in the bronze, some surface wear.

12in (30.5cm) high

£1,200-1,600   **CHEF**

An Art Deco bronze figurine of a scarf dancer, by Josef Lorenzl, signed, on onyx plinth.

4¾in (12cm) high

£400-500   **FLD**

A 1920s French Art Deco spelter figurine, by Roland, Paris, of an exotic dancer in Egyptian revival-style costume, on a marble base.

14¼in (36cm) high

£200-250   **FLD**

A 1920s Vienna gilded and silvered painted bronze 'Musette' figurine, on a marble base.

7½in (19cm) high

£500-600   QU

A 1930s Art Deco patinated bronze figurine of a female nude standing provocatively in a fur coat, by Bruno Zach, on a variegated black marble base, unsigned.

11½in (29cm) high

£2,000-2,500   FLD

A CLOSER LOOK AT A SPELTER FIGURINE

Although often thought of as much inferior to bronze, spelter figurines can be highly desirable.

The beauty of its finished patina (when spelter is cast it is produced without flaws) creates sculptural works that are perfect in form.

Spelter was first introduced to Europe from Asia by Dutch and Portuguese traders in the 17thC.

This figurine has all the movement and style that typifies Art Deco.

An Art Deco silvered spelter figurine of a female dancer, on a marble base, figurine loose to base, some rubbing to paint.

20in (50.5cm) high

£600-700   APAR

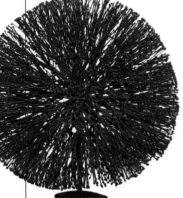

An untitled patinated bronze and copper sculpture, by Harry Bertoia, some oxidation.

Italian-born Harry Bertoia (1915-78) attended and taught at the Cranbrook Academy of Art in Michigan, USA. Bertoia is known for his sculpture, prints, jewellery and furniture. He died in 1978.

16in (40.5cm) high

£35,000-40,000   DRA

A patinated bronze figurine of a woodcock, by Nick Bibby (b.1960), Britain, limited edition no.11 of 12.

9in (23cm) long

£1,500-2,000   CHOR

A patinated bronze figurine of a partridge, by Geoffrey Dashwood (b.1947), Britain, limited edition no.12 of 12.

8½in (21.5cm) long

£2,000-2,500   CHOR

A bronze figurine of a nude woman in a deck chair, by Desmond Fountain (b.1946), limited edition no.9 of 9, signed, numbered.

17in (43cm) long

£3,000-4,000   GORL

A chrome-plated steel 'Eight Elbows' sculpture, by William Pye, stamped 'PYE' signature, dated, numbered '2/6' and '25', Redfern Gallery label to underside, light surface pitting.

'Eight Elbows' was part of a series of sculptures first exhibited by Pye in his second solo show at the Redfern Gallery, London. Although an abstract composition it was influenced by the rapidly evolving cultural production and industrial terrain of the 1960s. Consisting of eight 90-degree steel elbows welded together, Pye's use of 'the tube' was a conscious departure from modelling in order to lower 'immediate sensuality' and mask the effort involved in its production. See William Pye, Rupert Brown and Oliver Brown, 'William Pye, his work and words', Brown & Brown (2010), pp.52-53.

1968   *13in (33cm) high*

£5,000-6,000   CHEF

SEWING

QUICK REFERENCE - SEWING

- Most sewing accessories available to collectors date from the 19thC and early 20thC. Items from the 18thC and earlier, before mass production made these items common, are especially prized.
- Collectors tend to focus on one type of sewing tool or accessory, such as thimbles, pin cushions or needle cases. Pin cushions were very widely produced and remain popular with collectors, in part due to the aesthetic appeal of novelty pin cushions.
- Sewing accessories and tools were made from a range of materials, including silver, gold, ivory, bone, mother-of-pearl, tortoiseshell and wood. Silver pieces became increasingly common in the Edwardian period as the price of silver dropped.

An Edwardian silver duck pin cushion, by Abrahall & Bint, Birmingham.

1905   *4in (10cm) long*

£350-400   WW

An Edwardian silver goat pin cushion, by Adie & Lovekin Ltd., Birmingham, one green glass eye.

1909   *1¾in (4.5cm) high*

£500-550   WW

An Edwardian silver swan pin cushion, by Adie & Lovekin Ltd., Birmingham, set with glass eyes.

1909   *3in (7.5cm) long*

£300-350   WW

A late-Victorian silver 'flying swallow' pin cushion, by James Samuel Bell & Louis Willmott, London.

1895   *5in (12.5cm) long*

£750-850   WW

A Edwardian silver shoe pin cushion, by S. Blanckensee & Son, Chester.

S. Blanckensee & Son was founded by Solomon Blanckensee in Bristol in the early 19thC. The firm went on to acquire silversmiths Nathan & Hayes, Albion Chain Co. and J.W. Tiptaft Ltd. among others.

1910

£140-180   HAN

An Edwardian silver gondola pin cushion, by Adie & Lovekin Ltd., Birmingham, velvet cushion.

1906   *3¾in (9.5cm) long*

£180-220   WW

An Edwardian silver camel and cart pin cushion, by Adie & Lovekin Ltd., Birmingham, the camel pulling a mother-of-pearl cart, one wheel damaged.

1909   *5in (12.5cm) long*

£450-500   WW

An Edwardian silver billy goat and cart pin cushion, by Adie & Lovekin Ltd., Birmingham, the goat pulling a mother-of-pearl cart.

1909   *4¾in (12cm) long*

£700-800   WW

A silver Newfoundland dog pin cushion, by Adie & Lovekin Ltd., Birmingham, with green glass eyes, date letter worn.

2¼in (5.5cm) long

£950-1,100   WW

A silver pin cushion, by S. Blanckensee & Sons Ltd., Chester, modelled as the ship 'Royal George', with a rudder and propeller.

1910   *5¼in (13.5cm) long*

£450-550   WW

An Edwardian silver bulldog pin cushion, by Adie & Lovekin Ltd., Birmingham, later cushion.

Adie & Lovekin was established in Birmingham in the latter half of the 19thC by Alfred Lovekin and James Adie. The company, which produced silver items including pin cushions, buckles, button hooks and baby rattles, became Adie & Lovekin Ltd. in 1889. The company closed in the late 1920s.

1906   *2in (5cm) high*

£320-400   WW

An Edwardian silver hare pin cushion, by Boots Pure Drug Co., Birmingham.

1907   *2¼in (5.5cm) long*

£400-500   WW

A silver lizard pin cushion, by Crisford & Norris Ltd., Birmingham, with red cabochon eyes.

1913   *4¼in (11cm) long*

£600-650   **WW**

A late Victorian silver moon pin cushion, by Deakin and Sons, London, set with five stars, velvet cushion.

1894   *3in (7.5cm) long*

£230-300   **WW**

An Edwardian silver pin cushion, by Jones & Crompton, Birmingham, modelled as a tennis racket leaning against a tennis net.

1909   *1½in (4cm) high*

£600-700   **WW**

An Edwardian silver camel pin cushion, by Levi & Salaman, Birmingham.

Levi & Salaman was founded in c1870 in Birmingham by Phineas Harris Levi and Joseph Wolff Salaman. The company produced jewellery and silver items. In 1878, Levi & Salaman bought Potosi Silver, a manufacturer of silverplate cutlery. The company became Levi & Salaman Ltd. in 1910.

1903   *4in (10cm) long*

£700-800   **WW**

An Edwardian silver hedgehog pin cushion, by Levi & Salaman, Birmingham.

1905   *1¾in (4.5cm) long*

£300-350   **WW**

An Edwardian silver bull pin cushion, by Levi & Salaman, Birmingham.

1905

£400-450

2¼in (5.5cm) long

WW

A silver robin pin cushion, by Levi & Salaman Ltd., Birmingham, modelled as a robin holding a golf club, with original red padded chest.

1910   *4in (10cm) high*

£700-800   **WW**

An Edwardian silver arched cat pin cushion, by Levi & Salaman, Birmingham.

This is an unusual pin cushion and also appeals to cat collectors.

1905   *2¼in (5.5cm) long*

£1,200-1,600   **WW**

An Edwardian silver donkey pin cushion, by Robert Pringle, Birmingham.

1909   *2½in (6.5cm) high*

£600-700   **WW**

A silver hatching chick pin cushion, by S. Mordan & Co., Chester, dent to front, replaced fabric.

1907   *2½in (6.5cm) high*

£150-200   **DN**

An Edwardian silver-mounted leather boot pin cushion, hallmarked Samuel M. Levi, Birmingham 1909, Rd 556959.

1909   *3in (7.5cm) long*

£120-160   **FELL**

An Edwardian silver tortoise pin cushion, by Saunders and Shepherd, Birmingham.

1906   *2in (5cm) long*

£400-500   **WW**

SEWING

An Edwardian silver pig and cart pin cushion, by Sydney & Co., Birmingham, the pig pulling a mother-of-pearl cart.

1909   *3¾in (9.5cm) long*
£450-550   **WW**

A silver donkey and cart pin cushion, by Sydney & Co., Birmingham, the donkey pulling a mother-of-pearl cart.

1910   *3¼in (8.5cm) long*
£450-550   **WW**

An Edwardian silver fox pin cushion, by Walker & Hall, Birmingham.

1906   *2½in (6.5cm) long*
£500-600   **WW**

An Edwardian silver cat pin cushion, maker probably W.J. Myatt & Co. Ltd.

1908   *1¼in (3cm) high*
£380-450   **HT**

A Victorian silver butterfly pin cushion, with spread velvet wings, maker's mark worn.

1894   *5in (12.5cm) long*
£350-450   **WW**

An Edwardian silver chicken pin cushion, importer's mark of S. Landeck, import marks for Chester.

1901   *4¼in (11cm) long*
£400-500   **WW**

An Edwardian silver porcupine pin cushion, maker's mark worn.

1902   *2¾in (7cm) long*
£300-400   **WW**

A silver elephant pin cushion, maker's mark 'A. & L. LTD.', Birmingham.

1905   *2½in (6.5cm) long*
£200-250   **JN**

An Edwardian silver bulldog pin cushion, no maker's mark.

1906   *2in (5cm) high*
£300-400   **WW**

An Edwardian silver ox and cart pin cushion, the ox pulling a polished shell cart on fixed wheel axle, maker's mark rubbed.

1909   *6in (15cm) long*
£300-400   **HT**

A Victorian silver sewing egg, the gilded interior with holes for pins, a central column for cotton reels, maker's mark worn, and a later thimble.

1891   *2¼in (5.5cm) long*
£300-400   **WW**

A Victorian sewing machine, designed by Elias Howe, serial no.1401266.

£35-45   LOCK

A Singer '222k Featherweight' electric sewing machine, with original instructions, in original case.

£500-600   LOCK

A 'Shakespear Victorian' sewing machine, with plaque that reads 'Not for an Age, But for All Time, The Royal Sewing Machine Co. Birmingham'.
c1870

£130-180   LOCK

A possibly American folding enamel thimble, with floral decoration.

£60-70   LOCK

A Victorian 15 carat gold thimble, maker's mark partially worn, Birmingham 1899, in a later case.

0.15oz
WW

A 19thC French etui, the ivorine case opening to interior with six silver sewing implements, with a matched thimble.

£200-250   FLD

£200-250

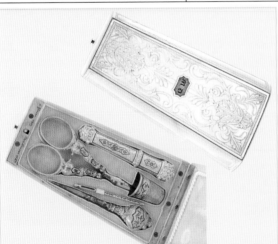

A 19thC French etui, the mother-of-pearl case opening to fitted interior, with five sewing implements with enamel highlights, case engraved 'Paris Chez Alph Giroux et Cie'.

£700-800   FLD

A pair of scissors, in the shape of a lady's legs.

£60-70   LOCK

A Victorian William Francis Garrud silver chatelaine, with a tape measure case, Levi & Salaman, Birmingham 1888, a vesta case, George Unite, Birmingham 1875, a scent bottle, Edwin Culver, London 1876, and a notepad case, Heinrich Levinger, Birmingham 1900.

12½in (32cm) long 7½oz

£120-180   APAR

SILVER

A George III silver-gilt vinaigrette, probably by John Bough, London.
1803   1¾in (4.5cm) long 0.7oz
£300-400   **WW**

A George III silver-gilt vinaigrette, possibly by William Thompson II, London, maker's mark 'WT'.
1804
£250-300   **FLD**

A George III silver vinaigrette/ whist marker, by Matthew Linwood, Birmingham, the hinged cover with a turning wheel and numbered 1-10, lacking pin.
1805   1¼in (3cm) diam 0.8oz
£600-700   **WW**

A George III silver-gilt pocket watch vinaigrette, by Samuel Pemberton, Birmingham, the reverse a glass locket compartment.
1816   1¼in (3cm) diam 0.8oz
£500-600   **WW**

A George III silver-gilt purse vinaigrette, by Joseph Willmore, Birmingham.
1816   1¼in (3cm) long 0.4oz
£300-350   **WW**

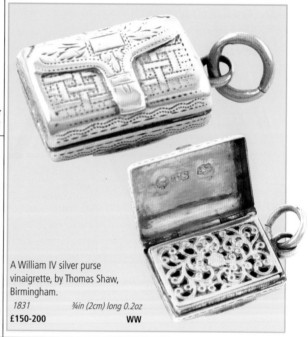

A William IV silver purse vinaigrette, by Thomas Shaw, Birmingham.
1831   ¾in (2cm) long 0.2oz
£150-200   **WW**

A George III silver reticulated fish vinaigrette, by Lea & Co., Birmingham.
1817   3¼in (8.5cm) long 0.6oz
£1,200-1,500   **WW**

A Victorian silver 'castle-top' vinaigrette, by Nathaniel Mills, Birmingham, of Kenilworth Castle.
1837   1½in (4cm) long 0.7oz
£600-650   **WW**

A silver vinaigrette, by Nathaniel Mills, Birmingham.
1841   1¾in (4.5cm) long 0.6oz
£200-250   **WW**

A silver 'castle top' vinaigrette, by Nathaniel Mills, of Abbotsford House.
1848   1½in (4cm) long
£650-750   **FLD**

A 19thC New Zealand silver tobacco/vesta box, by Stewart Dawson and Co., Dunedin and Wellington.

See p.338 for other vesta cases.

2¾in (7cm) long 1.1oz

£250-300　　　　　　　　　　WW

A silver horseshoe vesta case, with base metal striking plate, the side to be threaded with a wick operated by a spoked wheel, maker's mark mis-struck, Birmingham.

1871　　　　　2in (5cm) long

£125-150　　　　　　　　　　DN

A silver mussel shell vesta case, by Hilliard and Thomason, Birmingham.

1888　　　2¼in (5.5cm) long 0.5oz

£500-600　　　　　　　　　　WW

An Art Nouveau silver vesta case, by Charles Lyster & Son, Chester, with an embossed portrait of Queen Victoria, inscribed with 'RD274173 '.

1900　　　　2in (5cm) high 1oz

£300-350　　　　　　　　　　MART

A silver football vesta case, maker possibly J.H. Hillcox, retailed by George Maurice & Co., Birmingham.

1907　　　　　　　　0.81oz

£400-450　　　　　　　　　　BELL

A silver sovereign/vesta case, by H. Matthews, Birmingham, lid with striker.

1911　　　3in (7.5cm) long 1oz

£150-200　　　　　　　　　　WW

A silver dog and kennel table vesta case, by L. Emmanuel, Birmingham, back with a striker.

1917　　　2in (5cm) long 2.5oz

£450-500　　　　　　　　　　WW

A silver card case, by Nathaniel Mills, Birmingham, with figure leaning on a lyre, some damages.

1846　　　　4in (10cm) long

£300-350　　　　　　　　　　FLD

A silver 'castle-top' card case, by Nathaniel Mills, Birmingham, of The Scott Memorial.

1848　　　　4in (10cm) long 2.5oz

£900-1,100　　　　　　　　　WW

A silver card case, by Owen & Boon, Birmingham.

1856　　　4in (10cm) high 1.9oz

£110-150　　　　　　　　　　PW

An Edwardian silver 'castle-top' card case, of Battle Abbey, Sussex, maker's mark 'T&W', possibly for Birmingham maker Tongue & Walker.

3¾in (9.5cm) long

£220-280　　　　　　　　　　DN

SILVER

A George II silver and agate snuff box.

c1750　　　3¼in (8.5cm) long

£180-220　　　**WW**

A George III silver and parcel gilt Neo-Classical snuff box, maker 'TP ER', London.

1810　　　3¾in (9.5cm) long

£300-350　　　**WHP**

A George III silver-gilt snuff box, by Robert Mitchell & Co., Birmingham.

1811　　　2in (5cm) long 0.7oz

£400-450　　　**WW**

A George III silver snuff box, by Thomas Shaw, Birmingham, the cover with men around a table with a harp player.

1828　　　2¾in (7cm) long 3.4oz

£300-350　　　**WW**

An early 19thC silver and mother-of-pearl snuff box.

2¼in (5.5cm) long

£200-250　　　**WW**

A William IV silver snuff box, by Nathaniel Mills, Birmingham, with two coats of arms with mottos, rubbing to marks.

1831　　　6oz

£800-900　　　**ECGW**

A Russian silver and niello snuff box, by Ivan Kaltikov, Moscow, 84 zolotniki, engraved with the Bronze Horseman statue of Peter the Great in the Senate Square, Saint Petersburg.

1836　　　3¼in (8.5cm) long 3.2oz

£150-200　　　**DN**

An early Victorian 'castle-top' snuff box, by Edward Smith, Birmingham, of Abbotsford House, the underside engraved 'Elma'.

3in (7.5cm) wide 2.6oz

£400-450　　　**CHEF**

A snuff box, by Nathaniel Mills, Birmingham.

1843　　　2½in (6.5cm) wide 1.8oz

£350-400　　　**PSA**

A silver-mounted snuff mull, the horn body carved as a stylised horse's head, with a plaque inscribed 'Mrs J. Gourlay, 1852'.

c1850　　　3½in (9cm) long

£500-550　　　**WW**

A silver naval snuff box, by Asprey and Co. Ltd., London, engraved with a battleship, interior engraved with the badge of the Women's Royal Navy Service and inscribed '14 Oct. 42', and 'Evelyn'.

1940　　　3in (7.5cm) long 2.7oz

£200-250　　　**WW**

A silver owl pepperette, by George Fox, London, with glass eyes and stylised foliate piercing.

1863   *3¼in (8.5cm) high 2oz*

£450-500   **FELL**

A silver owl pepperette, by Hawksworth, Eyre & Co., with glass eyes.

1867   *3¼in (8.5cm) high 2oz*

£450-500   **FLD**

Two pairs of matching Victorian silver owl casters, by Richards & Brown, London, with glass eyes, stamped '7433', '7432', '6939', '6938', some denting.

1871   *3¼in (8.5cm) high 5.6oz*

£900-1,000   **CHEF**

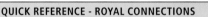

A pair of silver owl salt and pepper pots, by Francis Higgins and Sons Ltd., London.

1938   *2¾in (7cm) high 6oz*

£700-800   **WW**

QUICK REFERENCE - ROYAL CONNECTIONS

- Queen Charlotte, of Mecklenburg-Strelitz, was the Queen Consort of George III. Between 1789 and 1805, the Royal Family visited Weymouth. Sea bathing was thought to benefit the King's health. In 1789, the family stayed with the King's brother, the Duke of Gloucester, at Gloucester Lodge (later called Royal Lodge). They visited regularly until 1805, when the King's deteriorating health prevented them from travelling.

- The initials 'RH' are reputed to have been those of the daughter of the King's physician, Sir William Heberden junior. He was the Queen's personal doctor and would likely have visited Dorset with the family.

An Austrian silver elephant salt pot, by Georg Adam Scheid, blue stone eyes, later resin tusks, stamped 'Ges Gesch'.

3in (7.5cm) high 1.7oz

£550-600   **WW**

A George III silver mustard pot, by Hester Bateman, London, engraved with a crest, with a glass liner.

The crest is that of Mortlock, for John George Mortlock, of Melbourn and Meldreth, Cambridgeshire.

1787   *4in (10cm) long 2.4oz*

£400-450   **WW**

A George III silver barrel mustard pot, maker's mark worn, with a blue glass liner and a spoon, London.

1800

£150-200   **WW**

A George III silver mustard pot, by Robert Hennell I, London, with a blue glass liner, engraved 'The Gift of the Queen, Weymouth 1796' and 'RH', with an old English salt spoon, by Thomas Wallace, London 1794.

1795   *2½in (6.5cm) high 3.65oz*

£750-850   **DN**

A William IV silver mustard pot, by William Bateman, London, engraved with a crest.

1835   *4in (10cm) 6.2oz*

£600-650   **WW**

A silver drum mustard pot, by Samuel Whitford, London, with a later blue glass liner.

1867   *3in (7.5cm) high 5.5oz*

£250-300   **WW**

SILVER

A silver mouse box, by Thomas Johnson, London.
1885 *3in (7.5cm) long 2oz*
£650-700 **WW**

A silver duck cream jug, by George Fox, London.
1869 *4in (10cm) long 2.6oz*
£800-900 **WW**

An electroplated silver bee honey pot, by Mappin and Webb, screw-out glass body.
6¼in (16cm) long
£400-500 **WW**

A silver koi carp, with inset red paste eyes, unmarked.
7in (18cm) long 2.9oz
£350-400 **FELL**

A Zimbabwean silver model of a hippo, by Patrick Mavros, signed, and Zimbabwean hallmarks.
5¼in (13.5cm) long 7.7oz
£800-900 **WW**

A silver-gilt biscuit box, by Atkin Brothers, Sheffield, engraved '1881-1931, 16th Feb from C.M.B.', some wear.
1928 *7¼in (18.5cm) long 24.1oz*
£650-750 **DN**

A George III silver filigree toothpick box, cover with a wheatsheaf under glass.
c1790 *3¼in (8.5cm) long 1oz*
£400-450 **WW**

A French silver and pink enamel toothpick box, retailed by E. Dreyfous, Paris.
3¼in (8.5cm) long 1.1oz
£200-250 **WW**

A silver box, sponsor's mark David Bridge, London import marks.
1896 *6¼in (16cm) wide 4.3oz*
£120-160 **CHEF**

A Portuguese silver toothpick holder, maker's mark 'IM'.
6¾in (17cm) high
£200-250 **WW**

A silver 'diver's helmet' inkwell, by E.H. Stockwell, London, retailed by Percy Edwards and Co.
1890 *2¾in (7cm) high*
£550-600 **WW**

A Victorian silver-mounted aide-mémoire, by William & Edward Turnpenny, Birmingham, of Emmanuel College to one side and King's College to the other.
1844 *3¼in (8cm) long*
£650-700 **BELL**

A pair of Edwardian silver napkin rings, by S. Glass, Birmingham, embossed with the bust of Shakespeare.

1903   *1.7oz*

£150-200   **WW**

An Edwardian silver Arts and Crafts enamel decorated napkin ring, with stylised floral decoration, maker's mark 'L.C. & C.LD.', some wear.

2in (5cm) diam 1.25oz

£200-250   **APAR**

An Edwardian Arts and Crafts silver napkin ring, by Ramsden and Carr, London.

1909   *2¼in (5.5cm) diam 1.1oz*

£250-300   **WW**

An Arts and Crafts silver napkin ring, by Amy Sandheim, London, with central pink cabouchon flanked by Celtic knot motifs.

1930   *1.39oz*

£250-300   **HAN**

A silver duck napkin ring, by Crisford and Norris, Birmingham.

1913   *3¼in (8.5cm) long*

£200-250   **WW**

A George III silver jockey cap caddy spoon, by Joseph Taylor, Birmingham.

1800   *2in (5cm) long 0.3oz*

£650-700   **WW**

A George III silver eagle's wing caddy spoon, by Joseph Willmore, Birmingham.

1814   *3in (7.5cm) 0.2oz*

£2,000-2,500   **WW**

A George III silver caddy spoon, by Josiah Snatt, London.

1807   *2¾in (7cm) long 0.2oz*

£450-500   **WW**

A cast silver caddy spoon, by George Adams, London, initialled.

1848   *3¼in (8.5cm) long 0.6oz*

£450-500   **WW**

A cast silver caddy spoon, by George Adams, London.

1862   *3in (7.5cm) long 0.5oz*

£450-500   **WW**

A Scottish Provincial caddy spoon, by William Robb, Ballater, Edinburgh, of Balmoral Castle.

1905   *3½in (9cm) long 0.74oz*

£400-500   **L&T**

A parcel-gilt silver and enamel commemorative caddy spoon, by Stuart Devlin, London, limited edition no.38, celebrating the birth of Prince William, in case.

1982   *2¾in (7cm) long 0.9oz*

£200-250   **WW**

SILVER

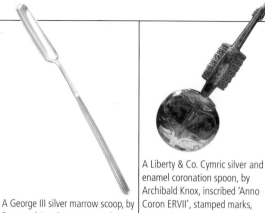

A George III silver marrow scoop, by Peter and Ann Bateman, London.

1799 9in (23cm) long 1.2oz

£100-150 WW

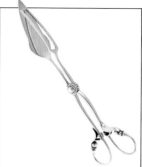

A Liberty & Co. Cymric silver and enamel coronation spoon, by Archibald Knox, inscribed 'Anno Coron ERVII', stamped marks, Birmingham, repaired.

1901 8in (20.5cm) long

£750-850 WW

A pair of sandwich tongs, by Georg Jensen, no.141, with berry and leaf motif grips, maker's mark.

8¼in (21cm) long 3.73oz

£250-300 FELL

A silver page marker, by S. Mordan and Co., London, the terminal with a magnifying glass and a miniature copy of 'The English Dictionary'.

1894 8in (20.5cm) long

£250-300 WW

A silver paper knife, by Sebastian Garrard, London, inscribed 'Presented by H.R.H. Prince and Princess of Wales A.C. Bully Esq. HMS Renown Indian 1905-6'.

On 19 October 1905, Prince George and his wife set out on a tour to India. There they travelled to Genoa, where they boarded HMS Renown to Bombay. They spent four months in India and often slept on a special train.

1905 9½in (24cm) long 3.8oz

£1,600-2,200 WW

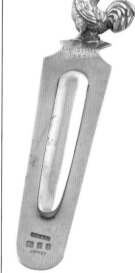

A silver cockerel page marker, by S. Mordan and Co., retailed by Asprey, London.

1930 3¼in (8.5cm) long 0.4oz

£200-250 WW

A silver mermaid ruler, by William Hutton and Sons, Sheffield.

1923 12in (30.5cm) long 9.4oz

£600-650 WW

An English silver bridge card suit marker.

1946 3¼in (8.5cm) high

£100-150 FLD

A 19thC Russian silver spice tower, impressed assay marks for St Petersburg, with an Assay Master Mark 'O.C.' over '1888'.

12¼in (31cm) high 10oz

£1,300-1,600 FELL

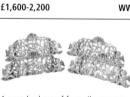

A matched set of four silver menu card holders, two by Brook & Son, Edinburgh, two unmarked, inscribed.

1891 3¼in (8.5cm) long 3.6oz

£300-350 WW

An Edwardian silver and enamel menu card holder, by Ramsden and Carr, London.

1907 3¼in (8.5cm) long 1.2oz

£400-450 WW

A silver pin stand, by Cornelius Desormeaux Saunders & James Francis Hollings (Frank) Shepherd.
1904   *5½in (14cm) high*
£55-65   **WHP**

A silver hatpin stand.
1905   *2½in (6.5cm) high*
£50-60   **WHP**

A silver butterfly hatpin, by Charles Horner, with glass inset.
1913   *8¼in (21cm) long*
£90-110   **WHP**

A silver hatpin, by Charles Horner, set two cabochon green beads.
1923 11½in (29cm) long
£120-160   **WHP**

An early 19thC filigree silver inkstand, probably made in Birmingham, with two silver-mounted glass inkwells.
3¼in (8.5cm) long
£300-350   **WW**

An Atkin Brothers silver toast rack, the divisions spelling 'TOAST', retailed by Thornhill & Co., Bond St.
1889   *5¼in (13.5cm) high 7oz*
£300-350   **DUK**

A miniature Spinning Jenny, with articulated wheel and foot pedal, possible Hanau pseudo-marks and Austria-Hungary import marks.
c1891-1901   *2¼in (5.5cm) high 0.75oz*
£130-160   **FELL**

An Edwardian silver import miniature steam engine train, by Singleton, Benda & Co Ltd., London, with Foreign mark, and Hanau psuedo-marks for Karl Kurz.
1903   *6½in (16.5cm) long 2.82oz*
£400-450   **FELL**

A silver miniature 'Owl and The Pussy Cat', by Sarah Jones, London.
1981   *2¼in (5.5cm) long 1.38oz*
£550-600   **BE**

A late 19thC Austro-Hungarian silver and enamel Moor hatpin, in later Cartier box.
£450-500   **WW**

A pair of thistle hatpins, with set polished stone.
9in (23cm) long
£75-85   **WHP**

SILVER

A set of 12 beakers, by Stuart Devlin, London.

Born in Gelong, Australia, Stuart Devlin (1931-2018) studied goldsmithing and silversmithing at the Royal Melbourne Technical College, before studying at the Royal College of Art, London, and Columbia University, New York. In 1965, Devlin set up a goldsmithing and silversmithing workshop, the first of seven, in London. Devlin was granted a royal warrant in 1982, and between 1996 and 1997 he worked as prime warden for the Goldsmith's Company.

1969-72   *4¼in (11cm) high 3oz*
£6,500-7,500   **L&T**

A set of four parcel-gilt-silver candle holders, by Stuart Devlin, with three glass liners and four detachable pierced wirework spherical shades.

1970   *5½in (14cm) high 41oz*
£5,500-6,500   **SOU**

A Bristol '600' silver goblet, by Stuart Devlin, with gilt-washed interior, stamped to underside and numbered '12/600', London.

1973   *6in (15cm) high 13¼oz*
£300-400   **LSK**

A parcel-gilt-silver rose bowl centrepiece, by Stuart Devlin, the pierced silver-gilt wirework cover with six holders, mounted with bark effect finial inset with an amethyst crystal, London.

1975   *6¼in (16cm) high 19oz*
£3,000-3,500   **SOU**

A matched set of seven Elizabeth II silver and gilt champagne flutes, by Stuart Devlin, London, with gilded stems.

1977-81   *8¾in (22.5cm) high 46¼oz*
£2,200-2,800   **BE**

A silver-gilt 'Surprise' easter egg, by Stuart Devlin, the exterior reveals five enamelled flowers.

1978   *2¾in (7cm) high 2¾oz*
£500-600   **DUK**

A silver-gilt 'Surprise' egg, by Stuart Devlin, no.279, opening to reveal a turtle with enamel decoration, hallmarked London.

1979   *3in (7.5cm) high*
£250-300   **WW**

A silver candlestick, by Stuart Devlin, with pierced stem raised on a conical foot, maker's marks 'SD', hallmarked London.

1980   *9in (23cm) high 0.17oz*
£400-500   **L&T**

A gold ring, by Stuart Devlin, London, set with tourmalines, aquamarines and sapphires within cornucopia design and a cherub.

1981   *size O*
£2,500-3,000   **WW**

A silver cigarette box, by Stuart Devlin, London, with gilt highlighted raised mosaic-shaped lined top, with a stained wooden interior.

1989   *6¾in (17cm) wide 29oz*
£1,000-1,500   **GYM**

A Victorian four sectional silver cigar case, with engraved floral decoration, Birmingham.
1901
£200-250 **FLD**

A Continental silver and enamel cigarette case, depicting a semi-nude female, hallmarked 'Birmingham import 1904', with '925' standard mark, maker's mark worn, with scratches and wear.
3½in (9cm) long
£350-450 **FELL**

A silver and enamel cigarette case, with an enamel panel landscape scene, hallmarked 'London import 1929', sponsor's mark 'FBR', probably F.B. Reynolds, and '925', with wear and tarnishing.
3½in (9cm) long
£400-500 **FELL**

A George VI hallmarked silver and guilloche enamel cigarette case, by Henry Clifford Davies, Birmingham.
1950 *3¼in (8.5cm) high*
£400-450 **WM**

A CLOSER LOOK AT A CIGARETTE CASE

This an unusual and desirable subject in exceptional condition.

It has dual function – that of a cigarette case and snuff box.

The hinged cover enamelled with a cartoon of a man on bended knee with a woman in Islamic dress, with a man peeping round a corner.

It has import marks for London 1930, importer's mark of H.C. Freeman, with Irish import marks for 1940.

A silver and enamel box, signed 'H.M. Bateman, Copyright'.
3in (7.5cm) long
£1,300-1,600 **WW**

An Austrian silver and enamel cigarette case, maker's mark possibly 'CD', with a panel of a lady in hunting dress.
3¼in (8.5cm) long
£500-600 **WW**

A Persian metalware and enamel cigarette box, with buildings in a landscape.
7¼in (18.5cm) long
£250-350 **WW**

A Russian silver-gilt and enamel cigarette case.
1896-1908 *4in (10cm) long*
£900-1,100 **WW**

A novelty oak smokers' compendium, modelled as a Great Western Railway coal truck, slight damage.

This appeals to railwayana collectors as well as those interested in smoking memorabilia.
13in (33cm) long
£300-400 **FLD**

SMOKING

A Victorian silver and enamel vesta case, by
S. Mordan and Co., London, retailed by Percy
Edwards and Co., with a huntsman being
thrown from his horse, the reverse initialled
'J.W.D'.

1885   *1¾in (4.5cm) long*
£1,000-1,400   **WW**

A Victorian enamel vesta case, with foxes, a
lady and hound and wild bird.

                                          2in (5cm) high
£600-650   **BELL**

A Continental silver and enamel vesta case,
with a naked lady, the hinged lid stamped '935'
to reverse.

**Match cases, commonly called vesta cases,
were popular from the late 1830s until the
1920s, when pocket lighters had begun to
replace matches. Early matches were likely
to ignite accidentally when they rubbed
against each other, so were placed in a small
box, usually made of metal. Vesta cases often
contained a textured surface on which to
strike matches.**

                                          2¼in (5.5cm) high
£650-750   **FELL**

A 20thC silver-plated dog vesta case, wear and
tarnishing.

                                          2¾in (7cm) long
£100-150   **FELL**

A French late 19thC gold-mounted vesta case,
enamelled with a lady and gentleman, the sides
with 'Allumettes - Chimiques' and 'Paris 15c',
some damage.

                                          2in (5cm) long
£350-400   **FLD**

A late 19thC Russian silver-gilt and enamel
cigarette and vesta case, maker's mark 'K.A.', St
Petersburg.

c1890   *3¾in (9.5cm) long*
£1,300-1,800   **WW**

A Victorian silver fish bowl table vesta holder,
'London 1891', retailed by Asprey.

                                          2in (5cm) high
£300-350   **WW**

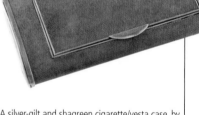

A silver-gilt and shagreen cigarette/vesta case, by
Thomas Callow and Sons Ltd., London, inscribed
'With Best Love From Tones, Xmas 1918'.

1918   *3¾in (9.5cm) long*
£200-300   **WW**

A Henry Howell & Co. 'YZ' rabbit vesta case,
with phenolic resin ears and feet, with glass
eyes, on Macassar ebony tray, impressed marks.

                                          4in (10cm) high
£110-150   **WW**

A Dunhill 18ct yellow gold cigarette lighter, no.340, stamped marks, in original wooden case.

Dunhill was formed in London in 1893 when Alfred Dunhill took over his father's saddler business, changing its focus to luxury car accessories. Dunhill's 1905 'Windshield Pipe' proved very popular and the company moved into the tobacco business, producing pipes and smoking accessories. Dunhill was bought by Richemont in the 1990s.

2½in (6.5cm) long

£950-1,100   **DUK**

A Dunhill silver unique golf ball table lighter, limited edition no.332, in fitted case, and a hand signed copy of 'Golf Studios, Harold Riley at Dunhill, Publ. Alfred Dunhill Limited, 2001'.

£1,500-2,000   **DUK**

A Dunhill 'Longitude' stainless steel and chrome-plated table lighter, inset with a clock, impressed marks, in fitted case.

2¾in (7cm) high

£350-400   **DUK**

A Dunhill 'Great Golf Courses of the World' silver lighter, designed by Harold Riley, limited edition no.271 of 288, with original case, outer-sleeve and booklets.

c1999   *2¾in (7cm) high*

£900-1,100   **DUK**

A Dunhill silver and wood grain effect Rollagas lighter, the base stamped 'US24163 Patented, Made in Switzerland, Dunhill', with import hallmarks, boxed with paperwork.

2½in (6.5cm) high

£500-600   **APAR**

A Dunhill 'The Aldunil' silver and rose gold-plated lighter, stamped 'Dunhill Paris', with import marks.

2½in (6.5cm) high

£350-400   **APAR**

A Dunhill 9ct gold-cased cigarette lighter, marked '9 375', surface scratches, wear.

2½in (6.5cm) high

£500-600   **FELL**

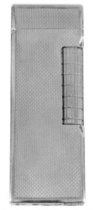

A Dunhill 9ct gold-cased cigarette lighter, marked '9 375 AD', surface scratches, wear.

2½in (6.5cm) high

£450-550   **FELL**

A Dunhill 9ct gold-cased cigarette lighter, marked '9 375', with scratches and wear.

2½in (6.5cm) high

£800-900   **FELL**

A Dunhill Aquarium table lighter, each side with reverse-painted intaglio fish and rock decoration on lucite panels, silver-plated mounts, registration no.737418, signed to arm.

4in (10cm) long

£3,500-4,000 BE

A mid-20thC pilot's Dunhill silver-plated 'Goliath' table lighter, inscription 'To W.H. Fell 1953' and signatures from other test pilots including Brian Trubshaw.

£650-750 SWO

A Dunhill silver-plated 'foot rule' table lighter, engraved with centimetres and inches, no.0001, impressed marks, in a fitted box.

13in (33cm) long

£500-600 DUK

A Cartier gold-plated cigarette lighter, no. E89285, 20 microns, in fitted case.

£250-350 DUK

A Colibri Monogas 9ct gold-cased cigarette lighter, marked '9 375', surface scratches, wear.

1¾in (4.5cm) high

£300-400 FELL

An S.T. Dupont gold-plated cigarette lighter, no.9039B, 20 microns, in fitted case.

1¾in (4.5cm) long

£200-250 DUK

A novelty terrier lighter, some damage and wear.

5¼in (13.5cm) high

£50-60 LOCK

A 9ct gold lighter, with engine-turned body, hallmarked 'London 1929 by GS*FS'.

0.63oz

£400-500 LOCK

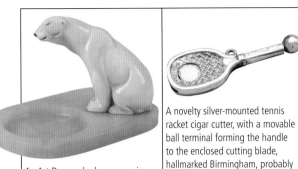

An Art Deco polar bear ceramic ashtray, with painted features, on a marble base, stamped 'Made in England', with serial number.

5¾in (14.5cm) high

£150-200 DUK

A novelty silver-mounted tennis racket cigar cutter, with a movable ball terminal forming the handle to the enclosed cutting blade, hallmarked Birmingham, probably William Oliver.

1887 *2½in (6.5cm) long*

£200-250 FELL

A CLOSER LOOK AT AN ASHTRAY

An ashtray in the popular Art Deco style.

The circular green onyx tray has an asymmetric dished centre.

It is surmounted to the edge with six various cold-painted bronze dogs in very good condition.

They include an Airedale, Scottie and Irish Setter.

An onyx ashtray, with bronze dog figurines.

tray 7¾in (19.5cm) diam

£1,000-1,200 HT

A 9ct gold cigar cutter, with suspension loop.

£120-180 FLD

An early 20thC German match striker, the base marked 'Gesetzl. Geschutzt'.

6¼in (16cm) high

£50-60 LOC

An early 20thC briar pipe, carved as a man's head wearing a straw hat, with inset two-colour glass eyes, with a vulcanite mouthpiece.

8in (20.5cm) long

£300-400 DN

A 19thC meerschaum pipe, the bowl carved as a human skull, with animal horn mouthpiece, with case.

1½in (4cm) high

£200-250 BELL

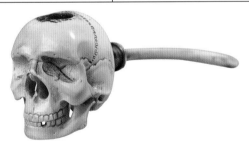

A 19thC large carved meerschaum pipe, of a lady with plumed hair, engraved gold band and amber stem, some damage, cased.

£80-100 FLD

A 19thC treen snuff box, with a dog carrying a dead rabbit, titled 'To Be delivered immediately', wear and rubbing, foil lining missing to interior.

3in (7.5cm) wide

£80-100 FELL

A Black Forest carved tobacco jar, in the form of a standing bear holding a bough and a brass bowl, inset glass eyes, some damage.

11¾in (30cm) high

£250-300 FLD

A Frank Roberts England international football shirt, season 1924-25, woollen button-up neck, with embroidered FA three lions badge.

Frank Roberts (1894-1961),an English professional footballer, played from the 1910s to 1928.

£2,700-3,000   GBA

A white England no.4 international jersey, worn by Bobby Robson in the England v Wales match at Ninian Park 14 October 1961, by Bukta, with a signed handwritten card 'THIS IS THE SHIRT THAT I WORE AGAINST WALES AT NINIAN PARK IN CARDIFF ON OCTOBER 14th 1961 WE DREW 1-1, BOBBY ROBSON'.

£3,000-3,500   GBA

A rare 1966 England World Cup winners replica shirt, signed by ten players, mounted with Bobby Moore signature on card in frame with two photos.

1966

£500-600   LOCK

A Pelé match-worn jersey and boots, the jersey a signed white Santos no.10 jersey worn in the match v Roma 3 March 1972, with a letter of authenticity from the son of Nocaute Jack, the Brazil team masseur 1970-94, and two dealer issued certificates of authenticity from JSA and Jersey14, with a pair of match-worn black and white Puma Pelé Santos boots, with a certificate of authenticity from BidAMI Auctions, together with Pelé memorabilia comprising a Pelé featured rosette issued for the Santos v Fulham game 3 December 1973, an Original Pelé Match Flyer Advertising Santos FC v Washington Darts 1970, and an NY Cosmos Official Pelé Farewell Programme 1 October, 1977 Cosmos v Santos.

£7,500-8,500   GBA

A match-worn Santos no.10 match jersey, signed by Pelé to the reverse no.10 as 'Edson Pelé', the signature is certified by a PSA/DNA sticker.

£2,000-2,500   GBA

A Lionel Messi blue and white striped Argentina v Colombia international jersey, from 15 November 2016, FIFA Russia 2018 qualifiers and Fair Play sleeve badges, the reverse lettered 'MESSI', with a certificate of authenticity issued by BidAMI Auctions.

£2,000-3,000   GBA

A photograph montage, signed by Ian Wright, Arsenal and England striker.

12in (30.5cm) wide

£40-50   LOCK

A Manchester United black and white photograph, signed by George Best and Dennis Law.

8in (20.5cm) wide

£60-70   LOCK

A 1966 World Cup winners image, signed by Geoff Hurst, Roger Hunt, Martin Peters, Ray Wilson and George Cohen.
1966
£50-60   LOCK

A Jimmy Ashcroft debut England v Ireland international 1905-06 cap, with gold wire rose, tear above rose, dated.

This match was played at the Solitude Ground, Belfast, 17 February 1906. England won 5-0.
1906
£2,000-2,500   GBA

A Frank Roberts England international debut cap, England v Belgium, orange and purple quartered, dated.

This match was played at West Bromwich Albion's Hawthorns ground, 8 December 1924. England won 4-0.
1924
£1,100-1,500   GBA

A football, signed by Brazilian footballer Pelé.
£120-160   LOCK

A UEFA Super Cup Competition silver-plated replica trophy, with UEFA inset logo, on a marble base with 'SUPER COMPETITION' band.

The UEFA Super Cup is an annual super cup football match organised by UEFA and contested by the reigning champions of the two main European club competitions, the UEFA Champions League and the UEFA Europa League.
pre-2006   18in (45.5cm) high
£2,000-2,500   GBA

A football programme, published for Bootle v Bolton Wanderers 25 March 1889, sellotape repairs.

This is the earliest known Bootle programme.
1889
£750-850   GBA

An England v Scotland international programme, played at Sheffield United 4 April 1903, some paper loss.
£1,500-2,000   GBA

A souvenir programme for the Everton v Newcastle United FA Cup Final, played at Crystal Palace 21 April 1906, 8-pager published by the London Evening News.
£1,800-2,200   GBA

A Southampton v Watford programme FA Cup tie, 12 January 1907, in the form of bi-fold match card.
1907
£650-750   GBA

An FA Cup Final Replay programme, Barnsley v Newcastle United played at Goodison Park, Everton, on Thursday 28 April 1910, Everton and Liverpool Official Programme, vol.6 no.54, 16 pages, typo in the team line-ups heading reading 'BARNSLEY v NEWCANTLE UNITED', with illustrations.

The programme is in good, stable condition, which is uncommon as the paper from these period Everton/Liverpool issues is often in a fragile state.
1910
£8,500-10,000   GBA

A World War I period football programme, for the England and Wales v Scotland and Ireland grand international charity football match, played in Salonika, 26 December 1918.

1918

£250-350   GBA

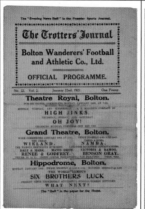

A football programme, Bolton Wanderers v Oldham Athletic, Div 1, 22 January 1921.

£250-300   LOCK

An FA Cup football programme, Hull City v Bolton Wanderers, 12 January 1924.

£200-250   LOCK

A football programme, Scotland v England, 2 April 1927 at Hampden Park.

£300-400   LOCK

An FA Cup final programme, Birmingham v West Bromwich Albion, 25 April 1931.

£350-450   LOCK

A football programme, Leicester City v Newcastle, 29 March 1932.

£200-250   LOCK

An FA Cup final programme, Everton v Manchester City, 29 April 1933.

1933

£350-400   LOCK

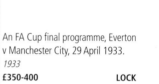

A football programme, England v Scotland, Wembley, 14 April 1934.

1934

£150-200   LOCK

An official programme for the first European Cup Final, Real Madrid v Reims, on 13 June 1956 at Parc des Princes, the 27-page programme with centre page of the team sheets of Real Madrid and Reims.

The European Cup, now known as the UEFA Champions League, was played at the Parc des Princes in Paris in front of 38,000 people on 13 June 1956, resulting in Real Madrid beating Reims 4-3.

1956

£3,000-4,000   GBA

An Irish Football Association Cup gold medal, awarded to William Gouk in 1882 QIFC, boxed.

Queen's Island FC won 1-0 against Cliftonville on 13 May 1882 at Prospect (Ballynagagh).
1in (2.5cm) wide
£800-1,200 GBA

A 9ct. gold FA Cup runners-up medal, awarded to a Manchester City player, with fitted case, recipient unknown, dated.

The Bolton Wanderers defeated Manchester City 1-0.
1926
£2,000-3,000 GBA

A Football League Division One Championship silver-gilt medal, awarded to Allenby Chilton of Manchester United in season 1951-52, inscribed 'THE FOOTBALL LEAGUE, CHAMPIONS DIVISION 1, SEASON 1951-52, MANCHESTER UNITED FC, A. CHILTON', in original case.

Allenby Chilton (1918-96), played briefly for Liverpool and then Manchester United from 1938 to 1955. Chilton served with the Durham Light Infantry. Post war he was centre-half for Matt Busby's team and was a key member in the 1951/52 league championship. In 1955, he went on to become player/manager for Grimsby Town, then as manager for both Wigan Athletic and Hartlepool United.
£27,000-30,000 GBA

A 9ct. gold Football League v Scottish Football League victory match representative medal, awarded to Frank Womack, inscribed 'VICTORY MATCH, ENGLAND v SCOTLAND, THE FOOTBALL LEAGUE, St ANDREWS, BIRMINGHAM, FEBRUARY 22nd 1919, F. WOMACK'.

Frank Womack (1888-1968) represented the Football League in the match v the Scottish F.L. in 1918-19. The Football League won 3-1.
1918-19
£300-400 GBA

QUICK REFERENCE - JIMMY ASHCROFT

● **James (Jimmy) Ashcroft (1878-1943) was an English football goalkeeper and Arsenal's first England international footballer. Ashcroft signed as a professional footballer in June 1900 for Woolwich Arsenal; his debut match was on 15 September 1900 against Burton Swifts. With Woolwich Arsenal he made 303 appearances in eight seasons until 1908. Ashcroft was the first Arsenal player to be capped for England, winning three caps in the British Home Nations Championship matches of 1906. In 1908, Ashcroft moved to Blackburn Rovers, leaving in 1913 on a free transfer and signing for Tranmere Rovers. He played one season before World War I halted first-class football.**

A Woolwich Arsenal 9ct. gold medal, awarded to goalkeeper Jimmy Ashcroft, during which Ashcroft kept a club record 20 clean sheets, inscribed 'WOOLWICH ARSENAL FOOTBALL CLUB, TO COMMEMORATE PROMOTION TO FIRST LEAGUE, PRESENTED TO J. ASHCROFT, 1903-4'.
£2,000-3,000 GBA

A bronze 1968 UEFA European Football Championship third-place medal, belonging to Roger Hunt, reverse inscribed 'UEFA CHAMPIONNAT D'EUROPE 1968 IIIe RANG', in original Huguenin fitted case.
1968
£3,000-3,500 GBA

A Tommy Docherty 1967 FA Cup runners-up medal, official FA retrospective presentation in 2010 to pre-1996 FA Cup Final managers, the medal in 9ct. gold by Toye, Kenning & Spencer Ltd., hallmarked Birmingham 2010, inscribed 'THE FOOTBALL ASSOCIATION, CHALLENGE CUP, RUNNERS-UP', the edge inscribed '1966-67', cased in 2010.

Following a campaign by Lawrie McMenemy, the FA agreed to honour the managers who took their clubs to an FA Cup final but at the time did not receive a medal. From 1996, managers joined the players and received medals on the day.
£3,500-4,000 GBA

A Fulham 1975 FA Cup Final runners-up 9ct. gold medal, belonging to John Mitchell, inscribed 'THE FOOTBALL ASSOCIATION, CHALLENGE CUP, RUNNERS-UP', the edge inscribed '1974-75', in original fitted case, with a 1975 FA Cup Final programme and ticket stub.
£4,500-5,000 GBA

A 1994 FIFA World Cup winners 14ct. gold medal, with 'FIFA WORLD CUP USA 1994' reverse, hallmarks and maker's mark Huguenin, recipient unknown.

This medal would have been awarded to a member of Brazil back room staff as opposed to a player.
1994 *2in (5cm) diam*
£14,000-20,000 GBA

'The INCOMPARABLE PRIZE FIGHT, JACK JOHNSON vs JIM JEFFRIES', framed, signs of watermarks in places.

Jeffries, 'The White Hope', was persuaded out of retirement to restore pride to the white race. He was, however, outclassed and defeated by the superior opponent.

1910　　*16½in (42cm) high*
£750-900　　　　　　**MM**

A Sunday Mirror newspaper, edition of 22 May 1966, signed in pen by Muhammad Ali the day after his defeat of Henry Cooper at Arsenal FC's Highbury Ground.

The seller of this lot obtained this autograph of Muhammad Ali on 22 May 1966, when he encountered Ali taking a Sunday stroll in St James's Park, London.

1966
£300-400　　　　　　**GBA**

A Muhammad Ali and Joe Frazier double signed poster, for their 1971 World Heavyweight Championship fight, poster has been rolled and has a series of creases.

£550-650　　　　　　**GBA**

An autographed Muhammad Ali training leather boxing glove, original yellow lace, signed in gold 'Muhammad Ali 19-78', with two letters of authenticity, dated.

This glove was signed by Muhammad Ali at his training camp at Deer Lake, Pennsylvania, during preparation for his fight against Leon Spinks. It was signed for Pete Morkovin, who visited the training camp during this time with his father. Subsequently sold to Craig Hamilton of JO Sports Inc. by Pete Morkovin. Includes two letters of authenticity from Pete Morkovin and Craig Hamilton.

1978　　*12in (30.5cm) long*
£3,000-4,000　　　　　**GBA**

A contact sheet, by Terry O'Neill CBE (b.1938), of Muhammad Ali preparing for his fight with Alvin Lewis in Dublin, 1972, printed later, signed and numbered '7/50', framed with plexi-glass.

sheet 48in (122cm) high
£2,000-3,000　　　　　**ROS**

A pair of Rocky Marciano leather boxing gloves, by Goldsmith of Cincinnati, with a wooden display plaque, with gilt titling from The National Sporting Club.

Thess gloves were in the Roland Dakin Collection. They were acquired from Mickey Duff via The National Sporting Club. Roland Dakin was a British Boxing Board of Control referee for 38 years and presided over 40 World Fight titles. He was an avid collector of boxing memorabilia and his professional capacity gave him wonderful access to leading boxing personalities.

£1,800-2,200　　　　　**GBA**

A boxing glove, signed by Evander Holyfield and Mike Tyson, in dome frame, mounted with replica fight poster behind.

£200-300　　　　　　**LOCK**

A former five weight World Boxing Champion Sugar Ray Leonard signed glove, in a dome frame.

£120-180　　　　　　**LOCK**

A World Boxing Champion Floyd Mayweather signed glove, in a box frame, with action image behind.

£180-220　　　　　　**LOCK**

A cricket bat, signed by the 1948 Australian 'Invincibles' cricket team, 17 signatures in ink, including Bradman, Morris, Hassett, Harvey, Barnes, Lindwall, Miller and Johnston.

£700-800 GBA

A cricket bat, signed by Packer Rebels, the face signed in ink by the World Team, the reverse signed by the West Indies and Australian teams of 1977.

£300-400 GBA

A Victorian silver-plated inkwell, modelled as a cricket ball, stamped 'EPNS'.

3¼in (8.5cm) diam

£180-220 GBA

A Gillette Cup Final cricket ball, set with a silvered shield inscribed 'GILLETTE CUP FINAL, 1973, GLOS. V SUSSEX, GLOS. 248-8. M.S. PROCTOR 94, A.S. BROWN 77 N.O.'.

1973

£200-250 GBA

An 18ct. gold Rothmans World Cup XI 1966 champions medallion, presented to the winners at Lord's September 1966, hallmarked, in a fitted Gregory & Nicholas Ltd. box.

A John Hampshire's Yorkshire County Cricket Club 1965 Gillette Cup Final winner's medal, silvered, in original case.

1965

£400-450 GBA

2in (5cm) diam

£2,500-3,000 GBA

A signed photograph of the Australian 2001 Ashes series winning cricket team, with 20 signatures including Fleming, Warne, Slater, the Waugh brothers, Langer, Gilchrist, Ponting, Katich, Gillespie, Hayden, McGrath and Martyn, framed, glazed.

2001

£120-180 GBA

A team-signed India ODI cricket shirt, from the 2006 Tour of Sri Lanka, 15 signatures including Dravid, Tendulkar, Sehwag, Yuvraj Singh, Kaif, Dhoni, Pathan, Agarkar, Harbhajan Singh, Powar and Patel.

2006

£160-200 GBA

A 19thC Staffordshire pottery figure, of the cricketer George Parr.

This figure was produced in 1861 to commemorate the first England trip to Australia.

13¾in (35cm) high

£650-750 CAN

A terracotta figure of Dr W.G. Grace, after Edwin Roscoe Mullins (1849-1907), signed, dated.

1885   32in (81.5cm) high

£13,000-16,000 CAN

A set of vintage racing silks, in the colours of Ada L. Rice.

These colours are associated with the 1940s and the racehorse Model Cadet, who won the 1949 Washington Futurity, ridden by Anthony Skoronski and trained by Seabiscuit's trainer Tom Smith.

£550-650   GBA

A Walter Swinburn horse racing saddle, with Bates Saddlery Perth label, signed.

19¾oz

£900-1,100   GBA

A racing plate worn by Seabiscuit in the Massachusetts Handicap 8 July 1937, mounted on a sterling silver hoof-shaped ashtray, engraved with 'JACK MCDONALD FROM C.S. HOWARD 1937', with sterling mark.

The US champion Seabiscuit (1933-47) recorded his seventh consecutive stakes victory in the 1937 Massachusetts Handicap in a track record time of 1 min 49 seconds. The winner's purse money of $51,780 was the highest amount he had won to date.

5in (12.5cm) long

£4,000-5,000   GBA

A silver cigar box, mounted with a racing plate worn by Mill Reef, hallmarked Birmingham 1968 by Padgett & Braham Ltd.

Mill Reef (1968-86) was bred in Virginia by his owner Mr Paul Mellon, but sent to be trained by Ian Balding at Kingsclere. In a career lasting three years, he raced 14 times, ridden exclusively by Geoff Lewis, winning 12 of his races.

1968   *7in (18cm) wide*

£4,500-5,000   GBA

A racing plate, on a mahogany shield, set with plaques inscribed 'Shergar' and 'WINNER, 1981 EPSOM DERBYRIDDEN BY WALTER SWINBURN, TRAINER MR STOUTE, OWNER THE AGA KHAN'.

Shergar (1978-c1983), a bay colt, was bred by HH The Aga Khan IV at his private stud in County Kildare and trained at Newmarket by (Sir) Michael Stoute. Shergar won his first race in September 1980 ridden by Lester Piggott. He was retired to Ballymany Stud in October 1981. Shergar had won six of his eight races. He was sydincated for £10 million at £250,000 for each of 40 shares, with a covering fee of £60,000-80,000. In 1983, Shergar was kidnapped and a ransom demanded. When this was refused, Shergar ended up dead. It is widely believed that the horse was killed by men inexperienced in handling stallions, yet speculation still surrounds his death.

1981   *10in (25.5cm) long*

£4,500-5,000   GBA

A photograph of the stallion Nearco, by equestrian photographer Anscomb, signed, inscribed 'Nearco', mounted, framed and glazed.

Nearco (1935-57) was bred by Federico Tesio and retired undefeated after 14 races, with his crowning glory being his facile win in the Grand Prix de Paris in 1938. He was bought by British bookmaker Martin Benson for £60,000 and sent to the Beech House Stud at Newmarket. He was thought so valuable that his own underground bomb shelter was constructed at Beech House.

1941   *8in (20.5cm) wide*

£400-500   GBA

A Royal Worcester porcelain figurine of Arkle, by Doris Lindner, factory marks, limited edition 447 of 500, with a framed certificate.

c1967   *10¾in (27.5cm) high*

£400-500   GBA

A sterling silver sculpture of Desert Orchid with Simon Sherwood up, modelled by Edwina Emery, hallmarked London 1990 by Garrard & Co. Ltd., agate and wooden base, facsimile signature of Edwina Emery, with a limited edition certificate no.2 of 9 in a leather frame.

£9,000-11,000   GBA

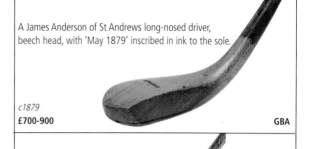

A James Anderson of St Andrews long-nosed driver, beech head, with 'May 1879' inscribed in ink to the sole.

c1879
£700-900   **GBA**

A rare square-toe blacksmith's general iron, with curved cut-off blade and heavy ash shaft, with a nail and saw-teeth nicking.

c1700   41¼in (105cm) long
£10,000-12,000   **GBA**

A George Forrester, Elie and Earlsferry, long-nosed club, long spoon, beach head, with hickory shaft.

c1880
£250-350   **GBA**

A Tom Morris St Andrews long-nosed driver head, the sole with ink signature of J. Anderson, dated.

1889
£2,500-3,000   **GBA**

A Jacobs Patent iron, by James Gourlay of Carnoustie, with vulcanite insert to face.

c1912
£300-350   **GBA**

A William Gibson Jack White civic putter, with original drilled holed face.

£180-220   **GBA**

A William & John Gourlay of Musselburgh feather golf ball, stamped with maker's name 'W. & J. GOURLAY' and inscribed in ink '31'.

c1840
£4,600-5,000   **GBA**

A red gutta-percha hand-hammered golf ball.

c1860
£400-500   **GBA**

A Tom Morris black rubber core bramble pattern golf ball.

c1896
£250-300   **GBA**

A Thornton Patent '27½' gutta-percha square mesh golf ball.

c1896
£180-220   **GBA**

A Taylor-Tunnicliffe pottery golfing tobacco jar and cover, with patent non-detachable fitting to airtight cover, the base stamped 'A.F.C. PATENT 17870'.

c1900   *6¼in (16cm) high*

£250-300   **GBA**

A Royal Doulton Kingsware golfing jug, designed by Crombie.

9in (23cm) high

£250-300   **GBA**

An Edwardian soft paste porcelain teapot, decorated with golfing scenes, marked '4271'.

5¼in (13.5cm) high

£200-250   **GBA**

A solid bronze golfer car mascot, by Louis Lejeune Ltd. of London.

c1935   *6½in (16.5cm) high*

£100-150   **GBA**

A rare Professional Golfers' Association medal for the Victory Tournament played at St Andrews in 1919, unhallmarked but probably silver-gilt, the obverse inscribed 'PROFESSIONAL GOLFERS ASSOCIATION, VICTORY TOURNAMENT 1919, PEACE BY VICTORY'.

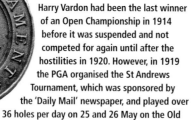

Harry Vardon had been the last winner of an Open Championship in 1914 before it was suspended and not competed for again until after the hostilities in 1920. However, in 1919 the PGA organised the St Andrews Tournament, which was sponsored by the 'Daily Mail' newspaper, and played over 36 holes per day on 25 and 26 May on the Old Course. As there had not been time to organise the usual qualifiers associated with an Open Championship, the field was restricted to 60 professionals. Despite this, it was referred to as the Victory Open. It was deemed to have resulted in a tie between George Duncan and Abe Mitchell, both with 312 strokes. There was no playoff.

£1,400-1,800   **GBA**

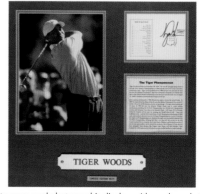

An Augusta score card photographic display, with a colour photograph of Tiger Woods, mounted next to an Augusta scorecard reverse mounted and signed by Woods, the reverse taped with a certificate of authenticity issued by ASA Accugrade Inc., limited edition numbered '18/25', framed and glazed.

29½in (75cm) wide

£150-200   **GBA**

A colour photograph, signed by Seve Ballesteros, mounted, framed and glazed.

£100-140   **GBA**

A pin flag from the 143rd Open Championship, signed in black permanent marker by the winning golfer Rory McIlroy, with certificate of authenticity and photo proof of golfer signing the flag.

2014

£180-220   **GBA**

A pin flag from the 147th Open Championship, signed in black permanent marker by the winning golfer Francesco Molinari, with certificate of authenticity and photo proof of golfer signing the flag.

2018

£150-200   **GBA**

A signed Michael Schumacher Ferrari Fila shirt, with Vodafone and Shell sponsors badges.

large (US)

£250-300   **APAR**

A Mercedes 2014 F1 World Championship season mini helmet, signed by Lewis Hamilton to the crown in black marker pen, with a photo proof dealer's certificate of authenticity.

£300-350   **GBA**

A print, signed by motor racing's Jack Brabham, chief Brabham designer Ron Tauranac and artist Randall Wilson, limited edition no.192/850, rolled.

£40-50   **LOCK**

A 2000 West McLaren-Mercedes Formula 1 racesuit, worn by David Coulthard, his name and Scottish Saltire stitched above the waistband.

Coulthard finished second behind his team mate, Mika Häkkinen, in that year's Spanish Grand Prix at Barcelona on 7 May.

£3,500-4,000   **GBA**

A Mercedes AMS Petronas 2012 F1 season 1:2 scale helmet, signed by Michael Schumacher in gold marker pen, with a photo proof dealer's certificate of authenticity.

£550-650   **GBA**

A 1965 National Sporting Club menu, signed by Jim Clark on the front cover above his Indianapolis 500 winning Lotus, for the dinner at the Cafe Royal on 18 November, the eight-page menu including a two-page celebration of his achievements, with a copy of 'Jim Clark At The Wheel'.

The 1965 World Champion and first-ever Formula 1 driver to win the 'Indy 500', signed this for club member Derrick Richard Hornby who sat on an adjacent table to him throughout the dinner.

£550-650   **GBA**

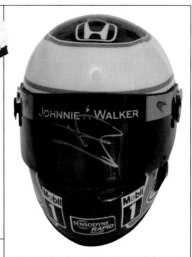

A McLaren Honda Japanese GP mini helmet, signed by Jenson Button to the visor in gold marker pen, sold with a photo proof dealer's certificate of authenticity.

£180-220   **GBA**

A photograph, signed in gold marker pen by Ayrton Senna, mounted in the colours of the Brazilian National Flag, in a wooden frame under glass, with a certificate of authenticity.

22½in (57cm) wide

£700-800   **GBA**

A French silver-plated motoring plaque, by A. Morlon, of a racing car and Hermes on a landscape setting.

3¼in (8.5cm) long

£350-400   **FLD**

SPORTING

A rare Paris 1900 Olympic Games programme for gymnastics, the booklet programme in French, 'CONCOURS INTERNATIONAUX, D'EXERCICES PHYSIQUES ET DE SPORTS, SECTION II, GYMNASTIQUES, PROGRAMME ET RÈGLEMENT'.

1900

£2,000-2,500   GBA

An Antwerp 1920 Olympic Games Football Prize Trophy, in the form of a bronze urn, by Henri Fugere, with a flying winged nude female figure of Victory holding Olympic rings.

This is the first time the Olympic rings were shown at the Games.

15¾in (40cm) high

£2,000-2,500   GBA

A London 1948 Olympic Games football official's badge, silvered, with Olympic Rings, Big Ben and the Houses of Parliament, ribbon stamped gilt 'FOOTBALL'.

1948

£320-380   GBA

A vest worn by Great Britain's Terry Spinks when winning the flyweight boxing division gold medal at the Melbourne 1956 Olympic Games, the white Ampro vest with Union Jack cloth badge inscribed 'OLYMPIC GAMES 1956, GREAT BRITAIN', framed and glazed.

Terence (Terry) George Spinks MBE (1938-2012), a Great British featherweight boxer, won the gold medal in the flyweight division at the 1956 Melbourne Summer Olympics. Spinks had two hundred amateur bouts and was the 1956 ABA flyweight champion, turning professional in April 1957 with a bout against Jim Loughrey at Harringay Arena, North London, which he won on a stoppage for a cut eye. He won his last bout against Johnny Mantle in December 1962 and became a trainer and coach on retirement, going on to coach the South Korean team in the 1972 Munich Summer Olympics.

1956   *28¼in (72cm) long*

£1,300-1,600   GBA

A Jamaica athletics running vest, signed in black marker pen by Usain Bolt, a replica of his Rio 2016 Olympic Games Vest, sold with a certificate of authenticity.

2016

£500-600   GBA

A CLOSER LOOK AT AN OLYMPIC TORCH

This is a rare example of a Rome 1960 Olympic Games bronzed aluminium bearer's torch.

The design is based on drawings of torches on ancient Etruscan ceramics.

It was designed by Professor Maiure and his team from the National Museum of Archeology in Naples.

Unusually, it is still complete with its original burner.

A British Olympic Asscociation car grille badge, chrome metal and enamel, inscribed 'BRITISH OLYMPIC ASSOCIATION'.

£200-250   GBA

A badge for the International Olympic Committee 62nd Session, inscribed '62 IOC SESSION, TOKYO', double white ribbon suspension.

1964

£1,500-2,000   GBA

A bronzed aluminium bearer's torch.

1960   *15½in (39.5cm) high*

£5,000-6,000   GBA

A Tokyo 1964 Olympic Games stainless steel bearer's torch, blackened aluminium alloy bowl inscribed 'XVIII OLYMPIAD TOKYO 1964'.

1964   25½in (65cm) high
£6,000-7,000   **GBA**

A Munich 1972 Olympic Games steel bearer's torch, by Krupp.

1972   28¾in (73cm) high
£1,500-2,000   **GBA**

A Moscow 1980 Olympic Games aluminium alloy bearer's torch, designed by Boris Tuchin, Moscow Games logo and legend in red.

1980   22in (56cm) high
£850-950   **GBA**

An Atlanta 1996 Olympic Games official bearer's torch, designed by Peter Mastrogiannis, in aluminium and Georgia pecan wood, with 22 reeds representing the cities where Olympic Games had taken place since 1896.

1996   31½in (80cm) high
£1,500-2,000   **GBA**

A silver 'B' winner's prize medal for the 2nd National Greek Olympic Games ('Zappas Olympics') held in Athens in 1870, struck by Paris Mint, designed by Barre, stamped 'ARGENT' on edge, obverse with head of King George I, reverse with Greek legend.

These Games were made possible through the sponsorship of the Greek businessman Evangelis Zappas. The first Games had been held in 1859. As such the Zappas Olympics were among the first revivals of the ancient Games, the other notable example being the Wenlock Olympian Games, organised by William Penny Brookes in England from 1850.
£1,500-2,000   **GBA**

An 1896 Olympic Games participation gilt-bronze medal, designed by N. Lytras, struck by Honto-Poulus.
1896
£600-700   **GBA**

A London 1908 Olympic Games Committee member's silvered bronze badge, by Vaughton of Birmingham, with inscribed blue enamel band.
£1,200-1,600   **GBA**

A London 1908 Olympic Games unawarded second prize bronze medal for the 7-metre yacht race, designed by Bertram Mackennal, the rim inscribed 'SECOND PRIZE 7 METRE YACHT RACE'.

Only two boats entered the competition, both with British crews. The race was in the Solent from the Royal Victoria Yacht Club, Ryde, Isle of Wight. However, only one boat 'Heroine' made the start line and the gold medal was awarded by a 'sail-over'. The second boat, which did not make the start, was 'Mignonette'.
£3,000-3,500   **GBA**

A Helsinki 1952 Olympic Games participant's bronze medal, designed by K. Rasanen, in original paper box.
1952
£150-200   **GBA**

SPORTING

A Westmorland County Rugby Football Union cap, gold cap, dated '1895-6-7-8'.

1895-1898

£150-200   GBA

A North of Scotland RFU representative cap, awarded to William Gladstone Falconer of Dollar Academy, Aberdeen Nomads and North of Scotland, embroidered dates for 1897-8-9, 1899-1900 and 1900-1901, pinned name tag to interior.

Falconer later became a Scotland RFU administrator.

£280-320   GBA

A Bath Rugby Football Club cap, dated.

1903

£200-250   GBA

A Neath Rugby Football Club cap, awarded to Gryff Bevan in season 1931-32, named to interior.

Gryff Bevan was a versatile player (centre, wing, outside-half) who played for Neath between 1929-30 and 1932-33. Bevan scored a total of 15 tries and was occasionally a goalkicker.

£150-200   GBA

A G.H. 'Mick' Exley England Rugby League International cap, rose emblem, inscribed in ink to the label inside 'G.H. EXLEY', dated.

Wakefield Trinity's Mick Exley played three times for England between 1932 and 1939.

1932-33

£200-250   GBA

A Northampton Rugby Football Club cap.

1933-37

£220-280   GBA

A Wales retro rugby jersey, signed by Gareth Edwards, J.P.R. Williams, Barry John, John Dawes and Phil Bennett.

£150-200   GBA

A rare Ireland v South Africa rugby union programme, played at Lansdowne Road, Dublin, 30 November 1912.

This was the second ever international between Ireland and South Africa and the first to be played in the south. The tourists won the game 38-0.

1912

£2,000-2,500   GBA

A Rugby League Challenge Cup Final programme, Dewsbury v Wigan played at Wembley Stadium 4 May 1929.

1929

£250-300   GBA

A Rugby League Challenge Cup Final programme, York v Halifax played at Wembley Stadium 2 May 1931, covers restored.

1931

£200-250   GBA

A Rugby League Challenge Cup Final programme, Huddersfield v Warrington played at Wembley Stadium 6 May 1933.

1933

£150-200   GBA

A rare Feltham's Climax tennis racket, stamped R. Whitty, 14 Tythebarn St Liverpool and H. Faulkner to the wedge and frame, the frame is also stamped with a registered number '49148', dating it to 1886, breaks to the original string.

This innovative frame is special because it has a very early laminated hoop with ash on the outside and cane to the inside.
c1886
£300-350   **GBA**

A 'Birmal' tennis racket, aluminium frame, wire stringing and leather/whipped handle, patents stamped on frame by the Birmingham Aluminium Company.
c1923
£450-550   **GBA**

A Wilson 'Indestruts' tennis racket, made in steel by Dayton, Ohio, with original steel stringing.
c1928
£220-280   **GBA**

An oversized tennis racket, by Greaves & Thomas, in the style of an early 20thC convex wedge racket ironically named 'Extra Light'.

It has faithfully reproduced features such as shoulder reinforcement, grooved handle and stringing pattern.
c1980s   *55½in (141cm) long*
£450-550   **GBA**

A tennis shirt, worn by Andy Murray when winning his second Wimbledon men's singles title in the match against Milos Raonic 10 July 2016, in a frame, with a certificate of authenticity signed by Matt Gentry, Managing Director of Murray's management company, a photograph of Murray hugging the trophy on Centre Court, and a title plaque.

Sir Andrew (Andy) Barron Murray OBE (b.1987) British Tennis Professional Player and former World Tennis No.1, represented Great Britain in the 2012 and 2016 Olympics, wining gold medals for the singles titles, and was on the winning Davis Cup Team in 2015. He became the first British player to win a Grand Slam Singles title since 1977 in the 2012 US Open Final, and the first British man since 1936 to win a Grand Slam singles title. In 2016, Murray became the first British man to win two Wimbledon singles titles since Fred Perry, and the first Scot to win a Wimbledon singles title since Harold Mahony in 1896. Murray's management company confirmed by letter that Andy wore two shirts on court during the 2016 final, this being one of them. The other shirt was donated by Murray to the Wimbledon Lawn Tennis Museum.
£9,000-11,000   **GBA**

An Andre Agassi and John McEnroe double-signed Nike Air Challenge Court windbreaker jacket.
1990s
£150-200   **GBA**

A Kayzerzinn silver-plated tennis figurine, by W. Zwick.
13in (33cm) high
£400-500   **GBA**

A Karl Ens Volkstedt porcelain lady tennis figurine, model no.3031 2, 'KVE' mark to base.
c1910   *11½in (29cm) high*
£500-600   **GBA**

A Victorian silver tennis racket bangle.
c1880
£250-300   **GBA**

A chrome eight-day tennis racket-shaped desk clock, by C.M. Depose.
c1930s   *9in (23cm) long*
£500-600   **GBA**

TAXIDERMY

A taxidermy cased Pike (Esox), with W. Howlett Newmarket label, reed and gravel base in glazed bow front case.

42in (106.5cm) wide

£250-300

CHEF

A set of three F.W. Anstiss stuffed roach, trade label to interior and handwritten detail to rear.

c1908

35in (89cm) wide

£900-1,100

BELL

A taxidermy brace of Perch (Perca) and a Rudd (Scardinius erythrophthalmus), W.B. Griggs, London, label and another label, 'Perch and Rudd, caught by Aldborough, M. Bourne at Stamford Waters, Norfolk August 1928'.

31½in (80cm) wide

£1,200-1,500

CHEF

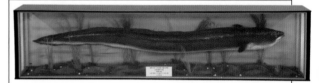

A British record Conger Eel, plaque states 'British Shore Record Conger Eel 68lb 8oz, captured Plymouth - Nov 1991 by M. Larkin'.

94½in (240cm) wide

£2,000-2,500

SWO

A late 19thC full-mount brown bear, grasping a tree branch and trunk frame, previously a stick stand.

75½in (192cm) high

£1,500-2,000

L&T

An early 20thC tiger head mount, attributed to Theobald Bros, from Mysore, India.

**As this tiger's head mount dates from earlier than 1947, it needs no certification for sale in this country.
May be subject to CITES regulations if exported.**

30¾in (78cm) high

£2,000-2,500

SWO

A late Victorian preserved Indian sun or sloth bear head mount, by James Gardner, the verso with a printed paper trade label.

16¼in (41.5cm) high

£800-900

WW

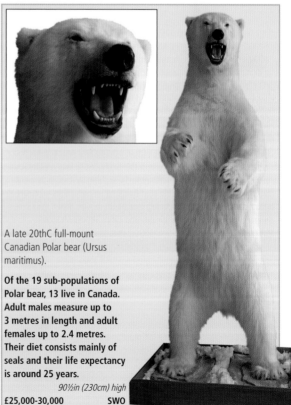

A late 20thC full-mount Canadian Polar bear (Ursus maritimus).

Of the 19 sub-populations of Polar bear, 13 live in Canada. Adult males measure up to 3 metres in length and adult females up to 2.4 metres. Their diet consists mainly of seals and their life expectancy is around 25 years.

90½in (230cm) high

£25,000-30,000

SWO

QUICK REFERENCE - TYPEWRITERS

- In the 19thC, there were various bids to develop writing machines, but it was Christopher Latham Sholes' 1867 model that is considered the first practical typewriter. Sholes patented his second typewriter model in 1868. After design improvements, in 1873, E. Remington and Sons began manufacture of the typewriter. The machine was called the Remington.

- In 1872, the first electrically operated typewriter was invented by Thomas A. Edison.

- Portable typewriters were sold from the late 19thC, but those considered truly portable did not appear until 1909. Portable electric typewriters appeared in 1956. Following the invention of the modern computer, the need for typewriters declined.

A German Frolio no.5 typewriter, 41007, cased.
c1929
£55-65   WHP

A German Gundka Junior Model 3 tinplate typewriter, with roller inking, cased.
c1920
£50-60   WHP

An American Blickensderfer no.7 typewriter, 93606, cased.
c1899
£200-250   WHP

An Imperial B typewriter, no.22795.
c1915
£200-250   WHP

An Oliver no.5 typewriter, no.322588.
c1908
£70-80   WHP

An American Remington Portable, serial no.NL 56808.
c1925
£55-65   WHP

An American Royal Standard no.5 typewriter, no.275306.
c1912
£95-110   WHP

A German Triumph Weke Perfekt typewriter, no.2190.
c1928
£75-85   WHP

A Canadian 'The Empire' typewriter, no.8812, cased.
c1917
£150-200   WHP

A Yost 'Light Running' no.10 typewriter, no.107563.
c1903
£150-200   WHP

TECHNOLOGY

An early 20thC refurbished 'Skeleton' telephone, by L.M. Ericsson & Co., no.16, for the UK market, signed, numbered on the ebonite insulation stage 'No.16', with original silk-covered cable to handset and wall.

11½in (29cm) high

£1,000-1,500   **CM**

An ebonised cradle telephone.
1940s
£90-110   **FLD**

A cream GPO model 300 Bakelite telephone, numbered to handset underside '164 57', later converted, slight damage.
1950s
£120-160   **FLD**

A Bush DAC 90A valve radio in ivory Bakelite.
1950s   *12in (30.5cm) long*
£50-60   **FLD**

An E.K. Cole Ltd. 'Ekco' all-electric model SH25 radio, in Bakelite case, with a fret 'Willow Tree' design to the speaker, slight damage.
1932   *18¼in (46.5cm) high*
£250-300   **FLD**

An Ekco model M23 radio, in a Bakelite case, medium wave/long wave metres, slight damage.
1931   *15¾in (40cm) high*
£70-80   **FLD**

A perspex-cased television, of globular translucent 'Sputnik' form, on a circular chrome foot.
1970s(?)   *18¼in (46.5cm) high*
£400-500   **BELL**

A pre-war RCA uni-directional type KU-3A ribbon microphone, with metal bracket.

Property of the late Ray Merrin film re-recording sound mixer, part of the Oscar winning Best Sound team for 'The Last Emperor' (1987) and recipient of the Bafta Lifetime Achievement Award for outstanding contribution to sound design. Merrin's filmography includes 'A Clockwork Orange', 'The Shining', 'Tommy', 'Alien', 'The Killing Fields', 'Little Voice', 'Hilary & Jack', 'Trainspotting' and the two first 'Harry Potter' films.

£1,400-1,800   **BELL**

An AKG D25 dynamic microphone, with metal boom bracket.

Property of the late Ray Merrin.
c1960
£400-500   **BELL**

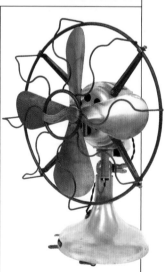

A Metropolitan-Vickers desk fan.
17¼in (44cm) high
£260-300   **SWO**

QUICK REFERENCE - STEIFF BEARS

- Steiff was founded by Margarete Steiff (1847-1909) in Giengen, Germany, in 1880.
- Margarete's nephew Richard Steiff (1877-1939) joined the company in 1897.
- In 1902 he designed his 'Steiff Bär 55PB', the first soft toy bear with jointed arms and legs. Over 3,000 bears were sold at the first trade fair and Steiff's new 'Teddy' bear was an international success. The name 'Teddy' supposedly comes from an incident on a 1902 hunting trip, where president Theodore 'Teddy' Roosevelt refused to kill an injured bear tied to a tree.
- Margarete's nephews took over the business following her death in 1909.
- Materials, colour, form and labels can all be used to identify and accurately date bears. Check for the distinctive 'Button-in-Ear' trademark, which Steiff used from 1904 to distinguish its bears from those of its rivals.
- Damaged bears can usually be restored by professionals but tears, stains, replaced pads or worn fur can all reduce value.

A very rare Steiff 35PB rod-jointed bear, with black boot button eyes, replacement gutta-percha nose, swivel head with seam from ear to ear across top of head, five claws in thick wool, hump, firm stuffing and rare elephant button with s-shaped trunk, about 10% of the plush has been rewoven, small patched hole in tip of muzzle and slight repair to pads.

1904   *19in (48.5cm) high*
£6,000-7,000   **SAS**

A CLOSER LOOK AT AN EARLY STEIFF BEAR

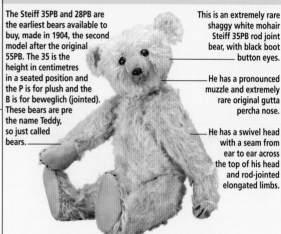

The Steiff 35PB and 28PB are the earliest bears available to buy, made in 1904, the second model after the original 55PB. The 35 is the height in centimetres in a seated position and the P is for plush and the B is for beweglich (jointed). These bears are pre the name Teddy, so just called bears.

This is an extremely rare shaggy white mohair Steiff 35PB rod joint bear, with black boot button eyes.

He has a pronounced muzzle and extremely rare original gutta percha nose.

He has a swivel head with a seam from ear to ear across the top of his head and rod-jointed elongated limbs.

A Steiff bear, excellently replaced felt pads, thick wool five claws, hump and firm stuffing, neat repair to right wrist, small patch to tip of right toe and slight general wear and thinning.

1904   *21in (53.5cm) high*
£8,000-10,000   **SAS**

An early Steiff cinnamon centre-seam teddy bear, with black boot button eyes, swivel head, jointed elongated limbs with felt pads, hump, working large side-squeezed squeaker, soft stuffing and FF button.

1908   *20in (51cm) high*
£4,500-5,500   **SAS**

An early Steiff white centre-seam teddy bear, with black boot button eyes, swivel head, jointed elongated limbs with felt pads, hump, inoperative growler, soft stuffing and FF button.

1908   *20in (51cm) high*
£4,500-5,500   **SAS**

An early Steiff teddy bear, with black boot button eyes, swivel head, jointed elongated limbs with felt pads, hump, inoperative growler and FF button, some slight thinning and damage to pads.

c1909   *20in (51cm) high*
£5,500-6,500   **SAS**

An early Steiff teddy bear, with blonde mohair, black boot button eyes, swivel head, jointed elongated limbs with felt pads, inoperative growler and FF button, slight general wear and thinning.

This bear is known as 'Irene' from the Wendy Jaques Collection.

c1909   *13½in (34.5cm) high*
£2,200-2,800   **SAS**

A Steiff blonde mohair teddy bear, straw stuffed, some sparse areas, feet pads replaced, lacks button.

c1909   *10¼in (26cm) high*
£450-550   **C&T**

An early 20thC Steiff dachshund on wheels, brown velveteen with black boot button eyes and four cast spoked wheels, well loved.

11¾in (30cm) long

£550-650   FLD

A Steiff bear, with movable head, collar and plush fur, on metal spoked wheels.

c1909   *13¾in (35cm) high*

£600-700   CHOR

A Steiff dark blonde plush straw-filled teddy bear, with swivel joints, brown button eyes and cloth pads.

c1910   *13½in (34.5cm) high*

£550-650   HT

A Steiff large plush teddy bear.

c1910   *29¼in (74.5cm) high*

£3,500-4,000   ROS

An early 20thC teddy bear, probably Steiff, with dark golden brown mohair, black boot button eyes, swivel head, jointed elongated limbs, hump and inoperative growler, slight damage.

c1910   *15¾in (40cm) high*

£1,800-2,200   FLD

A Steiff World War I substitute plush teddy bear, with unusual fine blonde corduroy material body, black boot button eyes, swivel head, jointed elongated limbs, woven paper plush (or nettle) fabric feet pads, inoperative side squeaker, missing most of left and half of right feet pads, some general wear.

As resources ran out during the war, Steiff came up with some unusual substitute plush to continue production including a paper-plush material made from nettles. Stylistically, this is a typical Steiff 8/9in teddy bear with a side squeaker and no hand pads, but this is the first time seen in this, possibly unique, corduroy.

8½in (21.5cm) high

£2,000-3,000   SAS

An early 20thC Steiff 'Bully' dog, swivelling head with velveteen forehead and muzzle with airbrushed detail, glass eyes, retains button to ear and label.

8in (20.5cm) high

£500-600   FLD

A Steiff white mohair teddy bear, with clear and black glass eyes with brown backs, swivel head, jointed elongated limbs with felt pads, hump, inoperative growler and FF button with remains of red tag, slight wear.

1920s   *20in (51cm) high*

£2,000-3,000   SAS

A Steiff golden mohair teddy bear, with glass eyes, stitched nose and claws, a pronounced hump, Steiff underlined F button, both ears requiring restitching.

16in (40.5cm) high

£600-700   **BER**

A Steiff teddy bear, with golden mohair, brown and black glass eyes, swivel head, jointed elongated limbs, hump, growler and small FF button, replaced pads, slight thinning and a little faded.

1920s   25in (63.5cm) high

£2,500-3,000   **SAS**

A rare Steiff cinnamon mohair 'Treff' dog, with brown and black glass eyes inserted into heavy eye lids, swivel head, inoperative squeaker and FF button, slight thinning and general wear.

1920s   10½in (26.5cm) high

£350-450   **SAS**

A Steiff 'Young Riding Bear' on wheels, with brown and black glass eyes, inoperative pull-growler, on metal frame, pull cord, some wear and fading.

1960s   39in (99cm) long

£400-500   **SAS**

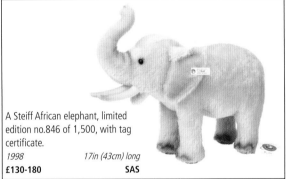

A Steiff African elephant, limited edition no.846 of 1,500, with tag certificate.

1998   17in (43cm) long

£130-180   **SAS**

A Steiff Netherlands Exclusive 'Tomato Teddy Bear', limited edition no.848 of 1,500, in original window box with certificate.

2000

£200-300   **SAS**

A Steiff 'Millennium Musical Band', limited edition no.793 of 2,000, in original box with certificate, the bears' heads could do with a firm brush, box flattened and worn.

2000

£350-450   **SAS**

A Steiff 'Harley Davidson 100th Anniversary Bear', limited edition no.3,424 of 5,000, in original box with certificate, some scuffing to box.

2003

£120-180   **SAS**

A Steiff large teddy bear 1906 replica, limited edition no.549 of 1,906, in original box with certificate, a slight musty odour.

2005

£250-350   **SAS**

A rare BMC large teddy bear, orange and black glass eyes, swivel head, jointed elongated limbs with felt pads, large rounded hump, inoperative squeaker and remains of black and gold woven label on foot pad, very minimal thinning.

The Bruin Manufacturing Company (BMC), based in New York, produced bears from 1907 to 1909. It is believed that this is the first time this bear has appeared in such a large size.

1907   28in (71cm) high
£2,500-3,500   SAS

A rare British United Toy Manufacturing Co. Ltd World War I 'Highlander Soldier' teddy bear, with clear and black oily glass eyes with brown painted backs, swivel head, jointed limbs with felt pads, original khaki jacket with brass buttons and leather Sam Brown belt, felt Glengarry bonnet, wool tartan kilt, loss of mohair from moth attack.

This is the only known example of this bear, probably dating from around World War I and very similar to Harwin's example. This bear was found with a fair amount of moth damage, but whatever the material used in the jacket, fortunately it was not attractive to the moth.

14½in (37cm) high
£1,300-1,600   SAS

A Chad Valley teddy, with orange and black glass eyes, swivel head, jointed limbs, inoperative squeaker, celluloid covered metal button in ear and woven red and white label on foot, some thinning, some wear.

This bear is known as 'Bradman' as the vendor was told that he was originally presented as a prize after a cricket match.

1920s   26in (66cm) high
£350-450   SAS

A Chad Valley clown teddy bear, with orange and black glass eyes, swivel head, jointed limbs, HM Queen and woven blue and white label on feet pads, inoperative squeaker, one ear split to make two ears with new halves, replaced pom-poms.

1930s   16in (40.5cm) high
£200-250   SAS

QUICK REFERENCE - CHILTERN BEARS

- The Chiltern Toy Works was founded in 1908 in Buckinghamshire by Josef Eisenmann and Leon Rees. Originally called Eisenmann & Co., it traded under the name Einco.
- The first teddy bear, 'Master Teddy', was produced in 1915. The 'Hugmee' bear was produced in 1923, becoming the company's most popular bear.
- Registered in 1924, the Chiltern Toys trademark was formed from a collaboration between Rees and founder of H.G. Stone & Co. Ltd., Harry Stone (previously of J.K. Farnell).
- Pam Howells worked for Chiltern between 1957 and 1967, designing the seated, unjointed bear.
- The company was taken over by Chad Valley in 1967.

A Chad Valley 'Navy Week Bulldog', for HMS Revenge, of cream velvet, orange and black glass eyes, oil-cloth collar, sailor's hat with HMS Revenge hat band, unusual label 'CHAD VALLEY PRODUCTS BRITISH SELLICKS, PLYMOUTH', celluloid covered blue button and card tag, slight discolouration.

8in (20.5cm) long
£200-250   SAS

A large plush teddy bear, probably Chad Valley, with interior bells to the ears, vacant patch for label to foot.

25¼in (64cm) high
£150-200   ROS

A Chiltern large 'Hugmee' teddy bear, with orange and black glass eyes, swivel head, jointed limbs, rounded hump and inoperative squeaker, known as 'Honey Bear', pads recovered, some slight thinning.

1930s   26in (66cm) high
£350-450   SAS

A Chiltern sheepskin 'Hugmee' teddy bear, with orange and black glass eyes, swivel head, jointed limbs with leather pads, label in side seam 'Chiltern Hugmee Toys Real Sheep Skin Made in England', some slight wear.

1940s   13½in (34.5cm) high
£100-150   SAS

A rare Chiltern 'Home Guard' teddy bear, with orange and black glass eyes, khaki velvet integral uniform with stripes on arms, black velvet feet and replacement felt helmet, some thinning to mohair.

This is believed to be the second known example of this bear, the other is in the Teddy Bears of Witney Collection and was later replicated by Merrythought.

1940s   *13in (33cm) high*
£2,000-2,500   **SAS**

An early FADAP teddy bear, with clear and black glass eyes, swivel head, jointed elongated limbs with felt pads, slight hump and inoperative growler, worn, faded and slight damage to pads.

This actual bear appears on page 55 of Eric Petit's book on FADAP and was the childhood toy of a lady from Divonne-les-Bains who later worked at the FADAP factory. This bear is known as 'Pradalet' from the Eric Petit Collection.

French company Fabrication Artistique d'Animaux en Peluche (FADAP) began producing teddy bears in 1925. Early FADAP bears had a metal button in one ear, embossed with 'FADAP' and 'France'. The bears were chubby, with thick paws. They typically had a seam under the chin and an upturned nose. FADAP closed in 1978.

1926/27   *15½in (39.5cm) high*
£200-300   **SAS**

An early FADAP teddy bear, with black boot button eyes, swivel head, jointed limbs with cloth pads, small hump and growler, fairly worn.

This actual bear appears on page 57 of Eric Petit's book on FADAP and is known as 'Theuyis' from the Eric Petit Collection.

1928/29   *23in (58.5cm) high*
£250-300   **SAS**

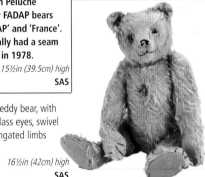

An early FADAP teddy bear, with clear and black glass eyes, swivel head, jointed elongated limbs with felt pads.

1926/27   *16½in (42cm) high*
£200-250   **SAS**

An early FADAP teddy bear, with black boot button eyes, swivel head, jointed limbs with cloth pads, hump, inoperative squeaker and original ribbon on chest.

This bear is known as 'Mazuc' from the Eric Petit Collection.

1930   *22½in (57cm) high*
£200-250   **SAS**

A Farnell teddy bear, with orange and black glass eyes, swivel head, jointed limbs with felt pads, hump and inoperative growler, stitched repairs to feet pads.

This bear is known as 'Maurice' from the Wendy Jaques Collection.

1920s   *21½in (54.5cm) high*
£1,200-1,600   **SAS**

A Farnell teddy bear, with orange and black glass eyes, swivel head, jointed limbs with cloth pads, hump and inoperative growler, balding to face and ear, general wear.

1920s   *16½in (42cm) high*
£250-300   **SAS**

A Farnell teddy bear, with orange and black glass eyes, swivel head, jointed limbs with painted cloth pads, rounded hump, inoperative growler, blue and white woven label on foot, known as 'Edward', slight wear.

1930s   *28in (71cm) high*
£500-600   **SAS**

A rare MAP purple wool plush teddy bear, with clear and black glass eyes, swivel head, jointed limbs with plush pads, hump and inoperative growler, slight wear.

This bear is known as 'Esquine' from the Eric Petit Collection.

1950/55   *23½in (59.5cm) high*
£200-300   **SAS**

A MAP large teddy bear, with clear and black glass eyes with brown backs, swivel head, jointed limbs with velvet pads, rounded hump and inoperative growler, very minor wear.

Manufacture D'animaux en Peluche (MAP) was a Parisian company run by Emile Lang. This bear is known as 'Peyreret' from the Eric Petit Collection.

                           31½in (80cm) high
£500-600   **SAS**

A large Merrythought 'Cheeky' teddy bear, with unusual cinnamon dralon plush, orange and black plastic eyes, ears with bells, swivel head, jointed limbs and printed yellow label on foot, some ageing.

1960s   *26in (66cm) high*
£90-110   **SAS**

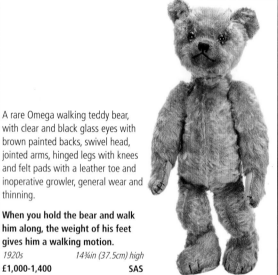

A rare Omega walking teddy bear, with clear and black glass eyes with brown painted backs, swivel head, jointed arms, hinged legs with knees and felt pads with a leather toe and inoperative growler, general wear and thinning.

When you hold the bear and walk him along, the weight of his feet gives him a walking motion.

1920s   *14¾in (37.5cm) high*
£1,000-1,400   **SAS**

A Peacock large teddy bear, orange and black glass eyes, swivel head, jointed limbs, slight rounded hump, squeaker and red and white label on foot, known as 'Percy', general thinning and wear.

1920s   *29in (73.5cm) high*
£250-300   **SAS**

A Pintel teddy bear, clear and black glass eyes, swivel head, chunky body, jointed arms and inoperative growler, fairly worn.

Pintel bears look very like FADAP bears at this time. This bear is known as 'Esquinle' from the Eric Petit Collection.

1930/35   *23in (58.5cm) high*
£150-200   **SAS**

An early 20thC Gebruder Sussenguth 'Peter' teddy bear, with swivelling black and white eyes and open mouth with teeth and moving tongue, jointed limbs, his neck with original ribbon and metal rimmed card tag 'Peter Ges. gesch. Nr.895257', within an original part box.

                   14in (35.5cm) high
£1,200-1,800   **ROS**

A plush teddy bear, in the Steiff style, with elongated arms and legs.

                  14½in (37cm) high
£150-200   **ROS**

An Arnold tinplate 'KLM Flying Dutchman', friction-powered aeroplane, boxed.

c1950   *18½in (47cm) long*

£250-300   **BELL**

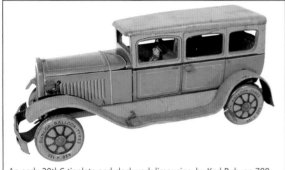

An early 20thC tinplate and clockwork limousine, by Karl Bub, no.788, number plate to both front and rear reads 'KB-788', fitted with a single fixed key and with battery compartment for front light operation.

15½in (39.5cm) long

£700-800   **LSK**

A Carette tinplate clockwork limousine, interior with fold down seats, and a roof rack, sporadic paint wear, lacking carriage lamps.

16in (40.5cm) long

£12,000-16,000   **POOK**

A Jep Darrack painted tinplate clockwork Talbot coupé, with operable headlights, opening doors and bonnet that reveals engine, restored.

17¼in (44cm) long

£1,200-1,600   **POOK**

A Japanese tinplate 'BATTERY OPERATED Fire Tricycle', made by T.N. (Nomura), in original box.

c1960s

£220-280   **LOCK**

A Japanese tinplate 'INTERPLANETARY SPACE FIGHTER', made by T.N. (Nomura), in original box, play worn.

c1960s

£500-600   **LOCK**

An Alps Television Spaceman tinplate robot.

c1960s

£200-250   **PSA**

A Cragstan SSS Tokyo tinplate battery-powered Cadillac 'Cragstan SSS', boxed.

17in (43cm) long

£300-350   **BELL**

A Japanese Shasta tinplate Bandai 'Rambler' travel trailer, no.523.
c1960   *11in (28cm) long*
£160-200   **BELL**

A Yoshiya tinplate 'Planet Robot', in need of attention.
c1960s
£60-80   **PSA**

A Lehmann tinplate 'St. Vincent 672' clockwork battleship, not in working order.
13¼in (33.5cm) long
£130-180   **LOCK**

A Marx tinplate 'Flying Fortress 2095' clockwork military aeroplane, boxed.
c1940   *13¼in (34cm) long*
£140-180   **BELL**

A Schuco 'Examico 4001' tinplate clockwork car, boxed with instructions, slight damage.
£100-140   **FLD**

A Schuco 'ELEKTRO-PHANOMENAL' 5503 Mercedes 190SL tinplate, with opening boot, chrome fittings, black tonneau and Mercedes badges, boxed, with instructions, lacking control and accessories.
8¼in (21cm) long
£100-150   **FLD**

A Spot-On 'Austin Prime Mover with Articulated Flat Float', no.106A/OC, in original box.
£350-400   **LOCK**

A painted tin paddle wheel clockwork steamboat, attributed to The Stevens & Brown Mfg. Co., Cromwell, Connecticut, stencilled 'COLUMBIA', with key.
c1870-80   *15in (38cm) long*
£2,500-3,000   **NA**

A tinplate and clockwork fire brigade engine, tyres read 'CONTINENTAL-BALLOON CORD 895 x 135'.
11½in (29cm) long
£75-85   **LOCK**

QUICK REFERENCE - CORGI

● In 1956, the Mettoy company launched a range of diecast models, partly inspired by the success of Dinky Supertoys. Diecast toys are made from a metal alloy that can be cast in a mould, also known as a die.

● Corgi cars were more realistic than Dinky cars, with clear windows, detailed interiors, 'Glidamatic' spring suspension and opening doors and boots. The earliest cars produced were modelled after contemporary British-built saloon cars.

● In the 1960s and 1970s, Corgi produced models inspired by TV programmes and films, including James Bond and Batman. These are often highly sought-after by collectors.

● Unusual colours increase the value, as do unusual combinations of wheel, interior and body colours. Condition is important for collectors of Corgi cars. Mint boxed examples tend to fetch the highest prices.

● Today, Corgi produces most of its cars and trucks as one-off limited-edition pieces.

A Corgi 'FORD CONSUL CORTINA SUPER ESTATE CAR', no.440, boxed, with inner display and inner card packaging.
£180-220   WM

A Corgi 'THE GREEN HORNET "BLACK BEAUTY" CRIME FIGHTING CAR', no.268, with two interior figures and accessories, in picture card box, with display stand.
£240-280   WM

A near-mint Corgi Toys 'JAMES BOND 007 TOYOTA 2000GT', no.336, in the original all-card sliding tray box with packing piece, packing ring, lapel badge, secret instructions, with eight various missiles.
£180-220   LSK

A mint Corgi 'MORRIS MINI MINOR WHIZZWHEELS', no.204, boxed.
£140-180   W&W

A near-mint Corgi Toys '251 HILLMAN IMP', in original all-card box, with luggage piece, with Corgi Model Club leaflet.
£90-110   LSK

A Corgi Toys 'TRIUMPH HERALD COUPE', no.231, in original all-card box with Model Club leaflet.
£80-90   LSK

A near-mint Corgi Toys 'JAMES BOND'S ASTON MARTIN DB5', no.261, with James Bond figure and bandit figure, in original all-card sliding tray box with secret instructions envelope, secret instructions leaflet and a spare bandit figure, pencil '9/11D' on box, base slightly collapsed.
£240-280   LSK

A near-mint Corgi Toys 'CHRYSLER IMPERIAL', no.246, with two figures, with golf trolley in boot, in original all-card box.
£120-160   LSK

A near-mint Corgi Toys 'THE 'SAINT'S' CAR VOLVO P.1800', no.258, in original all-card box.
£250-300   LSK

A near-mint Corgi Toys ''E' TYPE JAGUAR WITH DETACHABLE HARD TOP', no.307, in the original all-card box.
£220-260   LSK

A Corgi Toys 'Chitty Chitty Bang Bang', no.266, in original box, some damage.

£85-95   **LOCK**

A Corgi Toys 'Charlie's Angels Custom Van', no.434, in the original window box with header card.

£40-50   **LSK**

A Corgi Toys, 'MORRIS MINI COOPER', no.227, competition model.

£130-160   **LSK**

A Corgi Toys, Triumph TR3 Sports Car, no.305, in original all-card box, with leaflet.

£60-70   **LSK**

A near-mint Corgi Toys 'NEVILLE CEMENT MIXER', no.460 ERF, in original all-card box.

£55-65   **LSK**

A Corgi Toys 'HEINKEL ECONOMY CAR', no.233, in original all-card box.

£70-80   **LSK**

A Corgi 'CIRCUS GIRAFFE TRANSPORTER WITH GIRAFFES', no.503, boxed, with original inner card packaging.

£120-160   **WM**

A Corgi Major Toys Gift set, no.27, in original box, loss to polystyrene.

£70-80   **LOCK**

A Corgi 'COMMER "WALLS" REFRIGERATOR VAN', no.453, boxed.

£70-80   **BELL**

A near-mint Corgi Toys 'ECURIE ECOSSE RACING CAR TRANSPORTER', no.1126, in original lift-off lid all-card box, with three packing pieces, with Corgi Model Club leaflets.

£130-160   **LSK**

A Corgi Toys 1:76 scale 'GUY PANTECHNICON TESCO VAN', in original plastic packed box, limited edition with certificate no.0839/2000 released.

£20-25 LSK

A near-mint Corgi Toys 'BATBOAT AND TRAILER', no.107, boat with tinplate fin, in original all-card box.

£250-300 LSK

A Corgi 'DOLPHIN 20 CRUISER' boat, no.104, in card picture box.

£65-75 WM

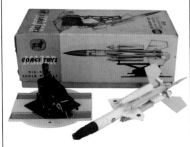

A Corgi Major Toys 'Bristol BLOODHOUND GUIDED MISSILE WITH LAUNCHING RAMP', no.1108, in original box, some wear.

£35-40 LOCK

A Corgi Major Toys 'MASSEY FERGUSON "780" COMBINE HARVESTER', no.1111, in original box, hole to lid.

£45-50 LOCK

A near-mint Corgi Toys 'FORD 5000 SUPER MAJOR TRACTOR', no.67, in original all-card box, with original packing piece and model club leaflet.

£110-150 LSK

A Corgi Toys 'CHIPPERFIELDS CIRCUS CRANE TRUCK', no.1126, in original all-card box, with original hook.

£65-75 LSK

A Corgi Toys Gift Set, no.24, Constructor Set GS/24, complete, in original box.

£50-60 LOCK

A Corgi Toys 'The Beatles Yellow Submarine', no.803, with two red hatches, boxed.

£350-400 WM

A Corgi 'Magic Roundabout' carousel, no.852, with Swiss musical movement, boxed.

£250-300 WM

QUICK REFERENCE - DINKY

- Starting out as Model Miniatures in 1931, Dinky toys were designed to accompany the Hornby railway sets. The majority of models were produced in a scale of 1:48.
- The first car, no.23a, was produced in 1934. In the same year, the range was renamed Dinky.
- After World War II, Dinky expanded its ranges, introducing Supertoys. This range of lorries was modelled to the standard Dinky scale of 1:48. Supertoys were typically sold in blue and white horizontally striped boxes. They were marketed as separate to Hornby's railways. To many diecast collectors these are the most desirable Dinkys. Rare variations and models fetch high prices. Production at Dinky's Binns Road factory stopped in the 1970s.

A near-mint Dinky Toys 'VOLKSWAGEN KARMANN GHIA COUPE', no.187, in original panel box.
£85-95　　　LSK

A Dinky Toys 'VOLKSWAGEN SALOON', no.181, in original correct colour spot all-card box, with unusual 'MY' decal to passenger side door.
£70-80　　　LSK

A near-mint Dinky Toys 'M.G. MIDGET SPORTS' car, no.102, in original correct colour spot all-card box.
£400-450　　　LSK

A Dinky Toys 'MORRIS MINI TRAVELLER', no.197, in original box.
£40-50　　　LOCK

A near-mint Dinky Toys 'VAUXHALL VIVA', no.136, in original all-card box.
£55-65　　　LSK

A Dinky Toys 'VAUXHALL VICTOR' estate car, no.141, in original all-card picture sided box.
£50-60　　　LSK

A Dinky Toys 'FORD "FORDOR" SEDAN' trade box, no.139A, in original all-card trade box, split to one end.
£55-65　　　LSK

A Dinky Toys 'ROLLS-ROYCE SILVER WRAITH', no.150, in original all-card box, one end flap missing.
£35-45　　　LSK

A near-mint Dinky Toys 'JAGUAR XK120 COUPÉ', no.157, in original all-card box, missing one end flap.
£120-160　　　LSK

A Dinky Toys 'ATLAS BUS', no.295, in original all-card box.
£30-40   LSK

A Dinky Toys 'CADILLAC TOURER', no.131, with driver, in original all-card spot box.
£55-65   LSK

A Dinky Junior '2 CV CITROËN', no.105, original chassis mounting with game.
This car is one of the rarest in the series.
1961
£1,300-1,600   IVN

A pre-war Dinky 'Trade Box (A1009)', no.28/2, with six 'Type 2 Delivery Vans', including; no. 28D 'OXO', 'OXO BEEF IN BRIEF' to side; no.28G 'Kodak Film', 'Use Kodak Film To Be Sure' on both sides; no.28H 'Dunlop Tyres', 'DUNLOP TYRES' to both sides; no.28K 'Marsh's Sausages', 'Marsh's Sausages' to both sides; no.28M 'Wakefield Castol', 'Wakefield Castol Motor Oil' to both sides; no.28P 'Crawford's', 'CRAWFORD'S BISCUITS' to both sides, minor crazing and minimal paint loss throughout, contained in trade box with dividers.
c1935
£14,000-18,000   M&M

A near-mint Dinky Toys 'FERRARI RACING CAR', no.234, with racing number '5', in original all-card box.
£360-400   LSK

A Dinky Toys 'AUSTIN-HEALEY "100" SPORTS', no.109, with racing number '23', in original correct colour spot all-card box.
£95-110   LSK

A Dinky Toys 'ASTON MARTIN DB3 SPORTS' car, no.110, racing number '20', with driver, in original all-card box.
£120-160   LSK

A Dinky Toys 'SUNBEAM ALPINE SPORTS' car, no.107, with driver and racing number '34', in original all-card box.
£80-100   LSK

A Dinky Toys 'TRIUMPH TR2 SPORTS' car, no.111, with driver and racing number '25', in original all-card box.
£120-160   LSK

A Dinky Toys 'CONNAUGHT RACING CAR', no.236, with driver and racing number '32', in original all-card box.

£75-85   LSK

A Dinky Toys pre-war 'Mobiloil' petrol tank wagon, no.25D, some playwear.

£220-280   LSK

A Dinky Toys 'SPRATT'S GUY VAN', no.917, in original box.

£70-80   LOCK

A Dinky Toys 'GUY FLAT TRUCK', no.512, in original box.

£60-70   LOCK

A near-mint Dinky Toys, 'FODEN 14-TON TANKER "MOBILGAS"', no.504, in original all-card box.

£720-800   LSK

A Dinky Toys 'TANK TRANSPORTER', no.660, in original lift-off lid all-card box, with one packing piece.

£70-80   LSK

A near-mint Dinky Toys 'SHELL B.P. FUEL TANER', no.944, with windows version, in original pictorial all-card box.

£220-280   LSK

A Dinky Toys 'BEDFORD 10 CWT. Van Kodak', no.480, in original box.

£65-75   LOCK

A Dinky Toys 'BEDFORD END TIPPER' trade box and contents, no.25M, in original all-card trade box.

£70-80   LSK

A near-mint Dinky Toys 'AUSTIN COVERED WAGON' trade box, no.30S.

£60-70   LSK

A near-mint Dinky Toys Trojan delivery van, no.454, with 'CYDRAX' livery.

£95-115　　　**LSK**

A Dinky Toys 00 'AUSTIN LORRY', no.064, playworn, in original all-card box.

£20-30　　　**LSK**

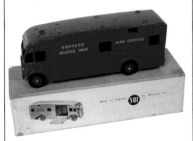

A Dinky Toys 'EXPRESS HORSE VAN', no.581, USA export version, in original Hudson Dobson labelled box, with packing pieces, box lid faded.

£130-180　　　**LSK**

A Dublo Dinky Toys 'LANSING BAGNALL TRACTOR & TRAILER', no.076.

£55-65　　　**LSK**

A near-mint Dinky Toys 'Souvenir Set London Scene', no.300, with 'London Taxi' and 'London Bus', in original polystyrene sliding tray pictorial box.

£25-35　　　**LSK**

QUICK REFERENCE - FRENCH DINKY

● **French Dinky began in Bobigny, Paris, in the early 1930s. At first, model trains and cars were produced in line with its British parent company, but French Dinky's range became increasingly different, focusing on commercial vehicles, aircraft and cars by French makers. It continued production into the 1970s after Dinky had declined in England. Production was transferred to the Pilen factory in Spain in 1977 and the company closed in 1981.**

A Dinky Toys 'Blaw Knox' bulldozer, no.561, in rare blue with tan driver and original tracks, playworn.

£45-55　　　**LSK**

A French Dinky Toys 'MASERATI SPORT 2000', no.22A, in original all-card box.

£90-120　　　**LSK**

A near-mint French Dinky Toys 33AN 'DÉMÉNAGEUR SIMCA "CARGO"' truck, in original all-card box.

£200-250　　　**LSK**

A French Dinky Toys 'ALFA ROMEO 1900 SUPER SPRINT' coupé, no.24J, in original all-card box.

£50-60　　　**LSK**

A French Dinky toys single-axle covered trailer, no.25T, with tinplate draw bar and rear hook.

£15-20　　　**LSK**

A French Dinky Toys 'C'EST UNE FABRICATION MECCANO' Unic Articulated BP tanker, no.887, with five hoses for filling tank, with electrical lights operated by spare wheel, in original Supertoys box.
£200-250   LSK

A mint French Dinky Toys 'AUTOBUS PARISIEN OU URBAIN', no.889, in original pictorial lift-off lid Supertoys box.
£160-200   LSK

A Dinky Toys 'FODEN 14-TON TANKER', no.504, in original Supertoys box.
£95-110   LOCK

A near-mint Dinky Supertoys 'BIG BEDFORD VAN "HEINZ"' delivery van, no.923, in original Supertoys all-card box.
£160-200   LSK

A Dinky Toys 'Weetabix GUY VAN', no.514, yellow Supertoys hubs, in original pictorial labelled all-card box.
£1,600-2,000   LSK

A near-mint Dinky Toys 'GUY FLAT TRUCK WITH TAILBOARD', no.513, in original Supertoys all-card box.
£140-180   LSK

A Dinky Supertoys 'CAR CARRIER WITH TRAILER', no.983, with matching trailer and Dinky Auto Service livery, in original Supertoys all-card box.
£200-300   LSK

A Dinky Toys 'PULLMORE CAR TRANSPORTER WITH FOUR CARS' gift set, no.990, with four cars, no.582 Pullmore Transporter, with a Hillman Minx no.154, repainted no.161 Austin Somerset, a Rover 75 and a Ford Zephyr, in original all-card box with packing piece and upper deck ramp.
£1,100-1,400   LSK

A Dinky Supertoys 'LEYLAND OCTOPUS WAGON', no.934, in original Supertoys box.
£150-200   LSK

A Bandai 'Rolls-Royce SILVER CLOUD Sedan', no.767, friction drive, boxed.
c1960
10½in (26.5cm) long
£150-200   **BELL**

A Bing painted tin fire pumper, with composition driver, copper boiler, battery-operated headlights.
19½in (49.5cm) long
£450-550   **POOK**

A near-mint Brian Norman Farm Miniatures 1/32 scale model of a David Brown Cropmaster tractor, no.FM05, in original all-card labelled box.
£120-160   **LSK**

A Buddy L pressed steel 'WRIGLEY'S SPEARMINT CHEWING GUM RAILWAY EXPRESS AGENCY' tractor trailer, with battery-operated headlights, minor paint loss.
23in (58.5cm) long
£500-600   **POOK**

A Buddy L yellow pressed steel Coca-Cola delivery truck, no.5426, with trays of bottles and two trollies, in original box.
c1960s
£180-220   **LOCK**

A Bura & Hardwick stop-frame animation prison truck and driver, the 1920s style G.A.D. truck with prison bars back and a foam rubber articulated man wearing denim dungarees, some perishing.
38in (96.5cm) long
£300-350   **SAS**

A Chestnut Miniatures 'MASSEY FERGUSON 510 COMBINE', 1:32 scale, with driver, limited edition no.11/500, in original foam-packed box, as issued with specification leaflet and certificate.
£600-700   **LSK**

A CIJ of France Renault Autobus, no.3/40, in original all-card box.
£55-65   **LSK**

A Citroën friction-powered tinplate four-door saloon, on the base faintly marked 'Jouet a Propulsion Andre Citroen Made-In-France', minor paint loss.
1930s
£200-250   **W&W**

A CMC M-098 'Mercedes-Benz W154' diecast model, 1:18 scale, boxed.
1938
£150-200   **FLD**

A Japanese Cragstan 'RAMBLER CLASSIC STATION WAGON', boxed.

c1960

£75-85 BELL

A mint Exoto Porsche 934 RSR racing car, 1:18 scale, with Jägermeister livery and racing no.24, in original polystyrene packed box.

£200-250 LSK

A rare Exoto 1966 Ford GT 40 Mk2, 1:10 scale, with racing no.2 and silver racing stripes with gold hubs, as driven by Amon/Maclaren, limited edition no.573, with dedication plaque addressing the men and women of the Ford Motor Company as signed by the President of Exoto Incorporated, in original polystyrene packed all-card box, with envelope with return response card to Exoto, Moor Park, California.

£1,800-2,200 LSK

A JRD Miniatures refuse truck, no.131, in original all-card box, play worn.

£60-70 LSK

A Lehmann Spielzeug 'Gnom' tinplate open-back truck, no.813, an Opel Blitz-style vehicle, with some rusting, boxed, some wear, one outer end flap missing.

1930s

£120-160 W&W

A near-mint Matchbox 1/75 series 'Morris J2 pickup', no.60, in the original type B all-card box.

£75-80 LSK

A near-mint Matchbox 1/75 Series Bedford tipper, no.40, in the original B2 all-card box.

£45-50 LSK

A near-mint Matchbox 1/75 series Foden 'CEMENT LORRY', no.26, in original type D all-card box.

£45-55 LSK

A Meccano pre-war constructor kit no.2 model car and driver, play worn with chips to paintwork, rear left wheel loose, some bolts missing.

13in (33cm) long

£650-750 APAR

A Mercury Models 'KEHRLI & OELER BERNE' Saurer advertising van, no.88, made for a company in Switzerland, TIR decal under headlight, some wear on decals, boxed.

Founded in 1932, Mercury manufactured machine parts. After World War II, the company made 1:43 scale diecast models. Mercury closed in 1978.

£1,000-1,500 BTA

A Taylor & Barratt 'AIR MAIL' van, in RAF blue, with silver livery, with some minor play wear.

£100-140   LSK

A Tipp Co. Steamlined Racing Car, no.959, with driver, fitted with fixed key mechanism, number plate to read 'TC 959', missing rear spare wheel.

14¼in (36cm) long

£950-1,100   LSK

A Tonka Toys large pressed steel Aerial Ladder Fire Engine/Truck, no.1348, in original box. *c1960s*

£140-180   LOCK

A Tri-ang Spot-On models 1/42 scale model of an ERF 68G, no.109/3B, with nine plastic barrels, in original box with packing piece, box lid reinforced.

£300-350   LSK

A Tri-ang Spot-On models Aston Martin DB3, no.113, in original all-card box.

£250-300   LSK

A Tri-ang pressed steel London Transport double-decker bus, no. 93, with working bell, number plate reads 'LIB 4242'.

12in (30.5cm) high

£160-200   LOCK

Judith Picks

I do love a toy with a story! And this racing car is also in excellent condition. This model was made to celebrate the record breaking MG Magic Midget, which was the first baby car to do over 100 mph, and the first to do over 120 mph, driven by Captain G.E. Eyston. Eyston's photo appears on the side of the box. It is tinplate with rubber tyres, wind-up mechanism and comes with original box and key. The winding and spinning mechanism still works well. No wonder it made almost three times the estimate price.

A Tri-ang 'MAGIC MIDGET' record breaking car, *c1933*

£3,000-4,000   GIL

An early 20thC Tri-ang large pressed steel and metal pedal car, number plate to read 'LIB.4242', with original steering wheel and windscreen with original glazing, requires extensive restoration.

£950-1,100   LSK

An Ugo Fadini handbuilt 1954 Cooper MkV record car, 1:43 scale, limited edition no.43 of 150, in original card box.

£150-200   LSK

A CIJ Alfa Romeo P2 Clockwork Racing Car, pressed steel body, racing no.2, original pneumatic tyres with tread, with CIJ manufacturer's mark to base, with original key, missing fuel and radiator caps.

CIJ (Compagnie Industrielle Du Jouet) produced this Alfa Romeo P2. It was based on the Grand Prix racing car designed by Vittorio Jano that raced between 1924 and 1930. Three of these Alfa Romeo P2s sold in the UK in March 2019.

1930s *21in (53.5cm) long*
£5,500-6,000 C&T

A CIJ Alfa Romeo P2 tinplate clockwork racing car.
21in (53.5cm) long
£6,000-7,000 BRI

A CLOSER LOOK AT A CIJ RACING CAR

This is a scarce example of an iconic toy car with a pressed steel body.

It has a working clockwork motor, driving the rear wheels and later issue original Michelin pneumatic tyres.

It has spoked wheels, knock-off hub caps, with drum brakes, rack and pinion steering, handbrake, starter handle, fuel and radiator caps.

Although it is missing the key and has some paint flaking, it's rarity still commands a strong price.

A CIJ Alfa Romeo P2 racing car, racing no.2.
1930s *21in (53.5cm) long*
£6,500-7,500 C&T

A Märklin construction set limousine, no.1101, with clockwork motor.
c1930 *15½in (39.5cm) long*
£400-500 BELL

A Meccano Constructors Car, no.1, with key and fixed clockwork mechanism.
£500-600 LSK

A Shackleton Toy 'Foden F.G.' clockwork flatbed Lorry, in original box, one front wheel detached.
£450-500 LOCK

A Tri-ang 'MINIC' tinplate and clockwork model of a traction engine, in original line drawing all-card box.
£25-35 LSK

A Gunthermann tin clockwork fire ladder truck, with hand-crank ladder, tin lithograph driver and two seated firemen, missing one fireman, old re-solder to fender, clicker tab on one gear is replaced.
14in (35.5cm) long
£800-1,000 POOK

A rare Märklin rear-entry clockwork limousine, with glass windscreen, nickel headlamps, clockwork motor and worm-gear steering system, restored.
11in (28cm) long
£7,500-8,500 BER

A Gunthermann eight-man scull, clockwork driven with synchronised rowing action like an actual racing skull.

29in (73.5cm) long

£14,000-16,000 **BER**

A Kuramochi celluloid clockwork 'Circus Elephant', holding bell and 'WELCOME! SEE OUR CIRCUS' sign, the mechanism causing the elephant to move his head and arms, damage to shoulder of one arm.

10in (25.5cm) high

£200-250 **SAS**

A Roullet & Decamps clockwork tiger, the fabric-covered tiger balances on a wood ball with applied paper stars, age crack in ball.

12¼in (31cm) high

£12,000-14,000 **POOK**

A Schuco clockwork monkey, no.985, with dancing baby mouse, some damage.

£70-80 **LSK**

A Schuco clockwork mouse, swinging a baby mouse, key present.

4¼in (11cm) high

£70-80 **LOCK**

An early English Perry & Co. 'Dancing Scotsman' automaton, dancing on a paper-covered wooden box housing the clockwork mechanism, with maker's labels, slight wear.

1860-70s *10¼in (26cm) high*

£600-700 **SAS**

A Mohr and Krauss, Nuremburg, clockwork motorcycle, with driver, reproduces a twin-cylinder, lithographed blue flywheel engine operated by a crank launching.

1900 *5½in (14cm) high*

£4,500-5,000 **IVN**

An Ives clockwork butter churner, appears to be original outfit, some paint loss to face and losses to back of bonnet, currently working.

10½in (26.5cm) high

£900-1,100 **POOK**

A scarce American clockwork ball and mallet player, possibly Ives, remains of original label on underside, one of three examples extant, working, figure is re-dressed.

18¾in (47.5cm) long

£7,500-8,500 **POOK**

QUICK REFERENCE - BRITAINS

- The William Britain Company manufactured lead mechanical toys from 1845. In 1893, William Britain Jr developed a method of hollowcasting lead die-cast toys, decreasing the production costs of toy soldiers. By 1900, the company had produced more than 100 different sets of toy lead figures.
- Britains also made toy cars and diecast military trucks. After World War I it made civilian figures, including footballers and Disney characters, and began its 'Home Farm' series.
- In the late 1950s, Britains launched its plastic 'Swoppet' series and its production of lead hollowcast figures ceased in 1966. The company was bought by The Dobson Park Group in 1984 and the name was changed to Britain Petite Ltd. After a series of acquisitions, the company was bought by The Good Soldier LLC company in 2016.

A Britains Fordson 'TRACTOR & REAR DUMP', no.9630, with original spade, rear fitting and puppet steering control attachments with string, in original box.

£1,500-2,000   LSK

A near-mint Britains Model Farm 128F 'Fordson Major TRACTOR', with driver, in original box, with Britains complaints leaflet and packing piece.

£250-300   LSK

A Britains 'FORD SUPER MAJOR 5000 DIESEL TRACTOR', no.9527, air filter and exhaust attachment and jewelled headlights, in original sliding tray all-card box, some wear.

£110-140   LSK

A Britains 'Home Farm' series farm wagon, no.5F, in original labelled all-card box.

£45-55   LSK

A Britains 'Premier' series Thornycroft AA truck with service detachment, created by Charles Biggs, no.8926, in original foam packed all-card box.

£80-100   LSK

A near-mint Britains 'ARMY LORRY', no.1334, with tipper action, with driver, in original all-card box.

£160-200   LSK

A Britains Military 155mm field gun, no.2064, in original labelled all-card box, with missiles and packing pieces.

£90-110   LSK

A Britains height finder, no.1729, with operator figure.

£30-40   LSK

A Britains Military 'BEETLE LORRY', no.1877, with driver, in original picture sided all-card box, with complaints leaflet.

£100-150   LSK

A scarce Britains 'CIVILIANS' set, no.168, in red box with grey-green Fred Whisstock picture label showing street scene, some wear.
1920s
£500-600   **W&W**

A scarce Britains 'POLICE' set, no.319, in red box with purple Fred Whisstock picture label showing the three types of figures, minor wear and tape repair to one end of lid, '428' stamped on label suggesting the box was possibly intended for the US Police set.
1920s
£600-700   **W&W**

A Britains 'COMPLETE RAILWAY STATION SET', no.158, with 13 figures and 12 accessories, re-tied into green box with picture label and inner card, some wear.
£450-550   **W&W**

A scarce set of Britains 'The CHANGING of the GUARD at BUCKINGHAM PALACE', no.1555, contains 84 Guards, with two sentry boxes complete with sentries, in a presentation display case, minor wear.
£600-700   **W&W**

A rare 'TIMPO STATION FIGURES' Railway Series set, no.850, with 15 figures and five accessories, re-tied into blue-green box with picture label and inner card, some wear and tape repair to all corners of the lid.
1950s
£350-400   **W&W**

A Britains first issue 'Soldiers of the British Empire' Madras Native Infantry, no.67, in original replacement Infantry in Steel Helmets, no.1794 box.

These examples have the very early oval bases.
c1900
£100-150   **LSK**

A Britains British Soldiers 'DRUMS AND BUGLES of the LINE' set, no.30, comprising eight figures, boxed, minor wear.
£120-160   **W&W**

A Britains 'TYPES of the WORLD'S ARMIES' Seaforth Highlanders set, no.88, boxed, with insert, minor wear, contents in mint condition, unused and still tied in.
£130-170   **W&W**

TOYS & GAMES

A French 19thC rocking horse, made by the Auguste Reidmeister Studio, carved wood with metal head and fittings, with a removable handlebar and wheels that drop down to make a pull-along toy.

42¼in (107.5cm) wide

£900-1,100　　　　　　　　SWO

An early 20thC Baby Carriages of Liverpool pine rocking horse, painted dapple grey, with original saddle, bears 'BCL Rambler Liverpool' label on the base.

40¼in (102cm) wide

£600-700　　　　　　　　FLD

A White Horses 'Linford-Christmas 1994' twin-pillar rocking horse.

48¾in (124cm) high

£400-500　　　　　　　　WHP

A Victorian carved wood and painted rocking horse.

£1,000-1,500　　　　　　　　JN

An early 20thC rocking horse, with horse hair mane and tail, mounted on a frame.

36¼in (92cm) long

£120-200　　　　　　　　LOCK

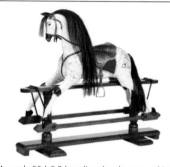

An early 20thC Edwardian dapple-grey rocking horse, with horse hair mane and tail, leather bridle and reins, on a wood trestle base with painted iron hardware.

59in (150cm) long

£800-900　　　　　　　　L&T

An original wooden Lines Juvenile fairground 'Jake' dobby horse, a hole where the pole would have been fitted.

c1900

27½in (70cm) high

£800-1,200　　　　　　　　LSK

An original wooden Lines Juvenile fairground 'Fizz' dobby horse, a hole where the pole would have been fitted.

c1900

27½in (70cm) high

£1,300-1,600　　　　　　　　LSK

A Phalibois trio of performing composition clowns musical automaton, under a glass dome, with clowns dressed in fanciful outfits, performing a balancing act, one twirling a chair on his nose, another with a bass drum and cymbals, with a small poodle and monkey, working, glass repair to side of dome.

26in (66cm) high

£5,500-6,500 **POOK**

A possibly French mid-19thC HMS Franklin papier mâché automaton, depicting the HMS Franklin trapped on an iceberg, with a sailor on deck swinging an axe at a polar bear, as a second sailor climbs the rigging while a second polar bear chases after him, as they disappear in the iceberg they reappear to resume the chase, with a Plexiglass display case.

This scene was inspired by the Arctic Expedition of Sir John Franklin who sailed ships to the Arctic in 1845 and mysteriously disappeared.

19½in (49.5cm) high

£4,000-5,000 **POOK**

A scarce Hubley cast iron Beach Patrol surfer boy pull toy.

7½in (19cm) high

£3,000-4,000 **POOK**

A Lehmann painted tin wind-up figurine of Heavy Swell, with the original cane and key, working.

8¾in (22cm) high

£1,200-1,600 **POOK**

A rare early G. & J. Lines pedal car, 'L.457' number plate, pedal and chain driven, original finish, general wear and rusting to grille.

c1912

36¾in (93.5cm) long

£2,000-2,500 **SAS**

A Märklin central station, for the English market, with real glass windows, missing one lead finial and bell.

18in (45.5cm) wide

£1,200-1,500 **BER**

A Martin 'Le Cherif Arab on camel', with lead feet, with wheels and rubber band mechanism, feet possibly replaced.

7¾in (20cm) high

£7,500-8,500 **BER**

A Meccano pre-war wooden constructor car garage, left door not shutting, some loss to decal, wear to paintwork.

14¼in (36cm) long

£350-400 **APAR**

A pre-war Meccano Outfit no.10, complete, in an original green enamelled wooden cabinet, with a correct set of manuals, numbers 6, 7/8 and 9/10 plus an edition of 'How to Use Meccano Parts'.

1937-41

£1,800-2,200 **LSK**

A post-war Meccano no.8 set, restrung on original cards.

c1949-53

£300-350 **LSK**

TOYS & GAMES

A Marx plastic battery-operated 'BIG LOO GIANT MOON ROBOT', with original box and instruction sheet, to include two rockets, four balls, four darts, a syringe, and a moon grenade, with a hand crank that operates the voice.

38in (96.5cm) high

£1,200-1,600   **POOK**

An early 20thC carved and painted wood fox hunting group, attributed to Frank Whittington of Forest Toys, comprising six horses and riders, seven hound dogs and a fox.

Frank Whittington (1876-1973) established a toy company at the end of World War I in the New Forest, making carved animals and people. Whittington began production from his home, but, in 1922, as demand increased he built a factory on the edge of the New Forest. Queen Mary ordered two dozen of Whittington's Noah's Arks after seeing them at the British Industries Fairs during the inter war period.

highest 9in (23cm) high

£1,000-1,400   **WW**

A pre-war Taylor & Barrett 'ZOO SERIES VISITORS AT TEA', set 30, of hollowcast figurines, in plain card box, with illustrated label.

£550-650   **FLD**

A painted Noah's Ark, with 83 carved and painted whimsical animals, some paint and paper losses to the ark.

ark 17in (43cm) long

£750-850   **POOK**

An early 20thC German wooden Noah's Ark, polychrome painted with 'bluebird' to the roof, 40 pairs of original painted wooden animals.

24¾in (63cm) wide

£1,100-1,400   **BELL**

A German large painted wood Noah's Ark, the interior with six stalls and an aviary under the lift lid, with 18 large-scale carved and painted animals, minor wear.

1987   *16¾in (42.5cm) high*

£1,500-2,000   **POOK**

A German composition 'Walking Santa', with rabbit-fur beard, some flaking to boot paint.

13in (33cm) high

£2,200-2,800   **BER**

A Zero-X Thunderbirds space toy, by Century 21 Toys Ltd., Hong Kong, (China), battery operated, boxed.

£550-650   **FLD**

TOYS & GAMES

QUICK REFERENCE - VENTRILOQUISM

- While evidence of forms of ventriloquism, at the time a ritual or religious practice, have been found in Egyptian and Hebrew archaeology, the first known ventriloquist was Louis Brabant, valet to King Francis I of France, in the 16thC.
- The term comes from the Latin 'venter' and 'loqui' to mean 'belly-speaking'. To create the illusion of the speaker's voice coming from somewhere else, the speaker opens their mouth as little as possible, releases their breath slowly and withdraws the tongue, reducing its movement. Today, ventriloquism is used for popular entertainment.

An early 20thC ventriloquist dummy of a girl, papier-mâché head with glass eyes and mouth, was used professionally.

35in (89cm) long

£140-200   **LOCK**

A Bob Bura's 'Mr Punch' marionette, probably by Gordon Murray, a papier-mâché large stage puppet with moving lower jaw, jointed wooden limbs, papier mâché torso and original costume, and a photographic montage including an image of Bob Bura with Mr Punch and David Jacobs.

Bob Bura (1924-2018) was a London-born animator and puppeteer. In the 1930s, he worked as a ventriloquist and entertainer in London's West End. Bura went on to work on children's TV programmes including 'Camberwick Green', 'Captain Pugwash' and 'Chigley' with Alan Hardwick.

38in (96.5cm) high

£300-350   **SAS**

A ventriloquist puppet, 'Cassy' (William Casanova) from Whirligig, made by Francis Coudrill, a composition or papier-mâché head with fixed blue striated glass eyes, articulated jaw revealing front teeth, the ears converted to alien points, a jointed body and some old and some new clothing, some wear.

With a letter from Joanna Coudrill, on Francis Coudrill headed paper, dated 13 July 1990, stating, 'received the sum of £1,000 (cheque) from Bob Bura for one ventriloquial puppet 'William'.

30in (76cm) high

£850-950   **SAS**

An old lady character ventriloquist dummy, with papier-mâché head, articulated jaw with single tooth and wart on chin, carved wooden hands, wooden jointed legs, knitted jumper, felt skirt, shopping bag and papier mâché bottle of stout, some wear.

A video available online shows Bob Bura entertaining a young girl with this character, calling the girl a 'silly sausage'.

28in (71cm) high

£420-500   **SAS**

An Effanbee Charlie McCarthy ventriloquist doll, with button, monocle and original outfit, in original box.

19¾in (50cm) high

£150-200   **POOK**

A Hooray Henry-type character ventriloquist dummy, with papier-mâché head, articulate jaw, large Roman nose, protruding two top teeth, the right eyebrow raised and eye shaped possibly for a monocle, hair moustache and side parted hair, wooden articulated body, foam stuffing, some wear.

36in (91.5cm) high

£350-450   **SAS**

An unusual Insull ventriloquist character jug, papier mâché or composition, handpainted with levers to operate eyes, top lip and bottom lip.

8in (20.5cm) high

£700-800   **SAS**

A magician's two-tiered stand, inscribed 'STROMBOLI Presents THE VICTORIAN CABINET of CURIOSITIES'.

36¼in (92cm) high

£350-450   **APAR**

A set of French early 20thC Grand Etteilla tarot reader's cards, numbered 1-78 with two blank cards, in used condition.

£400-500   SWO

A 19thC set of carved agate dominoes, probably Italian, in a leather case.

1¾in (4.5cm) wide

£250-350   WW

A scarce McLoughlin Bros. 'BULLS AND BEARS The GREAT WALL ST. GAME', patented 1883, with a lithograph box lid of a dressed bull and bear standing on Wall Street, a spinning board, play money and contracts, as well as the original instruction booklet.

1883

box 15¼in (38.5cm) wide

£18,000-22,000   POOK

A Milton Bradley 'Whirligig of Life' animated praxinoscope, with 9 full-colour strips and 18 larger strips.

7in (18cm) high

£450-550   POOK

A Jaques solitaire board game, the mahogany board with 16 recesses and corresponding numbered white glazed pottery marbles, impressed maker's marks 'JAQUES LONDON'.

c1858

7in (18cm) diam

£700-800   L&T

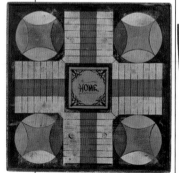

A 19thC painted pine Parcheesi game board, with polychromed blocks centring a 'HOME' block on blue background.

21in (53.5cm) square

£2,500-3,000   POOK

A Renzo Romagnoli black leather and gilt-metal games box, of modern manufacture.

18½in (47cm) wide

£400-500   ROS

A mahogany games compendium, with a set of boxwood and hardwood chess pieces, dominoes, cribbage and bezique scorers, draughtsmen, die-cast horses, dice and shakers, and a 'Rules Booklet' by J.W. Spear and Sons.

13.5in (34cm) wide

£100-150   DA&H

A French Jeu De Course horse race game, with interior and exterior rows of painted lead horses, lacking box lid.

14¾in (37.5cm) wide

£250-350   POOK

A Bing gauge I LNER green 4-4-2 c/w Precursor tank loco, top section of coal rail detached, with a key.

Founded by Ignatz and Adolf Bing in 1863, wholesalers Gebrüder Bing began producing its own toys in 1879. The company produced toy boats, cars, trains, train tracks and railway buildings. Bing also manufactured for Bassett-Lowke. In 1933, Bing was taken over by Karl Bub.
£500-600   LSK

A Bing 0-4-0 'APOLLO' c/w loco and six-wheel LMS red tender, tender no.513, crazing to paintwork.
£150-200   LSK

A Bing 0-4-0 live steam loco, spirit-fired single cylinder.
£150-200   LSK

A Bing 0-6-0 loco 12v DC three-rail, fitted with Bonds Motor, with an earlier Bing tender, loco has been repainted.
£110-150   LSK

A Bing for Bassett-Lowke 4-4-0 'GEORGE THE FIFTH' c/w loco and LMS tender no.5320, crazing to paintwork, droplinks missing from couplings, box faded, water stained and without labels.
£180-220   LSK

A Bing for Bassett-Lowke GNR 4-4-0 Atlantic loco, with tender 4-6v DC original mechanism, repainted in LNER livery no.3274, with coal added to tender.
£350-400   LSK

A Bing for Bassett-Lowke LNER D class 4-4-0 loco and tender no.504 12v DC three-rail, fitted with Leeds Model Co. mechanism.
£220-280   LSK

A Bing gauge 1 Br/3rd corridor bogie coach, no.1921.
£260-300   LSK

A Bing teak LNER bogie coach, no.2568, with repainted hinged roof and set of tables and chairs.
£55-65   LSK

A near-mint Bassett-Lowke post-war LMS Standard Compound 4-4-0 12v DC, no.1036, with six-wheel LMS tender.

£300-400   LSK

A Bassett-Lowke L&NWR 'GEORGE THE FIFTH' 4-4-0 c/w loco, cab roof distorted, corrosion to rods, handrails and couplings.

£80-100   LSK

A Bassett-Lowke 4-4-0 c/w 'GEORGE THE FIFTH' loco and six-wheel tender, no.2663.

£160-200   LSK

A Bassett-Lowke compound 4-4-0 loco and tender, LMS no.1108 red, base marked '12v DC', not Bassett-Lowke pick-up fitted.

£110-140   LSK

A Bassett-Lowke gauge I 0-4-0 c/w loco, L&NER re-numbered no.114, crazing to paintwork, corrosion to one coupling rod, not a Bassett-Lowke key.

£250-300   LSK

A Bassett-Lowke lithographed LMS Royal Scot class 4-6-0 8v DC, no.6100, with a six-wheel Fowler LMS tender, with Permag instructions.

£500-600   LSK

A Märklin clockwork LNER 0-6-0 tank loco, with 'TM1020' to rear of bunker, with speed control.

£300-400   LSK

A Märklin 0-4-2 loco and tender gauge 1, '1021D' on cabsides, six-wheel tender, key fits but is not Märklin.

£150-200   LSK

A Märklin DB green crocodile electric loco.

£180-220   LSK

A Märklin for Gamages gauge 1 'NE 2883' meat van.

£110-150   LSK

QUICK REFERENCE - HORNBY

- Hornby began in 1901, when Frank Hornby (1863-1936) applied for a patent for 'Improvements in Toy or Educational Devices for Children and Young People'. He went on to found Meccano Ltd. in 1907.
- Meccano produced toy trains from 1920. These Hornby trains were made of metal and were 0 gauge in size. They were powered first with a clockwork motor, then joined by an electric range in 1925.
- Hornby Dublo, of 00 gauge, was launched in 1938. These models were often decorated in the liveries of the then largest rail companies in Britain, such as London and North Eastern Railway and Great Western Railway.
- In 1964, Hornby was bought by Lines Bros., the parent company of Tri-ang. Trains were produced as Tri-ang Hornby, then Hornby Railways in 1972 after the Tri-ang Group was disbanded.
- In 1980, the company, then known as Hornby Hobbies Ltd., became independent. In 1986, it became a public company. Hornby, as the company is now known, moved its manufacturing to China in 1995.

A Hornby green LNER E220 20v AC 4-4-0 'THE BRAMHAM MOOR', no.201, with six-wheel LNER tender, scratches to cab roof.
1935-36
£500-600   LSK

A Hornby LNER no.1 Special Tank loco 0-4-0, no.8123, eight boiler bands, link missing from front coupling, corrosion to rods.
1929-30
£110-140   LSK

A Hornby LNER green 0-4-0 clockwork loco, no.623, chips to front buffers, box in poor condition, heavily taped.
1926-27
£70-80   LSK

A Hornby 1929-39 Metropolitan 6v AC, with repainted roof.
1929-39
£300-400   LSK

A Hornby 1929-30 'UNITED DAIRIES MILK TANK' wagon, chips and scratches.
1929-30
£90-120   LSK

A Hornby 'MECCANO' coal wagon, minute chips, boxed.
1931-32
£60-70   LSK

A Hornby 'CARR'S Biscuits' van, black standard base, sliding door, revised transfers, roof and box in poor condition.
1934-41
£75-85   LSK

A Hornby E2E engine shed, fold to one door.
1935-41
£180-240   LSK

A Hornby 'WINDSOR' station, no.2E, some chips on platform, one lamp bracket broken.
1933-34
£110-150   LSK

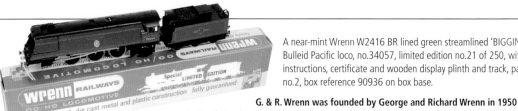

A near-mint Wrenn W2416 BR lined green streamlined 'BIGGIN HILL' Bulleid Pacific loco, no.34057, limited edition no.21 of 250, with instructions, certificate and wooden display plinth and track, packer no.2, box reference 90936 on box base.

G. & R. Wrenn was founded by George and Richard Wrenn in 1950 in South London. It specialised in producing track for model railways. In 1955, the company moved to Basildon, Essex. Wrenn began producing 00-guage model railway and later two-rail track for TT-gauge models. In 1965, Lines Brothers Ltd. bought shares in Wrenn and the company began producing Hornby Dublo models and Tri-ang's TT line, under the name Tri-ang Wrenn. Dapol bought Wrenn in 1992. Production ceased in 2001.

£600-700   LSK

A Wrenn W2219 LMS standard class 2-6-4 tank engine, no.2679, boxed.
£75-85   LSK

A near-mint Wrenn Railways W2217 LNER green 0-6-2 tank engine, with instructions, packer no.3 on box base.
£65-75   LSK

A Wrenn W2269 rebuilt BR green 'Golden Arrow', 'SIR KEITH PARK'.
£260-300   LSK

A Wrenn W2212 LNER blue 'Sir Nigel Gresley' engine and tender, packer no.3 on box base.
£55-65   LSK

A Wrenn Railways W2228 BR 'City of Birmingham' engine and tender, packer no.3 on box base, with instructions.
£90-120   LSK

A Wrenn Railways W2268 BR streamlined 'Bulleid Pacific', no.34004, 'Yeovil' packer no.3, ref.05320 on box base, with instructions, c230 made.
£400-500   LSK

A Wrenn Railways W2226 BR 'City of London' engine and tender, with box.
£80-100   LSK

A Tri-ang Wrenn W2227 LMS post-war 'City of Stoke on Trent' engine and tender, packer no.6 on box base.
£75-95   LSK

An Ace Trains maroon LMS freelance 4-4-4 tank loco E/1 standard 20v AC/DC, with test tag and operating instructions.
1996
£250-300　　　　　　　　　　　　　　**LSK**

An Aster GI live steam black Japanese 4-6-2 VR 0276, no. C575, on cab sides with bogie eight-wheel tender, VR0276T.
£2,200-3,000　　　　　　　　　　　　**LSK**

A mint Aster gauge one American outline two-rail electric tender New York Central System 4-6-4 'COMMODORE VANDERBILT' streamlined loco, with its 12-wheeled bogie tender with 'NEW YORK CENTRAL' to sides, boxed with instruction manual.
£1,500-2,000　　　　　　　　　　　　**W&W**

An Aster gauge 1 live steam GWR 0-6-0 Pannier Tank loco, serial no.0232, with instructions, in original box.
12¼in (31cm) long
£1,800-2,200　　　　　　　　　　　**LOCK**

A mint Aster Hobby Co. gauge 1 live steam loco and tender LNWR 'Jumbo' Hardwicke, no.16 of 220, appears unsteamed, with small amount of G1 track.
£1,800-2,200　　　　　　　　　　　**LSK**

A Bachmann OO-gauge 'MIDLAND PULLMAN' six-car DMU set 31-255DC, with two powered driving cars, two kitchen/dining cars and two dining cars, boxed, minor wear.
£250-300　　　　　　　　　　　　　**W&W**

A near-mint Fine Art Models PRR T1 engine and tender, in plexiglas and wood display case.
51¼in (130cm) long
£5,000-6,000　　　　　　　　　　　**MORP**

A near-mint Finescale Locomotive Co. gauge 1 coach LMS D1917 vestibule, first class period II livery.
£500-600　　　　　　　　　　　　　**LSK**

An American Flyer Lines 'Shasta' 0-4-0 Standard GI blue/green electric loco, no. 4637.
£400-500　　　　　　　　　　　　　**LSK**

A near-mint Keith Murray green SR 4-4-2 12v DC electric tank loco, no.2025, O-gauge finescale, two spoon pick-up, not a skate.
£350-400　　　　　　　　　　　　　**LSK**

TOYS & GAMES

A Kit/Scratch built finescale maroon LMS 4-6-2 'DUCHESS OF DEVONSHIRE' streamlined loco, no.6227, with six-wheel LMS tender.

£250-300   LSK

A mint KTM ready-to-run unpainted brass Pacific 'Big Boy' 4-8-8-4 engine and tender, Japanese made for Westside Model Company.

£750-850   LSK

A Lionel no.42 black 'Locomotive Outfit', missing one step and both couplers, no track, with early box.

The Lionel Manufacturing Company was founded by Joshua Lionel Cowen (1877-1965) in 1900 in New York city. In 1915, Lionel's O-gauge trains and track were launched. The company was renamed The Lionel Corporation in 1918. In 1970, Lionel opened a new plant in Michigan. The Lionel factory was briefly moved to Mexico in 1982, but after this proved unsuccessful, production was resumed in Michigan. Lionel moved its headquarters to Concord, North Carolina, in 2014.

15in (38cm) long

£900-1,100   BER

A near-mint Lionel three-rail Southern Pacific 'Daylight' 4-8-4 engine, ref 6-8307, with electronic steam sound, in near-mint box.

£130-160   LSK

A Lionel black cast steam outline 4-6-4 electric Hudson-type 700E, no.5344, with a bogie Pennsylvania tender.

£550-650   LSK

A Lionel Lines O-gauge dark/light umber 0-4-4-0 electric loco, no.256, motors turn freely.

£300-350   LSK

A Lionel Lines Standard 'BILD-A-LOCO' GI 2-4-2 green electric outline loco, no.9E.

£220-280   LSK

A McCoy wide-gauge 'SAN FRANCISCO MUNICIPAL RAILWAY' no.8 street car, with electric motor.

£200-250   LSK

An MTH Legionnaire passenger set, with 10-186E locomotive and 4380, 4381 and 4382 passenger cars.

£450-550   LSK

A Sunset models 'CANADIAN PACIFIC' brass 2-10-4 Selkirk-type engine and tender, no.5931.

£450-550   LSK

A Suydam Japanese painted 'PACIFIC ELECTRIC EXPRESS' Portland combine car, no.1872, motorised, with box.
£100-140   **LSK**

A Suydam Japanese unpainted brass powered Portland combine car, no decals, with box.
£90-110   **LSK**

A classic GI green/red steam outline 4-6-0, no.1108, fitted with electric can motor, with a bogie Southern tender.
£120-180   **LSK**

An exhibition-quality model of a 5in-gauge Great Western Railway Castle Class 4-6-0 'G.J. CHURCHWARD' loco and tender no.7017, built by Gold medal-winning builder Mr Graham Hawkins of Bristol, built mainly in stainless steel, with name plates, numbers and beading cut from brass plate by hand.

Castle Class no.7017 was never fitted with a double chimney.
Boiler History: Kingswood Boilers Bristol. Boiler Identity no.KB93003. Original boiler test Certificate and confirmation of copper materials. Southern Federation of Model Engineering Societies Boiler Test Record SF109076. Hydraulic test expired 24 August 2012. Test pressure 150 psi. Steam test expired 2 July 2011. Test pressure 100 psi.
£20,000-25,000   **DN**

A handmade wooden model of the Flying Dutchman Pullman Parlor Car, carpeted and wallpapered interior, in a glass display case, with a section of track.

Pullman, who was more famous for sleeping cars, produced parlor cars from the 1880s through the 1960s. This model exemplifies their production from the Gilded Age.
30½in (77.5cm) long
£4,500-5,500   **POOK**

A live steam 3½in-gauge 2-6-2 loco and tender LNER 3401 'BANTAM COCK'.
£2,000-2,500   **LSK**

A detailed 0-gauge two-rail electric BR rebuilt Battle of Britain Class 4-6-2 tender loco, Lord Dowding, RN 34052.
£900-1,100   **W&W**

A 7¼in-gauge 0-6-0 tender loco, no.904, Great Eastern Railway (Stratford Works 1891).
£8,500-9,500   **LSK**

A 5in-gauge model of Great Western Railway King Class 4-6-0 tender loco 'KING GEORGE V' no.6000, built by Mr W.E. Wilks of Bourton, with a copper super-heated boiler, with transportation case.

Boiler History: Western Steam Boiler no. WSME 073.03.2000. Test pressure 160 psi. Working pressure 80 psi. Southern Federation of Model Engineering Societies Boiler Test Certificate no.8911 Crawley ME. Hydraulic Test 160 psi expired 5 August 2002. Steam test 80 psi expired 6 August 2000.
72¾in (185cm) long
£8,500-9,500   **DN**

TOYS & GAMES

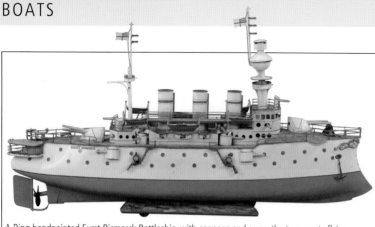

A Bing handpainted Furst Bismarck Battleship, with cannons and guns, the two masts flying British flags, professionally restored.

32in (81.5cm) long

£15,000-16,000   **BER**

A Bing painted tin clockwork ocean liner, four lifeboats and twin screws, with fore and aft 42-star American flags, restoration to paint, working, rigging replaced.

16½in (42cm) long

£800-1,000   **POOK**

A Carette painted tin clockwork gunboat, with four cannons, and swivel gun, with fore and aft French flags, restored, working.

13in (33cm) long

£450-550   **POOK**

A Märklin battleship, 'BALTIMORE', with ornamental castings to bow, with two masts and various cannons, professionally restored.

34in (86.5cm) long

£18,000-20,000   **BER**

A steam-powered model boat, with teak deck.

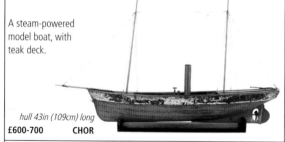

hull 43in (109cm) long

£600-700   **CHOR**

An early 20thC scale-model wooden steam ship, with an internal 'Stuart' steam-powered engine and boiler.

37¾in (96cm) long

£350-450   **BELL**

A cased model of the seven-masted schooner 'Thomas W. Lawson', carved and painted, with cloth sails, base inscribed '1902 – Collier – Thomas W. Lawson – Lost 1907'.

case 28¾in (73cm) long

£1,100-1,400   **NA**

A 1:5 scale Royal Navy cadet training model, for a sailing and pulling cutter gig, constructed in pine and oak.

c1890   *35½in (90cm) high*

£4,000-5,000   **CM**

A 20thC wooden pond yacht, fully rigged over a planked deck, on a wooden stand.

77½in (197cm) high

£500-600   **BELL**

A large pond yacht, with canvas sails and clinker built hull, brass mounts, on a carved wooden stand.

67¾in (172cm) long

£300-400   **DUK**

A medium pond yacht, with canvas sails and clinker built hull, brass mounts, on a carved wooden stand.

40½in (103cm) long

£250-300   **DUK**

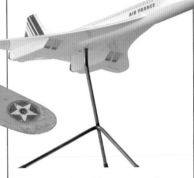

A Kyosho Fairwind plastic hulled racing yacht, radio control fitted for steering and sail, with Bermuda rigging, on purpose-built model stand, with an Apex R. radio control hand unit.

64½in (164cm) high

£75-95   **LSK**

A possible Vindex/Hubley prototype areoplane toy, inscribed 'AMERICA' and 'Fokker', with pilots and seated passengers.

17in (43cm) wide

£1,800-2,200   **BER**

A Concorde scale model, in Air France livery, with accompanying certificate to certify that 'Madame et Monsieur Winch broke the sound barrier aboard Concorde on 12th May 1997', signed by the Captain Monsieur Contresty.

33in (84cm) long

£550-650   **DUK**

A large composite model of the BOAC Concorde G-BOAC, on a purpose-made chrome-plated tripod stand.

96½in (245cm) long

£2,500-3,000   **DUK**

An early model of a Curtiss Jenny aeroplane.

32in (81.5cm) long

£750-850   **CHOR**

A model Martin B-26 Marauder aeroplane.

34¼in (87cm) long

£350-400   **CHOR**

TOYS & GAMES

A Becker painted tin windmill steam toy accessory, no.257, with a gentleman prodding a lithograph tin mule.

9¾in (24.5cm) high

£350-450   POOK

An unusual German painted tin carousel steam toy accessory, attributed to Bing, with three hanging dirigibles and four two-passenger seats, light wear.

12in (30.5cm) high

£1,500-2,000   POOK

A Bing tin lithograph enclosed tailor and shoe repair shop steam toy accessory, probably an early prototype, one window lacking pane. *c1900*   *8¼in (21cm) wide*

£750-950   POOK

A Bing painted tin weaving loom steam toy accessory, on a wood base, with complex action that simulates weaving, minor wear.
c1890   *8¼in (21cm) high*

£500-600   POOK

QUICK REFERENCE - THE FERRIS WHEEL

- The Ferris wheel was invented by George Washington Gale Ferris Jr, an engineer from Pittsburgh, Pennsylvania. Despite scepticism that the wheel was too tall and fragile, Ferris built a 250ft-diameter wheel for the 1893 World's Fair in Chicago, Illinois. It had 36 cars, which could each hold 60 people. The wheel proved a success at the fair, with 1.4 million people riding it.

- However, following the fair, Ferris struggled financially. He died from typhoid fever in 1896. The Ferris wheel was sold to the 1904 Louisiana Purchase Exposition, Missouri, before being scrapped.

- Ferris wheels have since cropped up all over Europe, as well as being copied in toy form.

A Bing painted tin deluxe roller coaster steam toy accessory, no.9956/336, with two four-passenger cars and a ticket gate, some wear.

16in (40.5cm) high

£4,500-5,500   POOK

A Bowman 'SWALLOW' steam boat, boxed.
1930s
£160-200   PSA

A Doll & Cie painted and embossed tin Ferris wheel steam toy accessory, no.729/2, with six gondolas, with painted composition riders, some older repaint.

15in (38cm) high

£1,200-1,600   POOK

A Doll & Cie painted and embossed tin lighthouse steam toy accessory, no.711, with a reservoir and two composition Native American figures in sailboats, during operation the top of the lighthouse rotates and the boats pitch back and forth, flags replaced.

14½in (37cm) high

£4,000-5,000   POOK

A CLOSER LOOK AT A STEAM TOY ACCESSORY

Ernst Plank & Company started out in 1866 in Nüremberg Germany as a toy-repair shop. Named after the company founder, they made magic lanterns, steam engines, diecast metal planes, boats, cars, steamboats and sewing machines produced from pressed tin plate.

Plank's toys were notable for their quality, often being ornate in design and more finely finished than other manufacturers of that era.

This very topical toy Ferris wheel has six gondolas.

Each gondola has two painted composition dressed sailors and two flags.

It has a stepped platform base, and a hand crank on flywheel.

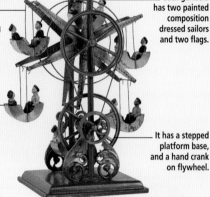

An Ernst Plank painted tin Ferris wheel steam toy accessory, platform overpainted.

16in (40.5cm) high

£1,500-2,000   **POOK**

An Eberl painted and lithographed tin Indian elephant steam toy accessory, with plink-plank-plunk music box.

9in (23cm) wide

£1,500-2,000   **POOK**

A Märklin painted tin and metal oval water fountain steam toy accessory, with six fish and dolphin spouts, paint loss.

7in (18cm) high

£600-800   **POOK**

EISLAUFBAHN

A Mohr & Krauss painted tin ice-skating rink steam toy accessory, with skaters that twirl about a mica flecked rink, the sign inscribed 'Eislauf Bahn'.

12in (30.5cm) wide

£2,500-3,000   **POOK**

A Schoenner painted tin horse carousel steam toy accessory, no.11/2, in original condition, some paint loss, a horse's leg is bent.

c1875   *12in (30.5cm) high*

£2,500-3,000   **POOK**

A German dolls' trestle-style Ferris wheel, with elaborate suspended gondolas, hand-crank or steam-powered engine, professionally restored.

18in (45.5cm) high

£1,500-2,000   **BER**

A painted and embossed tin wheelwright shop steam toy accessory, with three figures working, sporadic paint loss.

11in (28cm) wide

£650-750   **POOK**

QUICK REFERENCE - TREEN

- The term 'treen' refers to small items made from turned wood, usually beech, elm or chestnut. They were designed to be used around the home, on a farm or in a workshop. Common items include snuff and spice boxes, drinking vessels, spoons, measures, salts, bowls and utensils.
- The earliest pieces available to collectors today date from the 17thC and the most desirable pieces date from c1720 to c1800. Many of the pieces on the market now date from the 19thC; as there are many of them and they are often ignored by collectors, values tend to be lower.
- As the 19thC progressed, fewer items were made from wood as advances in technology meant they could be made more quickly and economically from pottery or metal.
- When buying treen, look carefully at the quality of the carving, the type of wood and the age of the item. The more decorative the piece, the more desirable it is likely to be. A warm, rich patina, built up over years of use, will add value.

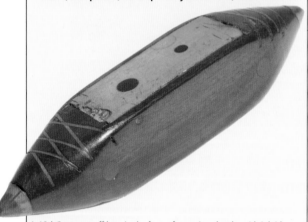

A 19thC treen snuff box, in the form of a sewing shuttle, with inlaid decoration and a hinged lid.

4½in (11.5cm) long

£150-200   WW

An early 19thC French carved coquilla nut snuff box, carved with two female missionaries, one holding a cross, the other the Bible.

3in (7.5cm) wide

£180-220   WW

A 19thC Tyrolean carved boxwood snuff box, carved with a girl feeding cattle, full length wooden hinge.

3¾in (9.5cm) wide

£200-250   BLEA

A 19thC pressed treen snuff box, the cover with Masonic symbolism to include a Temple and emblems, tortoiseshell simulated interior, inventory label no.583.

3¼in (8.5cm) diam

£300-350   HAN

A 19thC French carved coquilla nut snuff box, in the form of a basket, carved with a wheelbarrow filled with baskets of flowers and fruit and a watering can.

3in (7.5cm) wide

£180-220   WW

A carved treen 'Tam-o'Shanter' blind man's snuff box, the lid with relief carved scene of Tam being chased by a Nellie the witch, the sides carved with animals.

6¾in (17cm) wide

£450-500   BE

A Scottish 'blind man' wooden snuff box, the lid with two male figures (Tam and Souter) centred by a woman with child, sides and front carved with dogs and sheep, base branded 'W. Ward', chip to hat of one figure.

6¼in (16cm) long

£450-550   BLEA

A coquilla nut snuff box, carved with motifs and figures.

3¼in (8.5cm) long

£220-280   JN

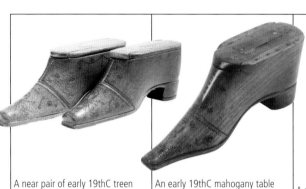

A near pair of early 19thC treen snuff shoes, with brass tack inlay, each with a sliding cover and a vacant plaque.

6½in (16.5cm) long

£1,200-1,500 **WW**

An early 19thC mahogany table shoe snuff box, decorated in brass pins, the toe with a thistle, the sliding lid with soft metal plaque.

5¾in (14.5cm) long

£300-350 **BLEA**

A rare 19thC large treen fruitwood table snuff shoe, with brass laces and tack decoration and inlaid with ivory and mother-of-pearl rondels.

This item may be subject to CITES regulations when exported.

10¼in (26cm) long

£4,000-5,000 **WW**

A late Victorian lacquered floral painted snuff box, modelled as a shoe.

3¼in (8.5cm) long

£60-80 **MART**

A 19thC treen snuff shoe, with pewter stringing and tack inlay, the hinged lid inset with a carved bone portrait medallion.

4¾in (12cm) long

£350-400 **WW**

A 19thC treen sailor's valentine snuff shoe, with brass tack inlay, the hinged lid with an inset pewter panel decorated with a love heart, the body with ships, fish and an anchor.

5¼in (13.5cm) long

£500-600 **WW**

An early 19thC pressed horn lidded snuff box, the cover with Masonic symbolism to include a beehive and swarm, inventory label no.602, some damage.

3¼in (8.5cm) diam

£300-400 **HAN**

A Victorian four-tier spice tower, each section labelled 'Mace', 'Cloves', 'Cinnamon' and 'Nutmegs', large split to top and wear and tear.

8in (20.5cm) high

£180-220 **APAR**

An early 19thC treen urn, the cover decorated with bands of leaves, above a pineapple-shaped body.

7in (18cm) high

£500-600 **WW**

An early 19thC Scottish Mauchline ware sycamore and penwork snuffbox, decorated with a scene of lovers on a garden bench, inscribed 'PRESENTED To M.J.R. Williams late of the Theatre Royal by several young Gentlemen of ABERDEEN as a mark of respect for his private character and admiration of his Theatrical Talents'.

3in (7.5cm) wide

£1,200-1,600   WW

An early 19thC Mauchline ware sycamore and penwork snuff box, with a scene of returning Highland soldier greeting his loved one, the body decorated with thistles.

3in (7.5cm) wide

£400-500   WW

An early 19thC Scottish Mauchline ware small sycamore and penwork snuff box, by George Sliman of Catrine, the foil-lined interior stamped 'G. SLIMAN CATRINE'.

2in (5cm) wide

£250-300   WW

An early 19thC Scottish Mauchline ware sycamore and penwork snuff box, with a tavern scene.

3in (7.5cm) wide

£200-300   WW

A late 19thC Mauchline ware penwork snuff box, the lid with handpainted scene of a curling match.

5¼in (13.5cm) wide

£950-1,100   L&T

A late 19thC Mauchline tartanware snuff box, the top with a bird, the body in Davidson tartan, stamped maker's marks for Smith, Mauchline.

The success of 'Mauchline ware' is due, in part, to the Smiths of Mauchline – it being initially manufactured by Andrew and William Smith, who produced wares from the 1820s. It became an industry that was to dominate the market for wooden souvenirs during most of the Victorian era. During the course of the 19thC, the factory developed new pieces, shapes, sizes and finishes. The company responded to the new Victorian taste for holidays and souvenirs, as commercial railways were developed and seaside trips became increasingly popular. Their wares were despatched to all parts of the British Isles, Europe, North and South America, South Africa, Australia and New Zealand. The Smiths' innovations earned them the Royal Warrant, enabling them to dominate the 'fancy goods' market. The business rejuvenated the local economy in Mauchline, and inspired many other makers of similar wares in Scotland. It closed in the 1930s.

1½in (4cm) wide

£450-500   L&T

A Mauchline tartanware photograph album, the boards in Stuart tartan, with a portrait of Mary, Queen of Scots, the interior with gilt-edged pages having blank apertures for photographs.

c1890   *12in (30.5cm) high*

£500-600   L&T

A late 19thC Mauchline tartanware necklace, with eleven links on a later thread.

19¼in (49cm) long

£300-400   L&T

Judith Picks

As with all Black Forest carvings, this begging dog is full of character, and I do have a soft spot for dogs! 'Black Forest' carvings were once thought to have been made in the Black Forest region of Bavaria, Germany, hence the name. In fact, most were produced in Brienz, Switzerland, over the course of the 19thC. These carvings were a key part of the town's economy and were highly popular with tourists.

The craftsmen of Brienz carved figures, furniture, boxes and clock cases from tree trunks, often linden or walnut. The most popular subjects were bears. Many carved bear figures were depicted engaging in human activities, including playing musical instruments, socialising or hiking. Dogs are rarer.

A 19thC Black Forest begging dog stick stand.

36¼in (92cm) high

£4,000-5,000   **HANN**

A Black Forest linden wood tobacco or match holder, carved as a dog in Tyrolean dress and holding an Alpine horn.

c1860   *8¼in (21cm) high*

£1,000-1,500   **L&T**

A late 19thC Black Forest carved wood table wine coaster, with three Bacchanalian cherubs, on serpent spoke wheels and bone castors.

18¼in (46.5cm) wide

£2,000-2,500   **WW**

A late 19thC Black Forest table gong, in the form of a standing bear, with a brass gong and a beater.

12½in (32cm) high

£600-700   **WW**

An early 20thC Black Forest carved wooden bear, with glass eyes, on a later separate wooden plinth.

15½in (39.5cm) wide

£450-500   **BELL**

A pair of late 19th/early 20thC Black Forest carved spill vases, with carved figures of a bull and cows.

11¾in (30cm) high

£800-900   **L&T**

A near pair of late 19thC Black Forest carved wood epergnes, each with a glass vase, one with remains of a printed paper trade label 'A.M. ... FABRIC. Grand-...'.

14¾in (37.5cm) high

£200-300   **WW**

A late 19thC Black Forest carved and painted wood royal stag head mount, applied with a set of real 13-point antlers.

48¾in (124cm) high

£1,000-1,500   **WW**

A late 19thC/early 20thC treen screw-action nutcracker, in the form of a squirrel eating a nut.

6¾in (17cm) high

£350-400   **WW**

A 19thC carved treen nutcracker, in the form of Mr Punch, with a tapered and faceted screw handle, slight damage.

7¾in (19.5cm) long

£120-160   **FLD**

An early 20thC carved walnut nutcracker, in the form of a Breton-style smiling character wearing a hat.

7in (18cm) high

£80-100   **FLD**

A 19thC treen dairy bowl.

23in (58.5cm) diam

£350-400   **WW**

A painted wood dummy board, in the form of a Hussar soldier.

60¾in (154.5cm) high

£400-500   **WW**

An early 20thC French wooden carousel fighting bull, with carved ornamental saddle, sword and banderillas.

27¼in (69cm) high

£1,300-1,800   **SWO**

A 19thC Tunbridge ware cottage money box, of painted white wood.

5in (12.5cm) high

£300-350   **WW**

A 19thC Tunbridge ware box, the cover with a scene of a castle.

10¾in (27.5cm) wide

£150-200   **L&T**

A Victorian Tunbridge ware and rosewood sewing box.

7¼in (18.5cm) wide

£250-300   **WW**

A 19thC Tunbridge ware rosewood table cabinet, the top panel inset with a castellated building.

12in (30.5cm) wide

£700-800   **L&T**

QUICK REFERENCE - TRIBAL ART

- The term 'tribal art' is used to describe the cultural, ritual and functional items produced by the indigenous peoples of Africa, Oceania, South East Asia and the Americas. Many of these items were originally functional rather than decorative. Today, pieces are collected both for their historic and ethnographic interest and for their visual impact and appeal. Many collectors choose to focus on one tribe or region or one type of item.
- Interest in tribal pieces began in the Western world in the 18thC and 19thC as explorers reached new places and cultures. This interest grew in the 20thC due to the influence tribal art had on European artists such as Pablo Picasso.
- Pieces from the 19thC and before with verifiable history tend to be the most valuable. Look for signs of use and age, such as wear or patina, but examine carefully, as patina can be easily faked. From the early 20thC, some tribes made large quantities of items purely for export or to sell as souvenirs. These pieces can be variable in quality and tend to be less valuable.
- In the past 20 years, the value of tribal art has been steadily increasing. Older pieces with clear provenances are often only accessible to wealthy collectors or museums.

A Bamana carved wood door lock, with stylised head finial and long ears, mounted.

18in (45.5cm) high

£900-1,100   **L&T**

A 20thC cast Benin-style bronze leopard's head, with five clearly defined whiskers.

15in (38cm) high

£650-750   **DUK**

A Dan mask, Ivory Coast, with a beak and applied metal strips.

13in (33cm) high

£250-300   **WW**

A Jokwe carved wood dancing mask, Central Congo, with scarification marks carved to cheeks, the crown with trade beads and plaited grass hair.

Collected between 1898 and c1920 by Major Ian Kelsey.

11in (28cm) high

£500-600   **WHYT**

A Nigerian Yoruba Ibeji figure, with a tiered coiffure, facial scarifications, with a bead and shell necklace, with brass bangles.

10in (25.5cm) high

£3,000-3,500   **WW**

A wooden mancala gaming board, possibly Mbala, Republic of Congo, a seated figure supporting the board.

26in (66cm) long

£450-550   **DUK**

A Nigerian Mama masked dancer figure, with a stylised bird mask with abrus seed eyes.

22in (56cm) high

£1,800-2,200   **WW**

A Songye kifwebe mask, pronounced disc coiffure, on stand.

23½in (60cm) high

£550-650   **MOR**

A Songye mask, Congo, with protruding, lozenge-shaped lips, incised cross-hatched design to brow and cheeks, with woven cowl.

Collected between 1898 and c1920 by Major Ian Kelsey.

15in (38cm) high

£600-700   **WHYT**

A Zulu carved and wired horn snuff bottle, with delicate neck and rounded lip.

3¼in (8.5cm) high

£950-1,100   **L&T**

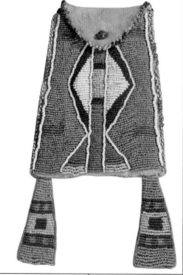

A pair of Blackfeet beaded buffalo hide moccasins, the soft-sole forms with multicoloured floral designs, traces of cloth at the ankle, minor bead loss.

1870s   *10½in (26.5cm) long*

£800-900   **SK**

A pair of Blackfeet beaded hide moccasins.

c1890   *10½in (26.5cm) long*

£1,800-2,200   **SK**

A Blackfoot part-beaded knife sheath rawhide, brass wire, coloured glass beads and paint.

15½in (39.5cm) long

£1,300-1,600   **WW**

A Kwakiutl puppet figure, British Columbia, with remains of fibre to the head, on a stand.

9in (23cm) high

£1,500-2,000   **WW**

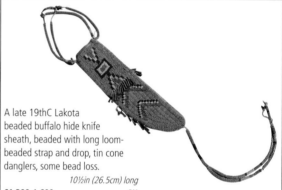

A late 19thC Crow beaded buffalo hide pouch, beaded with classic crow designs.

8½in (21.5cm) wide

£2,500-3,000   **SK**

A late 19thC Lakota beaded buffalo hide knife sheath, beaded with long loom-beaded strap and drop, tin cone danglers, some bead loss.

10½in (26.5cm) long

£1,300-1,600   **SK**

An early 20thC Navajo canvas apron, Southern North America, with an applied leather cut-out stag with a red glass bead, hung with tin cones.

10¼in (26cm) high

£200-250   **WW**

A North American roach spreaderbone, carved with two bears and nine tines, with sinew and metal wire.

6¼in (16cm) long

£400-450   **WW**

A Zuni carved stone bear fetish, Southwest USA, with a band of glass beads, shell, quill and a carved stone hare.

3¼in (8.5cm) high

£650-750   **WW**

A pair of Southern Cheyenne buckskin leggings, Southern Plains, with a border of coloured glass beads.

25½in (65cm) long

£800-900   WW

A Sioux feather dance bustle, Plains, cloth, rawhide and ribbon.

48½in (123cm) high

£300-400   WW

A Costa Rica metate grinding stone, Central America, with a jaguar head terminal, raised on three legs, with an oblong pestle.

Collected by a charity worker in Honduras in the 1950s.

14in (35.5cm) long

£300-400   WW

A set of four 20thC Peruvian dolls, with AD 1000-1400 textile fragments.

10¼in (26cm) wide

£120-160   WW

A pair of Chancay pottery male and female figures, Peru.

1100-1400   *largest 11¾in (30cm) high*

£300-400   WW

A Chimu weaving shuttle, Peru, with a carved figure finial and a tapering blade.

1100-1400   *14½in (37cm) long*

£200-300   WW

A probably 15thC/16thC Inca effigy container stone conopa, Peru, in the form of an alpaca, with a layered mane, mouth, snout and ear, with a chevron tail.

2½in (6.5cm) high

£90-120   WW

An Inca-style pottery vessel, Peru, decorated with four standing figures.

Provenance: Mr & Mrs John Pert, Lima, Peru, 1965-75.

8in (20.5cm) high

£200-250   WW

A Pima coiled basketry plaque, with squash blossom design.

11in (29cm) diam

£550-650   SK

TRIBAL ART

QUICK REFERENCE - INUIT ART

- Much of what is considered to be 'Inuit art' today has been made since the 1950s, when the work of Alaskan and North Canadian artists and sculptors was promoted by a young Canadian artist called James Houston. In the last few decades, the market has dramatically increased in size.
- Many sculptures are carved in local soapstone, then embellished with whalebone, ivory, antler, sinew and other materials.
- It is chiefly the artist that brings value to a work of Inuit art, although the visual appeal also plays a key role. Sculptures tend to be signed on the base, sometimes in Roman letters or syllabics, but often with a combination of numbers and letters assigned to the artist as an identifier, as there is no tribal tradition of written language.

A 'Polar Bear' stone figurine, by Henry Evaluardjuk (1923-2007), Frobisher Bay/Iqaluit.

2in (5cm) high

£300-400　　　　**WAD**

A 'Kneeling Man' stone figurine, by Joanasie Lyta (b.1921), Lake Harbour/Kimmirut, signed in syllabics, dated.

1976　　　7¾in (19.5cm) high

£90-120　　　　**WAD**

A 'Musk Ox' stone figurine, by Barnabus Arnasungaaq (1924-2017), E2-213, Baker Lake/Qamani'tuaq, signed syllabics.

2011　　　16in (40.5cm) long

£2,000-3,000　　　　**WAD**

A 'Polar Bear Swimming with Cubs' stone figurine, by Bill Nasogaluak (b.1953), Yellowknife, signed in Roman, dated.

2007　　　9in (23cm) long

£600-700　　　　**WAD**

A 'Dog' antler figurine, by Andy Miki (1918-83), Eskimo Point/Arviat.

9½in (24cm) long

£500-600　　　　**WAD**

A 19thC Alaskan Inuit sea otter marine ivory amulet, in feeding posture, with incised ribs and spine with inlay, with two pierced attachment holes.

3¼in (8.5cm) long

£9,000-11,000　　　　**WW**

An Alaskan Inuit carved whalebone snow goggle, with asymmetrical encrusted wooden panels over each eye, mounted.

5½in (14cm) wide

£1,000-1,500　　　　**L&T**

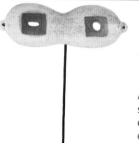

A lidded woven basket with bear knop, by John Harrow, Point Barrow, Alaska, of grass, baleen and ivory, signed in Roman.

5in (12.5cm) diam

£450-550　　　　**WAD**

A 'Two Birds Guard Sleeping Kiviiuk' linocut and stencil, by Jessie Oonark O.C. R.C.A. (1906-85), Baker Lake/Qamani'tuaq, no.35/50.

1981　　　37in (94cm) high

£700-900　　　　**WAD**

A 'Small Tundra Bird' stencil, by Kenojuak Ashevak C.C. R.C.A. (1927-2013), Cape Dorset/Kinngait, no.37/50.

1996　　　23in (58.5cm) high

£1,500-2,000　　　　**WAD**

An Aboriginal wunda shield, Western Australia, the back with linear carved decoration and an integral handle.

35in (89cm) long

£1,200-1,600 **WW**

A Fijian-Ula throwing club, head inset with tooth fragment and evidence of charring, on a shaft with geometric decorated handle.

After battle, a victim's tooth was hammered into the head of the club and it was then hung in a priest hut and used for ritualistic purposes.

15¾in (40cm) long

£500-600 **BE**

A 19thC Fijian ula or throwing club, with lobe carved head and zig zag carved grip section.

15in (38cm) long

£800-900 **HT**

A Fiji trumpet davui, Melanesia, shell and coconut fibre sennit, the shell with a pierced mouthpiece, with handwritten sticker 'Major Douglas-Jones, High Salvington Mill, Worthing, Sx'.

Provenance: Admiral Sir Crawford Caffin (1812-83); Major Douglas-Jones, Sussex, UK; James T. Hooper, Arundel, UK, acquired in 1956.

15¾in (40cm) long

£3,500-4,000 **WW**

A Batak medicine horn, Indonesia, buffalo horn with carved wood finials of mounted ancestor figures.

20½in (52cm) wide

£100-150 **WW**

A Dayak baby carrier, Indonesia, fibre, coloured wire and fabric, hung with strands of teeth, glass beads, figural amulets and metal bells, with beaded and teeth-mounted straps.

11½in (29cm) high

£500-600 **WW**

A Lake Sentani male figure, Irian Jaya, Indonesia, with carved motifs to the abdomen.

65½in (166.5cm) high

£1,000-1,500 **WW**

A Humboldt Bay figure, Irian Jaya.

18in (45.5cm) high

£300-350 **WW**

A Kanak bamboo flute, New Caledonia, with incised and stained pictorial decoration of a chief's house and two smaller houses with figural roof finial, with a figure hunting with bow and arrow, with three figures below, three two-masted ships, a large turtle, linear geometric decoration and a band of animals, with seven pierced holes.

28¼in (72cm) long

£2,000-2,500 **WW**

TRIBAL ART

An early 19thC Maori hei-tiki, green nephrite.

5in (12.5cm) high

£7,500-8,500   **JN**

A Maori hei-tiki nephrite pendant, New Zealand, with a sticking out tongue and suspension hole.

2¾in (7cm) high

£4,000-5,000   **WW**

A Maori bowl, New Zealand, with all-over carved linear and notched decoration, with end figural handles, the eyes and rim inlaid with haliotis shell.

15¼in (38.5cm) wide

£2,500-3,000   **WW**

A Papua New Guinea mask, Melanesia, with pigment decoration.

16¾in (42.5cm) high

£350-400   **WW**

A Ramu River ancestor mask, Papua New Guinea, with gum and hair and with painted decoration.

19½in (49.5cm) high

£350-450   **WW**

A Bontoc shield, Luzon Island, Philippines, with an integral handle and fibre binding.

34in (86.5cm) high

£450-550   **WW**

A Cook Islands ceremonial adze, Mangaia Island, Polynesia, with a faceted stone blade sennit.

31¾in (80.5cm) long

£1,200-1,600   **WW**

A Hawaii kou wood bowl, Polynesia.

9in (23cm) diam

£1,400-1,800   **WW**

A Tonga headrest kali hahapo, Polynesia, with a faceted underside.

14¾in (37.5cm) long

£3,000-3,500   **WW**

A standing 'Harlequin - The Politician' figurine of Tony Blair, by Ian Norbury, supported by four gargoyles depicting Peter Mandelson, Gordon Brown, John Prescott and Cherie Blair, limewood, walnut, bog oak and other woods, each side set with a carved face representing the artist's interpretation of Blair's different characteristics.

39¾in (101cm) high

£3,500-4,500   **CHOR**

An aluminium scale model of the Stautue of Liberty, after the original designed by Frédéric Auguste Bartholdi (1834-1904), fitted for electricity.

90½in (230cm) high

£5,000-6,000   **DUK**

A life-size plaster and fibreglass model of Arnold Schwarzenegger.

74in (188cm) high

£500-600   **DUK**

A collection of seven Lube Paris shop display mannequins, painted features and painted marks.

24in (61cm) high

£700-800   **DUK**

A life-size fibreglass emperor penguin, painted in polychrome.

34¾in (88.5cm) high

£220-280   **DUK**

A large vintage fibreglass and painted 'Flying Dumbo', painted in polychrome.

95¼in (242cm) long

£1,200-1,600   **DUK**

A 20thC large painted 'Shamu' whale shop advertising mascot.

98½in (250cm) long

£1,100-1,400   **DUK**

A rare mid-20thC privately owned cast iron Guernsey Post post box, with 'GR' cypher to front, manufactured by the Carron Company, Stirlingshire, with Chubb lock with key and interior cage and chute fitments.

66in (167.5cm) high

£30,000-35,000   **MART**

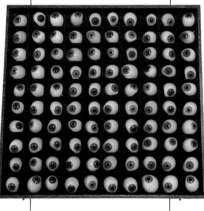

An early 20thC collection of one hundred prosthetic glass eyes, from the Jackson Cox Practice in Cambridge, shell grey, cased.

£2,000-2,500   **HAN**

WINE & DRINKING

QUICK REFERENCE - WINE LABELS

- Produced in silver from c1740, wine labels were hung around the neck of a bottle on a chain or wire hoop, replacing parchment labels.
- After the Licensing Act of 1860 required wine merchants to label individual bottles prior to selling them, very few wine labels were made.
- Wine labels from the 18thC and 19thC are usually made of silver or silver-plate. However, enamel, pottery, porcelain, ivory, bone and mother-of-pearl were also used.

A silver wine label, by Hester Bateman, London, incised 'SHERRY'.

c1780　　　　*3in (7.5cm) long 0.3oz*

£300-350　　　　**WW**

A silver wine label, by Hester Bateman, London, incised and blackened 'RUM'.

c1780　　*2¼in (5.5cm) long 0.3oz*

£550-650　　　　**WW**

A silver wine label, by George Adams, London, modelled as an heraldic Talbot, engraved decoration, incised and blackened 'PORT'.

1866　　*1¾in (4.5cm) long 0.4oz*

£600-700　　　　**WW**

A Scottish provincial silver wine label, by James Erskine, Aberdeen, incised 'BRANDY'.

c1795　　*1¾in (4.5cm) long 0.3oz*

£500-600　　　　**WW**

A silver-gilt armorial wine label, by Robert Garrard, London, incised 'CLARET'.

1864　　*2in (5cm) long 0.8oz*

£500-600　　　　**WW**

A silver wine label, by Robert and Samuel Hennell, London, incised 'PORT'.

1806　　*1½in (4cm) long 0.9oz*

£500-600　　　　**WW**

An early 19thC Maltese silver wine label, by Gioacchino Lebrun, incised 'SHERRY'.

c1805　　　　*2¼in (5.5cm) long 0.2oz*

£750-850　　　　**WW**

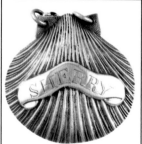

A silver wine label, by Matthew Linwood, Birmingham, incised 'SHERRY'.

1810　　*1½in (4cm) long 0.4oz*

£300-350　　　　**WW**

A silver wine label, by Stephen Noad, London, incised 'W.PORT'.

1826　　*2¾in (7cm) long 0.5oz*

£300-350　　　　**WW**

A silver wine label, by Phipps and Robinson, London, with an armorial mythical fish, incised 'PORT'.

1799　　　　*2in (5cm) long 0.5oz*

£1,000-1,400　　　　**WW**

A silver armorial wine label, by Phipps, Robinson and Phipps, London, modelled as an eagle's head with spread wings, pierced 'MADEIRA'.

1812   1¾in (4.5cm) long 0.8oz

£550-600   WW

A silver wine label, by Charles Rawlings, London, with bacchanalian putti, pierced 'L.CHRISTIE'.

1818   2¼in (5.5cm) long 0.8oz

£350-400   WW

A silver-gilt 'Lady Bountiful' wine label, by Charles Rawlings, London, pierced 'BURGUNDY', with a heavy chain.

1822   2¾in (7cm) long 1.2oz

£600-650   WW

A silver-gilt wine label, by Paul Storr, London, with bacchanalian cherubs, incised 'ZERRY'.

1824   2¼in (5.5cm) long 0.7oz

£650-750   WW

A silver wine label, by Paul Storr, London, incised 'BRANDY'.

1827   2½in (6.5cm) long 0.6oz

£400-450   WW

A silver armorial wine label, by John Terrey, London, modelled as a dragon head, incised 'MADEIRA'.

1828   1¾in (4.5cm) long 0.6oz

£700-750   WW

A pair of silver wine labels, by George Unite, Birmingham, incised 'THE DUKE 1812' and 'RIOTORTO "1820"'.

1844   2¼in (5.5cm) long 5.4oz

£400-500   WW

A silver wine label, by Joseph Willmore, Birmingham, incised 'SHERRY'.

1825   1½in (4cm) diam 0.3oz

£220-300   WW

A silver armorial wine label, unmarked, modelled as two demi-greyhounds, pierced 'MADEIRA'.

The crest is that of Bratt, Lysons and Atkins.

1½in (4cm) long

£600-700   WW

A George III silver wine label, unmarked, incised 'PORT'.

c1800   2¼in (5.5cm) long 0.5oz

£600-700   WW

A silver armorial wine label, unmarked, modelled as a mythical dolphin, incised 'PORT'.

c1800   2in (5cm) long 2oz

£600-700   WW

WINE & DRINKING

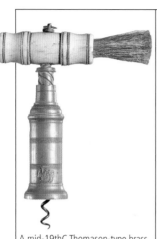

A mid-19thC Thomason-type brass barrel corkscrew, with turned bone handle and brush, badge marked 'Patent'.

£150-200   **BELL**

A mid-19thC twin-pillar open rack corkscrew, with turned bone handle and brush.

£320-400   **BELL**

A 19thC brass Cope and Cutler rack corkscrew, with turned bone handles, with an applied plaque.

7½in (19cm) long

£300-400   **WW**

A Lund's Queen's Patent corkscrew, with a King's screw, the rosewood handle originally with a brush, the plaque, inscribed 'LUND'S PATENT 57 CORNHILL,' the triple bottle grips stamped with three crowns and 'THE QUEENS PATENT GRANTED TO T. LUND LONDON'.

7¼in (18.5cm) long

£3,000-3,500   **WW**

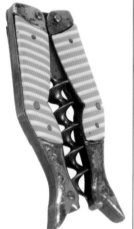

A German corkscrew, depicting a pair of female legs.

c1930s   *2½in (6.5cm) long*

£200-250   **LOCK**

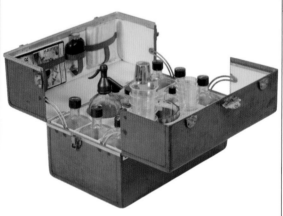

A Pendragon 'porta-bar' set, with a leather case, with 12 glasses, a soda siphon, silver-plated cocktail shaker, ice bucket, 5 quart bottles for spirits and 2 bottles for flavourings and essences.

18½in (47cm) long

£1,800-2,200   **DUK**

A barside cocktail 'shaker' recipe menu, with a flick menu of thirty-five recipes, stamped patent number '186582'.

5½in (14cm) high

£200-300   **SWO**

An American 'Price-O-Mat' bartender's icemaker.

9½in (24cm) high

£100-150   **SWO**

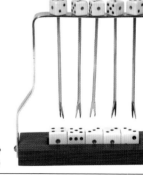

A pair of five novelty dice cocktail sticks, with five further dice to the plinth.

5in (12.5cm) wide

£200-300   **SWO**

QUICK REFERENCE - WRISTWATCHES

- Over the last two decades, interest in wristwatches has grown. The trend has been prompted in part by men's magazines and the popularisation of formal appearance and retro looks in men's fashion. Watches can be status symbols as well as investment pieces. The style, maker, complexity of the movement, date of manufacture and condition affect value.

- The first wristwatch, the Santos, was developed by Cartier in c1904 and is still produced today. Prior to this, pocket watches were adapted into wristwatches using a leather pocket and strap or wire strap 'lugs' soldered onto the case.

- Wristwatches became popular shortly after World War I, during which some (such as the Trench watch, identifiable by the protective grille over the glass dial cover) were issued to servicemen.

- Wristwatches can be dated from the case, hands, numbers and general design.

- After 1920, the range of case shapes developed to include rectangular, octagonal, oval and square wristwatches, having previously been predominantly circular. By the 1930s, wristwatches had nearly replaced pocket watches. In the 1940s, the cocktail watch was developed, influenced by fashions of the time. Simple, circular styles with pared down dials were popular in the 1950s. Bulkier, more sculptural and futuristic watches are often from the late 1960s-70s.

A gentleman's Audemars Piguet wristwatch, no.10462.
£3,500-4,000　　　JN

A mid-size Blancpain 'Villeret' chronograph wristwatch, 18ct yellow gold case, numbered '107', signed automatic movement with quick date set, signed crocodile strap, stamped '750'.
12½in (32cm) diam
£3,000-3,500　　　FELL

A gentleman's Breitling 'Navitimer Chrono-Matic' chronograph steel wristwatch, Breitling monogrammed crown, steel bracelet strap.
1970s　　dial 1¾in (4.5cm) diam
£1,800-2,200　　　HAN

A gentleman's steel Breitling 'Chrono Superocean' wristwatch, integral steel bracelet, ref. A1334011, serial no.2012053, boxed with paperwork and certificate.
c2005　　1½in (4cm) diam
£2,000-2,500　　　HAN

A Cartier 18ct yellow gold diamond-faced 'Pasha' wristwatch, stamped '18K 1035 CC715855', in original box.
£5,000-6,000　　　JN

A Cartier 'Santos' 18ct yellow gold wristwatch, in original box, with papers.
£4,000-5,000　　　JN

A Cartier 'Ronde Solo' wristwatch, ref.2934, serial no.740069PX, signed quartz calibre 115A with quick date set, stainless steel case, with signed alligator strap.
1½in (4cm) wide
£1,300-1,600　　　FELL

A Cartier 'Quadrant' wristwatch, stamped '750' with poincon, numbered 'A100772'.
1in (2.5cm) diam
£1,200-1,600　　　FELL

A Cartier 'Must De Cartier Ronde' wristwatch, ref.1810, serial no.006400, signed quartz calibre 01401/1.
1¼in (3cm) wide
£550-600　　　FELL

A gentleman's Chopard 'Mille Miglia Competitor Edition 2017' chronograph wristwatch, ref.8585, serial no.2014064, signed automatic calibre 109558 stainless steel case with tachymeter bezel, on a signed rubber strap with stainless steel pin buckle.

1¾in (4.5cm) wide

£2,000-2,500   **FELL**

A Corum 'Admirals Cup' wristwatch, ref.285.630.20, no.797310, automatic chronograph movement, 30-minute and 12-hour recording, date aperture at 6 o'clock, rotating bezel with enamelled signal flags for the numerals and degrees in-between, stainless steel, dial and movement signed, on a Corum black rubber strap.

c2005   *1¾in (4.5cm) diam*

£1,400-1,800   **DN**

A Dubois gentleman's chronograph wristwatch, gold-plated case with stainless steel case back, numbered '0194/1499', automatic movement with quick date set, subsidiary recorder dials to 6, 9 and 12, day and date aperture to 3, outer tachymeter track, on an unsigned leather strap.

1½in (4cm) diam

£500-600   **FELL**

A gentleman's Roger Dubuis 'Acqua Mare Just For Friends' wristwatch, limited edition no.25 of 888, signed automatic calibre 4565, stainless steel case, on a signed black rubber strap with stainless steel pin buckle.

1½in (4cm) wide

£3,000-3,500   **FELL**

A Girard-Perregaux 'Traveller' 21ct gold wristwatch, ref.4980 OJNO394, with leather strap.

£6,000-7,000   **JN**

A gentlemans's Hamilton 'Khaki' Automatic T2 wristwatch, series no.H775450, the twenty one jewel movement with exhibition case back, crowns at 2, 4 and 9 positions, on original rubber strap, cased and boxed with instruction manual and warranty, dated.

2010

£400-500   **HT**

A lady's Hermès 'Cape Cod Deux Zones' wristwatch, ref.CC3-210, serial no.1739837, signed movements, stainless steel case, on a signed green lizard strap with stainless steel pin buckle.

¾in (2cm) wide

£1,000-1,400   **FELL**

A gentleman's Tag Heuer 'Carrera Calibre 1887' chronograph wristwatch, ref.CAR2110-3, serial no.EKQ8238, signed automatic calibre 1887 with quick date set, stainless steel case with exhibition case back, on a signed leather strap with stainless steel deployant clasp, box and papers.

1½in (4cm) wide

£1,800-2,200   **FELL**

An International Watch Co. stainless steel mark 'II Military' gun camera watch, marked on back case '10AF/807 N.I 064'.

1½in (4cm) diam

£1,500-2,000   **LOCK**

A gentleman's Jacob & Co. 'Five Time Zone' wristwatch, stainless steel factory diamond set bezel, on a signed crocodile strap with stainless steel deployant clasp, with box and papers, some scratches.

1¾in (4.5cm) diam

£1,800-2,200   **FELL**

A gentleman's 9ct gold Swiss Jaeger-LeCoultre wristwatch, jewelled movement detailed 'Jaeger-le Coultre Swiss 119321', retailed by Cartier, on an associated 9ct gold oval link bracelet, with a foldover clasp, Birmingham 1961, case maker W.T. & Co., London. *1956*

£1,000-1,400   **BELL**

A British military issue Jaeger-LeCoultre stainless steel cased wristwatch, stamped to case with broad arrow '6b/346 2278/48'.

£6,000-7,000   **LOCK**

A gentleman's Jaeger-LeCoultre stainless steel 'Grandsport Reverso' wristwatch, original strap, inner and outer box, booklets, and certificate from purchase, scratches. *1999*

£1,800-2,200   **APAR**

A gentleman's Romain Jerome 'Octopus Titanic-DNA' wristwatch, ref.RJTAUDI003, serial no.5005578, limited edition no.002 of 888, stainless steel case with oxidised bezel containing trace metal from the Titanic, on a signed rubber strap with stainless steel pin buckle. *2in (5cm) wide*

£3,500-4,000   **FELL**

A gentleman's Maurice Lacroix 'Pontos Décentrique GMT' wristwatch, ref.PT6118, serial no.AO54888, signed automatic calibre ML121 with quick date set, stainless steel case on a signed black crocodile strap with stainless steel deployant clasp. *1¾in (4.5cm) wide*

£900-1,200   **FELL**

A gentleman's Longines 'Evidenza' automatic wristwatch, model no.L2.670.4, leather strap, with box and papers.

£550-650   **FLD**

A gentleman's Franck Muller 'Crazy Hours Colour Dreams' wristwatch, ref.1200 CH, numbered '255', signed automatic calibre 2800 V, stainless steel case, on a signed alligator strap with stainless steel pin buckle. *1¼in (3cm) wide*

£3,500-4,000   **FELL**

An Omega 'Speedmaster Automatic Michael Schumacher' wristwatch, limited edition no.4563 of 11111, with original boxes and papers, dated. *2003*

£1,800-2,200   **AST**

A gentleman's Omega 'Speedmaster Professional' steel bracelet wristwatch, no.861, the caseback detailed 'First watch worn on the moon, flight-qualify by Nasa, for all manned space missions', slight wear to clasp, case back key missing. *dial 1½in (4cm) diam*

£3,000-4,000   **BELL**

A gentleman's Omega 'Speedmaster Co-Axial' chronometer wristwatch, with stainless steel case, visible rear movement, original strap, both inner and outer box, tags, booklet, international warranty card, chronometer certificate card and pictogram card, minor surface scratches.

£2,200-2,800   **APAR**

An Omega 'Seamaster' wristwatch, ref.105.005-65, manual wind chronograph movement, 17 jewels, cal.321, no.24012161, stainless steel, screw down back, case, dial and movement signed, on an unsigned leather strap.

c1965   1½in (4cm) diam
£2,000-2,500   **DN**

A gentleman's Omega wristwatch, ref.2643S.C, serial no.11162322, stamped 0.750 with poinçon, yellow metal case, on an unsigned crocodile strap with gold-plated pin buckle.

1¼in (3cm) wide
£650-750   **FELL**

A gentleman's Omega 'Seamaster 300 M' stainless steel bracelet watch, with automatic movement, on Omega bracelet, in original box and outer box.

£1,800-2,200   **DUK**

An Omega 'Speedmaster Professional' MKII stainless steel bracelet wristwatch, tachymeter, Omega crown, on Omega 'Speedmaster' bracelet.

c1970s   1½in (4cm) diam
£2,500-3,000   **DUK**

A gentleman's Omega stainless steel cased wristwatch, serial no.8998565.

c1930s
£250-300   **LOCK**

A gentleman's Omega wristwatch, 9ct gold case, hallmarked Birmingham, numbered '224432', signed bumper automatic calibre 28.10RA, numbered '11306393', on an unsigned leather strap with gold-plated pin buckle, some scratches.

1948   1¼in (3cm) diam
£600-700   **FELL**

A lady's Patek Philippe wristwatch, strap stamped 'Patek Philippe Geneve', with a signed maroon leather case, with certificate of origin confirming date of purchase.

1997
£3,000-3,500   **BE**

A World War II military issue Vertex wristwatch, 'Dirty Dozen' type, inscribed on the back '^w.w.w A 8082 3520998'.

£800-900   **LOCK**

A gentleman's Raymond Weil 'Maestro' wristwatch, reference 2827, serial no.VI36309, signed automatic movement, stainless steel case with exhibition case back, on an unsigned leather strap.

1½in (4cm) diam
£450-500   **FELL**

A gentleman's Zenith Defy Xtreme El Primero chronograph bracelet wristwatch, numbered '96.0525.4000', automatic movement on a signed titanium bracelet with double folding clasp, with box and papers.

1¾in (4.5cm) diam
£3,000-3,500   **FELL**

QUICK REFERENCE - ROLEX

- In 1905, Hans Wilsdorf founded a company in London that focused on the distribution of timepieces. The company then began producing wristwatches, using pieces manufactured in Bienne, Switzerland. In 1908, Wilsdorf came up with the name 'Rolex'.

- A Rolex watch was awarded the Swiss Certificate of Chronometric Precision, in 1910. In 1914, Kew Observatory, UK, awarded a Rolex wristwatch a class A precision certificate. This certificate had previously only been awarded to marine chronometers. In 1919, Wilsdorf moved the company to Geneva, Switzerland. The company was renamed Rolex Watch Co. Ltd. in 1915, before becoming Montres Rolex S.A. in 1920.

- The company went on to develop the first waterproof watch in 1926 and, in 1931, patented the world's first self-winding mechanism with a perpetual rotor. By 1978, Rolex had developed a wristwatch that was waterproof to a depth of 1,220 metres. In 2012, the 'Oyster Perpetual Rolex Deepsea Challenge' wristwatch, waterproof to a depth of more than 10,000 metres, was launched.

- Wilsdorf died in 1960, leaving the company to his charitable trust. From the early 2000s, Rolex began laser etching its trademark crown on its wristwatch crystals in an attempt to reduce counterfeiting.

A gentleman's Rolex 'Oyster Perpetual' bracelet watch, reference 6582, serial no.329565, signed automatic calibre 1030, silvered 'Zephyr' dial, on a signed bi-metal Jubilee bracelet with Oysterclasp, movement worn, marks and scratches to dial.

c1957 1½in (4cm) diam

£1,500-2,000 **FELL**

A lady's Rolex 'Precision' wristwatch, with a 1401 calibre 13-jewel movement, the case back marked inside 'RW co', on a tricoloured textured bracelet, in 9ct hallmarked London 1966, with box.

1966

£1,000-1,400 **ECGW**

A gentleman's Rolex 'Oyster Perpetual' chronometer bubble-back steel wristwatch, later strap, case with light wear.

1950s

£1,200-1,600 **HAN**

A gentleman's Rolex 'Oyster Perpetual Air King' stainless steel wristwatch, integral steel bracelet, serial number.

1967

£1,500-2,000 **HAN**

A gentleman's Police 18ct Rolex 'Oyster Perpetual' day-date wristwatch, serial no.7397902, fitted 'President' bracelet and after-market diamond set dial and bracelet.

c1982-83

£5,000-5,500 **AST**

A lady's stainless steel Rolex 'Datejust' wristwatch, serial no.L478430, with jubilee bracelet and aftermarket diamond dial and bezel.

c1989-90

£1,800-2,200 **AST**

A gentleman's Rolex 'Oyster Perpetual Date Explorer II' bracelet watch, ref.16570, serial no.Y998359, signed automatic calibre 3185, stainless steel case, replacement dial, on a signed stainless steel Oyster bracelet with Oysterlock clasp.

c2002 1½in (4cm) diam

£3,500-4,000 **FELL**

A gentleman's 18ct yellow gold Rolex day-date chronometer, with dial set with diamonds, in a Rolex box.

£8,000-9,000 **JN**

A lady's 18ct gold Rolex wristwatch, 'President' bracelet stamped 'Rolex', with Rolex box, guarantee pamphlet and spare link.

2oz

£3,500-4,000 **BE**

KEY TO ILLUSTRATIONS

Every item illustrated has a letter code that identifies the dealer, auction house or private collector that owns or sold it.

AB
ALDRIDGES OF BATH
www.aldridgesofbath.com

AJ&S
ARTHUR JOHNSON AND SONS
www.arthurjohnson.co.uk

APAR
ADAM PARTRIDGE
www.adampartridge.co.uk

AST
ASTON'S AUCTIONEERS AND VALUERS
www.astonsauctioneers.co.uk

BBR
BBR AUCTIONS
www.onlinebbr.com

BE
BEARNES HAMPTON & LITTLEWOOD
www.bhandl.co.uk

BELL
BELLMANS
www.bellmans.co.uk

BER
BERTOIA AUCTIONS
www.bertoiaauctions.com

BLEA
BLEASDALES LTD.
www.bleasdalesltd.co.uk

BLO
BLOOMSBURY
(now part of Dreweatts 1759)
www.bloomsburyauctions.com

BMN
AUKTIONSHAUS BERGMANN
www.auction-bergmann.de

BOL
BOLDON AUCTION GALLERIES
www.boldonauctions.co.uk

BRI
BRIGHTWELLS
www.brightwells.com

BTA
BRITISH TOY AUCTIONS
www.britishtoyauctions.co.uk

C&T
C&T AUCTIONEERS AND VALUERS
www.candtauctions.co.uk

CAN
THE CANTERBURY AUCTION GALLERIES
www.thecanterburyauctiongalleries.com

CHEF
CHEFFINS
www.cheffins.co.uk

CHOR
CHORLEY'S
www.chorleys.com

CHT
CHARTERHOUSE AUCTIONEERS & VALUERS
www.charterhouse-auction.com

CLAR
CLARS
www.clars.com

CM
CHARLES MILLER LTD.
www.charlesmillerltd.com

CUTW
CUTTLESTONES AUCTIONEERS & VALUERS
www.cuttlestones.co.uk

DA&H
DEE ATKINSON & HARRISON
www.dee-atkinson-harrison.co.uk

DAWS
DAWSONS AUCTIONEERS & VALUERS
www.dawsonsauctions.co.uk

DN
DREWEATTS 1759
www.dreweatts.com

DRA
RAGO AUCTIONS
www.ragoarts.com

DUK
DUKE'S
www.dukes-auctions.com

ECGW
EWBANK'S
www.ewbankauctions.co.uk

FELL
FELLOWS
www.fellows.co.uk

FIS
AUKTIONSHAUS DR FISCHER
www.auctions-fischer.de

FLD
FIELDINGS AUCTIONEERS LTD.
www.fieldingsauctioneers.co.uk

FOM
FONSIE MEALY AUCTIONEERS
www.fonsiemealy.ie

FRE
FREEMAN'S
www.freemansauction.com

GHOU
GARDINER HOULGATE
www.gardinerhoulgate.co.uk

GBA
GRAHAM BUDD AUCTIONS
www.grahambuddauctions.co.uk

GIL
GILDINGS AUCTIONEERS
www.gildings.co.uk

GORL
GORRINGE'S
www.gorringes.co.uk

GRV
GEMMA REDMOND VINTAGE
www.gemmaredmondvintage.co.uk

GWA
GREAT WESTERN AUCTIONS LTD.
www.greatwesternauctions.com

GWRA
GW RAILWAYANA AUCTIONS
www.gwra.co.uk

GYM
GOLDING YOUNG & MAWER
www.goldingyoung.com

HALL
HALLS
www.fineart.hallsgb.com

HAN
HANSONS AUCTIONEERS AND VALUERS LTD.
www.hansonsauctioneers.co.uk

HANN
HANNAM'S
www.hannamsauctioneers.com

HT
HARTLEYS AUCTIONEERS AND VALUERS
www.hartleysauctions.co.uk

HUTC
HUTCHINSON-SCOTT AUCTIONEERS
www.hutchinsonscott.co.uk

IVN
IVOIRE NIMES
www.ivoire-nimes.fr

JDJ
JAMES D JULIA INC.
(now part of Morphy Auctions)
www.morphyauctions.com

JN
JOHN NICHOLSON'S FINE ART AUCTIONEERS & VALUERS
www.johnnicholsons.com

JNEW
JOHN NEWTON ANTIQUES
www.johnnewtonantiques.com

K&O
KINGHAM & ORME AUCTIONEERS VALUERS
www.kinghamandorme.com

KEY
KEYS AUCTIONEERS AND VALUERS
www.keysauctions.co.uk

KT
KERRY TAYLOR AUCTIONS
www.kerrytaylorauctions.com

L&T
LYON & TURNBULL
www.lyonandturnbull.com

LC
LAWRENCES AUCTIONEERS
www.lawrences.co.uk

LOC
LOCKE & ENGLAND
www.leauction.co.uk

LOCK
LOCKDALES AUCTIONEERS & VALUERS
www.lockdales.com

LPA
LEITZ PHOTOGRAPHICA AUCTION
www.leitz-auction.com

LSK
LACY SCOTT & KNIGHT
www.lsk.co.uk

LYN
LYNWAYS
www.lynways.com

M&DM
M&D MOIR
www.manddmoir.co.uk

M&K
MELLORS & KIRK
www.mellorsandkirk.com

M&M
M&M AUCTIONS
www.mm-auctions.com

MAB
MATTHEW BARTON LTD.
www.matthewbartonltd.com

MART
MARTEL MAIDES AUCTIONS
www.martelmaidesauctions.com

MM
MULLOCK'S
www.mullocksauctions.co.uk

MOR
MORPHETS
www.morphets.co.uk

MORP
MORPHY AUCTIONS
www.morphyauctions.com

NA
NORTHEAST AUCTIONS
northeastauctions.com

PC
PRIVATE COLLECTION

POOK
POOK & POOK INC.
www.pookandpook.com

PSA
POTTERIES AUCTIONS
www.potteriesauctions.com

PW
PETER WILSON FINE ART AUCTIONEERS
www.peterwilson.co.uk

QU
QUITTENBAUM
www.quittenbaum.de

ROS
ROSEBERY'S
www.roseberys.co.uk

SAS
SPECIAL AUCTION SERVICES
www.specialauctionservices.com

SK
SKINNER
www.skinnerinc.com

SOU
CATHERINE SOUTHON AUCTIONEERS & VALUERS LTD.
www.catherinesouthon.co.uk

SWA
SWANN AUCTION GALLERIES
www.swanngalleries.com

SWO
SWORDERS FINE ART AUCTIONEERS
www.sworder.co.uk

T&F
TAYLER & FLETCHER
www.taylerandfletcher.co.uk

TDM
THOMAS DEL MAR LTD.
www.thomasdelmar.com

TEN
TENNANTS AUCTIONEERS
www.tennants.co.uk

THER
THERIAULT'S
www.theriaults.com

TRI
TRING MARKET AUCTIONS
www.tringmarketauctions.co.uk

VEC
VECTIS
www.vectis.co.uk

W&W
WALLIS & WALLIS
www.wallisandwallis.co.uk

WAD
WADDINGTON'S
www.waddingtons.ca

WES
WESCHLER'S AUCTIONEERS & APPRAISERS
www.weschlers.com

WHP
W&H PEACOCK
www.peacockauction.co.uk

WHYT
WHYTE'S
www.whytes.ie

WM
WRIGHT MARSHALL
www.wrightmarshall.co.uk

WW
WOOLLEY & WALLIS
www.woolleyandwallis.co.uk

The following list of general antiques and collectables centres, markets, shops and shows has been organised by region. It is followed by a list of the major fair and show organisers. Any owner who would like to be listed in our next edition, space permitting, or who wishes to update their contact information, should email publisher@octopusbooks.co.uk

LONDON

Alfie's Antiques Market
www.alfiesantiques.com

Camden Passage Antiques Market
www.camdenpassageislington.co.uk

Covent Garden Antiques Market
www.jubileemarket.co.uk/antiques

Grays Antiques Market
www.graysantiques.com

Kensington Church Street Antiques Centre
58-60 Kensington Church Street, W8 4DB

Northcote Road Antiques Market
www.northcoteroadantiques.co.uk

Portobello Road Market
www.portobelloroad.co.uk

Spitalfields Antiques Market
www.oldspitalfieldsmarket.com

BEDFORDSHIRE

Ampthill Antiques Emporium
www.ampthillantiquesemporium.co.uk

BERKSHIRE

The Collectors Centre
www.collectorscentrereading.co.uk

Great Grooms at Hungerford
www.greatgrooms.co.uk

BUCKINGHAMSHIRE

Antiques at... Wendover
www.antiquesatwendover.co.uk

CAMBRIDGESHIRE

Cambridge Antiques Centre
www.cambsantiques.com

Waterside Antiques Centre
www.watersideantiques.co.uk

DERBYSHIRE

Alfreton Antique Centre
11 King Street, Alfreton, DE55 7AF

Bakewell Antiques & Works of Art
Tel: 01629 812 496

Heanor Antiques Centre
www.alscar.co.uk/heanor

Matlock Antiques & Collectables
www.matlockantiques.co.uk

DEVON

The Quay Antiques Centre
www.quayantiques.com

ESSEX

Debden Barns
www.debdenbarns.co.uk

GLOUCESTERSHIRE

Durham House Antiques
www.durhamhouseantiques.co.uk

Long Street Antiques
www.longstreetantiques.com

Lorfords
www.lorfordsantiques.com

Top Banana Antiques Mall
www.topbananaantiques.com

HEREFORDSHIRE

The Secondhand Warehouse & Antique Centre
www.secondhandwarehouseleominster.co.uk

HERTFORDSHIRE

By George Antique Centre
Tel: 01727 853032

KENT

Bagham Barn Antiques
www.baghambarnantiques.com

Fontaine
www.fontainedecorative.com

Junk Deluxe
www.junkdeluxe.co.uk

Otford Antiques and Collectors Centre
Tel: 01959 522025

LANCASHIRE

GB Antiques Centre
www.gbantiquescentre.com

Heskin Hall Antiques
www.heskinhallantiques.com

Karlen Antiques Centre & Interiors
www.antiquesshipper.co.uk

LINCOLNSHIRE

Christopher Pye Antiques
www.christopherpye.com

Hemswell Antique Centres
www.hemswell-antiques.com

St Martins Antiques Centre
www.st-martins-antiques.co.uk

NORTHAMPTONSHIRE

Brackley Antique Cellar
www.brackleyantiquecellar.co.uk

NOTTINGHAMSHIRE

Newark Antiques Centre
www.newarkantiquescentre.com

OXFORDSHIRE

Deddington Antiques Centre
www.deddingtonantiquecentre.co.uk

The Lamb Arcade Antiques & Lifestyle Centre
www.thelambarcade.co.uk

The Quiet Woman Antiques Centre
www.quietwomanantiques.co.uk

The Swan at Tetsworth Antiques Centre
www.theswan.co.uk

SOMERSET

Old Bank Antiques Centre
www.oldbankantiquescentre.com

STAFFORDSHIRE

Compton Mill Antique Emporium
Tel: 01538 373396

Potteries Antique Centre
www.potteriesantiquecentre.com

SURREY

Christique
www.christique.com

Kingston Antiques Centre
www.kingstonantiques.com

The Packhouse
www.packhouse.com

Talbot House Antique Centre
www.talbothouseantiques.com

EAST SUSSEX

The Brighton Lanes Antique Centre
www.brightonlanesantiques.co.uk

Brighton and Lewes Flea Market
www.flea-markets.co.uk

WEST SUSSEX

Arundel Bridge Antiques
Tel: 01903 884164

WEST MIDLANDS

Yoxall Antiques and Fine Arts
www.yoxallantiques.co.uk

WORCESTERSHIRE

Foley House Antiques
www.foleyhouseantiquesmalvern.co.uk

YORKSHIRE

The Antiques Centre York
www.theantiquescentreyork.co.uk

The Ginnel Antiques Centre
Tel: 01423 508857

SCOTLAND

Georgian Antiques
www.georgianantiques.net

Now and Then
www.oldtoysandantiques.wordpress.com

Rait Village Antiques Centre
www.rait-antiques.webnode.com

Scottish Antiques & Arts Centre
www.scottish-antiques.com

WALES

Afonwen Antiques
www.afonwen.co.uk

IRELAND

Powerscourt Centre
www.powerscourtcentre.ie

MAJOR FAIRS & SHOWS

Adam Antiques Fairs
www.adamsantiquesfairs.com

Antique Fairs Cornwall
www.antiquefairscornwall.co.uk

Antiques for Everyone
www.antiquesforeveryone.co.uk

B2B Events
www.b2bevents.info

Bentleys Fairs
www.bentleysfairs.co.uk

Cooper Antiques Fairs
www.cooperevents.com

The Decorative Antiques & Textiles Fair
www.decorativefair.com

IACF
www.iacf.co.uk

LAPADA
www.lapada.org

Love Fairs
www.lovefairs.com

Olympia International Art & Antiques Fair
www.olympia-antiques.co.uk

P&A Antiques
www.pa-antiques.co.uk

Penman Fairs
www.penman-fairs.co.uk

Sunbury Antiques Market
www.sunburyantiques.com

Arthur Swallow Fairs
www.arthurswallowfairs.co.uk

Take Five Fairs
www.antiquefairs.co.uk

If you wish to have any item valued, it is advisable to contact the dealer or specialist in advance to check that they will carry out this service and whether there is a charge. While most dealers will be happy to help you with an enquiry, do remember that they are busy people with businesses to run. Telephone valuations are not possible. Please mention the 'Miller's Collectables Handbook & Price Guide' by Judith Miller when making an enquiry. The following list is organised by the type of collectable.

ADVERTISING
Junktion Antiques Ltd.
www.junktionantiques.co.uk

ANTIQUITIES
Ancient Art
www.antiquities.co.uk

Finch & Co.
www.finch-and-co.co.uk

John A. Pearson
Tel: 01753 682136

Rupert Wace Ancient Art Ltd.
www.rupertwace.co.uk

ARCADE MACHINES
Liberty Games
www.libertygames.co.uk

ASIAN
Guest & Gray
www.chinese-porcelain-art.com

Roger Bradbury
Tel: 01692 538 293

Robert McPherson Antiques
www.orientalceramics.com

AUSTRIAN BRONZES
Hickmet Fine Arts
www.hickmet.com

AUTOMOBILIA
Richard Edmonds Auctions Ltd.
www.richardedmondsauctions.com

Finesse Fine Art
www.finesse-fine-art.com

Junktion Antiques Ltd.
www.junktionantiques.co.uk

BOOKS
Barter Books
www.barterbooks.co.uk

Bloomsbury
(now part of Dreweatts 1759)
www.bloomsburyauctions.com

George Bayntun
www.georgebayntun.com

Dominic Winter
www.dominicwinter.co.uk

Forum Auctions
www.forumauctions.co.uk

Zardoz Books
www.zardozbooks.co.uk

BOXES
Bleasdales
www.bleasdalesltd.co.uk

Mostly Boxes
www.mostlyboxesantiques.com

CAMERAS
Peter Loy
www.peterloy.com

West Yorkshire Cameras
wycameras.com

CANES
Michael German Antiques
www.antiquecanes.com

CERAMICS
Beth Adams, Alfies
www.alfiesantiques.com

AD Antiques
www.adantiques.com

Central Collectables
www.centralcollectablescom

China Search
www.chinasearch.co.uk

Tony Horsley
www.tonyhorsley.co.uk

KCS Ceramics
www.kcsceramics.co.uk

Lynways
www.lynways.com

Andrew Muir
www.andrew-muir.com

John Newton Antiques
johnnewtonantiques.com

Sue Norman
www.blueandwhitepotterysuenormanlondon.co.uk

Retroselect
www.retroselect.com

Geoffrey Robinson
www.robinsonantiques.co.uk

Vintage Interiors
www.vintagelifestyle.co.uk

CLOCKS
The Clock Clinic Ltd.
www.clockclinic.co.uk

Brian Loomes
www.brianloomes.com

Pendulum of Mayfair
www.pendulumofmayfair.co.uk

Raffety & Walwyn Ltd.
www.raffetyantiqueclocks.com

COMICS
The Book Palace
www.bookpalace.com

Comic Book Auctions
www.compalcomics.com

Phil-Comics
www.phil-comics.com

DOLLS
British Doll Showcase
www.britishdollshowcase.co.uk

Glenda O'Connor
www.glenda-antiquedolls.co.uk

FANS
Mad About Fans
www.madaboutfans.com

Mendes
www.mendes.co.uk

FASHION
Linda Bee
www.graysantiques.com

Beyond Retro
www.beyondretro.com

Rokit
www.rokit.co.uk

David Saxby
www.davidsaxby.co.uk

Kerry Taylor Auctions
www.kerrytaylorauctions.com

Vintage Modes
www.alfiesantiques.com

Vintage to Vogue
www.vintagetovoguebath.co.uk

FILM & TV
Prop Store
www.propstore.com

GLASS
Antique Glass
www.antique-glass.co.uk

Artius Glass
www.artiusglass.co.uk

Cloud Glass
www.cloudglass.com

Glass Etc.
www.decanterman.com

Grimes House Gallery
www.cranberryglass.co.uk

Jeanette Hayhurst Fine Glass
www.jeanettehayhurst.net

Andrew Lineham Fine Glass
www.antiquecolouredglass.com

Francesca Martire
www.francescamartire.com

M&D Moir
www.manddmoir.co.uk

Newsum Antiques
www.newsumantiques.co.uk

JEWELLERY
N. Bloom & Son (1912) Ltd.
www.nbloom.com

J.H. Bonnar
Tel: 0131 226 2811

Cristobal
www.cristobal.co.uk

Eclectica
www.eclectica.biz

Gemma Redmond Vintage
www.gemmaredmondvintage.co.uk

Scarab Antiques
www.scarabantiques.com

William Wain
www.williamwain.com

MECHANICAL MUSIC
On the Air Ltd.
www.vintageradio.co.uk

Stephen T.P. Kember
www.antique-musicboxes.co.uk

The Talking Machine
www.thetalkingmachine.co.uk

METALWARE
Adams Antiques
www.adamsantiquesfairs.com

Keith Hockin Antiques
www.keithhockin.com

Wakelin & Linfield
www.wakelin-linfield.com

MILITARIA
Jim Bullock Militaria
www.jimbullockmilitaria.com

The Old Brigade
www.theoldbrigade.co.uk

Garth Vincent
www.garthvincent.com

West Street Antiques
www.antiquearmsandarmour.com

PAPERWEIGHTS
Alan and Helen Thornton
www.pwts.co.uk

Weights-n-things
www.weights-n-things.com

PENS & WRITING
Battersea Pen Home
www.penhome.co.uk

Hans's Vintage Pens
07850 771183

The Pen & Pencil Gallery
www.penpencilgallery.com

POSTCARDS & CIGARETTE CARDS
PC Postcards
www.pcpostcards.co.uk

Intercol London
www.intercol.co.uk

POSTERS
At The Movies
www.atthemovies.co.uk

Dodo
www.dodoposters.com

Limelight Movie Art
www.limelightmovieart.com

The Reel Poster Gallery
www.reelposter.com

Rennies Seaside Modern
www.rennart.co.uk

Barclay Samson
www.barclaysamson.com

RAILWAYANA
GW Railwayana Auctions
www.gwra.co.uk

Sheffield Railwayana Auctions
www.sheffieldrailwayana.co.uk

ROCK & POP
Briggs
www.usebriggs.com

Sweet Memories
www.vinylrecords.co.uk

Tracks
www.tracks.co.uk

SCENT BOTTLES
Richard Hoppé
www.richardhoppe.co.uk

SCIENTIFIC INSTRUMENTS
Charles Miller
www.charlesmillerltd.com

Flea Glass Ltd.
www.fleaglass.com

SCULPTURE
Hickmet Fine Arts
hickmet.com

SEWING
Bleasdales
www.bleasdalesltd.co.uk

SILVER
B. Silverman
www.silverman-london.com

Mary Cooke Antiques
www.marycooke.co.uk

Paul Bennett
www.paulbennettonline.com

Sanda Lipton
www.antique-silver.com

Smith & Robinson
www.smithandrobinson.com

Steppes Hill Farm Antiques
www.steppeshillfarm.com

William Walter Antiques
www.williamwalter.co.uk

Daniel Bexfield Antiques
www.bexfield.co.uk

SMOKING
Richard Ball
www.lighter.co.uk

SPORTING
Graham Budd
www.grahambuddauctions.co.uk

Knights Sporting Auctions
www.knights.co.uk

Rhod McEwan Golf
www.rhodmcewangolf.com

Mullock's
www.mullocksauctions.co.uk

Manfred Schotten Antiques
www.sportantiques.co.uk

Sporting Antiques
www.sportingantiques.co.uk

TAXIDERMY
London Taxidermy
www.londontaxidermy.com

The Taxidermy Emporium & Son
www.taxidermyemporium.co.uk

TECHNOLOGY
Candlestick & Bakelite
www.candlestickandbakelite.co.uk

Junktion Antiques Ltd.
www.junktionantiques.co.uk

Telephone Lines
www.telephonelines.net

TOYS & GAMES
Collectors Old Toy Shop
www.collectorsoldtoyshop.com

Garrick Coleman
www.antiquechess.co.uk

Mike Delaney
www.vintagehornby.net

Donay Games
www.donaygames.com

The House of Automata
thehouseofautomata.com

Collectors Loft
www.collectorsloft.co.uk

Metropolis Toys
www.metropolistoys.co.uk

Sue Pearson
www.suepearson.co.uk

Special Auction Services
www.specialauctionservices.com

Teddy Bears of Witney
www.teddybears.co.uk

Toydreams
www.toydreams.co.uk

Vectis Auctioneers
www.vectis.co.uk

Wallis & Wallis
www.wallisandwallis.co.uk

TREEN & CARVING
J. Collins & Sons
www.collinsantiques.co.uk

TRIBAL ART
Jean-Baptiste Bacquart
www.jbbacquart.com

Michael Graham Stewart
Tel: 020 7495 4001

WATCHES
70s Watches
www.70s-watches.com

Kleanthous Antiques
www.kleanthous.com

The Watch Gallery
www.thewatchgallery.com

AUCTIONEERS

The following list of auctioneers who conduct regular sales by auction is organised by region. Any auctioneer who would like to be listed in our next edition, space permitting, or to update their contact information, should email publisher@octopusbooks.co.uk

LONDON

Altea Maps
www.alteagallery.com

Angling Auctions
angling-auctions.co.uk

Bainbridge's
www.bainbridges.auction

Baldwins
www.baldwin.co.uk

Barnes Auctions
www.barnesauctions.com

Dreweatts 1759
www.dreweatts.com

Matthew Barton Ltd.
www.matthewbartonltd.com

Bonhams
www.bonhams.com

Bromley Country Auctions
www.bromleycountryauctions.com

Graham Budd Auctions
www.grahambuddauctions.co.uk

Chiswick Auctions
www.chiswickauctions.co.uk

Christie's
www.christies.com

Criterion Auctioneers
www.criterionauctioneers.com

Dix Noonan Webb
www.dnw.co.uk

Forum Auctions
www.forumauctions.co.uk

Greenwich Auctions Partnership
www.greenwichauctions.co.uk

Hampstead Auctions
www.hampsteadauctions.com

London Auctions
www.londonauctions.co

Lots Road Auctions
www.lotsroad.com

Lynways
www.lynways.com

Charles Miller
www.charlesmillerltd.com

The Pedestal
www.thepedestal.com

Phillips
www.phillips.com

Roseberys
www.roseberys.co.uk

Sotheby's
www.sothebys.com

Southgate Auction Rooms
www.southgateauctionrooms.com

Spink & Son Ltd.
www.spink.com

Kerry Taylor Auctions
www.kerrytaylorauctions.com

Thomas Del Mar Ltd.
www.thomasdelmar.com

BEDFORDSHIRE

Locke & England
www.leauction.co.uk

W&H Peacock
www.peacockauction.co.uk

Charles Ross Auctioneers
charles-ross.co.uk

BERKSHIRE

Berkshire Auction Rooms
www.berkshireauctionrooms.co.uk

Dawson's Auctioneers
www.dawsonsauctions.co.uk

Dreweatts 1759
www.dreweatts.com

Historical & Collectable
www.historicalandcollectable.com

Martin & Pole
www.martinpole.co.uk

Special Auction Services
www.specialauctionservices.com

Thimbleby & Shorland
tsauction.co.uk

Wokingham Auctions
www.wokinghamauctions.com

BRISTOL

East Bristol Auctions
www.eastbristol.co.uk

BUCKINGHAMSHIRE

Amersham Auction Rooms
www.amershamauctionrooms.co.uk

Bourne End Auction Rooms
www.bourneendauctionrooms.co.uk

Dickins Auctioneers
www.dickinsauctioneers.com

Kings Auction Amersham
www.kingsauctionamersham.co.uk

CAMBRIDGESHIRE

Cheffins
www.cheffins.co.uk

Clifford Cross Auctions
www.cliffordcrossauctions.co.uk

Harrisons Auction Centre
www.harrisonsauctions.co.uk

Hyperion Auctions Ltd.
hyperion-auctions.co.uk

Rowley's Fine Art Auctioneers
www.rowleyfineart.com

Willingham Auctions
www.willinghamauctions.com

CHANNEL ISLANDS

Channel Islands Auctions
www.channelislandsauctions.com

Martel Maides
www.martelmaidesauctions.com

CHESHIRE

Adam Partridge Auctioneers & Valuers
www.adampartridge.co.uk

The Auction Centre
www.theauctioncentre.co.uk

British Toy Auctions
www.britishtoyauctions.co.uk

Byrne's Fine Art Auctioneers & Valuers
www.byrnesauctioneers.co.uk

Capes Dunn Fine Art Auctioneers
www.capesdunn.com

Andrew Hilditch & Son
andrewhilditchauctioneers.co.uk

Maxwells of Wilmslow
www.maxwells-auctioneers.co.uk

Omega Auctions
www.omegaauctions.co.uk

Warrington Auctions
www.warringtonauctions.co.uk

Peter Wilson Fine Art Auctioneers
www.peterwilson.co.uk

CLEVELAND

Vectis Auctioneers
www.vectis.co.uk

CORNWALL

Clarks Auction Rooms
clarksauctionrooms.com

Jefferys
www.jefferys.uk.com

Barbara Kirk Auctions
www.barbarakirkauctions.com

W.H. Lane & Son
www.whlane.auction

David Lay FRICS
www.davidlay.co.uk

Lodge & Thomas
www.lodgeandthomas.co.uk

The Truro Auction Centre
cornwallauction.co.uk

CUMBRIA

1818 Auctioneers
www.1818auctioneers.co.uk

Laidlaw Auctioneers & Valuers
www.laidlawauctioneers.co.uk

Mitchells
www.mitchellsantiques.co.uk

PFK Auctioneers
www.pfkauctions.co.uk

Thomson Roddick Auctioneers & Valuers
www.thomsonroddick.com

DERBYSHIRE

Bamfords Auctioneers & Valuers
www.bamfords-auctions.co.uk

Hansons
www.hansonsauctions.co.uk

DEVON

Bearnes Hampton & Littlewood
www.bhandl.co.uk

Chilcotts
www.chilcottsauctioneers.co.uk

Drake's Auctions
drakesauctions.co.uk

Eldreds Auctioneers & Valuers
www.eldreds.net

Kivells
www.kivells.com

Lyme Bay Auctions
www.lymebayauctions.co.uk

Michael J. Bowman
www.michaeljbowman.co.uk

Okehampton Auctions
www.okehamptonauctions.co.uk

Ottery Auction Rooms
www.otteryauctionrooms.co.uk

Piers Motley Auctions
www.piersmotleyauctions.co.uk

The Plymouth Auction Rooms
www.plymouthauctions.co.uk

Potburys
www.potburysauctions.co.uk

Queens Road Auctions
www.queensroadauctions.com

Rendells
www.rendells.co.uk

Whitton & Laing Auctions
www.whittonandlaingauctioneers.co.uk

Whittons
www.whittonsauctions.co.uk

DORSET

Bridport Auctions
bridportauctionhouse.com

Bulstrodes Auction Rooms
www.bulstrodes.co.uk

Busby
www.busby.co.uk

Charterhouse
www.charterhouse-auction.com

Clarke's Auctions
clarkesauctions.co.uk

Cottees Auctions Ltd.
www.cottees.co.uk

Dalkeith Auctions
www.dalkeithcatalogue.com

Duke's
www.dukes-auctions.com

Elliotts UK Auctioneers
www.elliottsuk.co.uk

House & Son
www.houseandson.com

Onslows
www.onslows.co.uk

Semley Auctioneers
www.semleyauctioneers.com

Thomas Watson
www.thomaswatson.com

DURHAM
Vectis Auctions Limited
www.vectis.co.uk

ESSEX
Frederick Andrews Ltd.
www.frederickandrews.uk

Boningtons Auctioneers
www.boningtons.com

Chalkwell Auctions
www.chalkwellauctions.co.uk

Reeman Dansie
www.reemandansie.com

Stacey's Auctioneers & Valuers
www.staceyauction.com

Sworders
www.sworder.co.uk

GLOUCESTERSHIRE
British Bespoke Auctions
www.bespokeauctions.co.uk

Chorley's
www.chorleys.com

Clevedon Salerooms
www.clevedon-salerooms.com

The Cotswold Auction Company
www.cotswoldauction.co.uk

David Hancock & Co.
www.davidhancock-co.co.uk

Mallams Fine Art Auctioneers
www.mallams.co.uk

Moore, Allen & Innocent
www.mooreallen.co.uk

Smiths Newent Auctions
www.smithsnewentauctions.co.uk

Stroud Auctions Ltd.
www.stroudauctions.com

Tayler & Fletcher
www.taylerandfletcher.co.uk/fine-art

Dominic Winter Auctions
www.dominicwinter.co.uk

Wotton Auction Rooms Ltd.
www.wottonauctionrooms.co.uk

HAMPSHIRE
Andrew Smith & Son
www.andrewsmithandson.com

George Kidner & Andrew Reeves Auctioneers
www.georgekidner.co.uk

Jacobs & Hunt Auctioneers
www.jacobsandhunt.com

Manor House Auctions
www.manorhouseauctions.co.uk

Nesbits Auctions Ltd.
www.nesbits.co.uk

Hannam's
www.hannamsauctioneers.com

Pump House Auctions
www.pumphouseauctions.co.uk

Ringwood Auctions
www.ringwoodauctions.co.uk

HEREFORDSHIRE
Brightwells
www.brightwells.com

R.G. & R.B. Williams
www.rgandrbwilliams.co.uk

John Goodwin
www.johngoodwin.co.uk

Nigel Ward & Co.
www.nigel-ward.co.uk

HERTFORDSHIRE
Sworders
www.sworder.co.uk

Tring Market Auctions
www.tringmarketauctions.co.uk

Bushey Auctions
www.busheyauctions.com

ISLE OF MAN
Murray's
www.murrays.im

ISLE OF WIGHT
Hose Rhodes Dickson
www.hose-rhodes-dickson.co.uk

KENT
Bentley's Fine Art Auctioneers
www.bentleysfineartauctioneers.co.uk

C&T Auctioneers and Valuers
www.candtauctions.co.uk

Gordon Day & Partners
www.gordondayauctions.com

Gorringe's
www.gorringes.co.uk

Grand Auctions
www.grandauctions.co.uk

Ibbet Mosely
www.ibbettmosely.co.uk

Kent Auction Galleries Ltd.
kentauctiongalleriesltd.co.uk

Pettmans
www.pettmans.com

Catherine Southon Auctioneers & Valuers
www.catherinesouthon.co.uk

J. Stuart Watson
www.jstuartwatson.com

The Canterbury Auction Galleries
www.thecanterburyauctiongalleries.com

Tunbridge Wells and Hastings Auctioneers
twauctionhouse.com

Watermans Auction Rooms
www.watermansauctionrooms.co.uk

Westenhanger Auctioneers
www.westenhangerauctioneers.com

LANCASHIRE
Bank Hall Auctions
www.bank-hall-auctions.co.uk

Silverwoods of Lancashire
silverwoods.co.uk

Smythes Fine Art
www.smythes.net

Warren & Wignall
www.warrenandwignall.co.uk

LEICESTERSHIRE
David Stanley Auctions
www.davidstanley.com

Gilding's Auctioneers & Valuers
www.gildings.co.uk

Shouler & Son
www.shoulers.co.uk

Sutton Hill Farm Country Auctions
suttonhillfarmcountryauctions.com

Tennants
www.tennants.co.uk

LINCOLNSHIRE
Batemans
www.batemans.com

Golding Young & Mawer
www.goldingyoung.com

Jackson, Green & Preston
www.jacksongreenpreston.co.uk

Longstaff
www.longstaff.com

Perkins George Mawer & Co.
www.perkinsgeorgemawer.co.uk

The Stamford Auction Rooms
www.stamfordauctionrooms.com

John Taylors Auction Rooms
www.johntaylors.com

M&M Auctions
www.mm-auctions.com

Unique Auctions
www.unique-auctions.com

MANCHESTER
Bolton Auction Rooms
boltonauction.co.uk

MERSEYSIDE
Adam Partridge
www.adampartridge.co.uk

Cato Crane & Co.
www.cato-crane.co.uk

NORFOLK
Beeston Auctions
beestonauctions.co.uk

Blyths Auctioneers & Valuers
www.blyths.com

T.W. Gaze
www.twgaze.com

Barry L. Hawkins
www.barryhawkins.co.uk

Holt's Auctioneers
www.holtandcompany.co.uk

Horners Valuers & Auctioneers
www.horners.co.uk

James & Sons Auctioneers
jamesandsonsauctioneers.com

Keys
www.keysauctions.co.uk

Knights Sporting Auctions
www.knights.co.uk

Landles Auctioneers 1856 Ltd.
www.landlesauctioneers1856.co.uk

NORTHAMPTONSHIRE
J.P. Humbert Auctioneers
01327 359595

NORTHUMBERLAND
Alnwick Auctions
alnwickauctions.co.uk

Railtons
www.jimrailton.com

NOTTINGHAMSHIRE
Arthur Johnson & Sons Auctioneers
www.arthurjohnson.co.uk

Mellors & Kirk
www.mellorsandkirk.com

Northgate Auction Rooms
www.northgateauctionrooms-newark.co.uk

John Pye
www.johnpye.co.uk

OXFORDSHIRE
Holloway's
www.hollowaysauctioneers.co.uk

Jones & Jacob Ltd.
www.jonesandjacob.com

JS Fine Art
www.jsfineart.co.uk

Mallams
www.mallams.co.uk

RUTLAND
Oakham Auction Centre
www.oakhamauctioncentre.co.uk

SHROPSHIRE
Brettells Antiques & Fine Art
www.brettells.com

Halls Fine Art
hallsgb.com/fine-art/

Hendersons Auctions
www.hendersonsauctions.co.uk

Mullock's
www.mullocksauctions.co.uk

Nock Deighton
www.nockdeighton.co.uk

Perry & Phillips
www.perryandphillips.co.uk

Trevanion & Dean
www.trevanionanddean.com

SOMERSET
Aldridges of Bath Ltd.
www.aldridgesofbath.com

Clevedon Salerooms
www.clevedon-salerooms.com

Dore & Rees
www.doreandrees.co.uk

Greenslade Taylor Hunt
www.gth.net

Gardiner Houlgate
www.gardinerhoulgate.co.uk

Killens Mendip Auction Rooms
www.mendipauctionrooms.co.uk

Lawrences of Crewkerne
www.lawrences.co.uk

McCubbing & Redfern
www.mccubbingandredfern.co.uk

Tamlyns
www.tamlynsprofessional.co.uk

STAFFORDSHIRE
Bury & Hilton
www.buryandhilton.co.uk

Cuttlestones Auctioneers
www.cuttlestones.co.uk

Potteries Auctions
www.potteriesauctions.com

Louis Taylor Auctioneers
www.louistaylorfineart.co.uk

Richard Winterton Auctioneers
www.richardwinterton.co.uk

SUFFOLK
Nick Barber Auctions
www.nickbarberauctions.com

Bishop & Miller Auctioneers Ltd.
www.bishopandmillerauctions.co.uk

Clarke & Simpson Auctions
www.clarkeandsimpson.co.uk

Diamond Mills & Co.
www.diamondmills.com

Durrants
www.durrants.com

Lacy Scott and Knight
www.lsk.co.uk

Lockdales
www.lockdales.com

Lowestoft Auction Rooms
www.lowestoftauctionrooms.com

Lowestoft Porcelain Auctions
www.lowestoftchina.co.uk

Mander Auctioneers
www.manderauctions.co.uk

Tony Murland Antique Tools
www.antiquetools.co.uk

SURREY
Crow's Auction Gallery
www.crowsauctions.co.uk

Ewbank's
www.ewbankauctions.co.uk

John Nicholson's
www.johnnicholsons.com

Lawrences of Bletchingley
www.lawrencesbletchingley.co.uk

Sterling Vault Auctioneers
www.sterlingvault.co.uk

Wellers of Guildford
wellersofguildford.com

P.F. Windibank
www.windibank.co.uk

Young's Auction
youngsauctions.co.uk

EAST SUSSEX
Brighton & Hove Auctions
brightonandhoveauctions.co.uk

Burstow & Hewett
www.burstowandhewett.co.uk

Pippa Deeley Auctions
www.pippadeeley.com

Eastbourne Auction Rooms
www.eastbourneauction.com

Falmer Auctions
falmerauctions.co.uk

Gorringe's
www.gorringes.co.uk

Inmans
www.inmansauctioneers.co.uk

Rosan Reeves Auctions
www.rosanreevesauctions.co.uk

Rye Auction Galleries
www.ryeauctiongalleries.com

Wallis & Wallis
www.wallisandwallis.co.uk

Watsons
watsonsauctioneers.co.uk

WEST SUSSEX
Henry Adams Fine Art
www.henryadamsfineart.co.uk

Bellmans
www.bellmans.co.uk

Campbells
campbellsauctions.co.uk

Denhams
www.denhams.com

Stride & Son
stridesauctions.com

Summers Place Auctions
www.summersplaceauctions.com

Toovey's
www.tooveys.com

TYNE AND WEAR
Anderson & Garland
www.andersonandgarland.com

Boldon Auction Galleries
www.boldonauctions.co.uk

Corbitts
www.corbitts.com

Featonby's
featonbys.co.uk

Jarrow Auction Rooms
www.jarrowauctions.co.uk

Thomas N. Millet
www.millersauctioneers.co.uk

WARWICKSHIRE
Bleasdales
www.bleasdalesltd.co.uk

Bigwood Auctioneers Ltd.
www.bigwoodauctioneers.co.uk

W&H Peacock
www.peacockauction.co.uk

WEST MIDLANDS
Aston's Auctioneers & Valuers
www.astonsauctioneers.co.uk

Biddle & Webb
www.biddleandwebb.com

Fellows
www.fellows.co.uk

Fieldings
www.fieldingsauctioneers.co.uk

Warwick Auctions of Coventry
www.warwickauctions.co.uk

WILTSHIRE
Henry Aldridge & Son
www.henry-aldridge.co.uk

Chippenham Auction Rooms
www.chippenhamauctionrooms.co.uk

Richard Edmonds Auctions Ltd.
richardedmondsauctions.com

Harrison Auctions Ltd.
jubileeauctions.com

Gardiner Houlgate
www.gardinerhoulgate.co.uk

Robert Finan
www.robertfinan.co.uk

Kidson-Trigg
www.kidsontrigg.co.uk

Netherhampton Salerooms
www.salisburyauctioncentre.co.uk

Wessex Auction Rooms
wessexauctionrooms.co.uk

Woolley & Wallis
www.woolleyandwallis.co.uk

WORCESTERSHIRE
GW Railwayana Auctions
www.gwra.co.uk

Kingham & Orme
www.kinghamandorme.com

Littleton Auctions
www.littletonauctions.com

Philip Serrell
www.serrell.com

EAST YORKSHIRE
Clubleys
www.clubleys.com

Dee Atkinson & Harrison
www.dee-atkinson-harrison.co.uk

Gilbert Baitson
gilbert-baitson.co.uk

Hawley's Auctioneers
hawleys.info

NORTH YORKSHIRE
Boulton & Cooper
www.boultoncooper.co.uk

David Duggleby Auctioneers
www.davidduggleby.com

Hutchinson-Scott
www.hutchinsonscott.co.uk

Lithgow Sons & Partner
www.lithgowsauctions.com

Morphets
www.morphets.co.uk

Richardson & Smith
www.richardsonandsmith.co.uk

Ryedale Auctioneers
www.ryedaleauctions.com

Summersgills Auctions
www.summersgills.com

Tennants
www.tennants.co.uk

Thompsons Auctioneers (Harrogate) Ltd.
www.thompsonsauctioneers.com

D. Wombell & Son
wombells.co.uk

SOUTH YORKSHIRE
BBR Auctions
www.onlinebbr.com

Paul Beighton Auctioneers
www.pbauctioneers.co.uk

Sheffield Auction Gallery
www.sheffieldauctiongallery.com

Sheffield Railwayana Auctions
www.sheffieldrailwayana.co.uk

Wilby's
www.wilbys.net

Wilkinson's Auctioneers Ltd.
www.wilkinsons-auctioneers.co.uk

WEST YORKSHIRE
Calder Valley Auctioneers
www.caldervalleyauctioneers.com

Gary Don
garydon.co.uk

Hartleys
www.hartleysauctions.co.uk

KLM Auctions
www.klmauctioneers.com

Thomson Roddick Auctioneers & Valuers
www.thomsonroddick.com

John Walsh & Co. Auctioneers
www.john-walsh.co.uk

SCOTLAND

Bonhams
www.bonhams.com

Border Auctions
borderauctions.co.uk

Franklin Browns
franklinbrowns.co.uk

Thomas R. Callan
www.trcallan.com

Cluny Auctions
www.clunyauctions.co.uk

Curr & Dewar Auctioneers
www.curranddewar.com

Great Western Auctions
www.greatwesternauctions.com

H&H Auction Rooms
www.hhauctionrooms.co.uk

Huntly Auctions
www.huntlyauctions.co.uk

Lindsay Burns & Company
www.lindsayburns.co.uk

Lyon & Turnbull
www.lyonandturnbull.com

D.J. Manning Auctioneers
www.djmanning.co.uk

McTear's Auctioneers
www.mctears.co.uk

John Milne
www.johnmilne-auctioneers.com

Mulberry Bank Auctions
www.mulberrybankauctions.com

Ramsay Cornish
www.ramsaycornish.com

Robertsons of Kinbuck
kinbuckauctions.co.uk

Thomson Roddick Auctioneers & Valuers
www.thomsonroddick.com

Shapes
www.shapesedinburgh.co.uk

Sotheby's
www.sothebys.com

L.S. Smellie & Sons Ltd.
www.hamiltonauctionmarket.com

Taylor's Auction Rooms
www.taylors-auctions.com

WALES

Anthemion Auctions
www.anthemionauction.com

Bonhams
www.bonhams.com

J. Straker Chadwick & Sons
www.jschadwick.co.uk

Morgan Evans & Co. Ltd.
www.morganevans.com

Peter Francis
www.peterfrancis.co.uk

Rogers Jones & Co.
www.rogersjones.co.uk

Wingetts
www.wingetts.co.uk

NORTHERN IRELAND

Bangor Auctions
bangorauctions.co.uk

Bloomfield Auctions
www.bloomfieldauctions.co.uk

McAfee Auctions
www.mcafeeauctions.com

North Coast Auction Rooms
www.northcoastauctionrooms.com

Ross's Auctioneers & Valuers
www.rosss.com

INTERNATIONAL

AUSTRIA

Lietz Photographica
www.leitz-auction.com

CANADA

Waddington's
www.waddingtons.ca

FRANCE

Ivoire Nîmes
www.ivoire-nimes.fr

GERMANY

Auktionhaus Dr Fischer
www.auctions-fischer.de

Auktionshaus Bergmann
www.auction-bergmann.de

Quittenbaum
www.quittenbaum.de

IRELAND

Adam's
www.adams.ie

Cobwebs
cobwebs.ie

Danker Antiques
www.dankerantiques.com

De Veres Art Auctions
www.deveres.ie

Sean Eacrett Antiques
www.ashgrovegroup.ie

Fonsie Mealy Auctioneers
fonsiemealy.ie

Lynes & Lynes
www.lynesandlynes.com

Matthews Auction Rooms
matthewsauctionrooms.com

Victor Mitchell's Auctioneers
www.victormitchell.com

Mullen's Laurel Park
www.mullenslaurelpark.com

Larry O'Keeffe Auctioneers
www.larryokeeffeauctions.com

O'Reilly's Auction Rooms 1948 Ltd.
www.oreillysfineart.com

Purcell Aucitoneers
www.purcellauctioneers.ie

Sheppard's Irish Auction House
www.sheppards.ie

John Weldon Auctioneers
www.jwa.ie

Whyte's
www.whytes.ie

USA

Bertoia Auctions
www.bertoiaauctions.com

Clars
www.clars.com

Freeman's
www.freemansauction.com

Morphy Auctions
www.morphyauctions.com

Northeast Auctions
northeastauctions.com

Pook & Pook Inc.
www.pookandpook.com

Rago Arts
www.ragoarts.com

Skinner
www.skinnerinc.com

Swann Auction Galleries
www.swanngalleries.com

Theriault's
www.theriaults.com

Weschler's Auctioneers & Appraisers
www.weschlers.com

INTERNET RESOURCES

Miller's Antiques & Collectables
www.millersguides.com

@millersantiques

1stdibs
www.1stdibs.com

The Antiques Trade Gazette
www.antiquestradegazette.com

Auction.fr
www.auction.fr

BADA
www.bada.org

Barnebys
www.barnebys.co.uk

Collectors Weekly
www.collectorsweekly.com

eBay
www.ebay.com

Go Antiques
www.goantiques.com

La Gazette du Drouot
www.drouot.com

Invaluable
www.invaluable.co.uk

LAPADA
www.lapada.org

Live Auctioneers
www.liveauctioneers.com

Maine Antique Digest
www.maineantiquedigest.com

Rubylane
www.rubylane.com

Rubylux
www.rubylux.com

The Saleroom
www.the-saleroom.com

WorthPoint
www.worthpoint.com

CLUBS & SOCIETIES

The following list is organised by the type of collectable. If you would like your club, society or organisation to appear in our next edition, or would like to update your details, please contact us at publisher@octopusbooks.co.uk

GENERAL
The Arts Society
theartssociety.org

ADVERTISING
The Street Jewellery Society
www.streetjewellery.org

ARCADE MACHINES
Vintage Arcade Preservation Society
www.arcade-museum.com/vaps

AUTOMOBILIA
Brmm Brmm Classic Network
www.brmmbrmm.com

BOOKS
The Enid Blyton Society
www.enidblytonsociety.co.uk

The Followers of Rupert
www.rupertbear.co.uk

CERAMICS
Carlton Ware World
www.carltonwareworld.com

Clarice Cliff Collectors Club
www.claricecliff.com

Fieldings Crown Devon Collectors Club
www.fieldingscrowndevonclub.co.uk

Friends of Blue
www.fob.org.uk

Goss Collectors' Club
www.gosscollectorsclub.org

Moorcroft Collectors' Club
www.moorcroft.com/members

Myott Collectors Club
www.myottcollectorsclub.com

Poole Pottery Collectors' Club
www.poolepotterycollectorsclub.co.uk

Royal Doulton Collector's Club
www.royaldoultoncollectorsclub.com

The Shelley Group
www.shelley.co.uk

International Wade Collectors Club
www.wadecollectorsclub.co.uk

CLOCKS
Antiquarian Horological Society
www.ahsoc.org

COMICS
The Beano & Dandy Collectors' Club
www.phil-comics.com/collectors_club.php

DOLLS
The Doll Club of Great Britain
www.dollclubgb.com

The Fashion Doll Collectors Club
www.fashiondollcollectorsclubgb.co.uk

FANS
Antique Fan Collectors Association
www.fancollectors.org

The Fan Circle International
www.fancircleinternational.org

FASHION
The British Compact Collectors' Society
www.compactcollectors.co.uk

The Costume Society
www.costumesociety.org.uk

GLASS
British Bottle Review
www.onlinebbr.com

The Carnival Glass Society
www.thecgs.co.uk

The Glass Association
www.glassassociation.org.uk

JEWELLERY
Costume Jewelry Collectors International
www.costumejewelrycollectors.com

MECHANICAL MUSIC
Musical Box Society of Great Britain
www.mbsgb.org.uk

METALWARE
Antique Metalware Society
www.antiquemetalwaresociety.org.uk

The Old Hall Club
www.oldhallclub.co.uk

MILITARIA
Military Historical Society
www.themilitaryhistoricalsociety.co.uk

The Orders & Medals Research Society
www.omrs.org

PAPERWEIGHTS
Paperweight Collectors Circle
www.paperweightcollectorscircle.com

Caithness Glass Paperweight Collectors Members Society
www.caithnessglass.co.uk/collectors

PENS & WRITING
The Writing Equipment Society
www.wesonline.org.uk

POSTCARDS & CIGARETTE CARDS
Cartophilic Society of Great Britain
www.card-world.co.uk

Postcard Pages
www.postcard.co.uk

RAILWAYANA
Railwayana Collectors Journal
www.prorail.co.uk

SCENT BOTTLES
International Perfume Bottle Association
www.ipba-uk.co.uk

SCIENTIFIC INSTRUMENTS
Scientific Instrument Society
www.scientificinstrumentsociety.org

SEWING
International Sewing Machine Collectors' Society
www.ismacs.net

The Thimble Society
www.thimblesociety.com

SILVER
Association of Small Collectors of Antique Silver (ASCAS)
www.ascasonline.org

SMOKING
The Lighter Club of Great Britain
www.lighterclub.co.uk

SPORTING
International Football Hall of Fame
www.ifhof.com

Programme Monthly & Football Collectable
www.pmfc.co.uk

British Golf Collectors Society
www.golfcollectors.com

Rugby Memorabilia Society
www.rugby-memorabilia.co.uk

TECHNOLOGY
British Vintage Wireless Society
www.bvws.org.uk

TEDDY BEARS
Merrythought International Collectors Club
www.merrythought.co.uk

Steiff Club
www.steiff.com

TOYS & GAMES
William Britain Collectors Club
www.wbritain.com/collectors-club

The British Model Soldier Society
www.bmssonline.com

Corgi Collector Club
www.corgi.co.uk/club

Hornby Collectors Club
www.hornby.com/uk-en/club-portal-hornby

TREEN
Mauchline Ware Collectors Club
www.mauchlineware.com

WATCHES
Antiquarian Horological Society
www.ahsoc.org

WINE & DRINKING
The Wine Label Circle
www.winelabelcircle.org

INDEX

A
Abrahall & Bint 324
accessories 201–4
Ace Trains 391
Acier 116
'Action Man' dolls 193
Adams, George 333, 410
Adams, John 136
Adiamec, Paul 90
Adie & Lovekin 324
advertising 9–13, 77
Aesthetic Movement 178
African tribal art 403
Agfa 51
Ainstable Pottery 174
aircraft, model 395
Akai 275
AKG 357
Alcock, Martyn 103
Aldermaston Pottery 170
Alo (Charles Hallo) 301
Alps 365
Amberina 252
American
  advertising 12
  glass 249
  mechanical banks 273
  mechanical music 274
  metalware 277
  toys 379
  tribal art 404–5
  typewriters 357
  wine and drinking 412
American Flyer Lines 391
American Sewing
  Machine Co. 273
amusement machines 16
Andersen, Michael & Sons 147
Anderson, James 349
Ando 29
Andrews, Denise 103
Andrews, Kirk 310
Andrews, Martin 253
animals
  advertising 10
  Beswick 57–64, 66–7
  Black Forest 401
  bronze 31, 34–5
  Bunnykins 103
  Burmantofts 73–4
  car mascots 36–7
  Charles Vyse 151
  Chinese 22, 24
  clockwork 379
  Coalport 89
  Doulton 95
  glass 226, 238, 242
  Japanese 30
  jewellery 259
  Lorna Bailey 114
  Minton 118
  netsuke 30
  pencils 288, 290, 291
  pin cushions 324–6
  Royal Cophenhagen 8
  Royal Crown Derby 142
  Royal Doulton flambé
    104–5
  Royal Worcester 143
  Scandinavian ceramics
    148–9
  silver 332
  smoking accessories
    340, 341
  sporting 348
  studio pottery 173, 176
  taxidermy 356
  teddy bears & stuffed toys
    359–64
  toys 384
  tribal art 404, 406
  Wade 152

weird & wonderful 409
Wemyss 154
West German stoneware
  157, 158
see also birds
annuals & comics 181–4
Anscomb 348
Anstiss, F.W. 356
antiquities 14–15
apothecary boxes 50
Arenburg, Mark von 303
Argy-Rousseau, Gabriel 247,
  270
Arita 27, 28
Armani Collezioni 205
Arnasungaaq, Barnabus 406
Arnold 365
Art Deco
  advertising 13
  ceramics 75–7
  clocks 179–80
  compacts 202
  glass 247, 248, 250, 251
  lighting 270–1
  metalware 276
  posters 299
  sculpture 321–3
Art Nouveau
  ceramics 132
  clocks 178
  frames 294
  jewellery 261
  lighting 269
  postcards 298
Arte Vetraria Muranese
  (A.V.E.M.) 237, 238
Arts and Crafts
  ceramics 68
  clocks 178
  frames 294
  jewellery 258, 260–1, 263
  lighting 269
Artzybasheff, Boris 44
Asbury, Lenore 139, 140
Ashcroft, Jimmy 345
Ashevak, Kenojuak 406
ashtrays 341
Aspinal of London 208
Asprey and Co. 330
Aster 396
Atkin Brothers 332, 335
Atkins, Lloyd 242
atomisers 229
Attwell, Mabel Lucie 40,
  152, 167
Audemars Piguet 413
Aulenti, Gae 272
Austrian
  bronzes 31–5
  cigarette cases 337
  clocks 179
  compacts 202
  silver 331
Austro Hungarian militaria 280
autographs, rock & pop 312
automata 274, 383
automobilia 36–40
  motor racing 351
awards, rock & pop 310
Ayrton, H. 143

B
Baby Carriages of Liverpool
  382
Baccarat 247, 283–4
Bachmann 391
Backström, Monica 239
badges
  automobilia 38
  militaria 280
  sporting 352
bags 208–12

Bahlsen, H. 50
Bailey, David 309
Bailey, Lorna 114
Bakalowits 225
Bakelite
  jewellery 267, 268
  telephones 358
Baker, Bevans and Irwin 68
Balenciaga 204, 265
Ball, E. 89
ballpoint pens 292, 293
balls, golf 349
Bally's 16
Balzar-Kopp, Elfriede 157
Bamforth, Vic 253
Bandai 375
bangles 262, 268, 355
banks, mechanical 273
Barbini, Alfredo 235
Barlow, Arthur 94
Barlow, Hannah 94
barometers 320
Barovier, Ercole 235
Barovier & Toso 235
Barre 353
Barrère, Adrian 306
Barrois 185
Bartholdi, Frédéric Auguste
  409
Bartlett, Robert 299
Bassett-Lowke 388
Bateman, H.M. 337
Bateman, Hester 331, 410
Bateman, Peter and Ann 334
Bateman, William 331
Batterham, Richard 170
Baxter, Geoffrey 245–6
beadwork, tribal art 404
beakers
  antiquities 14
  glass 234
  silver 336
The Beano 184
Beard, Peter 170
bears
  Black Forest 401
  teddy bears 359–64
The Beatles 308
Beck, R. and J. 319
Becker 396
Bedin, Martine 272
beds 310
Bell, James Samuel 324
Bell, Quentin 164
belt buckles 203, 263, 268
belts 204
Benson, W.A.S. 276
Bentley 36, 39
Bergman, Franz 31–5
Berluti 208
Bernhard, Robert 196–7
Bertoia, Harry 323
Besouw, Guido van 253
Beswick 57–67
Bianconi, Fulvio 234
Bibby, Nick 323
Biggs, David B. 101
Bing 375, 387, 394, 396
Bing & Grøndahl 162
binoculars 319
birdcages 50
birds
  Beswick 65–6
  bronze 32–4
  glass 235, 237, 238, 241
  Meissen 116
  pin cushions 325–6
  Scandinavian ceramics
    147–8
  sculpture 323
  silver 332, 333

studio pottery 171, 175,
  177
weird & wonderful 409
Wemyss 155
West German stoneware 157
Birdsall, Laura 253
biscuit boxes 50, 332
biscuit tins 11
Bishop, Rachel 127
bisque dolls 185, 186–9
Black, Penny 150
Black Forest carvings 401
  canes 354–6
  clocks 178
  tobacco jars 341, 401
Black Ryden 162
Blahnik, Manolo 201
Blanckensee, S. & Son 324
Blancpain 413
Blickensderfer 357
Blixen, Karen 41
Bloch, Bernard 162
blue & white ceramics 17–18,
  68–70
BMC 362
Boa-Rodrigues & Company 38
boats, toy 366, 379, 394–5
Bohemian glass 252
Bolton, Beatrice 138
Bond, James 219, 304
Bongaard, Hermann 241
bookends 136, 162
books 41–6
  automobilia 39
  children's books 44–6
  first editions 41–3
  rock & pop 308
Boots Pure Drug Co. 324
Borské Sklo 225
Bossons, Emma 90, 130
Boswell, Tim 253
Bottega Veneta 208
bottles 27, 222
Bouchaud, Michel 299
Bough, John 328
Boullemier, A. 117
Boullemier, Lucien Emile 117
Boulton, Enoch 75, 164
Bouraine, Marcel-André 321
Bourne, Henry 47
Bourne, Victoria 110
Bourne Denby 163
Bowen, Dylan 170
bowls
  antiquities 14
  Carlton Ware 77
  Chinese ceramics 17,
    19–20
  Clarice Cliff 79, 80, 83–5
  Coalport 89
  glass 226, 227, 229, 235,
    237, 239–41, 243, 245,
    249, 252–4
  Japanese ceramics 26, 27
  Minton 117
  Poole Pottery 137
  Scandinavian ceramics
    147, 149
  silver 23
  studio pottery 170, 171,
    173, 176, 177
  treen 402
  tribal art 408
  Wedgwood 153
  Wemyss 155, 156
Bowman 396
boxes 47–50
  Chinese ceramics 19
  Coalport 89
  glass 226, 247, 250
  silver 332, 336, 348
  snuff boxes 330, 341,
    398–400

tea caddies 47
Tunbridge ware 402
boxing 346
boxwood carvings 24
bracelets 262, 267–8
Bradbury, Arthur 137
Bragin, A.S. 317
Braham, E.F. 294
Brangwyn, Frank 88
Brannam, C.H. 162
brass
  candlesticks 276
  clocks 307
  dog collars 276
  doorstops 277
  trench art 276
  vesta cases 276
Brau, Casimir 36
Breitling 413
Bretby Art Pottery 162
Brideshead 255
Bridge, David 332
Brigden, Alison 150
Brindley, D. 98
Bristol glass 315, 318
Britains 380–1
British National Dolls 190
British United Toy
  Manufacturing Co. 362
bronze
  Austrian 31–5
  candlesticks 278
  car mascots 36
  Chinese 24
  desk sets 278
  doorstops 277
  Japanese 30
  lamp bases 278
  medals 345, 353
  picture frames 278
  sculpture 321–3
brooches 258–9, 264, 266
Brook & Son 334
Brooker, Teresa 93
Brown, Harry 136
Brown, Margaret Wise 44
Brown, Palmer 44
Brownett, Abraham 315
Browning, John 319
Bru Bébé 185
Brunhoff, Jean de 44
Bub, Karl 365
Buchan, John 41
Buckle, Claude 299
buckles 203, 263, 268
Buddy L 375
Bunnykins 103
Bura, Bob 385
Bura & Hardwick 375
Burberry 205, 208
Burham, Jeremy 218
Burmantofts 71–4
Burne-Jones, Edward 166
Burnett, W.R. 41
Burton, Virginia Lee 44
Bush 357
busts, ceramic 132, 135
Butler, Frank 94
buttons 155, 203
Buzzi, Tomaso 234

C
cabinets, table 402
caddy spoons 333
Caiger-Smith, Alan 170
calendars, advertising 13
Callow, Thomas and Sons 338
cameo brooches 258
cameras 51–2
Canadian typewriters 357
candle boxes 48
candlesticks

INDEX

bronze 278
ceramic 142
Clarice Cliff 88
copper 276
glass 241
Ruskin Pottery 146
silver 336
Wemyss 156
canes 53–6
Canon 51
Cantagalli 162
Cantonese fans 200
Capewell, Will 243
Cappellin & Co. 237
caps, sporting 343, 354
card cases 329
Carder, Frederick 242
Cardew, Michael 170
Carette 365, 394
Carlier, Émile 321
Carlton Ware 75–7
carpets 220
Carron Company 409
cars
  automobilia 36–40
  mascots 36–7, 350
  motor racing 351
  pedal cars 40
  toy 8, 365–8, 370–3, 375–8
Carter, Truda 136
Carter & Co. 9–10
Cartier 289
  belts 204
  cigarette lighters 340
  clocks 180
  handbags 208
  jewellery 261, 263
  pencils 289
  sunglasses 203
  vanity cases 214
  wristwatches 413
Cartlidge, George 165
carvings see treen & carvings;
  sculpture
Cary 320
cast iron see iron
Castel, Raoul Eric 299
casters, ceramic 70
Castiglioni, Achille and Pier 271
Caulden 162
ceiling lights 271, 272
Céline 208
celluloid dolls 190
censers 24
centrepieces 88, 336
Century 21 Toys 384
ceramics 57–177
  Bernard Moore 132
  Beswick 57–67
  blue & white 68–70
  Burmantofts 71–4
  Carlton Ware 75–7
  Charles Vyse 151
  Chinese ceramics 17–23
  Clarice Cliff 78–88
  Coalport 89
  Cobridge 90
  De Morgan tiles 91
  Dennis Chinaworks 92–3
  Doulton 94–5
  Fornasetti 221
  Fulper 106
  George Ohr 133–4
  Goldscheider 107–9
  Japanese 25–8
  Kevin Francis/Peggy
    Davies 110
  Lenci 111
  Lladró 112–13
  Lorna Bailey 114
  Martin Brothers 115
  Meissen 116
  Minton 117–18

Moorcroft 119–31
Parkinson Pottery 135
Poole Pottery 136–8
Rookwood 139–40
Roseville 141
Royal Crown Derby 142
Royal Doulton 96–105
Royal Worcester 143
Ruskin Pottery 144–6
Scandinavian 147–9
  sporting 348, 350
  studio pottery 170–7
  tribal art 405
Troika 150
Wade 152
Wedgwood 153
Wemyss 154–6
West German stoneware
    157–61
Chad Valley 190, 362
chambersticks 73
champagne flutes 336
champagne swizzle sticks 278
Chance, W.M. 62
chandeliers 271, 272
Chandler, Raymond 41
Chanel 209
  belts 204
  clothes 205
  costume jewellery 263,
    265, 267
  handbags 209
character jugs 100–2, 385
Character Novelty Co. 190
chargers
  Carlton Ware 77
  Clarice Cliff 87, 88
  cloisonné 29
  Cobridge 90
  Dennis Chinaworks 93
  Doulton 94
  Japanese ceramics 28
  Minton 117
  Poole Pottery 136–8
Chase, Martha 190
chatelaines 327
Chaumet 263
Chestnut Miniatures 375
Chihuly, Dale 253
Child & Child 258, 263, 294
children's books 44–6
Chiltern 362–3
Chinese
  ceramics 17–23
  fans 199–200
  tea caddies 47
  works of art 23–4
Chiparus, Demetre H. 321
Chloe 209
Chopard 414
chronometers 320
Churchill, Sir Winston 41
cigar boxes 348
cigar cutters 341
cigarette boxes and cases
    336, 337
CIJ (Compagnie Industrielle du
  Jouet) 375, 378
Ciner 267
Cinque Ports Pottery 171
Ciro 266
Citroën 375
Clarke, Norman Stuart 253
Clichy 284
Cliff, Clarice 8, 78–88
clocks 178–80
  advertising 10
  ceramic 126
  glass 226
  railwayana 307
  sporting 355
clockwork toys 377–9

cloisonné 24, 29, 53
clothes 205–7
  militaria 281
  sporting 342, 347, 348,
    351, 352, 355
CMC 375
coal bins 276
Coalport 89
coasters 221, 401
coats 205–7, 310
Cobridge 90
Coca-Cola 222
cocktail glasses 252
cocktail shakers 250, 412
coffee pots 80
coffee services 79, 83, 85,
    87, 153
Colan, Gene 183
Cole, E.K. 357
Coleman, Rebecca 117
Colibri 340
Colinet, Claire Jeanne Roberte
    321
Colletta, Vince 182
Collins, Albert 299
Collins, Nic 171
Collis, Charles 163
Colt 282
Columbia Graphophone Co.
    275
comics & annuals 181–4
commemoratives 68, 153, 168
compacts 202
compasses 320
Compton Potters' Art Guild
    162
Constantinidis, Joanna 171
Continental
  cigarette cases 337
  jewellery 259
  lighting 269
  mechanical music 275
  scent bottles 318
  vesta cases 338
Conway Stewart 292
Cooper, Carl 171
Cooper, Susie 168
Cope and Cutler 412
Copeland, W.T. & Sons 162
Coper, Hans 171
copper
  candlesticks 276
  letter racks 276
  pencils 291
  vases 276
Coppola e Toppo 265
Corfield 51
Corgi Toys 367–9
corkscrews 412
Coro 266
Corum 414
costume jewellery 265–8
Coudrill, Francis 385
Couper, James & Sons 247
Cousins, Joseph 276
Cowan, Sarah 254
Coyard 209
Coyne, Sallie 140
Cragstan 365, 376
Craighead and Kintz 269
Crane, Walter 163
cream jugs 332
creamware 68
cricket 347
Crisford & Norris 325, 333
Crolly 190
Crooks, Bob 253
Crosby, F. Gordon 36
Crown Devon 164, 169
cufflinks 203
Culver, Edwin 327
Cuneo, Terence 299
cups

Minton 117
  see also coffee services
Czech
  ceramics 169
  glass 223–5
  jewellery 268
  paperweights 285

D
Dadd, Caroline 101–2
Dahl, Roald 44
Dakon, Stephan 108, 109, 166
Danelectro 256
Danish see Scandinavian
Dapol 220
Darby, Gavin 310
Dartington 247
Dasent, Tony 171
Dashwood, Geoffrey 323
Daum 247
Davenport 68, 198
Davenport, Anji 130
Davidson, Peter Wylie 178
Davies, Henry Clifford 337
Davies, Iestyn 253
Davies, Peggy 110
Davis, Derek 171
Davis, Harry 143
Dawson, Stewart and Co. 329
Day, Lewis 178
De Morgan, William 91
de Waal, Edmund 171
Deakin & Francis 202, 294
Deakin and Sons 325
decanters 160, 225, 241, 243
Décorchement, François-Émile
    247
Degué 270
Della Robbia 163
Delle Site, Domenico 300
Dennis Chinaworks 92–3
DEP 185
DePalma, Tony 284
Depose, C.M. 179, 355
desk lamps 272
desk sets 278
Devez 247
Devlin, Stuart 333, 336
Di Fausto, Florestano 300
diamond jewellery 258, 259,
    261–3
Dickens, Charles 41
Diederich, William Hunt 277
Diers, Ed 139
Dietz 38
Dietz, Heinz Theo 158
Dinky Toys 8, 370–4
dinner services, dolls' 198
Dior, Christian 201, 209, 265–7
dioramas, dolls' 197
dishes
  blue & white 68
  Chinese ceramics 17, 18,
    20, 22
  Clarice Cliff 85
  cloisonné 29
  glass 224
  Japanese ceramics 25,
    27, 28
  Minton 117
  Moorcroft 126
  studio pottery 170–2
Ditko, Steve 183
dog collars 276
Dolce & Gabbana 204
Doll & Cie 396
dolls 185–93, 405
dolls' dioramas 197
dolls' furniture 198
dolls' houses 194–6
dominoes 386
Donaldson, Robert 64

D'Onofrio, Jim 284
doorstops 277
Dorfi (Albert Dorfinant) 306
Doulton 94–105
  see also Royal Doulton
Doyle, A. Conan 41
Dresser, Christopher 247
dresses 205–7
Dreyfous, E. 332
drinking glasses 243, 248
DuBois 414
Dubuis, Roger 414
Dudson 163
Dulac, Edmund 44
Dumenil, Charles 55
dummies, ventriloquist 385
dummy boards 402
Dunderdale, Mabson & Labron
    282
Dunhill
  briefcases 210
  cigarette lighters 339–40
  cufflinks 203
  pens 292
  photograph frames 294
Dupont, S.T. 292, 340

E
earrings 263, 265
earthenware see ceramics
Eberl 397
Edison 275
Edward and Son 289
Effanbee 385
eggs, silver 336
Egyptian jewellery 259
Ekco 357
Eker, Anna Greta 268
Elliott, F.W. 180
Elmer, Violet 75
Elzingre, Edouard 300
Emanuel, Max & Co. 163
Emery, Edwina 348
Emmanuel, L. 329
enamel
  badges 280
  cigarette cases 337
  cloisonné 24, 29, 53
  compacts 202
  frames 294
  jewellery 258–61
  pencils 286, 288–91
  scent bottles 317
  signs 9–13
  thimbles 327
  vesta cases 338
Englund, Eva 240
Ens, Karl 163, 355
epergnes 401
Epiphone 256
equestrian sports 348
Erickson, Ruth 165
Ericsson, L.M. & Co. 357
Erskine, James 410
Etruscan style jewellery 262
etuis 320, 327
Eudel, Jacques 201
Evaluardjuk, Henry 406
Evans of America 202
Everett, Bill 183
ewers
  Burmantofts 74
  cloisonné 24
  Coalport 89
  Moorcroft 128
Exoto 376
eyes, prosthetic 409

F
FADAP 363
Fadini, Ugo 377
faience 71–4

famille rose 19–20
fans 199–200
Fantoni, Marcello 163
Farnell 363
fashion 201–14
    accessories 201–4
    clothes 205–7
    handbags 208–12
    trunks 213–14
Fender 256
Fendi 203, 210
Fenton, Harry 100
fern pots 78, 80, 86
Ferris wheels 396, 397
Feure, Georges de 248
Fiddes Watt, A.G. 152
Fielding's 164
figures
    advertising 11, 13, 77
    Britains 380–1
    bronze 31–2
    car mascots 36–7
    Charles Vyse 151
    Chinese ceramics 20, 22
    Clarice Cliff 88
    Coalport 89
    film & television 215–16,
       218, 220
    Goldscheider 107–9
    Katzhütte 166
    Kevin Francis/Peggy Davies
       110
    Lenci 111
    lighting 270, 271
    Lladró 112–13
    Meissen 116
    Parkinson Pottery 135
    pencils 288, 290, 291
    Royal Doulton 96–9
    Scandinavian ceramics 147,
       149
    sculpture 321–3
    sporting 347, 355
    studio pottery 174
    toys 384
    tribal art 403–5, 407
    ventriloquist dummies 385
    Wade 152
    Wedgwood 153
    weird & wonderful 409
    West German stoneware 157
    see also animals; birds
film & television 215–20
    posters 304–5
    'Star Wars' 215–17
Finch, Ray 172
Fine Art Models 391
Finescale Locomotive Co. 391
Finnish see Scandinavian
fire grenades 222
first editions 41–3
Fischer, Vilhelm Theodor 147
fish, taxidermy 356
Flagg, James Montgomery 306
flags, sporting 350
flambé ceramics 104–5
flasks
    antiquities 14
    automobilia 39
    Burmantofts 72
    glass 224
    West German stoneware 161
Fleming, Ian 42
Fletcher, Harry 163
Flint, Keith 310
floor lamps 271
Flos 271
Flygfors 241
Fog, Astrid 264
Fog and Mørup 271
Foley 167, 178
folk art, treen 53
Fontana Arte 271

football 342–5
football tables 16
footbaths 68
Forest Toys 384
Fornasetti 221
Forrester, George 349
Forster, E.M. 41
Forsyth, Gordon 163
Fountain, Desmond 323
fountain pens 292–3
Fournier, Robert 172
Fox, George 331, 332
frames 278, 294
Francis, Kevin 110
Franck, Kaj 241
Fraser, Norman 300
Fratelli Toso 236
Freeman, Henry Charles 294
French
    advertising 10, 12
    clocks 179–80
    Dinky Toys 373–4
    dolls 185–7, 189
    lighting 270
    mechanical music 275
    militaria 281, 282
    pencils 290
    posters 299
    scent bottles 317
    sewing 327
    silver 332
    snuff boxes 398
    toys & games 382, 383, 386
    vesta cases 338
Frew, Adam 154
Frith, David 172
Frolio 357
Frost, Sir Terry 137
fruit bowls 69, 70, 85, 117
Fueller, Paul 274
Fugere, Henri 352
Fulham Pottery 164, 175
Fulper 106
fur coats 207
furniture, dolls' 198

G
Gallé, Émile 164, 248
Galli, Stan 300
Galliano, John 205
Gambeauche 109
games see toys & games
Gardner, James 356
Garrard, Robert 410
Garrard, Sebastian 334
Garrard & Co. 348
Garrud, Francis 327
Gaudin, Louis (Zig) 306
Gaultier, Jean Paul 205
Gaunt, J.R. 38
German
    boxes 50
    clocks 178
    compacts 202
    corkscrews 412
    dolls 186–9, 198
    dolls' houses 194–6
    mechanical music 274
    militaria 281
    toys 384, 396, 397
    trains 387–8
    typewriters 357
    West German stoneware
       157–61
Ghion, Christian 237, 254
Gibson 257
Gibson, Philip 129
Gibson, William 349
Giefer, Roland 158
Giefer-Bahn, Klotilde 158
Gilbert, Walter 251
Gillies, Stephen 254

ginger jars 19, 75, 128
Girard-Perregaux 414
glass 222–55
    antiquities 14–15
    bottles 222
    car mascots 37
    Czech 223–5
    Isle of Wight 231
    Lalique 226
    Loetz 227–9
    Mdina 230
    Monart 232–3
    Murano 234–8
    paperweights 226, 242,
       283–5
    prosthetic eyes 409
    Scandinavian 8, 239–41
    scent bottles 313–18
    snuff bottles 23
    Steuben 242
    Stevens & Williams 243
    studio glass 253–5
    Webb 244
    Whitefriars 245–6
Glass, S. 333
globes 320
glove boxes 50
gloves 204
    boxing gloves 346
Gmundner Keramik 164
goblets 245, 336
Godard, A. 321
Goebel, Kurt 109, 169
gold
    antiquities 15
    canes 53, 56
    jewellery 258, 260–4
    lighters 339–40
    medals 345
    pencils 286–7, 289–91
    pens 292–3
    thimbles 327
    wristwatches 413–17
Goldberg, Carl 225
Golding, Richard P. 254
Golding, William 43
Goldscheider 107–9
Goldsmith of Cincinnati 346
Goldsmiths & Silversmiths Co.
    214, 294
golf 349–50
gongs 401
Goodwin, Kerry 129, 162
Goss, W.H. 164
Göttschalk, Moritz 194
Gotz 191
Gourlay, James 349
Gourlay, William & John 349
Goyard 214
Grahame, Kenneth 43, 44
gramophones 275
Graphophone 275
gravy boats 350
Graydon-Stannus, Elizabeth 248
Grays Pottery 168
Gredington, Arthur 57–61, 63–7
Greenaway, Kate 313
Gregory, Mary 252, 315
Greiffenhagen, Maurice 300
Griffiths, E.J. 98
Griggs, W.B. 356
Grueby 165
Grut, Vivian Jeanne 167
Gucci 201, 210
Guerbe 301
Guillerme et Chambron 180
Guinness 77
guitars 256–7
Gundka 357
Gunthermann 378–9
Gustavsberg 147
Gyokuri 26

H
Hadeland 241
Hagenauer, Carl 179
hair clips 263
hairwork jewellery 260
Hald, Edvard 240
Hallam, Albert 61, 65–7
Hamilton 414
Hammerborg, Jo 271
Hammond, Creak and Co. 243
Hammond, Henry 172
Hancock & Sons 165
handbags 208–12
Handley, A. 89
Hanna, Ashraf 172
Harper, William K. 98, 101
Harrach 223
Harradine, L. 96–7
Harris, Jonathan 254, 318
Harris, Michael 230–1
Harrods 180
Harrow, John 406
Harwin 191
Hasbro 215
Haskell, Miriam 266, 267
Haskins, Gwen 137, 138
Hassall, John 36
hat pins 335
Hatchard, Anne 136, 137
Hawksworth, Eyre & Co. 331
Hayes, Peter 173
Hayes, Shirley 90
Haywards 222
Heckert, Fritz 248
Heinrich Handwerck 186
Heller, Paul 247
helmet plates 280
helmets
    militaria 281
    sporting 351
Hemingway, Ernest 43
Henk, Mark 100
Hennell, Robert 331, 410
Hennell, Samuel 410
Henry, Paul 301
Hentschel, William 140
Herman, Sam 254
Hermès 201, 204, 210, 414
Herold, Peter 147
Heron, François 201
Hertwig and Co. 166
Higgins, Francis and Sons 331
Hildebrand & Schramm 319
Hildebrandt, Tim & Greg 305
Hilditch, Paul 130
Hill, Mike 218
Hillcox, J.H. 329
Hilliard and Thomason 329
Himstedt, Annette 191
Hine, Margaret 'Margi' 173
Hobé 266
hock glasses 243
Hogan, James 245
Holder, Margaret 137
Holmegaard 241
honey pots 86, 332
Hooper & Son 320
Hornby 389
Horner, Charles 261, 335
horses
    equestrian sports 348
    rocking horses 382
hot water bottles 163
Howe, Elias 327
Howell, Henry & Co. 338
Howlett, W. 356
Howson 165
Hubley 383
Hudnut, Richard 202
Hudson's Soap 11
Huggins, Vera 95

Hughes-Lübeck, Amanda
    62, 64
humidors 213
Huntley & Palmer 11
Hussmann, H. 224
Hutton, William and Sons 334

I
Iittala 241
Imari 27
Imperial 357
incense burners 106
Indian
    jewellery 261, 262
    medals 279
inkwells
    bronze 33–5
    car mascots 37
    Fornasetti 221
    glass 245
    silver 332, 335
    sporting 347
International Watch Co. 414
Inuit tribal art 406
iron
    doorstops 277
    signs 307
    weathervanes 277
Isle of Wight glass 231
Italian
    fans 199
    lighting 272
    scent bottles 318
Ives 379
Ives, Blakeslee & Co. 273
ivory
    canes 53–5
    dominoes 386
    fans 199–200
    tribal art 406

J
jackets 205–7, 281, 355
Jackson, M. 110
Jacob & Co. 414
Jacopi, Abele 111
jade 23, 203
Jaeger-LeCoultre 180, 415
Jakks Pacific 220
Janus Company 218
Japanese
    ceramics 25–8
    dolls 190
    fans 199
    toys 365–6, 376, 393
    works of art 29–30
Jaques 386
jardinières
    Burmantofts 72
    Chinese ceramics 19
    Clarice Cliff 83
    Fulper 106
    Minton 117
    Moorcroft 127
    Poole Pottery 138
    Roseville 141
    Wemyss 156
jars
    Carlton Ware 75
    Chinese ceramics 19
    Dennis Chinaworks 92, 93
    glass 225, 242
    Moorcroft 128
    Rookwood 140
    Royal Worcester 143
    Ruskin Pottery 144, 146
    studio pottery 170, 171
    tobacco jars 341, 350
    West German stoneware
       160, 161
Jasperware 153
Jennens & Bettridge 50

Jennings, Walter 276
Jensen, Georg 264, 334
Jensen, Lauritz 162
Jensen, Sven Aage 149
Jep Darrack 365
Jesson Birkett & Co. 269
Jeu De Course 386
jewellery 258–68
   antiquities 15
   bracelets 262, 267–8
   brooches 258–9, 264, 266
   costume jewellery 265–8
   earrings 263, 265
   Georg Jensen 264
   necklaces 15, 260–1, 264,
      267–8, 400
   pendants 260–1
   rings 15, 262–3, 268, 336
Jogetsu 30
Johansen, Einar 149
Johnson, Crockett 45
Johnson, Thomas 332
Jomaz 265, 267
Jones, Don 173
Jones, Jenifer 173
Jones, Kate 254
Jones, Smith 335
Jones, W. and S. 320
Jones & Crompton 325
Joseff of Hollywood 266, 267
JRD Miniatures 376
jugs
   antiquities 15
   Burmantofts 71
   character jugs 100–2, 385
   Clarice Cliff 79, 80, 82–4, 86
   Dennis Chinaworks 92
   glass 252
   Lorna Bailey 114
   Moorcroft 124, 130
   Ruskin Pottery 144
   silver 332
   sporting 350
   Toby jugs 168
   Wemyss 155
   West German stoneware
      157–61
jukeboxes 274
Jumeau 186–7
Jung, Tom 304

K
Kage, Wilhelm 147
Kähler Keramik 147
Kalff, Louis Christian 271
Kaltikov, Ivan 330
Kämmer & Reinhardt 187
Katzhütte 166
Kayzerzinn 355
Kefford, Darren 218
Kelvin, White & Hutton 320
Kenner 215
Keramos Pottery 166, 169
Kestner 187–8
Keswick School of Industrial
   Art 276
Killarney ware 49
Killburn, Simone 150
King, Jessie M. 203
King, Leonard 71
Kinkozan 25
Kirby, Jack 182, 183
Knoll and Pregizer 266
Knox, Archibald 334
Kodak 51
Kohler, Robert 180
koros 25, 72
Kors, Michael 205
Koshida 26
Kosta 8, 239
Kosta Boda 239
Kralik 224

Kramer 265
Kruse, Kathy 191
KTM 392
Kuramochi 379
Kutchinsky 263
Kwan Ho 23
Kyhn, Knud 148
Kyser & Rex 273

L
labels, wine 410–11
lacquer
   fans 199
   screens 211
   snuff boxes 399
   tea caddies 47
Lacroix, Christian 265
Lacroix, Maurice 415
Lalique 226
Lambart, Alfred 301
lamp bases
   bronze 278
   ceramic 126, 129, 141,
      150, 165
   Doulton 94
   glass 233
   see also lighting
Landeck, S. 326
Lang, Andrew 45
Lang, Faust 152
Langley, Siddy 255
Lantiner Cherie 190
Laurence, Sturgis 140
Laverick, Tony 173
Lawrence 301
Layton, Peter 255
Lea & Co. 328
Leach, David 174
Leach, Janet 173
Leach, John 174
Lebrun, Gioacchino 410
Lee, Stan 182
Leeper, Sian 128
Leete, Alfred 306
LEGO 'Star Wars' 217
Legras 248
Lehmann 366, 376, 383
Leica 51–2
Leitz, E. 319
Lejeune, Augustine & Emile 37
Lejeune, Louis 37, 350
Lenci 111, 191
Lenhart, Franz 301
Lennon, John 308
letter boxes 48
letter racks 155, 276
Leuchars 290
Levi, Samuel M. 325
Levi & Salaman 318, 325, 327
Levinger, Heinrich 327
Liberty & Co. 203, 261
Lichfield, Patrick 311
Liddard, Steve 310
Liebenthron, Gerhard 159
lighters 339–40
lighting 269–72
   automobilia 38
   glass shades 249
   railwayana 307
   see also lamp bases
Limoges 268
Linares, Henri de 201
Lincoln, Elizabeth 140
Lindner, Doris 143, 348
Lindstrand, Vicke 8, 239
Lines, G. & J. 194–5, 383
Lines Juvenile 382
Linley, David 294
Linwood, Matthew 328, 410
Lionel 392
liqueur sets 225
Live Aid 309

Lladró 112–13
Lobmeyr 248
lockets 260–1
Lockwood Brothers 282
Loco Glass 254
Loetz 224, 227–9, 249
Logan, Maurice 301
Lone Star 219
Longines 415
Lorenzl, Josef 107–9, 270,
   321–2
Loro Piana 206
Lovatt, Vicky 128
Love Moschino 206
Lowe, Sue 150
Lowerdown Pottery 174
Lüber, J. 271
Lucas 38, 39
Lumitron 272
Lundberg, Theodor 149
Lundin, Ingeborg 240
Lund's 412
Lupton, Edith 94
Luther 257
Lutken, Per 241
Lyster, Charles & Son 329
Lyta, Joanasie 406
Lytras, N. 353
Lyttleton, David 67

M
Mcarthy, Frank 305
McCoy 392
McDermott, Elizabeth 140
MacDonald, George 45
McDonald, Margaret 139
Macfarlane, Alasdair 301
McGinnis, Robert 305
McGowan, Laurence 175
Machin, Arnold 153
McLaren, Malcolm 206
McLeod, Rory 92–3
McLoughlin Bros. 386
Madoura 175
Madsen, Theodor 147, 148
Madziva, Obediar 310
Maer, Mitchel 267
majolica 118
Malayan medals 279
Malcolm, Allister 255
Malinowski, Arno 264
Malone, Jim 174
Malone, Kate 174
Maltby, John 174
Maltese silver 410
Mamiya 52
mannequins, display 409
MAP 364
Mappin & Webb 269, 332
Margold, Emanuel Josef 50
Märklin 198, 378, 383, 388,
   394, 397
Marquis, Richard 255
Marseille, Armand 188
Marshall, William 'Bill' 175
Martens, Dino 236, 237
Martin 383
Martin, Benjamin 320
Martin Brothers 115
Martinelli Luce 272
Marvel Comics 181–3
Marx 219, 366, 384
mascots, car 36–7
masks, tribal art 403, 408
Maslankowski, Alan 61, 66, 67
Mastrogiannis, Peter 353
match strikers 341
Matchbox Toys 376
Matthews, H. 329
Mauchline ware 400
Mavros, Patrick 332

Mdina 230
meat plates 17, 68
Meccano 376, 378, 383
mechanical banks 273
mechanical music 274–5
medals
   militaria 279
   sporting 345, 347, 350, 353
meerschaum pipes 341
Meissen 116, 167
Melbourne, Colin 67
Melting Pot Glassworks 255
Memphis 272
menu card holders 334
Mercury Models 376
Merriott, Jack 301
Merrythought 364
Merton Abbey 91
Messel, Oliver 272
metalware 276–8
   Chinese 24
   Japanese 30
   see also bronze; silver
Metropolitan-Vickers 357
Mettes, Franciscus J.E. 302
Metz, Joachim 201
Meyer 52
Meyr's Neffe 225
micro-mosaic jewellery 260
microphones 358
microscopes 319
Miki, Andy 406
militaria 279–82
   medals 279
   weapons 282
Millar & Lang 297
Mills, Nathaniel 314, 328–30
Millville 284
Milne, A.A. 45
Milton Bradley 386
miniatures, Moorcroft 121
Minton 117–18
mirrors 9–13, 276, 294
Missoni 206
Mitchell, Robert & Co. 330
Miu Miu 211
moccasins 404
Moen, Louis 302
Mohr & Krauss 379, 397
Moko 195
Monart 232–3
Moncrieff Glassworks 232–3
money banks 152, 273
money boxes 162, 402
Mont Joye 248
Montblanc 292–3
Montegrappa 293
Moorcroft 119–31
Moorcroft, Lise B. 131
Moore, Bernard 132
Moore, Fred 94, 105
Mordan, S. and Co.
   page markers 334
   pencils 286–9
   pin cushions 325
   scent bottles 313
   vesta cases 338
Morlon, A. 351
Morris, Tony 138
Morris and Co. 166
Moser 50, 224
mother-of-pearl
   boxes 49
   etuis 327
   fans 200
   snuff boxes 330
   tea caddies 47
motor racing 351
MTH 392
Mucha, Alphonse 298
Muchelney Pottery 174
mugs
   blue & white 68

Clarice Cliff 85
Wedgwood 153
Wemyss 156
Mühlendyck, Johannes 161
Mühlendyck, Wim 160–1
Muir, Arthur G. 302
Mulberry 211, 214
Muller, Franck 415
Mullins, Edwin Roscoe 347
Murano 234–8, 272
Murphy, Doug 310
Murray, Keith (ceramicist)
   153, 243
Murray, Keith (toy trains) 391
Murrle Bennett & Co. 261
music
   guitars 256–7
   mechanical 274–5
   musical boxes 274
   rock & pop 308–12
mustard pots 331
Myatt, W.J. & Co. 326
Mycro 52

N
Napier 265
napkin rings 333
Nasogaluak, Bill 406
Nason, Aldo 237
Native Americans
   jewellery 261
   tribal art 404–5
navigation 320
Neale, William 294
necklaces 260–1
   antiquities 15
   costume jewellery 267–8
   Georg Jensen 264
   tartanware 400
Negretti & Zambra 320
Negro Travelers' Green Book 43
Nekola, Joseph 166
Nekola, Karel 155, 156
netsuke 30
Neue Munchner Kinderpuppen
   191
Newbound, Frank 306
newspapers, sporting 346
Nichols, Maria Longworth 139
Nicole Frères 274
Nielson, Kai 147
Nikon 52
Noad, Stephen 410
Noah's Arks 384
Noke, Charles 96, 98, 100,
   103–5
Nomura 365
Norbury, Ian 409
Norman, Brian 375
Norwegian see Scandinavian
Nossiter, Doris 258
Novy Bor 225
Nugent, Frank 218
nutcrackers 402
Nuutajörvi Notsjo 241
Nymolle 147

O
Obediar Creations 310
Oceania tribal art 407–8
octants 320
Ohr, George 133–4
Öhrström, Edvin 240
oil lamps 15, 269
Okra 254
Oliver 357
Oliver, Kermit 201
Olympic Games 352–3
Omas 293
Omega 364, 415–16
O'Neill, Terry 346
Onoto Magna 293

Oonark, Jessie 406
Orrefors 240
Orwell, Graham 59, 67
Osiris Studio 253
Ovchinnikov, Pavel 316
Owen & Boon 329

P
Padgett & Braham 348
page markers 334
Painlevé, Jean 268
paintings, automobilia 40
Palitoy 216
Palmer & Co. 269
Palmqvist, Sven 240
panels, Chinese ceramics 19, 20
Panton, Verner 271
pap boats 68
paper knives 334
paperweights
   ceramic 142
   glass 226, 242, 283–5
papier mâché
   automata 383
   boxes 50
   dolls 185
   pencils 290
   ventriloquist dummies 385
Parker 293
Parkinson Pottery 135
Parsons, P. 98–9
Patek Philippe 204, 416
Pathé 275
Pavely, Ruth 136, 137
Peacock 364
pearlware 68
Pears, Dion 40
Pedigree 192
Pemberton, Samuel 328
pendants 260–1
Pendragon 412
pens & writing 286–93
   pencils 286–91
   pens 292–3
Pentax 52
penwork 400
pepper pots 331
perfume bottles see scent bottles
Perichon, Henry 266
Perry & Co. 379
Persian cigarette cases 337
Petersen, Armand 148
Phalibois 383
Phillips, Clarence Coles 306
Phipps and Robinson 410–11
phonographs 275
photograph frames 294
photographs
   cameras 51–2
   postcards 295–7
   rock & pop 308, 309, 311
   sporting 342–3, 346–8,
      350, 351
Pianon, Alessandro 238
Picasso Pottery 175
picture frames 278, 294
Piel Frères 268
Pierre, Roger Jean 266
pin cushions 324–6
pin stands 335
pinball machines 16
Pintel 364
Piper, John 175
pipes 341
pistols 282
pitchers
   blue & white 68, 70
   Scandinavian ceramics 147
   studio pottery 175
Plank, Ernst 397
plaques
   Burmantofts 71, 72

Carlton Ware 77
Clarice Cliff 78, 82, 83
   militaria 280
   Minton 117
   Poole Pottery 138
   Royal Worcester 143
   sporting 351
   studio pottery 174
   Troika 150
   West German stoneware 157
plates
   blue & white 68, 69
   Chinese ceramics 17
   Clarice Cliff 78–9, 81, 86, 87
   Fornasetti 221
   Japanese ceramics 26
   Minton 117
   Moorcroft 126, 130
   Wemyss 155
Platt, Warren 103
platters
   blue & white 69
   Chinese ceramics 17
   studio pottery 170, 173
Pleydell-Bouverie, Katharine 175
Plichta, Jan 166
Plusczok, Heidi 191, 192
Poli, Flavio 235, 237
polyphons 274
pond yachts 395
Pongratz, Elisabeth 191
Ponti, Gio 234
Poole Pottery 136–8
porcelain see ceramics
Portobello 166
Porzellanfabrik Mengersgereuth 188
Poschinger 249
post boxes 409
postcards 295–8
   rock & pop 308, 312
posters 299–306
   advertising 9
   film 304–5
   rock & pop 308
   sporting 346
   travel 299–303
pot pourri jars
   Rookwood 140
   Royal Worcester 143
   Ruskin Pottery 144, 146
Potter, Beatrix 45
Potter, Harry 8, 45–6, 220
pottery see ceramics
powder boxes 250
Powell, Harry 245
Powell, James & Sons 245
Powolny, Michael 168
Prada 211
preserve pots 77, 79, 84
Pringle, Robert 325
programmes
   rock & pop 311, 312
   sporting 343–4, 352, 354
Prutscher, Otto 225
Pucci, Emilio 206
Pye 275
Pye, William 323

Q
quaiches 156
Quezal 249

R
Rade, Max 248
Radi, Giulio 237
radios 358
Ragan, Leslie 302
railwayana 307
   cigarette cases 337
   posters 299–302
   toy trains 387–93

Ramos, Antonio 113
Ramsden, Omar 261
Ramsden & Carr 261, 263,
   333, 334
Ransome, Arthur 43
Rasanen, K. 353
Ravilious, Eric 153
Rawlings, Charles 411
Ray-Ban 203
RCA 357
Read, Alfred 138
records, rock & pop 311–12
Reichert, C. 319
Reidmeister (August) Studio 382
Reilly, E.M. & Co. 282
Reinicke, Peter 116
Remington 357
Retrosi, Virgilio 302
Revivalist jewellery 260
revolvers 282
Reynolds, F.B. 337
Rhythm and Hues Studio 220
Richards, J.M. 43
Richards & Brown 331
Richardson's 249
Ridge, S. 99
Rie, Lucie 175
Rigon, Roberto 176
Riker Bros. 260
Riley, Harold 339
Rindskopf 249
rings 15, 262–3, 268, 336
Robb, William 333
Rock & Graner 249
rock & pop 308–12
   The Beatles 308
   guitars 256–7
   Keith Flint 310
   Live Aid 309
rocking horses 382
Rodica 202
Roland, Paris 322
Rolex 203
Rolls-Royce 37, 39
Romagnoli, Renzo 386
Romain Jerome 415
Roman antiquities 14–15
Rookwood 139–40
Rose, John 68
Rosenthal Studio 249
Roseville 141
Ross & Co. 52
Rothenbusch, Fred 139
Roullet & Decamps 379
Rousselet, Louis 265, 267
Rowling, J.K. 8, 45–6, 220
Royal Bonn 167
Royal Brierley 243
Royal Copenhagen 8, 147–9,
   167
Royal Crown Derby 142
Royal Doulton 96–105, 350
   Bunnykins 103
   character jugs 100–2
   figures 96–9
   flambé 104–5
Royal Dux 169
Royal Standard 357
Royal Worcester 143, 348
Roycroft 276
Ruckl 225
rugby 354
Ruhlmann, Émile Jacques 276
rulers 334
Ruocco, Chris 312
Rushbrook, Karlin 255
Rushton, Morris 164
Ruskin Pottery 144–6, 269
Russian
   canes 53, 56
   scent bottles 316, 317
   silver 330, 334

smoking 337, 338
Ryumin 30

S
Saino 37, 250
sabretaches 281
Saint Laurent, Yves 202,
   205, 266
St Louis 285
sake bottles 27
Sales, Harry 103
salt boxes 48
salt pots 88
Salto, Axel 149
Saltykov, Ivan 317
Salviati 254
Samson 167
Sandheim, Amy 333
Sandland, Edwin 156
Sands End Pottery 91
Sangster, Jimmy 218
Sassoon, Siegfried 43
Satsuma 25–6
saucer dishes 18, 171
Saunders, Cornelius
   Desormeaux 335
Saunders & Shepherd 316,
   317, 325
Savinsky, V. 316
Sax, Sara 139, 140
Scandinavian
   boxes 48
   ceramics 147–9
   glass 239–41
Scarpa, Carlo 234, 237
scarves 201–2
Scavini, Helen König 111
scent bottles 290, 313–18
   Isle of Wight 231
   Lalique 226
   Moorcroft 121
   Ruskin Pottery 144
Scheid, Georg Adam 331
Schiaparelli, Elsa 268
Schmidt, Bruno 188
Schneider 250, 319
Schoenau & Hoffmeister 189
Schoenner 397
Schuco 366, 379
Schulz, Charles M. 46
scientific instruments 319–20
Sciolari, Gaetano 272
scissors 276, 327
sconces 278
Scottish
   Mauchline ware 400
   silver 333, 410
   snuff boxes 398
screens, lacquer 211
scripts, film 218, 220
sculpture 321–3
   glass 242, 251, 254, 255
   Inuit 406
   studio pottery 173, 174
seals, glass 226
Sebastian of London 193
Secor, Jerome B. 273
Secretan 319
Seguso, Archimede 238, 267
Seguso Vetri d'Arte 237
Selby, Gwendoline 136
Selro 268
Sendak, Maurice 46
Seuss, Dr 46
sewing 324–7
sewing boxes 49, 402
sewing machines 327
SFBJ 189
Shackelford, Jan 193
Shackleton Toys 378
Shasta 366
Shaw, Thomas 328, 330

Shelley 167
Shepherd, James Francis
   Hollings 335
shirts
   rock & pop 312
   sporting 342, 347, 351, 355
shoes 204
signs
   advertising 9–13
   automobilia 40
   railwayana 307
silk postcards 298
silver 328–36
   boxes 332, 336, 348
   buckles 203
   caddy spoons 333
   canes 54–6
   card cases 329
   Chinese 23
   cigarette cases 337
   compacts 202
   cufflinks 203
   frames 294
   Japanese 30
   jewellery 258, 261, 263–6,
      268
   lighters 339, 340
   musical boxes 274
   napkin rings 333
   pencils 286–91
   pepper and mustard pots 331
   pin cushions 324–6
   scent bottles 313–18
   snuff boxes 330
   Stuart Devlin 336
   tea caddies 47
   vesta cases 329, 338
   vinaigrettes 328
   wine labels 410–11
Simeon, Harry 95
Simon & Halbig 186, 187, 189
Sindy dolls 192
Singer 327
Singleton, Benda & Co. 335
Sinnott, Joe 182
Sirota, Benny 150
Slaney, Nicola 90, 128
Slater, Walter 167
Slil, Kenneth 302
Sliman, George 400
Smith, Annie 163
Smith, Edward 330
Smith, Laura 302
Smith, Robin 255
Smith, W.H. 13
smoking 337–41
Snatt, Josiah 333
snuff bottles 17, 19, 23, 403
snuff boxes 330, 341, 398–400
soapstone 24
Soholm 149
solitaire 386
Solven, Pauline 255
South African medals 279
spelter, sculpture 320
Spencer, Browning & Rust 320
Spencer Edge 168
spice towers 399
spill vases 18, 163, 401
Spode 168
spoon racks 48
spoons, silver 333–4
sporting 342–5
   boxing 346
   cricket 347
   equestrian 348
   football 342–5
   golf 349–50
   motor racing 351
   Olympics 352–3
   rugby 354
   tennis 355
Spot-On 366

Stabler, Harold 136
Staffordshire pottery 68–70, 347
Stahl, Rudi 161
Stair, Julian 176
Staite-Murray, William 176
Stålhane, Carl-Harry 147
standard lamps 272
'Star Wars' 215–17, 305
steam toys 396–7
Steel, Kenneth 303
Steiff 193, 359–61, 364
stem cups 21
stereoscopic viewers 319
Steuben 242
Stevens, J. & E. Co. 273
Stevens & Brown Mfg. Co. 366
Stevens & Williams 243
Stevenson, Ralph 70
stick stands 72
Stickland, E.E. 137
Stickley Brothers 276
Stilnovo 272
Stockwell, E.H. 332
stoneware see ceramics
Storr, Paul 411
Stourbridge 249, 250
stoves, ceramic 72
straw work 30
strawberry sets 250
string boxes 48
Strode, Jackie 90
Stuart & Sons 250
studio glass 253–5
studio pottery 170–7
stuffed toys 359–64
suffragette postcards 297
sugar bowls 80, 84
sugar casters 124
sugar sifters
    Clarice Cliff 79, 81, 84, 85
    Lorna Bailey 114
suitcases 213–14
Summers, Pat 137
Sumner, George Heywood 276
sunglasses 203
Sunset Models 392
supper sets 68
Sussenguth, Gebruder 364
Sutcliffe, Clare 176
Suydam 393
Swatch 219
Swedish see Scandinavian
Swiss
    mechanical music 274
    wristwatches 415
swizzle sticks 278
swords 282
Sydenham, Guy 138
Sydney & Co. 326
symphonions 274
Synyer & Beddoes 294

T
Tabbelor, Robert 110
table lamps 270–2, 278
Tag Heuer 414
tankards 124, 160
tarot cards 386
tartanware 400
Tauschek, Otto 224
taxidermy 356
Taylor, Horace 303
Taylor, Joseph 333
Taylor, Leonard Campbell 299
Taylor, Stanley J. 100
Taylor, Sutton 176

Taylor, William Howson 145, 146
Taylor & Barrett 377, 384
Taylor-Tunnicliffe 350
tea caddies 18, 47, 160
tea cups, Minton 117
tea sets 80
teapots
    automobilia 40
    Chinese ceramics 22
    Clarice Cliff 78, 80, 86
    George Ohr 134
    glass 255
    Japanese ceramics 26
    Minton 118
    Royal Crown Derby 142
    Royal Doulton 103
    silver 23
    sporting 350
technology 357–8
teddy bears & stuffed toys 359–64
telephones 358
telescopes 55, 319
television see film & television
television sets 358
Ten Broek, Willem Frederik 303
tennis 355
Terrey, John 411
Theobald Bros 356
theodolites 319
thermometers 13
thimbles 327
Thompson, William II 328
Thomsen, Christian 148
Thornhill, W. 290
Thornton 349
Thorogood, S. 98
Tiffany, L.C. 251
Tiffany & Co. 203, 278, 290
Tiffany Studios 278
tiles
    advertising 9–10
    De Morgan 91
    Poole Pottery 137
    studio pottery 175
tin
    biscuit tins 11
    tinplate toys 365–6
    weathervanes 277
Tinworth, George 95
Tipp Co. 377
Tittensor, Harry 96, 97, 303
toast racks 335
tobacco jars 341, 350
Toby jugs 168
Toikka, Oiva 241
Tomschick, Franz 224
tongs, silver 334
Tongue, Graham 61, 62, 66
Tongue & Walker 329
Tonka Toys 377
toothpick boxes 332
torches, Olympic 352–3
tortoiseshell
    boxes 50
    canes 53
    fans 200
    scent bottle stands 318
    tea caddies 47
Toso, Aureliano 236
Toso, Ermanno 236
Tower 282
toys & games 365–97
    boats 394–5
    Britains 380–1
    clockwork 377–9
    games 386

other vehicles 375–7
pond yachts & model planes 395
rocking horses 382
'Star Wars' 215–16
steam 396–7
teddy bears & stuffed toys 359–64
tinplate 365–6
trains 387–93
ventriloquist dummies 385
trains
    toy 387–93
    see also railwayana
transfer-printed wares 68
travel posters 299–303
travelling boxes 49
Travers, P.L. 46
trays, ceramic 70, 77, 123, 154
treen & carvings 398–402
    Black Forest 401
    canes 53
    Mauchline ware 400
    snuff boxes 341, 398–400
Treidler, Adolph 303
trench art 276
Trendon 193
Tri-ang 377, 378
tribal art 403–8
Trifari 265, 268
Triumph 357
Troika 150
trophies, sporting 352
trunks 213–14
Tuchin, Boris 353
Tuffin, Sally 92–3, 126
tumblers, Clarice Cliff 85
Tunbridge ware 402
tureens 70, 85
Turnpenny, William & Edward 332
typewriters 357
Tyrolean snuff boxes 398

U
umbrella stands 221
umbrellas 56
Underhill, Craig 177
Unite, George 327, 411
Universal Studios 218
urns 106, 399

V
Vacchetti, Sandro 111
Val St Lambert 251
Valentien, Anna Maria 139
Valentino 206, 211
Valery 179
Vallien, Bertil 239
vanity cases 49, 214
vanity jars 242
vases
    Bernard Moore 132
    Burmantofts 71–3
    Carlton Ware 76
    Charles Vyse 151
    Chinese ceramics 18–21
    Clarice Cliff 8, 78–88
    cloisonné 24, 29
    Coalport 89
    Cobridge 90
    copper 276
    Dennis Chinaworks 92–3
    Doulton 94–5
    Fulper 106
    George Ohr 133–4

glass 8, 223–5, 227–37, 239–55
Grueby 165
Hancock & Sons 165
Japanese ceramics 25–8
Lorna Bailey 114
Martin Brothers 115
Minton 117
Moorcroft 119–31
Poole Pottery 136–8
Rookwood 139–40
Roseville 141
Royal Crown Derby 142
Royal Doulton 105
Ruskin Pottery 144–6
Scandinavian ceramics 147, 149
silver 23, 30
studio pottery 171–7
Troika 150
Wedgwood 153
Wemyss 156
West German stoneware 157–9, 161
Vaughton of Birmingham 353
Vauzelles, Christiane 201
Venini, Paolo 234
Venini & C. 234
Verart 251
Le Verre Français 269
Versace, Gianni 204, 234
Vertex 416
vesta cases 40, 276, 329, 338
Vienna, sculpture 323
vinaigrettes 313–15, 328
Vistosi 238
vitrines 50
Volkstedt 355
Vox 257
Vrba, Lawrence 267
Vuitton, Louis 202, 204, 212–13
Vyse, Charles 151

W
Wade 152
Wagner, Richard 46
Wain, Louis 163, 298
Walker, Jeff 255
Walker & Hall 326
wall masks 88, 109, 169
wall plaques see plaques
Wallace, Thomas 331
Wallace, U.K.C. 168
wallets 204
Walmsley, Joseph 71
Walsh Walsh, John 251–2
Walters, Annette 150
Ward, John 177
Warhol, Andy 249
waste bins 221
watches 219
water pots 22
wax dolls 185
weapons 282
weathervanes 277
Webb, Thomas & Sons 244, 313, 317, 318
Wedgwood 153
Weil, Raymond 416
weird & wonderful 409
Weiss, Claire 109
Welch, Robert 272
Wellings, Norah 193
Wells, H.G. 43
Welz 225

Wemyss 154–6
Wentoy 219
Werkstätte Hagenauer Wien 179
West German stoneware 157–61
Westerwald 157, 160–1
Westwood, Vivienne 206, 310
whistles, railwayana 307
Whitaker, Robert 308
White, Adam 93
White Horses 382
Whitefriars 245–6
Whitford, Samuel 331
Whiting, Geoffrey 177
Whittington, Frank 384
Wiener Werkstätte 168
Wiinblad, Bjørn 147
Wilcox, Harriet 140
Wileman & Co. 167, 178
Wilkinson, Henry 282
Wilkinson, Norman 306
Williams, Arthur 141
Willmore, Joseph 314, 328, 333, 411
Willmott, Louis 324
Wills, Peter 177
Willson, G. 55
Wiltshaw and Robinson 75–7
Winchcombe Pottery 170, 172
wine and drinking
    bottles 222
    corkscrews 412
    silver cups 23
    wine labels 410–11
Wirkkala, Tapio 241
WMF 252
wood
    boxes 48–9
    canes 53–6
    netsuke 30
    tea caddies 47
    treen & carvings 398–402
    tribal art 403–8
Wood, E.G. 319
Wood, Enoch & Sons 70
Wood, Harley 303
Wood, T.E. 243
Woodman, Rachael 255
Wren, Rosemary 177
Wrenn 390
Wright, R. John 190
wristwatches 413–17
writing see pens & writing
Wünsch, Karel 225
Wurlitzer 274

Y
yachts, pond 395
Yagher, Jeff 218
Yeats, William Butler 43
Yorkshire ceramics 168
Yoshiya 366
Yost 357
Yozan 26
Ysart, Paul 285

Z
Zach, Bruno 323
Zalmen, Pal 60
Zenith 416
Zettel, Josephine 139
Zhitomirsky, Alexander 303
Zwick, W. 355